NEET PG

Entrance Exam

Latest Edition
Practice Kit

11 Tests
08 Mock Test
03 Previous Year Paper

Based On Real Exam Pattern

✓ Thoroughly Revised and Updated

✓ Sample Papers with Answer Keys

Title	: NEET PG Entrance Exam
Author Name	: Mr. Rohit Manglik
Published By	: EduGorilla Community Pvt. Ltd.
Publishers Address	: 12/651, First Floor Opp. Arvindo Park, Near Jama Masjid, Indira Nagar, Lucknow, Uttar Pradesh-226016, India

Copyright EduGorilla

Disclaimer EduGorilla

Compiled and created by EduGorilla Community Pvt. Ltd

Printed By EduGorilla Community Pvt. Ltd.

ROHIT MANGLIK
CEO, EduGorilla

Dear Applicants,

People say *"Success comes to those who work hard."* But I've seen people working hard for their exams day in and day out for marginal success. While others succeed in their examinations by putting in just half the work. So are they God Gifted? No! I believe that it's because they work *smart* and not just *hard*. Similarly, for your exams, you should strategize your preparation so as to increase the likelihood of success. Well with EduGorilla get ready to increase your *chances of selection* in your exam by *16x*.

EduGorilla helps you in not only working *hard* but also working in a *smart and strategic* manner. With EduGorilla's preparation package, you get a chance to make your exam preparation easy, and a fun learning path towards selection. Finding the right path to your preparations can be difficult if you don't know in which direction to head. Don't worry, we have you covered! EduGorilla will be your guide to success in your journey. With our Preparation Package, you can prepare strategically and beat the exam in just one attempt.

EduGorilla's Preparation Package includes-

- **Test Series**
- **Books**

Our preparation package is handcrafted as per the latest changes, expert opinions, and students' discretion. Thus, enabling you to get through each stage of the selection process for your exam.

Our Books are designed by the teachers and experts of the respective exam with a combined 150+ years of experience; to provide you with easy, efficient, and effective learning. Our books are smart, in the sense that not only do they give you the answers to the questions but also provide similar questions for practice.

EduGorilla's competent Test Series gives you real-time experience and confidence through which you can clear your offline or online exam in just one attempt. We currently host 83,000+ mock tests for 1,440+ competitive and academic exams.

Thus, EduGorilla misses no chance to assist you in your preparation and covers all stages of the exam, so that you don't have to look anywhere else.

We provide complete preparation packages for defense, banking, teaching, and other National & State-Level exams. Hence, it doesn't matter which exam you aspire to because you will reach your success.

ALL THE BEST !

Let EduGorilla be your Guide to Success.

Rohit Manglik,
Founder and CEO, EduGorilla

INTRODUCTION

EduGorilla focuses on guiding students to succeed in their examinations. With that in mind, our book, titled "NEET PG : Entrance Exam", has been drafted through the collective efforts of our distinguished experts with 150+ years of combined experience. This book consists of questions that are created following the latest changes in the syllabus and exam pattern. We compiled the book on the basis of questions that are most likely to appear in the NEET PG. Through EduGorilla's "NEET PG : Entrance Exam" your chances of success will increase 16x.

EduGorilla does this through our Complete Preparation Package. This package consists of well-conceptualized and structured content in the form of questions that are tailor-made according to your needs and will help you practice for exams in a smart way by pinpointing all the necessary information. It also provides smart answer sheet for your self-evaluation. You can assess your shortcomings and work accordingly on areas that may require more of your attention.

EduGorilla promises to help you succeed in your examination and accomplish your dream goals. We believe in our aspirants and see them at the top of the merit list. And the first step towards the top is to start preparing with us. EduGorilla's "NEET PG : Entrance Exam" includes the following attributes.

➤ Well-Researched Content

➤ Top-Notch Quality

➤ Smart Answer Sheet

➤ Exam Relevant Questions

Therefore, EduGorilla fortifies your preparation and makes it durable enough to help you stand tall and beat the examination.

NEET PG
Scan QR code for Eligibility, Exam Pattern, Syllabus and more.

Book ID: 0783

TABLE OF CONTENTS

Mock Test	1-169
Mock Test - 1	1-20
Mock Test - 2	21-41
Mock Test - 3	42-60
Mock Test - 4	61-79
Mock Test - 5	80-99
Mock Test - 6	100-118
Mock Test - 7	119-147
Mock Test - 8	148-169

Previous Year Paper	170-243
Memory Based Previous Year Paper 2018	170-191
Memory Based Previous Year Paper 2019	192-217
Memory Based Previous Year Paper 2020	218-243

Mock Test 01

PART A

Q.1 Which of the following muscular valve controls the flow of digestive juice from the hepatopancreatic duct to the duodenum?

A. Sphincter of Oddi **B.** Semilunar valve
C. Ileocaecal valve **D.** Pyloric sphincter

Q.2 The movement at the following joint permits a person to look towards the right or left:

A. Atlanto-occipital joint
B. Atlanto-axial joint
C. C2-C3 joint
D. C3-C4 joint

Q.3 The intricately and prodigiously looped system of veins and arteries that lie on the surface of the epididymis is known as :

A. Choroid plexus **B.** Tuberal plexus
C. Pampiniform plexus **D.** Pectiniform septum

Q.4 While exposing the kidney from behind, all of the following nerves are liable to injury except:

A. Lateral cutaneous nerve of thigh
B. Ilioinguinal nerve
C. Subcostal nerve
D. Iliohypogastric nerve

Q.5 Which of the following movements will not be affected by the involvement of the L5 Nerve root?

A. Thigh adduction **B.** Knee Flexion
C. Knee Extension **D.** Toe Extension

Q.6 Barr body is found in the following phase of the cell cycle:

A. Interphase **B.** Metaphase
C. G^1 phase **D.** Telophase

Q.7 All of the following physiological processes occur during the growth at the epiphyseal plate except:

A. Proliferation and hypertrophy
B. Calcification and ossification
C. Vasculogenesis and erosion
D. Replacement of red bone marrow with yellow marrow

Q.8 The type of joint between the sacrum and the coccyx is a:

A. Symphysis **B.** Synostosis
C. Synchondrosis **D.** Syndesmosis

Q.9 Single uriniferous tubule does not contain

A. Loop of Henle
B. Collecting duct
C. Distal convoluted tubule
D. Bowman's capsule

Q.10 All of the following are branches of the external carotid artery except:

A. Superior thyroid artery
B. Anterior Ethmoidal artery
C. Occipital artery
D. Posterior auricular artery

Q.11 The maximum amount of urea is present in:

A. Dorsal Aorta **B.** Hepatic Vein
C. Renal Vein **D.** Hepatic Portal Vein

Q.12 Polar bodies are formed during:

A. Spermatogenesis **B.** Organogenesis
C. Oogenesis **D.** Morphogenesis

Q.13 Upper limb weight is transmitted to axial skeleton by all except?

A. Coracoacromial ligament
B. Claviculoclavicular [interclavicular] ligament
C. Costoclavicular ligament
D. Acromioclavicular ligament

Q.14 Which of the following among axillary lymph nodes is a terminal group?

A. Pectoral **B.** Central **C.** Lateral **D.** Apical

Q.15 Which one ofthe following is the correct statement during operation on the submandibular gland?

A. The submandibular gland is seen to wrap around the posterior border of mylohyoid.
B. The facial artery rind vein are divided as they course through the deep part of the gland,
C. The hypoglossal nerve is seen to loop under the submandibular duct
D. Damage to the lingual nerve will cause loss of sensation to the posterior third of the tongue

Q.16 A midline cleft lip is due to the failure of fusion between:

A. Maxillary processes
B. Medial nasal processes
C. Medial and lateral nasal process
D. Medial nasal and maxillary process.

Q.17 Lumbar hemivertebra results due to the abnormal development of:

A. Dorsal sclerotome
B. Intermdiate cell mass
C. Notocord
D. Ventral sclerotome

Q.18 Which of the following organs is not involved in calcium homeostasis?

A. Kidneys **B.** Skin
C. Intestines **D.** Lungs

Q.19 The cell bodies of orexinergic neurons are present in:

A. Locus ceruleus
B. Dorsal raphe
C. Lateral hypothalamic area
D. Hippocampus

Q.20 The hyperkinetic features of Huntington's disease are due to the loss of:
A. Nigrostriatal dopaminergic system
B. Intrastriatal cholinergic system
C. GABA-ergic and cholinergic system
D. Intrastriatal GABA-ergic and cholinergic system

Q.21 On electromyography, all of the following features suggest denervation, except:
A. Unrgulated firing of individual muscle fibres
B. Small short-duration polyphasic action potentials
C. Presence of positive sharp waves
D. Spontaneous firing of motor units

Q.22 Follicular stimulating hormone receptors are present on:
A. Theca cells
B. Granulosa cells
C. Leydig cells
D. Basement membrane of ovarian follicle

Q.23 Which of the following organs secretes zinc in large amount in man?
A. Seminal vesicle   **B.** Prostate
C. Epididymis   **D.** Vas

Q.24 Which of the following favours filtration at the arteriolar end of the capillary bed.
A. Decrease in hydrostatic pressure of capillaries
B. Increase in hydrostatic pressure of capillaries
C. Increase in oncotic pressure of capillaries
D. Decrease in oncotic pressure of interstitium

Q.25 For PCR which of the following is not required:
A. Taq polymerase
B. dNTP
C. Primer
D. Radiolabelled DNA probe

Q.26 In isometric exercise all are increased except :
A. Heart rate
B. Cardiac output
C. Mean arterial pressure
D. Systemic vascular resistance

Q.27 Renin is secreted by -
A. PCT
B. DCT
C. Collecting duct
D. Juxatglomerular apparatus

Q.28 Juxtaglomerular apparatus lies in relation to:
A. Proximal convoluted tubule
B. Ascending loop of Henle
C. Descending loop of Henle

D. Glomerulus

Q.29 Cerebral blood flow is regulated by all except:
A. Blood pressure
B. Arterial PCO2
C. Potassium ions
D. Cerebral metabolic rate

Q.30 Which of the following hormone is not secreted by the kidney:
A. Renin   **B.** Angiotensin I
C. Erythropoietin   **D.** 1, 25 DHCC

Q.31 Toxic effects of high oxygen tension include all of the following except:
A. Pulmonary edema
B. Decreased cerebral blood flow
C. Retinal damage
D. CNS excitation and convulsion

Q.32 Delta waves are seen in:
A. Deep sleep
B. REM sleep
C. Awake state
D. Stage I NREM sleep

Q.33 The processing of short term memory to long term memory is done in:
A. Prefrontal cortex   **B.** Hippocampus
C. Neocortex   **D.** Amygdala

Q.34 Broca's area is concerned with:
A. Word formation   **B.** Comprehension
C. Repetition   **D.** Reading

Q.35 Mitochondrial DNA is:
A. Closed circular   **B.** Nicked circular
C. Linear   **D.** Open circular

Q.36 Which type of RNA has the highest percentage of modified base?
A. mRNA   **B.** tRNA   **C.** rRNA   **D.** snRNA

Q.37 Microsatellite sequence is:
A. Small satellite
B. Extra chromosomal DNA
C. Short sequence (2-5) repeat DNA
D. Looped-DNA

Q.38 The type of enzyme inhibtion in which succinate dehydrogenase reaction is inhibited by malonate is an example of:
A. Noncompetitive   **B.** Uncompetitive
C. Competitive   **D.** Allosteric

Q.39 Which of the following estimates blood creatinine level most accurately.
A. Jaffe method
B. Kinetic jaffe method
C. Technicon method

D. Enzyme assay

Q.40 Chymotrypsinogen is a:

A. Zymogen **B.** Carboxypeptidase
C. Transaminase **D.** Elastase

Q.41 Same aminoacid is coded by multiple codons. This property is known as:

A. Degeneracy
B. Frame-shift mutation
C. Transcription
D. Mutation

Q.42 Increased level of lipoprotein(a) predisposes to:

A. Liver cirrhosis
B. Atherosclerosis
C. Nephrotic syndrome
D. Pancreatitis

Q.43 Increased copper excretion in urine is seen in all except:

A. Primary sclerosing cholangitis
B. Wilson's disease
C. Primary biliary cirrhosis
D. Hepatocellular carcinoma

Q.44 End product of purine metabolism in non primate mammals is:

A. Uric acid **B.** Ammonia
C. Urea **D.** Allantoin

Q.45 SYBR Green Dye is used for:

A. HPLC
B. Immunofluorescence
C. PCR
D. ELISA

Q.46 Rapid method of chromosome identification in intersex is:

A. FISH (Fluorescent in situ hybridization)
B. PCR (Polymerase chain reaction)
C. SSCP (Single stranded conformation polymorphism)
D. Karyotyping

Q.47 Enzyme responsible for complete oxidation of glucose to Carbon dioxide and water is present in:

A. Cytosol
B. Mitochondria
C. Lysosomes
D. Endoplasmic reticulum

Q.48 Dinitrophenol causes:

A. Inhibition of ATP synthase
B. Inhibition of electron transport
C. Uncoupling of oxidation and phosphorylation
D. Accumulation of ATP

Q.49 Within the RBC, hypoxia stimulates glycolysis by which of the following regulating pathways?

A. Hypoxia Stimulates pyruvate dehydrogenase by increased 2,3 DPG
B. Hypoxia inhibits hexokinase
C. Hypoxia stimulates release of all Glycolytic enzymes from Band 3 on RBC membrane
D. Activation of the regulatory enzymes by high PH

Q.50 Study of multiplication of proteins in disease process is called:

A. Proteomics **B.** Genomics
C. Glycomics **D.** Nucleomics

PART B

Q.51 Serum C_3 is persistently low in the following?

A. Post streptococcal glomerulonephritis
B. Membranoproliferative glomerulonephritis
C. Lupus nephritis
D. Glomerulonephritis related to bacterial endocarditis

Q.52 All of the following are associated with low complement levels except:

A. Lupus nephritis
B. Mesangio capillary glomerulonephritis
C. Diarrhea-associated hemolytic uremic syndrome
D. Post—infections glomerulonephritis

Q.53 Males who are sexually under developed with rudimentary testes and prostate glands, sparse pubic and facial hair, long arms and legs and large hands & feet are likely to have the chromosome complement of:

A. 45, XYY **B.** 46, XY **C.** 46, XXY **D.** 46, X

Q.54 Which of the following gene defect is associated with development of medullary carcinoma of thyroid?

A. RET protooncogene **B.** FAP gene
C. Rb gene **D.** BRCA 1 gene

Q.55 To which of the following family of chemical mediators of inflammation, the Lipoxins belong?

A. Kinin system
B. Cytokines
C. Chemokines
D. Arachidonic acid metabolite

Q.56 The membrane protein, clathrin is involved in:

A. Cell motility
B. Receptor-mediated endocytosis
C. Exocytosis
D. Cell shape

Q.57 Differential expression of same gene depending on parent of origin is referred to as:

A. Genomic imprinting **B.** Mosaicism
C. Anticipation **D.** Nonpenetrance

Q.58 Which one of the following is not a feature of liver histology in Non cirrhotic portal fibrosis (NCPF)?

A. Fibrosis in and around the portal tracts
B. Thrombosis of the medium and small portal vein branches
C. Non specific inflammatory cell infiltrates in the portal tracts
D. Bridging fibrosis

Q.59 Characteristic feature in kidney biopsy from a child with hemolytic uremic syndrome is:

A.   Thrombotic microangiopathy

B.   Proliferative glomerulonephritis

C.   Focal segmental glomerulosclerosis

D.   Minimal change disease

Q.60 In which of the following conditions bilateral contracted kidneys are characteristically seen?

A.   Amyloidosis

B.   Diabetes mellitus

C.   Rapidly progressive (crescentic) glomerulonephritis

D.   Benign nephrosclerosis

Q.61 Atypical pneumonia can be caused by the following microbial agents except?

A.   Mycoplasma pneumoniae

B.   Legionella pneumophila

C.   Human Coronavirus

D.   Klebsiella pneumoniae

Q.62 Aschoff' s nodules are seen in:

A.   Subacute bacterial endocarditis

B.   Libman-Sacks endocarditis

C.   Rheumatic carditis

D.   Non—bacterial Thrombotic endocarditis

Q.63 Which of the following statements pertaining to leukemia is correct?

A.   Blasts of acute myeloid leukemia are typically sudan black negative.

B.   Blasts of acute lymphoblastic leukemia are typically myeloperoxidase positive.

C.   Low leucocyte alkaline phosphatase score is characteristically seen in blastic phase of chronic myeloid leukemia.

D.   Tartrate resistant acid phosphatase positivity is typically seen in hairy cell leukemia.

Q.64 The subtype of Hodgkin's disease, which is histologically distinct from all the other subtypes. is:

A.   Lymphocyte predominant

B.   Nodular sclerosis

C.   Mixed cellularity

D.   Lymphocyte depleted

Q.65 The classification proposed by the International Lymphoma Study Group for non Hodgkin's lymphoma is known as:

A.   Kiel classification

B.   REAL classification

C.   WHO classification

D.   Rappaport classification

Q.66 In familial Mediterranean fever, the gene encoding the following protein undergoes mutation:

A.   Pyrin

B.   Perforin

C.   Atrial natriuretic factor

D.   Immunoglobulin light chain

Q.67 Which type of Amyloidosis is caused by mutation of the transthyretin protein?

A.   Familial Mediterranean fever

B.   Familial amyloidotic polyneuropathy

C.   Dialysis associated amyloidosis

D.   Prion protein associated amyloidosis

Q.68 One of the following stains is specific for Amyloid?

A.   Periodic Acid schiff (PAS)

B.   Alizarin red

C.   Congo red

D.   Von—Kossa

Q.69 Which one of the following is not used as a tumor marker in testicular tumours?

A. AFP   **B.** LDH   **C.** HCG   **D.** CEA

Q.70 An example of a tumour suppressor gene is:

A. Myc   **B.** Fos   **C.** Ras   **D.** Rb

Q.71 All endothelial cells produce thrombomodulin except those found in:

A.   Hepatic circulation

B.   Cutaneous circulation

C.   Cerebral microcirculation

D.   Renal circulation

Q.72 In apoptosis, Apaf-1 is activated by release of which of the following substances from the mitochondria?

A. Bcl 2   **B.** Bax

C. Bcl-XL   **D.** Cytochrome C

Q.73 Fibrinoid necrosis may be observed in all of the following, except:

A.   Malignant hypertension

B.   Polyarteritis nodosa

C.   Diabetic glomerulosclerosis

D.   Aschoff's nodule

Q.74 A peripheral smear with increased neutrophils, basophils, eosinophils, and platelets is highly suggestive of:

A.   Acute myeloid leukemia

B.   Acute lymphoblastic leukemia

C.   Chronic myelogenous leukemia

D.   Myelodysplastic syndrome

Q.75 Which of the following is characteristically not associated with the development of interstitial lung disease?

A.   Organic dusts

B.   Inorganic dusts

C.   Toxic gaes e.g. chlorine, sulphur dioxide

D.   Inhalation of tobacco smoke

Q.76 Inhaled nitric oxide is used:

A.   For stabilizing systemic hemodynamics

B.   In case of jaundice

C.   To prevent CNS complication

D.   For reducing pulmonary hypertension

Q.77 A patient of peptic ulcer was prescribed ranitidine and sucralfate in the morning hours. Why is this combination incorrect:

A. Ranitidine combines with sucralfate and prevents its action.

B. Combination of these two drugs produces serious side effects like agranulocytosis.

C. Ranitidine decreases the gastric pH so sucralfate is not able to act.

D. Sucralfate inhibits absorption of ranitidine.

Q.78 All the following statements regarding interactions of levodopa are correct except:

A. In Parkinsonism, phenothiazines reduce its efficacy.

B. It is a prodrug.

C. Pyridoxine reduces effect of levodopa in parkinsonism.

D. Domperidone blocks levodopa induced emesis and its therapeutic potential.

Q.79 Which of the following action is ascribed to delta type of opioid receptors?

A. Supraspinal analgesia

B. Respiratory depression

C. Euphoria

D. Reduced intestinal motility

Q.80 Morphine can be used in all the following conditions except:

A. Head injury

B. Asthma

C. Hypothyroidism

D. Diabetes

Q.81 Which of the following statements is not true regarding sulfonamides:

A. Sulfasalazine is absorbed well from GIT.

B. Crystalluria can occur with sulfonamide administration.

C. Sulfonamide administration to Newborn may cause Kernicterus.

D. Sulfonamides are of value in treatment of infections due to Nocardia species.

Q.82 A 60 year old man with rheumatic mitral stenosis with atrial fibrillation is on therapy for a fast ventricular rate. While on treatment, he developed a regular pulse of 64/min. The most likely drug being administered was:

A. Verapamil

B. Digoxin

C. Carvedilol

D. Propranolol

Q.83 Which of the following does not bind to GABA receptor chloride channels?

A. Ethanol

B. Alfaxalone

C. Zolpidem

D. Buspirone

Q.84 All of the following Anticancer agents cause bone marrow depression except?

A. Chlorambucil

B. Daunorubicin

C. Doxorubicin

D. Flutamide

Q.85 All of the following statements about an alpha-glucosidase inhibitor are true except:

A. Reduces intestinal absorption of carbohydrates.

B. Effective in both type I & 2 diabetes.

C. Hypoglycemia is a common & serious side effect.

D. Can be used with other oral Hypoglycemic drugs.

Q.86 Which one of the following statements about biguanides is not true?

A. Don't stimulate insulin Release

B. Decrease hepatic glucose production

C. Renal Dysfunction is not a contraindication for their use

D. Can be combined with sulfonylureas

Q.87 Sympathomimetic drugs are useful in the therapy of all of the following conditions except?

A. Acute decompensated heart failure

B. Hypotension

C. Hypertension

D. Erectile dysfunction

Q.88 In which of the following phases of clinical trial of drug, ethical clearance is not required?

A. Phase I   **B.** Phase II   **C.** Phase III   **D.** Phase IV

Q.89 A highly ionized drug:

A. Is excreted mainly by the kidneys

B. Crosses the placental barrier easily

C. Is well absorbed from the intestine

D. Is highly protein bound

Q.90 A young pregnant woman presents with fulminant hepatic failure. The most likely aetiological agent is:

A. Hepatitis B virus

B. Hepatitis C virus

C. Hepatitis E virus

D. Hepatitis A virus

Q.91 Etarcept acts by one of the following mechanisms:

A. By blocking tumor necrosis factor

B. By blocking bradykinin synthesis

C. By inhibiting cyclo-oxygenase-2

D. By blocking lipoxygenase

Q.92 Nevirapine is a:

A. Protease inhibitor

B. Nucleoside reverse transcriptase inhibitor

C. Non-nucleoside reverse transcriptase inhibitor

D. Fusion inhibitor

Q.93 The group of antibiotics which possess additional anti-inflammatory and immunomodulatory activity is:

A. Tetracyclines

B. Polypeptide antibiotics

C. Fluoroquinolones

D. Macrolides

Q.94 One of the following is not penicillinase susceptible:

A. Amoxicillin

B. Penicillin G

C. Piperacillin

D. Cloxacillin

Q.95 Inverse agonist of benzodiazepine receptor is:

A. Phenobarbitone

B. Flumazenil

C. Beta-carboline

D. Gabapentin

Q.96 A woman with infertility receives an ovary transplant from her sister who is an identical Twin. What type of graft it is?

A. Xenograft **B.** Autograft
C. Allograft **D.** Isograft

Q.97 The capsule of Cryptococcus neoformans in a CSF sample is best seen by:

A. Gram stain
B. India ink preparation
C. Giemsa stain
D. Methenamine-Silver stain

Q.98 Which of the following is not a neuroparasite?

A. Taenia solium **B.** Acanthamoeba
C. Naegleria **D.** Trichinella spiralis

Q.99 Viruses can be isolated from clinical samples by cultivation in the following except:

A. Tissue culture
B. Embryonated eggs
C. Animals
D. Chemically defined media

Q.100 Which one of the following statements is true regarding Chlamydia pneumoniae:

A. Fifteen serovars have been identified as human pathogens.
B. Mode of transmission is by the airborne bird excreta.
C. The Cytoplasmic inclusions present in the sputum specimen are rich in glycogen.
D. The group specific antigen is responsible for the production of complement fixing antibodies.

Q.101 Chlamydia trachomatis is associated with the following except:

A. Endemic trachoma
B. Inclusion conjunctivitis
C. Lymphogranuloma venereum
D. Community acquired pneumonia

Q.102 The most common pathogens responsible for nosocomial pneumonias in the ICU are:

A. Gram positive organisms
B. Gram negative organisms
C. Mycoplasma
D. Virus infections

Q.103 The following statements are true regarding melioidosis except:

A. It is caused by Burkholderia mallei.
B. The agent is a gram negative aerobic bacteria.
C. Bipolar staining of the aetiological agent is seen with methylene blue stain.
D. The most common form of melioidosis is pulmonary infection.

Q.104 A child was diagnosed to be suffering from diarrhoea due to Campylobacter jejuni. Which of the following will be the correct environmental conditions of incubation of the culture plates of the stool sample:

A. Temperature of 42°C and microaerophilic
B. Temperature of 42°C and 10% carbon dioxide
C. Temperature of 37°C and microaerophilic
D. Temperature of 37°C and 10% carbon dioxide

Q.105 All of the following Vibrio sp. are halophilic, except:

A. V. cholerae **B.** V. parahaemolyticus
C. V. alginolyticus **D.** V. fluvialis

Q.106 A vitreous aspirate from a case of metastatic endophthalmitis on culture yields Gram-positive round to oval cells, 12-14 microns in size. The aspirate on Gram staining shows the presence of pseudohyphae. Which of the following is the most likely aetiological agent?

A. Aspergillus **B.** Rhizopus
C. Candida **D.** Fusarium

Q.107 Which of the following parasitic infestation can lead to malabsorption syndrome?

A. Amoebiasis
B. Ascariasis
C. Hookworm infestation
D. Giardiasis

Q.108 With reference to Bacteroides fragilis the following statements are true, except:

A. B. fragilis is the same frequent anaerobe isolated from clinical samples.
B. B. fragilis is not uniformly sensitive to metronidazole.
C. The lipopolysaccharide formed by B. fragilis is structurally and functionally different from the conventional endotoxin.
D. Shock and disseminated intravascular coagulation are common in Bacreriodes bacteremia.

Q.109 A young male patient presented with urethral discharge. On urine examination pus cells were found but no organisms. Which method would be the best for culture.

A. Mc coy cell line
B. Thayer martin medium
C. L J medium
D. Levinthal medium

Q.110 Which of the following bacteria act by increasing cAMP.

A. Vibrio cholera
B. Staphylococcus aureus
C. E. coli heat stable toxin
D. Salmonella

Q.111 A person working in an abattoir presented with a pustule on his hand which turned into ulcer, which will best help in diagnosis.

A. Trichrome methylene blue
B. Carbel fuschin
C. Acid fast stain
D. Calcoflour white

Q.112 A elderly male presented with fever, chest pain and dry cough. Sputum was cultured on charcoal yeast medium, the organism identified will be -

A. H.influenza
B. Moraxella catarrhalis

C. Legionella

D. Burkholderia cepacia

Q.113 Most common cause of Traveller's diarrhoea:

A. Enterotoxigenic E. coli

B. Enterohemorrhagic E. coli

C. Enteropathogenic E. coli

D. Enreroinvasive E. coli

Q.114 A farmer presents with pustules, which show Gram Positive Cocci on smear. Culture shows Beta hemolysis, and organisms are Catalase negative. To show that the identified organism is group A streptococci, which of the following test should be done?

A. Bacitracin sensitivity

B. Optochin sensitivity

C. Novobiocin sensitivity

D. Bile solubility

Q.115 Components of Innate immunity that are active against viral cells includes:

A. NK cells

B. Cytotoxic T cells

C. B cell

D. Memory B cell

Q.116 Preservation of brain is not required in:

A. Alkaloid poisoning

B. Organophosphorus poisoning

C. Volatile organic poisoning

D. Heavy metal poisoning

Q.117 Sexual asphyxia is associated with which of the following sexual behaviour.

A. Masochism

B. Sadism

C. Fetichism

D. Voyeurism

Q.118 Abortion stick used in criminal abortion causes abortion by the mechanism of:

A. Uterine contraction

B. Stimulation of uterine nerves

C. Uterine infection & necrosis

D. Placental separation

Q.119 Hemoperfusion with charcoal is useful in poisoning with:

A. Barbiturate poisoning

B. Methyl alcohol

C. Lithium

D. Ethylene glycol

Q.120 Dialysis is useful in poisoning with all of the following except:

A. Methyl alcohol

B. Barbiturates

C. Ethylene glycol

D. Copper sulphate

Q.121 Which is not an aryl phosphate.

A. Parathion

B. Tik-20

C. Malathion

D. Paraoxon

Q.122 Spalding's sign is seen in:

A. Drowning

B. Mummification

C. Adipocere

D. Maceration

Q.123 Acrodynia is associated with:

A. Mercury

B. Phenolic acid

C. Oxalic acid

D. Carbolic acid

Q.124 The most fixed part of the intestine is

A. Duodenum

B. Jejunum

C. Colon

D. Ileum

Q.125 "Nutmeg liver" refers to

A. Amoebic hepatitis

B. Pyogenic abscess

C. Chronic venous congestion

D. Portal cirrhosis

Q.126 The required temperature for sterilization against spores in a Hot-air oven is:

A. 120-140°C for one hour

B. 140-160°C for one hour

C. 160-180°C for one hour

D. 180-200°C for one hour

Q.127 Juvenile Justice (Care and Protection of Children) Act was passed by the Government of India in?

A. 1984

B. 1993

C. 2000

D. 2004

Q.128 True statement about Himalayan Goitre Belt:

A. 2400 Km wide.

B. Largest goitre belt in the world.

C. Extends from Kashmir in the west to Naga hills in the east.

D. All of them.

Q.129 Toxoid is prepared from:

A. Exotoxin

B. Endotoxin

C. Both of above

D. None of these

Q.130 If prevalence of diabetes is 10%, the probability that three people selected at random from the population will have diabetes is:

A. 0.01

B. 0.03

C. 0.001

D. 0.003

Q.131 If each value of a given group of observations is multiplied by 10 the standard deviation of the resulting observations is:

A. Original std. Deviation x 10

B. Original std. Deviation /10

C. Original std. Deviation – 10

D. Original std. Deviation itself

Q.132 The National Population Policy of India has set the following goals except:

A. To bring down Total Fertility Rate (TFR) to replacement levels by 2015.

B. To reduce the Infant Mortality Rate to 30 per l000 live births.

C. To reduce the Maternal Mortality Rate to 100 per 100000 live births.

D. 100 percent registration of births, deaths, marriages and pregnancies.

Q.133 Sullivan's index indicates

A. Life free of disability

B. Pregnancy rate per HWY

C. Hookworm eggs/gm of stool

D. Standard of living

Q.134 Which one of the following is not included in the elements of Primary Health Care?

A. Immunization services

B. Family planning services

C. Specialized services

D. Health education regarding water and sanitation

Q.135 The events A and B are mutually exclusive, so:

A. Prob (A or B) = Prob (A) + Prob (B)

B. Prob (A and B) = Prob (A) * Prob (B)

C. Prob (A) = Prob (B)

D. Prob (A) + Prob (B) = 1

Q.136 The PEFR of a group of 11 year old girls follow a normal distribution with mean 300 l/min and standard deviation 20 l/min:

A. About 95% of the girls have PEFR between 260 and 340 l/min

B. The girls have healthy lungs

C. About 5% of girls have PEFR below 260 l/min

D. All the PEFR must be less than 340 l/min

Q.137 The standard normal distribution:

A. Is skewed to the left

B. Has mean = 1.0

C. Has standard deviation = 0.0

D. Has variance = 1.0

Q.138 All of the following statements are true about Congenital Rubella except:

A. It is diagnosed when the infant has IgM antibodies at birth.

B. It is diagnosed when IgG antibodies persist from more than 6 months.

C. Most common congenital defects are deafness, cardiac malformations and cataract.

D. Infection after 16 weeks of gestation results in major congenital defects.

Q.139 For the treatment of case a of class III dog bite, all of the following are correct except:

A. Give Immunoglobulins for passive immunity.

B. Give ARV.

C. Immediately stitch wound under antibiotic coverage.

D. Immediately wash wound with soap and water.

Q.140 'Endemic Disease` means that a disease:

A. Occurs clearly in excess of normal expectancy.

B. Is constantly present in a given population group.

C. Exhibits seasonal pattern.

D. Is prevalent among animals.

Q.141 Infant mortality does not include:

A. Early neonatal mortality

B. Perinatal mortality

C. Post neonatal mortality

D. Late neonatal mortality

Q.142 While applying chi-square test to a contingency table of 4 rows and 4 columns, the degrees of freedom would be:

A. 1   **B.** 4   **C.** 9   **D.** 8

Q.143 The highest percentages of polyunsaturated fatty acids are present in:

A. Groundnut oil   **B.** Soyabean oil

C. Margarine   **D.** Palm oil

Q.144 The following statements are true regarding leptospirosis, except:

A. It is zoonosis

B. Man is the dead end host

C. Man is an accidental host

D. Lice act as reservoirs of infection

Q.145 Which epidemiological study gives the most accurate result.

A. Meta analysis

B. Cross-sectional study

C. Randomized control trial with double blinding

D. Cohort study

Q.146 True about ASHA (accredited social health activist) is:

A. Mental health worker

B. Involved in minimum need program

C. Deployed $\frac{1}{1000}$ population

D. To replace Anganwadi worker in ICDS

Q.147 Causative toxin for endemic ascites is:

A. Pyrrolizidine

B. Beta-oxalyl amino-alanine

C. Ergot

D. Aflatoxin

Q.148 Vision 2020 "The right to sight" includes all except:

A. Trachoma

B. Epidemic conjunctivitis

C. Cataract

D. Onchocerciasis

Q.149 Chlorine demand of water is measured by-

A. Horrock's appratus   **B.** Chlorimeter

C. Double pot   **D.** Berkfeld filter

Q.150 Comprehensive emergency obstetric care does not include:

A. Manual removal of placenta

B. Hysterectomy

C. Blood transfusion

D. Cesarean section

PART C

Q.151 Immunosuppressant drugs are consumed with:

A. Major viruses   **B.** Peritoneal dialysis

C. Kidney transplant   **D.** Hemodialysis

Q.152 All of the following conditions are known to cause diabetes insipidus except:

A. Multiple sclerosis **B.** Head injury
C. Histiocytosis **D.** Viral encephalitis

Q.153 40 year old female came to the OPD with complaints of with depressed mood, insomnia, loss of appetite and lack of interest in surroundings for the past 1 year. These symptoms appeared after loss in a business deal 1 year ago. Which is correct regarding the management?

A. Selective Serotonin Reuptake Inhibitors (SSRI's) are the most effective drugs

B. Antidepressants should be given based on the side effect profile

C. No treatment is required as it is due to loss in a business deal

D. Combination therapy with 2 or more antidepressants

Q.154 A 25 year old female presents with 2 year history of repetitive, irresistible thoughts of contamination with dirt associated with repetitive hand washing. She reports these thoughts to be her own and distressing; but is not able to overcome them along with medications. She is most likely to benefit from which of the following therapies?

A. Exposure and response prevention
B. Systematic desensitization
C. Assertiveness training
D. Sensate focusing

Q.155 One of the following usually differentiates hysterical symptoms from hypochondriacal symptoms:

A. Symptoms do not normally reflect understandable physiological or pathological mechanism

B. Physcial symptoms are prominent which are not explained by organic factors

C. Personality traits are significant

D. Symptoms run a chronic course

Q.156 Bright light treatment has been found to be most effective in treatment of:

A. Anorexia nervosa
B. Seasonal affective disorder
C. Schizophrenia
D. Obsessive compulsive disorder

Q.157 Mutism and akinesis in a person, who appears awake and even alert, is best described as:

A. Twilight state **B.** Oneiroid state
C. Stupor **D.** Delirium

Q.158 Intense nihilism, somatization and agitation in old age are the hallmark symptoms of:

A. Involutional melancholia
B. Atypical depression
C. Somatized depression
D. Depressive stupor

Q.159 Loosening of association is an example of:

A. Formal thought disorder
B. Schneiderian first rank symptoms

C. Perseveration
D. Concrete thinking

Q.160 5-HIAA is a metabolite of:

A. Serotonin **B.** Dopamine
C. Epinephrine **D.** Histamine

Q.161 A middle aged person reported to Psychiatric OPD with the complaints of the fear of leaving home, fear of travelling alone and fear of being in a crowd. He develops marked anxiety with palpitations and swelling if he is in these situations. He often avoids public transport to go to his place of work. The most likely diagnosis is:

A. Generalised anxiety disorder
B. Schizophrenia
C. Personality disorder
D. Agoraphobia

Q.162 The following is not an atypical antipsychotic.

A. Thioridazine **B.** Clozapine
C. Olanzapine **D.** Resperidone

Q.163 Most common substance abuse in India is:

A. Tobacco **B.** Cannabis
C. Alcohol **D.** Heroin

Q.164 Naltrexone is used in opioid addiction because:

A. To treat withdrawl symptoms
B. To treat overdose of opioids
C. Prevent relapse
D. Has addiction potential

Q.165 Delusion is a disorder of:

A. Thought **B.** Perception
C. Insight **D.** Cognition

Q.166 Which of the following is responsible for drug induced pulmonary fibrosis?

A. Phenytoin **B.** Bleomycin
C. Actinomycin D **D.** Cisplatin

Q.167 Conditions associated with thymoma are all except?

A. Myasthenia gravis
B. Cushing's syndrome
C. SIADH
D. Hypogammaglobulinemia

Q.168 Bence Jones proteinuria is seen in?

A. Alpha heavy chain disease
B. Gamma heavy chain disease
C. Mu heavy chain disease
D. Epsilon heavy chain disease

Q.169 Which of the following is false regarding delirium tremens?

A. Tremors
B. Ophthalmoplegia
C. Visual hallucinations
D. Clouding of consciousness

Q.170 Coarctation of aorta is most commonly seen with?

A. ASD
B. VSD
C. PDA
D. Bicuspid aortic valve

Q.171 Disseminated intravascular coagulation (DIC) differs from thrombotic thrombocytopenic purpura. In this reference the DIC is most likely characterized by:
A. Significant numbers of schistocytes
B. A brisk reticulocytosis
C. Decreased coagulation factor levels
D. Significant thrombocytopenia

Q.172 The most sensitive test for the diagnosis of myasthenia gravis is:
A. Elevated serum ACh-receptor binding antibodies
B. Repetitive nerve stimulation test
C. Positive edrophonium test
D. Measurement of jitter by single fibre electromyography

Q.173 All of the following are neurologic channelopathies except:
A. Hypokalemic periodic paralysis
B. Episodic ataxia type 1
C. Familial hemiplegic migraine
D. Spinocerebellar ataxia 1

Q.174 EEG is usually abnormal in all of the following, except:
A. Subacute sclerosing panencephalitis
B. Locked — in state
C. Creutzfeldt — Jakob disease
D. Hepatic encephalopathy

Q.175 Which of the following is a cause of reversible dementia?
A. Subacute combined degeneration
B. Picks disease
C. Creutzfeldt — Jakob disease
D. Alzheimers disease

Q.176 Normal CSF glucose level in the normoglycemic adult is:
A. 20-40 mg/dl
B. 40-70 mg/dl
C. 70-90 mgdl
D. 90-110 mg/dl

Q.177 Which one of the following is the most common location of hypertensive bleed in the brain?
A. Putamen/external capsule
B. Pons
C. Ventricles
D. Lobar white matter

Q.178 Which of the following features are seen in lower motor lesions?
A. Flaccid paralysis
B. Hyperactive stretch reflex
C. Spasticity
D. Muscular incordination

Q.179 Cluster headache is characterized by all, except:
A. Affects predominantly females
B. Unilateral headache
C. Onset typically in 20-50 years of life
D. Associated with conjunctival congestion

Q.180 Discriminant function is used for determining the prognosis of?
A. Alcoholic hepatitis
B. Cirrhosis
C. Viral hepatitis
D. Fulminant hepatic failure

Q.181 5'-Nucleotidase activity is increased in:
A. Bone diseases
B. Prostate cancer
C. Chronic renal failure
D. Cholestatic disorders

Q.182 Which one of the following conditions commonly predisposes to Colonic carcinoma?
A. Ulcerative colitis
B. Crohn's disease
C. Diverticular disease
D. Ischaemic colitis

Q.183 Serum angiotensin converting enzyme may be raised in all of the following, except:
A. Sarcoidosis
B. Silicosis
C. Berylliosis
D. Bronchogenic carcinoma

Q.184 The abnormal preoperative pulmonary function test in a patient with severe kyphoscoliosis includes:
A. Decreased RV and TLC
B. Reduced FEV1/ FVC ratio
C. Reduced FEF 25-75%
D. Increased FRC

Q.185 All of the following are the causes of relative polycythemia except:
A. Dehydration
B. Dengue haemorrhagic fever
C. Gaisbock syndrome
D. High altitude

Q.186 In which of the following conditions Splenectomy is not useful?
A. Herediatary spherocytosis
B. Porphyria
C. Thalassemia
D. Sickle cell disease with large spleen

Q.187 The presence of anti Saccharomyces cerevisae antibody is a surrogate marker of one of the following:
A. Celiac disease
B. Crohn's disease
C. Ulcerative colitis
D. Tropical sprue

Q.188 Anticentromere antibodies are most commonly associated with:
A. Diffuse cutaneous systemic sclerosis
B. Mixed connective tissue disease
C. CREST syndrome
D. Polymyositis

Q.189 Smoking is not a risk factor for development of?

A. Small cell carcinoma

B. Respiratory bronchiolitis

C. Emphysema

D. Bronchiolitis obliterans organizing pneumonia

Q.190 Mycotic abscesses are due to:

A. Bacterial infection

B. Fungal infection

C. Viral infection

D. Mixed infection

Q.191 Which of the following is least likely to cause infective endocarditis?

A. Staphylococcus albus

B. Streptococcus faecalis

C. Salmonella typhi

D. Pseudomonas aeruginosa

Q.192 All of the following are true for mitral valve prolapse, except:

A. Transmission may be as an autosomal dominant trait

B. Majority of the cases present with features of mitral regurgitation

C. The valve leaflets characteristically show myxomatous degeneration

D. The disease is one of the common cardiovascular manifestations of Marfan's Syndrome

Q.193 All of the following may occur due to hyperkalemia except:

A. Prolonged PR interval

B. Prolonged QRS interval

C. Prolonged QT interval

D. Ventricular asystole

Q.194 All of the following are major complications of massive transfusion, except:

A. Hypokalemia

B. Hypothermia

C. Hypomagnesemia

D. Hypocalcemia

Q.195 All of the following statements regarding primary effusion lymphoma are true except:

A. It generally presents in elderly patients

B. There is often an association with HHV 8

C. The proliferating cells are NK cells

D. Patients are commonly HIV positive

Q.196 Laparoscopic procedure patient develops shoulder pain due to:

A. Subphrenic abscess

B. Positional pain during surgery

C. Subdiaphragmatic migration of gas

D. Injury to liver

Q.197 Gangrene not caused by -

A. Frostbite

B. Burger's disease

C. Varicose veins

D. Atherosclerosis

Q.198 The defective migration of neural crest cells results in:

A. Congenital megacolon

B. Albinism

C. Adrenogenital hypoplasia

D. Dentinogenesis imperfecta

Q.199 Which one of the following statements is incorrect in regard to stones in the gallbladder?

A. Pigment stones are due to increased excretion of conjugated bilirubin

B. Are considered a risk factor for the development of gallbladder carcinoma

C. 10% of gallstones are radio-opaque

D. A mucocele of the gallbladder is caused by a stone impacted in Hartman's pouch

Q.200 In which of the following conditions acquired (secondary) megacolon is seen?

A. Fissure in-ano

B. Complete absence of parasympathetic ganglion cells

C. Absence of sympathetic ganglion cells

D. Rectal malignancy

Q.201 A patient has carcinoma of right tongue on its lateral border of anterior $\frac{2^{rd}}{3}$, with lymph node of size 4 cm in level 3 on the side of the neck, stage of disease is:

A. N0

B. N1

C. N2

D. N3

Q.202 Tumor marker for primary hepatocellular carcinoma are all except:

A. Alpha feto protein

B. Alpha 2 macroglobulin

C. PIVKA-2

D. Neurotensin

Q.203 Which of the following colonic polyps is not premalignant.

A. Juvenile polyps

B. Hamartomatous polyps associated with Peutz-Jegher's syndrome

C. Villous adenoma

D. Tubular adenomas

Q.204 Severity of acute pancreatitis correlate with levels of all of the following except:

A. Glucose

B. Amylase

C. Transaminase

D. Calcium

Q.205 Stone which is resistant to lithotripsy.

A. Calcium oxalate

B. Triple phosphate stone

C. Cystine stone

D. Uric acid stone

Q.206 Which of the following is not a complication of surgery for thoracic outlet syndrome.

A. Pneumothorax

B. Brachial plexus injury

C. Lymphocutaneous fistula

D. Long thoracic nerve injury

Q.207 Colonic diverticulosis is best diagnosed by -

A. Colonoscopy **B.** Nuclear scan

C. Barium enema **D.** CT scan

Q.208 Most common complication after ERCP is:

A. Acute pancreatitis

B. Acute cholangitis

C. Acute cholecystitis

D. Duodenal perforation

Q.209 Which of the following statements related to gastric injury is not true?

A. Mostly related to penetrating trauma

B. Treatment is simple debridement and suturing

C. Blood in stomach is always related to gastric injury

D. Heals well and fast

Q.210 Most common hormone deficiency seen after intracranial radiation therapy?

A. Prolactin **B.** Gonadotropins

C. ACTH **D.** Growth hormone

Q.211 Which of these tumors is least radiosensitive.

A. Ewing's sarcoma **B.** Osteosarcoma

C. Wilm's tumor **D.** Neuroblastoma

Q.212 In which one of the following conditions is sialography contraindicated?

A. Ductal calculus

B. Chronic parotitis

C. Acute parotitis

D. Recurrent sialadenitis

Q.213 Gardner's syndrome is a rare hereditary disorder involving the colon. It is characterized by:

A. Polyposis colon, cancer thyroid, skin tumours

B. Polyposis in jejunum, pituitary adenoma and skin tumours

C. Polyposis colon, osteomas, epidermal inclusion cysts and fibrous tumours in the skin

D. Polyposis of gastrointestinal tract, Cholangiocarcinoma and skin tumours

Q.214 Apart from Escherichia coli. the other most common organism implicated in acute suppurative bacterial peritonitis is:

A. Bacteroides **B.** Klebsiella

C. Peptostreptococcus **D.** Pseudomonas

Q.215 Referred pain from all of the following conditions may be felt along the inner side of right thigh, except:

A. Inflamed pelvic appendix

B. Inflamed ovaries

C. Stone in pelvic ureter

D. Pelvic abscess

Q.216 Which is not elevated in a child presenting with jaundice, icterus, pruritus & clay coloured stools.

A. Gamma glutanyl transpeptidase

B. Alkaline phosphatase

C. 5'-nucleotidase

D. Glutamate dehydrogenase

Q.217 Barrett's esophagus is diagnosed by:

A. Squamous metaplasia

B. Intestinal metaplasia

C. Squamous dysplasia

D. Intestinal dysplasia

Q.218 This type of thalassemia disease is Cooley anaemia:

A. Alloimmunization **B.** Beta-thalassemia

C. Alpha-thalassemia **D.** None of these

Q.219 Pigmented villonodular synovitis most commonly affects :

A. Shoulder

B. Ankle

C. Knee

D. Metatarsophalangeal joint

Q.220 Meralgia paresthetica is due to involvement of:

A. Medical cutaneous nerve of thigh

B. Lateral cutaneous nerve of thigh

C. Sural nerve

D. Femoral nerve

Q.221 Rickets in infancy is characterized by the following except :

A. Craniotabes

B. Rachitic rosary

C. Wide open fontanelles

D. Bowlegs

Q.222 Which is not a deep heat therapy?

A. Short wave diathermy

B. Ultrasound therapy

C. Infrared therapy

D. Microwave therapy

Q.223 Bohler's angle is decreased in fracture of:

A. Calcaneum **B.** Talus

C. Navicular **D.** Cuboid

Q.224 Which of the following statements is true of primary grade IV-V vesicoureteric reflux in young children?

A. Renal scarring usually begins in the mid polar regions

B. Postnatal scarring may occur even in the absence of urinary tract infections

C. Long term outcome is comparable in patients treated with either antibiotic prophylaxis or surgery

D. Oral amoxicillin is the antibiotic of choice for prophylaxis

Q.225 The most common site of Morgagni hernia :

A. Right anterior **B.** Right posterior

C. Left anterior **D.** Left posterior

Q.226 Prognosis in head injury is best given by:

A. Glasgow coma scale

B. Age of patient

C. Mode of injury

D. CT head

Q.227 Adjuvant chemotherapy is of definite value in:

A. CA colon

B. CA pancreas

C. CA gall bladder

D. CA esophagus

Q.228 A patient has carcinoma of right tongue on its lateral border of anterior 2/3rd, with lymph node of size 4 cm in level 3 on the side of the neck, stage of disease is:

A. N0   **B.** N1   **C.** N2   **D.** N3

Q.229 True about Branchial cyst is:

A. Cysts are more common than sinuses

B. Mostly arises from 2nd branchial system

C. Causes dysphagia and hoarseness

D. Sinus should always be operated

Q.230 Carcinoembryonic antigens (CEA) is increased in all except:

A. Lung cancer

B. Breast cancer

C. Colon cancer

D. Osteogenic sarcoma

Q.231 True about solitary rectal ulcer syndrome is all/except:

A. Increased muscle layer proliferation

B. Crypt distortion

C. Lamina propria infiltration with lymphocyte

D. Subepithelial fibrosis

Q.232 A patient comes with hematemesis and melena. On the upper GI endoscopy, there was no significant lesion. 2 days later the patient rebleeds. The next line of investigation is:

A. Emergency angiography

B. Repeat upper GI endoscopy

C. Enteroscopy

D. Laparotomy

Q.233 All of the following are true about Lymphoma of the thymus except:

A. More common in females

B. Slow growing

C. Clinically confused with undifferentiated tumors

D. May present with respiratory distress and dysphagia

Q.234 Which of the following is not a histological variant of thyroid neoplasm?

A. Follicular

B. Merkel cell

C. Insular

D. Anaplastic

Q.235 All of the following are complications of supracondylar fracture of humerus in children, except:

A. Compartment syndrome

B. Myositis ossificans

C. Malunion

D. Non-Union

Q.236 The lesions associated with recurrent dislocation of shoulder include all, except:

A. Hill-Sach's lesion

B. Bankart's lesion

C. Capsular laxity

D. Supraspinatus tear

Q.237 The malunion of supracondylar fracture of the humerus most commonly leads to:

A. Flexion deformity

B. Cubitus varus

C. Cubitus valgus

D. Extension deformity

Q.238 Bankarts lesion involves which part of the glenoid labrum:

A. Anterior

B. Superior

C. Anterosuperior

D. Anteroinferior

Q.239 A 7-year-old child presents with a lesion in the upper tibia. X-ray shows the radiolucent area with Codman's triangle and Sunray appearance. Diagnosis is :

A. Ewing's sarcoma

B. Osteosarcoma

C. Osteoid osteoma

D. Chondrosarcoma

Q.240 All of the following mechanisms of action of oral contraceptive pill are true, except:

A. Inhibition of ovulation

B. Prevention of fertilization

C. Interference with implantation of a fertilized ovum

D. Interference with placental function

Q.241 The investigation of choice in a 55-year-old postmenopausal woman who has presented with postmenopausal bleeding is:

A. Pap smear

B. Fractional curettage

C. Transvaginal ultrasound

D. Ca 125 estimation

Q.242 The cysts in Polycystic Ovarian syndrome are formed by:

A. Failure of atretic follicles to undergo apoptosis

B. Oocyte proliferation

C. Multiple corpus lutea

D. Cystic degeneration of ovarian cortex

Q.243 In which of the following heart diseases maternal mortality is found to be highest?

A. Eisenmenger's complex

B. Coarctation of aorta

C. Mitral stenosis

D. Aortic stenosis

Q.244 A female with recurrent abortion and isolated prolonged APTT is most likely associated with:

A. Lupus anticoagulant

B. DIC

C. Von Willebrand disease

D. Hemophilia

Q.245 PAP smear shows Ca in situ-what is the best next logical procedure

A. Conisation

B. Colposcopy & biopsy

C. Hysterectomy

D. HPV viral D.N.A. testing

Q.246 HRT is useful in all except

A. Flushing

B. Osteoporosis
C. Vaginal atrophy
D. Coronary heart disease

Q.247 Most common heart disease which is associated with maximum mortality during pregnancy
A. Eisenmenger syndrome
B. MS
C. AS
D. VSD

Q.248 After the coming head of breach will have difficulty in delivery in all of the following conditions except
A. Hydrocephalus
B. Placenta previa
C. Incomplete dilatation of cervix
D. Extension of head

Q.249 A premature baby of 34 weeks was delivered. The baby had a bullous lesion on the body. X ray shows periostitis. What is the next investigation?
A. VDRL for mother & baby
B. ELISA for HIV
C. PCR for T.B.
D. Hepatitis surface antigen for mother

Q.250 The most common site of ligation in female sterilisation is:
A. Isthmus
B. Ampullary
C. Cornual
D. Fimbrial

Q.251 A lady presents with Jaundice, abdominal distension and pedal edema after delivering a normal baby. Her clinical condition deteriorates with increasing abdominal distension and severe ascites. Her bilirubin is 5 mg/dl, S.alkaline phosphatase was 450 u/L and ALT 345 u/L. There is tender hepatomegaly 6 cm below the costal margin and ascitic fluid show protein less than 2 mg%. Diagnosis is:
A. Acute fatty liver of pregnancy
B. HELLP syndrome
C. Acute fulminant liver failure
D. Budd Chiari syndrome

Q.252 Ovarian tumour which is bilateral:
A. Dysgerminoma
B. Endodermal sinus tumour
C. Immature teratoma
D. Embryonal cell carcinoma

Q.253 During Pregnancy, deficiency of which of the following leads to neural tube defects?
A. Folic acid
B. Iron
C. Calcium
D. Zinc

Q.254 Shape of a nulliparous cervix is:
A. Circular
B. Transverse
C. Longitudinal
D. Fimbriated

Q.255 Which of the following condition is screened by "Pap Smear"?
A. Ovarian cancer
B. Endometrial cancer
C. Cervical cancer
D. Breast Cancer

Q.256 Prolonged second state of Labour may occur due to:
A. Uterine inertia
B. Epidural analgesia
C. Cephalopelvic disproportion
D. All of the above

Q.257 Prerequisites for internal rotation of the head – A/E:
A. Well – flexed head
B. Efficient uterine contraction
C. Favourable shape of the pelvis
D. Tone of the abdominal muscles

Q.258 The first Movements of the baby felt by the mother are known as?
A. Lightening
B. Engagement
C. Quickening
D. Ballottement

Q.259 A 13-year old girl came to the casualty with acute lower abdominal pain. She had cyclical pain for the last 6 months. She has not yet attained her menarche. On examination, a tense bulge was seen in the region of the hymen. The most probable diagnosis is?
A. Mayer-Rokitansky-Küster-Hauser syndrome
B. Imperforate hymen
C. Asherman's syndrome
D. Congenital adrenal hyperplasia

Q.260 Which one is the hazard of induction of labor with Pitocin?
A. Elevation in blood pressure
B. Infection
C. Rupture of uterus
D. Early rupture of membrane

Q.261 What is the commonest cause of Postpartum Hemorrhage?
A. Atonicity of uterus
B. Subinvolution
C. Birth Injury
D. Puerperal sepsis

Q.262 The absence of which of the following development milestones in a 12-week -old child indicates a grave prognosis(LQ):
A. Babbling (monosyllables)
B. Vocalization
C. Raise the head to 90% in prone posture
D. Hand-to-hand transfer to the object

Q.263 Pincer grasp develops by months:
A. 5-7
B. 9-12
C. 8-9
D. 12-24

Q.264 Which of the following cannot be done by a 3-year-old child
A. Draw a triangle
B. Draw a circle
C. Can arrange 9 cubes
D. Can go up and down

Q.265 A normally developing 10 months old child should be able to do all the following except:

A. Standalone
B. Play peak to boo
C. Pick up a pellet with thumb and index finger
D. Build a tower of 3-4 cubes

Q.266 A child is below the third percentile for height in growth velocity is normal, but chronological age is more the skeletal age. The most likely diagnosis is:

A. Constitutional delay in growth
B. Genetic short stature
C. Primordial dwarfism
D. Hypopituitarism

Q.267 Generally, a person with Down syndrome has an IQ of

A. 20-30
B. 40-50
C. 60-70
D. None of the above

Q.268 Peak growth velocity in an adolescent girl is seen just after

A. The appearance of pubic & axillary hair
B. Breast enlargement
C. Onset of menstruation
D. Enlargement of external genitalia

Q.269 A female child has recently learned to eat with a spoon without spilling, to dress and undress herself with supervision and to understand that she is a girl. These skills are the first mastered between the ages of-

A. 2 and 3 years
B. 3 and 4 years
C. 4 and 5 years
D. 5 and 6 years

Q.270 Which one of the following is the most common cause of congenital hydrocephalus?

A. Craniosynostosis
B. Intra uterine meningitis
C. Aqueductal stenosis
D. Malformations of the great vein of Galen

Q.271 The most common presentation of a child with Wilms tumor is:

A. An asymptomatic abdominal mass
B. Haematuria
C. Hypertension
D. Hemoptysis due to pulmonary secondary

Q.272 The most common laser used in laryngeal surgery is?

A. Argon laser
B. Nd YAG laser
C. CO_2 laser
D. KTP laser

Q.273 Hyperacusis in Bell's palsy is due to the paralysis of the following muscle:

A. Tensor tympani
B. Levator veli palatini
C. Tensor veli palatini
D. Stapedius

Q.274 A lady has bilateral hearing loss for 4 years which worsened during pregnancy. Type of impedance audiometry graph will be:

A. Ad
B. As
C. B
D. C

Q.275 Rhinolalia clausa is associated with all of the following except?

A. Allergic rhinitis
B. Palatal paralysis
C. Adenoids
D. Nasal polyps

Q.276 Structure not seen in bronchoscopy?

A. Vocal cords
B. Trachea
C. First segmental division of bronchi
D. Subcarinal lymph nodes

Q.277 The most common site of a leak in CSF rhinorrhoea is:

A. Sphenoid sinus
B. Frontal sinus
C. Cribriform plate
D. Tegmen tympani

Q.278 The most common and earliest manifestation of carcinoma of the glottis is:

A. Hoarseness
B. Haemoptysis
C. Cervical lymph nodes
D. Stridor

Q.279 A 5-year-old patient is scheduled for a tonsillectomy. On the day of surgery, he had a running nose, a temperature of 37.5°C, and a dry cough. Which of the following should be the most appropriate decision for surgery?

A. Surgery should be cancelled
B. Can proceed for surgery if chest is clear and there is no history of asthma
C. Should get Xray chest before proceeding for surgery
D. Cancel surgery for 3 weeks and patient to be put on antibiotics

Q.280 Which is the investigation of choice in assessing hearing loss in neonates?

A. Impedance audiometry
B. Brainstem Evoked Response Audiometry (BERA)
C. Free field audiometry
D. Behavioral audiometry

Q.281 Ophthalmoplegic migraine is best characterised as?

A. Recurrent headache with transient palsy of the ophthalmic nerve
B. Headache associated with irreversible palsy of 3rd nerve
C. Recurrent headache with transient palsy of 3, 4 and/or 6th cranial nerves
D. Headache with optic neuritis

Q.282 Which of the following is false regarding intraocular retinoblastoma?

A. 94% cases are sporadic
B. Individuals with sporadic retinoblastoma do not pass their genes to their children
C. Reese Ellsworth classification is used for predicting visual prognosis following radiotherapy
D. Tumour calcification can be detected by an ultrasound scan

Q.283 Bitemporal hemianopia is a characteristic feature of?

A. Glaucoma

B. Optic neuritis

C. Pituitary tumor

D. Retinitis pigmentosa

Q.284 The most common type of scleritis:

A. Non-necrotizing anterior scleritis

B. Necrotizing anterior scleritis

C. Posterior scleritis

D. None of these

Q.285 Arden index is used for interpretation of?

A. Visual evoked response

B. Electrooculogram

C. Electroretinogram

D. Visual field chartin

Q.286 All of the following are involved in endophthalmitis except?

A. Retina   **B.** Vitreous   **C.** Sclera   **D.** Uvea

Q.287 An 18-year-old boy comes to the eye casualty with a history of injury with a tennis ball. On examination, there is no perforation but there is hyphema. The most likely source of the blood is

A. Iris vessels

B. Circulus iridis major

C. Circulus iridis minor

D. Short posterior ciliary vessels

Q.288 In Von Hippel Lindau Syndrome, retinal vascular tumors are often associated with intracranial hemangioblastoma. Which one of the following regions is associated with such vascular abnormalities in this syndrome?

A. Optic radiation   **B.** Optic tract

C. Cerebellum   **D.** Pulvinar

Q.289 The most common cause of vitreous hemorrhage in adults is:

A. Retinal hole   **B.** Trauma

C. Hypertension   **D.** Diabetes

Q.290 Which drug can cause macular toxicity when given intravitreally?

A. Gentamicin   **B.** Vancomycin

C. Dexamethasone   **D.** Ceftazidime

Q.291 Which is the main source of estrogen and progesterone after the 3 months of pregnancy?

A. Hypothalamus   **B.** Pituitary gland

C. Placenta   **D.** Ovary

Q.292 The following drug is not helpful in the treatment of ectopic pregnancy:

A. Methotrexate   **B.** Misoprostol

C. Actinomycin-D   **D.** RU 486

Q.293 Which pituitary hormone is to stimulate the secretion of breast milk from the mammary gland?

A. Prolactin   **B.** Vasopressin

C. L.H.   **D.** H.C.G.

Q.294 In the Manning scoring system of biophysical profile for fetal monitoring, which parameter is not included

A. Fetal tone

B. Fetal gross body movements

C. Oxytocin challenge test

D. Non-stress test

Q.295 The pseudomyxoma peritonei occurs as a complication of the following ovarian tumor:

A. Serous cystadenoma

B. Mucinous cystadenoma

C. Dysgerminoma

D. Gonadoblastoma

Q.296 Which of the following is the least likely physiological change in pregnancy?

A. Increase in intravascular volume

B. Increase in cardiac output

C. Increase in stroke volume

D. Increase in peripheral vascular resistance

Q.297 Hypothyroidism in pregnancy is least likely to be associated with

A. Recurrent abortions   **B.** Polyhydramnios

C. PIH   **D.** Preterm labour

Q.298 Late hyperglycemia in pregnancy is associated with

A. Macrosomia

B. IUGR

C. Postmaturity

D. Congenital malformation

Q.299 Endolymph is present in?

A. Bony labyrinth   **B.** Scala media

C. Scala vestibule   **D.** Scala tympani

Q.300 What is the name of the first secretion from the mother's breast following delivery?

A. Sequestrum   **B.** Colostrum

C. Lochia   **D.** Leucorrhoea

// Smart Answer Sheet //

Correct Indicates percentage of students who answered questions correctly.

Skipped Indicates percentage of students who skipped questions.

Q.	Ans.	Correct / Skipped	Q.	Ans.	Correct / Skipped	Q.	Ans.	Correct / Skipped	Q.	Ans.	Correct / Skipped	Q.	Ans.	Correct / Skipped
1	A	51.16 % / 16.28 %	17	D	13.02 % / 27.91 %	33	B	33.95 % / 20.0 %	49	C	13.95 % / 27.91 %	65	B	10.7 % / 59.53 %
2	B	36.74 % / 29.31 %	18	D	33.49 % / 29.3 %	34	A	32.09 % / 29.31 %	50	A	31.16 % / 29.77 %	66	A	7.44 % / 53.49 %
3	C	46.05 % / 26.97 %	19	C	19.53 % / 16.75 %	35	A	33.95 % / 24.65 %	51	A	6.05 % / 56.74 %	67	B	13.95 % / 54.89 %
4	A	21.86 % / 29.77 %	20	D	19.53 % / 24.19 %	36	B	24.65 % / 28.37 %	52	C	13.95 % / 53.03 %	68	C	17.67 % / 61.4 %
5	A	18.6 % / 21.4 %	21	B	18.14 % / 21.86 %	37	C	34.42 % / 27.44 %	53	C	22.33 % / 59.07 %	69	D	10.23 % / 59.07 %
6	A	19.53 % / 28.84 %	22	B	21.4 % / 29.3 %	38	C	26.51 % / 28.84 %	54	A	19.53 % / 55.82 %	70	D	11.63 % / 40.93 %
7	D	21.86 % / 26.51 %	23	B	24.19 % / 17.21 %	39	A	16.28 % / 29.77 %	55	D	9.3 % / 61.86 %	71	C	14.42 % / 54.42 %
8	A	21.4 % / 28.83 %	24	B	28.84 % / 30.23 %	40	A	24.19 % / 28.83 %	56	B	15.35 % / 51.63 %	72	D	7.91 % / 54.42 %
9	B	19.53 % / 27.45 %	25	D	18.14 % / 24.65 %	41	A	26.98 % / 20.93 %	57	A	15.35 % / 58.6 %	73	C	10.7 % / 59.07 %
10	B	27.91 % / 29.3 %	26	D	33.49 % / 29.77 %	42	B	32.09 % / 29.31 %	58	D	4.19 % / 56.28 %	74	C	16.74 % / 46.05 %
11	B	17.21 % / 26.05 %	27	D	54.88 % / 19.54 %	43	D	19.53 % / 27.45 %	59	A	11.16 % / 58.61 %	75	D	7.44 % / 60.47 %
12	C	40.0 % / 28.84 %	28	D	26.98 % / 29.3 %	44	D	19.53 % / 28.84 %	60	D	8.84 % / 60.46 %	76	D	12.09 % / 58.61 %
13	A	20.93 % / 20.0 %	29	C	30.23 % / 24.65 %	45	C	15.81 % / 24.66 %	61	D	9.77 % / 59.07 %	77	D	8.84 % / 60.93 %
14	D	26.98 % / 29.76 %	30	B	30.23 % / 28.84 %	46	A	14.88 % / 29.31 %	62	C	19.07 % / 57.21 %	78	D	12.09 % / 53.03 %
15	A	12.56 % / 23.72 %	31	B	22.79 % / 28.84 %	47	B	30.7 % / 27.44 %	63	D	6.05 % / 58.6 %	79	A	5.58 % / 61.86 %
16	B	20.93 % / 27.44 %	32	A	25.58 % / 25.12 %	48	C	29.3 % / 28.37 %	64	A	11.16 % / 52.56 %	80	A	12.09 % / 56.75 %

Q.	Ans.	Correct / Skipped
81	A	6.05 % / 58.6 %
82	B	13.95 % / 56.75 %
83	D	8.37 % / 55.82 %
84	D	12.56 % / 52.56 %
85	C	6.51 % / 60.0 %
86	C	13.02 % / 53.96 %
87	D	6.51 % / 55.82 %
88	D	9.3 % / 60.47 %
89	A	9.77 % / 59.07 %
90	C	12.56 % / 62.79 %
91	A	5.12 % / 60.46 %
92	C	13.02 % / 53.49 %
93	D	7.91 % / 60.0 %
94	D	11.63 % / 55.81 %
95	C	4.65 % / 61.4 %
96	D	19.53 % / 55.82 %

Q.	Ans.	Correct / Skipped
97	B	15.81 % / 60.93 %
98	D	12.09 % / 56.28 %
99	D	14.42 % / 60.93 %
100	D	5.12 % / 60.0 %
101	D	19.07 % / 59.07 %
102	B	14.42 % / 54.42 %
103	A	4.65 % / 54.42 %
104	A	5.58 % / 60.47 %
105	A	6.51 % / 59.54 %
106	C	11.16 % / 55.82 %
107	D	6.51 % / 62.33 %
108	D	3.72 % / 59.54 %
109	A	5.58 % / 58.61 %
110	A	15.81 % / 55.82 %
111	A	13.95 % / 56.28 %
112	C	10.7 % / 58.6 %

Q.	Ans.	Correct / Skipped
113	A	18.6 % / 58.61 %
114	A	16.28 % / 54.42 %
115	A	12.09 % / 59.54 %
116	D	7.91 % / 61.86 %
117	A	15.81 % / 58.61 %
118	A	12.56 % / 60.93 %
119	A	13.49 % / 61.39 %
120	D	9.3 % / 60.0 %
121	C	9.3 % / 61.4 %
122	D	15.81 % / 48.38 %
123	A	16.28 % / 54.88 %
124	A	13.49 % / 63.72 %
125	C	17.67 % / 60.0 %
126	C	11.63 % / 57.67 %
127	C	6.98 % / 61.39 %
128	D	24.19 % / 59.53 %

Q.	Ans.	Correct / Skipped
129	A	12.09 % / 51.63 %
130	C	9.3 % / 57.21 %
131	A	6.05 % / 53.48 %
132	A	10.7 % / 59.53 %
133	A	14.88 % / 60.0 %
134	C	26.51 % / 58.14 %
135	A	3.72 % / 61.86 %
136	A	8.37 % / 59.54 %
137	D	5.12 % / 61.86 %
138	D	10.7 % / 60.46 %
139	C	21.4 % / 60.93 %
140	B	21.86 % / 60.93 %
141	B	16.74 % / 60.47 %
142	C	6.51 % / 60.0 %
143	B	16.74 % / 55.35 %
144	D	10.7 % / 61.39 %

Q.	Ans.	Correct / Skipped
145	A	7.44 % / 57.21 %
146	C	16.28 % / 58.6 %
147	A	3.26 % / 62.32 %
148	B	12.56 % / 59.53 %
149	A	25.12 % / 55.81 %
150	B	15.35 % / 56.28 %
151	C	18.14 % / 62.33 %
152	A	2.79 % / 66.51 %
153	B	8.84 % / 67.44 %
154	A	6.98 % / 68.37 %
155	A	3.26 % / 60.46 %
156	B	8.84 % / 66.51 %
157	C	7.44 % / 65.58 %
158	A	6.05 % / 66.04 %
159	A	9.3 % / 66.05 %
160	A	12.56 % / 66.51 %

Q.	Ans.	Correct	Skipped
161	D	9.77 %	65.11 %
162	A	11.16 %	65.58 %
163	A	17.67 %	62.8 %
164	C	7.91 %	66.51 %
165	A	13.02 %	62.33 %
166	B	9.3 %	65.58 %
167	C	6.51 %	66.98 %
168	C	4.65 %	66.98 %
169	B	13.95 %	57.68 %
170	D	7.44 %	64.19 %
171	C	12.09 %	63.72 %
172	C	10.23 %	66.51 %
173	D	4.19 %	60.46 %
174	B	6.51 %	66.51 %
175	A	6.05 %	65.11 %
176	B	8.37 %	66.98 %

Q.	Ans.	Correct	Skipped
177	A	13.49 %	62.79 %
178	A	10.23 %	68.37 %
179	A	7.91 %	64.65 %
180	A	5.58 %	66.51 %
181	D	3.72 %	66.51 %
182	A	11.63 %	65.58 %
183	D	9.3 %	61.86 %
184	A	4.65 %	66.98 %
185	D	4.19 %	62.79 %
186	B	7.44 %	65.12 %
187	B	6.51 %	65.58 %
188	C	11.63 %	66.51 %
189	D	9.3 %	67.91 %
190	B	14.88 %	66.05 %
191	C	11.63 %	63.25 %
192	B	5.12 %	66.97 %

Q.	Ans.	Correct	Skipped
193	C	5.58 %	66.05 %
194	A	9.3 %	67.91 %
195	C	4.65 %	65.12 %
196	C	14.88 %	66.98 %
197	C	14.42 %	66.98 %
198	A	6.05 %	67.44 %
199	D	5.12 %	66.51 %
200	D	7.91 %	66.04 %
201	C	9.77 %	66.97 %
202	B	6.51 %	63.72 %
203	A	10.7 %	65.11 %
204	B	4.65 %	66.51 %
205	C	10.23 %	66.05 %
206	C	6.98 %	66.97 %
207	C	15.81 %	66.52 %
208	A	8.37 %	66.05 %

Q.	Ans.	Correct	Skipped
209	C	10.23 %	64.65 %
210	D	6.98 %	66.04 %
211	B	7.91 %	66.51 %
212	C	9.3 %	66.51 %
213	C	9.77 %	63.72 %
214	A	4.65 %	66.05 %
215	D	6.51 %	67.91 %
216	D	3.72 %	66.51 %
217	B	6.98 %	66.97 %
218	B	12.09 %	66.98 %
219	C	6.98 %	67.44 %
220	B	14.42 %	67.91 %
221	D	8.84 %	60.46 %
222	C	6.05 %	64.18 %
223	A	8.84 %	68.37 %
224	B	5.58 %	66.98 %

Q.	Ans.	Correct	Skipped
225	A	5.12 %	64.65 %
226	A	16.28 %	66.05 %
227	A	7.44 %	67.44 %
228	C	7.91 %	66.97 %
229	B	14.42 %	63.25 %
230	D	10.23 %	67.44 %
231	C	8.84 %	63.25 %
232	D	5.12 %	66.51 %
233	B	3.72 %	67.44 %
234	B	9.77 %	66.04 %
235	D	8.37 %	67.44 %
236	D	6.51 %	66.51 %
237	B	9.77 %	67.9 %
238	A	3.72 %	66.51 %
239	B	11.63 %	66.51 %
240	D	16.74 %	67.45 %

Q.	Ans.	Correct / Skipped	Q.	Ans.	Correct / Skipped	Q.	Ans.	Correct / Skipped	Q.	Ans.	Correct / Skipped	Q.	Ans.	Correct / Skipped
241	B	6.98 % / 66.51 %	253	A	19.53 % / 67.91 %	265	D	10.7 % / 65.58 %	277	C	19.53 % / 63.26 %	289	D	4.65 % / 66.05 %
242	A	9.3 % / 66.05 %	254	A	10.23 % / 65.58 %	266	A	11.16 % / 66.05 %	278	A	13.49 % / 67.91 %	290	A	5.12 % / 66.51 %
243	A	8.37 % / 64.65 %	255	C	21.4 % / 66.51 %	267	B	11.63 % / 62.32 %	279	D	11.63 % / 64.18 %	291	C	17.21 % / 64.65 %
244	A	5.58 % / 68.37 %	256	D	15.81 % / 67.45 %	268	A	10.23 % / 66.98 %	280	B	18.6 % / 66.52 %	292	B	9.3 % / 67.44 %
245	B	11.16 % / 66.98 %	257	D	6.51 % / 66.05 %	269	A	8.37 % / 62.33 %	281	C	12.56 % / 62.32 %	293	A	17.67 % / 66.52 %
246	D	11.63 % / 66.51 %	258	C	18.6 % / 67.45 %	270	C	7.91 % / 66.04 %	282	B	5.12 % / 65.11 %	294	C	13.95 % / 66.98 %
247	A	9.77 % / 66.97 %	259	B	18.6 % / 63.26 %	271	A	13.95 % / 63.26 %	283	C	12.09 % / 68.38 %	295	B	13.95 % / 61.86 %
248	B	9.3 % / 66.98 %	260	C	10.23 % / 66.51 %	272	C	5.12 % / 67.9 %	284	A	5.58 % / 67.91 %	296	D	9.3 % / 66.51 %
249	A	12.09 % / 65.58 %	261	A	20.0 % / 63.26 %	273	D	6.51 % / 66.51 %	285	B	9.3 % / 62.79 %	297	B	6.98 % / 66.51 %
250	A	9.3 % / 66.05 %	262	B	6.05 % / 66.51 %	274	B	12.09 % / 66.51 %	286	C	12.09 % / 67.44 %	298	A	14.88 % / 66.05 %
251	D	1.86 % / 66.51 %	263	B	11.16 % / 61.4 %	275	B	12.09 % / 66.98 %	287	B	7.91 % / 62.32 %	299	B	9.77 % / 64.65 %
252	A	8.37 % / 67.44 %	264	A	5.12 % / 67.44 %	276	D	13.95 % / 66.52 %	288	C	3.26 % / 67.9 %	300	B	18.6 % / 67.91 %

Performance Analysis

Avg. Score (%)	8.5%
Toppers Score (%)	68.33%
Your Score	

Mock Test 02

PART A

Q.1 Deficiency of lysyl hydroxylase causes?

A. Alport syndrome

B. Menkes disease

C. Epidermolysis bullosa

D. Osteogenesis imperfecta

Q.2 The enzyme used for the mapping of hypersensitive sites in recombinant DNA research is?

A. DNA ligase

B. DNA polymerase

C. DNase I

D. Polynucleotide kinase

Q.3 Deficiency of argininosuccinate synthase causes?

A. Hyperargininemia

B. Hyperammonemia type II

C. Argininosuccinicaciduria

D. Citrullinemia

Q.4 All are disorders due to peroxisomal abnormalities except?

A. Pfeiffer syndrome

B. Zellweger syndrome

C. Hyperoxaluria type 1

D. Acatalasemia

Q.5 Rothera's test is utilized for detection of?

A. Glucose   **B.** Proteins

C. Urea   **D.** Ketone bodies

Q.6 Sphingomyelinase deficiency is characteristic of?

A. Fabry disease

B. Krabbe's disease

C. Tay Sachs disease

D. Niemann Pick disease

Q.7 Nonenzymatic glycosylation or glycation creates glycoproteins by:

A. Chemical addition of sugars to polypeptides

B. Extracellular synthesis

C. Attaching 20 amino acids

D. Secretion into the extracellular matrix

Q.8 All are inhibitors of oxidative phosphorylation except?

A. Carboxin   **B.** Oligomycin

C. Valinomycin   **D.** Atractyloside

Q.9 Proteins targeted for destruction in eukaryotes are covalently linked to :

A. Clathrin   **B.** Pepsin

C. Laminin   **D.** Ubiquitin

Q.10 Process used in an expression vector to increase yield of recombinant protein synthesis ?

A. Translation initiation

B. Promoter induction

C. Transcription terminators

D. Multiple cloning sites

Q.11 The structural proteins are involved in maintaining the shape of a cell or in the formation of matrices in the body. The shape of these proteins is:

A. Globular   **B.** Fibrous

C. Stretch of beads   **D.** Planar

Q.12 Which of the following amino acids has to be supplemented in the diet?

A. phenylalanine   **B.** cysteine

C. glutamine   **D.** asparagine

Q.13 In which of the following conditions the level of creatinine kinase 1 increase?

A. Myocardial ischemia

B. Brain Ischemia

C. Kidney damage

D. Electrical cardioversion

Q.14 Which of the following substances acts to increase the release of Ca2+ from endoplasmic reticulum?

A. Inositol triphosphate

B. Parathyroid hormone

C. 1,25 dihydroxy cholecalciferol

D. Diacylglycerol

Q.15 The transmembrane region of protein is likely to have:

A. A stretch of hydrophilic amino acids

B. A stretch of hydrophobic amino acids

C. A disulphide loop

D. Alternating hydrophilic and hydrophobic amino acids

Q.16 Shine Dalgarno sequence in bacterial mRNA is near:

A. AUG codon   **B.** UAA codon

C. UAG codon   **D.** UGA codon

Q.17 Claw hand occurs due to paralysis of:

A. Adductor paralysis

B. Flexor digitorum profundus

C. Extensor Digitorium Longus

D. Extensor Digitorum Communis

Q.18 The posterior interosseous nerve is a continuation of:

A. Anterior interosseous nerve

B. Median nerve

C. Radial nerve

D. Ulnar nerve

Q.19 The powerful supinator of the semi – flexed elbow:

A. Brachialis   **B.** Brachioradialis

C. Supinator   **D.** Biceps brachii

Q.20 Which of the following is an example of hyaline cartilage:

A. epiglottis

B. tip of nose

C. the apex of arytenoid cartilage

D. pinna

Q.21 Single unit smooth muscles are seen in:

A. Iris

B. Ductus deferens

C. Ureter

D. Trachea

Q.22 Hairpin bends of end arteries are present in abundance in which part of the long bone?

A. epiphysis

B. metaphysis

C. diaphysis

D. all the above

Q.23 The characteristic feature of compact bone:

A. Volkmann canal

B. Haversian system

C. lamellar arrangement

D. trabeculae

Q.24 Deepest layer of scalp is:

A. Connective tissue

B. Aponeurosis (Epicranial Aponeurosis)

C. Loose areolar tissue (Danger area of scalp)

D. None of these

Q.25 Which of the following movements will not be affected by involvement of the L5 Nerve root?

A. Thigh adduction

B. Knee Flexion

C. Knee Extension

D. Toe Extension

Q.26 The Couinaud's segmental nomenclature is based on the position of the

A. Hepatic veins and portal vein

B. Hepatic veins and biliary ducts

C. Portal vein and biliary ducts

D. Portal vein and hepatic artery

Q.27 The first costo-chondral joint is a :

A. Fibrous joint

B. Synovial joint

C. Syndesmosis

D. Synchondrosis

Q.28 After radical mastectomy there was injury to the long thoracic nerve. The integrity of the nerve can be tested at the bedside by asking the patient to :

A. Shrug the shoulders

B. Raise the arm above the head on the affected side

C. Touch the opposite shoulder

D. Lift a heavy object from the ground

Q.29 An inhaled foreign body is likely to lodge in the right lung due to all of the following features except:

A. Right lung is shorter and wider than left lung

B. Right principal bronchus is more vertical than the left bronchus

C. Tracheal bifurcation directs the foreign body to the right lung

D. Right inferior lobar bronchus is in continuation with the principal bronchus

Q.30 The following statements concerning chorda tympani nerve are true except that it:

A. Carries secretomotor fibers to submandibular gland

B. Joins lingual nerve in infratemporal fossa

C. Is a branch of facial nerve

D. Contains postganglionic parasympathetic fibers

Q.31 The superior oblique muscle is supplied by:

A. 3rd cranial nerve

B. 4th cranial nerve

C. 5th cranial nerve

D. 6th cranial nerve

Q.32 Benign Prostatic hypertrophy results in obstruction of the urinary tract. The specific condition is associated with enlargement of the:

A. Entire prostate gland

B. Lateral lobes

C. Median lobe

D. Posterior lobes

Q.33 While doing thoracocentesis, it is advisable to introduce needle along:

A. Upper border of the rib

B. Lower border of the rib

C. In the center of the intercostal space

D. In the anterior part of the intercostal space

Q.34 Cause of death in cyanide poisoning is:

A. Anoxic anoxia

B. Anemia anoxia

C. Histotoxic anoxia

D. Stagnant anoxia

Q.35 The volume of air taken into the lungs in normal respiration is known as:

A. Vital capacity

B. Timed vital capacity

C. Tidal volume

D. Inspiratory reserve volume

Q.36 Retinal isomerase catalyses the conversion of?

A. 11-cis retinal to rhodopsin

B. All trans retinal to 11-cis retinal

C. Lumirhodopsin to metarhodopsin

D. Bathorhodopsin to lumirhodopsin

Q.37 Which is a true statement regarding inhibin?

A. Increases the secretion of GnRH.

B. Molecular weight is between 5000 and 10,000.

C. It is secreted by hypothalamus.

D. It is a glycoprotein.

Q.38 Juxtamedullary nephrons:

A. Have smaller sized glomeruli

B. Possess short loops of Henle

C. Have slow rate of filtration

D. Both descending and ascending limbs of loop of Henle contain thin segments.

Q.39 Regarding somatomedin, which is true?

A. Reduced glucose oxidation in fat

B. Increases chondrogenesis

C. Activity is increased in protein deficiency

D. Activity is increased by glucocorticoids

Q.40 Action of calcitonin is?

A. Increases bone resorption

B. Increases calcium and phosphate absorption from GIT

C. Increases renal formation of 1-25 DHCC

D. Increases renal excretion of calcium and phosphate

Q.41 Through which of the following activities does an organism maintain homeostasis by Regulation processes?

A. Sweating and shivering

B. Formation of thick-walled spores to survive unfavorable conditions

C. Changing body temperature with ambient nature

D. Temporarily moving away from stressful habitat

Q.42 The function of axonemal dynein is?

A. Moves particles to the 'minus' end of microtubule.

B. Binds to actin and produce motion by bending their neck region.

C. Responsible for the beating of flagella and cilia.

D. Moves particles towards 'plus' end of microtubule.

Q.43 Which among the following is the primary action of nitric oxide in the GIT?

A. Contraction of gastrointestinal smooth muscle

B. Relaxation of gastrointestinal smooth muscle

C. Vasodilation

D. Vasoconstriction

Q.44 Pulmonary compliance is not decreased in?

A. COPD

B. Decreased surfactant production

C. Pulmonary congestion

D. Pulmonary fibrosis

Q.45 A newly posted junior doctor had difficulty in finding out base deficit/excess for blood in a given patient. An experienced senior resident advised a quick method to determine acid base composition of blood based onPCO2. Which of the following is the likely method he suggested to predict acidbase composition of blood?

A. Red ford nonuogram

B. DuBio's normogram

C. Goldman constant Field equation

D. Siggard Andersen normogram

Q.46 During the cardiac cycle the opening of the aortic valve takes place at the:

A. Beginning of systole

B. End of isovolumetric contraction

C. End of diastole

D. End of diastasis

Q.47 Patients having acute cardiac failure do not show pedal oedema, because :

A. The plasma oncotic pressure is high

B. There is renal compensation

C. There is an increase in cardiac output

D. There is a fall in the systemic capillary hydrostatic pressure

Q.48 During acclimatization to high altitude all of the following take place except:

A. Increase in minute ventilation

B. Increase in the sensitivity of central chemoreceptors

C. Increase in the sensitivity of carotid body to hypoxia

D. Shift in the oxygen dissociation curve to the left

Q.49 Neuronal degeneration is seen in all of the following except:

A. Crush nerve injury

B. Fetal development

C. Senescence

D. Neuropraxia

Q.50 The fibers from the contralateral nasal hemiretina project to the following layers of the lateral geniculate nucleus:

A. Layers 2, 3 & 5

B. Layers 1, 2 & 6

C. Layers 1, 4 & 6

D. Layers 4, 5 & 6

PART C

Q.51 Which of the following is false regarding neoplastic compressive myelopathy?

A. Most neoplasms are subdural in origin

B. Thoracic spine is most commonly involved

C. Tumor does not cross the disk space to involve adjacent vertebral body

D. Prognosis is poor when motor deficits are established for > 48 hours

Q.52 Identify the wrong statement regarding Bell's palsy:

A. It is the most common form of facial paralysis

B. Paralysis is usually preceded by pain behind the ear

C. MRI reveals swelling and enhancement of gasserian ganglion

D. Presence of incomplete paralysis in first week is the most favourable prognostic sign

Q.53 Which nutritional deficiency is associated with hereditary ataxia?

A. Vitamin B12

B. Vitamin B1

C. Vitamin E

D. Vitamin C

Q.54 Kayser Fleischer Ring is seen in what proportion of Wilson's disease patients with neurologic features?

A. 10% **B.** 50% **C.** 80% **D.** 100%

Q.55 Which of the following is not a feature of right heart failure?

A. Jugular venous distension

B. Hepatomegaly

C. Basal crepitations

D. Ascites

Q.56 Riociguat is used in the treatment of:

A. Gouty arthritis

B. Rheumatoid arthritis

C. Chronic thromboembolic pulmonary hypertension

D. Obesity

Q.57 Which of the following is not a component of Syndrome Z?

A. Obstructive sleep apnoea

B. Blood pressure more than 130/85 mm Hg

C. Fasting triglyceride more than 150mg/dl

D. LDL more than 100mg/dl

Q.58 Most common cause of lobar hemorrhage in elderly age group ?

A. Hypertension

B. Vascular malformation

C. Coagulopathy

D. Amyloid angiopathy

Q.59 Which is the most common preceding infection in bone marrow failure syndromes?

A. Parvo B19

B. EBV

C. HIV

D. Hepatitis

Q.60 Which among the following statements is wrong :

A. Light chains are synthesised in slight excess normally in plasma cells

B. Qualitative assessment of M component can be done by electrophoresis

C. M components are detected in chronic myeloid leukaemia

D. In 20% myelomas, only light chains are produced

Q.61 Most specific symptom of temporal arteritis?

A. Visual loss

B. Jaw claudication

C. Temporal headache

D. Polymyalgia rheumatica

Q.62 The artery that is spared in polyarteritis nodosa?

A. Bronchial artery

B. Renal artery

C. Coronary artery

D. Pulmonary artery

Q.63 Generalised painless lymphadenopathy is seen in?

A. Rocky mountain spotted fever

B. Scrub typhus

C. Epidemic typhus

D. Q fever

Q.64 Bacillary angiomatosis is caused by?

A. Bartonella bacilliformis

B. Bartonella rochalimae

C. Rickettsia japonica

D. Bartonella henselae

Q.65 Lipoatrophy can occur in patients treated with?

A. Abacavir

B. Tenofovir

C. Stavudine

D. Maraviroc

Q.66 Severe muscle weakness is seen in?

A. Cori disease

B. Andersen disease

C. McArdle disease

D. Tarui disease

Q.67 Protein losing enteropathy with mucosal erosion is seen in?

A. Lymphoma

B. Coeliac disease

C. Menetrier's disease

D. Systemic lupus erythematosus

Q.68 All are true regarding hepatitis C infection except?

A. Serum transaminase level is a good predictor of the level of liver fibrosis

B. Telaprevir is effective in management

C. 3% risk of vertical transmission

D. Sharing toothbrushes is a risk factor for transmission

Q.69 Sausage digit is seen in?

A. Rheumatoid arthritis

B. Juvenile idiopathic arthritis

C. Enteropathic arthritis

D. Psoriatic arthritis

Q.70 Ehrlichiosis is a common coinfection with?

A. Lyme disease

B. Louse borne relapsing fever

C. Tick borne relapsing fever

D. Leptospirosis

Q.71 Which of the following is seen in Churg-Strauss syndrome?

A. Sinusitis

B. Raynaud's phenomenon

C. Allergic rhinitis

D. Epistaxis

Q.72 All are true regarding Scheuermann's osteochondritis except?

A. Dorsal kyphosis

B. Autosomal recessive inheritance

C. Predominantly affects adolescent boys

D. Irregular ossification of vertebral endplates

Q.73 Which of the following substances produced by osteoclasts is responsible for digestion of minerals during bone resorption?

A. Hydrochloric acid

B. Acetic acid

C. Cathepsin K

D. Sclerostin

Q.74 Collagen fibrils in bone are crosslinked with?

A. Osteopontin

B. Laminin

C. Fibrillin

D. Pyridinium

Q.75 Most abundant protein of bone is?

A. Laminin

B. Osteocalcin

C. Type 1 collagen

D. Type 2 collagen

Q.76 Which of the following increases bone resorption?

A. Osteoprotegerin (OPG)

B. Oestrogen / testosterone

C. Mechanical loading

D. Interleukin 1

Q.77 Which of the following decreases bone resorption?

A. Receptor activator of nuclear factor kappa B ligand (RANKL)

B. Interleukin 1

C. Osteoprotegerin

D. Tumour necrosis factor

Q.78 Sclerostin is produced by?

A. Osteocytes   **B.** Osteoblasts
C. Osteoclasts   **D.** Chondrocytes

Q.79 Most common form of arthritis is?

A. Rheumatoid arthritis
B. Psoriatic arthritis
C. Seronegative arthritis
D. Osteoarthritis

Q.80 Which of the following has a male female ratio of 1:1?

A. Rheumatoid arthritis
B. Gout
C. Seronegative spondyloarthritis
D. Polymyalgia rheumatica

Q.81 Triad of skin lesions, asymmetric mononeuritis multiplex and eosinophilia are seen in?

A. Cryoglobulinemic vasculitis
B. Polyarteritis nodosa
C. Churg Strauss Syndrome
D. Giant cell arteritis

Q.82 Which of the following genetic mutation has been described in aortic stenosis?

A. KCNH2   **B.** KCNQ1
C. NOTCH1   **D.** SCN5A

Q.83 Which of the following is not a feature of complete heart block onthe ECG:

A. Constant RR interval
B. Constant PP interval
C. Constant PR interval
D. PP interval shorter than RR interval

Q.84 Mitral annular area in systole:

A. Decreases by 10%   **B.** Decreases by 25%
C. Increases by 10%   **D.** Increases by 25%

Q.85 Dominant right coronary artery means?

A. Right coronary artery supplies major portion of the myocardium
B. Right coronary artery crosses the crux and gives rise to posterior left ventricular branches
C. Right coronary artery supplies major portion of the left ventricle
D. None of the above

Q.86 Sokolow-Lyon electrocardiographic criteria is for the diagnosis of:

A. Left atrial enlargement
B. Left ventricular hypertrophy
C. Right atrial enlargement
D. Right ventricular hypertrophy

Q.87 Prominent upper lobe vessels in X-ray chest in mitral stenosis indicate:

A. Antler sign

B. Pulmonary venous hypertension
C. Cephalization
D. All of the above

Q.88 Which of the following is not an ideal indication for bioprosthetic valve (compared to mechanical prosthetic valve)?

A. Female planning pregnancy
B. Young adult male
C. Elderly female
D. History of endocarditis

Q.89 Most commonly used route for emergency pericardiocentesis in cardiac tamponade is:

A. Left parasternal   **B.** Right parasternal
C. Apical   **D.** Subxiphoid

Q.90 Which of the following is not an Acute aortic syndrome?

A. Acute aortic dissection
B. Acute occlusion of aortic bifurcation
C. Intramural hematoma of aorta
D. Perforating ulcer of aorta

Q.91 A 60 year old man presented to the OPD with symptoms suggestive of acute pancreatitis. He consumes high quantities of alcohol regularly. His symptoms started 4 days ago. But he continued to consume alcohol. He was admitted for further evaluation. Presently, he has severe vomiting. He also complains of dizziness when standing. Examination revealed tenderness in the epigastrium and right hypochondrium. A reddish discolouration is noted in the flanks. Which of the following statements regarding the patient is most accurate?

A. The patient should be evaluated for concomitant appendicitis
B. USG is likely to demonstrate pseudocyst of pancreas
C. Contrast CT scan of the abdomen will reveal severe necrotising pancreatitis
D. Pancreatic calcification will be seen in X-ray abdomen

Q.92 A 30 year old woman presented to the OPD with proximal muscle weakness, ptosis and easy fatigability. Which of following is the most sensitive test to arrive at a diagnosis?

A. Single fiber electromyography
B. Muscle biopsy
C. Measurement of creatinine phosphokinase levels
D. Edrophonium test

Q.93 Symmetric, high voltage, triphasic, slow wave EEG pattern is seen in?

A. Uremic encephalopathy
B. Hypoxic ischemic encephalopathy
C. Hypercapnic encephalopathy
D. Hepatic encephalopathy

Q.94 Use of streptokinase is contraindicated in?

A. Pulmonary embolism
B. AV fistula
C. Thrombophlebitis
D. Intracranial tumour

Q.95 Kayser Fleischer ring is characteristic of ?

A. Pterygium
B. Scleritis
C. Hemochromatosis
D. Wilson's disease

Q.96 Androphonia can be corrected by doing:
A. Type I Thryoplasty
B. Type 2 Thryoplasty
C. Type 3 Thryoplasty
D. Type 4 Thryoplasty

Q.97 Use of seigel's speculum during examination of the ear provides all except:
A. Magnification
B. Assessment of movement of the tympanic membrane
C. Removal of foreign body from the ear
D. As applicator for the powdered antibiotic of ear

Q.98 Sensorineural deafness may be feature of all, except:
A. Nail patella syndrome
B. Distal renal tubular acidosis
C. Bartter syndrome
D. Alport syndrome

Q.99 Which of the following conditions causes the maximum hearing loss?
A. Ossicular disruption with intact tympanic membrane
B. Disruption of malleus and incus as well tympanic membrane
C. Partial fixation of the stapes footplate
D. Ottitis media with effusion

Q.100 A 30 year old male is having Attic cholesteatoma of left ear with lateral sinus thrombophlebitis. Which of the following will be the operation of choice?
A. Intact canal wall mastoidectomy
B. Simple mastoidectomy with Tympanoplasty
C. Canal wall down mastoidectomy
D. Mastoidectomy with cavity obliteration

Q.101 Which of the following is not a typical feature of malignant otitis externa?
A. Caused by Pseudomonas aeruginosa
B. Patients are usually old
C. Mitotic figures are high
D. Patient is immune compromised

Q.102 Which of the following is not a typical feature of Ménière's disease?
A. Sensorineural deafness
B. Pulsatile tinnitus
C. Vertigo
D. Fluctuating deafness

Q.103 Which of the following is the most common etiological agent in paranasal sinus mycoses?
A. Aspergillus spp
B. Histoplasma
C. Conidiobolus coronatus
D. Candida albicans

Q.104 Treatment of choice for glue ear is
A. Myringotomy with cold knife
B. Myringotomy with diode laser
C. Myringotomy with ventilation tube insertion
D. Conservative treatment with analgesics & antibiotics

Q.105 Rhinophyma is associated with:
A. Hypertrophy of the sebaceous glands
B. Hypertrophy of sweat glands
C. Hypertrophy of endothelial cells
D. Hypertrophy of epithelial cells

Q.106 Drug of choice in eclampsia:
A. Oral magnesium sulphate
B. Intravenous magnesium sulphate
C. Oral phenytoin sodium
D. Intravenous phenytoin sodium

Q.107 Patients of Rectovaginal fistula should be initially treated with:
A. Colostomy
B. Primary repair
C. Colporrhaphy
D. Anterior resection

Q.108 Drug of choice for treatment of intrahepatic cholestasis in pregnancy is?
A. Ursodeoxycholic acid
B. Dexamethasone
C. Antihistamines
D. Cholestyramine

Q.109 The most common side effect of IUCD insertion is:
A. Bleeding
B. Pain
C. Pelvic infection
D. Ectopic pregnancy

Q.110 In a case of Dysgerminoma of ovary one of the following tumor markers is likely to be raised.
A. Serum HCG
B. Serum alphafetoprotein
C. Serum lactate dehydrogenase
D. Serum inhibin

Q.111 The most common pure germ cell tumor of the ovary is:
A. Choriocarcinoma
B. Dysgerminoma
C. Embryonal cell tumor
D. Malignant Teratoma

Q.112 The most common cause of secondary amenorrhoea in India is:
A. Endometrial tuberculosis
B. Premature ovarian failure
C. Polycystic ovarian syndrome
D. Sheehan's syndrome

Q.113 All of the following appear to decrease hot flushes in menopausal women except:
A. Androgens
B. Raloxifene
C. Isoflavones
D. Tibolone

Q.114 Aspermia is the term used to describe:
A. Absence of semen
B. Absence of sperm in ejaculate
C. Absence of sperm motility

D. Occurrence of abnormal sperm

Q.115 Which one of the following is the ideal contraceptive for a patient with heart disease:

A. IUCD

B. Depo-Provera

C. Diaphragm

D. Oral contraceptive pills

Q.116 Use of one of the following vaccination is absolutely contraindicated in pregnancy:

A. Hepatitis B

B. Cholera

C. Rabies

D. Yellow fever

Q.117 Which of the following statements is incorrect in relation to pregnant women with epilepsy?

A. The rate of congenital malformation is increased in the offspring of women with epilepsy

B. Seizure frequency increases in approximately 70% of women

C. Breast feeding is safe with most anticonvulsants

D. Folic acid supplementation may reduce the risk of neural tube defect

Q.118 Infants of diabetic mother are likely to have the following cardiac anomaly:

A. Coarctation of aorta

B. Fallot's tetrology

C. Ebstein's anomaly

D. Transposition of great arteries

Q.119 All are the risk factors associated with macrosomia except:

A. Maternal obesity

B. Prolonged Pregnancy

C. Previous large infant

D. Short Stature

Q.120 All are the causes of intrauterine growth retardation except:

A. Anemia

B. Pregnancy induced hypertension

C. Maternal heart disease

D. Gestational diabetes

Q.121 The smallest diameter of the true pelvis is:

A. Interspinous diameter

B. Diagonal conjugate

C. True conjugate

D. Intertuberous diameter

Q.122 Which one of the following biochemical parameters is the most sensitive to detect open spina bifida?

A. Maternal serum alpha fetoprotein

B. Amniotic fluid alpha fetoprotein

C. Amniotic fluid acetyl cholinesterase

D. Amniotic fluid glucohexaminase

Q.123 The best period of gestation to carry out chorion villous biopsy for prenatal diagnosis is?

A. 8-10 weeks

B. 10-12 weeks

C. 12-14 weeks

D. 14-16 weeks

Q.124 The following complications during pregnancy increase the risk of postpartum hemorrhage (PPH) except:

A. Hypertension

B. Macrosomia

C. Twin pregnancy

D. Hydramnios

Q.125 A primigravida presents to casualty at 32 weeks gestation with acute pain abdomen for 2 hours, vaginal bleeding and decreased fetal movements. She should be managed by:

A. Immediate cesarean section

B. Immediate induction of labor

C. Tocolytic therapy

D. Magnesium sulphate therapy

Q.126 Which of the following tumors is not commonly known to increase in pregnancy?

A. Glioma

B. Pituitary adenoma

C. Meningioma

D. Neurofibroma

Q.127 Which of the following ovarian tumor is most prone to undergo torsion during pregnancy?

A. Serous cystadenoma

B. Mucinous cystadenoma

C. Dermoid cyst

D. Theca lutein cyst

Q.128 All of the following mechanisms might account for a reduced risk of upper genital tract infection in users of progestin releasing IUDs, except:

A. Reduced retrograde menstruation

B. Decreased ovulation

C. Thickened cervical mucus

D. Decidual changes in the endometrium

Q.129 Prenatal diagnosis at 16 weeks of pregnancy can be performed using all of the following, except:

A. Amniotic fluid

B. Maternal blood

C. Chorionic villi

D. Fetal blood

Q.130 Emergency contraception prevents pregnancy by all of the following mechanisms, except:

A. Delaying/inhibiting ovulation

B. Inhibiting fertilization

C. Preventing implantation of the fertilized egg

D. Interrupting an early pregnancy

Q.131 Which of the following statements is incorrect regarding levonorgestrel releasing intrauterine system:

A. There is increased incidence of menorrhagia

B. This system can be used as hormone replacement therapy

C. This method is useful for the treatment of endometerial hyperplasia

D. Irregular uterine bleeding can be problem initially

Q.132 The most common cause of tubal block in India is

A. Gonorrhea infection

B. Chlamydia infection

C. Tuberculosis

D. Bacterial vaginosis

Q.133 Which surgical procedure has the highest incidence of ureteric injury?

A. Vaginal hysterectomy

B. Abdominal hysterectomy

C. Weitheim's hysterectomy

D. Anterior colporrhaphy

Q.134 The risk of Asherman syndrome is the highest if Dilatation and Curettage (D & C) is done for the following condition:

A. Medical termination of pregancy

B. Missed abortion

C. Dysfunctional uterine bleeding

D. Post partum haemorrhage

Q.135 All are true about separation anxiety disorder except:

A. The prevalence is 3.5% to 5.4%

B. Comorbidity is common

C. Prevalence is higher in girls

D. Average age of onset is 4 years

Q.136 All of the following are example of peripheral neuropathies except?

A. Abetalipoproteinemia

B. Charcot-Marie-Tooth disease

C. Werdnig Hoffman disease

D. Dejerine Sottas disease

Q.137 CA-125 is a marker antigen for the diagnosis of:

A. Colon cancer

B. Breast cancer

C. Brain cancer

D. Ovarian cancer

Q.138 Least common cause of ambiguous genitalia in females?

A. 21 hydroxylase deficiency

B. 11 hydroxylase deficiency

C. WNT4 gene mutation

D. Foetal placental steroid sulfatase deficiency

Q.139 Earliest sign of pathological gastroesophageal reflux in infants is?

A. Upper GI bleeding

B. Respiratory symptoms

C. Oesophageal stricture

D. Postprandial regurgitation

Q.140 Blalock and Taussig's shunt is done between:

A. Aorta to the pulmonary artery

B. Aorta to pulmonary vein

C. Subclavian artery to pulmonary vein

D. Subclavian vein to an artery

Q.141 Right sided isomerism is found in association with?

A. Asplenia

B. Single spleen

C. Two spleens

D. Multiple spleens

Q.142 Most common cause of meningoencephalitis in children is?

A. HSV

B. Measles

C. Arbovirus

D. Enterovirus

Q.143 Which one of the following drugs is used for fetal therapy of congenital adrenal hyperplasia?

A. Hydrocortisone

B. Prednisolone

C. Fludrocortisone

D. Dexamethasone

Q.144 The following features are true for tetralogy of Fallot, except:

A. Ventricular septal defect

B. Right ventricular hypertrophy

C. Atrial septal defect

D. Pulmonary stenosis

Q.145 In a child, non functioning kidney is best diagnosed by:

A. Ultrasonography

B. IVU

C. DTPA renogram

D. Creatinine clearance

Q.146 All of the following are anterior dystrophies except?

A. Reis-Buckler's dystrophy

B. Meesmann's dystrophy

C. Schnyder's dystrophy

D. Stocker-Holt's dystrophy

Q.147 False about Argyll Robertson Pupil is?

A. Accommodation reflex normal

B. Direct pupillary reflex absent

C. Indirect pupillary reflex normal

D. Visual acuity normal

Q.148 Enlarged corneal nerves may be seen in all of the following except:

A. Keratoconus

B. Herpes simplex keratitis

C. Leprosy

D. Neurofibromatosis

Q.149 Horner's syndrome is characterized by all of the following except:

A. Miosis

B. Enopthalmos

C. Ptosis

D. Cycloplegia

Q.150 Which one of the following statements is incorrect about Optic glioma?

A. Has a peak incidence in first decade

B. Arises from oligodendrocytes

C. Causes meningeal hyperplasia

D. Is associated with type I neurofibromatosis

Q.151 Typically bilateral inferior subluxation of lens is seen in:

A. Marfan's syndrome

B. Homocystinuria

C. Hyperinsulinemia

D. Ocular trauma

Q.152 When should a case of Non-Insulin dependent diabetes mellitus (NIDDM) with a history of diabetes for one year have an ophthalmic examination?

A. As early as feasible

B. After 5 years

C. After 10 years

D. Only after visual symptoms develop

Q.153 SAFE strategy is recommended for the control of :

A. Trachoma

B. Glaucoma

C. Diabetic retinopathy

D. Cataract

Q.154 Band shaped keratopathy is caused by:

A. Amyloid

B. Calcium

C. Monopolysaccharide

D. Lipid

Q.155 The laser procedure, most often used for treating iris neovascularization, is:

A. Goniophotocoagulation

B. Laser trabeculoplasty

C. Panretinal photocoagulation (PRP)

D. Laser iridoplasty

Q.156 Commonest site of urethral carcinoma in males is?

A. Prostatic urethra

B. Penile urethra

C. Bulbomembranous urethra

D. Navicular fossa

Q.157 First autologous renal transplantation was performed by?

A. Hardy   **B.** Higgins   **C.** Studor   **D.** Kavosis

Q.158 Lord's plication is used in the treatment of ?

A. Hydrocele

B. Inguinal hernia

C. Testicular malignancy

D. Varicocele

Q.159 Which of the following structures are connected by Grayhack shunt?

A. Corpora cavernosa and saphenous vein

B. Corpora cavernosa and dorsal vein

C. Corpora cavernosa and corpus spongiosum

D. Corpora cavernosa and glans

Q.160 Which of the following conditions is associated with multiple cutaneous sebaceous adenomas?

A. Turcot's syndrome

B. Cowden syndrome

C. Gardner's syndrome

D. Muir Torre syndrome

Q.161 Which of the following renal calculi is seen associated with proteus infection?

A. Calcium Oxalate   **B.** Triple Phosphate

C. Xanthine   **D.** Uric Acid

Q.162 Which of the following is the most troublesome source of bleeding during a radical retropubic prostatectomy?

A. Dorsal venous complex

B. Inferior vesical pedicle

C. Superior vesical pedicle

D. Seminal vesicular artery

Q.163 Which of the following catheter materials is most suited for long-term use?

A. Latex   **B.** Silicone

C. Rubber   **D.** Polyurethane

Q.164 A new born presented with bloated abdomen shortly after birth with passing of less meconium. A full thickness biopsy of the rectum was carried out. Which one of the following rectal biopsy findings is most likely to be present?

A. Fibrosis of submucosa

B. Hyalinisation of the muscular coat

C. Thickened Muscularis propria

D. Lack of ganglion cells

Q.165 Abbey Estlander flap is used in the reconstruction of:

A. Buccal mucosa   **B.** Lip

C. Tongue   **D.** Palate

Q.166 The most common complication seen in hiatus hernia is:

A. Oesophagitis

B. Aspiration pneumonitis

C. Volvulus

D. Esophageal stricture

Q.167 In which one of the following head and neck cancer, perineural invasion is most commonly seen?

A. Adenocarcinoma

B. Adenoid cystic carcinoma

C. Basal Cell Adenoma

D. Squamous cell carcinoma

Q.168 Lumbar sympathectomy is of value in the management of:

A. Intermittent claudication

B. Distal ischaemia affecting the skin of the toes

C. Arteriovenous Fistula

D. Back pain

Q.169 A blood stained discharge from the nipple indicates one of the following:

A. Breast abscess

B. Fibroadenoma

C. Duct Papilloma

D. Fat Necrosis of Breast

Q.170 The most preferred approach for pituitary surgery at the present time is:

A. Transcranial   **B.** Transethmoidal

C. Trans-sphenoidal   **D.** Transcallosal

Q.171 Which of the following is not a preferred site for planning vascular access for maintenance hemodialysis?

A. Nondominant extremity

B. Upper limb

C. Radiocephalic AV fistula

D. Saphenofemoral fistula

Q.172 Dacron vascular graft is:

A. Nontextile synthetic
B. Textile synthetic
C. Nontextile biologic
D. Textile biologic

Q.173 Allen's test is useful in evaluating:

A. Thoracic outlet compression
B. Presence of cervical rib
C. Integrity of palmar arch
D. Digital blood flow

Q.174 The most common cause of acquired arteriovenous fistula is:

A. Bacterial infection
B. Fungal infection
C. Blunt trauma
D. Penetrating trauma

Q.175 Which of the following statements is true regarding testicular tumors?

A. Are embryonal cell carcinomas in 95% of cases
B. Bilateral in up to 10% cases
C. Teratomas are more common than seminomas
D. Usually present after 50 years of age

Q.176 The treatment of choice for squamous cell anal cancer is:

A. Abdominoperineal resection
B. Laser fulgaration
C. Chemoradiotherapy
D. Platinum—based chemotherapy

Q.177 Which of the following drugs is not a part of the 'Triple Therapy' immunosuppression for post-renal transplant patients?

A. Cyclosporine
B. Azathioprine
C. FK 506
D. Prednisolone

Q.178 All of the following modalities can be used for in situ ablation of liver secondaries, except?

A. Ultrasonic waves
B. Cryotherapy
C. Alcohol
D. Radiofrequency

Q.179 Biliary stricture developing after laparascopic cholecystectomy usually occurs at which part of the common bile duct?

A. Upper
B. Middle
C. Lower
D. All sides with equal frequency

Q.180 Which one of the following statements is incorrect regarding stones in the common bile duct?

A. Can present with Charcot's triad
B. Are suggested by a bile duct diameter >6 mm in ultrasound
C. ERCP, sphincterotomy and balloon clearance is now the standard treatment
D. When removed by exploration of the common bile ducts the T-tube can be removed after 3 days

Q.181 A patient of post cholecystectomy biliary stricture has undergone an ERCP three days ago. Following this she has developed acute cholangitis. The most likely organism is:

A. Escherichia coli
B. Bacillus fragilis
C. Streptococcus viridans
D. Pseudomonas aeruginosa

Q.182 The tumor, which may occur in the residual breast or overlying skin following wide local excision and radiotherapy for mammary carcinoma, is:

A. Leiomyosarcoma
B. Squamous cell carcinoma
C. Basal cell carcinoma
D. Angiosarcoma

Q.183 In which of the following types of breast carcinoma, would you consider biopsy of opposite breast?

A. Adenocarcinoma-poorly differentiated
B. Medullary carcinoma
C. Lobular carcinoma
D. Comedo carcinoma

Q.184 The most important prognostic factor in breast carcinoma is:

A. Histological grade of the tumor
B. Stage of the tumor at the time of diagnosis
C. Status of estrogen and progesterone receptors
D. Over expression of p53 tumour suppressor gene

Q.185 One of the following is not correct in papillary carcinoma of thyroid:

A. Can be reliably diagnosed using fine needle aspiration cytology
B. Always unifocal
C. Typically spreads to the cervical lymph nodes
D. Requires a total thyroidectomy for large tum

Q.186 Which of the following brain tumours is highly vascular in nature?

A. Glioblastoma
B. Meningiomas
C. C P angle epidermoid
D. Pituitary adenomas

Q.187 Early postoperative complication of ileostomy:

A. Obstruction
B. Prolapse
C. Diarrhoea
D. Necrosis

Q.188 Most common biochemical abnormality in congenital pyloric stenosis.

A. Hyperkalemic metabolic acidosis
B. Hypokalemic metabolic acidosis
C. Hyperkalemic metabolic alkalosis
D. Hypokalemic metabolic alkalosis

Q.189 Hypotension in acute spinal injury is due to:

A. Loss of sympathetic tone
B. Loss of parasympathetic tone

C. Orthostatic hypotension

D. Vasovagal attack

Q.190 Least risk of CA breast is seen in:

A. BRCA1

B. BRCA2

C. Li-Fraumeni syndrome

D. Ataxia telangiectasia

Q.191 External hemorrhoids below the dentate line are –

A. Painful

B. Ligation is done as management

C. Skin tag is not seen in these cases

D. May turn malignant

Q.192 The technique employed in radiotherapy to counteract the effect of tumour motion due to breathing is known as:

A. Arc technique

B. Modulation

C. Gating

D. Shunting

Q.193 Plethoric lung fields are seen in all of the following conditions, except:

A. Atrial septal defect (ASD)

B. TAPVC (Total Anomalous Pulmonary venous connection)

C. Ebsteins' anomaly

D. Ventricular septal defect

Q.194 On MRI the differential diagnosis of spinal cord edema is:

A. Myelodysplasia

B. Myelomalacia

C. Myeloschisis

D. Cord tumors

Q.195 The diagnostic procedure not done in case of pheochromocytoma.

A. CT scan

B. MRI

C. FNAC

D. MIBG scan

Q.196 A young male is brought unconscious to the hospital with external injuries. CT brain showed no midline shift. Basal cistern was compressed with multiple small haemorrhages. What is the likely diagnosis?

A. Cerebral contusion

B. Cerebral laceration

C. Multiple infarcts

D. Diffuse axonal injuries

Q.197 Metabolic abnomiality seen in congenital hypertrophic pyloric stenosis is:

A. Hypochloremic hypokalemic metabolic alkalosis

B. Hyperchloremic hypokalemic metabolic alkalosis

C. Hypochloremic hypokalemic metabolic acidosis

D. Hyperchloremic hypokalemic metabolic acidosis

Q.198 A patient sustained Traumatic injury to major abdominal vessels. It has been planned to explore the Suprarenal Aorta. the Celiac Axis, the Superior Mesentric Artery, and the Left Renal Artery. What maneuver for exposure is recommended:

A. Cranial Visceral Rotation

B. Caudal Visceral Rotation

C. Left Medial Visceral Rotation

D. Right Medical Visceral Rotation

Q.199 The following is a marker of Paget's disease of breast

A. S- 100

B. HMB 45

C. CEA

D. Neuron specific enolase

Q.200 Chronic burrowing ulcer is caused by:

A. Microaerophilic streptococci

B. Peptostreptococcus

C. Streptococcus viridans

D. Streptococcus pyogenes

PART B

Q.201 Which of the following is true regarding nuclear fluorescence in systemic lupus erythematosus?

A. Rim staining pattern indicates antibodies to double stranded DNA

B. Homogenous staining reflects antibodies specific to centromeres

C. Speckled pattern reflects the presence of antibodies to histones

D. Nucleolar pattern reflects antibodies to chromatin

Q.202 Which of the following is true regarding lymphangioleiomyomatosis?

A. Primarily seen in old age

B. Commonly associated with persistent cough

C. Proliferation occurs in perivascular epithelioid cells

D. Disease is rapidly progressive

Q.203 The proto oncogene associated with Burkitt lymphoma is?

A. ABL

B. BRAF

C. HGF

D. MYC

Q.204 All are true regarding desmoid tumours except?

A. Consist of large infiltrative masses that do not metastasize

B. Most frequent in old age

C. Mutations occur in the APC gene

D. Predominantly seen in women

Q.205 All of the following diseases are caused by trinucleotide repeat mutations affecting non-coding regions except?

A. Fragile X syndrome

B. Myotonic dystrophy

C. Spinocerebellar ataxia

D. Friedreich ataxia

Q.206 Rupture of Charcot Bouchard aneurysm usually causes?

A. Extradural haemorrhage

B. Subdural haemorrhage

C. Subarachnoid haemorrhage

D. Intracerebral haemorrhage

Q.207 Anti LKM antibodies are found in?

A. Inflammatory myopathies

B. Behcet's syndrome

C. HCV infection

D. Primary biliary cirrhosis

Q.208 Which of the following is not an anterior mediastinal tumour?

A. Thymoma
B. Lymphoma
C. Neurogenic tumour
D. Teratoma

Q.209 Not an action of bradykinin?

A. Bronchodilation
B. Vasodilatation
C. Pain
D. Increase in vascular permeability

Q.210 Marker for langerhans cell histiocytosis is?

A. CD 5
B. CD 1a
C. CD 22
D. CD 30

Q.211 A person who is heterozygous for sickle cell anemia has increased resistance for?

A. Malaria
B. Filariasis
C. Dengue haemorrhagic fever
D. Thalassemia

Q.212 Caspases are involved in ?

A. Apoptosis
B. Necrosis
C. Neoplasia
D. Inflammation

Q.213 Most common cause of Down's syndrome is?

A. Translocation
B. Mosaicism
C. Paternal nondisjunction
D. Maternal nondisjunction

Q.214 Which stain is used to study fungal morphology in tissue sections?

A. Periodic acid–Schiff
B. Alizarin Red
C. Masson's Trichrome
D. Von Kossa

Q.215 Psammoma body is not seen in ?

A. Papillary carcinoma of thyroid
B. Follicular carcinoma of thyroid
C. Serous cystadenocarcinoma of ovary
D. Meningiom

Q.216 Which among the following is not a neuronal tumour?

A. Ependymoma
B. Ganglioglioma
C. Neurocytoma
D. Gangliocytoma

Q.217 Necrotizing lymphadenitis is a characteristic feature of?

A. Hodgkin's disease
B. Kikuchi disease
C. Kimura disease
D. Castleman disease

Q.218 Which among the following is not an autoimmune disease?

A. Myasthenia gravis
B. Systemic lupus erythematosus
C. Grave's disease
D. Sickle cell disease

Q.219 True statement regarding platelet function defects?

A. Normal platelet count with increased bleeding time
B. Decreased platelet count with increased bleeding time
C. Increased platelet count with increased bleeding time
D. Normal platelet count with normal bleeding time

Q.220 HbH is seen in which of the following conditions?

A. Deletion of 3 beta genes
B. Deletion of 3 alpha genes
C. Deletion of 4 beta genes
D. Deletion of 4 alpha genes

Q.221 All are true about Xanthogranulomatous inflammation except?

A. Associated with tuberculosis
B. Foam cells are present
C. Yellow nodules are present
D. Multi-nucleated giant cells are present

Q.222 Which of the following is most characteristic feature of acute inflammation?

A. Vasodilatation and increased vascular permeability
B. Margination of leukocytes
C. Vasoconstriction
D. Vascular stasis

Q.223 Which of the following enzymes are responsible for generating 'oxygen burst' within neutrophils for killing intracellular bacteria?

A. Superoxide dismutase
B. Glutathione peroxidase
C. Oxidase
D. Catalase

Q.224 Which of the following organelles plays a pivotal role in Apoptosis?

A. Mitochondria
B. Endoplasmic Reticulum
C. Nucleus
D. Golgi Apparatus

Q.225 The blood in the vessels normally does not clot because:

A. Vitamin K antagonists are present in plasma
B. Thrombin has a positive feedback on plasminogen
C. Sodium citrate in plasma chelates calcium ions
D. Vascular endothelium is smooth and coated with glycocalyx

Q.226 Which of the following is not a long acting muscarinic antagonist?

A. Glycopyrronium
B. Aclidinium
C. Indacaterol
D. Umeclidinium

Q.227 Ibrutinib is used for the management of?

A. Chronic Myelogenous Leukemia
B. Acute Lymphoblastic Leukemia
C. Mantle Cell Lymphoma
D. Lymphocyte rich Hodgkin's Lymphoma

Q.228 Patients suffering from multidrug resistant tuberculosis can be treated with all the following drugs except:

A. Tobramycin

B. Amikacin

C. Ciprofloxacin

D. Clarithromycin

Q.229 All are true regarding leflunomide except?

A. Inhibits proliferation of stimulated lymphocytes

B. Depresses antibody production by B lymphocytes

C. Can be used in children

D. Can cause thrombocytopenia

Q.230 Which of the following drugs have a narrow therapeutic index?

A. Lithium

B. Diazepam

C. Penicillin

D. Desipramine

Q.231 Which of the following is an integrase inhibitor currently in use for the treatment of HIV infection?

A. Indinavir

B. Elvitegravir

C. Saquinavir

D. Raltegravir

Q.232 MAO inhibitors are contraindicated in a patient taking?

A. Pethidine

B. Buprenorphine

C. Morphine

D. Pentazocin

Q.233 Ethosuximide is the drug of choice for treatment of ?

A. Generalized tonic clonic seizures

B. Absence seizures

C. Simple partial seizures

D. Complex partial seizures

Q.234 Which of the following is not an adverse effect of chronic amiodarone therapy?

A. Pulmonary fibrosis

B. Hypothyroidism

C. Hyperthyroidism

D. Systemic lupus erythematosus

Q.235 Alkalinization of urine is done during the administration of which of the following chemotherapeutic drugs?

A. Ara-C (Cytarabine)

B. Methotrexate

C. Cisplatin

D. Ifosfamide

Q.236 Which of the following is used in the treatment of meningococcal meningitis in patients allergic to penicillin?

A. Ciprofloxacin

B. Teicoplanin

C. Meropenem

D. Chloramphenicol

Q.237 Not true about Na+ K+ 2Cl- Co-transporter:

A. It is a glycoprotein

B. 12 membrane spanning domains

C. There are distinct isoforms for secretory and absorptive function

D. The secretory form is found exclusively in thick segment of ascending limb of loop of Henle

Q.238 Which of the following has a uricosuric action:

A. Allopurinol

B. Losartan

C. Ramipril

D. Atenolol

Q.239 All of the following are known adverse effects of thalidomide, except:

A. Diarrhoea

B. Teratogenicity

C. Deep Vein Thrombosis

D. Peripheral Neuropathy

Q.240 Which of the following antihypertensive drugs should not be used in a patient on Lithium in order to prevent Lithium Toxicity?

A. Clonidine

B. Beta blockers

C. Calcium Channel Blockers

D. Diuretics

Q.241 All of the following statements about Aprepitant are true except?

A. Agonist at Neurokinin receptor (NK1)

B. Crosses blood brain barrier

C. Metabolised by CYP3A4 pathway

D. Ameliorates nausea and vomiting of chemotherapy

Q.242 All of the following statement s about 'Erlotinib' are true except?

A. Tyrosine kinase inhibitor

B. Food decreases its absorption

C. Rashes may occur

D. Used in non small cell lung carcinoma

Q.243 A patient who was given primaquine develops dark coloured urine one day after administration of the drug. The likely diagnosis is:

A. Glucose-6-phosphate dehydrogenase deficiency

B. Glucose-6- phosphatase deficiency

C. Galactose-6-phosphate dehydrogenase deficiency

D. Galactose-6-phosphatase deficiency

Q.244 All of the following statements about serotonin syndrome are true, except:

A. It is not an idiosyncratic reaction

B. Can be caused by SSRI

C. Dantrolene is the drug of choice

D. Associated with hyperthermia and hypertension

Q.245 BAL is useful in treating poisoning due to all except?

A. Lead

B. Organic mercury

C. Cadmium

D. Arsenic

Q.246 Which of the following statements is true regarding ARBO viruses :

A. Yellow fever is endemic in India

B. Dengue virus has only one serotype

C. Kyasanur Forest disease (KFD) is transmitted by ticks

D. Mosquito of culex vishnui complex is the vector of Dengue fever

Q.247 Draughtsman appearance is seen with colonies of:

A. Pneumococcus

B. Streptococcus

C. Staphylococcus

D. None of the above

Q.248 The most sensitive method for detecting cervical Chlamydia trachomatis infection is:

A. Direct fluorescent antibody test
B. Enzyme immunoassay
C. Polymerase chain reaction
D. Culture on irradiated McConkey cells

Q.249 Epstein Barr (EB) virus has been implicated in the following malignancies except:

A. Hodgkin's disease
B. Non-Hodgkin's lymphoma
C. Nasopharyngeal carcinoma
D. Multiple myeloma

Q.250 A 20 years old male patient presents to the STD clinic with a genital ulcer. The gram stain of the smear from the ulcer shows gram-negative coccobacilli. The most appropriate media for culture would be:

A. Thayer Martin Medium
B. Blood agar with X & V factors
C. Chocolate agar with IsoVitaleX
D. Teilurite blood agar

Q.251 Regarding gas gangrene one of the following is correct:

A. It is due to Clostridium Botulinum infection
B. Clostridial species are gram-negative spore-forming anaerobes
C. The clinical features are due to the release of protein endotoxin
D. Gas is invariably present in the muscle compartments

Q.252 A man, after skinning a dead animal, developed a pustule on his hand. A smear prepared from the lesion showed the presence of Gram-positive bacilli in long chains which were positive for McFadyean's reaction. The most likely aetiological agent is :

A. Clostridium tetani
B. Listeria monocytogenes
C. Bacillus anthracis
D. Actinomyces sp

Q.253 A microbiologist wants to develop a vaccine for the prevention of attachment of diarrhoeagenic E. coli to the specific receptors in the gastrointestinal tract. All of the following fimbrial adhesions would be appropriate vaccine candidates except :

A. CFA-I   B. P-Pili   C. CS-2   D. K 88

Q.254 Which of the following infestation leads to malabsorption?

A. Giardia lamblia
B. Ascaris lumbricoides
C. Necator americanus
D. Ancylostama duodenale

Q.255 Which one of the following statements is true regarding Chlamydia pneumonia:

A. Fifteen serovars have been identified as human pathogens
B. Mode of transmission is by the airborne bird excreta
C. The Cytoplasmic inclusions present in the sputum specimen are rich in glycogen
D. The group-specific antigen is responsible for the production of complement-fixing antibodies

Q.256 A child was diagnosed to be suffering from diarrhoea due to Campylobacter jejuni. Which of the following will be the correct environmental conditions of incubation of the culture plates of the stool sample:

A. The temperature of 42°C and microaerophilic
B. The temperature of 42°C and 10% carbon dioxide
C. The temperature of 37°C and microaerophilic
D. The temperature of 37°C and 10% carbon dioxide

Q.257 A bacterial disease that has been associated with the 3 "Rs" i.e., rats, ricefields, and rainfall is:

A. Leptospirosis   B. Plague
C. Melioidosis   D. Rodent bite fever

Q.258 All can cause pulmonary eosinophilia except-

A. Necator americanus
B. Ankylostoma duodenale
C. Trichinella spiralis
D. Ascaris lumbricoides

Q.259 The following diseases are associated with Epstein-Barr virus infection, except:

A. Infectious mononucleosis
B. Epidermodysplasia verruciformis
C. Nasopharyngeal carcinoma
D. Oral hairy leukoplakia

Q.260 Which one of the following is true

A. Agar has nutrient properties
B. Chocolate medium is a selective medium
C. Addition of selective substances in a solid medium is called enrichment media
D. Nutrient broth is basal medium

Q.261 An elderly male presented with fever, chest pain and dry cough. Sputum was cultured on charcoal yeast medium, the organism identified will be

A. H.influenza
B. Moraxella catarrhalis
C. Legionella
D. Burkholderia cepacia

Q.262 A person working in an abattoir presented with a papule on hand, which turned into an ulcer. Which will best help in diagnosis?

A. Trichrome Methylene Blue
B. Carbol Fuschin
C. Acid Fast Stain
D. Calcofluor White

Q.263 A patient in an ICU is on a central venous line for the past week. He is on ceftazidime and amikacin. After 7 days of antibiotics, he develops a spike of fever and his blood culture is positive for gram-positive cocci in chains, which are catalase-negative. Following this vancomycin was started but the culture

remained positive for the same organism even after 10 days of therapy. The most likely organism causing this infection is

A. Staphylococcus aureus A

B. Virdans streptococci

C. Enterococcus faecalis

D. Coagulase-negative staphylococcus

Q.264 A young male patient presented with UTI. On urine examination, pus cells were found but no organisms. Which method would be best used for culture?

A. Mc Coy culture

B. Thayer martin medium

C. LJ Medium

D. Levinthal Medium

Q.265 A child presents with infective skin lesions of the leg. Culture was done which showed gram-positive cocci in chains and hemolytic colonies. Which of the following tests will best identify the organism?

A. Bile solubility

B. Optochin sensitivity

C. Bacitracin sensitivity

D. Catalase positive

Q.266 In India, magistrate inquest is done in the following cases except:

A. Exhumation cases

B. Dowry deaths within 5 years of marriage

C. Murder cases

D. Death of a person in police custody

Q.267 Sparrow's footmarks are characteristic of?

A. Vitriolage

B. Windshield glass injury

C. Lightning strike

D. Stab injury

Q.268 A 34-year old rickshaw puller has been using heroin for the past ten years. One evening his family members found him unconscious. He was brought to the casualty. On examination, he had tachycardia, shallow breathing, constricted pupils. His blood pressure was 100/70 mm of Hg. He had brisk bilateral deep tendon reflexes. The plantar reflexes were flexor on both sides. Which of the following is the best treatment for him?

A. Buprenorphine   **B.** Flumazenil

C. Methadone   **D.** Naloxone

Q.269 A middle-aged man presents with paraesthesia of hand and feet. Examination reveals the presence of 'Mees' lines in the nails and raindrop pigmentation in the hands; The most likely causative toxin for the above-mentioned symptoms is :

A. Lead   **B.** Arsenic   **C.** Thallium   **D.** Mercury

Q.270 In which of the following conditions, postmortem caloricity is seen?

A. Massive haemorrhage

B. Cyanide poisoning

C. Corrosive poisoning

D. Septicemia

Q.271 Deep blue colour of hypostasis is seen in death due to poisoning by

A. Potassium cyanide   B. Phosphorus

C. Aniline dyes   D. Carbon monoxide

Q.272 The cephalic index of the Indian population is between:

A. 70-75   **B.** 75-80   **C.** 80-85   **D.** 85-90

Q.273 Auto-Rikshaw ran over a child's thigh, there is a mark of the tyre tracks, it is an

A. Contact bruise   B. Patterned bruise

C. Imprint abrasion   D. Ectopic bruise

Q.274 In methyl alcohol poisoning there is CNS depression, cardiac depression and optic nerve atrophy. These effects are produced due to:

A. Formaldehyde and formic acid

B. Acetaldehyde

C. Pyridine

D. Acetic acid

Q.275 Mercury will affect which part of the renal tubule

A. PCT   B. DCT

C. CT   D. Loop of Henle

Q.276 Safe yield of a water supply source is the yield that is adequate for?

A. 80% of the year

B. 90% of the year

C. 95% of the year

D. The whole of the year

Q.277 Minimum depth for the lining of a sanitary well is?

A. 10 feet   **B.** 20 feet   **C.** 35 feet   **D.** 50 feet

Q.278 Quantity of water available per capita considered adequate to meet the needs of all urban domestic purposes?

A. 100-150 L   B. 150-200 L

C. 200-250 L   D. 250-300 L

Q.279 Screening test specificity is the ability of a test to correctly identify:

A. False positives   B. True positives

C. True negatives   D. False negatives

Q.280 Non-deliberate cultural practice with the anti-mosquito effect is?

A. Use of mosquito repellents

B. Use of bed nets

C. Use of alkaline detergent for washing clothes

D. Use of larvicides

Q.281 A sewage worker with fever and jaundice presented to the emergency department. Lab investigations revealed increased blood urea nitrogen and serum creatinine – indicative of renal failure. Which of the following antibiotics is preferred in this patient?

A. Erythromycin   B. Doxycycline

C. Penicillin G   D. Ciprofloxacin

Q.282 Modes of disease transmission by vectors are all except?

A. Regurgitation
B. Biting
C. Ingestion
D. Rubbing of infected excrement

Q.283 JSY is an acronym for?

A. Janani Suraksha Yojana
B. Jeevan Suraksha Yojana
C. Jeevan Shakthi Yojana
D. Jan Suraksha Yojana

Q.284 Movement across socioeconomic levels is known as?

A. Social insurance
B. Social mobility
C. Social equality
D. Social upliftment

Q.285 The usefulness of a 'screening test' in a community depends on its :

A. Sensitivity
B. Specificity
C. Reliability
D. Predictive value

Q.286 "Five clean practices" under strategies for elimination of neonatal tetanus include all except :

A. Clean surface for delivery
B. Clean hand of the attendant
C. New blade for cutting the cord
D. Clean airway

Q.287 The following statements about breast milk are true except :

A. The maximum milk output is seen at 12 months
B. The coefficient of uptake of iron in breast milk is 70%
C. Calcium absorption of human milk is better than that of cow's milk
D. It provides about 65 kcals per 100 ml

Q.288 A 10-month-old child weighing 8kg has Bitot spots in both eyes. Which of the following is the most appropriate schedule to prescribe vitamin A to this child?

A. 2 lakh units intramuscular (IM) on day 0, 14
B. 1 lakh units IM on day 0, 14
C. 2 lakh units IM on day 0, 1 and 14
D. 1 lakh units IM on day O, 1 and 14

Q.289 All of the following are the mode of transmission of leprosy except?

A. Breast milk
B. Insect bite
C. Transplacental spread
D. Droplet infection

Q.290 According to International Health Regulations, there is no risk of spread of yellow Fever if the Aedes aegypti index remains below:

A. 1%   **B.** 5%   **C.** 8%   **D.** 10%

Q.291 The following statements are true about DPT vaccine except:

A. Aluminium salt has an adjuvant effect
B. Whole killed bacteria of Bordetella pertussis has an adjuvant effect
C. Presence of acellular pertussis component increases its immunogenicity
D. Presence of H. influenzae type B component increases its immunogenicity

Q.292 A study began in 1970 with a group of 5000 adults in Delhi who were asked about their alcohol consumption. The occurrence of cancer was studied in this group between 1990-1995. This is an example of :

A. Cross-sectional study
B. Retrospective cohort study
C. Concurrent cohort study
D. Case-control study

Q.293 Which one of the following is not source of manager's power:

A. Reward
B. Coercive
C. Legitimate
D. Efferent

Q.294 Under the WHO 'Vision 2020' program. the 'SAFE' strategy is adopted for which of the following diseases?

A. Trachoma
B. Glaucoma
C. Diabetic retinopathy
D. Onchocerciasis

Q.295 Total cholesterol level = a + b (calorie intake) + c (physical activity) + d (body mass index); is an example of:

A. Simple linear regression
B. Simple curvilinear regression
C. Multiple linear regression
D. Multiple logistic regression

Q.296 The PEFR of a group of 11-year-old girls follow a normal distribution with a mean of 300 l/min and standard deviation of 20 l/min:

A. About 95% of the girls have PEFR between 260 and 340 l/min
B. The girls have healthy lungs
C. About 5% of girls have PEFR below 260 l/min
D. All the PEFR must be less than 340 l/min

Q.297 The following tests are used to check the efficiency of pasteurization of milk except:

A. Phosphatase test
B. Standard plate count
C. Coliform count
D. Methylene blue reduction test

Q.298 Which of the following viral infections is transmitted by tick?

A. Japanese encephalitis
B. Dengue fever
C. Kyasanur forest disease (KFD)
D. Yellow fever

Q.299 Which one of the following is a good index of the severity of an acute disease?

A. Cause specific death rate
B. Case fatality rate

C. Standardized mortality ratio

D. Five year survivial

Q.300 Eicosapentaenoic acid is present in

A. Soyabean oil   B. Corn oil

C. Safflower oil   D. Fish oil

// Smart Answer Sheet //

Correct   Indicates percentage of students who answered questions correctly.

Skipped   Indicates percentage of students who skipped questions.

Q.	Ans.	Correct / Skipped	Q.	Ans.	Correct / Skipped	Q.	Ans.	Correct / Skipped	Q.	Ans.	Correct / Skipped	Q.	Ans.	Correct / Skipped
1	B	84.38 % / 10.59 %	17	A	77.35 % / 17.32 %	33	A	76.84 % / 21.31 %	49	D	49.98 % / 37.94 %	65	C	54.58 % / 32.05 %
2	C	49.55 % / 50.26 %	18	C	77.78 % / 12.21 %	34	C	79.89 % / 12.46 %	50	C	89.66 % / 10.28 %	66	B	64.39 % / 35.22 %
3	D	15.21 % / 70.77 %	19	D	43.37 % / 34.91 %	35	C	87.7 % / 10.24 %	51	A	45.38 % / 49.36 %	67	A	82.98 % / 15.46 %
4	A	79.15 % / 15.61 %	20	B	87.57 % / 10.96 %	36	B	89.95 % / 10.0 %	52	C	22.42 % / 67.48 %	68	A	64.94 % / 33.35 %
5	D	78.14 % / 19.68 %	21	C	84.87 % / 12.44 %	37	D	56.14 % / 40.41 %	53	C	51.4 % / 44.25 %	69	D	77.41 % / 14.33 %
6	D	78.11 % / 12.61 %	22	B	76.98 % / 14.01 %	38	D	43.07 % / 44.78 %	54	D	62.17 % / 33.23 %	70	A	45.26 % / 50.35 %
7	A	88.64 % / 10.31 %	23	B	78.71 % / 11.85 %	39	B	80.58 % / 18.3 %	55	C	78.47 % / 11.02 %	71	C	13.24 % / 85.19 %
8	A	80.73 % / 10.01 %	24	D	78.03 % / 17.2 %	40	D	83.39 % / 10.22 %	56	C	58.92 % / 31.0 %	72	B	63.72 % / 30.3 %
9	D	78.49 % / 18.81 %	25	A	62.89 % / 36.06 %	41	A	89.98 % / 10.02 %	57	D	58.98 % / 31.85 %	73	A	53.63 % / 41.57 %
10	B	83.63 % / 12.61 %	26	A	81.97 % / 12.51 %	42	C	85.88 % / 12.47 %	58	D	55.31 % / 30.05 %	74	D	67.34 % / 31.39 %
11	B	44.73 % / 43.92 %	27	D	89.83 % / 10.16 %	43	B	27.21 % / 68.34 %	59	D	17.13 % / 80.55 %	75	C	13.04 % / 79.11 %
12	A	68.26 % / 30.85 %	28	B	21.07 % / 78.8 %	44	A	83.73 % / 12.59 %	60	B	60.41 % / 37.71 %	76	D	58.46 % / 34.2 %
13	B	83.21 % / 13.8 %	29	A	66.8 % / 30.09 %	45	D	84.8 % / 12.79 %	61	B	42.31 % / 32.35 %	77	C	66.28 % / 33.34 %
14	A	60.88 % / 38.28 %	30	D	89.72 % / 10.14 %	46	B	69.13 % / 30.74 %	62	D	86.25 % / 10.02 %	78	A	56.9 % / 33.72 %
15	B	79.18 % / 10.54 %	31	B	79.07 % / 15.22 %	47	D	52.88 % / 42.87 %	63	B	12.81 % / 78.93 %	79	D	69.61 % / 30.18 %
16	A	80.42 % / 14.81 %	32	C	41.77 % / 32.91 %	48	D	19.41 % / 78.7 %	64	D	42.15 % / 57.83 %	80	C	24.96 % / 70.81 %

Q.	Ans.	Correct / Skipped	Q.	Ans.	Correct / Skipped	Q.	Ans.	Correct / Skipped	Q.	Ans.	Correct / Skipped	Q.	Ans.	Correct / Skipped
81	C	61.36 % / 36.84 %	97	C	60.54 % / 38.65 %	113	B	50.34 % / 40.24 %	129	D	44.62 % / 37.92 %	145	C	47.51 % / 34.07 %
82	C	69.71 % / 30.01 %	98	A	84.7 % / 10.87 %	114	A	64.93 % / 31.22 %	130	D	53.11 % / 43.62 %	146	C	23.29 % / 69.81 %
83	C	63.33 % / 30.33 %	99	A	48.74 % / 46.79 %	115	C	86.97 % / 11.0 %	131	A	41.5 % / 57.14 %	147	C	65.36 % / 31.48 %
84	D	78.37 % / 16.15 %	100	C	63.15 % / 30.41 %	116	D	48.54 % / 30.06 %	132	C	61.89 % / 36.97 %	148	B	48.07 % / 38.69 %
85	B	76.32 % / 20.04 %	101	C	51.42 % / 34.27 %	117	B	43.78 % / 52.56 %	133	C	14.54 % / 80.55 %	149	D	57.12 % / 33.69 %
86	B	14.14 % / 81.95 %	102	B	58.81 % / 34.27 %	118	D	63.59 % / 36.27 %	134	D	88.94 % / 10.66 %	150	C	59.0 % / 34.02 %
87	D	55.38 % / 30.79 %	103	A	60.35 % / 39.62 %	119	D	16.77 % / 82.99 %	135	D	62.72 % / 34.41 %	151	B	14.95 % / 83.87 %
88	B	40.29 % / 45.95 %	104	C	11.84 % / 67.8 %	120	D	67.36 % / 32.11 %	136	C	67.2 % / 32.46 %	152	A	49.26 % / 49.05 %
89	D	60.55 % / 30.59 %	105	A	40.73 % / 31.67 %	121	A	68.98 % / 30.53 %	137	D	46.18 % / 36.45 %	153	A	62.99 % / 34.05 %
90	B	48.84 % / 34.13 %	106	B	46.88 % / 33.95 %	122	C	53.09 % / 36.59 %	138	D	52.35 % / 37.35 %	154	B	89.88 % / 10.12 %
91	C	56.5 % / 32.45 %	107	A	40.71 % / 49.4 %	123	B	80.19 % / 13.44 %	139	B	81.33 % / 15.16 %	155	C	47.61 % / 38.46 %
92	A	56.72 % / 41.04 %	108	A	60.34 % / 33.63 %	124	A	26.66 % / 68.15 %	140	A	50.83 % / 35.14 %	156	C	67.25 % / 30.93 %
93	D	51.56 % / 44.36 %	109	A	15.14 % / 71.13 %	125	A	66.13 % / 31.79 %	141	A	27.86 % / 69.32 %	157	A	13.18 % / 69.65 %
94	D	58.16 % / 40.04 %	110	C	42.58 % / 48.12 %	126	A	45.5 % / 36.39 %	142	D	62.53 % / 31.02 %	158	A	40.86 % / 46.46 %
95	D	51.26 % / 47.24 %	111	B	45.28 % / 31.5 %	127	C	82.43 % / 17.39 %	143	D	51.97 % / 39.03 %	159	A	52.34 % / 37.77 %
96	D	67.99 % / 30.32 %	112	C	49.92 % / 34.36 %	128	B	18.14 % / 77.81 %	144	C	64.83 % / 33.15 %	160	D	56.16 % / 43.08 %

Q.	Ans.	Correct / Skipped	Q.	Ans.	Correct / Skipped	Q.	Ans.	Correct / Skipped	Q.	Ans.	Correct / Skipped	Q.	Ans.	Correct / Skipped
161	B	78.19 % / 21.01 %	177	C	49.14 % / 49.84 %	193	C	26.87 % / 70.97 %	209	A	85.68 % / 12.42 %	225	D	40.72 % / 36.4 %
162	A	11.6 % / 75.08 %	178	A	48.51 % / 44.41 %	194	B	57.39 % / 39.33 %	210	B	78.42 % / 21.33 %	226	C	78.82 % / 17.71 %
163	B	43.04 % / 38.16 %	179	A	26.99 % / 72.47 %	195	C	62.15 % / 31.71 %	211	A	87.96 % / 10.87 %	227	C	79.92 % / 18.81 %
164	D	59.66 % / 35.06 %	180	D	43.37 % / 46.66 %	196	D	26.07 % / 71.95 %	212	A	68.23 % / 30.37 %	228	A	86.36 % / 10.7 %
165	B	15.96 % / 80.67 %	181	A	64.27 % / 32.07 %	197	A	85.38 % / 10.11 %	213	D	87.85 % / 10.21 %	229	C	81.55 % / 13.37 %
166	A	65.23 % / 32.6 %	182	D	14.37 % / 72.17 %	198	C	43.94 % / 32.36 %	214	A	87.06 % / 11.09 %	230	A	12.72 % / 68.74 %
167	B	50.96 % / 30.47 %	183	C	41.32 % / 51.12 %	199	C	52.0 % / 38.99 %	215	B	65.27 % / 30.79 %	231	D	84.57 % / 13.45 %
168	B	10.53 % / 74.63 %	184	B	45.78 % / 36.78 %	200	A	48.98 % / 46.11 %	216	A	19.19 % / 79.47 %	232	A	81.34 % / 10.4 %
169	C	53.52 % / 30.36 %	185	B	47.16 % / 45.71 %	201	A	77.44 % / 20.4 %	217	B	68.12 % / 31.09 %	233	B	55.33 % / 40.5 %
170	C	52.67 % / 34.52 %	186	A	52.24 % / 45.19 %	202	C	76.51 % / 10.62 %	218	D	82.19 % / 12.38 %	234	D	76.75 % / 21.19 %
171	D	11.86 % / 83.49 %	187	A	53.23 % / 37.73 %	203	D	76.17 % / 17.45 %	219	A	77.58 % / 21.67 %	235	B	28.99 % / 70.67 %
172	B	65.67 % / 30.95 %	188	D	63.81 % / 31.8 %	204	B	44.36 % / 38.09 %	220	B	41.52 % / 33.77 %	236	D	88.32 % / 11.39 %
173	C	31.18 % / 68.22 %	189	A	85.19 % / 11.09 %	205	C	79.05 % / 12.69 %	221	A	67.32 % / 31.3 %	237	D	81.43 % / 16.02 %
174	D	76.78 % / 12.55 %	190	D	60.23 % / 38.83 %	206	D	87.13 % / 11.84 %	222	A	67.36 % / 32.27 %	238	B	77.52 % / 15.72 %
175	B	52.02 % / 44.74 %	191	A	28.14 % / 70.34 %	207	C	89.29 % / 10.37 %	223	C	15.62 % / 67.25 %	239	A	85.98 % / 10.47 %
176	C	51.8 % / 46.17 %	192	C	65.67 % / 31.14 %	208	C	49.43 % / 37.64 %	224	A	85.93 % / 13.77 %	240	D	76.17 % / 14.14 %

Q.	Ans.	Correct / Skipped	Q.	Ans.	Correct / Skipped	Q.	Ans.	Correct / Skipped	Q.	Ans.	Correct / Skipped	Q.	Ans.	Correct / Skipped
241	A	12.54 % / 76.22 %	253	B	28.26 % / 69.21 %	265	C	43.03 % / 49.49 %	277	B	44.2 % / 54.98 %	289	C	88.64 % / 10.3 %
242	B	14.65 % / 77.38 %	254	A	81.05 % / 11.63 %	266	C	55.13 % / 32.19 %	278	B	54.17 % / 40.47 %	290	A	57.1 % / 34.87 %
243	A	78.25 % / 16.88 %	255	D	76.23 % / 22.49 %	267	B	57.95 % / 31.39 %	279	C	56.77 % / 33.48 %	291	D	45.61 % / 43.35 %
244	C	32.17 % / 67.12 %	256	A	86.68 % / 11.03 %	268	D	64.77 % / 30.24 %	280	C	19.25 % / 69.7 %	292	C	27.95 % / 70.08 %
245	C	81.04 % / 16.29 %	257	A	40.04 % / 52.08 %	269	B	89.89 % / 10.11 %	281	C	41.81 % / 57.1 %	293	D	63.65 % / 33.21 %
246	C	77.36 % / 15.88 %	258	C	49.04 % / 39.94 %	270	D	51.24 % / 36.75 %	282	C	85.07 % / 10.72 %	294	A	41.41 % / 49.09 %
247	A	77.59 % / 16.14 %	259	B	55.33 % / 33.69 %	271	C	59.0 % / 30.03 %	283	A	21.54 % / 75.49 %	295	C	51.32 % / 31.34 %
248	C	77.72 % / 21.99 %	260	D	80.29 % / 11.41 %	272	A	63.45 % / 34.73 %	284	B	53.18 % / 40.19 %	296	A	43.13 % / 51.74 %
249	D	28.74 % / 69.81 %	261	C	86.42 % / 10.83 %	273	C	80.21 % / 11.9 %	285	A	84.25 % / 10.37 %	297	D	87.77 % / 10.5 %
250	C	85.6 % / 10.84 %	262	A	81.46 % / 16.84 %	274	A	81.97 % / 15.83 %	286	D	69.74 % / 30.0 %	298	C	44.68 % / 47.65 %
251	D	23.08 % / 72.62 %	263	C	45.58 % / 39.25 %	275	A	89.59 % / 10.27 %	287	A	88.02 % / 10.02 %	299	B	83.54 % / 15.7 %
252	C	65.85 % / 31.94 %	264	A	51.25 % / 47.63 %	276	C	62.49 % / 33.15 %	288	D	62.61 % / 33.39 %	300	D	55.9 % / 42.12 %

Performance Analysis	
Avg. Score (%)	48.17%
Toppers Score (%)	57.0%
Your Score	

PART A

Q.1 The cavernous sinus does not communicate with the:

A. Ophthalmic vein

B. Internal jugular vein

C. External jugular vein

D. Pterygoid plexus

Q.2 The artery, which runs along the lower border of posterior belly of digastric is :

A. Lingual

B. Ascending hypophyseal

C. Occipital

D. Palatine

Q.3 Little's area constitutes:

A. Anastomosis between branch of maxillary artery and the branch of facial artery

B. Anastomosis between two branches of facial artery

C. Anastomosis between two branches of maxillary artery

D. None of the above

Q.4 Ophthalmic artery is a branch of:

A. Maxillary artery

B. Sphenopalatine artery

C. ICA

D. ECA

Q.5 All of the following are branches of external carotid artery except:

A. Superior thyroid artery

B. Anterior ethmoidal artery

C. Posterior auricular artery

D. Occipital artery

Q.6 The blood supply of tonsils is:

A. Lingual artery

B. Superior thyroid artery

C. Facial artery

D. Pharyngeal artery

Q.7 Facial artery is the branch of the :

A. Internal carotid artery

B. External carotid artery

C. Superficial temporal

D. Maxilary artery

Q.8 First branch of external carotid artery is:

A. Facial artery

B. Ascending pharyngeal artery

C. Occipital artery

D. Lingual artery

Q.9 Which of the following arteries does not supply the Circle of Willis?

A. Anterior cerebral

B. Middle cerebral

C. Posterior inferior cerebral

D. Posterior communicating

Q.10 The papillae present on margins of the tongue:

A. Fungiform papillae

B. Filiform papillae

C. Vallate papillae

D. Foliate papillae

Q.11 Main arterial supply to the tongue is:

A. Lingual artery

B. Facial Artery

C. Ascending palatine artery

D. Ascending pharyngeal artery

Q.12 Ptosis may occur due to damage to:

A. Trochlear nerve

B. Oculomotor

C. Trigeminal nerve

D. Superior oblique muscle

Q.13 Safety muscle of tongue is:

A. Palatoglossus

B. Styloglossus

C. Genioglossus

D. Hyoglossus

Q.14 Paralysis of the upper eyelid is due to paralysis of:

A. III

B. IV

C. V

D. VII

Q.15 TMJ is supplied mainly by:

A. Masseteric and auriculotemporal nerve

B. Superficial temporal nerve

C. Facial nerve peripheral branch

D. Posterior auricular nerve

Q.16 The otic ganglion:

A. Is in relation to maxillary nerve

B. Receives preganglionic parasympathetic fibers, through the greater superficial petrosal nerve

C. Sends postganglionic parasympathetic fibers to the auriculotemporal nerve

D. Is related to the tensor tympani

Q.17 The Tongue:

A. Separated from the epiglottis by glossoepiglottic folds

B. Contains 6-10 circumvallate papilla located posterior to sulcus terminals

C. Embryologically derives from 1st branchial arch only

D. Contains foramen caecum which is present on the dorsum of frenulum

Q.18 In jaundice, there is an unconjugated hyperbilirubinemia which is most likely due to :

A. Hepatitis

B. Cirrhosis

C. Obstruction of bile canaliculi

D. Increased breakdown of red cells

Q.19 Which of the following body secretion is maximum?

A. Salivary   **B.** Gastric   **C.** Sweat   **D.** Lacrimal

Q.20 Bile acids are derived from:

A. Bile salts

B. Bile pigments

C. (A) and (B)

D. Cholesterol

Q.21 Intrinsic factor which helps in absorption of vitamin B12 is produced by :

A. Parietal cells of stomach

B. Chief cells of stomach

C. Beta cells of pancreas

D. Goblet cells

Q.22 Pharyngeal phase of deglutition :

A. Is a reflex mechanism

B. Vocal cords are closed

C. Is a voluntary mechanism

D. (A) and (B)

Q.23 Nutrients are mainly absorbed in:

A. Small intestine

B. Large intestine

C. Liver

D. Stomach

Q.24 All of the following are autocoids except:

A. Histamine

B. Eicosanoids

C. Serotonin

D. Insulin

Q.25 Drug receptors for steroids are present in the:

A. Nuclear chromatin

B. Cell membrane

C. Cytoplasm

D. Nucleus

Q.26 Which of the following is not a glycoprotein?

A. FSH

B. LH

C. Human chorionic gonadotropin

D. Prolactin

Q.27 Growth hormone is also called as:

A. Somatostatin

B. Somatomedin

C. Somatocrinin

D. Somatotropin

Q.28 Function of ADH (Antidiuretic hormone) is:

A. Water reabsorption

B. Water excretion

C. Na^+ absorption

D. K^+ secretion

Q.29 Maximum amount of glucose absorption occurs at?

A. PCT

B. DCT

C. Loop of Henle

D. None

Q.30 Brush border is seen in?

A. Bowman's capsule

B. Proximal convoluted tubule

C. Distal convoluted tubule

D. Loop of Henle

Q.31 Ammonia in the kidney tubules is excreted in exchange for?

A. $HCO3^-$ **B.** Na^+ **C.** Cl^- **D.** $PO4^{--}$

Q.32 Tidal volume in an adult is:

A. 125 ml   **B.** 500 ml   **C.** 1500 ml   **D.** 2200 ml

Q.33 Surfactant is secreted by:

A. Pneumocyte

B. Pneumocyte

C. Goblet cells

D. Pulmonary vessels

Q.34 Smoking causes:

A. Ciliary motility

B. Cellular hyperplasia

C. Mucous secretion

D. All of the above

Q.35 Which vitamin is synthesized by intestinal Bacteria?

A. Vitamin B

B. Vitamin D

C. Vitamin E

D. Vitamin K

Q.36 Vitamin C is present in largest amount in the body in:

A. Eye

B. Kidneys

C. Testes

D. Adrenal Cortex

Q.37 Which of the following is the poorest source of vitamin C?

A. Milk   **B.** Guava   **C.** Cabbage   **D.** Radish

Q.38 The 3 D's, Dermatitis, Diarrhea, Dementia are seen in the deficiency of:

A. Thiamine

B. Riboflavin

C. Niacin

D. Pyridoxine

Q.39 Which of the following enzymes require Vitamin C for their activity?

A. Procollagen proline hydroxylase

B. Procollagen amino peptidase

C. Procollagen carboxyl peptidase

D. Lysyl oxidase

Q.40 The following Vitamin is important in non-oxidative decarboxylation, transamination and trans-sulfuration reaction:

A. Riboflavin

B. Thiamine

C. Pyridoxine

D. Pantothenic acid

Q.41 Coenzyme A contains which of the following Vitamins?

A. Biotin

B. Pyridoxine

C. Pantothenic acid

D. Niacin

Q.42 Vitamin K antagonizes:

A. Corticosteroids

B. Thrombin Formation

C. Bishydroxy Coumarin

D. Production of clotting factors by liver

Q.43 Which of the following is not a polymer of glucose?

A. Glycogen

B. Cellulose

C. Amylase

D. Inulin

Q.44 An essential for the conversion of glucose to glycogen in the liver are:

A. UTP

B. GTP

C. Pyruvate kinase

D. Guanosine

Q.45 Enzymes concerned with the citric acid cycle are found in the :

A. Nucleus
B. Ribosomes
C. Mitochondria
D. Nonparticulate cytoplasm

Q.46 Cane sugar is:

A. Glucose   **B.** Sucrose   **C.** Fructose   **D.** Maltose

Q.47 Which acid is formed in the citric acid cycle?

A. Oxaloacetic acid   **B.** Glutamic acid
C. Nitric acid   **D.** Butyric acid

Q.48 Which of the following is an abnormal constituent of urine:

A. Glucose   **B.** Creatine
C. Urea   **D.** None of the above

Q.49 Which of the following is a non reducing sugar?

A. Glucose   **B.** Maltose   **C.** Lactose   **D.** Sucrose

Q.50 The end product of glycolysis under anaerobic conditions is:

A. Lactic acid   **B.** Pyruvic acid
C. Acetoacetic acid   **D.** Oxaloacetic acid

PART B

Q.51 The reversible change including the replacement of one type of adult cells with the other type is called:

A. Hyperplasia   **B.** Metaplasia
C. Dysplasia   **D.** Neoplasia

Q.52 Lack of differentiation of cells is known as:

A. Anaplasia   **B.** Metaplasia
C. Dysplasia   **D.** Hypertrohpy

Q.53 A simple bacterial test for mutagenic carcinogens is:

A. Ames test   **B.** Redox test
C. Bacteriophage   **D.** Gene splicing

Q.54 Cellular and flagellar movement is carried out by all of the following except:

A. Intermediate filaments
B. Actin
C. Tubulin
D. Myosin

Q.55 Presence of dermoid cyst in the ovary is an example of:

A. Choristoma   **B.** Hamartoma
C. Neoplasia   **D.** Teratoma

Q.56 Which of the following is not a feature of malignant neoplasm?

A. Invasion   **B.** Encapsulation
C. Metastasis   **D.** Anaplasia

Q.57 The most common malignancies found in males are:

A. Lung and oral cavity
B. Brain and parotid
C. Prostate and parotid
D. Brain and prostate

Q.58 Which of the following has best prognosis?

A. Malignant melanoma
B. Squamous cell carcinoma
C. Basal cell carcinoma
D. Osteosarcoma

Q.59 Burkitt's lymphoma is associated with the proliferation of:

A. T cells   **B.** B cells
C. Lymph vessels   **D.** Lymph nodes

Q.60 The wasting syndrome associated in cancer is called:

A. Achalasia   **B.** Cachexia
C. Atelexis   **D.** Cacogeusia

Q.61 Onion skin appearance is seen in:

A. Ewing's sarcoma   **B.** Osteosarcoma
C. Osteoma   **D.** Fibrosarcoma

Q.62 Sunburst appearance and Codman's triangle are seen in:

A. Osteosarcoma   **B.** Fibrosarcoma
C. Chondrosarcoma   **D.** None of the above

Q.63 Coagulative necrosis is:

A. Characteristic of focal bacterial infections
B. Characteristic of hypoxic death
C. Characterized by loss of tissue architecture
D. None of the above

Q.64 Diabetic gangrene is caused by:

A. Vasospasm   **B.** Peripheral neuritis
C. Atherosclerosis   **D.** None of the above

Q.65 Liquefactive necrosis is commonly seen in:

A. Brain   **B.** Lung   **C.** Liver   **D.** Spleen

Q.66 Which of the following is correct?

A. Pyknosis - Shrinkage of Nucleus
B. Karyolysis - Dissolution of Nucleus
C. Karyorrhexis - Fragmentation of Nucleus
D. All of the above

Q.67 Stain used for demonstration of amyloid is:

A. Congo Red   **B.** Masson's Trichrome
C. Vonkosa   **D.** Reticulin

Q.68 The hormone dependent shedding of endometrium is an example of :

A. Necrosis   **B.** Autolysis
C. Apoptosis   **D.** None of the above

Q.69 Synthesis of DNA occurs in which phase?

A. G1   **B.** G2   **C.** S   **D.** M

Q.70 'Physiologic programmed cell death' is termed as:

A. Apoptosis   **B.** Lysis
C. Autolysis   **D.** Autopsy

Q.71 Anasarca means

A. Abnormal inflammatory process
B. Severe generalized swelling
C. Absence of proliferation of vessels following inflammation
D. Presence of pus

Q.72 Nutmeg liver occurs in:
A. Jaundice
B. Chronic venous congestion
C. Cirrhosis
D. Hepatocellular carcinoma

Q.73 Infarcts are not common in:
A. Both Liver and Lung
B. Liver
C. Kidney
D. Lung

Q.74 Which of the following is true regarding lymphangioleiomyomatosis?
A. Primarily seen in old age
B. Commonly associated with persistent cough
C. Proliferation occurs in perivascular epithelioid cells
D. Disease is rapidly progressive

Q.75 Risk factor for atherosclerosis:
A. Hypertension
B. Diabetes
C. Smoking
D. All of them

Q.76 Which of the following is primarily a bactericidal drug?
A. Chloramphenicol
B. Gentamicin
C. Sulphadiazine
D. Tetracycline

Q.77 Penicillin is effective against:
A. Neisseria meningitidis
B. Neisseria gonorrhoeae
C. Treponema pallidum
D. All of the above

Q.78 The drug of choice for typhoid is:
A. Tetracycline
B. Metronidazole
C. Ciprofloxacin
D. Cefotaxime

Q.79 Desfuroxamide is a drug used for:
A. Kala-azar
B. Pernicious anemia
C. Pain control
D. Thalassemia

Q.80 A patient taking which of the following drug should not eat cheese?
A. Tetracycline
B. Amoxycillin
C. Doxycycline
D. Triamterene

Q.81 The drug which gives orange-red color to the urine is:
A. Rifampicin
B. Ethambutol
C. Isoniazid
D. Streptomycin

Q.82 Bacitracin is a :
A. Oral antibiotic
B. Topical antibiotic
C. Parenteral antibiotic
D. All of these

Q.83 Phototoxicity is the side effect of:
A. Penicillin
B. Demeclocycline
C. Erythromycin
D. Streptomycin

Q.84 Agent used in oral thrush:
A. Miconazole
B. Clobetasol
C. Clotrimazole
D. Amoxycillin

Q.85 Aminoglycosides is :
A. Accumulate in renal failure
B. Inhibit protein synthesis
C. Effective against gram-negative infections
D. All of the above

Q.86 Which of the following is a sign of deep anesthesia?
A. Appearance of tears in eyes
B. Resistance to passive inflation of lungs
C. Fall in blood pressure
D. Patient makes swallowing movements

Q.87 The minimal alveolar concentration (MAC) of halothane is:
A. 75%
B. 25%
C. 7.5%
D. 0.75%

Q.88 Which of the following is used mainly for the induction of general anesthesia?
A. Fentanyl + Droperidol.
B. Ketamine
C. Thiopentone sodium
D. All of the above

Q.89 The general anesthetic having significant cardio depressant activity is:
A. Halothane
B. Enflurane
C. Ether
D. Nitrous oxide

Q.90 The immobility produced by general anesthetics in response to painful surgical stimuli is primarily due to their action on:
A. Motor cortex
B. Basal ganglia
C. Thalamus
D. Spinal cord

Q.91 The most common side effect of the oral administration of ampicillin is:
A. Anaphylactic shock
B. Diarrhea
C. Oral candidiasis
D. Renal failure

Q.92 Which of the following drugs is likely to damage the eighth cranial nerve when administered for a long period of time?
A. Ethambutol
B. Isoniazid
C. Rifampicin
D. Streptomycin

Q.93 Mechanism of action of quinolones is:
A. Inhibits DNA gyrase
B. Inhibits bacterial protein synthesis
C. Inhibits bacterial cell wall synthesis
D. Inhibits intake of folic acid

Q.94 Fluconazole is used for the treatment of:
A. Pemphigus
B. Herpes simplex
C. Candidiasis
D. Syphilis

Q.95 Ototoxicity and nephrotoxicity is caused by:

A. Antibiotic

B. Antiemetic

C. Antifungal

D. Antiviral

Q.96 On a stained slide, Clostridium tetani has the appearance of a:

A. Bunch of grapes

B. Chain of beads

C. Drum stick

D. Safety pin

Q.97 In initial stages of typhoid, salmonella can be detected in:

A. Feacus

B. Urine

C. Blood

D. All of the above

Q.98 The following are applicable to bacterial genome except:

A. It is composed of DNA

B. It does not contain histones

C. It is circular

D. Its DNA has both introns and extrons

Q.99 Each of the following can cause food poisoning except:

A. Cl. difficile

B. Staphylococcus

C. Cl. welchii

D. Cl. botulinum

Q.100 Organ of locomotion in bacteria is:

A. Fimbria

B. Flagella

C. Capsule

D. Cell wall

Q.101 Wasserman test is diagnostic of:

A. Syphilis

B. Gonorrhea

C. TB

D. Typhoid

Q.102 In a patient with typhoid, diagnosis after 15 days of onset of fever is best done by:

A. Blood culture

B. Widal test

C. Stool culture

D. Urine culture

Q.103 Bacteria with potent exotoxin is:

A. Clostridium tetani

B. Pseudomonas

C. Shigella

D. Klebsiella

Q.104 Grape bunch shaped colonies are seen in:

A. Streptococcus

B. Staphylococcus

C. E.coli

D. Gonococci

Q.105 Inactivated microorganisms are used in the manufacture of which of the following:

A. Salk vaccine

B. Tetanus toxoid

C. Sabin's oral vaccine

D. All of the above

Q.106 The major intestinal pathogens which are non-lactose fermenters are:

A. Salmonella

B. Klebsiella

C. Escherichia

D. Paracolons

Q.107 A protoplast is best characterized as a bacterial cell:

A. With a cell wall but free of a capsule

B. Containing a cell wall and a capsule

C. Free of a cell wall and a capsule

D. Uniquely sensitive to penicillin

Q.108 With regards to temperature requirement, most pathogenic bacteria are:

A. Psychrophiles

B. Mesophiles

C. Cryophiles

D. Thermophiles

Q.109 Which of the following is anaerobic:

A. E.coli

B. Bacteroides

C. Pseudomonas

D. Klebsiella

Q.110 One of the following is a treponemal test for diagnosis of syphilis:

A. FAB

B. Widal test

C. Wasserman test

D. Kahn test

Q.111 The vaccine for Japanese Encephalitis is?

A. Live (mutant) vaccine

B. Killed vaccine

C. Live (attenuated) vaccine

D. Live (recombinant) vaccine

Q.112 The mechanism by which most fungi cause disease is:

A. Exotoxin production

B. Lecithinase production

C. Hypersensitivity

D. Coagulase production

Q.113 Germ tubes are formed mainly by:

A. Candida albicans

B. Candida stellatoidea

C. Candida tropicalis

D. Candida pseudotropicalis

Q.114 Fungal infection of human beings is called as:

A. Mucorsis

B. Mycosis

C. Fungosis

D. Micromia

Q.115 The culture media for fungus is:

A. Tellurite medium

B. NNN medium

C. Chocolate agar medium

D. Sabourauds medium

Q.116 The brick red color of post mortem lividity is seen in poisoning due to?

A. Carbon monoxide

B. Hydrogen sulfide

C. Phosphorus

D. Cyanide

Q.117 Lichtenberg figures are seen in?

A. Heatstroke

B. Radiation injury

C. Lightning

D. Electrocution

Q.118 'Paradox gun' is a?

A. Revolver

B. Shotgun

C. Automatic pistol

D. Machine gun

Q.119 Danbury tremor is seen in?

A. Mercury poisoning

B. Iron poisoning

C. Lead poisoning

D. Arsenic poisoning

Q.120 Kevorkian sign is seen in?

A. Cornea

B. Retinal vessels

C. Pupil

D. Vitreous humor

Q.121 Which of the following is true regarding superfecundation?

A. Fertilization of the second ovum in a woman who is already pregnant

B. Occurs in the bipartite uterus

C. Both ova do not always develop to maturity

D. The second fetus is born later as a mature child

Q.122 Scorching results from:

A. The flame emerging from the muzzle

B. Grains of gunpowder being driven into the skin

C. Superficial deposit of smoke on the skin

D. Deposition of lead or other metal in the skin

Q.123 The test to determine blood groups in a bloodstain is:

A. Luminol Spray

B. Haemin crystal test

C. Kastle-Meyer test

D. Lattes crust method

Q.124 Which among the following is a waxy, luminous & translucent poison?

A. Yellow phosphorous

B. Cobra venom

C. Organophosphates

D. Iodine

Q.125 Regarding rugoscopy, all are true except?

A. Palatal rugae are used as a method of identification

B. Palatoprints do not change during growth

C. Primary rugae are less than 3 mm

D. Secondary rugae are 3-5 mm

Q.126 Which theory of social health puts profit ahead of health?

A. Parsonian

B. Foucauldian

C. Marxist

D. Feminist

Q.127 The purpose is to limit the incidence of disease by controlling causes and risk factors:

A. Primordial prevention

B. Primary prevention

C. Secondary prevention

D. Tertiary prevention

Q.128 The property of a test to identify the proportion of truly ill persons in a population who are identified as ill by a screening test.

A. Sensitivity

B. Specificity

C. Positive predictive value

D. Negative predictive value

Q.129 A study that measures the number of persons with influenza in a calendar year:

A. Cohort study

B. Case-control

C. Cross-sectional

D. Case report

Q.130 The leading cause of Diarrheal disease is:

A. Enterotoxigenic Escherichia col

B. Salmonella (non-typhoid)

C. Rotavirus

D. Campylobacter jejuni

Q.131 Mammography should be done annually in women of what age?

A. 50 years old and above

B. 60 years old and above

C. 45 years old and above

D. 30 years old and above

Q.132 Samuel Hahnemann is referred to as founding Father of:

A. Ayurveda

B. Allopathy

C. Homeopathy

D. Yoga

Q.133 Origin of SPM dates back to:

A. 17th Century

B. 18th Century

C. 19th Century

D. 20th Century

Q.134 Benefits of Socialization of medicine are all except:

A. It eliminates competition among physicians in search of clients

B. It ensures social equity and universal coverage

C. Medical care becomes free for the patients, which is supported by the state

D. Patients can get a good quality of treatment without cost

Q.135 Socialization of medicine means:

A. Study of man as a social being in his total environment

B. Provision of medical services and professional education by the state but operated and regulated by the government

C. Provision of medical services and professional education by the state but operated and regulated by professional groups rather than by the government

D. Study of man as a social being in his whole life

Q.136 Who introduced the concept of social medicine?

A. Rene Sand

B. Neumann

C. Jules Guerin

D. A Grotjahn

Q.137 Which military surgeon successfully evolved the principle of preventing non-communicable disease with specific diet therapy?

A. Major Walter Reed

B. James Lind

C. Major Ronald Ross

D. Bruce

Q.138 Who propounded the germ theory of disease?

A. Leeuwenhoek

B. Robert Koch

C. Ambroise Pare

D. Louis Pasteur

Q.139 Who among the following introduced the concept of the relationship of the environment with human health?

A. Avicenna

B. Charaka

C. Hippocrates

D. Paracelsus

Q.140 The system of medicine currently not recognized by the Government of India is:

A. Ayurveda/Siddha

B. Homeopathy

C. Acupuncture

D. Unani

Q.141 The concept of health in Ayurvedic medicine is a state of balance between:

A. Four primary senses of humor
B. Three primary senses of humor
C. Five natural elements
D. None of the above

Q.142 A most common cause of maternal death in India:

A. Severe bleeding
B. Unsafe abortion
C. Obstructed labor
D. Eclampsia

Q.143 The incidence of tuberculosis in a community is measured by:

A. Sputum smear examination
B. Tuberculin test
C. Mass miniature radiography
D. Mantoux test

Q.144 Kuppuswamy scale for socioeconomic status is used for:

A. Urban population
B. Rural population
C. Urban slum population
D. Any population

Q.145 "Bhopal Gas Tragedy" is an example of:

A. Continuous or repeated exposure epidemic
B. Point source epidemic
C. Slow epidemic
D. Propagated epidemic

Q.146 Tuberculin positive means:

A. Immuno deficient patient
B. Allergic to tuberculin protein
C. The patient is suffering from the disease
D. The patient is infected with mycobacterium

Q.147 Who is known for the discovery of the prevention of scurvy?

A. John Snow
B. Louis Pasteur
C. James Lind
D. Joseph Lister

Q.148 The most common cancer affecting Indian women is:

A. Cervical cancer
B. Breast cancer
C. Ovarian cancer
D. Uterine cancer

Q.149 The best parameter to measure air pollution is:

A. SO_2
B. CO_2
C. CO
D. All of the above

Q.150 All of the following diseases are transmitted by the Aedes mosquito except:

A. Yellow fever
B. Dengue
C. Chikungunya fever
D. Japanese encephalitis

PART C

Q.151 All of the following are seen in tuberous sclerosis except?

A. Civatte bodies
B. Koenen tumors
C. Ash leaf macules
D. Shagreen patch

Q.152 An absence of pigment in the skin is called

A. Acanthosis nigricans
B. Albinism
C. Melanism
D. Xanthoderma

Q.153 Pseudo-isomorphic phenomenon is characteristic of?

A. Vitiligo
B. Psoriasis
C. DI F
D. Plane warts

Q.154 Blaschko's lines represent?

A. Lines of development
B. Dermatomes
C. Lines along blood vessels
D. Lines along lymphatics

Q.155 Most common type of vitiligo is?

A. Segmental vitiligo
B. Focal vitiligo
C. Generalized vitiligo
D. Mucosal vitiligo

Q.156 Which of the following would be prescribed for acne?

A. Actiq
B. Actonel
C. Accu-Check
D. Accutane

Q.157 A 36 year old factory worker developed itchy, annular scaly plaques in both groins. Application of a corticosteroid ointment led to temporary relief but the plaques continued to extend at the periphery. The most likely diagnosis is:

A. Erythema annulare centrifugum
B. Granuloma annulare
C. Annular lichen planus
D. Tinea cruris

Q.158 Which of the following is not a cutaneous marker of internal malignancy?

A. Bullous pemphigoid
B. Acanthosis nigricans
C. Dermatomyositis
D. Erythema chronicum migrans

Q.159 An 8-year-old boy from Bihar presents with a 6 months history of an ill-defined, hypopigmented slightly atrophic macule on the face. The most likely diagnosis is:

A. Pityriasis alba
B. Indeterminate leprosy
C. Morphea
D. Calcium deficiency

Q.160 A 6-month-old infant had itchy erythematous papules and exudative lesions on the scalp, face, groins, and axillae for one month. She also had vesicular lesions on the palms. The most likely diagnosis is:

A. Congenital syphilis
B. Seborrheic dermatitis
C. Scabies
D. Psoriasis

Q.161 Airborne contact dermatitis can be diagnosed by:

A. Skin biopsy

B. Patch test

C. Prick test

D. Estimation of serum IgE levels

Q.162 A 3 year old child has eczematous dermatitis on extensor surfaces, His mother has a history of Bronchial asthma Diagnosis should be -

A. Atopic dermatitis

B. Contact dermatitis

C. Seborrhoeic dermatitis

D. Infantile eczematous dermatitis

Q.163 Tuberculids are seen in:

A. Lupus vulgaris

B. Scrofuloderma.

C. Lichen scrofulosorum

D. Erythema nodosum

Q.164 True regarding Pityriasis Rosea is:

A. Self-limiting

B. Chronic relapsing

C. Life-threatening infection

D. Caused by dermatophytes

Q.165 'Chancre redux' is a clinical feature of:

A. Early relapsing syphilis

B. Late syphilis

C. Chancroid

D. Recurrent herpes simplex infection

Q.166 Treatment of alcohol dependence is by all except?

A. Disulfiram

B. `Naltrexone

C. Flumazenil

D. Acamprosate

Q.167 A 45-year-old farmer has itchy erythematous papular lesions on the face, neck, 'V' area of the chest, dorsum of hands, and forearms for 3 years. The lesions are more severe in summer and improve by 75% in winter. The most appropriate test to diagnose the condition would be:

A. Skin biopsy

B. Estimation of IgE levels in blood

C. Patch test

D. Intradermal prick test

Q.168 Drug used for treatment of nocturnal enuresis is?

A. Trazodone

B. Imipramine

C. Chlorpromazine

D. Sertraline

Q.169 Most common cause of premature death in schizrenia is?

A. Drug toxicity

B. Nosocomial infection

C. Homicide

D. Suicide

Q.170 Which is not a cognitive dysfunction?

A. Overgeneralization

B. Thought block

C. Catastrophic thinking

D. Arbitrary inference

Q.171 Which of the following is seen associated with alcoholic paranoia?

A. Drowsiness

B. Delusions

C. Hallucinations

D. Impulsiveness

Q.172 An 18-year-old student complains of a lack of interest in studies for the last 6 months. He has frequent quarrels with his parents and has frequent headaches. The most appropriate clinical approach would be to:

A. Leave him as a normal adolescent problem

B. Rule out depression

C. Rule out migraine

D. Rule out an oppositional defiant disorder

Q.173 Somatic passivity is seen in?

A. Depression

B. Hypomania

C. Body dysmorphic disorder

D. Paranoid Schizophrenia

Q.174 All are features of autistic disorders except?

A. Stereotypic movements

B. Impairment of social interaction

C. Visual impairment

D. Delay in speech development

Q.175 40 year old female came to the OPD with complaints of depressed mood, insomnia, loss of appetite, and lack of interest in surroundings for the past 1 year. These symptoms appeared after a loss in a business deal 1 year ago. Which is correct regarding the management?

A. Selective Serotonin Reuptake Inhibitors (SSRI's) are the most effective drugs

B. Antidepressants should be given based on the side effect profile

C. No treatment is required as it is due to loss in a business deal

D. Combination therapy with 2 or more antidepressants

Q.176 Delusions in clear consciousness are seen in:

A. Dementia

B. Delirium

C. Schizophrenia

D. Neurosis

Q.177 Dementia is seen in all except:

A. Schizophrenia

B. Head injury

C. Huntington's chorea

D. Cannabis

Q.178 Impaired consciousness, visual hallucination, hyperactivity and fragmentary delusions are:

A. Delirium

B. Dementia

C. Paranoid psychosis

D. Schizophrenia

Q.179 Postural orthostatic tachycardia syndrome is characterised by all except?

A. Women affected more commonly than men

B. Heart rate >120/minute

C. Increase in heart rate >30/minute when standing

D. Usually presents with orthostatic hypotension

Q.180 Who introduced cocaine in psychiatry.

A. Freud　　**B.** Jung　　**C.** Miller　　**D.** Stanley

Q.181 Most common cause of mood congruent delusion is:

A. Schizophrenia　　　　**B.** Mania
C. OCN　　　　　　　　**D.** Dementia

Q.182 Which of the following is a mature defense mechanism:

A. Projection　　　　　**B.** Reaction formation
C. Anticipation　　　　**D.** Denial

Q.183 Not a proper match:

A. Auditory hallucination - Alcoholism
B. Thought broadcasting-schizophrenia
C. Delusion of infidelity - obsessive-compulsive neurosis
D. Delusion of grandeur - mania

Q.184 Suicidal tendencies are least common with:

A. Alone　　　　　　　**B.** Depression
C. Old age　　　　　　**D.** Married person

Q.185 Psychoanalysis was introduced by:

A. Freud　　　　　　　**B.** Schielder
C. Dale & Denicker　　**D.** Eugen Bluer

Q.186 Thematic perception test is named after:

A. Freud　　　　　　　**B.** Simon paul
C. Douglas　　　　　　**D.** Wechslers

Q.187 RANKL is produced by all except?

A. Osteocytes
B. Osteoclasts
C. Activated T cells
D. Bone marrow stromal cells

Q.188 The commonest cause of mental retardation is:

A. Alkaptonuria
B. Kluver-Bucy syndrome
C. Korsakoffs syndrome
D. Birth asphyxia

Q.189 Ego's defense mechanism "Undoing" is typically seen in:

A. Depression
B. Schizophrenia
C. Obsessive-compulsive neurosis
D. Hysteria

Q.190 The eight-stage classification of human life is proposed by -

A. Sigmund Freud　　　**B.** Pavel
C. Strauss　　　　　　**D.** Erikson

Q.191 The patient presents with altered behavior, delusions & hallucination suggest.

A. Psychotic disorder
B. Confirms schizophrenia
C. Korsakoff s psychosis
D. Obsessive-compulsive neurosis

Q.192 Commonest psychiatric illness in India is:

A. Schizophrenia

B. Endogenous depression
C. Neurotic depression
D. Anxiety neurosis

Q.193 Oedipus complex (given by Sigmund Freud) is seen in:

A. Boys of 1-3 years of age
B. Girls of 1-3 years of age
C. Boys of 3 - 5 years of age
D. Girls of 3-5 years of age

Q.194 Which of the following is a center for recent memory:

A. Parietal cortex
B. Temporal lobe
C. Hippocampus
D. Thalamus and subthalamus

Q.195 Biochemical etiology of Alzheimer's disease relates it to:

A. Acetylcholine　　　**B.** GABA
C. Serotonin　　　　　**D.** Dopamine

Q.196 Which is the most common cause of hypothyroidism?

A. Multinodular goitre
B. Lymphoma of thyroid
C. Hashimoto's thyroiditis
D. Reidel's thyroiditis

Q.197 The most common level of thyroglossal cyst is:

A. Lingual　　　　　　**B.** Infra-lingual
C. Supra-hyoid　　　　**D.** Infra-hyoid

Q.198 Hashimoto's disease is :

A. A granulomatous thyroiditis
B. An autoimmune thyroiditis
C. Fibrous thyroiditis
D. A viral infection of the thyroid gland

Q.199 A ranula is a:

A. Type of epulis
B. Sublingual thyroid
C. Thyroglossal cyst
D. Cystic swelling in the floor of the mouth

Q.200 Threshold radiation dose for haematological syndrome is?

A. 1 Gy　　**B.** 5 Gy　　**C.** 20 Gy　　**D.** 100 Gy

Q.201 Best investigation for the detection of bone metastases is?

A. X-ray　　　　　　　**B.** CT Scan
C. MRI　　　　　　　　**D.** Bone scan

Q.202 Which of the following contrast agents can be used in a patient with renal dysfunction for the prevention of contrast nephropathy?

A. Low osmolar contrast
B. Ionic contrast
C. Fenoldopam
D. Acetylcysteine

Q.203 Egg on side appearance is characteristic of?

A. Tetralogy of Fallot
B. Total anomalous pulmonary venous connection
C. Patent ductus arteriosus
D. Transposition of great arteries

Q.204 Most ionizing radiation among the following is?

A. X rays
B. Gamma rays
C. Alpha rays
D. Beta rays

Q.205 Which of the following substances are used to coat the walls of a CT scan room for radiation shielding?

A. Tungsten   **B.** Glass   **C.** Lead   **D.** Iron

Q.206 Which one of the following tumors shows calcification on CT Scan:

A. Ependymoma
B. Medulloblastoma
C. Meningioma
D. CNS Lymphoma

Q.207 Which one of the following is the most preferred route to perform cerebral angiography?

A. Transfemoral route
B. Transaxillary route
C. Direct carotid puncture
D. Transbronchial route

Q.208 Which of the following ultrasound marker is associated with the greatest increased risk for Trisomy 21 in fetus:

A. Echogenic foci in heart
B. Hyperechogenic bowel
C. Choroid plexus cysts
D. Nuchal edema

Q.209 The most sensitive imaging modality for diagnosis of ureteric stones in a patient with acute colic is:

A. X-ray KUB region
B. Ultrasonogram
C. Non-contrast CT scan of the abdomen
D. Contrast-enhanced CT scan of the abdomen

Q.210 The gold standard for the diagnosis of osteoporosis is:

A. Dual-energy X-ray absorptiometry
B. Single energy X-ray absorptiometry
C. Ultrasound
D. Quantitative computed tomography

Q.211 At $t = 0$ there are 6×10^{23} radioactive atoms of a substance, which decay with a disintegration constant equal to $0.01/\text{sec}$. What would be the initial decay rate?

A. 6×10^{23} **B.** 6×10^{22} **C.** 6×10^{21} **D.** 6×10^{20}

Q.212 The technique employed in radiotherapy to counteract the effect of tumor motion due to breathing is known as:

A. Arc technique
B. Modulation
C. Gating
D. Shunting

Q.213 Gamma camera in Nuclear Medicine is used for:

A. Organ imaging
B. Measuring the radioactivity
C. Monitoring the surface contamination
D. RIA

Q.214 The MR imaging in multiple sclerosis will show lesions in:

A. White matter
B. Grey matter
C. Thalamus
D. Basal ganglia

Q.215 The procedure of choice for the evaluation of an aneurysm is:

A. Ultrasonography
B. Computed tomography
C. Magnetic resonance imaging
D. Arteriography

Q.216 Complications of stellate ganglion block are all except?

A. Mediastinitis
B. Cardiac arrest
C. Pneumothorax
D. Mueller's syndrome

Q.217 Anaesthetic implication in Gaisbock's syndrome is?

A. Postoperative respiratory failure
B. Risk of deep vein thrombosis
C. Renal dysfunction
D. Risk of aspiration

Q.218 Thiopental is contraindicated in all of the following except?

A. Porphyria
B. Status asthmaticus
C. Pericardial tamponade
D. Penetrating eye injury

Q.219 Which of the following anaesthetic agents can induce epilepsy?

A. Sevoflurane
B. Isoflurane
C. Desflurane
D. Methoxyflurane

Q.220 Contraindications to vasoconstrictors in local anaesthesia?

A. Spinal anaesthesia
B. Epidural anaesthesia
C. Digital nerve block
D. Regional anaesthesia

Q.221 Which of the following is correct regarding colour coding of anaesthetic gases?

A. Oxygen - Black with grey shoulders
B. Nitrous oxide - Blue
C. Cyclopropane - Red
D. Helium - Orange

Q.222 Which of the following agents is not used to provide induced hypotension during surgery?

A. Sodium nitroprusside
B. Hydralazine
C. Mephentermine
D. Esmolol

Q.223 Which of the following agents is used for the treatment of postoperative shivering?

A. Thiopentone
B. Suxamethonium
C. Atropine
D. Pethidine

Q.224 Which of the following intravenous induction agents is the most suitable for daycare surgery?

A. Morphine   **B.** Ketamine
C. Propofol   **D.** Diazepam

Q.225 Which of the following statements is not true about etomidate?

A. It is an intravenous anesthetic
B. It precipitates coronary insufficiency
C. It inhibits cortisol synthesis
D. It causes pain at site of injection

Q.226 In case of reimplantation of an amputated digit, which of the following structures is fixed first?

A. Nerve   **B.** Artery   **C.** Vein   **D.** Bone

Q.227 Agents which decrease bone resorption in osteoporosis are all except?

A. Risedronate   **B.** Teriparatide
C. Strontium ranelate   **D.** Raloxifene

Q.228

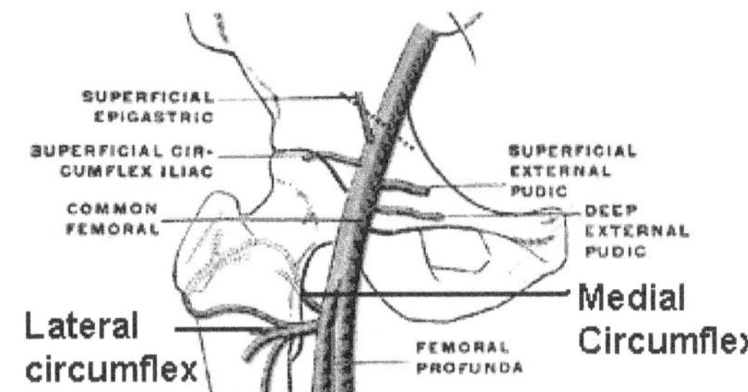

Arteries around the hip joint

Blood supply to head and neck of femur is mainly from?
A. Superficial epigastric artery
B. Medial circumflex femoral artery
C. Lateral circumflex femoral artery
D. Artery of ligamentum teres

Q.229 Which of the following is a characteristic feature of Blount's disease?

A. Genu valgum   **B.** Genu varum
C. Coxa vara   **D.** Coxa valga

Q.230 Agnes Hunt traction is used for?

A. Flexion deformity of hip
B. Trochanteric fracture
C. Fracture shaft of femur in adults
D. Low backache

Q.231 Triad of Klippel Feil syndrome consists of all except?

A. Low hair line
B. Elevated scapula
C. Short neck
D. Limited neck movements

Q.232 Brown tumor is characteristic of?

A. Hyperparathyroidism
B. Hypoparathyroidism
C. Hyperthyroidism
D. Hypopituitarism

Q.233 Which of the following is tested using the 'Lift off test'?

A. Teres Minor   **B.** Subscapularis
C. Supraspinatus   **D.** Infraspinatus

Q.234 All are true regarding synovial sarcoma except?

A. More common at extra articular sites
B. Knee and foot are commonly involved
C. Usually seen in individuals less than 50 years of age
D. Originates from the synovial lining

Q.235 Clavicular fracture is treated by?

A. Fixation with plate and screw
B. Open reduction and internal fixation
C. Skeletal traction
D. Figure of eight bandage

Q.236 A joint is innervated by the articular branches of the nerves which supply the muscles which move the joint. This law is known as:

A. Hilton's law   **B.** Andry's law
C. Wolff's law   **D.** Cushing's law

Q.237 Bone remodeling in response to stress was described by:

A. Harvey Cushing   **B.** William Osler
C. Julius Wolff   **D.** Nicolas Andry

Q.238 Most common nerve injured in supracondylar fracture humerus?

A. Median
B. Radial
C. Ulnar
D. Anterior interosseous nerve

Q.239 Heberden's Arthropathy affects:

A. Lumbar spine
B. Symmetrically large joints
C. Sacroiliac joints
D. Distal interphalangeal joints

Q.240 Gallow's traction is used for?

A. Fracture shaft of femur
B. Fracture neck of femur
C. Fracture humerus
D. Fracture tibia

Q.241 Duration of second state of labour in a multipara is:

A. 10 minutes   **B.** 30 minutes
C. 2 hours   **D.** 1 hour

Q.242 Most important conjugate during labour:

A. Anatomical conjugate
B. True conjugate
C. Obstetric conjugate
D. Diagonal conjugate

Q.243 Progression of labour is assessed by:

A. Partograph

B. Cervical dilatation

C. Fetal heart monitoring

D. Status of membranes

Q.244 In android pelvis:

A. Shape is triangular

B. Cavity is convergent

C. Sacral angle less than 90 degrees and inclined forward

D. All of the above

Q.245 All the fetal skull measurements are 9.5 cm except:

A. Bi - parietal

B. Sub mento bregmatic

C. Sub occipito bregmatic

D. Occipitofrontal

Q.246 The best intervention in I stage of labour is:

A. Artificial rupture of membranes with Oxytocin

B. Artificial rupture of membranes with methergine

C. Artificial rupture of membranes with sedation

D. Artificial rupture of membranes only

Q.247 In the partogram devised by WHO, the action line lies ___ hours to the right of the alert line.

A. 2　　　　**B.** 4　　　　**C.** 6　　　　**D.** 8

Q.248 The length of diagonal conjugate is:

A. 5 cm　　**B.** 13 cm　　**C.** 13 .5 cm　　**D.** 10 cm

Q.249 Obstetric conjugate is the distance between:

A. Sacral promontory & inner surface of pubic symphysis

B. Sacral promontory & outer surface of pubic symphysis

C. Sacral promontory & upper edge of pubic symphysis

D. Sacral promontory & lower edge of pubic symphysis

Q.250 A pregnant woman in her third trimester was in a motor vehicle accident presets to the ER. She is stable and no uterine bleeding or contractions. Fetal heart sounds are normal and placenta is intact.

Which of the following is the best next step?

A. Blood type and Rh testing

B. Cesarean section

C. Induction of labor

D. Send her home and follow up the next scheduled visit

Q.251 The highest incidence of Gestational Trophoblastic Disease is in:

A. Australia　　　　　　**B.** Asia

C. North America　　　　**D.** Westem Europe

Q.252 The quantity of hormone released by Progestasert per day is?

A. 25 μ g　　**B.** 45 μg　　**C.** 65 μg　　**D.** 85 μg

Q.253 Which of the following is true regarding Organ of Rosenmuller?

A. Forms paraovarian cyst

B. Consist of horizontal tubules in mesovarium

C. Tubules are lined by columnar cells

D. Represents cranial end of the Wolffian body

Q.254 An athletic girl presents with amenorrhea for 3 weeks. Pregnancy test is negative and her vital signs are within normal limits.

Which is the most likely cause of this amenorrhea?

A. Estrogen deficiency

B. Progesterone deficiency

C. Testosterone deficiency

D. Thyroid hormone deficiency

Q.255 All of the following are germ cell tumours except?

A. Mesonephroid tumors

B. Teratoma

C. Dysgerminoma

D. Endodermal sinus tumour

Q.256 Which of the following is not true regarding Large Loop Excision of the Transformation Zone (LLETZ)?

A. Uses low voltage diathermy

B. Applicable only to cervix

C. Loop size greater than 2cm gives a better cone

D. Shorter procedure time compared to laser ablation

Q.257 Solid tumour with cystic areas in between filled with haemorrhagic fluid a accounting for about 20% of all ovarian cancers is?

A. Cystadenocarcinoma

B. Mesonephroid tumors

C. Endometrioid tumour

D. Brenner tumour

Q.258 Moschcowitz repair is done for?

A. Vault prolapse

B. Enterocoele

C. Chronic inversion of uterus

D. Adenomyosis

Q.259 Which is true reqarding Savage syndrome?

A. Receptor defect to gonadotrophic hormones

B. Short stature

C. Ovaries do not contain follicles

D. FSH is normal

Q.260 Which of the following is true regarding RU 486 ?

A. Prevents fertilization

B. Has affinity for estrogen receptors

C. Single dose of 10 mg prevents pregnancy in 90% cases

D. Causes delayed menstruation

Q.261 Absence of corkscrew glands is seen in?

A. Halban's disease

B. Polycystic ovarian disease

C. Irregular ripening

D. Metropathia haemorrhagica

Q.262 All are true regarding medical treatment of endometriosis except?

A. Oral progestins cause decidualization of endometrial tissue

B. Injectable progestagen is used once in 3 months in the management of pain of endometriosis

C. Levonorgestrel releasing intrauterine system reduces dysmenorrhoea in endometriosis

D. Gestrinone is given orally 2.5-5 mg per day to induce endometrial atrophy

Q.263 Which of the following is not a contraindication to pregnancy?

A. Severe pulmonary hypertension

B. Severe obstructive valvular lesions

C. Large secundum atrial septal defect with left to right shunt

D. Marfan syndrome with dilated aorta

Q.264 Gold standard test for measuring B HCG levels in serum is?

A. ELISA

B. Bioassay

C. Radioimmunoassay

D. Latex agglutination test

Q.265 False regarding hormone levels in polycystic ovarian disease?

A. Increased Androgen

B. Increased Prolactin

C. Increased LH

D. Increased LH/FSH ratio

Q.266 Most specific marker for neural tube defects is?

A. Alpha-fetoprotein

B. Unconjugated estriol

C. Acetylcholinesterase

D. Pseudocholinesterase

Q.267 Please identify which of the following are true with regard to pubertal development.

A. Pregnancy is not possible until regular menstruation occurs.

B. Adrenarche is the beginning of breast development.

C. Menarche, or onset of menstruation, is the first manifestation of puberty in the female.

D. Development of a menstrual cycle is dependent upon GnRH pulses increasing in amplitude and frequency.

Q.268 Weight gain in pregnancy depends on all except?

A. Smoking

B. Pre pregnancy weight

C. Ethnicity

D. Maternal age

Q.269 A primigravida in the first trimester of pregnancy was found to be sputumb positive for acid fast bacilli. There is no prior history of tuberculosis. What is the treatment of choice for this patient?

A. Category I DOTS

B. Category II DOTS

C. Category III DOTS

D. Start ATT after delivery

Q.270 Virus responsible for non immune hydrops foetalis is?

A. Cytomegalovirus

B. Herpes simplex virus

C. Hepatitis B virus

D. Parvovirus

Q.271 Plasma retinol value which is considered as marginal in children is?

A. 0.25 to 0.35 µmol L

B. 0.35 to 0.7 µmol L

C. 0.7 to 1.05 µmol L

D. 1.05 to 1.45 µmol L

Q.272 All of the following are features of anorexia nervosa except:

A. Restriction of energy intake relative to requirement

B. Intense fear of gaining weight

C. Symptoms emerge in later adolescence

D. Individual has engaged in recurrent episodes of binging or purging behaviour

Q.273 Which of the following is the fastest growing developmental disorder?

A. Specific learning disorder

B. Intellectual developmental disorder

C. Childhood onset fluency disorder

D. Autism spectrum disorder

Q.274 Which of the following is an X linked disease?

A. Friedreich's ataxia

B. Fabry's disease

C. Osteogenesis imperfecta

D. Cystic fibrosis

Q.275 Differentiating an ASD from a VSD using a chest X-Rays is by detection of?

A. Enlargement of pulmonary artery

B. Enlarged left atrium

C. Dilated aorta

D. Pulmonary plethora

Q.276 A12 year old Boy with hematemesis, melena and mild splenomegaly presented to the paediatrics OPD. Examination revealed absence of jaundice/ascites. Most probable diagnosis is?

A. Extrahepatic Portal Venous Obstruction (EHPVO)

B. Cirrhosis

C. Non Cirrhotic Portal Fibrosis (NCPF)

D. Malaria with disseminated intravascular coagulation

Q.277 Most common malignant orbital tumor in children is?

A. Acute myeloid leukemia

B. Acute lymphoblastic leukemia

C. Rhabdomyosarcoma

D. Cavernous hemangioma

Q.278 An eight year old boy presented to the casualty with high fever, pruritic erythematous rash, joint pain and lymph node enlargement. There is a history of upper respiratory tract infection for which he was on cefaclor 8 days completed of a 10 day course. The most likely diagnosis is?

A. Serum sickness like illness

B. HSP

C. Type III hypersensitivity

D. Kawasaki disease

Q.279 The protective effects of breast milk are known to be associated with:

A. IgM antibodies

B. Lysozyme

C. Mast cells

D. IgA antibodies

Q.280 The appropriate approach to a neonate presenting with vaginal bleeding on day 4 or life is:

A. Administration of vitamin K

B. Investiaation for bleeding disorder

C. No specific therapy

D. Administration of 10ml/kg of fresh frozen plasma over 4 hours

Q.281 The incision used in endomeatal approach to the ear is?

A. Lempert I incision

B. Rosen's incision

C. Lempert II incision

D. Wilde's incision

Q.282 Hitzelberg's sign is:

A. Reduced corneal sensitivity

B. Hypoesthesia of the posterior meatal wall

C. Paraesthesia of face

D. Delayed blink reflex

Q.283 Orbital apex syndrome involves?

A. Olfactory nerve

B. Ophthalmic division of trigeminal nerve

C. Maxillary division of trigeminal nerve

D. Mandibular division of trigeminal nerve

Q.284 All are true regarding mucocele of frontal sinus except?

A. Cystic tender swelling

B. Eggshell crackling can be elicited

C. Displaces the eyeball downward and laterally

D. Treatment is frontoethmoidectpomy

Q.285 Pain in tonsillar fossa and upper neck is characteristic of ?

A. Eagle's syndrome

B. Apert's syndrome

C. Sickler's syndrome

D. Usher's syndrome

Q.286 The following is true for Gradenigo's syndrome?

A. Mastoid tenderness

B. Retro-orbital

C. Hearing loss

D. Sagging of posterosuperior meatal wall

Q.287 Most common site of origin of vestibular schwannoma is?

A. Cochlear nerve

B. Superior vestibular nerve

C. Inferior vestibular nerve

D. Facial nerve

Q.288 Pain pathway from ethmoid sinus is via?

A. Nasociliary nerve

B. Lacrimal nerve

C. Lateral pterygoid nerve

D. Frontal nerve

Q.289 Endolymphatic hydrops is characteristic of:

A. Cholesteatoma

B. Meniere's disease

C. Otosclerosis

D. Gradenigo's syndrome

Q.290 Secondary haemorrhage after tonsillectomy is most commonly seen?

A. 6 hours after surgery

B. 24 hours after surgery

C. 6 days after surgery

D. 14 days after surgery

Q.291 Which of the following is true regarding Mittendorf dot?

A. Glial tissue projecting from optic disc

B. Obliterated vessel running forward into the vitreous

C. Associated with posterior polar cataract

D. Commonest congenital anomaly of hyaloid system

Q.292 All of the following are seen in Favre-Goldman syndrome except?

A. Ectopia lentis

B. Retinoschisis

C. Nyctalopia

D. Pigmentary changes similar to retinitis pigmentosa

Q.293 Stocker's line is seen in?

A. Pinguecula

B. Trachoma

C. Pterygium

D. Concretions

Q.294 Cogan's syndrome is associated with?

A. Keratitis

B. Conjunctivitis

C. Iritis

D. Myopia

Q.295 Gun sign is?

A. Silver wiring of arterioles

B. Deflection of veins at arteriovenous crossing

C. Copper wiring of arterioles

D. Tapering of veins on either side of the crossings

Q.296 Retinoscopy is:

A. Visualization of retina alone

B. Visualization of retina and all other posterior segment contents

C. Objective measurement of the refractive error of the patient

D. Subjective measurement of the refractive error of the patient

Q.297 Bilateral granulomatous panuveitis is seen in?

A. Heerfordt's syndrome

B. Reiter's syndrome

C. Behcet's disease

D. Toxoplasmosis

Q.298 Appendages of the eyes include all except?

A. Lacrimal gland	B. Eyelids
C. Eyebrows	D. Extraocular muscles

Q.299 Diplopia in superior oblique palsy is
A.	Vertical diplopia on downward gaze
B.	Vertical diplopia on upward gaze
C.	Horizontal diplopia on inward gaze
D.	Horizontal diplopia on outward gaze

Q.300 Organism most commonly implicated in Late onset endophthalmitis after cataract surgery is?
A.	Pseudomonas aeruginosa
B.	staphylococcus epidermidis
C.	Candida albicans
D.	Propionibacterium acnes

// Smart Answer Sheet //

Correct — Indicates percentage of students who answered questions correctly.

Skipped — Indicates percentage of students who skipped questions.

Q.	Ans.	Correct / Skipped	Q.	Ans.	Correct / Skipped	Q.	Ans.	Correct / Skipped	Q.	Ans.	Correct / Skipped	Q.	Ans.	Correct / Skipped
1	C	87.21 % / 10.56 %	17	A	76.76 % / 13.08 %	33	B	77.93 % / 20.61 %	49	D	67.04 % / 30.24 %	65	A	63.1 % / 34.26 %
2	C	49.29 % / 49.74 %	18	D	78.01 % / 17.02 %	34	D	78.25 % / 15.37 %	50	A	47.79 % / 42.06 %	66	D	49.37 % / 44.38 %
3	A	23.52 % / 71.22 %	19	B	85.06 % / 12.53 %	35	D	78.39 % / 19.48 %	51	B	21.48 % / 69.16 %	67	A	55.37 % / 40.84 %
4	C	63.58 % / 33.42 %	20	D	79.47 % / 19.68 %	36	D	79.14 % / 19.1 %	52	A	87.92 % / 10.88 %	68	C	79.83 % / 17.41 %
5	B	58.29 % / 37.86 %	21	A	81.06 % / 14.6 %	37	A	89.46 % / 10.08 %	53	A	78.41 % / 10.62 %	69	C	66.45 % / 31.06 %
6	C	81.26 % / 11.09 %	22	D	19.27 % / 75.14 %	38	C	62.12 % / 34.77 %	54	A	65.41 % / 30.55 %	70	A	66.89 % / 30.41 %
7	B	28.85 % / 68.03 %	23	A	10.39 % / 87.33 %	39	A	82.05 % / 12.54 %	55	D	60.56 % / 32.85 %	71	B	89.69 % / 10.2 %
8	B	53.94 % / 39.03 %	24	D	78.26 % / 18.29 %	40	C	85.3 % / 12.45 %	56	B	88.53 % / 10.48 %	72	B	84.69 % / 11.32 %
9	C	76.34 % / 15.37 %	25	C	42.31 % / 52.43 %	41	C	58.09 % / 32.03 %	57	A	16.91 % / 78.77 %	73	A	89.46 % / 10.53 %
10	A	84.69 % / 12.08 %	26	D	83.07 % / 16.68 %	42	C	83.46 % / 15.77 %	58	C	58.1 % / 33.45 %	74	C	83.1 % / 13.57 %
11	A	85.17 % / 13.61 %	27	D	69.69 % / 30.27 %	43	D	87.79 % / 11.52 %	59	B	80.15 % / 13.04 %	75	D	89.55 % / 10.09 %
12	B	60.92 % / 34.89 %	28	A	53.43 % / 43.08 %	44	A	76.47 % / 22.09 %	60	B	45.49 % / 53.95 %	76	B	57.57 % / 37.41 %
13	C	85.0 % / 13.13 %	29	A	87.01 % / 11.43 %	45	C	62.57 % / 33.47 %	61	D	85.5 % / 11.58 %	77	D	87.11 % / 11.27 %
14	A	76.92 % / 20.05 %	30	B	76.29 % / 22.17 %	46	B	49.46 % / 47.1 %	62	A	82.99 % / 10.85 %	78	C	82.95 % / 10.37 %
15	A	88.13 % / 11.86 %	31	B	82.4 % / 15.46 %	47	A	41.48 % / 42.92 %	63	B	79.78 % / 16.41 %	79	D	88.58 % / 11.22 %
16	C	65.49 % / 32.63 %	32	B	54.67 % / 33.47 %	48	A	84.12 % / 14.99 %	64	C	46.36 % / 35.59 %	80	A	88.47 % / 10.59 %

Q.	Ans.	Correct / Skipped	Q.	Ans.	Correct / Skipped	Q.	Ans.	Correct / Skipped	Q.	Ans.	Correct / Skipped	Q.	Ans.	Correct / Skipped
81	A	79.3 % / 10.96 %	97	C	79.71 % / 13.44 %	113	A	59.55 % / 34.65 %	129	C	80.02 % / 18.49 %	145	B	77.12 % / 18.49 %
82	B	89.28 % / 10.55 %	98	D	52.5 % / 42.73 %	114	B	89.59 % / 10.25 %	130	C	83.28 % / 16.38 %	146	A	87.64 % / 10.31 %
83	B	65.27 % / 34.56 %	99	A	89.69 % / 10.03 %	115	D	79.05 % / 20.59 %	131	A	81.62 % / 18.29 %	147	A	79.2 % / 14.92 %
84	C	77.58 % / 12.54 %	100	B	81.75 % / 17.25 %	116	D	20.83 % / 77.86 %	132	C	79.02 % / 13.27 %	148	B	49.5 % / 32.61 %
85	D	17.6 % / 71.9 %	101	A	84.48 % / 12.08 %	117	C	20.56 % / 75.18 %	133	B	18.23 % / 71.97 %	149	D	43.51 % / 33.44 %
86	C	77.64 % / 14.24 %	102	B	65.17 % / 34.56 %	118	B	17.93 % / 75.83 %	134	D	52.16 % / 31.45 %	150	A	79.65 % / 14.87 %
87	D	40.96 % / 52.59 %	103	A	89.78 % / 10.1 %	119	A	77.93 % / 13.85 %	135	C	81.73 % / 10.74 %	151	A	89.82 % / 10.0 %
88	C	48.67 % / 32.73 %	104	B	41.14 % / 31.01 %	120	B	77.17 % / 21.48 %	136	C	87.76 % / 11.7 %	152	B	83.13 % / 13.86 %
89	A	12.04 % / 86.59 %	105	A	76.23 % / 21.05 %	121	C	82.95 % / 12.92 %	137	B	82.86 % / 10.92 %	153	D	40.24 % / 40.19 %
90	D	88.86 % / 11.12 %	106	A	78.72 % / 11.69 %	122	A	88.03 % / 11.81 %	138	D	82.86 % / 12.2 %	154	A	88.93 % / 10.17 %
91	B	46.07 % / 47.79 %	107	C	89.73 % / 10.13 %	123	D	83.25 % / 16.54 %	139	C	82.91 % / 13.24 %	155	C	87.21 % / 12.43 %
92	D	88.38 % / 10.54 %	108	B	47.95 % / 32.47 %	124	A	85.74 % / 11.66 %	140	C	83.5 % / 12.33 %	156	D	45.89 % / 43.06 %
93	A	40.88 % / 39.24 %	109	B	87.11 % / 10.68 %	125	B	43.88 % / 55.69 %	141	B	76.25 % / 18.55 %	157	D	87.53 % / 11.52 %
94	C	81.1 % / 14.84 %	110	A	44.83 % / 46.55 %	126	C	85.74 % / 12.4 %	142	A	84.44 % / 13.42 %	158	D	67.45 % / 30.27 %
95	A	77.64 % / 12.65 %	111	B	86.07 % / 12.98 %	127	B	80.5 % / 11.56 %	143	A	86.23 % / 13.73 %	159	B	83.76 % / 14.79 %
96	C	82.11 % / 16.43 %	112	C	69.25 % / 30.32 %	128	B	77.92 % / 14.53 %	144	A	89.09 % / 10.31 %	160	C	78.09 % / 15.41 %

Q.	Ans.	Correct / Skipped	Q.	Ans.	Correct / Skipped	Q.	Ans.	Correct / Skipped	Q.	Ans.	Correct / Skipped	Q.	Ans.	Correct / Skipped
161	B	84.85 % / 11.88 %	177	D	77.8 % / 12.52 %	193	C	79.67 % / 18.67 %	209	C	68.09 % / 30.86 %	225	B	55.61 % / 36.29 %
162	A	79.01 % / 19.15 %	178	A	78.43 % / 14.31 %	194	C	89.72 % / 10.17 %	210	A	87.1 % / 10.52 %	226	D	22.41 % / 70.54 %
163	C	80.55 % / 15.85 %	179	D	82.23 % / 10.34 %	195	A	81.76 % / 14.79 %	211	C	83.85 % / 11.76 %	227	B	86.67 % / 11.86 %
164	A	85.19 % / 13.22 %	180	A	42.15 % / 57.21 %	196	C	87.85 % / 10.92 %	212	C	76.48 % / 15.87 %	228	B	83.68 % / 12.4 %
165	A	59.7 % / 31.1 %	181	B	79.25 % / 16.28 %	197	D	80.11 % / 10.89 %	213	B	84.46 % / 11.94 %	229	B	11.89 % / 70.91 %
166	C	41.76 % / 38.66 %	182	A	89.08 % / 10.19 %	198	B	87.04 % / 10.69 %	214	A	81.97 % / 14.4 %	230	A	78.45 % / 20.74 %
167	C	60.75 % / 30.77 %	183	C	30.67 % / 68.17 %	199	B	77.24 % / 20.03 %	215	D	22.52 % / 75.92 %	231	B	53.84 % / 31.87 %
168	B	83.71 % / 15.51 %	184	D	26.29 % / 68.74 %	200	A	65.45 % / 30.56 %	216	D	78.86 % / 12.29 %	232	A	86.01 % / 13.84 %
169	D	76.01 % / 22.47 %	185	A	81.88 % / 12.85 %	201	D	83.84 % / 15.29 %	217	B	81.05 % / 11.23 %	233	B	76.71 % / 10.12 %
170	B	83.94 % / 13.26 %	186	D	28.94 % / 70.74 %	202	A	85.26 % / 13.59 %	218	C	79.93 % / 17.21 %	234	D	80.18 % / 17.27 %
171	B	28.75 % / 70.51 %	187	B	32.0 % / 67.13 %	203	D	79.33 % / 18.41 %	219	A	79.13 % / 10.9 %	235	D	86.26 % / 12.54 %
172	B	79.99 % / 11.87 %	188	D	87.33 % / 10.09 %	204	C	51.41 % / 35.84 %	220	C	82.91 % / 13.66 %	236	A	80.68 % / 12.44 %
173	D	87.92 % / 11.15 %	189	C	59.75 % / 35.35 %	205	C	77.51 % / 14.81 %	221	B	86.05 % / 12.74 %	237	C	84.83 % / 11.33 %
174	C	67.21 % / 32.51 %	190	D	20.83 % / 76.44 %	206	C	83.87 % / 13.9 %	222	C	80.58 % / 17.54 %	238	D	85.18 % / 13.38 %
175	B	59.56 % / 38.72 %	191	A	82.21 % / 16.15 %	207	A	57.66 % / 35.81 %	223	D	76.36 % / 15.65 %	239	D	83.7 % / 15.64 %
176	C	78.35 % / 12.32 %	192	C	77.82 % / 21.26 %	208	D	78.83 % / 19.73 %	224	C	83.99 % / 10.7 %	240	A	86.03 % / 13.91 %

Q.	Ans.	Correct / Skipped		Q.	Ans.	Correct / Skipped		Q.	Ans.	Correct / Skipped		Q.	Ans.	Correct / Skipped		Q.	Ans.	Correct / Skipped
241	B	79.3 % / 13.76 %		253	D	68.04 % / 30.72 %		265	B	87.29 % / 12.54 %		277	C	15.63 % / 80.69 %		289	B	63.32 % / 35.43 %
242	C	81.41 % / 16.65 %		254	A	87.91 % / 11.93 %		266	C	76.05 % / 10.39 %		278	A	67.67 % / 30.86 %		290	C	85.05 % / 12.46 %
243	A	83.22 % / 10.41 %		255	A	82.62 % / 15.41 %		267	D	87.84 % / 11.68 %		279	D	56.91 % / 39.35 %		291	C	78.2 % / 16.89 %
244	D	78.24 % / 16.54 %		256	C	81.77 % / 10.83 %		268	A	51.82 % / 43.94 %		280	C	85.76 % / 10.38 %		292	A	84.91 % / 12.44 %
245	D	87.74 % / 10.69 %		257	C	18.03 % / 69.39 %		269	A	29.63 % / 67.86 %		281	B	77.45 % / 11.72 %		293	C	84.09 % / 12.9 %
246	A	85.31 % / 10.22 %		258	B	58.55 % / 38.34 %		270	D	79.73 % / 18.0 %		282	B	46.68 % / 50.17 %		294	A	88.87 % / 10.85 %
247	B	85.76 % / 12.48 %		259	A	82.23 % / 15.56 %		271	C	45.8 % / 51.57 %		283	C	81.91 % / 10.81 %		295	D	88.52 % / 10.66 %
248	C	76.67 % / 17.05 %		260	D	81.24 % / 16.14 %		272	C	78.59 % / 13.58 %		284	A	87.61 % / 11.21 %		296	C	85.7 % / 13.32 %
249	A	84.6 % / 11.18 %		261	D	76.45 % / 21.19 %		273	D	60.93 % / 31.79 %		285	A	45.1 % / 39.09 %		297	A	81.05 % / 18.17 %
250	A	18.94 % / 67.03 %		262	D	41.56 % / 52.93 %		274	B	89.18 % / 10.77 %		286	B	78.87 % / 12.95 %		298	D	78.11 % / 14.06 %
251	B	53.66 % / 41.35 %		263	C	57.65 % / 34.36 %		275	B	84.87 % / 12.53 %		287	B	77.03 % / 20.82 %		299	A	85.28 % / 13.2 %
252	C	31.76 % / 67.13 %		264	C	85.7 % / 12.58 %		276	A	18.57 % / 67.69 %		288	A	84.33 % / 13.05 %		300	D	19.02 % / 78.63 %

Performance Analysis

Avg. Score (%)	63.67%
Toppers Score (%)	73.0%
Your Score	

PART A

Q.1 The most widely used method for determining the purity of a protein is?

A.   Isoelectric focusing

B.   Polyacrylamide gel electrophoresis

C.   Ion exchange chromatography

D.   High-pressure chromatography

Q.2 The enzyme catalyzing the production of orotidylic acid is?

A.   Dihydro orotate

B.   Aspartyl transcarbamoylase

C.   Dihydro orotate dehydrogenase

D.   Orotate phosphoribosyltransferase

Q.3 Deficiency of lysosomal maltase causes?

A. McArdle disease   **B.** Andersen disease

C. Cori disease   **D.** Pompe disease

Q.4 Which of the following is not a protein misfolding disorder?

A.   Tuberculosis

B.   Creutzfeldt Jakob disease

C.   Alzheimer's disease

D.   Cystic fibrosis

Q.5 Which of the following enzymes is responsible for the transfer of amino groups from an amino acid to an alpha-keto acid?

A. Transaminase   **B.** Transketolase

C. Deaminase   **D.** Lyase

Q.6   Which among the following is a cardioprotective fatty acid?

A. Oleic acid   **B.** Omega-3 fatty acid

C. Beta acid   **D.** Both A & B

Q.7 Alpha helix and the beta-pleated sheet are examples of:

A.   Primary structure

B.   Secondary structure

C.   Tertiary structure

D.   Quaternary structure

Q.8 Cytochrome C of the bacteria has 50% identity of amino acid sequence with that of human. Which of the following is the most conserved parameter in these two proteins?

A.   Quarternary structure

B.   Tertiary structure

C.   Amino acid sequence

D.   Loop and turn segments

Q.9 Which of the following elements is known to influence the body's ability to handle oxidative stress?

A. Calcium   **B.** Iron

C. Potassium   **D.** Selenium

Q.10 A person on a fat-free carbohydrate-rich diet continues to grow obese. Which of the following lipoproteins is likely to be elevated in his blood?

A. Chylomicrons   **B.** VLDL

C. LDL   **D.** HDL

Q.11 Which of the following is a membrane-bound enzyme that catalyzes the formation of cyclic AMP from ATP?

A. Tyrosine Kinase   **B.** Polymerase

C. ATP synthase   **D.** Adenylate cyclase

Q.12 Xeroderma pigmentosum is produced as a result of a defect in:

A.   DNA polymerase III

B.   DNA polymerase I

C.   DNA exonuclease

D.   DNA ligase

Q.13 Rothera's test is utilized for detection of?

A. Glucose   **B.** Proteins

C. Urea   **D.** Ketone bodies

Q.14 Site of the urea cycle is?

A. Liver   **B.** Kidney   **C.** GIT   **D.** Lungs

Q.15 The process used in an expression vector to increase the yield of recombinant protein synthesis?

A.   Translation initiation

B.   Promoter induction

C.   Transcription terminators

D.   Multiple cloning sites

Q.16 Decreased energy production in thiamine deficiency is due to?

A.   It is a cofactor for oxidative reduction

B.   It is required for transamination reactions

C.   It is a coenzyme for alpha-ketoglutarate dehydrogenase and pyruvate dehydrogenase in the citric acid cycle

D.   It is a coenzyme for transketolase in hexose monophosphate shunt

Q.17 Molecules of myoglobin will bind to:

A.   1 molecule of oxygen

B.   16 molecules of oxygen

C.   4 molecules of oxygen

D.   64 molecules of oxygen

Q.18 Which of the following decreases with age?

A. Vital capacity   **B.** Systolic BP

C. Pulse pressure   **D.** Residual volume

Q.19 Substance not filtered in the pulmonary circulation:

A. Blood clots   **B.** Cancer cells

C. Plasma proteins   **D.** Gas bubbles

Q.20 Maximum resistance during expiration is due to:

A. Alveolar collapse

B. Expiratory muscle fatigue

C. The dynamic collapse of airways

D. Breaking action of inspiratory muscles

Q.21 Sudden cessation of breathing with maximal expiratory effort is due to:

A. Dynamic airway compression

B. Alveolar collapse

C. Expiratory muscle fatigue

D. Breaking action of inspiratory muscles

Q.22 The maximum amount of carbon dioxide in the human body is transported as:

A. Bicarbonate

B. Carbide

C. Amylase

D. None of the above

Q.23 The primary function of the cerebrospinal fluid is to:

A. Protect the brain

B. Provide nutrients to the surrounding tissues

C. Remove waste products

D. All of the above

Q.24 Jellyfish breathe through:

A. Book lungs

B. Gills

C. Diffusion

D. None of the above

Q.25 _______ are functional units of food absorption.

A. Red blood cells

B. Small intestine

C. Villi

D. Aggregated lymphoid nodules

Q.26 Night blindness and xerophthalmia are generally conditions associated with the deficiency of which vitamin?

A. Vitamin B

B. Vitamin K

C. Vitamin B2

D. Vitamin A

Q.27 Stomach epithelial cells in the body secrete _______.

A. Hydrochloric acid

B. Oxytocin

C. Adrenaline

D. Testosterone

Q.28 Closing volume determines:

A. Transmural pressure

B. Residual volume

C. Small airway resistance

D. Dead space

Q.29 Elbow joint is an example of:

A. hinge joint

B. gliding joint

C. ball and socket joint

D. pivot joint

Q.30 A patient is generally advised to specially, consume more meat, lentils, milk, and eggs in the diet only when he suffers from?

A. Scurvy

B. Kwashiorkor

C. Rickets

D. Anemia

Q.31 Melatonin is produced by:

A. Thymus

B. Skin

C. Pituitary

D. Pineal gland

Q.32 Which part of the human brain is concerned with the regulation of body temperature?

A. Cerebellum

B. Cerebrum

C. Hypothalamus

D. Medulla Oblongata

Q.33 The junction between an axon and dendrite is called:

A. Cyton

B. Synapse

C. Relay

D. Conduction zone

Q.34 Which of the following muscle is supplied by the anterior division of the mandibular nerve?

A. Medial pterygoid

B. Lateral pterygoid

C. Mylohyoid

D. Anterior belly of digastric

Q.35 All are true regarding axillary artery except?

A. It is a continuation of the subclavian artery.

B. It is crossed by pectoralis minor muscle.

C. It extends from the outer border of the second rib to the lower border of the teres minor.

D. The second part of the axillary artery is posterior to the pectoralis minor muscle.

Q.36 Roof the fourth ventricle is formed by all of the following except?

A. Inferior medullary velum

B. Superior medullary velum

C. Obex

D. Median eminence

Q.37 The branch arising from the main trunk of the mandibular nerve is?

A. Nerve to medial pterygoid

B. Nerve to lateral pterygoid

C. Buccal nerve

D. Auriculotemporal nerve

Q.38 Deep perineal pouch in males does not include?

A. Pudendal nerve

B. Sphincter urethrae

C. Long peroneal nerve

D. Dorsal nerve of the penis

Q.39 Which is true regarding the suprarenal gland?

A. The posterior surface of the left suprarenal is related to the kidney.

B. The posterior surface of the right suprarenal is related to the inferior vena cava.

C. The lateral border of the left suprarenal is related to the left gastric artery.

D. The lateral border of the right suprarenal is related to the right coeliac ganglion.

Q.40 The Pisiform is considered as a sesamoid bone in the tendon of?

A. Flexor digitorum superficialis

B. Flexor digitorum profundus
C. Abductor digiti minimi
D. Flexor carpi ulnaris

Q.41 The largest bursa in the human body is?
A. Subacromial bursa **B.** Prepatellar bursa
C. Infrapatellar bursa **D.** Trochanteric bursa

Q.42 Which is not a part of the hypogastric sheath?
A. Transverse cervical ligament
B. Broad ligament
C. Lateral ligament of the bladder
D. Uterosacral ligament

Q.43 The Chief pronator of the forearm is?
A. Pronator quadratus **B.** Pronator teres
C. Gravity **D.** Flexor carpi radialis

Q.44 Oblique head of adductor pollicis arises from?
A. Trapezium **B.** Trapezoid
C. Capitate **D.** Hamate

Q.45 The Anterior choroidal artery is a branch of?
A. Anterior cerebral artery
B. Posterior cerebral arter
C. Internal carotid artery
D. Anterior communicating artery

Q.46 Which of the following is not a pneumatic bone?
A. Frontal bone **B.** Sphenoid
C. Maxilla **D.** Mandible

Q.47 Muscles supplied by anterior division of mandibular nerve are all except?
A. Medial pterygoid **B.** Lateral pterygoid
C. Temporalis **D.** Masseter

Q.48 Where is the urethral crest located?
A. Membranous urethra
B. Penile urethra
C. Prostatic urethra
D. Bulbar urethra

Q.49 Which is the type of joint seen in the growth plate?
A. Primary cartilaginous
B. Secondary cartilaginous
C. Fibrous joint
D. Plane Joint

Q.50 Which of the following gives rise to the muscular component of the dorsal aorta?
A. Intermediate mesoderm
B. Lateral plate mesoderm
C. Axial mesoderm
D. Paraxial mesoderm

PART B

Q.51 Rose-Waaler test is a?
A. Co-agglutination test
B. Latex agglutination test
C. Slide agglutination test
D. Haemagglutination test

Q.52 Which of the following is an intermediate level disinfectant?
A. Glutaraldehyde
B. Quaternary ammonium compound
C. Hydrogen peroxide
D. Iodophors

Q.53 The best culture medium for primary isolation of H. influenzae is?
A. Chocolate agar **B.** Fildes' agar
C. Levinthal's medium **D.** Nutrient agar

Q.54 Endemic relapsing fever is caused by all except?
A. Borrelia duttonii **B.** Borrelia hermsii
C. Borrelia parkeri **D.** Borrelia recurrentis

Q.55 Which of the following gastroenteritis viruses can spread by air?
A. Sapovirus **B.** Rotavirus
C. Norovirus **D.** Astrovirus

Q.56 Fildes technique is used for the culture of?
A. Clostridium perfringens
B. Clostridium tetani
C. Clostridium botulinum
D. Clostridium difficile

Q.57 Aflatoxin is produced by the fungus?
A. Aspergillus flavus
B. Aspergillus niger
C. Penicillium marneffei
D. Candida albicans

Q.58 All of the following are non-photochromogens except?
A. Mycobacterium ulcerans
B. Mycobacterium xenopi
C. Mycobacterium avium
D. Mycobacterium marinum

Q.59 Which of the following is an enrichment medium?
A. Alkaline peptone water
B. Loeffler serum slope
C. Deoxycholate citrate agar
D. MacConkey's agar

Q.60 Which of the following does not have a polysaccharide capsule related antigen-antibody response?
A. Haemophilus influenzae
B. Neisseria meningitidis
C. Streptococcus pneumonia
D. Bordetella pertussis

Q.61 Erythema chronicum migrans is caused by?
A. Borrelia japonica **B.** Borrelia burgdorferi
C. Borrelia andersonii **D.** Borrelia recurrentis

Q.62 Latent varicella-zoster infection is found in?

A. T cells   **B.** B cells

C. Macrophages   **D.** Trigeminal ganglion

Q.63 False statement about streptococcus:

A. Cell division occurs along a single axis

B. Part of normal flora in human beings

C. Causes localized infections which do not spread along tissue planes

D. Daughter cells after cell division form a string

Q.64 A patient presented to the OPD with clinical features of pneumonia. Sputum examination of the patient revealed gram-positive cocci with alpha hemolysis on sheep agar. Which test will you do to confirm the diagnosis?

A. Coagulase test

B. Bacitracin sensitivity

C. CAMP test

D. Bile solubility

Q.65 Ehrlich phenomenon is seen in:

A. Mycobacterium TB   **B.** Proteus

C. Staphylococcus   **D.** Corynebacterium

Q.66 Metachromatic granules are found in:

A. Diphtheria

B. Mycoplasma

C. Gardenerella vaginalis

D. Chlamydia

Q.67 Albert's staining is done for:

A. Clostridium   **B.** Corynebacterium

C. Brucella   **D.** Pneumococcus

Q.68 The incubation period of diphtheria is:

A. 2 - 6 days   **B.** 2 - 6 hours

C. 2 - 6 weeks   **D.** 2 - 6 months

Q.69 Brazilian purpuric fever is caused by?

A. Haemophilus haemolyticus

B. Haemophilus aphrophilus

C. Haemophilus aegyptius

D. Haemophilus parainfluenzae

Q.70 Skin test based on neutralization reaction is/are:

A. Casoni test   **B.** Lepromin test

C. Tuberculin test   **D.** Tuberculin test

Q.71 Most potent fluoroquinolone against Mycobacterium leprae is?

A. Levofloxacin   **B.** Ofloxacin

C. Moxifloxacin   **D.** Ciprofloxacin

Q.72 The antiretroviral drug combination to be avoided is?

A. Zidovudine + Stavudine

B. Zidovudine + Lamivudine

C. Didanosine + Abacavir

D. Didanosine + Zidovudine

Q.73 Basiliximab is:

A. Anti CD3 antibody

B. Anti CD25 antibody

C. IL1 receptor antagonist

D. TNF alpha inhibitor

Q.74 Shortest acting non-benzodiazepine hypnotic is?

A. Zaleplon   **B.** Zolpidem

C. Zopiclone   **D.** Eszopiclone

Q.75 Which of the following does not have significant first-pass metabolism?

A. Labetalol   **B.** Acebutolol

C. Atenolol   **D.** Metoprolol

Q.76 Which is associated with vaginal carcinoma in female offspring?

A. Diethylstilbestrol   **B.** Phenytoin

C. ACE inhibitors   **D.** Indomethacin

Q.77 Which of the following can cause discoloration of teeth in the fetus?

A. Lithium   **B.** Tetracycline

C. Warfarin   **D.** Isotretinoin

Q.78 Amylin analogue is?

A. Sitagliptin   **B.** Liraglutide

C. Nateglinide   **D.** Pramlintide

Q.79 Intake of which of the following is associated with neural tube defects?

A. Phenytoin   **B.** Lithium

C. Valproate   **D.** Phenobarbitone

Q.80 Phocomelia is an adverse effect of?

A. Diethylstilbestrol   **B.** Thalidomide

C. Valproate   **D.** Progestins

Q.81 Who is known as the Father of Pharmacology?

A. Oswald Schmiedeberg

B. J Langley

C. Rudolf Buchheim

D. Paul Ehrlich

Q.82 Which of the following is used to decrease the toxicity of amphotericin B?

A. Dose reduction

B. Liposomal delivery systems

C. Supplementing glucose

D. Giving it along with flucytosine

Q.83 Ethosuximide is the drug of choice for treatment?

A. Generalized tonic-clonic seizures

B. Absence seizures

C. Simple partial seizures

D. Complex partial seizures

Q.84 All of the following drugs cross the placenta except?

A. Phenytoin   **B.** Diazepam

C. Morphine   **D.** Heparin

Q.85 Which of the following is used for the treatment of chlamydia infection in pregnancy?

A. Tetracycline

B. Erythromycin

C. Azithromycin

D. Doxycycline

Q.86 Simeprevir is used for the treatment of?

A. HIV

B. CMV infection

C. Kaposi sarcoma

D. Chronic Hepatitis C

Q.87 Tyrosine kinase inhibitors are useful in the management of?

A. Acute myeloid leukemia

B. Small cell carcinoma of the lung

C. Gastrointestinal stromal tumors

D. Neurofibromatosis

Q.88 As a side effect the metabolic syndrome is most commonly associated with the following group of medications:

A. Anti-anxiety drugs

B. Anti-depressant drugs

C. Antipsychotic drugs

D. Anticholinergic drugs

Q.89 Mechanism of action of tianeptine in the brain is:

A. Selective serotonin reuptake inhibition

B. Selective serotonin reuptake enhancement

C. Selective dopamine reuptake inhibition

D. Selective norepinephrine reuptake inhibition

Q.90 Prolactin secretion is inhibited by:

A. Dopamine antagonist

B. GABA

C. Neurophysin

D. Bromocriptine

Q.91 Principle organelle involved in the execution of apoptosis is?

[NEET PG, 2014]

A. Nucleus

B. Lysosome

C. Mitochondria

D. Endoplasmic reticulum

Q.92 Some antigen was injected into a rabbit. What antibody will it produce initially?

[NEET PG, 2014]

A. IgG

B. IgM

C. IgA

D. IgD

Q.93 Psammoma bodies are seen in all except?

[NEET PG, 2014]

A. Follicular carcinoma thyroid

B. Papillary carcinoma thyroid

C. Cystadenocarcinoma

D. Meningioma

Q.94 Which complement component is the first common point between involved classical and alternate pathways?

A. C1

B. C2

C. C3

D. C4

Q.95 All are involved in generating free oxygen radical for the killing off bacteria except-

A. Superoxide Dismutase

B. Fenton's reaction

C. NADPH oxidase

D. Glutathione peroxidase

Q.96 Slide fixing in pathology most commonly done by–

A. Formaldehyde

B. Alcohol

C. Picric acid

D. Glutaraldehyde

Q.97 Various cells respond differently to a second messenger (such as increased cAMP) because they have different?

A. Receptors

B. Enzymatic composition

C. Nuclei

D. Membrane lipids

Q.98 The light brown perinuclear pigment seen on H&F staining of the cardiac muscle fibers in the grossly normal-appearing heart of an 83- year old man at autopsy is due to deposition of?

A. Hemosiderin

B. Lipochrome

C. Cholesterol metabolites

D. Anthracotic pigment

Q.99 The level of alpha-fetoprotein is raised in all of the following except?

A. Cirrhosis of liver

B. Hepatocellular carcinoma

C. Yolk sac tumor

D. Dysgerminoma

Q.100 Brain lipid-binding protein is expressed by which of the following?

A. Mature astrocytes

B. Oligodendrocytes

C. Purkinje cells

D. Pyramidal neurons

Q.101 A high amylase level in pleural fluid suggests a diagnosis of?

A. Tuberculosis

B. Malignancy

C. Rheumatoid arthritis

D. Pulmonary infarction

Q.102 Which of the following malignant tumors is radioresistant?

A. Ewing's sarcoma

B. Retinoblastoma

C. Osteosarcoma

D. Neuroblastoma

Q.103 The most important determinant of prognosis in Wilms tumor:

A. Stage of disease

B. Loss of heterozygosity of chromosome 1p

C. Histology

D. Age less than one year at a presentation

Q.104 Hypoglycemia occurs as a paraneoplastic syndrome in:

A. Bronchogenic carcinoma

B. CA pancreas

C. Fibrosarcoma

D. RCC

Q.105 Test for carcinogenicity:

A. Kveim's test   **B.** Ame's test

C. Schilling's test   **D.** Schick test

Q.106 Grading of cancers does not depend on:

A. Degree of differentiation

B. Number of mitoses

C. Architectural features

D. Size of the primary lesion

Q.107 Acid phosphatase is a tumor marker for:

A. Pancreatic carcinoma

B. Prostatic carcinoma

C. Papillary carcinoma of the thyroid

D. Renal cell carcinoma

Q.108 The hallmark change in cell physiology that determines the malignant phenotype:

A. Self-sufficiency in growth signals

B. Sustained angiogenesis

C. Resistance to apoptosis

D. Aerobic glycolysis

Q.109 CA-125 is used is the monitoring and treatment of:

A. Ovarian cancer   **B.** Colon cancer

C. Breast cancer   **D.** Pancreatic cancer

Q.110 Calcitonin is a marker of:

A. Prostate cancer

B. Medullary carcinoma of the thyroid

C. Pheochromocytoma

D. Pancreatic cancer

Q.111 Molecular profiling of cancer cells is obtained by:

A. Flow cytometry

B. Immunohistochemistry

C. DNA microarray analysis

D. PCR

Q.112 Which is not an antibody associated with retrograde degenerative cerebellar?

A. Anti-Yo   **B.** Anti-Hu   **C.** Anti-Ri   **D.** Anti-Tr

Q.113 An 8-year-old boy completed 8 out of a 10-day course of cefaclor. Now he developed a generalized erythematic rash which is mildly pruritic and lymphadenopathy. Diagnosis is?

A. Kawasaki disease

B. Type 3 hypersensitivity

C. Anaphylaxis

D. Infectious mononucleosis

Q.114 The commonest cause of death in a patient with primary amyloidosis is?

A. Renal failure

B. Cardiac involvement

C. Bleeding diathesis

D. Respiratory failure

Q.115 At the physiological pH, the DNA molecules are?

A. Positively charged   **B.** Negatively charged

C. Neutral   **D.** Amphipathic

Q.116 Disputed maternity can be solved by using the following tests except?

A. Blood grouping   **B.** HLA typing

C. Preciptin test   **D.** DNA fingerprinting

Q.117 Contre—coup injuries are seen in :

A. Brain   **B.** Diazepam

C. Flumazenil   **D.** Ethyl alcohol

Q.118 Paradox gun' is a?

A. Revolver   **B.** Shotgun

C. Automatic pistol   **D.** Machine gun

Q.119 The combination of alopecia & skin rash, painful peripheral neuropathy, and confusion with lethargy are seen in?

A. Copper poisoning   **B.** Nickel poisoning

C. Selenium poisoning   **D.** Thallium poisoning

Q.120 Rave drug is?

[NEET PG, 2014]

A. Cannabis   **B.** Hashish

C. Ecstasy   **D.** Heroin

Q.121 Which among the following is a waxy, luminous & translucent poison?

A. Yellow phosphorus   **B.** Cobra venom

C. Organophosphates   **D.** Iodine

Q.122 Visualization of gunpowder residue on blood-stained clothes can be facilitated by?

A. Ultraviolet rays   **B.** Infrared rays

C. Magnifying lens   **D.** Paraffin test

Q.123 Which of the following is used for narco analysis?

A. Atropine   **B.** Phenobarbitone

C. Pethidine   **D.** Scopolamine

Q.124 A person was brought by police from the railway platform. He is talking irrelevantly. He is having a dry mouth with hot skin, dilated pupils, a staggering gait, and slurred speech. The most probable diagnosis is:

A. Alcohol intoxication

B. Carbamates poisoning

C. Organophosphorus poisoning

D. Dhatura poisoning

Q.125 Hydrogen peroxide is used in all of the following chemical tests for blood except:

A. Benzidine test   **B.** Phenolphthalein test

C. Orthotolidine test   **D.** Teichmann's test

Q.126 The concept of social medicine was first introduced by:

A. Neuman and Virchow

B. Robert Grotjahrr

C. John Ryle

D. Rene sand

Q.127 The best method for collecting vital statistics in India:

A. Active surveillance

B. Passive surveillance

C. Sentinel surveillance

D. Contact tracing

Q.128 The dose of diphtheria antitoxin is:

A. 1000 to 5000 IU

B. 10000 to 100000 IU

C. 1000 to 2000 IU

D. None of them

Q.129 Which of the following is the tertiary level of prevention:

A. Health promotion

B. Specific protection

C. Early diagnosis & treatment

D. Disability limitation

Q.130 Which vaccine is used to prevent death from pneumonia in children?

A. Measles vaccine

B. Rubella vaccine

C. Chickenpox vaccine

D. Influenza vaccine

Q.131 In a country, socio-economic progress is best indicated by:

A. Gross net production

B. IMR

C. Annual per capita income of the family

D. Death rate

Q.132 Disease rate is:

A. Risk of susceptibility

B. Usually expressed as a percentage

C. The time period in a calendar year

D. Disease occurrence in a specific time period

Q.133 The concept of levels of prevention aims at:

A. Ascertaining the prognosis of a disease

B. Eradication of a disease

C. Preventing epidemics

D. Intervening in the natural history of a disease

Q.134 The disease which is known as "Father of Public health" is:

A. Smallpox

B. Rabies

C. Plague

D. Cholera

Q.135 Quarantine is for:

A. Infective period

B. Shortest incubation period

C. Generation time

D. Longest incubation period

Q.136 In the overhead tank of a hostel, cysts of entameba were found. The best method of disinfection is:

A. Ultraviolet radiation

B. Boiling

C. Lodination

D. Chlorination

Q.137 The diagnostic accuracy of a test is determined by:

A. Sensitivity

B. Specificity

C. Predictive value

D. None

Q.138 Which is the most economical and best screening?

A. Mosquitos

B. Direct contact

C. Droplet

D. Placenta

Q.139 Which of the following is the most powerful chemical disinfectant?

A. Phenol

B. Lysol

C. Dettol

D. Pot. permanganate

Q.140 Scientific proof of an etiological factor is given by:

A. Case-control study

B. Cohort study

C. Randomized clinical trial

D. Non-randomized trial

Q.141 Disease imported to a country not otherwise present:

A. Exotic

B. Enzootic

C. Epizootic

D. Endemic

Q.142 An odds ratio is derived from:

A. Case-control study

B. Cohort study

C. Randomized clinical trial

D. Non-randomized trial

Q.143 Longitudinal studies are:

A. Are easy to conduct

B. Can detect only one risk factor

C. Can find out the incidence of disease

D. Have increase bias

Q.144 Live attenuated vaccines are:

A. OPV

B. Hepatitis

C. Japanese B encephalitis

D. Chickenpox

Q.145 Vertical transmission is by:

A. Mosquitos

B. Direct contact

C. Droplet

D. Placenta

Q.146 Re morbidity indicators except:

A. Period of stay in hospital

B. Doctor: population ratio

C. Attendance of out-patient department

D. Notification rates

Q.147 A vaccine which is given at earliest:

A. BCG

B. OPV

C. MMR

D. DPT

Q.148 Transovarian transmission of infection occurs in:

A. Fleas

B. Ticks

C. Mosquitos

D. Sandfly

Q.149 AH is a live vaccine except:

A. 17-D

B. Rubella

C. Salk

D. Measles

Q.150 Descriptive epidemiology studies in relation to:

A. Time

B. Place

C. Person

D. All

<u>PART C</u>

Q.151 A patient presents to the emergency department with abdominal trauma with signs of shock and peritonitis. Airway and breathing were checked. 2 large bore cannulas were inserted to secure IV access. What is the next step in the management of this patient?

A. Immediate exploratory laparotomy with general anesthesia

B. Focused Assessment with Sonography in Trauma (FAST)

C. Laparoscopic visualization of the injury

D. Watch and wait

Q.152 The Abdominal approach is used in?

A. Thiersch operation

B. Delorme's operation

C. Altemier's procedure

D. Ripstein's operation

Q.153 Which of the following is true regarding hereditary pancreatitis?

A. Autosomal recessive disorder

B. Has 80% penetrance

C. Accounts for about 30% of cases of chronic pancreatitis

D. IgG4 concentrations are elevated

Q.154 Stemmer's sign is due to?

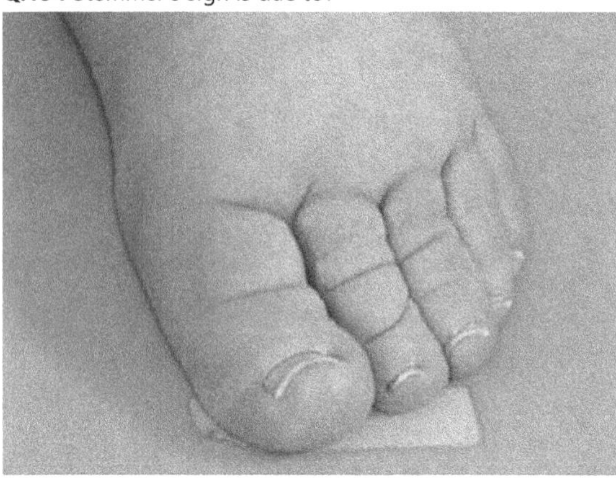

A. Lipodystrophy

B. Retroperitoneal fibrosis

C. Subcutaneous fibrosis

D. Deep vein thrombosis

Q.155 Migratory necrolytic skin rash is seen in?

A. ACTHoma

B. VIPoma

C. Glucagonoma

D. Somatostatinoma

Q.156 Delayed obstruction of the urinary tract after TURP is most commonly caused by?

A. Bladder neck stenosis

B. Penoscrotal stricture

C. Bulbar stricture

D. Membranous urethral stricture

Q.157 Which one of the following soft tissue sarcomas frequently metastasizes to lymph nodes?

A. Fibrosarcoma

B. Osteosarcoma

C. Embryonal Rhabdomyosarcoma

D. Alveolar soft part sarcoma

Q.158 Sclerotherapy is ideal for the treatment of:

A. External hemorrhoids

B. Internal hemorrhoids

C. Prolapsed hemorrhoids

D. Strangulated hemorrhoids

Q.159 The earliest manifestation of increased intracranial pressure following head injury is:

A. Ipsilateral pupillary dilatation

B. Contralateral pupillary dilatation

C. Altered mental status

D. Hemiparesis

Q.160 Lymphangiosarcoma was originally described in?

A. Stewart-Treves' syndrome

B. Klippel-Trenaunay's syndrome

C. Milroy's disease

D. Meig's disease

Q.161 Agnes Hunt traction is used for?

A. Flexion deformity of the hip

B. Trochanteric fracture

C. Fracture shaft of femur in adults

D. Low backache

Q.162 The most common type of teratoma of the testis is?

A. Teratoma differentiated

B. Malignant teratoma intermediate

C. Malignant teratoma anaplastic

D. Malignant teratoma trophoblastic

Q.163 Which of the following is tested using the 'Lift off test'?

A. Teres Minor

B. Subscapularis

C. Supraspinatus

D. Infraspinatus

Q.164 Which is not true regarding Schatzki's ring?

A. Seen at squamocolumnar junction

B. Associated with reflux disease

C. Circular ring in the proximal oesophagus

D. Respond to dilatation

Q.165 Gallow's traction is used for?

A. Fracture shaft of the femur

B. Fracture neck of the femur

C. Fracture humerus

D. Fracture tibia

Q.166 All are true regarding Caroli's disease except?

A. Intrahepatic stone formation

B. Biliary stasis

C. Commonly presents with ascites

D. Malignant change can occur

Q.167 Heberden's Arthropathy affects:

A. Lumbar spine

B. Symmetrically large joints
C. Sacroiliac joints
D. Distal interphalangeal joints

Q.168 The most common sequelae of tuberculous spondylitis in an adolescent is:
A. Fibrous Ankylosis
B. Bony Ankylosis
C. Pathological dislocation
D. Chronic osteomyelitis

Q.169 All of the following areas are commonly involved sites in pelvic fracture except:
A. Pubic rami
B. Alae of ileum
C. Acetabulum
D. Ischial tuberosities

Q.170 A 30-year-old man had a road traffic accident and sustained a fracture of the femur. Two days later he developed sudden breathlessness. The most probable cause can be:
A. Pneumonia
B. Congestive heart failure
C. Bronchial asthma
D. Fat Embolism

Q.171 The Best investigation for the detection of bone metastases is?
A. X-ray
B. CT Scan
C. MRI
D. Bone scan

Q.172 In the case of reimplantation of an amputated digit, which of the following structures is fixed first?
A. Nerve
B. Artery
C. Vein
D. Bone

Q.173 In Klippel-Feil syndrome, the patient has all of the following clinical features except:
A. Low hair-line
B. Bilateral Neck webbing
C. Bilateral shortness of sternomastoid muscles
D. Gross limitations of neck movements

Q.174 Most common type of teratoma of the testis is?
A. Teratoma differentiated
B. Malignant teratoma intermediate
C. Malignant teratoma anaplastic
D. Malignant teratoma trophoblastic

Q.175 Which of the following ultrasound marker is associated with the greatest increased risk for Trisomy 21 in the fetus:
A. Echogenic foci in the heart
B. Hyperechogenic bowel
C. Choroid plexus cysts
D. Nuchal edema

Q.176 A joint is innervated by the articular branches of the nerves which supply the muscles which move the joint. This law is known as:
A. Hilton's law
B. Andry's law
C. Wolff's law
D. Cushing's law

Q.177 In Radionuclide imaging, the most useful radiopharmaceutical for skeletal imaging is:
A. Gallium 67
B. Technetium sulfur colloid
C. Technetium-99m
D. Technetium—99m linked to Methylene diphosphonate

Q.178 The threshold radiation dose for the hematological syndrome is?
A. 1 Gyw
B. 5 Gy
C. 20 Gy
D. 100 Gy

Q.179 The most accurate investigation for assessing ventricular function is:
A. Multislice CT
B. Echocardiography
C. Nuclear scan
D. MRI

Q.180 Which of the following is a characteristic feature of Blount's disease?
A. Genu valgum
B. Genu varum
C. Coxa vara
D. Coxa valga

Q.181 The ideal timing of radiotherapy for Wilms tumor after surgery is:
A. Within 10 days
B. Within 2 weeks
C. Within 3 weeks
D. Any time after surgery

Q.182 Which one of the following imaging techniques gives maximum radiation exposure to the patient?
A. Chest X-ray
B. MRI
C. CT scan
D. Bone-scan

Q.183 The anesthetic implication in Gaisbock's syndrome is?
A. Postoperative respiratory failure
B. Risk of deep vein thrombosis
C. Renal dysfunction
D. Risk of aspiration

Q.184 Guttmann's sign is?
A. Flushing of the conjunctiva
B. Engorged veins of the arm
C. Stuffiness of the nostril
D. The warmth of the face

Q.185 Which of the following is true regarding type III neuroendocrine tumour of the stomach?
A. Most frequent neuroendocrine tumour of the stomach
B. Serum gastrin is normal
C. High-grade malignant tumour
D. Endoscopic resection is the treatment of choice

Q.186 Which of the following is not a definitive airway?
A. Tracheostomy
B. Orotracheal tube
C. Nasotracheal tube
D. Laryngeal mask airway

Q.187 The mechanism of action of everolimus is?
A. Blocks IL-2 gene transcription

B. Blocks IL-2 receptor signal transduction
C. Blockade of T cells
D. Prevents lymphocyte proliferation

Q.188 A patient presents to the emergency department with abdominal trauma with signs of shock and peritonitis. Airway and breathing were checked. 2 large bore cannulas were inserted to secure IV access. What is the next step in the management of this patient?

A. Immediate exploratory laparotomy with general anaesthesia
B. Focused Assessment with Sonography in Trauma (FAST)
C. Laparoscopic visualization of the injury
D. Watch and wait

Q.189 A most common type of teratoma of the testis is?
A. Teratoma differentiated
B. Malignant teratoma intermediate
C. Malignant teratoma anaplastic
D. Malignant teratoma trophoblastic

Q.190 Which is not true regarding Schatzki's ring?
A. Seen at the squamocolumnar junction
B. Associated with reflux disease
C. Circular ring in the proximal esophagus
D. Respond to dilatation

Q.191 Which of the following is true regarding type III neuroendocrine tumor of the stomach?
A. Most frequent neuroendocrine tumor of the stomach
B. Serum gastrin is normal
C. High-grade malignant tumor
D. Endoscopic resection is the treatment of choice

Q.192 True regarding obstructive azoospermia is?
A. Increased FSH and LH
B. Increased FSH and normal LH
C. Normal FSH and increased LH
D. Normal FSH and LH

Q.193 Areas involved in posterior cerebral artery infarct are all except?
A. Thalamus
B. Temporal lobe
C. Anterior cortex
D. Choroid plexus

Q.194 Which of the following is not a component of Total Parenteral Nutrition?
A. Amino acids
B. Fats
C. Vitamins
D. Fiber

Q.195 Tumour secreting placental alkaline phosphatase is?
A. Carcinoid tumor
B. Arrhenoblastoma
C. Granulosa cell tumour
D. Dysgerminoma

Q.196 Which of the following is not true regarding the Large Loop Excision of the Transformation Zone (LLETZ)?
A. Uses low voltage diathermy
B. Applicable only to the cervix
C. Loop size greater than 2cm gives a better cone
D. Shorter procedure time compared to laser ablation

Q.197 Solid tumor with cystic areas in between filled with hemorrhagic fluid and accounting for about 20% of all ovarian cancers is?
A. Cystadenocarcinoma
B. Mesonephroid tumors
C. Endometrioid tumor
D. Brenner tumor

Q.198 The characteristics of caput succedaneum – A/E:
A. Crosses midline
B. Crosses the suture line
C. It does not disappear with 2-3 days
D. It is diffuse edematous swelling of the soft tissues of the scalp

Q.199 Which is true regarding Savage syndrome?
A. Receptor defect to gonadotrophic hormones
B. Short stature
C. Ovaries do not contain follicles
D. FSH is normal

Q.200 The absence of corkscrew glands is seen in?
A. Halban's disease
B. Polycystic ovarian disease
C. Irregular ripening
D. Metropathia hemorrhagic

Q.201 Immediate cord ligation is done in:
A. Pre-term babies
B. Rh incompatibility
C. Both a and b
D. Anemia

Q.202 True for internal rotation of the head:
A. The Rotation occurs mostly in the cervix
B. In majority of rotation occurs in the pelvic floor
C. The rotation occurs commonly after the crowning of the head
D. Rotation is earlier in primipara than multipara

Q.203 The use of which of the following drugs for the treatment of menorrhagia is not supported by clinical evidence?
A. Tranexamic acid
B. Oral contraceptives
C. Ethamsylate
D. Progesterone only pills

Q.204 The Gold standard test for measuring ß HCG levels in serum is?
A. ELISA
B. Bioassay
C. Radioimmunoassay
D. Latex agglutination test

Q.205 Definition of crowning:
A. Biparietal diameter at the inlet of the pelvis
B. Biparietal diameter at the ischial spine
C. Biparietal diameter at the vulval outlet

D. Biparietal diameter just outside the vulval outlet

Q.206 The Most specific marker for neural tube defects is?

A. Alpha-fetoprotein

B. Unconjugated estriol

C. Acetylcholinesterase

D. Pseudocholinesterase

Q.207 Nodular tags of the hymen in the post-pregnancy period:

A. Carunculae myrtiformes

B. Vestibulae myrtiformes

C. Orficiae myrtiformes

D. Carunculae orificis

Q.208 Engagement of the head occurs when:

A. The greatest horizontal plane – bitemporal is above the pelvic brim

B. The greatest horizontal plane – bitemporal is below the pelvic brim

C. Shortest horizontal plane – biparietal is below the pelvic brim

D. None of the above

Q.209 Which of the following congenital malformations can be diagnosed in the first trimester?

A. Microcephaly

B. Anencephaly

C. Meningocele

D. Encephalocele

Q.210 Causes of primary amenorrhoea are all except:

A. Turner syndrome

B. Sheehan's syndrome

C. MRKH syndrome

D. Kallmann syndrome

Q.211 A primigravida in the first trimester of pregnancy was found to be sputum positive for acid-fast bacilli. There is no prior history of tuberculosis. What is the treatment of choice for this patient?

A. Category I DOTS

B. Category II DOTS

C. Category III DOTS

D. Start ATT after delivery

Q.212 The drug of choice for treatment of intrahepatic cholestasis in pregnancy is?

A. Ursodeoxycholic acid

B. Dexamethasone

C. Antihistamines

D. Cholestyramine

Q.213 Is the virus responsible for non-immune hydrops fetal is?

A. Cytomegalovirus

B. Herpes simplex virus

C. Hepatitis B virus

D. Parvovirus

Q.214 Increased nuchal translucency in 13th-week fetal ultrasound characteristic of?

A. Turner syndrome

B. Down's syndrome

C. Hydrocephalus

D. Klinefelter syndrome

Q.215 Which of the following is a Low grade squamous intraepithelial lesion as per the Bethesda system?

A. CIN I

B. CIN II

C. CIN III

D. Squamous metaplasia

Q.216 Which among the following is most commonly associated with carcinoma cervix?

A. HPV 35   **B.** HPV 33   **C.** HPV 18   **D.** HPV 16

Q.217 Estrogen administration in a menopausal woman increases the:

A. Gonadotropin secretion

B. LDL cholesterol

C. Bone mass

D. Muscle mass

Q.218 Which of the following maneuvers is not used for the management of shoulder dystocia?

A. McRoberts maneuver

B. Suprapubic pressure

C. Woods corkscrew maneuver

D. Mauriceau Smellie Veit maneuver

Q.219 Decreased motility of the Fallopian tube is seen associated with?

A. Noonan syndrome

B. PCOD

C. Churg Strauss syndrome

D. Kartagener's syndrome

Q.220 The obstetric conjugate is the distance between:

A. Sacral promontory & inner surface of the pubic symphysis

B. Sacral promontory & outer surface of the pubic symphysis

C. Sacral promontory & upper edge of the pubic symphysis

D. Sacral promontory & lower edge of the pubic symphysis

Q.221 The Sensitivity of uterine musculature:

A. Enhanced by progesterone

B. Enhanced by estrogen

C. Inhibited by estrogen

D. Enhanced by estrogen and inhibited by progesterone

Q.222 Which vitamin deficiency is most commonly seen in a pregnant mother who is on phenytoin therapy for epilepsy?

A. Vitamin B6

B. Vitamin B12

C. Vitamin A

D. Folic acid

Q.223 Which is not included in active management of III state of labor to prevent PPH?

A. Direct oxytocin injection after delivery of shoulder

B. Immediate cutting and cord clamping

C. Prophylactic misoprostol

D. Controlled and sustained cord traction

Q.224 Progression of labor is assessed by:

A. Partograph

B. Cervical dilatation

C. Fetal heart monitoring

D. Status of membranes

Q.225 Most important conjugate during labor:

A. Anatomical conjugate

B. True conjugate

C. Obstetric conjugate

D. Diagonal conjugate

Q.226 The incision used in the endometrial approach to the ear is?

A. Lempert I incision

B. Rosen's incision

C. Lempert II incision

D. Wilde's incision

Q.227 Hitzelberger's sign is?

A. Reduced corneal sensitivity

B. Hypoesthesia of the posterior meatal wall

C. Paraesthesia of face

D. Delayed blink reflex

Q.228 Does orbital apex syndrome involve?

A. Olfactory nerve

B. The ophthalmic division of a trigeminal nerve

C. Maxillary division of trigeminal nerve

D. Mandibular division of trigeminal nerve

Q.229 All are true regarding the use of sodium fluoride in otosclerosis except?

A. It inhibits proteolytic enzymes in the cochlea

B. Its use is contraindicated in patients with chronic nephritis

C. It acts by inhibition of osteoblastic activity

D. It is used in patients with positive Schwartz sign

Q.230 Prussak's space is bounded below by?

A. Fibers of a lateral malleolar fold

B. Shrapnell's membrane

C. The short process of malleus

D. Neck of malleus

Q.231 Pain in the tonsillar fossa and upper neck is characteristic of?

A. Eagle's syndrome

B. Apert's syndrome

C. Sickler's syndrome

D. Usher's syndrome

Q.232 Ipsilateral immobility of soft palate is seen in?

A. Lermoyez syndrome

B. Ortner's syndrome

C. Costen's syndrome

D. Trotter's syndrome

Q.233 The following is true for Gradenigo's syndrome?

A. Mastoid tenderness

B. Retro-orbital pain

C. Hearing loss

D. Sagging of posterosuperior meatal wall

Q.234 Secondary hemorrhage after tonsillectomy is most commonly seen?

A. 6 hours after surgery

B. 24 hours after surgery

C. 6 days after surgery

D. 14 days after surgery

Q.235 Otoacoustic emissions arise from?

A. Inner hair cells

B. Outer hair cells

C. Organ of Corti

D. None of the above

Q.236 A child climbs with alternate steps, builds a tower of 9 cubes, but can tell not his name and cannot say his age and sex, the probable age is:

A. 36 months

B. 24 months

C. 30 months

D. 48 months

Q.237 A child's growth variation is normal but bone development is not acc to the chronological age. What is the diagnosis?

A. Genetic

B. Dwarfism

C. Constitutional delay

D. Familial short stature

Q.238 Taste perception of the baby develops at:

A. Birth   **B.** 4 month   **C.** 6 month   **D.** 8 month

Q.239 A 3-month baby will have:

A. Pincer Grasp

B. Head control

C. Sitting with support

D. Transfer objects

Q.240 A two-month-old child likely to:

A. Show a positive parachute protective reflex

B. Hold head steady in a seated positive

C. Lift head chest off a flat surface with extended ventral

D. Sustain head level with the body when the placed suspension

Q.241 Adolescent starts at the age of:

A. 7 years   **B.** 10 years   **C.** 14 years   **D.** 17 years

Q.242 Child change rattle from one hand to another at:

A. 1 year

B. 6 months

C. 3 months

D. 2 years

Q.243 Short stature, secondary to growth hormone deficiency's associated with:

A. Normal body proportion

B. Low birth weight

C. Normal epiphyseal development

D. Height age equal to skeletal age

Q.244 Order of development of secondary sexual characteristic in male:

A. Testicular development-pubic hair-axillary hair-beard

B. Pubic hair- testicular development -axillary hair -beard

C. Testicular development -beard-pubic hair-axillary hair

D. Axillary hair- beard- pubic hair-testicular development

Q.245 The maximum growth spurt is seen in the girl at, time of:

A. Pubarche **B.** Thelarche
C. Menarche **D.** Adrenarche

Q.246 All of the following are seen in Favre-Goldmann syndrome except?

A. Ectopia lentis
B. Retinoschisis
C. Nyctalopia
D. Pigmentary changes similar to retinitis pigmentosa

Q.247 Axenfeld anomaly is seen in glaucoma associated with?

A. Aniridia
B. Phakomatosis
C. Ectopia lentis
D. Iridocorneal dysgenesis

Q.248 Stocker's line is seen in?

A. Pinguecula **B.** Trachoma
C. Pterygium **D.** Concretions

Q.249 Cogan's syndrome is associated with?

A. Keratitis **B.** Conjunctivitis
C. Iritis **D.** Myopia

Q.250 Which of the following is seen in Lowe's syndrome?

A. Glaucoma **B.** Choroiditis
C. Secondary cataract **D.** Myopia

Q.251 Gunn sign is?

A. Silver wiring of arterioles
B. Deflection of veins at an arteriovenous crossing
C. Copper wiring of arterioles
D. Tapering of veins on either side of the crossings

Q.252 Weiss operation is done for?

A. Cicatricial entropion
B. Senile entropion
C. Senile ectropion
D. Cicatricial ectropion

Q.253 Bilateral granulomatous panuveitis is seen in?

A. Heerfordt's syndrome
B. Reiter's syndrome
C. Behcet's disease
D. Toxoplasmosis

Q.254 Ophthalmoplegic migraine is best characterized as?

A. Recurrent headache with transient palsy of the ophthalmic nerve
B. Headache associated with irreversible palsy of 3rd nerve
C. Recurrent headache with transient palsy of 3, 4, and/or 6th cranial nerves
D. Headache with optic neuritis

Q.255 Which of the following is a topical NSAID for ophthalmic use?

A. Ibuprofen **B.** Diflunisal
C. Nepafenac **D.** Oxaprozin

Q.256 A 40-year old woman presents with a 2-year history of erythematous papulopustular lesions on the convexities of the face. There is a background of erythema and telangiectasia. The most likely diagnosis in the patient is:

A. Acne vulgaris
B. Rosacea
C. Systemic lupus erythematosus
D. Polymorphic light eruption

Q.257 Neoplastic dyskeratosis is seen in?

A. Darier's disease
B. Warty dyskeratoma
C. Familial benign pemphigus
D. Actinic keratosis

Q.258 The pseudo-isomorphic phenomenon is characteristic of?

A. Vitiligo **B.** Psoriasis
C. DLE **D.** Plane warts

Q.259 Blaschko's lines represent?

A. Lines of development
B. Dermatomes
C. Lines along blood vessels
D. Lines along lymphatics

Q.260 A 27-year-old sexually active male develops a vesiculobullous lesion on the glans soon after taking a paracetamol tablet for fever. The lesion healed with hyperpigmentation. The most likely diagnosis is:

A. Behcet's syndrome **B.** Herpes genitalis
C. Fixed drug eruption **D.** Pemphigus Vulgaris

Q.261 An otherwise healthy male presented to the OPD with a curdy white patch on the tongue. The most probable diagnosis is?

A. Candidiasis **B.** Lichen planus
C. Histoplasmosis **D.** Aspergillosis

Q.262
The only definite indication for giving systemic corticosteroids in pustular psoriasis is:

A. Psoriatic erythroderma with pregnancy
B. Psoriasis in a patient with alcoholic cirrhosis
C. Moderate arthritis
D. Extensive lesions

Q.263 Anemia with stippling of erythrocytes is seen commonly in which metal toxicity?

A. Lead **B.** Mercury
C. Manganese **D.** Arsenic

Q.264 A 45-year-old farmer has itchy erythematous papular lesions on the face, neck, 'V' area of the chest, dorsum of hands, and forearms for 3 years. The lesions are more severe in summer and improve by 75% in winter. The most appropriate test to diagnose the condition would be:

A. Skin biopsy
B. Estimation of IgE levels in the blood
C. Patch test
D. Intradermal prick test

Q.265 A patient had seven irregular hyperpigmented macules on the trunk and multiple small hyperpigmented macules in the axillae and groins since early childhood. There were no other skin lesions. Which is the most likely investigation to support the diagnosis?

A.	Slit-lamp examination of the eye
B.	Measurement of intraocular tension
C.	Examination of fundus
D.	Retinal artery angiography

Q.266 Ivermectin is indicated in the treatment of:

A. Syphilis	**B.** Scabies
C. Tuberculosis	**D.** Dermatophytosis

Q.267 Anagen phase of the hair indicates:

A.	The phase of activity and growth
B.	The phase of transition
C.	The phase of resting
D.	The phase of degeneration

Q.268 A patient had seven irregular hyperpigmented macules on the trunk and multiple small hyperpigmented macules in the axillae and groins since early childhood. There were no other skin lesions. Which is the most likely investigation to support the diagnosis?

A.	Slit lamp examination of eye
B.	Measurement of intraocular tension
C.	Examination of fundus
D.	Retinal artery angiography

Q.269 The drug used for the treatment of nocturnal enuresis is?

A. Trazodone	**B.** Imipramine
C. Chlorpromazine	**D.** Sertraline

Q.270 False statement regarding Complex Regional Pain Syndrome (CRPS) is?

A.	Type 1 CRPS occurs following a nerve injury
B.	Type 1 CRPS is also called Reflex Sympathetic Dystrophy
C.	It occurs due to adrenergic sensitivity of afferent nociceptors
D.	CRPS Type 1 resolves with symptomatic treatment

Q.271 Which of the following is not a feature of pseudohypoparathyroidism?

A.	Hyperparathyroidism
B.	Hypocalcemia
C.	Hypoparathyroidism
D.	Hyperphosphatemia

Q.272 Which of the following is a false statement?

A.	Acetaminophen does not have anti-inflammatory action
B.	NSAIDs with least cardiovascular risk in Naproxen
C.	Gastric irritation is more severe with NSAIDs compared to aspirin
D.	Non-selective COX-2 inhibitors are contraindicated in postoperative patients

Q.273 Wrong statement about SGLT (sodium-glucose linked transporter):

A.	SGLT1 is present in the intestine and kidneys
B.	SGLT1 has low capacity and high affinity
C.	SGLT2 inhibitors worsen heart failure
D.	SGLT2 inhibitors produce weight loss

Q.274 Which of the following is false regarding Multiple Sclerosis (MS)?

A.	More common in women and age of onset is between 20-40 years of age
B.	Risk factors include vitamin D deficiency and cigarette smoking
C.	Pathological hallmark is axonal degeneration
D.	HLA DRB1 in MHC class II is associated with 10% of disease risk

Q.275 The following drug is not used for the treatment of type II lepra reaction:

A. Chloroquine	**B.** Thalidomide
C. Cyclosporine	**D.** Corticosteroids

Q.276 The clinical picture is diagnostic of acne vulgaris. Isotretinoin is used in severe intractable acne. Pterygium of the nail is characteristically seen in:

A. Lichen planus	**B.** Psoriasis
C. Tinea unguium	**D.** Alopecia areata

Q.277 The main cytokine, involved in erythema nodusum leprosum (ENL) reaction is:

A.	Interleukin—2
B.	Interferon-gamma
C.	Tumor necrosis factor-alpha
D.	Macrophage colony-stimulating factor

Q.278 All of the following are true regarding CSF abnormalities in multiple sclerosis except?

A.	CSF protein concentration is more than 100 mg/dl
B.	CSF IgG index expresses the ratio of IgG to albumin in CSF divided by the same ratio in serum
C.	Oligoclonal bands may be absent at onset of multiple sclerosis
D.	The number of oligoclonal bands increases with time

Q.279 Max. Joseph's space is a histopathological feature of:

A. Psoriasis Vulgaris	**B.** Lichen planus
C. Pityriasis rosea	**D.** Parapsoriasis

Q.280 'Chancre redux' is a clinical feature of:

A.	Early relapsing syphilis
B.	Late syphilis
C.	Chancroid
D.	Recurrent herpes simplex infection

Q.281 All of the following drugs are effective in the treatment of pityriasis versicolor except:

A. Selenium sulphide	**B.** Ketoconazole
C. Griseofulvin	**D.** Clotrimazole

Q.282 A 16-year-old boy presented with asymptomatic, multiple, erythematous, annular lesions with a collarette of scales at the periphery of the lesions present on the trunk. The most likely diagnosis is:

A. Pityriasis Versicolor
B. Pityriasis alba
C. Pityriasis rosea
D. Pityriasis rubra pilaris

Q.283 In which of the following conditions Parakeratosis most frequently occurs?
A. Actinic keratoses
B. Seborrheic keratoses
C. Molluscum contagiosum
D. Basal cell carcinoma

Q.284 A 24-year old unmarried woman has multiple nodular, cystic, pustular, and comedonal lesions on the face, upper back, and shoulders for 2 years. The drug of choice for her treatment would be:
A. Acitretin
B. Isotretinoin
C. Doxycycline
D. Azithromycin

Q.285 All of the following drugs are effective in the treatment of pityriasis Versicolor except:
A. Selenium sulfide
B. Ketoconazole
C. Griseofulvin
D. Clotrimazole

Q.286 Mutation in malignant melanoma-
A. N-myc
B. CDK2A
C. RET
D. None

Q.287 Mycosis fungoides affects:
A. T Cells
B. B Cells
C. NK Cells
D. K Cells

Q.288 Civatte bodies are found in:
A. Lichen Planus
B. Psoriasis
C. Dermatophytosis
D. Vitiligo

Q.289 Broke's tumor is a tumor of:
A. Superficial dermal vessels
B. Sweat glands
C. Hair follicles
D. Sebaceous glands

Q.290 Reactivation tuberculosis is almost exclusively a disease of the:
A. Lungs
B. Bones
C. Joints
D. Brain

Q.291 Prolonged parasitism in malaria is due to:
A. Antigenic variation
B. Intracellularity of the parasite
C. Immunosuppression
D. Sequestration

Q.292 Which of the following cell types is not a target for the initiation and maintenance of HIV infection?
A. CD4 T cell
B. Macrophage
C. Dendritic cell
D. Neutrophil

Q.293 Pautriers abscess is mainly composed of which of the following cells:
A. Eosinophils
B. Lymphocytes
C. Neutrophils
D. Macrophages

Q.294 Simplex type of Epidermolysis Bullosa involves mutations in:
A. Keratin 5
B. Lamina Lucida
C. Type VII collagen
D. Dystrophin

Q.295 Selective granular IgA deposit at dermal papillae tips as seen in:
A. Bullous pemphigoid
B. Dermatitis Herpetiformis
C. Lichen planus
D. Pemphigus Vulgaris

Q.296 Linear band of immunofluorescence (due to immunoglobulin deposition) along the dermo-epidermal junction (Ribbon candy pattern) is seen in:
A. Bullous pemphigoid
B. Dermatitis Herpetiformis
C. Pemphigus Vulgaris
D. Lichen planus

Q.297 All are true about basal cell carcinoma except:
A. It is a locally aggressive tumor
B. They are slow-growing and rarely metastasize
C. Associated with mutations that activate Hedgehog pathway signaling
D. A most common site is acral parts

Q.298 Plasmodium falciparum affects all organs except:
A. Lung
B. Liver
C. Kidney
D. Heart

Q.299 Acantholytic cells in Pemphigus are derived from:
A. Stratum granulosum
B. Stratum basale
C. Langerhans cell
D. Stratum spinosum

Q.300 The most common cause of premature death in schizophrenia is?
A. Drug toxicity
B. Nosocomial infection
C. Homicide
D. Suicide

// Smart Answer Sheet //

| Correct | Indicates percentage of students who answered questions correctly. |

| Skipped | Indicates percentage of students who skipped questions. |

Q.	Ans.	Correct / Skipped	Q.	Ans.	Correct / Skipped	Q.	Ans.	Correct / Skipped	Q.	Ans.	Correct / Skipped	Q.	Ans.	Correct / Skipped
1	B	64.17 % / 33.63 %	17	A	79.61 % / 14.24 %	33	B	89.97 % / 10.02 %	49	A	87.29 % / 10.45 %	65	D	46.34 % / 48.77 %
2	D	28.47 % / 67.11 %	18	A	79.51 % / 17.13 %	34	B	78.29 % / 13.06 %	50	B	18.17 % / 74.47 %	66	A	81.29 % / 16.68 %
3	D	40.85 % / 53.43 %	19	C	88.07 % / 10.08 %	35	C	42.28 % / 51.88 %	51	D	59.57 % / 38.34 %	67	B	78.53 % / 13.57 %
4	A	81.38 % / 14.28 %	20	D	20.77 % / 69.52 %	36	D	78.74 % / 15.23 %	52	D	86.4 % / 12.72 %	68	A	79.22 % / 20.73 %
5	A	46.63 % / 50.6 %	21	A	41.26 % / 47.98 %	37	A	15.0 % / 74.61 %	53	B	47.51 % / 35.59 %	69	C	20.58 % / 73.26 %
6	D	64.13 % / 34.11 %	22	A	80.81 % / 16.54 %	38	C	43.77 % / 56.02 %	54	D	85.12 % / 12.14 %	70	D	85.27 % / 12.45 %
7	B	54.03 % / 38.9 %	23	D	82.81 % / 16.49 %	39	A	86.63 % / 10.29 %	55	C	77.88 % / 14.34 %	71	C	59.7 % / 33.92 %
8	B	60.07 % / 30.39 %	24	C	40.6 % / 59.22 %	40	D	88.2 % / 10.32 %	56	B	60.71 % / 33.48 %	72	A	83.79 % / 13.24 %
9	D	84.77 % / 11.14 %	25	C	80.16 % / 19.25 %	41	A	58.66 % / 31.59 %	57	A	25.68 % / 74.04 %	73	B	41.14 % / 41.37 %
10	B	80.12 % / 14.97 %	26	D	60.96 % / 36.1 %	42	B	89.82 % / 10.04 %	58	D	46.32 % / 45.79 %	74	A	83.78 % / 15.03 %
11	D	86.03 % / 13.88 %	27	A	47.72 % / 51.58 %	43	A	53.93 % / 42.03 %	59	C	82.63 % / 13.16 %	75	C	86.6 % / 11.0 %
12	B	41.62 % / 41.36 %	28	A	79.97 % / 10.52 %	44	C	89.89 % / 10.09 %	60	D	42.03 % / 41.44 %	76	A	27.1 % / 69.74 %
13	D	57.99 % / 35.78 %	29	A	86.88 % / 12.88 %	45	C	78.09 % / 14.49 %	61	B	76.95 % / 19.23 %	77	B	86.38 % / 13.51 %
14	A	78.23 % / 19.7 %	30	B	53.33 % / 31.46 %	46	D	41.49 % / 49.69 %	62	D	76.11 % / 22.58 %	78	D	83.38 % / 11.07 %
15	B	85.53 % / 13.12 %	31	D	80.57 % / 11.81 %	47	A	52.69 % / 40.29 %	63	C	82.75 % / 14.96 %	79	C	81.02 % / 17.45 %
16	C	86.41 % / 13.08 %	32	C	27.93 % / 67.77 %	48	C	65.14 % / 33.27 %	64	D	85.33 % / 11.74 %	80	B	81.08 % / 14.89 %

Q.	Ans.	Correct / Skipped
81	A	86.53 % / 12.56 %
82	B	27.45 % / 67.31 %
83	B	53.18 % / 36.69 %
84	D	87.43 % / 11.69 %
85	C	55.93 % / 30.05 %
86	D	79.23 % / 12.15 %
87	C	83.55 % / 15.2 %
88	C	88.35 % / 10.91 %
89	B	76.47 % / 14.06 %
90	A	89.73 % / 10.05 %
91	C	23.6 % / 67.73 %
92	B	81.05 % / 14.74 %
93	A	80.38 % / 14.72 %
94	C	61.65 % / 31.01 %
95	D	86.93 % / 11.46 %
96	A	88.08 % / 11.76 %
97	B	88.79 % / 10.9 %
98	B	87.35 % / 10.49 %
99	D	85.62 % / 13.84 %
100	B	68.89 % / 30.85 %
101	B	83.53 % / 15.71 %
102	C	53.93 % / 44.85 %
103	C	85.66 % / 12.6 %
104	C	62.81 % / 32.25 %
105	B	85.83 % / 12.89 %
106	D	87.4 % / 11.3 %
107	B	52.47 % / 38.65 %
108	D	87.28 % / 10.26 %
109	A	88.6 % / 11.38 %
110	B	53.57 % / 34.92 %
111	C	85.69 % / 13.81 %
112	B	80.35 % / 18.31 %
113	B	78.42 % / 14.91 %
114	B	79.71 % / 17.36 %
115	B	76.42 % / 14.69 %
116	C	12.24 % / 68.54 %
117	A	60.57 % / 34.3 %
118	B	63.89 % / 34.28 %
119	D	88.8 % / 10.95 %
120	C	66.49 % / 30.42 %
121	A	11.44 % / 82.12 %
122	B	17.99 % / 68.86 %
123	D	78.54 % / 19.17 %
124	D	87.61 % / 11.91 %
125	D	79.51 % / 10.36 %
126	A	77.3 % / 20.86 %
127	C	89.77 % / 10.09 %
128	B	15.82 % / 82.22 %
129	D	79.02 % / 18.75 %
130	A	84.02 % / 15.88 %
131	C	81.86 % / 12.63 %
132	B	54.16 % / 43.89 %
133	D	21.32 % / 70.77 %
134	D	77.14 % / 14.96 %
135	D	29.74 % / 68.69 %
136	D	69.34 % / 30.55 %
137	C	10.37 % / 85.97 %
138	D	83.94 % / 13.57 %
139	B	51.15 % / 46.3 %
140	C	56.99 % / 33.7 %
141	A	89.5 % / 10.11 %
142	A	89.22 % / 10.72 %
143	A	25.4 % / 71.04 %
144	A	77.67 % / 17.13 %
145	D	83.44 % / 14.69 %
146	B	24.14 % / 73.4 %
147	A	88.56 % / 10.17 %
148	B	76.54 % / 20.21 %
149	C	82.64 % / 12.01 %
150	D	46.04 % / 36.81 %
151	A	23.28 % / 73.97 %
152	D	78.83 % / 13.37 %
153	B	78.63 % / 19.47 %
154	C	81.89 % / 15.97 %
155	C	87.55 % / 10.79 %
156	A	87.29 % / 12.66 %
157	C	84.19 % / 10.15 %
158	B	87.48 % / 12.25 %
159	C	47.69 % / 51.32 %
160	A	88.52 % / 10.02 %

Q.	Ans.	Correct / Skipped	Q.	Ans.	Correct / Skipped	Q.	Ans.	Correct / Skipped	Q.	Ans.	Correct / Skipped	Q.	Ans.	Correct / Skipped
161	A	27.26 % / 70.87 %	177	D	76.17 % / 23.07 %	193	C	55.31 % / 30.87 %	209	B	86.53 % / 10.81 %	225	C	88.64 % / 10.99 %
162	B	82.16 % / 16.59 %	178	A	56.57 % / 41.73 %	194	D	82.98 % / 14.22 %	210	B	57.81 % / 37.78 %	226	B	88.33 % / 10.88 %
163	B	56.85 % / 31.16 %	179	B	88.75 % / 10.61 %	195	D	43.4 % / 42.41 %	211	A	79.7 % / 13.54 %	227	B	85.41 % / 13.99 %
164	C	31.6 % / 67.43 %	180	B	22.0 % / 73.53 %	196	C	31.95 % / 68.04 %	212	A	85.5 % / 10.03 %	228	C	48.22 % / 31.74 %
165	A	85.92 % / 13.83 %	181	A	88.19 % / 10.44 %	197	C	56.7 % / 41.81 %	213	D	89.73 % / 10.04 %	229	C	81.37 % / 15.39 %
166	C	48.35 % / 41.92 %	182	C	86.79 % / 10.07 %	198	C	16.07 % / 79.43 %	214	B	79.29 % / 12.9 %	230	C	79.13 % / 15.77 %
167	D	42.85 % / 36.96 %	183	B	83.49 % / 10.08 %	199	A	79.12 % / 17.76 %	215	A	13.38 % / 76.35 %	231	A	13.35 % / 76.34 %
168	B	86.81 % / 10.02 %	184	C	78.47 % / 11.27 %	200	D	83.59 % / 12.87 %	216	D	20.93 % / 74.6 %	232	D	76.61 % / 13.63 %
169	D	81.97 % / 12.57 %	185	B	51.59 % / 37.11 %	201	C	18.18 % / 74.62 %	217	C	23.72 % / 74.17 %	233	B	25.37 % / 69.92 %
170	D	87.67 % / 11.22 %	186	D	62.64 % / 32.55 %	202	B	81.4 % / 10.55 %	218	D	63.15 % / 36.49 %	234	C	42.57 % / 38.32 %
171	D	65.53 % / 32.09 %	187	B	85.87 % / 13.72 %	203	C	85.24 % / 14.15 %	219	D	88.78 % / 10.38 %	235	B	79.61 % / 17.36 %
172	D	88.71 % / 10.48 %	188	A	79.04 % / 12.73 %	204	C	42.37 % / 38.37 %	220	A	55.14 % / 32.89 %	236	C	64.83 % / 35.15 %
173	C	85.18 % / 13.47 %	189	B	20.62 % / 76.84 %	205	C	52.03 % / 32.3 %	221	D	64.94 % / 30.09 %	237	C	44.13 % / 40.81 %
174	B	15.99 % / 74.21 %	190	C	65.26 % / 33.93 %	206	C	48.82 % / 51.04 %	222	D	77.25 % / 10.79 %	238	A	16.17 % / 82.5 %
175	D	80.06 % / 10.79 %	191	B	79.49 % / 18.41 %	207	A	56.0 % / 37.78 %	223	C	60.79 % / 31.24 %	239	B	77.52 % / 21.68 %
176	A	66.86 % / 31.2 %	192	D	41.82 % / 32.22 %	208	D	57.92 % / 41.43 %	224	A	82.39 % / 13.92 %	240	D	58.64 % / 33.41 %

Q.	Ans.	Correct / Skipped
241	B	78.56 % / 20.1 %
242	B	62.88 % / 30.37 %
243	A	56.8 % / 40.6 %
244	A	84.03 % / 13.25 %
245	C	79.0 % / 18.26 %
246	A	76.25 % / 23.07 %
247	D	83.25 % / 15.51 %
248	C	43.74 % / 41.83 %
249	A	87.63 % / 10.41 %
250	A	77.23 % / 18.07 %
251	D	78.92 % / 13.83 %
252	B	83.91 % / 13.77 %

Q.	Ans.	Correct / Skipped
253	A	24.78 % / 74.96 %
254	C	80.31 % / 18.71 %
255	C	19.7 % / 67.68 %
256	B	86.35 % / 13.15 %
257	D	83.88 % / 15.13 %
258	D	40.91 % / 41.76 %
259	A	58.91 % / 32.85 %
260	C	69.74 % / 30.13 %
261	A	83.93 % / 13.98 %
262	D	68.65 % / 31.06 %
263	D	88.16 % / 11.43 %
264	C	83.13 % / 13.3 %

Q.	Ans.	Correct / Skipped
265	A	80.3 % / 12.72 %
266	B	88.48 % / 10.39 %
267	A	78.69 % / 15.62 %
268	A	87.02 % / 11.24 %
269	B	84.23 % / 10.57 %
270	A	77.68 % / 20.1 %
271	C	65.66 % / 31.57 %
272	C	78.04 % / 17.98 %
273	C	80.72 % / 14.72 %
274	C	84.64 % / 14.77 %
275	C	77.72 % / 14.4 %
276	A	66.22 % / 30.81 %

Q.	Ans.	Correct / Skipped
277	C	84.82 % / 14.5 %
278	A	77.09 % / 20.57 %
279	B	80.38 % / 11.25 %
280	A	79.78 % / 16.82 %
281	C	81.38 % / 17.77 %
282	C	86.56 % / 12.87 %
283	A	63.05 % / 32.26 %
284	B	82.52 % / 12.3 %
285	C	78.31 % / 19.97 %
286	B	76.0 % / 20.85 %
287	A	80.87 % / 10.07 %
288	A	83.75 % / 14.68 %

Q.	Ans.	Correct / Skipped
289	C	78.3 % / 21.58 %
290	A	60.37 % / 36.84 %
291	B	48.86 % / 44.51 %
292	D	87.15 % / 12.22 %
293	B	44.97 % / 35.66 %
294	A	76.31 % / 20.22 %
295	B	89.86 % / 10.1 %
296	A	11.11 % / 73.5 %
297	D	22.59 % / 68.51 %
298	A	88.32 % / 10.51 %
299	D	50.71 % / 35.62 %
300	D	85.33 % / 10.34 %

Performance Analysis

Avg. Score (%)	65.33%
Toppers Score (%)	69.0%
Your Score	

Part A

Q.1 A person is unable to extend his metacarpophalangeal joint. This can result from injury to which nerve -
A. Ulnar nerve injury
B. Radial nerve injury
C. Median nerve injury
D. Posterior Interosseous nerve injury

Q.2 Wrist drop is due to injury of -
A. Ulnar nerve
B. Radial nerve
C. Median nerve
D. Musculocutaneous nerve

Q.3 Which of the following is not supplied by C8 T1 -
A. Abductor pollicis brevis
B. Extensor indices
C. Palmar interossei
D. 3rd & 4th lumbricals

Q.4 Structure passing deep to flexor retinaculum is -
A. Post tibial artery
B. Long saphenous vein
C. Tibialis anterior tendon
D. Peroneus Tertius

Q.5 Which of the following structure is unable in crossing the dorsal surface of the ischial spine
A. Pudendal nerve
B. Nerve to obturator internus
C. Obturator nerve
D. Internal pudendal vessel

Q.6 Inferior most structure of right hilum is -
A. Bronchus
B. Inferior pulmonary vein
C. Pulmonary artery
D. Inferior bronchial vein

Q.7 In a case of chest pain with pericarditis and pericardial effusion, pain is referred by -
A. Phrenic nerve
B. Superficial cardiac plexus
C. Deep cardiac plexus
D. Vagus nerve

Q.8 What does not crossing midline mean?
A. Left gonadal vein
B. Left renal vein
C. Left brachiocephalic vein
D. Hemiazygos vein

Q.9 Ureteric constrictions are at all sites except -
A. Pelviureteric junction
B. Lesser pelvis
C. At ischial spine
D. Urinary bladder wall

Q.10 Which of the following is transmitted through foramen spinosum -
A. Middle meningeal artery
B. Internal carotid artery
C. Facial nerve
D. Mandibular nerve

Q.11 Incudomalleolar joint is an example of:
A. Saddle joint
B. Condylar joint
C. Pivot joint
D. Plane joint

Q.12 All are contents of the interpeduncular fossa except the part-
A. Trochlear nerve
B. Oculomotor nerve
C. Mamillary bodies
D. None of these

Q.13 Cerebellar connection to other parts of the brain is projected through which cell -
A. Golgi cells
B. Basket cells
C. Purkinje cells
D. Oligodendrocytes

Q.14 The cells are belonging to which of the following type of epithelium -
A. Transitional
B. Stratified squamous
C. Stratified cuboidal
D. Stratified columnar

Q.15 Which of the following is not lined by Urothelium
A. Urinary bladder
B. Minor calyx
C. Ureters
D. Membranous urethra

Q.16 The upper 3/4th of vagina develops from -
A. Wolfian duct
B. Mullerian duct
C. Sino vaginal bulb
D. Endoderm

Q.17 The most common cause of delayed umbilical cord separation is
A. Raspberry tumour
B. Leukocyte adhesion deficiency
C. Patent urachus
D. Umbilical granuloma

Q.18 The transition temperature of lipid bilayers of the cell membrane is increased by
A. Cholesterol
B. Saturated fatty acids
C. Hydrocarbons
D. Unsaturated fatty acids

Q.19 Most potent antioxidant -

A. Vitamine E   **B.** Vitamine A
C. Vitamine K   **D.** Vitamine C

Q.20 Which of the following does not occur in mitochondria :
A. Citric acid cycle (Kreb's cycle)
B. Glycogenolysis
C. Fatty acid oxidation
D. Electron transport chain

Q.21 Resting membrane potential is mainly due to
A. Na^+ **B.** K^+ **C.** Cl^- **D.** Mg^{++}

Q.22 Almost all transmissible electrically charged particle in excitable tissue is -
A. Na^+ **B.** K^+
C. Cl^- **D.** None of these

Q.23 Which is TRUE regarding nerve conduction
A. All or none phenomenon
B. Conduction independent of amplitude
C. The propagated action potential is generated in dendrites
D. Faster in unmyelinated fibres

Q.24 All are true regarding intrafusal fibres except
A. Nuclear chain fibres are shorter & thinner
B. Nuclear bag fibres are lesser
C. Primary endings excited by bag fibres only
D. Secondary endings excited by chain fibres only

Q.25 True about fatty acid synthesis
A. Occurs in mitochondria
B. Occurs in cytosol
C. Occurs in the endoplasmic reticulum
D. Occurs in ribosomes

Q.26 Where does protein synthesis occur?
A. Smooth ER   **B.** Golgi bodies
C. Rough ER   **D.** Lysosomes

Q.27 Physiological dead space is?
A. 150 ml   **B.** 200 ml   **C.** 250 ml   **D.** 100 ml

Q.28 Total alveolar ventilation volume (in L/min) is
A. 1.5   **B.** 3.5   **C.** 4.2   **D.** 5

Q.29 The pacemaker potential is due to
A. Fast Na^+ channel
B. Decrease in K^+ permeability
C. Slow Ca^{++} channel
D. Rapid repolarisation

Q.30 Einthoven's law
A. I + III = II   **B.** I − III = II
C. I + II + III = 0   **D.** I + III = avL

Q.31 Which of the following structures does not lie in the renal medulla-
A. Juxtaglomerular apparatus
B. Loop of Henle
C. Collecting duct

D. Vasa Recta

Q.32 Proteolytic enzyme Renin is present in?
A. Lungs   **B.** Liver   **C.** Kidney   **D.** Stomach

Q.33 Parietal cell secretes
A. Mucus   **B.** Pepsinogens
C. Gastrin   **D.** Intrinsic factor

Q.34 The cephalic phase of gastric secretion
A. 20%   **B.** 70%   **C.** 10%   **D.** 100%

Q.35 The mechanism by which pyruvate cytosol is transported to mitochondria is
A. Chloride antiport
B. Proton symport
C. ATP dependent antiport
D. Facilitated uniport

Q.36 Which of the following acts as co-enzymes and not as co-factors
A. Folic acid   **B.** Biotin
C. Thiamine   **D.** All of these

Q.37 Substrate level phosphorylation is catalysed by which enzyme?
A. Succinate dehydrogenase
B. Alpha-ketoglutarate dehydrogenase
C. Succinate thiokinase
D. Malate dehydrogenase

Q.38 The biosynthesis of the enzyme pyruvate carboxylase is repressed by
A. Insulin   **B.** Glucagon
C. Cortisol   **D.** Epinephrine

Q.39 Pompe's disease is due to deficiency of which enzyme storage disease
A. Branching enzyme
B. Glucose 6 phosphatase
C. Acid maltase deficiency
D. Muscle phosphorylase

Q.40 1st acetyl group donor in fatty acid synthesis is
A. Malonyl CoA   **B.** Palmitate
C. Acetyl CoA   **D.** Citrate

Q.41 Acetyl CoA carboxylase is activated by
A. Malonyl CoA   **B.** Citrate
C. Palmitoyl CoA   **D.** Acetoacetate

Q.42 Which of the following is/are a storage protein
A. Myoglobin   **B.** Ovalbumin
C. Ferritin   **D.** All of these

Q.43 The main source of energy derived from
A. Fat   **B.** Glycogen
C. Lactate   **D.** Acetone

Q.44 Thiamine acts as a cofactor in
A. Conversion of pyruvate to acetyl-CoA

B. Transamination reactions

C. Oxidation in the respiratory chain

D. Conversion of pyridoxal to pyridoxal phosphate

Q.45 Consumption of raw egg may lead to the deficiency of

A. Biotin
B. Riboflavin
C. Thiamine
D. Avidin

Q.46 True about the coding strand of DNA

a) Acts as a template for mRNA

b) Minus strand

c) Plus strand

d) Matches with RNA transcript that encodes a protein

A. ab
B. bc
C. bd
D. cd

Q.47 All statements are false regarding mature cytoplasmic messenger RNA except-

A. Transcribed from Nuclear DNA

B. Has Thiamine in place of Uracil

C. Sugar is Deoxy Ribose

D. Its molecular weight is more than hn-RNA

Q.48 Which of the following is related to the structure of a codon-

A. Two complementary base pairs

B. Three consecutive nucleotide units

C. An individual ribosome

D. Four individual nucleotides

Q.49 Nobel prize in 2006 was given for the discovery of

A. Lipoxins

B. RNAi

C. DNA

D. β-transcription factor

Q.50 All of these are required for PCR except-

A. Taq polymerase

B. d-NTP

C. Primer

D. Radiolabelled DNA probe

Part B

Q.51 Which of the following is the reason behind delayed prolonged bleeding?

A. Direct injury to endothelial cell

B. Histamine

C. Leukocyte dependent injury

D. IL-I

Q.52 Cardinal signs of Inflammation are all except?

A. Rubor
B. Tumour
C. Calor
D. Cyanosis

Q.53 The first step in the initiation of primary hemostasis for clot formation is?

A. Fibrin deposition
B. Vasoconstriction
C. Platelet adhesion
D. Thrombosis

Q.54 Hypoplasia of the gland shown in the Photograph is associated with

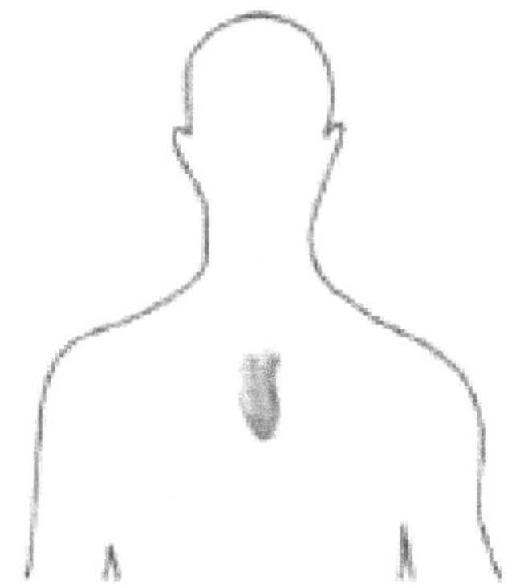

A. Wiskott Aldrich Syndrome

B. IgA deficiency

C. Digeorge syndrome

D. Agammaglobulinemia

Q.55 A 34-year-old, G, P0, presents for genetic counselling at 12 week's gestation. The patient has two sisters and a brother; her father has haemophilia. Her siblings are not affected, but she has a nephew that is:

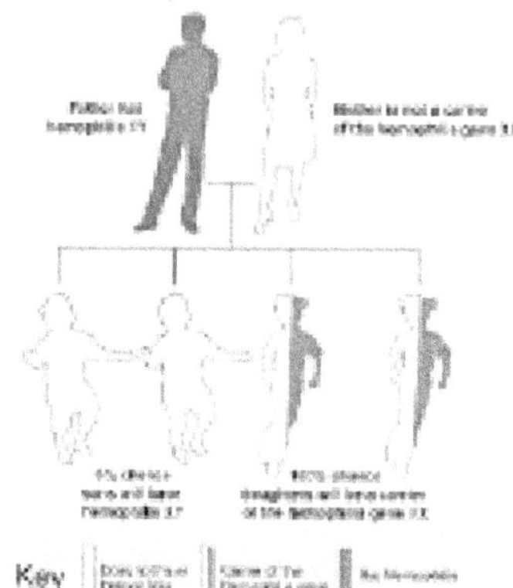

A. Autosomal recessive

B. X-linked inheritance

C. Mitochondrial inheritance

D. Multifactorial inheritance

Q.56 Tumour shown in Photograph is known as

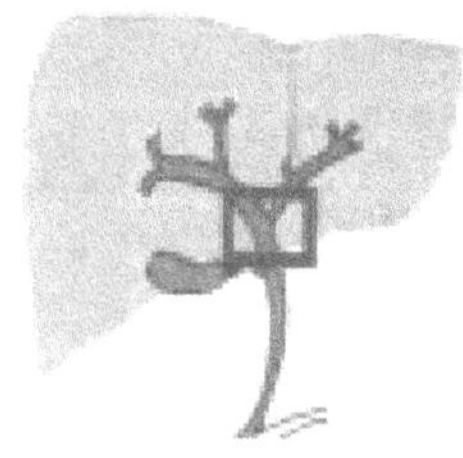

A. Krukenberg tumour

B. Signet ring cell carcinoma

C. Oncocytoma

D. Klatskin tumor

Q.57 Dystrophic calcification is seen in
A. Rickets
B. Atheromatous plaque
C. Hyperparathyroidism
D. Vitamin 'A' intoxication

Q.58 Progenitor hematopoietic stem cells originate in -
A. Bone Marrow
B. Thymus
C. Lymph node
D. Spleen

Q.59 Hemophilia manifest clinically as a rise in -
A. PTT
B. PT
C. CT
D. BT

Q.60 Reed Sternberg cells are found in

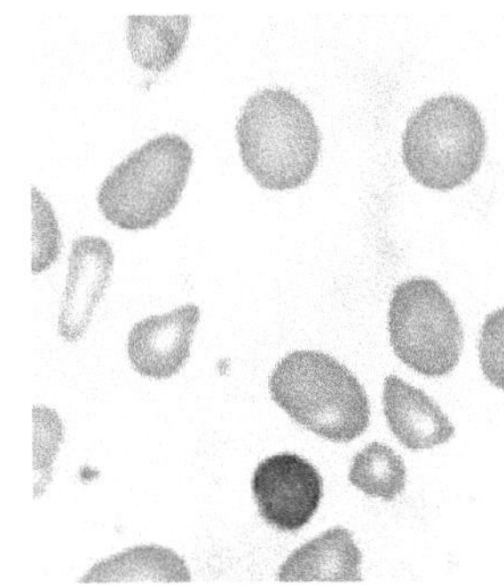 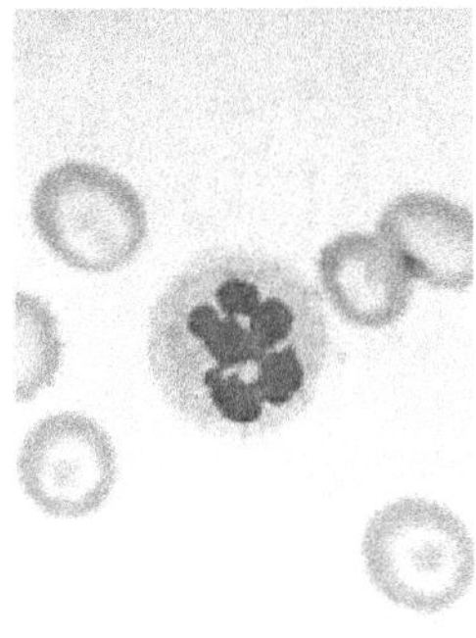

A. Hodgkin's disease
B. Sickle cell anaemia
C. Thalassemia
D. CML

Q.61 Best prognostic type of Hodgkin's lymphoma is -
A. Lymphocytic predominant
B. Lymphocytic depletion
C. Mixed cellularity
D. Nodular sclerosis

Q.62 The collapse of the lung is called
A. Emphysema
B. Bronchiectasis
C. Atelectasis
D. Bronchitis

Q.63 The protein in glomerular basement membrane responsible for charge-dependent filtration is -
A. Albumin
B. Collagen type IV
C. Proteoglycan
D. Fibronectin

Q.64 Mallory Weiss Syndrome is caused due to tear in -
A. The lower esophageal end
B. Crico pharyngeal junction
C. Gastroesophageal junction
D. None of the above

Q.65 Hepatic infarcts are seen in -
A. Pre-eclampsia
B. Chronic venous congestion
C. Shock
D. All of the above

Q.66 Which of the following testicular tumor is not a germ cell neoplasm -
A. Seminoma
B. Yolk sac tumor
C. Sertoli cell tumor
D. Teratoma

Q.67 Which of the following joint is characteristically involved in RA. -
A. Spine
B. Sacroiliac joint
C. Metacarpophalangeal joint and proximal interphalangeal joint
D. Wrist joint

Q.68 Neuroglia answerable for phagocytosis is -
A. Fibrous Astrocytes
B. Protoplasmic Astrocytes
C. Oligodendrocytes
D. Microglia

Q.69 Which of the following syndrome is related to Medullary carcinoma of the thyroid.
A. MEN I
B. MEN II
C. Li–Fraumeni syndrome
D. Hashimoto's thyroiditis

Q.70 The highest hurtful potential is in -
A. Epidermal naevus
B. Junctional naevus
C. Intradermal naevus
D. None of the above

Q.71 The commonest type of spinal T. B. is -
A. Posterior
B. Paradiscal
C. Pedicle
D. Anterior

Q.72 Which of the following is not seen in primary tuberculosis-
A. Cavitation
B. Caseation
C. Calcification
D. Giant cell

Q.73 Metastasis in neuroblastoma goes to -
A. Liver
B. Lung
C. Bone
D. All of the above

Q.74 Which events in neuroblastoma is associated as 'good' outcome
A. Diploidy
B. N-myc amplification
C. Chromosome 1 p deletion
D. Trk A expression

Q.75 Which of the following conditions is related to Aniridia and Hemihypertrophy -
A. Neuroblastoma
B. Wilm's tumour
C. Non-Hodgkin's lymphoma
D. Germ cell tumour

Q.76 Metabolism of drugs is mostly done by which enzyme
A. Cytochrome C
B. Cytochrome P450
C. Glucuronyl transferase
D. Acetylase

Q.77 100% bioavailability is seen with which route

A. Oral   **B.** Intravenous

C. Rectal   **D.** Subcutaneous

C. Redistribution

D. Rapid metabolism in the systemic circulation

Q.78 Which of the following is true?

A. As the concentration of the drug increases over the therapeutic range, only the bound form of the drug increases

B. The bound form is not available for metabolism but is available for excretion

C. Acidic drugs bind to beta globulin and basic drugs bind to albumin

D. Binding sites are non–specific and one drug can displace the other

Q.79 Cholinomimetic drugs can be used for the treatment of all the following conditions EXCEPT:

A. Closed-angle Glaucoma

B. Bradycardia

C. Cobra bite

D. Myasthenia gravis

Q.80 Lid retraction is caused by?

A. Bimatoprost   **B.** Latanoprost

C. Brimonidine   **D.** Apraclonidine

Q.81 A pupillary dilator is provided by:

A. Postganglionic parasympathetic from Edinger Westphal nucleus

B. Postganglionic sympathetic from cervical sympathetic chain

C. Third cranial nerve

D. Sympathetic fibres of the front-orbital branch of the trigeminal nerve

Q.82 Which of the following drugs can cause hypotension by the release of histamine from mast cells?

A. Aspirin   **B.** Procaine

C. Morphine   **D.** Sulfadiazine

Q.83 Which of the following drugs can prolong survival in patients with CHF?

A. Furosemide   **B.** Amrinone

C. Losartan   **D.** Digoxin

Q.84 The site of action of the furosemide is

A. Descending limb of the loop of Henle

B. Thick ascending limb of the loop of Henle

C. Proximal convoluted tubule

D. Distal convoluted tubule

Q.85 Which of the following is not an adverse effect of growth hormone therapy?

A. Carpal tunnel syndrome

B. Hypoglycemia

C. Intracranial hypertension

D. Slipped femoral epiphysis

Q.86 The result of thiopentone on the CNS is rapidly aborted by reason of:

A. Rapid metabolism in the CNS

B. Quick first-pass elimination

Q.87 To prevent exercise-induced bronchial asthma, a drug used is :

A. Sodium cromoglycate

B. Ipratropium bromide

C. Terbutaline

D. Epinephrine

Q.88 Which of the following drugs is not an antiemetic?

A. Ondansetron   **B.** Domperidone

C. Metoclopramide   **D.** Cinnarizine

Q.89 All of the following drugs are bactericidal except :

A. Isoniazid   **B.** Tigecycline

C. Daptomycin   **D.** Ciprofloxacin

Q.90 Remifentanil is :

A. Useful for short painful procedures

B. Metabolized by plasma esterases

C. Equipotent as fentanyl

D. All of these

Q.91 All are antithyroid drugs EXCEPT

A. Carbamazepine   **B.** Propylthiouracil

C. Methimazole   **D.** Carbimazole

Q.92 Bremelanotide is used for :

A. Erectile dysfunction

B. Lower urinary tract symptoms

C. Prostate Cancer

D. Metastatic renal cancer

Q.93 Which among the following does not cause hyperpyrexia?

[NEET PG, 2014]

A. MAO Inhibitors   **B.** Alcohol

C. Atropine   **D.** Amphetamine

Q.94 Which of the following drugs is NOT used in scabies?

A. Benzene hexachloride

B. Permethrin

C. Ciclopirox olamine

D. Crotamiton

Q.95 Prostaglandin analogues have therapeutic utility in the following EXCEPT :

A. Pulmonary hypertension

B. Palliative treatment of patent ductus arteriosus

C. Impotence

D. Inflammatory bowel disease

Q.96 Staining procedure shown in Photograph is used to visualize _______ of the bacterium

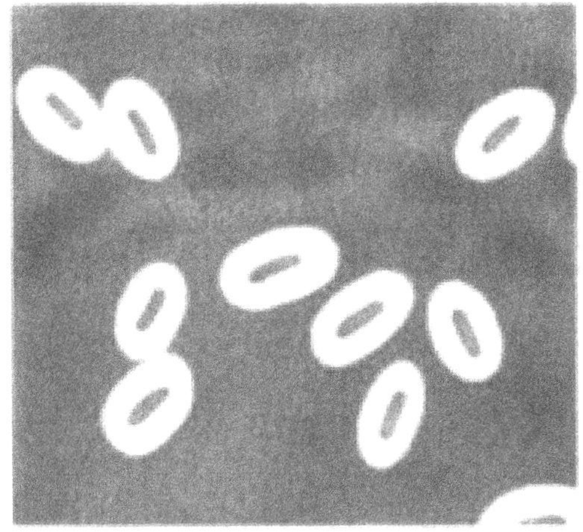

A. Nucleus
B. Motility
C. Capsule
D. Ribosomes

Q.97 Mycobacterium tuberculosis was discovered by -
A. Louis Pasteur
B. Robert Koch
C. Lister
D. Jenner

Q.98 To see the bacteria, the methods used are -
A. Microscopy
B. Stained preparations
C. Both
D. None of these

Q.99 All are peripheral lymphoid organs except -
A. Lymph nodes
B. Spleen
C. Thymus
D. Mucosa-associated lymphoid tissue

Q.100 B cell maturation takes place in -
A. Thymus
B. Lymph node
C. Bone marrow
D. Spleen

Q.101 Innate immunity active against viral cells -
A. NK cells
B. Cytotoxic T cells
C. B cell
D. Memory B cell

Q.102 In an inflammatory response, macrophages are usually derived from -
A. Monocytes
B. Reticuloendothelial cells
C. Neutrophils
D. Lymphocytes

Q.103 Which of the following is gram-positive bacillus-
A. Staphylococcus
B. Streptococcus
C. Listeria
D. Meningococci

Q.104 "Genital elephantiasis" is caused by all except
A. Lymphogranuloma venereum
B. Chancroid
C. Syphilis
D. Rickettsia

Q.105 Blood culture is positive in which infection of staph. aureus-
A. TSS
B. SSSS
C. Infective endocarditis
D. Impetigo

Q.106 DNA covering material in a virus is called as -
A. Capsomere
B. Capsid
C. Nucleocapsid
D. Envelope

Q.107 Both intranuclear and cytoplasmic inclusion is seen in -
A. Poxvirus
B. Herpesvirus
C. Measles virus
D. Mumps virus

Q.108 The appearance of cow dry type A inclusion bodies -
A. Granular
B. Circumscribed
C. In polio
D. None of these

Q.109 River blindness is caused by:
A. Trichomonas
B. Trichuris
C. Onchocerca volvulus
D. Dracunculus

Q.110 Non-gonococcal urethritis is mostly caused by:
A. Chlamydia and mycoplasma
B. Chlamydia and Streptococcus
C. Chlamydia and treponema
D. Chlamydia and ureaplasama

Q.111 Which of the following acts as an intermediate host of malaria a parasite?
A. Culex
B. Female anopheles
C. Human
D. Trombiculid mite

Q.112 The fungi which do not have a sexual phase belong to which of the following groups -
A. Phycomycetes
B. Fungi Imperfecti
C. Basidiomycetes
D. Ascomycetes

Q.113 Spherule is a feature of which of the following fungus
A. Blastomyces
B. Histoplasma
C. Paracoccidioides
D. Coccidioides

Q.114 Bacteria showing antigenic variation -
A. Yersinia
B. Bordetella
C. Brucella
D. Borrelia

Q.115 A most common organism which can contaminate crowded army camps is?
A. Klebsiella
B. E. coli
C. Neisseria meningitidis
D. Staphylococcus

Q.116 Dowry as a punishable offence under IPC act -
A. 304 A
B. 304 B
C. 420
D. 498

Q.117 Duret Haemorrhage is seen in:

A. Lung   **B.** Spleen   **C.** Liver   **D.** Brain

Q.118 Perjury means giving willful false evidence by a witness while under oath, the witness is liable to be prosecuted for perjury and the imprisonment may extend to 7 years. This falls under which section of IPC?

A.   190 of Indian Penal Code
B.   191 of Indian Penal Code
C.   192 of Indian Penal Code
D.   198 of Indian Penal Code

Q.119 Which of the following offence related to the 509-IPC act-

A.   Masturbation in a public place
B.   Inquest
C.   Dowry death
D.   Act intended to insult the modesty of a women

Q.120 Which of the following is related to "Tentative cuts"?

A. Homicide   **B.** Accidents
C. Fall from height   **D.** Suicide

Q.121 Heat stabilizing in muscles happens overhead temperature (°C) -

A. 30   **B.** 60   **C.** 40   **D.** 50

Q.122 In the case of Hanging neck ligature marks are an example of

A. Bruise   **B.** Pressure abrasion
C. Laceration   **D.** None of the above

Q.123 Lynching is -

A.   Practised in South America
B.   Practised by white people on Negros
C.   Hanging publically on a tree
D.   All of the above

Q.124 In which of the following BAL is not used to treat poisoning due to

A. Organic mercury   **B.** Arsenic
C. Lead   **D.** Cadmium

Q.125 Eonism is -

A.   Desire to identify with the opposite sex
B.   Intercourse with a lower animal
C.   Female homosexualism
D.   Oral sex

Q.126 An Optimal healthy life includes -

A.   Moderate physical exercise
B.   Sufficient nutrition
C.   Mental peace
D.   All of the above

Q.127 Missing cases are detected by?

A.   Active surveillance
B.   Passive surveillance
C.   Monitoring
D.   Sentinel surveillance

Q.128 All are measurements of mortality except -

A. Crude death rate   **B.** Survival rate
C. Incidence   **D.** Case fatality rate

Q.129 The Burden of disease is given by -

A.   Incidence
B.   Crude death rate
C.   Cause-specific death rate
D.   Proportional mortality rate

Q.130 Any abnormality of anatomical function is-

A. Disease   **B.** Impairment
C. Disability   **D.** Handicap

Q.131 There is a disease in which overall survival is increased by screening procedure is-

A. Prostate Cancer   **B.** Lung Cancer
C. Colon Cancer   **D.** Ovarian Cancer

Q.132 In the birth weight of each of the 10 babies born in a hospital in a day is found to be 2.8 kgs, then the standard deviation of this sample will be -

A. 2.8   **B.** 0   **C.** 1   **D.** 0.28

Q.133 A Scatter diagram is drawn to study

A.   The trend of a variable over a period of time
B.   Frequency of occurrence of events
C.   Relationship between two given variables
D.   Mean & median values of the given data

Q.134 Measles is infectious during -

A.   After 4 days of rash
B.   4 days before and 5 days after the rash
C.   Throughout disease
D.   Only in the incubation period

Q.135 Which is not a complication of chickenpox -

A. Pancreatitis   **B.** Pneumonia
C. Encephalitis   **D.** Thrombocytopenia

Q.136 From the following options given below, which one is recognized to do the screening of the school children firstly, under NPCB?

A.   Medical officer
B.   Ophthalmologic assistant
C.   Village health guide
D.   School teachers

Q.137 Under the National Programme for Control of Blindness, the goal is to reduce the prevalence of blindness to a level of -

A. 0.1%   **B.** 0.3%   **C.** 0.5%   **D.** 1%

Q.138 Widely practised method of family planning by capable partners in India is -

A. IUCD   **B.** OC Pill
C. Sterilization   **D.** Nirodh

Q.139 What is the mechanism of action of Glatiramer?

A. Antifungal   **B.** Immunomodulator
C. Antiviral   **D.** Antibacterial

Q.140 Which of the following statements is not true about breast milk-

A. The maximum milk output is seen at 12 months

B. The coefficient of uptake of iron in breast milk is 70%

C. Calcium absorption of human milk is better than that of cow's milk

D. It provides about 65 kcals per 100 ml

Q.141 The undersupply in weight for height in a 4 years old child specifies –

A. Acute malnutrition

B. Chronic malnutrition

C. Concomitant acute and chronic

D. Underweight

Q.142 Groundwater has the following advantages except –

A. Likely to be free from pathogenic organisms

B. Usually requires no treatment

C. Supply is likely to be certain even during the dry season

D. Likely to be hard

Q.143 The recommended concentration of iodine in iodised salt at the consumer level is:

A. 20 ppm   **B.** 15 ppm   **C.** 10 ppm   **D.** 5 ppm

Q.144 Additional daily energy requirement during the first six months of a lactating woman is -

A. 350 Kcalories   **B.** 600 Kcalories

C. 550 Kcalories   **D.** 450 Kcalories

Q.145 The incidence of mental illness is the maximum if the causal factors affect a particular period –

A. Perinatal period

B. First five years of life

C. School age

D. Adolescence

Q.146 Average hospital waste produced per bed per day in Government hospital –

A. 1.5-2.0 kg   **B.** 0.5–4 kg

C. 0.5–1 kg   **D.** 0.5–2 kg

Q.147 Following are used in the planning of Health education except –

A. Cover felt needs

B. Using simple words

C. Catchy slogans

D. Ensuring participation

Q.148 Which anti-cancer drug is eliminated by lung:

A. Cyclophosphamide   **B.** 5-FU

C. Enalapril   **D.** Cisplatin

Q.149 Follow–up of cataract operations in the national blindness control program is done by –

A. Active surveillance

B. Passive surveillance

C. Sentinel surveillance

D. Routine check-up

Q.150 The community is described as -

A. A conglomeration people

B. A group of people bound with social norms

C. An association with regulated membership

D. An association patterned the norms of interaction

Part C

Q.151 SIADH- all are features except -

A. Decreased sodium, maintaining the concentrating ability of the urine osmolality (> 100 mOsm)

B. Normal sodium balance maintained indicating excess urinary sodium is due to efficient sodium intake

C. Hypouricemia

D. Low blood pressure due to volume depletion

Q.152 Cardiogenic shock occurs as a result of:

A. Excessive vasodilation and possibly increased capillary permeability.

B. Severe central nervous system trauma that causes a rapid loss in sympathetic stimulation.

C. Reduction in intravascular fluid volume.

D. Myocardial dysfunction.

Q.153 Features of glomerular haematuria -

A. Full of R.B.C. in the high power field

B. Fragmented R.B.C.

C. Dysmorphic R.B.C.

D. Gross haematuria

Q.154 32-year-old AIDS-positive female presented with headaches and nuchal stiffness. On lumbar puncture examination clear CSF was obtained with leucocytes >100/cu.mm. India ink staining was positive. The most probable diagnosis is?

A. Candida Meningitis

B. Cryptococcus meningitis

C. Tubercular Meningitis

D. Cryptosporidium

Q.155 All are present in Fragile X syndrome-

a) FMR

b) Microorchidism

c) Large facies

d) Small ear

A. cd   **B.** ab   **C.** ac   **D.** bd

Q.156 The chance that a health worker gets HIV from an accidental needle prick is -

A. 1%   **B.** 10%   **C.** 95%   **D.** 100%

Q.157 Which is NOT a function of muscles?

A. Cause movement   **B.** Produce heat

C. Absorb nutrients   **D.** Maintain posture

Q.158 Pulsus Bigeminus is seen in therapy with -

A. Beta-blockers

B. ACE inhibitors

C. Digitalis

D. Calcium channel blockers

Q.159 Which of these statements regarding the conduction system of the heart is TRUE

A. The sinoatrial (SA) node of the heart acts as the pacemaker.

B. The SA node is located on the upper wall of the left atrium.

C. The AV node conducts action potentials rapidly through it.

D. Action potentials are carried slowly through the atrioventricular bundle.

Q.160 Which of the following stands for the statement, "Atrioventricular valves open and semilunar valves close during the Ventricular Systole"

A. True
B. False
C. Partially true
D. Partially false

Q.161 Which of these statements correctly applies to intrinsic regulation of the heart?

A. Starling's law of the heart has a major influence on cardiac output.

B. As venous return increases, cardiac output decreases.

C. In response to stretch, cardiac muscle fibers contract with less force.

D. In response to stretch, there is a slight decrease in heart rate.

Q.162 Management of essential hypertension is?

A. No need to treat
B. Diet modification alone
C. Diet modification and drug
D. Invasive surgery

Q.163 In Wilsons disease, copper deposition occurs in -

A. Pons
B. Medulla
C. Cerebellum
D. Basal ganglia

Q.164 The net diffusion of water from one solution of water from one solution through a semipermeable membrane to another solution containing a lower concentration of water is termed-

A. Filtration
B. Diffusion
C. Osmosis
D. Brownian motion

Q.165 CLL is characterized by?

A. Small lymphocytes in peripheral smear
B. Seen commonly in age >50 years persons
C. Hepatosplenomegaly
D. All of the above

Q.166 Desmosomes are helpful in connecting –

A. Keratinocytes
B. Melanocytes
C. Dermis and epidermis
D. Langerhans cells

Q.167 True about stratum lucidum –

a) Sandwiched between S. spinosum and S.granulosum
b) Sandwiched between S. corneum and S.granulosum
c) Contain hair follicle
d) Also known as prickle cell layer
e) Contain degenerated cells

A. ab
B. be
C. ad
D. ce

Q.168 Hypopigmented patches occur in -

A. Becker naevus
B. Freckles
C. Nevus anemicus
D. Nevus Ota

Q.169 An increased incidence of vitiligo is found is –

A. Psoriasis
B. Nutritional deficiency
C. Old age
D. Diabetes mellitus

Q.170 Dennie–Morgan line occurs in –

A. Dermatomyositis
B. SLE
C. Psoriasis vulgaris
D. Atopic dermatitis

Q.171 The most common cause of Airborn Dermatitis in India is –

A. Parthenium
B. Calotropis
C. Dust
D. None of these

Q.172 A most common type of psoriasis –

A. Plaque psoriasis
B. Psoriasis vulgaris
C. Both (A) and (B)
D. Penile psoriasis

Q.173 Auspitz sign is characteristically seen in –

A. Plaque psoriasis
B. Pustular psoriasis
C. Lichen planus
D. Inverse psoriasis

Q.174 A 30-year-old male had severely itchy papula–vesicular lesions on extremities, knees, elbows, and buttocks for one year. tired immunofluorescence staining of the lesions showed IgA deposition at the dermo-epidermal junction. The most probable diagnosis is –

A. Pemphigus vulgaris
B. Bullous pemphigoid
C. Dermatitis herpetiform
D. Nummular eczema

Q.175 A-85 year-old woman with Nikolsky sign–ve, blisters on thigh & trunk, lesions come on & off. What is the cause –

A. Pemphigus vulgaris
B. Pemphigoid
C. Lichen planus
D. Dermatitis herpetiformis

Q.176 Inverted saucer-shaped lesion is found in –

A. Lepromatous leprosy
B. Tuberculoid leprosy
C. Borderline leprosy
D. Indeterminate leprosy

Q.177 About tuberculoid leprosy, false is-

A. Pale-coloured skin
B. CMI is increased
C. A single anaesthetic patch
D. None of these

Q.178 Multiple painful ulcers over glans without in duration is suggestive of –

A. LGV

B. Granuloma inguinale

C. Chancroid

D. 2° syphilis

Q.179 The genital ulcer is seen in A/E –

A. Granuloma inguinale

B. Syphillis

C. LGV

D. Donovanosis

Q.180 Cafe au lait spots seen in?

A. NF

B. Gardner syndrome

C. Cockayne syndrome

D. Down syndrome

Q.181 The Stain used for staining fungal elements –

A. Acid-fast stain

B. Mucicarmic

C. Methenamine

D. Gram stain

Q.182 Which does not cause Tinea capitis –

A. Epidermophyton

B. Microsporum

C. Trichophyton rubrum

D. Trichophyton violaceum

Q.183 In which of the following, the disturbed orientation is observed

A. Schizophrenia

B. Neurosis

C. Paranoid personality

D. Organic mental disorder

Q.184 Which of the following behavioral problems would suggest an organic brain lesion -

A. Formal thought disorder

B. Auditory hallucinations

C. Visual hallucinations

D. Depression

Q.185 A 16-year-old boy suffering from drug abuse presents with a cross-over of sensory perceptions, such that, sounds can be seen and colors can be heard. Which of the following is that the most likely agent responsible for drug abuse

A. Cocaine

B. LSD

C. Marijuana

D. PCP

Q.186 Which of the following is not seen in morphine poisoning-

A. Cyanosis

B. Pinpoint pupil

C. Hypertension

D. Respiratory depression

Q.187 Somatic passivity is a feature of-

A. Depressive illness

B. Paranoid Schizophrenia

C. Hypochondriasis

D. Panic disorder

Q.188 Which of the following hallucinations is pathognomonic of schizophrenia -

A. Auditory hallucinations commanding the patient

B. Auditory hallucinations giving running commentry

C. Auditory hallucinations criticizing the patient

D. Auditory hallucinations talking to patient

Q.189 Which of the following conditions is classified under anxiety disorders according to DSM-III

A. Obsessive-compulsive disorder

B. Depression

C. Schizophrenia

D. Bipolar disorder

Q.190 Which of the following is not found in conversion disorder?

A. Jealousy

B. Paralysis

C. Anaesthesia

D. Abnormal gait

Q.191 Not true about narcolepsy -

A. Sleep sudden

B. Long duration (>3 hrs) of sleep

C. Cataplexy

D. All of the above

Q.192 All are features of autistic disorder except -

A. Mental retardation

B. Absent social smile

C. Onset before 21/2 years

D. Third-person hallucination

Q.193 Electroconvulsive therapy is currently advocated as a line of treatment in the following conditions except -

A. Catatonic schizophrenia

B. Severe depression with psychosis

C. Manic-depressive disorder

D. Obsessive-compulsive disorder

Q.194 Which of the following is a stage of intuitive thought appeared in the jean-Piaget scheme -

A. Sensorimotor

B. Concrete

C. Preoperational stage

D. Formal operations stage

Q.195 Best drug therapy for paranoid schizophrenia in a thinly built 21-years old young male would be-

A. Chlorpromazine

B. Risperidone

C. Olanzapine

D. Quetiapine

Q.196 March fracture is-

A. Fracture of 4th metatarsal

B. Fracture of 2nd metatarsal

C. Fracture of cuboids

D. Fracture of tibia

Q.197 Callus formation is seen between what duration of fracture healing

A. 0 - 2 weeks
B. 2 - 4 weeks
C. 4 - 12 weeks
D. 12 -16 weeks

Q.198 Most common muscle damaged in rotator cuff-

A. Supraspinatus
B. Infraspinatus
C. Subscapularis
D. Teres minor

Q.199 Bankart's lesion is seen at -

A. Post surface of the glenoid labrum
B. Anterior surface of glenoid labrum
C. The Anterior part of the head of the humerus
D. Post part of the head of the humerus

Q.200 If a patient with a suspected fracture of the pelvis has some bleeding from the urethra and is unable to pass urine -

A. He should be encouraged to pass urine after being given antibiotics and analgesics
B. He should be immediately catheterized in the ward
C. A hot water bottle should be given followed by an injection of corbachol
D. He should be prepared for surgery and catheterization attempted in the 0.T

Q.201 Which of the following is the main source to supply blood in the head and neck of the femur?

A. Lateral circumflex femoral Artery
B. Medial circumflex femoral Artery
C. Artery of Ligamentum Teres
D. Popliteal Artery

Q.202 For which fracture, the tube (cylinder) is applied-

A. Shoulder
B. Hip
C. Pelvis
D. Knee

Q.203 All are true regarding whiplash injury except -

A. The Lumbar spine is commonly involved
B. Fractures do not usually cause difficulties
C. A relatively common injury that occurs to a person's neck
D. Hyperextension injury

Q.204 Greenstick fracture is

A. Fracture in adults
B. Complete fracture
C. Incomplete fracture
D. Fracture spine

Q.205 An 11 years old male having pain in left hip & stumbling on examination constricted abduction & internal rotation, probable diagnosis is -

A. Septic arthritis of the hip
B. Tuberculous arthritis of the hip
C. Congenital dislocation of the hip
D. Perthes disease

Q.206 Reduced digestion of Epiphyseal plate in a growing child occurs in -

A. Rickets
B. Osteomalacia
C. Scurvy
D. Osteoporosis

Q.207 In Bony ankylosis, there is -

A. Painless, No movement
B. Painful complete movement
C. Painless complete movement
D. Painful incomplete movement

Q.208 The classification system of bone tumours is -

A. Enneking
B. Manchester
C. Edmonton
D. TNM

Q.209 Type of collagen found in bone is

A. Type 2
B. Type 3
C. Type 4
D. Type 1

Q.210 The contraindication to internal fixation -

A. Physical injury
B. Active infection
C. Intraarticular fracture
D. Fracture dislocation

Q.211 Safety pin index for oxygen cylinder is

A. 3,5
B. 1,5
C. 2,5
D. 1,4

Q.212 Bag and mask ventilation is absolutely contraindicated in –

A. Tracheoesophageal fistula with esophageal atresia and esophagus connected to the trachea
B. Diaphragmatic hernia
C. Meconium aspiration
D. All of the above

Q.213 All of the following are except- advantages of LMA

A. More reliable than a face mask
B. Prevent aspiration
C. Alternative to Endotracheal intubation
D. Does not require a laryngoscope & Visualization

Q.214 A Patient is on regular medications for co-existing medical problems. Which of the following drugs may be stopped safely with minimal risk of adverse effects before an abdominal surgery –

A. Statins
B. Beta Blockers
C. ACE inhibitors/ACE Receptor Blockers
D. Steroids

Q.215 Glycopyrrolate is beer than atropine because –

A. It crosses the blood-brain barrier
B. Not crosses the blood-brain barrier
C. More sedation
D. Antisialague

Q.216 Which of the following is the SAFEST test to be performed in a patient with acutely injured knee joint -

A. Lachmann test
B. Pivot shift test
C. McMurray's test
D. Apley's grinding test

Q.217 A 23-year-old lady with a past of hypersensitivity to neostigmine is displayed for a constituent caesarean part under general anaesthesia. The best muscle intoxicant of choice in this patient should be –

A. Pancuronium   **B.** Atracurium
C. Rocuronium   **D.** Vecuronium

Q.218 Succinylcholine is a muscle relaxant which acts by –

A. Persistent depolarisation
B. Competitive antagonist
C. Mechanism of action uncertain
D. Both (A) and (B)

Q.219 In a young patient who had extensive soft tissue and muscle injury, which of these muscle relaxants used for endotracheal intubation might lead to cardiac arrest –

A. Atracurium   **B.** Suxamethonium
C. Vecuronium   **D.** Pancuronium

Q.220 Commonly used route of administration for general anaesthesia is –

A. Inhalational   **B.** Intravenous
C. Intra-arterial   **D.** Subcutaneous

Q.221 Thiopentone is used for induction anaesthesia because it is –

A. An ultra-short-acting barbiturate
B. Rapidly redistributed to body fat
C. Rapid redistribution
D. Easy to monitor

Q.222 Among the following anaesthetic drug/inducing agents which should be avoided in a patient with a history of epilepsy-

A. Propofol   **B.** Thiopentone
C. Ketamine   **D.** Midazolam

Q.223 From which of the following routes absorption of local anaesthetic is maximum?

A. Intercostal   **B.** Epidural
C. Bronchial   **D.** Caudal

Q.224 Which of the following drugs are believed to be effective in the treatment of postoperative shivering?

A. Ondansetron   **B.** Diclofenac Sodium
C. Pethidine   **D.** Paracetamol

Q.225 End-tidal CO_2 is increased to the maximum level in –

A. Pulmonary embolism
B. Malignant hyperthermia
C. Extubation
D. Blockage of secretion

Q.226 The concentration of colour in Fetal Doppler is resolved by -

A. Direction flow
B. Velocity of flow
C. Strength of returning echo
D. None of the above

Q.227 True about MRI are all except

A. Not helpful in a breast implant
B. Not good for calcified lesions
C. No radiation exposure
D. Contraindicated in cardiac pacemaker

Q.228 Best investigation for Bronchiectasis is?

A. Chest X-Ray
B. MRI
C. Pulmonary Function Tests
D. HRCT

Q.229 Silhouetting of the left border of the heart (silhouette sign positive) on chest radiograph indicates what pathology

A. Upper lobe   **B.** Hilar
C. Lingula   **D.** Lower lobe

Q.230 In a Down's syndrome patient posted for surgery, the necessary preoperative investigation to be done is –

A. CT Brain
B. Echocardiography
C. Ultrasound Abdomen
D. X-ray cervical spine

Q.231 A symptomless old patient introduces noise in the carotid artery. Which of the following is the inspection of possibility?

A. Doppler ultrasonography
B. Internal carotid angiography
C. Aortic arch angiography
D. Spiral CT angiography

Q.232 Which of the following is the earliest sign of ulcerative colitis on double-contrast barium enema study -

A. Mucosal granularity
B. Loss of haustrations
C. 'Collar - button' ulcer
D. Lead pipe colon

Q.233 The string of beads appearance on abdominal X-ray is seen in –

A. Small bowel obstruction
B. Large bowel obstruction
C. Carcinoma of stomach
D. Gastric outlet obstruction

Q.234 In Renal cell carcinoma investigation of choice to evaluate inferior vena cava & renal vein for thrombus –

A. IVP   **B.** Coloured doppler
C. USG   **D.** CT scan

Q.235 The inspection of the solution for viewing of urinary tract tuberculosis (UTTB) is –

A. Plain film X-ray
B. Intravenous urography
C. Ultrasound
D. Computed tomography

Q.236 X-ray features of hypoparathyroidism are the following except –

A. Osteosclerosis
B. Calvarial thickening
C. Subperiosteol resorption
D. Subcutaneous calcification

Q.237 Hair-on end appearance is seen in –

A. Thalassemia
B. Sickle cell anemia
C. Hemochromatosis
D. Megaloblastic anemia

Q.238 Subdural hematoma most commonly results from –

A. Rupture of intracranial aneurysm
B. Injury to cortical bridging veins
C. Rupture of cerebral AVM
D. Haemophilia

Q.239 Phosphorous 32 emits

A. Beta particle
B. Alpha particle
C. Neutron
D. X-rays

Q.240 Which of the following is the best technique for differentiating repetition of brain tumour from dispersion therapy-convinced necrosis?

A. MRI
B. Contrast enhanced MRI
C. PET scan
D. CT scan

Q.241 Conjugate of the diagonal is taken as 'a' cm, then obstetric conjugate will be

A. a + 1 cm   **B.** a + 2 cm   **C.** a - 1 cm   **D.** a - 2 cm

Q.242 Time taken for spermatogenesis is (according to tritium-labeled biopsies)

A. 40-50 days
B. 60-70 days
C. 90-120 days
D. 70-80 days

Q.243 In which of the following transition meiosis occurs

A. Primary to secondary spermatocyte
B. Second spermatocyte to globular spermatid
C. Germ cells to spermatogonium
D. Spermatogonium to primary spermatocyte

Q.244 Blood transfusion is indicated in the following condition with sickle cell anemia

A. Frequent sickling episodes
B. Twin pregnancy
C. Poor obstetrical outcome
D. All of the above

Q.245 Most delicate test for the observation of iron exhaustion in pregnancy is-

A. Serum iron-binding capacity
B. Serum transferrin
C. Serum iron
D. Serum ferritin

Q.246 Chaser Moir surgery is done is a case of

A. Uterine inversion
B. Vesicovaginal fistula repair
C. Ureterovesical fistula repair
D. Retroverted uterus

Q.247 Post-term labor is seen in:

A. Anencephaly
B. PID
C. Hydramnios
D. Multiple pregnancy

Q.248 Best drug for a type of glaucoma shown in the photograph is:

A. Physostigmine
B. Pilocarpine
C. Latanoprost
D. Apraclonidine

Q.249 Risk of sear rupture in the classical cesarean section is –

A. 0.9%-12%
B. 5%-4%
C. 9%- 10%
D. 4%-9%

Q.250 IUGR is seen in:

A. Rubella
B. Syphilis
C. CMV
D. All of the above

Q.251 Best parameter for ultrasound evaluation of IUGR is:

A. Placental membrane
B. Length of femur
C. Abdominal circumference
D. BPD

Q.252 A large baby is born with which complication in pregnancy:

A. Gestational diabetes
B. Gestational hypertension
C. Anaemia
D. None of the above

Q.253 In which of the following, the Oxytocin challenge test for assessing fetal well-being is not contraindicated.

A. Placenta previa
B. Previous 2 LSCS
C. Breech
D. Premature labour

Q.254 Sinusoidal heart rate pattern is seen in:

A. Placenta previa
B. Vasa previa
C. Battledore placenta
D. Succenturiate placenta

Q.255 All are an explanation for decreased variability of the fetal heart tracing except-

A. Fetal "sleep state"
B. Prematurity
C. Barbiturate ingestion
D. Fetal stimulation

Q.256 All of the following pelvic structures support the vagina, except:

A. Perineal body
B. Pelvic diaphragm
C. Levator ani muscle
D. Infundibulopelvic ligament

Q.257 True about the timing of LH surge

A. Occur 12 hours before ovulation
B. Occur 12 hours after ovulation
C. Occur 24 hours before ovulation
D. Occur 24 hours after ovulation

Q.258 The cutoff point of serum estrogen level for the diagnosis of ovarian failure:

A. 10 pg/ml   **B.** 20 pg/ml   **C.** 30 pg/ml   **D.** 40 pg/ml

Q.259 False about PCOS:

A. Increased risk of diabetes mellitus
B. Bilateral ovarian cyst
C. Hirsutism
D. High FSH/LH ratio 1:2

Q.260 The vaginal epithelium is derived from:

A. Endoderm of genital ridge
B. Mesoderm of urogenital sinus
C. Endoderm of urogenital sinus
D. Mesoderm of genital ridge

Q.261 A 16-year-old girl with a height of 5 inches presents with primary amenorrhea and rising FSH. The histological finding most consistent with her conditions is?

A. Marfan syndrome
B. Corpus luteal hemorrhage
C. Low oocyte in ovary
D. Pituitary Apoplexy

Q.262 Minimum criteria to diagnose PID include(s):

A. Lower abdominal pain
B. Fever
C. Cervical motion tenderness
D. Leucocytosis

Q.263 Which of the following surgeries of stress incontinence has the long-term success rate is maximum with-

A. Stamey's repair
B. Burch's colposuspension
C. Kelly's stitch
D. Aldridge surgery

Q.264 What are the chances of a normally fertile couple having a baby in one month?

A. 80%   **B.** 25%   **C.** 60%   **D.** 45%

Q.265 Contraceptive vaginal foam tablet "today "contains:

A. Nonoxynol 9   **B.** Octoxynol 9
C. Menfegol   **D.** None of the above

Q.266 All are the complication of leiomyoma in pregnancy except?

A. Red degeneration   **B.** Obstructed labour
C. PPH   **D.** Placenta previa

Q.267 Best investigation endometriosis is:

A. Laparoscopy   **B.** USG
C. X-ray pelvis   **D.** CT Scan

Q.268 Endometrial hyperplasia is seen in-

A. Endodermal sinus tumor
B. Dysgerminoma
C. PCOD
D. Ca cervix

Q.269 CA 125 is elevated in all except :

A. Tuberculosis
B. Endometriosis
C. Ovarian tumor
D. Polycystic ovarian disease

Q.270 Menstruation is defined as precocious if it starts before the child reaches the age of:

A. 8 years   **B.** 10 years   **C.** 14 years   **D.** 20 years

Q.271 True about head circumference measurement –

A. Measured in supra–orbital ridge
B. Measured hydrocephalus/microcephaly
C. Serial measurement is useful
D. All of these

Q.272 Newborn phase expands up to –

A. 21 days of life   **B.** 30 days of life
C. 28 days of life   **D.** 35 days of life

Q.273 An infant presents with cardiac failure. Examination reveals a weaker femoral pulse when compared to the radial pulse. What is the probable diagnosis?

A. PDA
B. Aorto-iliac vasculitis
C. COA
D. VSD

Q.274 The most common cause of pneumonia in children less than 2 years is?

A. RSV
B. Streptococcus aureus
C. Staphylococcus aureus
D. Klebsiella

Q.275 Congenital hypertrophic pyloric stenosis usually presents –

A. Within 2 days after birth
B. Around 1 week after birth
C. Around 2 weeks after birth
D. Around 2 months after birth

Q.276 Toxic megacolon is seen in –

A. Chronic nonspecific ulcerative colititis
B. Crohn's disease
C. Colonic diverticulosis
D. Hamartomatous polyp

Q.277 % of children with simple febrile seizures developing epilepsy is –

A. 1–2%   **B.** 2–5%   **C.** 5–10%   **D.** 10–20%

Q.278 Which of the following statements is true regarding childhood hurtful is –

A. Wilm's tumour is the commonest
B. AML is the most common malignancy
C. Neuroblastoma arises in the first 4 years
D. None of the above

Q.279 "Haemoglobin E" (HbE) is common in –

A. Punjab **B.** Kerala
C. Bengal **D.** Maharashtra

Q.280 Multiple carboxylase deficiency is treated by-–
A. Biotin **B.** Pyridoxine
C. Thiamine **D.** Folic acid

Q.281 The first branch of the facial nerve is -
A. Greater petrosal nerve
B. Lesser petrosal nerve
C. Chorda-tympani nerve
D. Nerve to the stapedius

Q.282 Lacrimation is affected when facial nerve injury is at -
A. Geniculate ganglion
B. In semicircular canal
C. At sphenopalatine ganglion
D. None of these

Q.283 Dryness of the eye is caused by injury to the facial nerve at-
A. Chorda tympani
B. Cerebellopontine angle
C. Tympanic canal
D. Geniculate ganglion

Q.284 Killian's dehiscence is seen in -
A. Oropharynx **B.** Nasopharynx
C. Cricopharynx **D.** Vocal cords

Q.285 Treatment of Puberphonia is
A. Thyroplasty type III **B.** Thyroplasty type I
C. Thyroplasty type II **D.** Thyroplasty type IV

Q.286 The voice in a patient with Bilateral abductor paralysis of the larynx is
A. Puberphonia
B. Phonasthenia
C. Dysphonia plicae ventricularis
D. Normal or good voice

Q.287 Ranula is -
A. Hypertrophied lymphoid tissue
B. Arises from mucosa of floor of mouth
C. Hard and Hemorrhagic
D. An abscess

Q.288 All are precancerous lesions of oral cavity except -
A. Leukoplakia
B. Erythroplakia
C. Diffuse oral submucous fibrosis
D. Diffuse aphthous ulcers

Q.289 What is the treatment of choice for ethmoidal polyps?
A. Functional Endoscopic sinus surgery with polypectomy
B. Intranasal ethmoidectomy
C. Extra nasal ethmoidectomy
D. Transanal ethmoidectomy

Q.290 Radical mastoidectomy is done for -
A. ASOM
B. CSOM
C. Atticoantral cholesteatoma
D. Acute mastoiditis

Q.291 The axial length of the eyeball at birth is .... % of an adult eye –
A. 100 **B.** 90 **C.** 70 **D.** 40

Q.292 Pinhole can reduce refractive error up to -
A. 3 D **B.** 1 D **C.** 5 D **D.** 10 D

Q.293 A SAFE strategy is for?
A. Bacterial conjunctivitis
B. Viral conjunctivitis
C. Onchocercariasis
D. Trachoma

Q.294 Which of the following organism can penetrate the normal cornea –
a) Gonococcus
b) Pseudomonas
c) Diphtheria
d) Streptococcus
e) Staphylococcus epidermidis
A. a **B.** bc **C.** ad **D.** ac

Q.295 Signs of uveitis –
a) Generalized conjunctival congestion
b) Circumciliary congestion
c) Cells and flare in aqueous
d) Shallow anterior chamber
A. a **B.** c **C.** ac **D.** bc

Q.296 Which of the following statements is correct in regard to aqueous humour-
A. It is secreted at a rate of 2–3 microL/min
B. Secreted by ciliary process
C. Has less protein than plasma
D. All of the above

Q.297 Soft exudates are found in –
A. DM **B.** HTN
C. Toxemia **D.** All of these

Q.298 All are true about optic nerve except -
a) Arises from axons of bipolar neurons
b) 4 cm long
c) Covered by 3 layers continuous with meninges
d) Crossed by the ophthalmic artery
A. ac **B.** ab **C.** ad **D.** bc

Q.299 Bitemporal hemianopia field defect is characteristic of -
A. Glaucoma **B.** Optic neuritis
C. Pituitary tumour **D.** Retinal detachment

Q.300 The function of superior oblique muscle -
A. Intortion **B.** Extortion

C. Lateral rotation

D. Upward rotation

// Smart Answer Sheet //

Correct — Indicates percentage of students who answered questions correctly.

Skipped — Indicates percentage of students who skipped questions.

Q.	Ans.	Correct / Skipped	Q.	Ans.	Correct / Skipped	Q.	Ans.	Correct / Skipped	Q.	Ans.	Correct / Skipped	Q.	Ans.	Correct / Skipped
1	D	16.67 % / 5.55 %	17	B	16.67 % / 50.0 %	33	D	33.33 % / 50.0 %	49	B	11.11 % / 52.78 %	65	D	36.11 % / 58.33 %
2	B	41.67 % / 41.66 %	18	B	5.56 % / 50.0 %	34	A	22.22 % / 50.0 %	50	D	19.44 % / 50.0 %	66	C	25.0 % / 58.33 %
3	B	13.89 % / 44.44 %	19	A	38.89 % / 50.0 %	35	B	11.11 % / 50.0 %	51	A	25.0 % / 52.78 %	67	C	36.11 % / 58.33 %
4	A	22.22 % / 47.22 %	20	B	22.22 % / 50.0 %	36	D	33.33 % / 50.0 %	52	D	33.33 % / 55.56 %	68	D	19.44 % / 58.34 %
5	C	5.56 % / 47.22 %	21	B	25.0 % / 50.0 %	37	C	11.11 % / 52.78 %	53	B	25.0 % / 58.33 %	69	B	27.78 % / 58.33 %
6	B	19.44 % / 47.23 %	22	B	2.78 % / 50.0 %	38	A	19.44 % / 52.78 %	54	C	19.44 % / 58.34 %	70	B	19.44 % / 58.34 %
7	A	36.11 % / 44.45 %	23	A	36.11 % / 50.0 %	39	C	25.0 % / 50.0 %	55	B	25.0 % / 58.33 %	71	B	11.11 % / 58.33 %
8	A	16.67 % / 47.22 %	24	C	13.89 % / 52.78 %	40	C	22.22 % / 50.0 %	56	D	22.22 % / 58.34 %	72	A	22.22 % / 58.34 %
9	C	11.11 % / 44.45 %	25	B	30.56 % / 50.0 %	41	B	8.33 % / 50.0 %	57	B	16.67 % / 58.33 %	73	D	27.78 % / 58.33 %
10	A	30.56 % / 44.44 %	26	C	33.33 % / 50.0 %	42	D	30.56 % / 50.0 %	58	A	30.56 % / 58.33 %	74	D	8.33 % / 58.34 %
11	A	33.33 % / 44.45 %	27	A	38.89 % / 50.0 %	43	B	27.78 % / 50.0 %	59	A	22.22 % / 58.34 %	75	B	19.44 % / 58.34 %
12	D	5.56 % / 47.22 %	28	C	19.44 % / 52.78 %	44	A	33.33 % / 50.0 %	60	A	38.89 % / 58.33 %	76	B	36.11 % / 58.33 %
13	C	27.78 % / 50.0 %	29	B	5.56 % / 50.0 %	45	A	30.56 % / 50.0 %	61	A	22.22 % / 58.34 %	77	B	36.11 % / 58.33 %
14	A	8.33 % / 47.23 %	30	A	25.0 % / 52.78 %	46	D	11.11 % / 52.78 %	62	C	38.89 % / 58.33 %	78	D	11.11 % / 61.11 %
15	D	19.44 % / 47.23 %	31	A	33.33 % / 50.0 %	47	A	5.56 % / 52.77 %	63	C	8.33 % / 58.34 %	79	B	19.44 % / 58.34 %
16	B	25.0 % / 47.22 %	32	C	33.33 % / 50.0 %	48	B	27.78 % / 52.78 %	64	D	2.78 % / 58.33 %	80	D	2.78 % / 61.11 %

Q.	Ans.	Correct / Skipped
81	B	5.56 % / 58.33 %
82	C	11.11 % / 58.33 %
83	C	2.78 % / 61.11 %
84	B	19.44 % / 58.34 %
85	B	11.11 % / 58.33 %
86	C	13.89 % / 61.11 %
87	A	27.78 % / 58.33 %
88	D	38.89 % / 58.33 %
89	B	13.89 % / 58.33 %
90	D	30.56 % / 58.33 %
91	A	36.11 % / 58.33 %
92	A	13.89 % / 58.33 %
93	B	13.89 % / 58.33 %
94	C	30.56 % / 58.33 %
95	B	8.33 % / 58.34 %
96	C	27.78 % / 58.33 %

Q.	Ans.	Correct / Skipped
97	B	36.11 % / 58.33 %
98	C	36.11 % / 58.33 %
99	C	25.0 % / 58.33 %
100	C	25.0 % / 58.33 %
101	A	36.11 % / 58.33 %
102	A	22.22 % / 58.34 %
103	C	36.11 % / 58.33 %
104	D	19.44 % / 58.34 %
105	C	16.67 % / 58.33 %
106	B	22.22 % / 58.34 %
107	C	22.22 % / 58.34 %
108	A	19.44 % / 58.34 %
109	C	33.33 % / 58.34 %
110	D	22.22 % / 58.34 %
111	C	27.78 % / 58.33 %
112	B	13.89 % / 61.11 %

Q.	Ans.	Correct / Skipped
113	D	13.89 % / 58.33 %
114	D	5.56 % / 58.33 %
115	C	13.89 % / 58.33 %
116	B	22.22 % / 58.34 %
117	D	19.44 % / 58.34 %
118	D	8.33 % / 58.34 %
119	D	22.22 % / 58.34 %
120	D	33.33 % / 58.34 %
121	B	5.56 % / 58.33 %
122	B	25.0 % / 58.33 %
123	D	25.0 % / 58.33 %
124	D	22.22 % / 58.34 %
125	A	30.56 % / 58.33 %
126	D	36.11 % / 58.33 %
127	D	25.0 % / 58.33 %
128	C	25.0 % / 58.33 %

Q.	Ans.	Correct / Skipped
129	D	11.11 % / 61.11 %
130	B	25.0 % / 58.33 %
131	C	13.89 % / 58.33 %
132	B	11.11 % / 61.11 %
133	C	13.89 % / 61.11 %
134	B	33.33 % / 58.34 %
135	A	22.22 % / 58.34 %
136	D	30.56 % / 58.33 %
137	C	5.56 % / 58.33 %
138	D	19.44 % / 58.34 %
139	B	27.78 % / 58.33 %
140	A	30.56 % / 58.33 %
141	A	27.78 % / 58.33 %
142	D	16.67 % / 58.33 %
143	B	27.78 % / 58.33 %
144	B	13.89 % / 58.33 %

Q.	Ans.	Correct / Skipped
145	B	16.67 % / 58.33 %
146	B	22.22 % / 61.11 %
147	C	13.89 % / 61.11 %
148	B	27.78 % / 58.33 %
149	C	8.33 % / 58.34 %
150	B	36.11 % / 61.11 %
151	D	8.33 % / 47.23 %
152	D	22.22 % / 47.22 %
153	C	8.33 % / 50.0 %
154	B	41.67 % / 50.0 %
155	C	13.89 % / 50.0 %
156	A	36.11 % / 50.0 %
157	C	25.0 % / 50.0 %
158	C	16.67 % / 50.0 %
159	A	36.11 % / 50.0 %
160	B	13.89 % / 52.78 %

Q.	Ans.	Correct / Skipped	Q.	Ans.	Correct / Skipped	Q.	Ans.	Correct / Skipped	Q.	Ans.	Correct / Skipped	Q.	Ans.	Correct / Skipped
161	A	25.0 % / 52.78 %	177	B	13.89 % / 50.0 %	193	D	27.78 % / 50.0 %	209	D	13.89 % / 50.0 %	225	B	16.67 % / 50.0 %
162	C	33.33 % / 50.0 %	178	C	22.22 % / 50.0 %	194	C	8.33 % / 52.78 %	210	B	30.56 % / 50.0 %	226	B	11.11 % / 50.0 %
163	D	33.33 % / 50.0 %	179	C	2.78 % / 50.0 %	195	C	11.11 % / 52.78 %	211	C	27.78 % / 50.0 %	227	A	16.67 % / 50.0 %
164	C	27.78 % / 50.0 %	180	A	41.67 % / 50.0 %	196	B	30.56 % / 50.0 %	212	D	41.67 % / 50.0 %	228	D	36.11 % / 50.0 %
165	D	41.67 % / 50.0 %	181	C	11.11 % / 50.0 %	197	C	11.11 % / 52.78 %	213	B	8.33 % / 50.0 %	229	C	5.56 % / 52.77 %
166	A	16.67 % / 50.0 %	182	A	16.67 % / 50.0 %	198	A	33.33 % / 50.0 %	214	C	19.44 % / 52.78 %	230	B	30.56 % / 50.0 %
167	B	16.67 % / 50.0 %	183	D	13.89 % / 50.0 %	199	B	19.44 % / 50.0 %	215	B	16.67 % / 50.0 %	231	A	19.44 % / 50.0 %
168	C	16.67 % / 50.0 %	184	C	16.67 % / 50.0 %	200	D	38.89 % / 52.78 %	216	A	27.78 % / 50.0 %	232	A	5.56 % / 50.0 %
169	D	19.44 % / 50.0 %	185	B	22.22 % / 50.0 %	201	B	38.89 % / 50.0 %	217	B	27.78 % / 50.0 %	233	A	27.78 % / 52.78 %
170	D	19.44 % / 50.0 %	186	C	19.44 % / 50.0 %	202	D	16.67 % / 52.77 %	218	A	11.11 % / 50.0 %	234	B	13.89 % / 50.0 %
171	A	30.56 % / 50.0 %	187	B	19.44 % / 50.0 %	203	A	19.44 % / 50.0 %	219	B	27.78 % / 50.0 %	235	B	33.33 % / 50.0 %
172	C	19.44 % / 50.0 %	188	B	22.22 % / 50.0 %	204	C	36.11 % / 50.0 %	220	B	27.78 % / 50.0 %	236	C	11.11 % / 50.0 %
173	A	25.0 % / 50.0 %	189	A	27.78 % / 52.78 %	205	D	25.0 % / 50.0 %	221	A	25.0 % / 50.0 %	237	A	33.33 % / 50.0 %
174	C	13.89 % / 50.0 %	190	A	22.22 % / 50.0 %	206	A	36.11 % / 50.0 %	222	C	22.22 % / 50.0 %	238	B	22.22 % / 50.0 %
175	B	11.11 % / 50.0 %	191	B	11.11 % / 50.0 %	207	A	13.89 % / 50.0 %	223	A	13.89 % / 50.0 %	239	A	19.44 % / 50.0 %
176	C	8.33 % / 50.0 %	192	D	25.0 % / 50.0 %	208	A	16.67 % / 52.77 %	224	C	30.56 % / 50.0 %	240	C	13.89 % / 50.0 %

Q.	Ans.	Correct / Skipped	Q.	Ans.	Correct / Skipped	Q.	Ans.	Correct / Skipped	Q.	Ans.	Correct / Skipped	Q.	Ans.	Correct / Skipped
241	D	16.67 % / 52.77 %	253	C	22.22 % / 50.0 %	265	A	27.78 % / 52.78 %	277	A	8.33 % / 55.56 %	289	A	27.78 % / 55.55 %
242	D	13.89 % / 50.0 %	254	B	22.22 % / 50.0 %	266	D	27.78 % / 52.78 %	278	C	13.89 % / 52.78 %	290	C	25.0 % / 55.56 %
243	A	11.11 % / 52.78 %	255	D	16.67 % / 52.77 %	267	A	27.78 % / 52.78 %	279	C	11.11 % / 55.56 %	291	C	11.11 % / 58.33 %
244	D	41.67 % / 50.0 %	256	D	25.0 % / 52.78 %	268	C	13.89 % / 52.78 %	280	A	22.22 % / 52.78 %	292	A	13.89 % / 58.33 %
245	D	33.33 % / 50.0 %	257	C	27.78 % / 50.0 %	269	D	22.22 % / 52.78 %	281	A	19.44 % / 52.78 %	293	D	38.89 % / 55.55 %
246	B	19.44 % / 50.0 %	258	B	8.33 % / 50.0 %	270	B	19.44 % / 52.78 %	282	A	33.33 % / 55.56 %	294	D	22.22 % / 55.56 %
247	A	25.0 % / 50.0 %	259	D	22.22 % / 50.0 %	271	D	38.89 % / 52.78 %	283	D	25.0 % / 55.56 %	295	D	22.22 % / 55.56 %
248	C	8.33 % / 50.0 %	260	C	19.44 % / 50.0 %	272	C	30.56 % / 52.77 %	284	C	30.56 % / 55.55 %	296	D	38.89 % / 55.55 %
249	D	8.33 % / 50.0 %	261	C	11.11 % / 50.0 %	273	C	25.0 % / 52.78 %	285	A	16.67 % / 58.33 %	297	D	33.33 % / 55.56 %
250	D	44.44 % / 50.0 %	262	A	22.22 % / 50.0 %	274	A	25.0 % / 52.78 %	286	D	5.56 % / 55.55 %	298	B	2.78 % / 58.33 %
251	C	13.89 % / 50.0 %	263	B	27.78 % / 50.0 %	275	C	13.89 % / 52.78 %	287	B	33.33 % / 55.56 %	299	C	19.44 % / 55.56 %
252	A	44.44 % / 50.0 %	264	B	5.56 % / 55.55 %	276	A	30.56 % / 52.77 %	288	D	27.78 % / 55.55 %	300	A	25.0 % / 52.78 %

Performance Analysis

Avg. Score (%)	16.0%
Toppers Score (%)	81.0%
Your Score	

Part A

Q.1 Ape thumb malformation is seen in involvement of -

A. Median nerve   **B.** Ulnar nerve

C. Radial nerve   **D.** Axillary nerve

Q.2 Froment's sign is characteristically seen in -

A. Ulnar nerve injury

B. Median nerve injury

C. Radial nerve injury

D. Intercostobrachial nerve injury

Q.3 Atrophy of the intrinsic muscles of the hand can be awaited to follow injury of the -

A. Ulnar nerve   **B.** Radial nerve

C. Branchial nerve   **D.** Axillary nerve

Q.4 In a femoral triangle, the most medial structure seen is

A. Lymphatics   **B.** Artery

C. Vein   **D.** Nerve

Q.5 Adductor canal lies beneath the -

A. Adductor longus   **B.** Adductor magnus

C. Sartorius   **D.** Vastus medialis

Q.6 What lies anterior to transverse sinus -

A. Aorta   **B.** Pulmonary artery

C. IVC   **D.** SVC

Q.7 All the following openings in the right atrium are guarded by valve except -

A. Superior vena cava

B. Inferior vena cava

C. Coronary sinus

D. Atrioventricular opening

Q.8 Sphincter urethra is present in-

A. Prostatic urethra

B. bulbar urethra

C. Membranous urethra

D. Penile urethra

Q.9 The correct relationship of structures at the hilum of a kidney from anterior to posterior is -

A. Renal artery, renal vein, renal pelvis

B. Renal vein, renal artery, renal pelvis

C. Renal pelvis, ranal artery, renal vein

D. None of the above

Q.10 All of the following statements about Sternberg Canal are true, Except -

A. Located anterior and medial to Foramen Rotundum

B. Located posterior and lateral to Foramen Rotundum

C. Caused by incomplete fusion of greater wing of the sphenoid

D. Cause of intrasphenoidal meningocele

Q.11 Suture present between parietal & occipital bones is -

A. Lambdoid suture   **B.** Sagittal suture

C. Coronal suture   **D.** Metopic suture

Q.12 Falx cerebri contains-

A. Straight sinus

B. Occipital sinus

C. Transverse sinus

D. Anterior intercavernous sinus

Q.13 All the following branches of the Vth nerve supply the dura mater except -

A. Anterior ethmoidal   **B.** Posterior ethmoidal

C. Auriculotemporal   **D.** Mandibular

Q.14 The Lining epithelium of the vagina is -

A. Pseudostratified columnar epithelium

B. Keratinized stratified squamous epithelium

C. Non keratinized stratified squamous epithelium

D. Ciliated columnar epithelium

Q.15 The Windpipe is lined by -

A. Stratified squamous epithelium

B. Ciliated columnar epithelium

C. Simple columnar epithelium

D. Pseudostratified columnar epithelium

Q.16 The outer layer of the blastocyst forms -

A. Primitive streak   **B.** Yolk sac

C. Embryo proper   **D.** Trophoblast

Q.17 The development of diaphragm is from?

A. Septum Transversum

B. Pleuropericardial membranes

C. Pleuroperitoneal membranes

D. Both (A) and (C) are true.

Q.18 Enzymatic markers of plasma membrane include all except

A. 5'-nucleotidase

B. Adenylyl cyclase

C. Na^+-K^+-ATPase

D. Galactosyl transferase

Q.19 Among the following, the transmembrane region of the proteins have-

A. A stretch of hydrophilic amino acids

B. A stretch of hydrophobic amino acids

C. A disulphide loop

D. Alternating hydrophilic and hydrophobic amino acids

Q.20 In the cell membrane, the following is true -

A. Lipids are regularly arranged

B. Lipids are symmetrical

C. Protein displaced laterally

D. None

Q.21 Initiation of impulse starts in

A. Axon

B. Axon hillock + initial segment

C. Cell body

D. Dendritic tree

Q.22 Orthodromic conduction is

A. An axon can conduct impulse in one direction only

B. An axon can conduct impulse in both directions

C. The jumping of depolarization from node to node

D. The point at which a runaway spike potential occurs

Q.23 Pseudounipolar cells

A. Sympathetic ganglia

B. Parasympathetic

C. Cranial nerve ganglia

D. Dorsal Root Ganglia

Q.24 Skeletal muscle shrinking ends when

A. Ca^{++} move out of the cytoplasm

B. Ach is absorbed from the Neuromuscular junction

C. Closure and indrawing of receptors

D. Decreased calcium outside reticulum

Q.25 Which one of the following does not increase the force of muscle contraction?

A. Increasing the frequency of activation of motor units

B. Increasing the number of motor units activated

C. Increasing the amplitude of action potentials in the motor neurons

D. Recruiting larger motor units

Q.26 Increase in cytosolic calcium from intracellular storage, during smooth muscle contraction, is/are due to -

A. cAMP

B. cGMP

C. cCMP

D. IP3-DAG

Q.27 Pulmonary function changes seen in Emphysema are

A. ↑TLC

B. ↓RV

C. ↑FEV₁

D. ↑VC

Q.28 The normal intrapleural pressure at the start/beginning of inspiration is _______ cm of H_2O.

A. -8

B. -5

C. 1.5

D. 0

Q.29 Body temperature regulation centre is located at

A. Pituitary

B. Thalamus

C. Hypothalamus

D. Basal ganglia

Q.30 The opening of which channel is d/t Plateau phase of ventricular muscle?

A. Na^+ channel

B. K^+ channel

C. Ca–Na channel

D. Closure of Ca^{2+} channel

Q.31 During a complex mitral valve replacement, it is determined that the patient will benefit from brief protective

hypothermia. Of the options listed below, which is tend to be the poor substitute for core temperature.

A. Rectum

B. Bladder

C. Nasopharynx

D. None of these

Q.32 Which of the following does not form a filtration barrier in nephrons

A. Podocytes

B. Mesangium

C. Endothelial cell

D. Basement membrane

Q.33 Normal gastric juice contains all except

A. Na^+

B. K^+

C. Ca^{++}

D. Mg^{++}

Q.34 The intrinsic element of the citadel is discharged by which of the following cells in gastric glands

A. Chief cells

B. Parietal cells

C. Enterochromaffin cells

D. B cells

Q.35 Transport of ADP in and ATP out of mitochondria is inhibited by

A. Atractyloside

B. Oligomycin

C. Rotenone

D. Cyanide

Q.36 Chymotrypsinogen is a form of _________.

A. Zymogen

B. Carboxypeptidase

C. Transaminase

D. Clot lysing protein

Q.37 Which of the following is an aldose

A. Ribulose

B. Ribose

C. Erythrulose

D. None of these

Q.38 In glycolysis, the first committed step is catalysed by

A. 2, 3 DPG

B. Glucokinase

C. Hexokinase

D. Phosphofructokinase

Q.39 Which of the following metabolites is involved in glycogenolysis, glycolysis and gluconeogenesis?

A. Galactose–1–phosphate

B. Glucose–6–phosphate

C. Uridine diphosphoglucose

D. Fructose–6–phosphate

Q.40 Which organ does not utilise ketone bodies

A. Liver

B. Brain

C. Skeletal muscles

D. Cardiac muscles

Q.41 NADPH is required for

A. Gluconeogenesis

B. Glycolysis

C. Fatty acids synthesis

D. Glycogenolysis

Q.42 Which amino acid is scarce in pulses?

A. Lysine

B. Threonine

C. Methionine   **D.** Serine

Q.43 About Denaturation of protein, which is true

A.   Biological property persists
B.   Primary structure lost
C.   Always irreversible
D.   Mostly renders protein insoluble.

Q.44 Menkes Kinky hair syndrome is characterized by a congenital deficiency of

A.   Serum ceruloplasmin
B.   Serum copper
C.   Ferochelatase
D.   Copper binding ATPase.

Q.45 The pyruvate utilization in tissues is decreased in

A. Pernicious anemia   **B.** Scurvy
C. Beriberi   **D.** Pellagra

Q.46 Triple bonds are found between which base pairs

A. A–T   **B.** C–G   **C.** A–G   **D.** C–T

Q.47 mRNA is an approving version of

A.   tRNA
B.   rRNA
C.   Ribosomal of DNA
D.   A single strand of DNA

Q.48 Ends of chromosomes replicated by

A.   Telomerase
B.   Centromere
C.   Restriction endonuclease
D.   Exonuclease

Q.49 Nonsense codons bring about

A.   Elongation of the polypeptide chain
B.   Pre-translational modification of protein
C.   Initiation of protein synthesis
D.   Termination of protein synthesis

Q.50 Correct statement about restriction fragment gene -

A.   Detected by southern blot
B.   Used for identification of the gene for genomic mapping
C.   RFLP is a DNA variation sequence
D.   All of these

Part B

Q.51 True about Apoptosis include the following except:

A.   Inflammation is present
B.   DNA breakage
C.   Clumping of chromatin
D.   Cell shrinkage

Q.52 Complete wound strength is gained by?

A. Never regained   **B.** 1 month
C. 6 months   **D.** 1 year

Q.53 Virchow triad includes all except:

A.   Endothelial injury

B.   Abnormal blood flow
C.   Hypercoagulability
D.   Pulmonary embolism

Q.54 The most important source of the organic compound shown in the photograph is

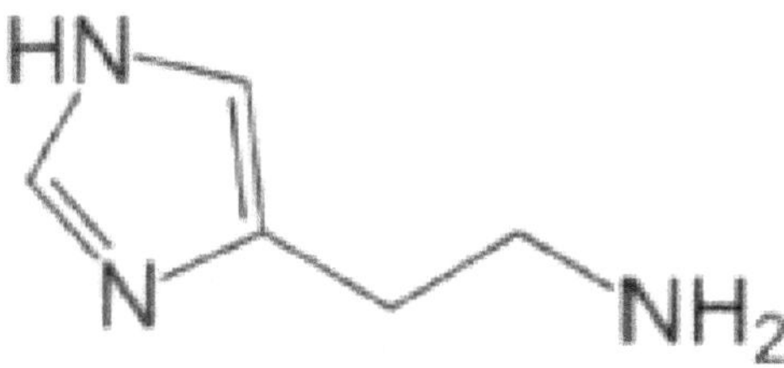

A. Eosinophil   **B.** Mast cells
C. Neutrophil   **D.** Macrophages

Q.55 Which of the following is the most likely inheritance pattern in the pedigree given below-

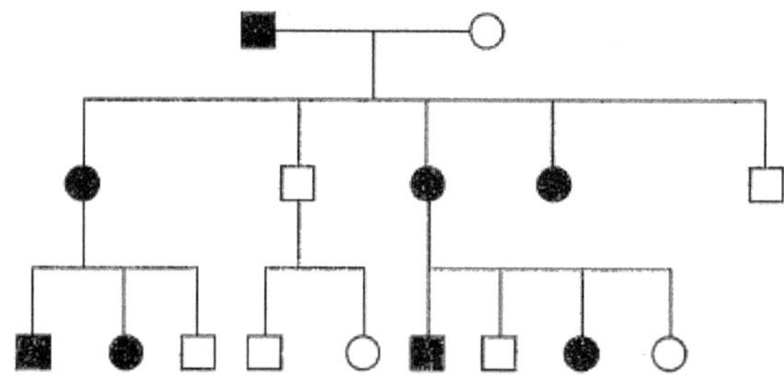

A.   Autosomal dominant
B.   Mitochondrial
C.   Autosomal recessive
D.   X-linked dominant

Q.56 Tumour marker for Carcinoma of Organ shown in Photograph is

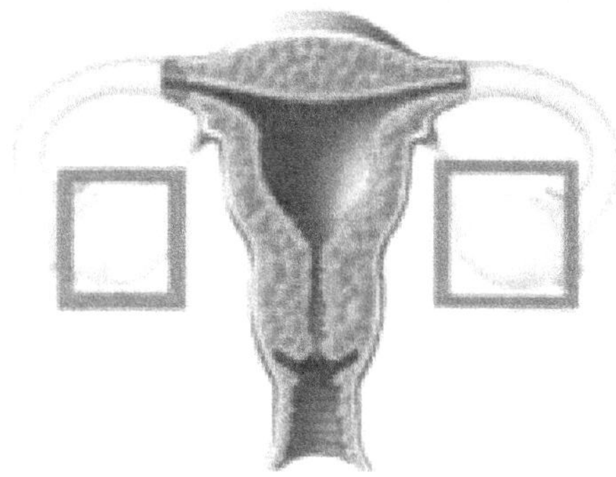

A. PSA   **B.** Fibronectin
C. Acid phosphatase   **D.** CA 125

Q.57 Solitary hypoechoic lesion of the liver without septate or debris is most likely to be-

A. Hydatid cyst   **B.** Caroli's disease

C. Liver abscess   **D.** Simple cyst

Q.58 A 22-year-old biker had a road traffic accident with severe injury, after admitting in the hospital his condition suddenly worsens and leads to death, the pathological specimen is provided, what could be likely cause of death?

A. Septic shock
B. Pulmonary thromboembolism
C. Deep vein thrombosis
D. Varicosities of the vein

Q.59 Which of the following is a chemotactic factor:

A. Thromboxanes   **B.** Leukotrienes
C. Prostacyclins   **D.** Prostaglandins

Q.60 Inability to perform the rapid alternating movement is -

A. Past-pointing   **B.** Dysmetria
C. Dysdiadochokinesia   **D.** None

Q.61 Annexin V is associated with:

A. Artherosclerosis   **B.** Inflammation
C. Necrosis   **D.** Apoptosis

Q.62 Which of the following is not component of acinus-

A. Pulmonary lobule
B. Respiratory bronchioles
C. Alveolar ducts
D. Alveolar sac

Q.63 Podocytes are seen in -

A. Bowman's capsule
B. Proximal convoluted tubule
C. Distal convoluted tubule
D. Collecting tubule of the kidney

Q.64 The following image shows:-

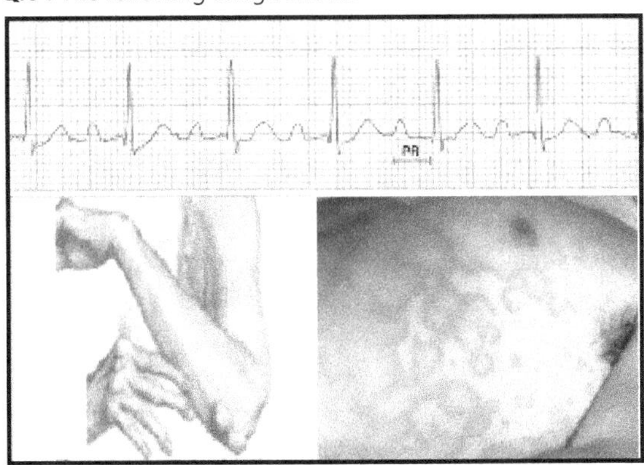

A. Second-degree heart block, Subcutaneous nodule, Erythema marginatum
B. First-degree heart block, Subcutaneous nodule, Erythema marginatum
C. First-degree heart block, Subcutaneous nodule, Erythema nodosum
D. None of these

Q.65 Nutmeg liver is seen in -

A. Right sided heart failure
B. Left sided heart failure

C. Increased pulmonary pressure
D. Decreased pulmonary pressure

Q.66 Carcinoma penis is rarest among -

A. Americans   **B.** Indians
C. Swedes   **D.** Jews

Q.67 Bone resorption markers are all except -

A. Tartrate resistant acid phosphatase
B. Osteocalcin
C. Cross linked-N-telopeptides
D. Urine total free deoxypyridinoline

Q.68 What are gitter cells -

A. Astrocytes
B. Macroglia
C. Modified macrophages in CNS
D. Oligodendrocytes

Q.69 Which of the followings are Anterior pituitary secretes except -

A. Growth hormone   **B.** Prolactin
C. FSH hormone   **D.** Oxytocin

Q.70 Dyskeratosis -

A. Leukoplakia
B. Hyperpigmentation
C. Nail dystrophy
D. Premature keratinisation

Q.71 In a congenital dystrophic variety of epidermolysis bullosa, the mutation is seen in the gene coding for?

A. Laminin 4   **B.** Collagen type 7
C. Alpha 6 integrin   **D.** Keratin 14

Q.72 In primary T.B. seen -

A. Ghon's focus   **B.** Pleural effusion
C. Miliary mottling   **D.** Fibrosis

Q.73 Which of the following is a reason of Bone affection in scurvy-

A. Bad mineralization of the osteoid tissue
B. Imperfect osteoid matrix formation
C. Defective calcification in osteoid
D. Increased degradation of osteoid tissue

Q.74 Sub-Acute radiation hepatic damage is most marked between-

A. 1-7 days   **B.** 7-21 days
C. 21-40 days   **D.** 40-100 days

Q.75 ESR depends on -

A. Viscosity   **B.** Fibrinogen
C. Rouleaux formation   **D.** All of above

Q.76 Which of the following acid poisoning treated by alkaline diuresis -

A. Morphine   **B.** Amphetamine
C. Phenobarbitone   **D.** Atropine

Q.77 Alkalinization of urine is required for decreasing the poisoning due to:

A. Barbiturates
B. Amphetamine
C. Alcohol
D. Morphine

Q.78 CYP–450 inducers are:

A. Cimetidine
B. Ketoconazole
C. Phenobarbitone
D. Theophylline

Q.79 Current ASA standards require that during anaesthesia, systemic blood pressure and heart rate be evaluated at least every

A. 3 minutes
B. 5 minutes
C. 7 minutes
D. 10 minutes

Q.80 What is the expected observation in a patient with an expanded pupil not reacting quickly to 1% pilocarpine?

A. Diabetic 3rd nerve palsy
B. Adie's tonic pupil
C. Uncal herniation
D. Pharmacological block

Q.81 Synaptic transmission in the autonomic ganglion is usually:

A. Adrenergic
B. Peptidergic
C. Cholinergic
D. Mediated by substance P

Q.82 Ergometrine is commonly used for :

A. PostPartum Hemorrhage
B. To shorten 2nd stage of labour
C. Dysmenorrhea
D. Toxemia of pregnancy

Q.83 Which of the following drugs is not used for the treatment of congestive heart failure -

A. Nitroglycerin
B. Spironolactone
C. Nesiritide
D. Trimetazidine

Q.84 The adverse effect of Losartan are all except:

A. Cough
B. Hyperkalemia
C. Headache
D. Angioedema

Q.85 Octreotide is used in all except:

A. Glucagonoma
B. Insulinoma
C. Carcinoid syndrome
D. Glioma

Q.86 Rizatriptan is a drug used for?

A. Prophylaxis of migraine
B. Acute migraine
C. Cluster headache
D. Chronic migraine

Q.87 An anti-emetic drug that also decreases acid secretion due to its action on H_1 receptors is :

A. Promethazine
B. Domperidone
C. Metoclopramide
D. Ondansetron

Q.88 An antacid drug that typically causes diarrhoea?

A. Sodium bicarbonate
B. Magnesium hydroxide
C. Calcium bicarbonate
D. Aluminium hydroxide

Q.89 Drug resistance transmitting factor present in bacteria is :

A. Plasmid
B. Chromosome
C. Introns
D. Centromere

Q.90 The minimal alveolar concentration of an inhalational anaesthetic is a measure of its :

A. Potency
B. Therapeutic index
C. Diffusibility
D. Oil : water partition coefficient

Q.91 Troglitazone is the drug used in the treatment of:

A. Type 2 diabetes mellitus
B. Petit mal epilepsy
C. Hyperlipidaemia
D. D. Osteoporosis

Q.92 Treatment of choice for SIADH is:

A. Vasopressin
B. Lithium carbonate
C. Hypertonic Saline
D. Demeclocycline

Q.93 Which of the following drugs is used for noninfectious uveitis in LUMINATE clinical trial program :

A. Steroid/Infliximab
B. Cyclosporin
C. Methotrexate
D. Voclosporin

Q.94 A 17-year-old girl had been taking a drug for the treatment of acne for the last 2 years, which has lead to pigmentation. Which drug could it be?

A. Doxycycline
B. Minocycline
C. Azithromycin
D. Chlorpromazine

Q.95 In which of the following Interstitial nephritis is not observed-

A. Diuretics
B. Beta lactams
C. Allopurinol
D. Isoniazid

Q.96 The instrument shown in Photograph is sterilized by

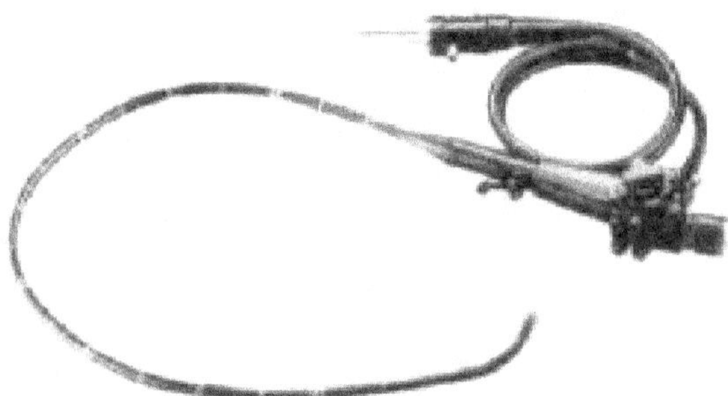

A. Formalin
B. Autoclaving
C. Boiling
D. Glutaraldehyde

Q.97 Which of the following statements is not related with Louis Pasteur-

A. Introduction of Complex media

B. Discovery of Rabies vaccine

C. Discovery of M.tuberculosis

D. Disproved spontaneous generation theory

Q.98 Treponema pallidum was innovated by -

A. Robert Koch

B. Twort

C. Schaudinn and Hoffman

D. Ellerman

Q.99 All are autoimmune disease except-

A. Myasthenia gravis

B. Systemic lupus erythematosus

C. Graves' disease

D. Sickle cell disease

Q.100 T cell-subjected to the field is -

A. Cortical follicles of lymph node

B. Medullary cords

C. Mantle layer

D. Paracortical area

Q.101 All of the following are functions of CD4 helper cells, except -

A. Immunogenic memory

B. Produce immunoglobulins

C. Activate macrophages

D. Activate cytotoxic cells

Q.102 All are mononuclear-macrophages except -

A. Histiocytes **B.** Microglia

C. Kupffer cells **D.** B-cells

Q.103 Staph aureus virulence is due to -

A. Pathogenicity correlated with coagulase

B. Endotoxin

C. Hemolysis

D. None of the above

Q.104 In carriers, staphylococci are found in the following sites except -

A. Throat **B.** Nose

C. Skin **D.** None of the above

Q.105 Which organism causes toxic shock syndrome -

A. Pneumococcus

B. E. coli

C. Staphylococcus aureus

D. Enterococcus

Q.106 All of the following are general properties of Viruses except -

A. May contain both DNA and RNA

B. Form extracellular infectious particles

C. Heat labile

D. Not affected by antibiotics

Q.107 Bollinger bodies are spot in -

A. Chickenpox **B.** Cowpox

C. Fowlpox **D.** Smallpox

Q.108 Which is not a DNA virus-

A. Parvovirus **B.** Papovavirus

C. Poxvirus **D.** Rhabdovirus

Q.109 Which of the following is true regarding trematodes-

A. Two host required **B.** Segmented

C. Anus present **D.** Body cavity present

Q.110 Stain with parasite having Charcot-Leyden crystals but no pus cells-

A. Giardia **B.** Taenia

C. E. histolytica **D.** Trichomonas

Q.111 Invasive amoebiasis can be best diagnosed by -

A. ELISA

B. Counter current immunoelectrophoresis

C. Indirect hemagglutination test

D. Complement fixation test

Q.112 Fungi are -

A. Prokaryotes **B.** Eukaryotes

C. Plant **D.** Animals

Q.113 Ascospore is -

A. Asexual spore **B.** Sexual spore

C. Conidia **D.** None of the above

Q.114 Nakayama strain used for which vaccine?

A. Typhoid

B. Chicken pox

C. Japanese encephalitis

D. Yellow fever

Q.115 In which of the following, the Maltese cross is seen on polarizing microscopy-

A. Cryptococcus neoformans

B. Penicillium marneffei

C. Blastomyces

D. Candida albicans

Q.116 Criminal negligence is punishable under Section 304 A for a maximum of -

A. 1 year **B.** 2 years **C.** 3 years **D.** 5 years

Q.117 Which of the following is shared out by CrPC Sec 174-

A. Inquest **B.** Inquiry

C. Murder **D.** Medical negligence

Q.118 Criminal responsibility of a person of Unsound mind in India is incorporated in the Indian Penal Code -

A. Section 302 **B.** Section 84

C. Section 85 **D.** Section 88

Q.119 A subpoena is a somewhat -

A. Decomposed body tissue

B. Designation

C. Document

D. Court tribunal

Q.120 The rate of cooling down of dead bodies in a tropical climate is -

A. 0.2°C/ hours

B. 0.5°C/ hours

C. 1.0°C/ hours

D. 1.5°C/ hours

Q.121 Cherry red colour of hypostasis is seen in-

A. CO poisoning

B. Burns

C. Sulphuric acid

D. Nitric acid

Q.122 Which of the following is not the part of shotgun -

A. Barrel

B. Choke bore

C. Bullets

D. Muzzle

Q.123 Hanging with the feet touching the ground is seen in-

A. Partial hanging

B. Complete hanging

C. Homicidal hanging

D. Suicidal hanging

Q.124 All are cardiotoxic except -

A. Aconite   **B.** Opium   **C.** Oleander   **D.** Nicotine

Q.125 Dopamine agonist

A. Clomiphene citrate

B. Bromocriptine mesylate

C. GnRH

D. Dexamethasone

Q.126 Definition of health given by WHO includes which of the following dimension -

A. Social

B. Economic

C. Mental

D. All of the above

Q.127 Which of the following is the current trend in Health Care -

A. Qualitative enquiry

B. Community participation

C. Equitable distribution

D. Primary Health Care

Q.128 Sipuleucel-T is used in the treatment of which cancer?

A. Breast   **B.** Prostate   **C.** Kidney   **D.** Pancreas

Q.129 Height in cms, by the cube root of body weight, is term as:

A. Quetelet index

B. Corpulence index

C. Broca's index

D. Ponderal index

Q.130 ELISA is executed on people with low generality. What would be the result of executing double screening ELISA tests -

A. Increased sensitivity and positive predictive value

B. Increased sensitivity and negative predictive value

C. Increased specificity and positive predictive value

D. Increased specificity and negative predictive value

Q.131 In a population of 10000 people, the prevalence of a disease is 20%. The sensitivity of a screening test is 95% and specificity is 80%. The positive predictive value of the test will be

A. 45.7%   **B.** 54.3%   **C.** 15.3%   **D.** 98.5%

Q.132 A group of experts discussing and interacting about a particular topic in the presence of an audience is:

A. Symposium

B. Seminar

C. Panel discussion

D. Workshop

Q.133 Confidence limit includes -

A. Range & standard deviation

B. Median and standard error

C. Mean and standard error

D. Mode and standard deviation

Q.134 The infectivity of chickenpox continues for -

A. Till the last scab falls off

B. 6 days after onset of rash

C. 3 days after onset of rash

D. Till the fever subsides

Q.135 Not true about varicella infection -

A. Secondary attack rate is 90%

B. Lesions occur on flexor surfaces

C. Only single stage of lesion is present at a time

D. Reactivation occur in 10-30% cases

Q.136 According to WHO, blindness is defined as visual acuity of the better eye, less than

A. 6/60.   **B.** 5/60.   **C.** 4/60.   **D.** 3/60.

Q.137 Which of the following is the least common reason for the heart disease in this country-

A. Rheumatic

B. Hypertensive

C. Ischaemic

D. Congenital

Q.138 Following age pyramid denotes

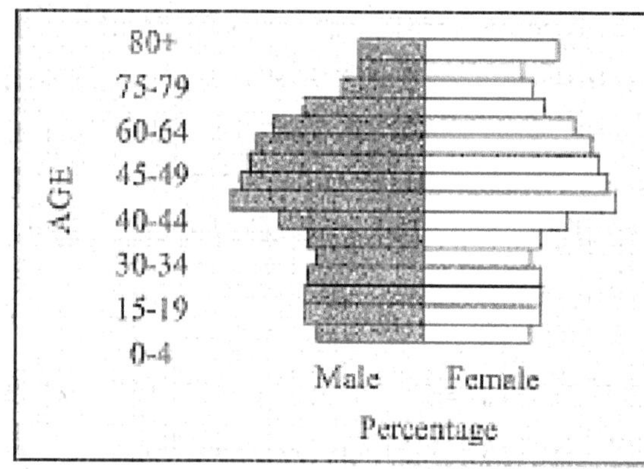

A. Developing country

B. Developed country

C. Underdeveloped country

D. Poor country

Q.139 Demography deals with all except-

A. Mortality

B. Fertility

C. Morbidity

D. Marriage

Q.140 Fatty acid characteristically present in breast milk and essential for baby growth –

A. Palmitic acid

B. Arachidonic acid

C. Docosahexaenoic acid

D. Both (B) and (C)

Q.141 MCH care is assessed by –

A. Death rate

B. Birth rate

C. Maternal mortality rate

D. Anemia in mother

Q.142 Daily per capita water consumption for all purposes is –

A. 50-100 litres **B.** 100-150 litres

C. 150–200 litres **D.** 200-250 liters

Q.143 Weight of an Indian reference woman is –

A. 45 kg **B.** 50 kg **C.** 55 kg **D.** 60 kg

Q.144 Energy requirement in late pregnancy –

A. 2500 cal **B.** 1400 cal **C.** 1000 cal **D.** 500 cal

Q.145 Objectives of the National Mental Health programme are all except –

A. Promote community participation

B. Promote the application of mental health knowledge

C. Provides free antipsychotic drugs to all

D. Provide accessibility of mental health care

Q.146 Amount of waste infectious produced in hospitals –

A. 45% **B.** 65% **C.** 80% **D.** 100%

Q.147 Health education –

A. Is health promotion

B. Is health distortion

C. Is delivered through public health agencies only

D. Does not help in prevention of cancer

Q.148 Elements of primary health care include all of the following except –

A. Adequate supply of safe water and basic sanitation

B. Providing essential drugs

C. Health Education

D. Sound referral system

Q.149 Which of the following is not included in Vision 2020 "The right to sight" ____?

A. Trachoma

B. Epidemic conjunctivitis

C. Cataract

D. Onchocerciasis

Q.150 Commonest among diseases with Mendelian inheritance is –

A. Autosomal dominant

B. Autosomal recessive

C. X–linked recessive

D. X–dominant

Part C

Q.151 Notching of ribs occurs in all except?

A. Coarctation of aorta

B. Neurofibromatosis

C. Hypothyroidism

D. Osteogenesis imperfecta

Q.152 Which of the following is measured by Automated Perimeters?

A. Total deviation box plot

B. Pattern deviation plot

C. Grey scale

D. All of the above

Q.153 Urine of a UTI patient has a pH of more than 8, the probable organism is:

A. Ecoli **B.** Proteus

C. Klebsiella **D.** Candida

Q.154 Which drug is used for Mvaesthenia Gravis testing

A. Adrenaline **B.** Phycostigmine

C. Acetylcholine **D.** Edrophonium

Q.155 Which of the following is an example of disorders of sex chromosomes

A. Marfan's syndrome

B. Testicular feminization syndrome

C. Klinefelter's syndrome

D. Down's syndrome

Q.156 False positive ELISA for HIV -

A. Multiple mycloma

B. Lepromatous leprosy

C. SLE

D. All of the above

Q.157 For preservation of alcohol Which chemical is being used ?

A. Potassium acetate **B.** Sodium sulphide

C. Sodium fluoride **D.** Glycerine

Q.158 Carney triad consists of

(A) Gastric carcinoma

(B) Paraganglioma

(C) Pulmonary Chordoma

(D) Carcinoma bronchus

(E) Chondromatosis

A. ABC **B.** CAB **C.** DAB **D.** EBD

Q.159 "Intraepidermal" IgG toppling is spot in:

A. Herpes genitalis **B.** Bullous pemphigoid

C. Pemphigus **D.** SLE

Q.160 This sound is produced during the closure of the semilunar valves-

A. Lubb **B.** Dupp

C. Lubb dupp **D.** Lubb duppshhh

Q.161 What is the prominant feature of ARDS true?

A. Type 2 respiratory failure

B. Lung compliance decreased

C. Increase in diffusion capacity

D. None

Q.162 In ARDS mechanical TV low volume ventilation is

A. 2-3ml/kg **B.** 5-7 ml/kg

C. 5-l0ml/kg

D. None of these

Q.163 HLA-DR4 is a marker of -

A. Sarcoidosis

B. Rheumatoid arthritis

C. Sero-negative gouty arthritis

D. Psoriasis

Q.164 Which of the following does not cause high anion gap metabolic acidosis -

A. Lactic acidosis

B. Salicylats poisoning

C. Ethylene glycol poisoning

D. Ureterosigmoidostomy

Q.165 The minimum concentration of reduced hemoglobin required for cyanosis is

A. 1gm/dl.   **B.** 3 gm/d   **C.** 7 gm/d   **D.** 5 gm/d

Q.166 Spaghetti and meatball appearance is seen in-

A. Dermatophytes   **B.** Pityriasis versicolor

C. Aspergillus   **D.** Candida

Q.167 All statements are true regarding skin except –

a. Skin is stratified squamous epithelium

b. Melanocyte & Merkel cells are immigrant cells

c. Keratin filaments are a hallmark of epidermal cells

d. Keratinization process cause hydration of cells

e. Spines of spinous cells are formed from housekeeping organelle

A. de   **B.** bc   **C.** cd   **D.** bd

Q.168 Piebaldism allude to –

A. Androgenetic alopecia

B. Erythema nodosum leprosum

C. Associated with white forelock

D. None of the above

Q.169 Acanthosis nigricans is seen in -

A. Diabetes   **B.** GIT cancer

C. Hypothyroidism   **D.** All of the above

Q.170 M.C. precipitant of contact dermatitis is –

A. Gold   **B.** Nickle   **C.** Silver   **D.** Iron

Q.171 Determination of Airborne contact dermatitis is possible–

A. Skin biopsy

B. Patch test

C. Prick test

D. Estimation of serum IgE levels

Q.172 Hanging curtain sign is seen in -

A. Pityriasis alba   **B.** Pityriasis versicolor

C. Pityriasis rosea   **D.** Pitryasis miliaris

Q.173 Typical silvery scales of psoriasis are absent in –

A. Scalp   **B.** Knee   **C.** Groin   **D.** Elbow

Q.174 All are true about erythema multiformis except –

A. Due to Herpes simples

B. Due to sulphonamide

C. Lesion are symmetrical

D. Mucous membrane is usually involved

Q.175 All of the following are bullous lesions except -

A. Pemphigus vulgaris

B. Dermatitis herpetiformis

C. Atopic dermatitis

D. Pemphigoid

Q.176 All are involved in Leprosy except–

A. CNS   **B.** Testis   **C.** Skin   **D.** Cornea

Q.177 Skin smear is negative in which leprosy –

A. Indeterminate   **B.** Neuritic

C. Lepromatous   **D.** Borderline

Q.178 The highest recurrent cause of frequent genital ulceration in a erotic vital male is –

A. Herpes genitalis   **B.** Aphthous ulcer

C. Syphilis   **D.** Chancroid

Q.179 Treponema pallidum causes –

A. Condyloma acuminata

B. Condyloma lata

C. Both

D. None

Q.180 Female presents with a history of color change from pallor to cyanosis on exposure to cold in fingers. This condition is mostly associated with?

A. Scleroderma

B. Leukemia

C. Lung infections

D. Hepatosplenomegaly

Q.181 Husband having a suspicion that his wife is having an affair with another man, diagnosis is

A. Delusion   **B.** Illusion

C. Hallucination   **D.** Delirium

Q.182 A patient gets tingling when his bed light is flashed suddenly. Which type of hallucination is this -

A. Hypnagogic hallucinations

B. Hypnopompic hallucinations

C. Reflex hallucinations

D. Functional hallucinations

Q.183 Features of delirium -

A. Deficit of attention

B. Autonomic instability

C. Altered sleep wake pattern

D. All of the above

Q.184 Fox Fordyce Disease effects:

A. Eccrine Glands   **B.** Apocrine glands

C. Pituitary gland   **D.** Sebaceous glands

Q.185 The following symptoms may be seen in opium withdrawal -

A. Tremors

B. Lacrimation

C. Dry nose and mouth

D. Constipation

Q.186 Which of the following drugs is not used in opioid dependence?

A. Disulfiram

B. Clonidine

C. Lorazepam

D. Naltrexone

Q.187 All are features of neurosis except -

A. Symptoms cause subjective distress

B. Contact with reality preserved

C. Personality disturbances

D. Insight is maintained

Q.188 One of the following drug abuse produces a psychosis closely resembling paranoid schizophrenia-

A. Barbiturates

B. Amphetamines

C. Opioids

D. Benzodiazepines

Q.189 Anxiety neurosis is manifested by -

A. Difficulty in breathing

B. Complete consciousness

C. Negative thinking

D. All of the above

Q.190 Differentiation of hysterical fits from epileptic fit -

A. Occurs in sleep

B. Injuries to person

C. Incontinence

D. Occurs when people are watching

Q.191 What are the EEG waves recorded for the parietooccipital region with subject awake & eye closed

A. Alpha waves

B. Beta waves

C. Delta waves

D. Theta waves

Q.192 Which of the following drugs are used in the treatment of ADHD?

A. Amphetamine

B. Modafinil

C. Methylphenidate

D. All

Q.193 ECT is advocated in following except -

A. Chronic schizophrenia

B. Catatonic schizophrenia

C. Severe depression

D. Severe psychoses

Q.194 According to Sigmund Freud, primary process thinking is-

A. Illogical & Bizarre

B. Rational

C. Absent during sleep

D. Logical & unconscious

Q.195 Treatment of depression with suicidal tendencies is?

A. Clozapine

B. Mitrazapine

C. ECT

D. Olenzapine

Q.196 Indicators of bone formation include all of the following except -

A. Osteocalcin

B. Alkaline phosphatase

C. Hydroxyproline

D. Type 1 procollegen

Q.197 What diaphysis fracture involve?

A. Skull bones

B. Long bone

C. Sternum

D. Ribs

Q.198 Which is true regarding shoulder dislocation -

A. Posterior dislocation is often over-looked

B. Pain is severe in anterior dislocation

C. Radiography may be misleading in posterior dislocation

D. All of the above

Q.199 Avascular necrosis is the commonest in one of the following fracture -

A. Garden 1 and 2 fracture of femoral neck

B. Garden 3 and 4 fracture of femoral neck

C. Sub-trochanteric fracture of femoral neck

D. Baso-trochanteric fracture

Q.200 In the case of a 70-year-old lady with an intracapsular fracture of the neck of femur, the ideal treatment would be -

A. Closed traction

B. Hemiarthropalsty

C. Internal fixation with nail

D. Internal fixation with nail and plate

Q.201 Trochanteric fracture of the femur is best treated by -

A. Dynamic hip screw

B. Inlay plates

C. Plaster in abduction

D. Plaster in abduction and internal rotation

Q.202 Which of the following Treatment of choice be used for old non-united fracture of shaft of the femur -

A. Compression plating

B. Bone grafting

C. Nailing

D. Compression plating with bone grafting

Q.203 The investigation of choice to detect a prolapsed intervertebral disc is?

A. CT Scan

B. MRI

C. Myelography

D. Radiograph

Q.204 Hangman's fracture is-

A. Subluxation of C_5 over C_6

B. Fracture dislocation of C_2

C. Fracture dislocation of ankle joint

D. Fracture of odontoid

Q.205 Regarding Perth's disease, which of the following is not correct- -

A. Osteonecrotic osteochondritis

B. Decreased bone age

C. Age of onset has no affect on course

D. Restricted abduction

Q.206 Which of these muscles undergoes wasting first in osteoarthritis knee-

A. Quadriceps only   **B.** Hamstrings only

C. Gastronemius   **D.** All of the above

Q.207 Chronic persistent neutrophilic discharge is seen in -

A. Chronic osteomyelitis

B. Acute osteomyelitis

C. Septic arthritis

D. None

Q.208 A 10-year child presented with a mid tibial swelling which an x-ray revealed a lytic lesion with sclerotic margins. What is the most likely diagnosis?

A. Eosinophilic granuloma

B. Osteoid osteoma

C. Fibrocortical defect

D. Fibrous dysplasia

Q.209 All are true for Dupuytren's contracture except -

A. Usually 4th finger is involved

B. Bilateral disease is rare

C. Surgical release is useful

D. May be associated with Pyronie disease

Q.210 During the surgical procedure -

A. Tendons should be repaired before nerves

B. Nerves should be repaired before tendons

C. Tendons should not be repaired at the same time

D. None of the above

Q.211 Color of oxygen cylinder is:

A. Black with white color

B. Blue with white color

C. Yellow with white color

D. Grey with grey

Q.212 Bain circuit is Mapleton type circuit –

A. Type A   **B.** Type F   **C.** Type D   **D.** Type E

Q.213 Nasal intubation is contraindicated in –

A. CSF Rhinorrhea

B. Fracture cervical spine

C. Fracture inaudible

D. Short neck

Q.214 All are features of difficult airway except

A. limited mouth opening

B. Micrognathia with macroglossia

C. TMJ ankylosis

D. Increased thyromental distance

Q.215 Malampatti grading is for –

A. Mobility of cervical spine

B. Mobility of atlanto axial joint

C. Assessment of free rotation of neck before intubation

D. Inspection of oral cavity before intubation

Q.216 Pre-anesthetic medication is given to -

A. Reducon of secreon of saliva

B. To prevent undesirable reflexes

C. Reduce anxiety and fear

D. All of the above

Q.217 Shortest acting non depolarizing muscle relaxant –

A. Mivacurium   **B.** Vercuronium

C. Atracurium   **D.** Succinyl choline

Q.218 The muscle relaxant from the following is responsible for maximum longevity of the action :

A. Atracurium   **B.** Vecuronium

C. Rocuronium   **D.** Doxacurium

Q.219 Skeletal muscle relaxant of choke in the liver and renal disease is?

A. Atracurium   **B.** Mivacurium

C. Gallium   **D.** Vecuronium

Q.220 A dentist notices that his 39yr lady patient has scattered, white, 0.2 to 1.5cm, reticulated areas on the buccal mucosa. She says that these lesions have been present for a year. She also has some 0.3cm, pruritic, purple papules on each elbow. A biopsy of a skin lesion shows a band-like infiltrate of lymphocytes at the dermal-epidermal junction along with degeneration of basal keratinocytes. What would you advise the patient?

A. A squamous cell carcinoma is likely to develop.

B. You have systemic lupus erythematosus.

C. You should stop taking all medications.

D. These lesions will probably resolve over time.

Q.221 Use of Thiopentone –

A. Seizure   **B.** Truth spell

C. Reduction of ICP   **D.** All of the above

Q.222 An intravenous anesthetic agent that is associated with hemodynamic stability, maintenance of CVP with postoperative nausea, vomiting, and myoclonus –

A. Ketamine   **B.** Etomidate

C. Propofol   **D.** Opioids

Q.223 True about local anesthetic agents-

A. Duration depends on protein binding

B. Potency depends upon lipid solubility

C. LA with low PKa is more active

D. All of the above

Q.224 Sodium bicarbonate, when given with local anesthetics has which of the following effect –

A. Increases speed and quality of anaesthesia

B. Decreases diffusion of the anaesthetic drug

C. Causes rapid elimination of the local anaesthetic

D. Decreases speed and quality of anaesthesia

Q.225 Cause of postoperative hypertension –

A. Pre-operative hypertension

B. Inadequate analgesia

C. Phaeochromocytoma

D. All of the above

Q.226 X - rays are modified -

A. Protons

B. Electrons

C. Neutrons

D. Positrons

Q.227 A patient is presented with a metallic foreign body in the eye. Which investigation should not be done:

A. USG

B. X - ray

C. CT

D. MRI

Q.228 Characteristics of BENIGN tumor of the lung in X-ray is

A. Size > 5 cms diameter

B. Cavitation

C. Peripheral location

D. Concentric dense calcification

Q.229 A 55-year-old man who has been on bed rest for the past 10 days, complain of breathlessness and chest pain. The chest X-ray is normal. The next step in the investigation should be –

A. Lung ventilation – perfusion scan

B. Pulmonary arteriography

C. Pulmonary venous wedge angiography

D. Echocardiography

Q.230 All are chest radiographic feature of left atrial enlargement except-

A. Double left heart border

B. Elevated left main bronchus

C. Splaying of carina

D. Enlargement of left atrial appendage

Q.231 Boot shaped heart on chest X-ray is seen in

A. TGA

B. TAPVC

C. Tetrofogy of fallot

D. PAPVC

Q.232 Which among the following is false regarding the need for chest radiograph in a patient of the acute abdomen –

A. Supine chest radiograph is the best radiograph for showing presence of a small pnetunoperitoneum

B. A number of chest conditions can present as acute abdominal condition

C. Acute abdominal condition may be complicated by the chest pathology

D. Even when the chest radiograph is normal it acts as a most valuable baseline

Q.233 Which one of the following hepatic lesions can be diagnosed with high accuracy by using nuclear imaging?

A. Hepatocellular carcinoma

B. Hepatic adenoma

C. Focal nodular hyperplacia

D. Cholangiocarcinoma

Q.234 Which of the following agents is used to measure glomerular filtration rate (GFR) –

A. Iodohippurate

B. Tc99m – DTPA

C. Tc99m – MAG3

D. Tc99m – DMSA

Q.235 Arthritis mutilans is seen in:

A. OA

B. Reiters syndrome

C. Psoriatic Arthropathy

D. Rheumatoid arthritis

Q.236 Expansile lytic lesion with fluid-fluid levels within the metaphysis of fibula seen on CT and MRI in an early adolescent female is typical of –

A. Giant cell tumor

B. Aneurysmal bone cyst

C. Hemangioma

D. Fibrous dysplasia

Q.237 Onion - peel appearance is seen in -

A. Ewing's sarcoma

B. Osteoma

C. Osteosarcoma

D. Osteoclastoma

Q.238 Which of the following is not an MRI feature of Mesial temporal sclerosis?

A. Atrophy of mammillary body

B. Atrophy of fornix

C. Blurring of Grey white matter junction of ipsilateral temporal lobe

D. Atrophy of hippocampus

Q.239 Investigation of choice for acute subarachnoid hemorrhage –

A. Enhanced MRI

B. MRI

C. CT-scan

D. Angiography

Q.240 Cozen's test is for:

A. Golfers elbow

B. Students elbow

C. Frozen elbow

D. Tennis elbow

Q.241 Fertilization usually occurs in which part of the fallopian tube

A. Fimbrial end

B. Ampulla

C. Interstitium

D. Isthumus

Q.242 The major contribution to the semen from:

A. Testes

B. Seminal vesicles

C. Prostate

D. Bulbourethral and urethral glands

Q.243 Absent fructose content in the seminal fluid suggests

A. Congenital absence of seminal vesicle

B. Partial duct obstruction

C. None

D. Both

Q.244 The diagnostic factor for Choriocarcinoma is:

A. Hypoplastic trophoblasts

B. HCG Level less than 35,000Miu/ml

C. Lung Metastasis

D. None of them

Q.245 Which of the following hematological criteria remains unchanged during pregnancy

A. MCHC

B. TIBC

C. Blood Volume   **D.** S. ferritin

Q.246 The dose of folic acid per day for treating megaloblastic anemia in pregnancy

A. 400 μg   **B.** 1 mg   **C.** 5 mg   **D.** 2 mg

Q.247 Partogram is not used to monitor -

A. Cervical dilatations   **B.** Uterine contractions
C. Fetal lung maturity   **D.** Descent of head

Q.248 A Patient at 22 weeks gestation is diagnosed as having LUD which occurred at 17 weeks but did not have a miscarriage. This patient is at increased risk for:

A. Septic abortion
B. Recurrent abortion
C. Future infertility
D. Consumptive coagulopathy with hypofibrinogenemia

Q.249 A G2P1 female at 35 weeks experiences uterine contractions. No fetal distress is seen and membranes are not ruptured. Which of the following is to be done?

A. 12 mg betamethasone injection
B. Tocolytic therapy
C. Vaginal swab culture
D. Cervical cerclage

Q.250 Meconium is excreted by a new born till _______ day.

A. 7   **B.** 3   **C.** 6   **D.** 4

Q.251 Fetal cardiac activity is detected with Transvaginal USG as early as?

A. 8 weeks   **B.** 6 weeks
C. 10 weeks.   **D.** 12 weeks

Q.252 IUGR is defined when:

A. Birth weight is below the tenth percentile of the average of gestational age
B. Birth weight is below the 20 percentile of the average of gestational age
C. Birth weight is below the 30 percentile of the average of gestational age
D. Weight of baby is less than 1000 gm

Q.253 Increased acidosis and hypoxemia are seen in:

A. Normal Doppler wave form
B. Increased fetal diastolic flow in the middle cerebral artery with absent diastolic flow in the aorta
C. Presence of the 'notch' in the uterine artery
D. Absent umbilical artery

Q.254 Consider the following

1. Reactive NST
2. Absence of deceleration
3. Sinusoidal pattern

Which of the above findings in an antepartum CTG indicate fetal well being :

A. 1 and 2 only   **B.** 2 and 3 only
C. 1 and 3 only   **D.** 1, 2 and 3

Q.255 In a female with appendicitis in pregnancy treatment of choice is:

A. Surgery at earliest
B. Abortion with appendectomy
C. Surgery after delivery
D. Continue pregnancy with medical Rx

Q.256 Regarding labia majora, all are correct except:

A. Is homologus to scrotum in males
B. Is supplied by branches of internal and external pudendal arteries
C. Drains into superficial inguinal lymph nodes
D. The broad ligament terminates at its anterior end

Q.257 The ovarian cycle is initiated by:

A. FSH   **B.** Estrogen
C. LH   **D.** Progesterone

Q.258 In PCOD which of the following drug is not used for infertility

A. Clomiphene   **B.** Tamoxifen
C. Spironolactone   **D.** Testosterone

Q.259 Regarding PCOS and hyperinsulinemia

A. Hyperinsulinemia is observed in about 40% to 80% of women with PCOS
B. Metformin has many other health benefits
C. Metformin causes hypoglycemia in normoglycaemic women
D. Hyperinsulinemia stimulates hepatic synthesis of SHBG

Q.260 About Mayer rokitansky Kuster Hauser syndrome

A. Uterus absent and ovaries present
B. Fallopian tubes are present
C. Typically ovaries are abnormal
D. Secondary sexual characters are not developed.

Q.261 Sensitivity of uterine musculature:

A. Enhanced by progesterone
B. Enhanced by estrogen
C. Inhibited by estrogen
D. Enhanced by estrogen and inhibited by progesterone

Q.262 Gonorrhea — which is not a presenting feature?

A. Hematuria
B. dysuria
C. Discharge
D. Reddened lips of vulva and vagina

Q.263 Postpartum VVF is best repaired after:

A. 6 weeks   **B.** 8 weeks
C. 3 months   **D.** 6 months

Q.264 Treatment of genuine stress incontinence:

a. Anterior colporrhaphy
b. Posterior colporrhaphy
c. colposuspension
d. Pelvic floor exercise
e. Sling operation

A. bce   **B.** bde   **C.** acde   **D.** abde

Q.265 Which is not an assisted reproduction technique:

A. GIFT

B. ZIFT

C. IVF and ET

D. Artificial insemination

Q.266 Not a barrier contraceptive:

A. Diaphragm   **B.** Centochroman

C. Condom   **D.** Today

Q.267 The most common cause of menorrhagia in the childbearing period:

A. Dysfunctional uterine bleeding

B. Fibroid

C. Pelvic endometriosis

D. Adenomyosis

Q.268 Stage-IIIB endometrial carcinoma true is/are:

a. Vaginal metastasis

b. Lymph node metastasis (paraaortic)

c. Pelvic lymph node involvement

d. Positive peritoneal cytology

e. Rectal invasion

A. c   **B.** ac   **C.** ab   **D.** ad

Q.269 The advantages of cryosurgery over electrocauterization are all except:

A. Less discomfort to the patient.

B. Postoperative bleeding is much less

C. Postoperative vaginal discharge is also much less

D. Cervical stenosis is extremely rare

Q.270 Corpus luteum cyst occurs due to:

A. HCG   **B.** Progesterone

C. Estrogen   **D.** None of the above

Q.271 A mother comes with her 3-year-old female child with the complaint that child is not eating anything. Her weight is 11 kg (50th percentile) and her height is 88 cm (75th percentile). What should be done next –

A. Vitamin rich tonic to be given

B. Forceful eating

C. Nothing should be done actively and assure the parent

D. Complete investigation for UTI

Q.272 Key features of kangaroo mother care are all the following except?

A. Skin to skin contact between mother and baby

B. Exclusive breast feeding

C. Done for babies with cyanosis

D. Initiated in a facility and continued at home

Q.273 True about fetal circulation –

A. Blood in SVC has more oxygen saturation

B. Pressure in left ventricle is more

C. Brain receives blood with low oxygen saturation

D. Heart receives blood with high oxygen saturation

Q.274 Approx 3-month-old child presents with irregular footer. what is the main reason of it? –

A. Laryngotracheobronchitis

B. Laryngomalacia

C. Respiratory obstruction

D. Foreign body aspiration

Q.275 Which of the following is not the most common renal cystic disease in infants, except ?

A. Polycystic kidney

B. Simple renal cyst

C. Unilateral renal dysplasia

D. Calyceal cyst

Q.276 A child comes with steroid-resistant nephrotic syndrome secondary to FSGS, not responsive to methylprednisolone. What next should be given –

A. Oral cyclophosphamide

B. Oral cyclosporine

C. Oral mycophenolate

D. IV cyclophosphamide

Q.277 Hypsarrhythmia in a child is due to –

A. Grandmal epilepsy   **B.** Petitmal epilepsy

C. Myoclonic epilepsy   **D.** Reflex epilepsy

Q.278 Common childhood tumors are –

a. Acute lymphoblastic leukemia

b. Chronic lymphoblastic leukemia

c. Chronic myeloid leukemia

d. Brain tumor

e. Wilm's tumor

A. ade   **B.** bde   **C.** abd   **D.** ad

Q.279 The hair on end appearance is seen in X–ray skull in –

a. Thalassemia

b. Hydrocephalus

c. Chronic malaria

d. Sickle cell anemia

A. ad   **B.** c   **C.** ac   **D.** ab

Q.280 Acute malnutrition is manifested by –

A. Weight for age   **B.** Weight for height

C. Age for height   **D.** Brocas index

Q.281 Adenoids are also called?

A. Nasopharyngeal tonsils

B. Palatine tonsils

C. Faucial tonsils

D. Lingual tonsils

Q.282 Otolith organs are involved with the role of?

A. Oculovestibular reflex

B. Rotary nystagmus

C. Linear acceleration

D. Angular acceleration

Q.283 Hyperacusis is caused by damage to?

A. Stapedius   **B.** T. palati

C. T. tympani   **D.** All

Q.284 Choana is -

A. Anterior nares

B. Posterior nares

C. Tonsils

D. Larynx

Q.285 Osteomeatal complex (OMC) connects-

A. Nasal cavity with maxillary sinus

B. Nasal cavity with sphenoid sinus

C. The two nasal cavities

D. Ethmoidal sinus with ethmoidal bulla

Q.286 Ethmoid bone forms A/E -

A. Superior turbinate

B. Middle turbinate

C. Inferior turbinate

D. Uncinate process

Q.287 Lyre sign in seen in-

A. Grave's disease

B. Meniere's disease

C. Lateral sinus thrombosis

D. Carotid body tumour

Q.288 Alternative for SMR -

A. Tympanoplasty

B. Septoplasty

C. Caldwell Luc operation

D. Turboplasty

Q.289 Passavant's ridge is formed by

A. Superior constrictor and palatopharyngeus

B. Inferior constrictor and palatopharyngeus

C. Superior constrictor and palatoglossus

D. Inferior constrictor and palatoglossus

Q.290 In which of the following locations there is a collection of pus in quinsy -

A. Peritonsillar space

B. Parapharyngeal space

C. Retropharyngeal space

D. Within the tonsil

Q.291 Avascular structure of the eye is -

A. Conjuctiva

B. Cornea

C. Ciliary body

D. Retina

Q.292 Visual axis is –

A. Center of cornea to retina

B. Object to fovea

C. Center of lens to cornea

D. None

Q.293 Which of the following is seen in chronic contact lens wearer:

A. Inclusion Conjuntivitis

B. Giant papillary Conjunctivitis

C. Vernal keratoconjuntivitis

D. Follicular conjunctivitis

Q.294 Satellite nodules are seen in –

A. Fungal corneal ulcer

B. Tuberculosis

C. Sarcoidosis

D. Viral ulcer

Q.295 Chorioretinitis is caused by –

A. Toxoplasmosis

B. CMV

C. Oncocerca volvulus

D. All of the above

Q.296 Treatment of choice for congenital cataract is –

A. Pharmacotherapy

B. Combined cataract surgery and Goniotomy

C. Cataract surgery

D. Pars plana lensectomy with no IOL implant

Q.297 Which of the following is primary glaucoma –

a. Juvenile glaucoma

b. Steroid-induced glaucoma

c. Pigmentary glaucoma

d. Congenital glaucoma

e. Infantile glaucoma

A. ade

B. bde

C. abd

D. ad

Q.298 Cotton wool spots are commonly seen in –

a. AIDS

b. DM

c. Hypertension

d. CMV

A. ab

B. bc

C. acd

D. abc

Q.299 In Holmes-Adie pupil all are true except -

A. There is absent or retarded pupil reactions to light and near

B. Most cases are bilateral

C. Causes reduced or absent accommodation

D. Constricts with 2.5% methacholine

Q.300 III nerve palsy causes all of the following except -

A. Ptosis

B. Mydriasis

C. Medial deviation of eyeball

D. Pupillary reflex lost

// Smart Answer Sheet //

Correct   Indicates percentage of students who answered questions correctly.

Skipped   Indicates percentage of students who skipped questions.

Q.	Ans.	Correct / Skipped
1	A	43.75 % / 4.17 %
2	A	20.83 % / 47.92 %
3	A	37.5 % / 50.0 %
4	A	31.25 % / 47.92 %
5	C	20.83 % / 47.92 %
6	A	22.92 % / 47.91 %
7	A	22.92 % / 47.91 %
8	C	14.58 % / 50.0 %
9	B	20.83 % / 52.09 %
10	B	10.42 % / 54.16 %
11	A	31.25 % / 54.17 %
12	A	25.0 % / 50.0 %
13	C	18.75 % / 52.08 %
14	C	37.5 % / 50.0 %
15	D	22.92 % / 54.16 %
16	D	27.08 % / 54.17 %

Q.	Ans.	Correct / Skipped
17	D	37.5 % / 52.08 %
18	D	14.58 % / 52.09 %
19	B	12.5 % / 54.17 %
20	C	14.58 % / 54.17 %
21	B	37.5 % / 52.08 %
22	A	29.17 % / 54.16 %
23	D	20.83 % / 52.09 %
24	D	14.58 % / 52.09 %
25	C	12.5 % / 54.17 %
26	D	20.83 % / 52.09 %
27	A	22.92 % / 52.08 %
28	B	29.17 % / 50.0 %
29	C	41.67 % / 52.08 %
30	C	18.75 % / 54.17 %
31	A	18.75 % / 52.08 %
32	B	20.83 % / 52.09 %

Q.	Ans.	Correct / Skipped
33	C	22.92 % / 52.08 %
34	B	27.08 % / 54.17 %
35	A	20.83 % / 52.09 %
36	A	33.33 % / 54.17 %
37	B	22.92 % / 54.16 %
38	D	20.83 % / 52.09 %
39	B	33.33 % / 52.09 %
40	A	25.0 % / 54.17 %
41	C	31.25 % / 54.17 %
42	C	22.92 % / 54.16 %
43	D	18.75 % / 56.25 %
44	D	14.58 % / 56.25 %
45	C	20.83 % / 54.17 %
46	B	29.17 % / 54.16 %
47	D	18.75 % / 54.17 %
48	A	33.33 % / 54.17 %

Q.	Ans.	Correct / Skipped
49	D	25.0 % / 54.17 %
50	D	27.08 % / 56.25 %
51	A	41.67 % / 47.91 %
52	A	20.83 % / 52.09 %
53	D	33.33 % / 50.0 %
54	B	35.42 % / 50.0 %
55	D	25.0 % / 52.08 %
56	D	43.75 % / 50.0 %
57	D	16.67 % / 50.0 %
58	B	33.33 % / 50.0 %
59	B	37.5 % / 50.0 %
60	C	41.67 % / 52.08 %
61	D	31.25 % / 52.08 %
62	A	31.25 % / 52.08 %
63	A	41.67 % / 52.08 %
64	B	18.75 % / 52.08 %

Q.	Ans.	Correct / Skipped
65	A	39.58 % / 54.17 %
66	D	31.25 % / 54.17 %
67	B	12.5 % / 54.17 %
68	C	33.33 % / 52.09 %
69	D	37.5 % / 52.08 %
70	D	22.92 % / 52.08 %
71	B	20.83 % / 54.17 %
72	A	43.75 % / 52.08 %
73	B	16.67 % / 54.16 %
74	D	14.58 % / 56.25 %
75	D	41.67 % / 52.08 %
76	C	27.08 % / 52.09 %
77	A	29.17 % / 52.08 %
78	C	14.58 % / 52.09 %
79	B	20.83 % / 54.17 %
80	D	14.58 % / 54.17 %

Q.	Ans.	Correct / Skipped	Q.	Ans.	Correct / Skipped	Q.	Ans.	Correct / Skipped	Q.	Ans.	Correct / Skipped	Q.	Ans.	Correct / Skipped
81	C	22.92 % / 54.16 %	97	C	22.92 % / 52.08 %	113	B	14.58 % / 52.09 %	129	D	20.83 % / 52.09 %	145	C	25.0 % / 56.25 %
82	A	39.58 % / 52.09 %	98	C	29.17 % / 54.16 %	114	C	31.25 % / 52.08 %	130	C	10.42 % / 56.25 %	146	A	25.0 % / 56.25 %
83	D	16.67 % / 54.16 %	99	D	37.5 % / 52.08 %	115	A	25.0 % / 52.08 %	131	B	8.33 % / 58.34 %	147	A	43.75 % / 54.17 %
84	A	22.92 % / 52.08 %	100	D	16.67 % / 54.16 %	116	B	10.42 % / 54.16 %	132	C	31.25 % / 52.08 %	148	D	22.92 % / 54.16 %
85	D	29.17 % / 52.08 %	101	B	33.33 % / 52.09 %	117	A	29.17 % / 52.08 %	133	C	10.42 % / 56.25 %	149	B	14.58 % / 52.09 %
86	B	25.0 % / 52.08 %	102	D	27.08 % / 52.09 %	118	B	35.42 % / 52.08 %	134	B	25.0 % / 52.08 %	150	A	31.25 % / 54.17 %
87	A	25.0 % / 52.08 %	103	A	35.42 % / 52.08 %	119	C	20.83 % / 54.17 %	135	C	20.83 % / 52.09 %	151	C	27.08 % / 47.92 %
88	B	20.83 % / 52.09 %	104	D	16.67 % / 52.08 %	120	B	22.92 % / 54.16 %	136	D	29.17 % / 54.16 %	152	D	25.0 % / 52.08 %
89	A	39.58 % / 52.09 %	105	C	41.67 % / 52.08 %	121	A	45.83 % / 52.09 %	137	D	29.17 % / 52.08 %	153	B	29.17 % / 50.0 %
90	A	18.75 % / 52.08 %	106	A	22.92 % / 52.08 %	122	C	14.58 % / 54.17 %	138	B	27.08 % / 52.09 %	154	D	39.58 % / 50.0 %
91	A	41.67 % / 52.08 %	107	C	29.17 % / 52.08 %	123	A	39.58 % / 52.09 %	139	C	14.58 % / 54.17 %	155	C	31.25 % / 50.0 %
92	D	25.0 % / 52.08 %	108	D	31.25 % / 52.08 %	124	B	18.75 % / 54.17 %	140	D	25.0 % / 52.08 %	156	C	4.17 % / 50.0 %
93	D	12.5 % / 54.17 %	109	A	16.67 % / 52.08 %	125	B	31.25 % / 52.08 %	141	C	33.33 % / 52.09 %	157	C	22.92 % / 52.08 %
94	B	29.17 % / 52.08 %	110	C	18.75 % / 52.08 %	126	D	39.58 % / 52.09 %	142	C	18.75 % / 56.25 %	158	A	25.0 % / 50.0 %
95	D	12.5 % / 56.25 %	111	A	20.83 % / 54.17 %	127	B	27.08 % / 54.17 %	143	C	29.17 % / 52.08 %	159	C	8.33 % / 50.0 %
96	D	37.5 % / 52.08 %	112	B	25.0 % / 52.08 %	128	B	20.83 % / 52.09 %	144	A	35.42 % / 52.08 %	160	B	29.17 % / 50.0 %

Q.	Ans.	Correct / Skipped	Q.	Ans.	Correct / Skipped	Q.	Ans.	Correct / Skipped	Q.	Ans.	Correct / Skipped	Q.	Ans.	Correct / Skipped
161	B	27.08 % / 50.0 %	177	B	10.42 % / 52.08 %	193	A	18.75 % / 50.0 %	209	B	14.58 % / 52.09 %	225	D	29.17 % / 52.08 %
162	B	16.67 % / 54.16 %	178	A	29.17 % / 50.0 %	194	A	16.67 % / 52.08 %	210	A	25.0 % / 52.08 %	226	B	16.67 % / 54.16 %
163	B	29.17 % / 50.0 %	179	B	18.75 % / 50.0 %	195	C	31.25 % / 50.0 %	211	A	37.5 % / 54.17 %	227	D	27.08 % / 52.09 %
164	D	14.58 % / 52.09 %	180	A	41.67 % / 50.0 %	196	C	12.5 % / 50.0 %	212	C	18.75 % / 54.17 %	228	D	18.75 % / 54.17 %
165	D	25.0 % / 50.0 %	181	A	35.42 % / 50.0 %	197	B	39.58 % / 52.09 %	213	A	33.33 % / 52.09 %	229	A	25.0 % / 52.08 %
166	B	25.0 % / 50.0 %	182	C	27.08 % / 52.09 %	198	D	27.08 % / 50.0 %	214	D	27.08 % / 54.17 %	230	A	12.5 % / 56.25 %
167	A	12.5 % / 52.08 %	183	D	37.5 % / 50.0 %	199	B	16.67 % / 54.16 %	215	D	27.08 % / 54.17 %	231	C	41.67 % / 52.08 %
168	C	22.92 % / 54.16 %	184	B	22.92 % / 50.0 %	200	B	25.0 % / 54.17 %	216	D	37.5 % / 52.08 %	232	A	20.83 % / 56.25 %
169	D	35.42 % / 50.0 %	185	B	20.83 % / 50.0 %	201	A	27.08 % / 54.17 %	217	A	20.83 % / 54.17 %	233	C	18.75 % / 52.08 %
170	B	43.75 % / 50.0 %	186	A	29.17 % / 50.0 %	202	D	31.25 % / 54.17 %	218	D	10.42 % / 52.08 %	234	B	20.83 % / 54.17 %
171	B	27.08 % / 50.0 %	187	C	18.75 % / 50.0 %	203	B	35.42 % / 52.08 %	219	A	27.08 % / 52.09 %	235	C	10.42 % / 54.16 %
172	C	16.67 % / 50.0 %	188	B	20.83 % / 50.0 %	204	B	31.25 % / 52.08 %	220	D	8.33 % / 52.09 %	236	B	25.0 % / 54.17 %
173	C	20.83 % / 50.0 %	189	D	39.58 % / 52.09 %	205	C	27.08 % / 52.09 %	221	D	25.0 % / 54.17 %	237	A	35.42 % / 54.16 %
174	D	8.33 % / 50.0 %	190	D	37.5 % / 50.0 %	206	A	18.75 % / 54.17 %	222	B	10.42 % / 54.16 %	238	C	10.42 % / 56.25 %
175	C	27.08 % / 50.0 %	191	A	25.0 % / 52.08 %	207	A	29.17 % / 52.08 %	223	D	27.08 % / 54.17 %	239	C	22.92 % / 54.16 %
176	A	10.42 % / 50.0 %	192	D	35.42 % / 50.0 %	208	B	22.92 % / 52.08 %	224	A	16.67 % / 54.16 %	240	D	22.92 % / 56.25 %

Q.	Ans.	Correct / Skipped		Q.	Ans.	Correct / Skipped		Q.	Ans.	Correct / Skipped		Q.	Ans.	Correct / Skipped		Q.	Ans.	Correct / Skipped
241	B	31.25 % / 54.17 %		253	B	20.83 % / 56.25 %		265	D	20.83 % / 54.17 %		277	C	20.83 % / 58.34 %		289	A	29.17 % / 60.41 %
242	B	29.17 % / 54.16 %		254	A	27.08 % / 54.17 %		266	B	22.92 % / 54.16 %		278	A	27.08 % / 58.34 %		290	A	22.92 % / 60.41 %
243	D	18.75 % / 56.25 %		255	A	25.0 % / 54.17 %		267	A	18.75 % / 54.17 %		279	A	31.25 % / 58.33 %		291	B	35.42 % / 58.33 %
244	D	4.17 % / 54.16 %		256	D	25.0 % / 54.17 %		268	D	10.42 % / 56.25 %		280	B	29.17 % / 58.33 %		292	B	10.42 % / 62.5 %
245	A	14.58 % / 54.17 %		257	A	18.75 % / 54.17 %		269	C	12.5 % / 56.25 %		281	A	37.5 % / 58.33 %		293	B	18.75 % / 60.42 %
246	B	8.33 % / 54.17 %		258	C	12.5 % / 54.17 %		270	A	16.67 % / 54.16 %		282	C	10.42 % / 58.33 %		294	A	27.08 % / 60.42 %
247	C	37.5 % / 54.17 %		259	B	16.67 % / 56.25 %		271	C	22.92 % / 54.16 %		283	A	29.17 % / 58.33 %		295	D	22.92 % / 60.41 %
248	D	27.08 % / 54.17 %		260	A	25.0 % / 56.25 %		272	C	31.25 % / 54.17 %		284	B	29.17 % / 58.33 %		296	C	10.42 % / 60.41 %
249	C	6.25 % / 54.17 %		261	D	22.92 % / 56.25 %		273	D	12.5 % / 58.33 %		285	A	25.0 % / 58.33 %		297	A	27.08 % / 62.5 %
250	B	22.92 % / 54.16 %		262	A	25.0 % / 54.17 %		274	B	16.67 % / 58.33 %		286	C	10.42 % / 58.33 %		298	D	16.67 % / 62.5 %
251	B	27.08 % / 54.17 %		263	C	8.33 % / 54.17 %		275	C	8.33 % / 56.25 %		287	D	20.83 % / 58.34 %		299	B	8.33 % / 62.5 %
252	A	18.75 % / 56.25 %		264	C	8.33 % / 56.25 %		276	B	14.58 % / 56.25 %		288	B	18.75 % / 58.33 %		300	C	12.5 % / 60.42 %

Performance Analysis

Avg. Score (%)	21.75%
Toppers Score (%)	82.58%
Your Score	

Part A

Q.1 Tyrosine kinase receptors

A. Have constitutively active tyrosine kinase domains

B. Phosphorylate and activate ras directly

C. Mediate cellular processes involved in growth and differentiation

D. Are not phosphorylated upon activation

Q.2 Physiological anemia of pregnancy is due to

A. Decrease in plasma iron binding capacity

B. Hypoactivity of bone marrow

C. Disproportionate increase in plasma volume

D. Deficiency of vitamin B_{12}

Q.3 Strawberry tongue can be seen in all except:

A. Kawasaki disease

B. Scarlet fever

C. Brucellosis

D. Toxic shock syndrome

Q.4 Clinical findings of which of the following typically includes a rash-like erythema, which spreads throughout the skin of the breast?

A. Inflammatory carcinoma

B. Medullary tumor

C. Colloid tumor

D. Paget's disease

Q.5 The radiographic appearance of the vertebra shown in the image is most common in ?

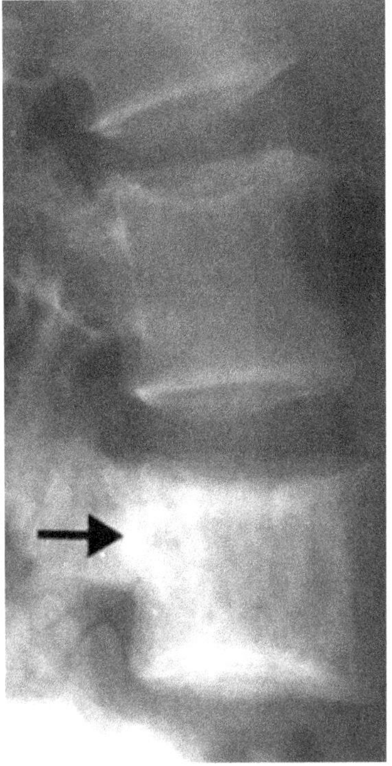

A. Eosininophilic Granuloma

B. Sickle cell anemia

C. Vertebral hemangioma

D. Paget's disease

Q.6 Which of the following isotopes is commonly used in teletherapy?

A. Pd-103   **B.** Co-60   **C.** Tc-99   **D.** Ir-19

Q.7 In a patient with back pain, CT spine reveals the following appearance of the vertebra. What is the diagnosis and the sign shown on CT?

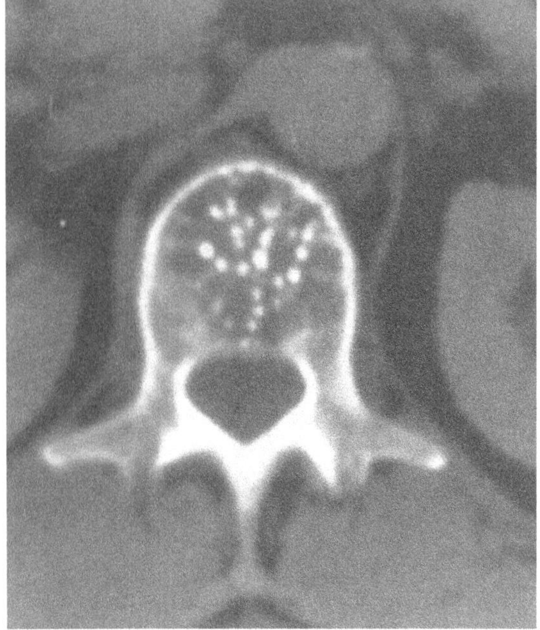

A. Hemangioma, corduroy appearance

B. Hemangioma, polka dot appearance

C. Osteoporosis, H-shape vertebrae

D. Osteoporosis, Polka dot appearance

Q.8 Divorce can be given if there is:

A. Impotence

B. Sterility

C. Premature ejaculation

D. None of the above

Q.9 A 35-year-old woman has been in a women's shelter for past 15 years. She spends most of her day rocking, muttering softly to herself, or looking at her reflection in a small mirror. She needs help with dressing and showering and she often giggles and laughs for no apparent reason. What is the appropriate diagnosis ?

A. Psychotic depression

B. Schizophrenia, paranoid type

C. Shared psychotic disorder

D. Schizophrenia, disorganized type

Q.10 Benzodiazepines those are useful as anticonvulsants have the following properties for increased efficacy

A. Long half-life, and slow entry into the brain

B. Short half-life, and slow entry into the brain

C. Long half-life, and rapid entry into the brain

D. Short half-life, and rapid entry into the brain

Q.11 Treatment of rectal prolapse in childhood is:

A. Lahaut's operation

B. Incision of prolapsed mucosa

C. Thiersch operation

D. Ripstein operation

Q.12 Which of the following changes is a frequent consequence of chronic rheumatic fever ?

A. Anitschkow cells in the endocardium

B. Aschoff bodies in the myocardium

C. Fibrin deposits in the pericardium

D. Stenosis of the mitral valve

Q.13 A patient complaining of having lost his wealth, status as well as his strength and internal body organs has

A. Capgrass Syndrome

B. Fregoli Syndrome

C. Cotard syndrome

D. De Clerambault's Syndrome

Q.14 Mode of action of fluoxetine is:

A. Inhibition of serotonin uptake

B. Inhibition of dopamine uptake

C. Facilitation of adrenergic impulse

D. Facilitation of cholinergic response

Q.15 All of the following are true about Warthin tumor except

A. It is a malignant salivary gland tumor

B. It arises almost always in the parotid gland

C. About 10% are bilateral

D. It has cystic spaces and dense lymphoid stroma

Q.16 Which of the following are characteristic of the secretory phase of the menstrual cycle ?

A. It precedes ovulation

B. It coincides with the development of ovarian follicles

C. It depends on progesterone secretion by the corpus luteum

D. It coincides with rapid drop in estrogen levels

Q.17 True statement about Infraglottic carcinoma larynx:

A. Commonly spreads to mediastinal nodes

B. Second most common carcinoma

C. Most common carcinoma

D. Spreads to submetal nodes

Q.18 Laboratory studies show an elevated serum B-type natriuretic peptide in a 70-year old man with poorly controlled diabetes mellitus, exertional chest pain, bilateral pulmonary rales and pitting edema of legs. Chest radiograph shows prominent right and left heart borders. Which of the following pathologic findings is most likely present in this man?

A. Critical coronary stenosis

B. Left atrial mural thrombus

C. Mitral and tricuspid valve thickening

D. Pericardial fibrinohemorrhagic exudate

Q.19 Under development of which of the following embryonic structures may be related to abnormally thin wall in the smooth part of right atrium in an infant?

A. Pulmonary trunk

B. Conus cordis

C. Sinus venosus

D. Truncus arteriosus

Q.20 The highest concentration of chyle is found in the lymphatics that drain which of the following organs?

A. Small intestine

B. Heart

C. Long bones

D. Spleen

Q.21 The probability of a test detecting a truly positive person from the population of diseased is the:

A. Sensitivity of the test

B. Specificity of the test

C. Positive predictive value of the test

D. Likelihood ratio

Q.22 Criteria for fetal growth are all EXCEPT

A. Height of the uterus

B. Maternal weight gain

C. Ultras onographic measurement of biparietal diameter

D. Ultrasonographic measurement of fetal abdominal circumference

Q.23 Which one of the following statements regarding megalocornea is false?

A. This condition is defined as a clear normal-appearing cornea with a diameter measuring greater than 13 mm

B. This condition is often associated with anterior megalophthalmos, an autosomal dominant disorder

C. The simple form of megalocornea is usually seen as a bilateral condition

D. Tearing and IOP are important factors in the workup

Q.24 Vitreous complications are least seen in surgery in

A. Mature cataract

B. Posterior polar cataracts

C. Nuclear sclerosis grade 2

D. Nuclear sclerosis grade 4

Q.25 An apathetic male child (Image) is having peripheral edema, a "moon" face, and an enlarged, fatty liver. Which of the following basic defects cause this change in the liver?

A. Decreased protein intake leads to decreased lipoproteins

B. Decreased caloric intake leads to hypoalbuminemia

C. Decreased fluid intake leads to hypernatremia

D. Decreased fat absorption leads to hypovitaminosis

Q.26 All are true regarding AFP Surveillance except:

A. WHO recommends it for age less than 15 years

B. Two stool samples are collected per case

C. Non polio AFP rate should be greater than 1 per 100,000 among less than 15 years old

D. Adequate stool specimens should be taken from 100 % AFP

Q.27 The most common premalignant condition of oral carcinoma is:

A. Leukoplakia

B. Erythroplakia

C. Lichen planus

D. Fibrosis

Q.28 Causes of metabolic alkalosis in a child include all of the following except : -

A. Recurrent vomiting

B. Mineralocorticoid deficiency

C. Bartter's syndrome

D. Thiazide diuretic therapy

Q.29 After receiving a drug to treat UTI (apparently due to Serratia marcescens) for 2 weeks, a 68 year old woman develops headache, nausea/vomiting, vertigo, tinnitus, and progressive loss of hearing. The drug used was most likely a member of which of the following antibiotic classes?

A. Macrolides

B. Tetracyclines

C. Cephalosporins

D. Aminoglycosides

Q.30 Verrucous carcinoma of the buccal mucosa is identified with which of the following characteristics ?

A. It is faster growing than the epidermoid form

B. It is not associated with tobacco chewing

C. It has a predilection for the gingivobuccal gutter

D. It rarely extends to the mandible

Q.31 Control of urea cycle involves the enzyme:

A. Carbamoyl phosphate synthetase

B. Ornithine transcarbamoylase

C. Argininosuccinase

D. Arginase

Q.32 Fetal sac can be seen using vaginal sonography from the last menstrual period between :

A. 25 - 30 days

B. 33 - 35 days

C. 36 - 40 days

D. 41 - 45 days

Q.33 Uncomplicated Alcohol withdrawal for patients should be treated with?

A. Diazepam

B. Chlordiazepoxide

C. Codeine

D. Disulfiram

Q.34 A 25 year old woman complains of nonpuritic and painless red splotchy rash on her chest during intercourse. It usually resolves within a few minutes to a few hours after intercourse. Which of the following is the most likely cause of the rash?

A. Allergic reaction to her partner's pheromones

B. Decreased systolic blood pressure during the plateau phase

C. Increased estrogen during the excitement phase

D. Vasocongestion during the excitement phase

Q.35 A healthy 42 year old woman is found to have a calcium level of 12 mg/dl. She feels well and her physical examination is normal. Further investigation reveals a parathormone (PTH) level of 750 pg/ml (230-630 pg/ml). Which of the following findings is also associated with this disorder ?

A. Osteoblastic lesion of bone

B. Lytic bone lesion

C. Polycythemia

D. Orthostatic hypotension

Q.36 Tzank smear was made from the scrapping of the lesion of a patient having painful tiny vesicular ulcers on lips. Identify the pathogen ?

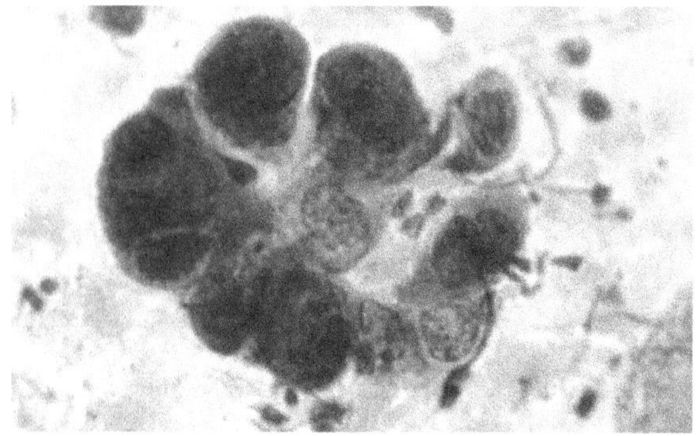

A. HPV
B. Parvovirus
C. Herpes simplex
D. Varicella zoster

Q.37 Tachyphylaxis is produced by all of the following drugs except :

A. Tyramine
B. Ephedrine
C. Amphetamine
D. Epinephrine

Q.38 Which of the following symptoms in a newborn infant would prompt a pediatrician to test for cystic fibrosis?

A. Pneumonia
B. Intrauterine growth retardation
C. Meconium ileus
D. Hypochloremic alkalosis

Q.39 An elderly man with end-stage renal disease from hypertensive nephrosclerosis that had been treated by hemodialysis for 14 years presented with a productive cough and fever, from which he recovered. On the basis of following findings (Images) diagnosis of brown tumour was made. Which of the following conditions it may be associated with ?

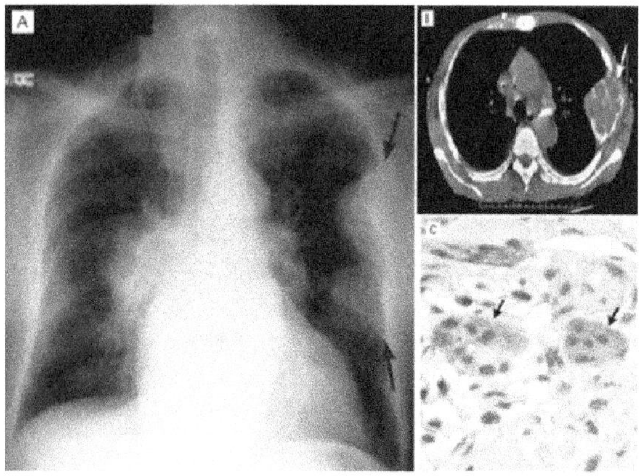

A. Hyperthyroidism
B. Hypothyroidism
C. Hyperparathyroidism
D. Hypoparathyroidism

Q.40 Which of the following laboratory tests would most likely confirm the diagnosis of Prader-Willi syndrome (PWS)?

A. Routine chromosome testing
B. Fluorescence in situ hybridization (FISH) study for subtelomeric rearrangements
C. FISH testing of the 15q11.2-q13 region
D. Lactic acid level

Q.41 Salkowski test is performed for the identification of:

A. Glycerol
B. Cholesterol
C. Fatty acids
D. Vitamin D

Q.42 The artery to the ductus deferens is a branch of

A. Inferior epigastric artery
B. Superior Epigastric Artery
C. Superior Vesical Artery
D. Cremasteric Artery

Q.43 Jejunal biopsy in coeliac disease shows

A. Leaf-shaped villi
B. Flattening of the crypts
C. Appearances resembling severe tropical sprue
D. Fissures penetrating into the submucosa

Q.44 Which of the following is not a significant risk factor for the development of heterotopic ossification:

A. Hypertrophic osteoarthritis
B. Ankylosing spondylitis
C. Posttraumatic arthritis
D. Previous osteonecrosis

Q.45 Naproxen is a weak acid with a pKa of 5.2. What percentage of the drug is most likely water soluble in a patient's plasma?

A. 50%
B. 76%
C. 99%
D. More than 99%

Q.46 A fracture of the femur occurs through the diaphysis of the femur involves which of the following?

A. Acetabulum
B. Midshaft
C. Medial condyle
D. Anterior cruciate ligament

Q.47 A 55 yrs. male presents with dysphagia, retrosternal discomfort and weight loss. Studies reveal achalasia. Which of the following is most likely recommended primary treatment?

A. Graded pneumatic dilation
B. Calcium channel blockers and nitrates
C. Intrasphincteric injection of botulinum toxin
D. laparoscopic Heller myotomy and partial fundoplication

Q.48 A 50-year-old woman with history of hypertension reported having difficulty reading, what clinical presentation would be expected in this patient?

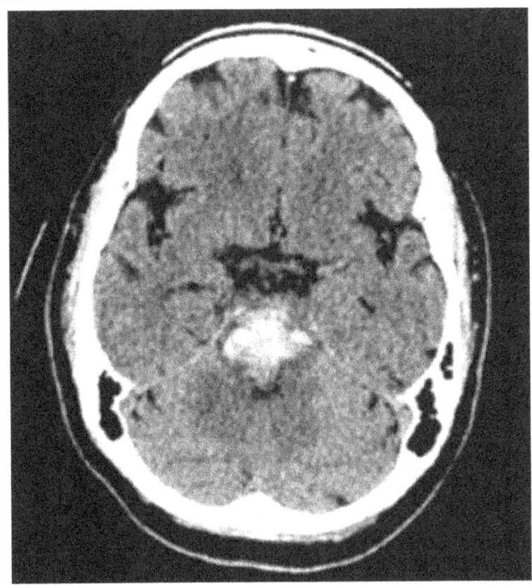

A. Asymmetrical mydriasis

B. Ataxic hemiparesis

C. Hypothermia

D. Quadriplegia

Q.49 Which type of sample can be used to isolate poliovirus earliest?

A. blood   B. Stool   C. throat   D. CSF

Q.50 Consider the following statements regarding mammography -

I - Exposure to low voltage, high amperage x rays.

II - Sensitivity to this test decreases with age.

III - 5 % of breast cancers are missed by population based mammographic screening programmes

A. I, II and III are true

B. I and II are true

C. II and III are true

D. I and III are true

Part B

Q.51 Triple therapy for post renal transplant patients include all except

A. Azathioprine

B. FK 506

C. Prednisolone

D. Cyclosporine

Q.52 Clinical features of nasopharyngeal angiofibroma are all except:

A. Adolescent male

B. Epistaxis and nasal obstruction is the cardinal symptom

C. Radiotherapy is the Rx of choice

D. Arises from posterior nasal cavity

Q.53 Which of the following is the most likely cause Budd-Chiari syndrome?

A. Obstruction of the intrahepatic sinusoids

B. Thrombosis of the hepatic artery

C. Thrombosis of the hepatic vein

D. Thrombosis of the portal vein

Q.54 Treatment of cord prolapse is based on all of the following factors except :

A. Fetal viability

B. Fetal maturity

C. Fetal weight

D. Cervical dilatation

Q.55 A 35-year-old woman has had episodes of light-headedness, irritability, palpitation and difficulty concentrating at her work for the past year. Her haemoglobin is 14.2 g/dL. An abdominal CT scan shows a 1 cm mass in the tail of the pancreas. Which of the following is the most likely diagnosis?

A. Cystadenoma

B. Insulinoma

C. Pseudocyst

D. Pheochromocytoma

Q.56 A 55-day-old infant born prematurely is brought with swelling as shown in the image. The swelling is not tender, firm, hot, or red, and it does not transilluminate. It seems to resolve with pressure, but returns when the infant cries or strains. Which of the following is the most appropriate course of action at this point?

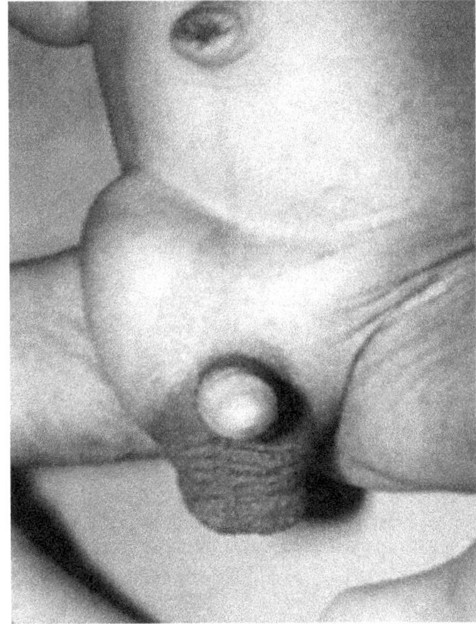

A. Obtain a surgical consultation

B. Perform a needle aspiration

C. Order a barium enema

D. Observe the patient and reassure the patient and family

Q.57 The typical movement of mitral valve calcification is :

A. Upwards and downwards

B. Counter clock wise

C. Side to side

D. Circular

Q.58 Mouse-nibbled appearance of vocal cord is seen in:

A. TB

B. Syphillis

C. Cancer

D. Papilloma

Q.59 All of the following are present in the given ECG EXCEPT:

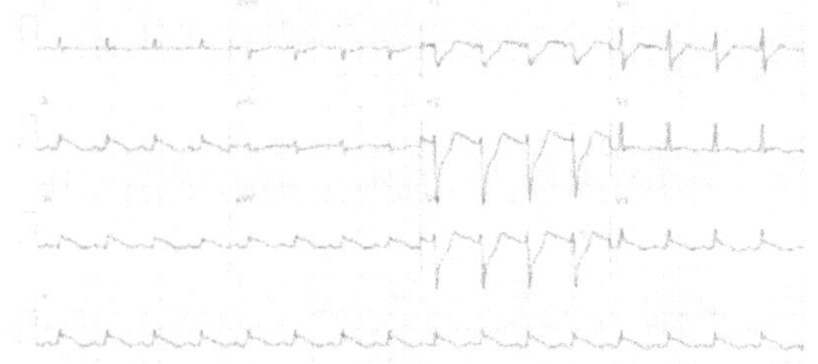

A. Ventricular tachycardia
B. Inferior myocardial ischemia
C. Posterior myocardial ischemia
D. Sinus tachycardia

Q.60 All are true regarding measles vaccine except:
A. Freeze dried live attenuated vaccine
B. Single intramascular dose of 0.5 ml
C. Is occasionally associated with TSS
D. Contraindicated in pregnancy

Q.61 In a pregnant woman, Deep Vein Thrombosis (DVT) is
A. More common in left leg as compare to right leg
B. More common in right leg as compare to left leg
C. Equally common in both the legs
D. An uncommon phenomenon

Q.62 All of the following may be associated with thymoma except
A. Myasthenia gravis
B. Paraneoplastic
C. Hypergammaglobulinemia
D. Pure red cell aplasia

Q.63 A patient having infertility is found to have bilateral cornual block on investigations. Best treatment that can be offered to her would be :
A. In vitro fertilization
B. Tuboplasty
C. Hydrotubation
D. Laparoscopy & hysteroscopy

Q.64 ECG recording of the patient shown below is due to?

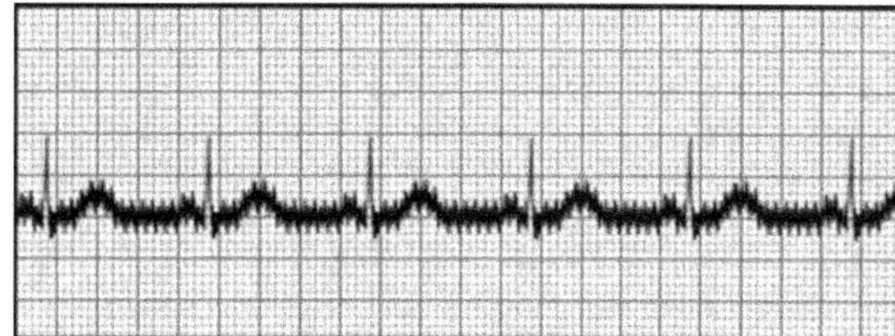

A. Sweating leading to poor electrode contact
B. Electrical interference
C. Restless patient
D. Cable failure

Q.65 A 48-year-old man presents with a three-month history of heartburn after meals which has not been settling with antacids and PPIs. The most appropriate investigation for diagnosing hiatus hernia is:

A. Ultrasound

B. Chest x-ray
C. Upper GI endoscopy
D. Barium meal

Q.66 Apoplexy is:
A. Learning disability
B. Insanity leading to commitment of a crime
C. Sudden onset of bleeding in the brain
D. Injury to the brain due to trauma

Q.67 Hardy Weinberg law states that
A. Relative frequencies of gene allele tends to remain constant from generation to generation
B. Human population and human gene pool is never static
C. Human gene pool changes occur mainly by mutation
D. Harmful genes are eliminated from the gene pool

Q.68 Which of the following structures would most likely be affected by the abscess located between the perineal membrane and the inferior fascia of the pelvic diaphragm within the deep perineal space?
A. Bulbourethral glands
B. Perineal body
C. Superficial transverse perineal muscles
D. Ischiocavernosus muscles

Q.69 The lipoprotein associated with activation of LCAT is
A. HDL　　**B.** LDL　　**C.** VLDL　　**D.** IDL

Q.70 Identify the organism given below?

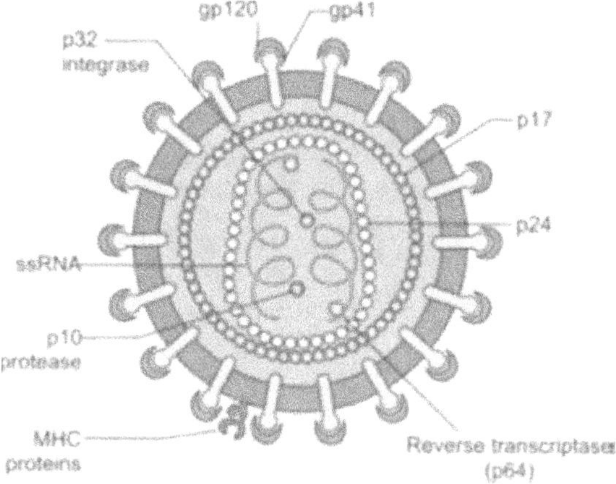

A. Rabies virus
B. Ebola virus
C. H1N1 virus
D. HIV virus

Q.71 A 25 year male is presented with pain in abdomen. On USG, mixed echogenicity was found at left renal hilum and a multifocal necrotic mass is detected. Probable diagnosis is ?
A. Metastatic germ cell tumour
B. Transitional cell carcinoma
C. Lymphoma
D. Metastatic malignant melanoma

Q.72 India belongs to which demographic trends:
A. High stationary
B. Low stationary
C. Early expanding
D. Late expanding

Q.73 Which of the following cytopathologic findings in pap smear is suggestive of HPV infection?

A. Donovan bodies   **B.** Koilocytes

C. Clear cells   **D.** Paget cells

Q.74 Risk factors for acalculous cholecystitis include:

A. Extensive burns   **B.** Sepsis

C. Multiple trauma   **D.** All of the above

Q.75 Cradle of civilization is:

A. Mesopotamia   **B.** Haddapa

C. Mohenjodaro   **D.** Sindhu ghati

Q.76 In which of the following conditions the serum alkaline phosphatase activities are likely to be reduced?

A. Osteomalacia   **B.** Paget's disease

C. Hypophosphatasia   **D.** All of the above

Q.77 A 35-year-old female complains of recurrent urticarial lesions she has had for the last 6 months, which occasionally leave a residual discoloration. She also has had arthralgias. The sedimentation rate now is 85 mm/h. The procedure most likely to yield the correct diagnosis in this case would be?

A. A battery of wheal-and-flare allergy skin tests

B. Measurement of total serum IgE concentration

C. Measurement of C1 esterase inhibitor activity

D. Skin biopsy

Q.78 Which of the following medications may most likely increase the uric acid levels in a patient?

A. Acetazolamide

B. Amiloride

C. Spironolactone

D. Hydrochlorothiazide

Q.79 Antihypertensive of choice in Marfans syndrome is:

A. Beta Blockers

B. Ace Inhibitors

C. Prazosin

D. Angiotensin receptor blockers

Q.80 Which of the following statements regarding stress ulceration is true ?

A. It is true ulceration, extending into and through the muscularis mucosa

B. It classically involves the antrum

C. Increased secretion of gastric acid has been shown to play a causative role

D. It frequently involves multiple sites

Q.81 Period of amenorrhea followed by massive bleeding is seen in premenopausal women with:

A. Irregular ripening

B. Irregular shedding

C. Metropathia hemorrhagica

D. All of the above

Q.82 A 2-year-old boy, is brought with multiple bony abnormalities, as shown in the image. A decrease in which of the following is characteristic of this condition?

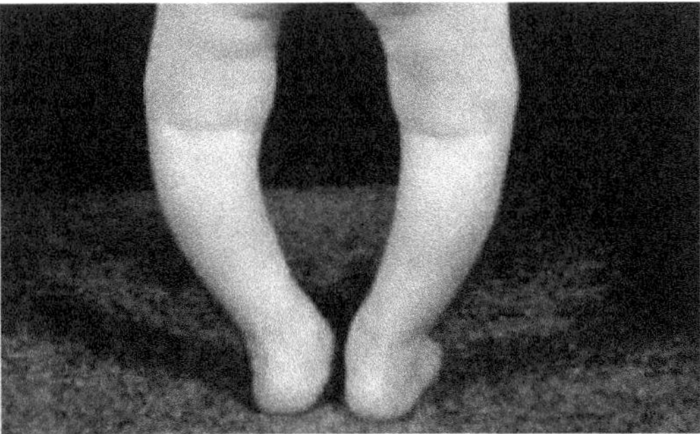

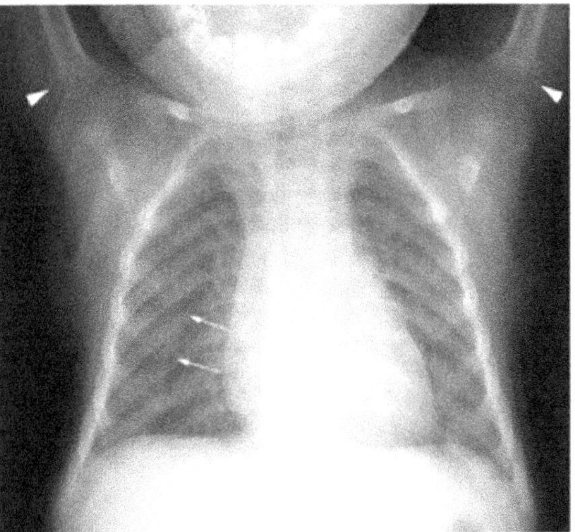

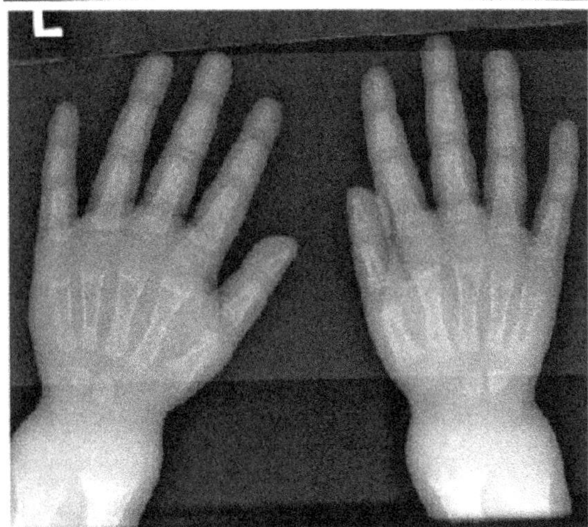

A. Bony osteoblastic activity

B. Calcification of osteoid

C. Serum alkaline phosphatase activity

D. Synthesis of osteoid

Q.83 Characteristics of Mittelschmerz are all except :

A. Pain is usually situated in the hypogastrium

B. It appears in mid menstrual period

C. Pain is usually located on both the ovarian sides irrespective of which ovary is ovulating

D. Probable factors include increased tension of graffian follicle just prior to rupture

Q.84 A woman presents with burning retrosternal chest pain, radiating to the sides of the chest that is aggravated by bending forward. The pain is most likely arising from

A. Heart   **B.** Intercostal nerves
C. Pancreas   **D.** Esophagus

Q.85 The epiglottis is example of

A. Elastic cartilage   **B.** Fibrocartilage
C. Hyaline cartilage   **D.** Articular

Q.86 Axillary sheath is the extention of

A. Prevertebral fascia
B. Pretacheal fascia
C. Carotid sheath
D. Bucco pharyngeal fascia

Q.87 The following are risk factors for puerperal infection, EXCEPT:

A. Prolonged rupture of the membranes
B. Prolonged pregnancy
C. Prolonged second stage
D. Caesarean section

Q.88 Which of the following is major fuel for brain after several weeks of starvation?

A. Beta hydroxyl butyrate
B. Glucose
C. Glycerol
D. Fatty acids

Q.89 Which of the following is Arachidonate 5-lipoxygenase inhibitor?

A. Zileuton
B. Montelukast
C. Sodium chromoglycate
D. Terbutaline

Q.90 Maximum absorption of bile occurs in :

A. Jejunum   **B.** Duodenum
C. Ileum   **D.** Colon

Q.91 A patient presents with right sided weakness of arm and leg. Drooping of the left side of his mouth also noted. Where is the lesion?

A. Left motor cortex   **B.** Right motor cortex
C. Left brainstem   **D.** Right brainstem

Q.92 Which of the following grows the colonies on Mac Conkey agar as shown in the image?

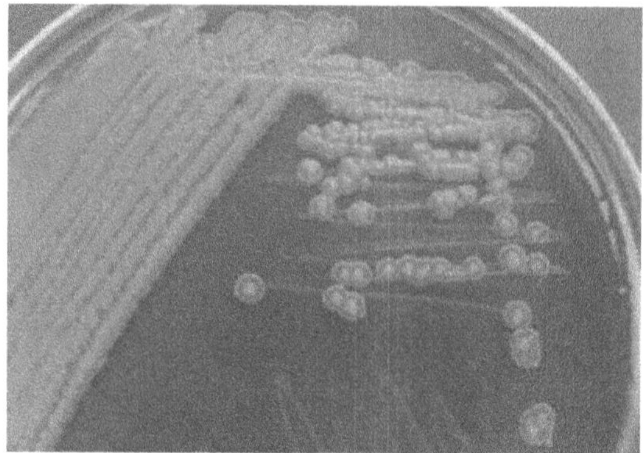

A. Shigella   **B.** Salmonella
C. Proteus   **D.** Klebsiella

Q.93 Commonest cause of female pseudohermaphroditism is:

A. Virilizing ovarian tumor
B. Ovarian dysgenesis
C. Exogenous androgen
D. Congenital adrenal hyperplasia

Q.94 The following are the complications of the HIV infection except

A. Cardiac tamponade   **B.** Pericardial effusion
C. Thromboembolism   **D.** Cardiomyopathy

Q.95 Iceberg phenomenon is a part of disease, which presents clinically, screening tests are used for:

A. To detect tip of iceberg
B. To detect clinical cases
C. To detect submerged part [clinical cases]
D. To detect submerged part [sub clinical cases]

Q.96 Which of the following is TRUE regarding the image provided?

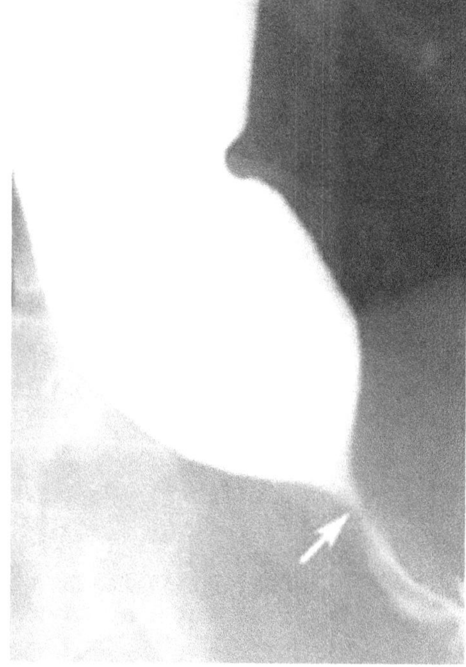

A. Increased tone of lower esophageal sphincter

B. Associated with vitamin A deficiency

C. Not a premalignant condition

D. It's a normal phenomenon

Q.97 Beta adrenergic antagonist are useful antihypertensive agent in all except -

A. Young patients with high renin levels

B. Patients with associated conditions like migraine

C. Patients receiving vasodilators to counteract tachycardia

D. Patients on oral hypoglycemic agents

Q.98 Which of this does not handle the free radicals in lens?

A. Vitamin A

B. Vitamin C

C. Vitamin E

D. Catalase

Q.99 Patients with Huntington disease may benefit from treatment with drugs that antagonize

A. GABA

B. Acetylcholine

C. Dopamine

D. Serotonin

Q.100 Production of the type of cell shown in Figure is increased by

A. Interleukin-2 (IL-2)

B. Granulocyte colony-stimulating factor (G-CSF)

C. Erythropoietin

D. Interleukin-4 (IL-4)

Q.101 A 52-year-old woman presented with indigestion and heartburn occurring shortly after meals. Physical examination revealed mild epigastric tenderness. A radiolabeled-urea breath test is positive. What is the most probable etiologic agent?

A. Campylobacter jejuni

B. Clostridium difficile

C. Helicobacter pylori

D. Shigella dysenteriae

Q.102 During removal of a neurogenic tumor in the posterior mediastinum, the structure indicated by arrow in the given diagram was damaged. What type of nerve fibers were affected by this iatrogenic injury?

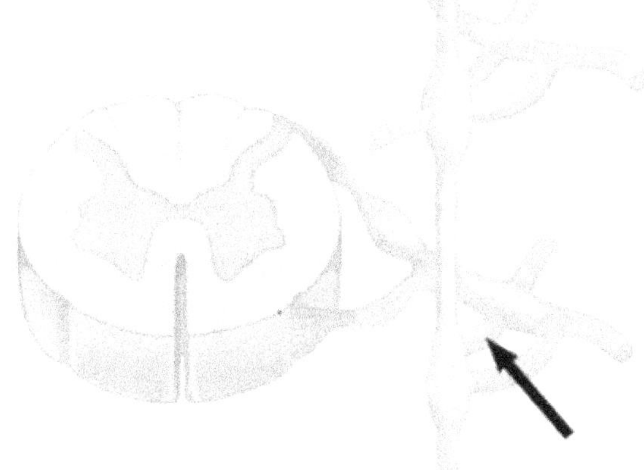

A. Presynaptic sympathetic axons

B. Presynaptic parasympathetic axons

C. Postsynaptic sympathetic axons

D. Postsynaptic parasympathetic axons

Q.103 Stimulation of which of the following might be expected to produce itching?

A. Dorsal root C fibers

B. B fibers in peripheral nerves

C. Dorsal columns of the spinal cord

D. Touch receptors

Q.104 Which of the following medications is most useful for the treatment of premenstrual syndrome?

A. Progesterone

B. Anxiolytics

C. Vitamins

D. Selective serotonin reuptake inhibitors (SSRIs)

Q.105 Which of the following statements concerning acute rheumatic fever is true?

A. Sydenham's chorea typically occurs early in the course of the disease

B. Erythema marginatum is a common finding, occurring in more than 50% of cases

C. Secondary prophylaxis should be initiated in order to decrease recurrent episodes of rheumatic fever

D. Group A streptococci can usually be recovered in the upper respiratory tract of patients with rheumatic fever

Q.106 Which of the following is most characteristic of Huntington disease?

A. Degeneration of upper and lower motor neurons

B. Dopamine depletion and depigmentation of the substantia nigra

C. Increased number of trinucleotide repeats in a gene on chromosome 4

D. Neurofibrillary tangles and amyloid plaques in the cerebral cortex

Q.107 Decrease in heart rate in response to rise in blood pressure is explained by -

A. Baroreflex

B. Chemoreflex

C. Bainbridge reflex

D. Hering-Bruer reflex

Q.108 The reliability of visual field testing becomes suspect when pupil diameter decreases below:

A. 4 mm **B.** 3 mm **C.** 2 mm **D.** 1 mm

Q.109 An elderly man presents with chronic fatigability, central obesity, diabetes mellitus. Purple skin pigmentation is noted as shown in the image. Also his knuckles showed evidence of hyperpigmentation. What is the Diagnosis?

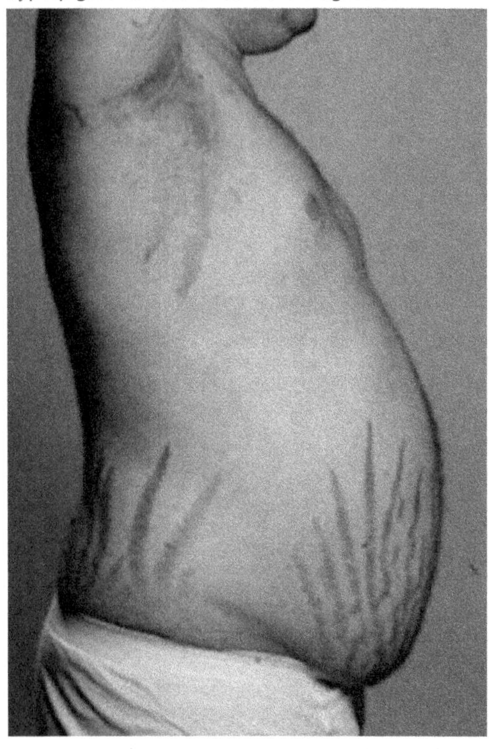

A. Acromegaly **B.** Graves' disease
C. Hyperprolactinemia **D.** Cushing's disease

Q.110 Imbert-Fick law is used in

A. Slit lamp examination
B. Pachymetry
C. Indirect ophthalmoscopy
D. Applanation tonometry

Q.111 The key function of component indicated by arrow in the given diagram of thin filament of skeletal muscle includes

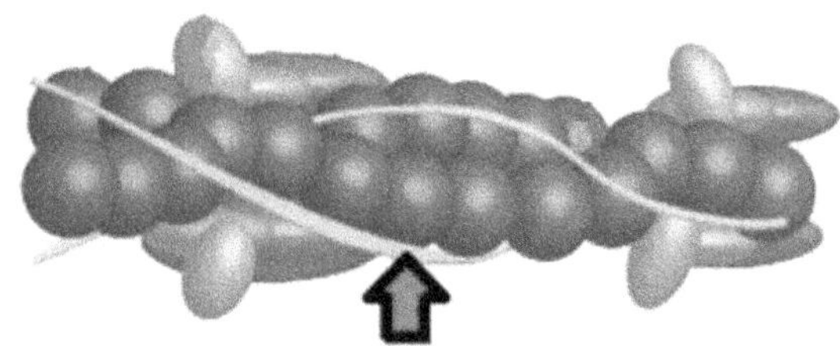

A. Sliding on actin to produce shortening
B. Releasing Ca^{2+} after initiation of contraction
C. Binding to myosin during contraction
D. Acting as a "relaxing protein" at rest by covering up the sites where myosin binds to actin

Q.112 Best test for diagnosis of Organic Mental Disorders :

A. Sentence completion test
B. Bender Gestalt test
C. Rorshach test
D. Thematic Appreciation test

Q.113 Which bacteria act by mechanism of cAMP activation?

A. V. cholerae **B.** B. Cereus
C. B. fragils **D.** Cl. Difficile

Q.114 Which of the following is used to treat digitalis induced ventricular arrhythmia:

A. Phenytoin **B.** Propranolol
C. Quinidine **D.** Diltiazem

Q.115 Which one of the following compound acts as strong inducer but do not act as substrate of β-galactosidase in Escherichia coli :

A. Allolactose
B. Isopropylthiogalactoside (IPTG)
C. Lactose
D. Glucose

Q.116 Shine Dalgarno sequence in prokaryotes is related to

A. Replication **B.** Translation
C. Translocation **D.** Transcription

Q.117 Which of the following diuretic is most likely to cause diabetes mellitus?

A. Acetazolamide **B.** Amiloride
C. Chlorothiazide **D.** Spironolactone

Q.118 What kind of chest radiograph findings might be seen with cyanoacrylate/lipiodol pulmonary embolization ?

A. Prominent pulmonary vasculature that seem to be outlined with a hyperdense coating (vascular cast sign).
B. A very deep costophrenic angle on one side of the chest (deep sulcus sign).
C. A white line at the apex of a lung.
D. More prominent pulmonary vessels in the upper lung zones than in the lower lung zones (cephalization).

Q.119 Aripiprazole an atypical antipsychotic drug, useful in treatment of schizophrenia, is a

A. D2 receptor antagonist
B. D2 receptor partial agonist
C. D2 receptor agonist
D. D2 receptor inverse agonist

Q.120 Rebound phenomenon in the cerebellar lesion occurs because of

A. Exaggerated inverse stretch reflex
B. Loss of cerebellar component of the stretch reflex
C. Loss of the reciprocal inhibition
D. None of the above

Q.121 AFP is a marker of

A. Seminoma
B. Hepatoblastoma
C. Sertoli-Leydig cell tumor

D. Choriocarcinoma

Q.122 An obese and playful 18 month old toddler presents with pallor. He drinks around 2 liters of milk per day. Which laboratory test would most likely reveal the diagnosis?

A. Chest x-ray
B. Examination of stool for ova and parasites
C. Complete blood count
D. Serum haptoglobin

Q.123 Which of the following histologic features would most likely be present in the biopsy specimen of medullary carcinoma of the thyroid?

A. Tumor cells embedded in an amyloid-laden stroma
B. Psammoma bodies
C. Tumor cells with "Orphan Annie" nuclei
D. Infiltrates of lymphocytes with germinal center formation

Q.124 A 74-year-old woman complains of vomiting and intermittent colicky abdominal pain. X rays reveal fluid levels and air in the biliary tree. What is the likely cause?

A. Abdominal adhesions
B. Gallstone ileus
C. Carcinoma of the right colon
D. Abdominal lymphosarcoma

Q.125 Such a presentation is most commonly seen in:

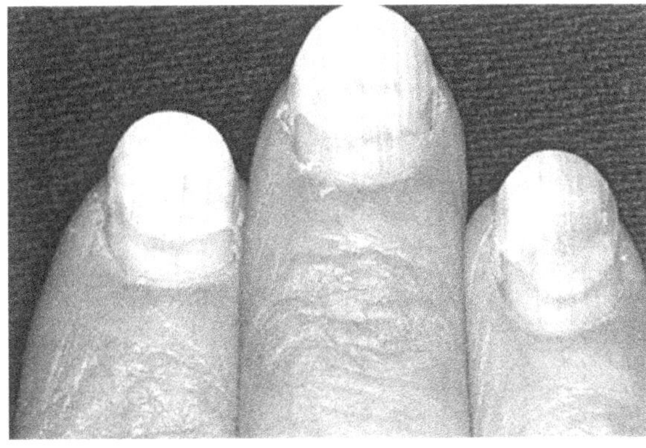

A. Lichen planus
B. Psoriasis
C. Pemphigus valgaris
D. Arsenic poisoning

Q.126 Which of the following actions most likely mediates the positive inotropic action of dobutamine?

A. Inhibition of phosphodiesterase
B. Protein kinase-mediated increase in cytoplasmic Ca^{2+} availability
C. Inhibition of the Ca^{2+}/Na^+ exchanger in cardiac cell membrane
D. Activation of phospholipase A2

Q.127 The risk factors for stroke in a patient with atrial fibrillation include all except :

A. Mitral stenosis
B. Age more than 75 years
C. Spontaneous echo contrast
D. Right ventricular dysfunction

Q.128 A 65-year-old man presents with a tender lump over his right popliteal fossa and severe pain in his leg for 2 days. The lump, which was there a couple of years, has become extremely tender over the last couple of days, the leg has become cold and he is unable to walk. Which of the following is most likely diagnosis?

A. Abdominal aortic aneurysm
B. Internal carotid artery (ICA) stenosis
C. Popliteal artery aneurysm
D. Abdominal compartment syndrome

Q.129 Which one of the following is false regarding Isosorbide mononitrate

A. It does not undergo significant first pass metabolism
B. It has excellent bioavailablity after oral administration
C. It is short acting with half-life of 1-3 min
D. It is one of the active metabolites of Isosorbide dinitrate

Q.130 What is the most common cause of a unilateral neck mass in patients older than 40 years?

A. Reactive lymphadenopathy
B. Hodkin's disease
C. Squamous cell carcinoma
D. Salivary gland infection

Q.131 An elderly patient receiving a blood transfusion develops tachypnea, lumbar pain, tachycardia, and nausea. Which of the following is the most likely explanation?

A. Acute leukemia
B. Fluid overload
C. Hemolysis
D. Pulmonary embolism

Q.132 Riedel's thyroiditis is clinically associated with all, except :

A. Intense fibrosis of thyroid with induration of the surrounding structure occurs
B. Associates with mediastinal and retroperitoneal fibrosis
C. It has to be differentiated from thyroid malignancy
D. Audible bruit present

Q.133 "Lymes Disease"- all are true except

A. Borellia bourgdorferi replicates locally and invades locally
B. Infection progress inspite of good humoral immunity
C. Polymorphonuclear lymphocytosis in CSF suggest meningeal involvement
D. Ig A intrathecally confirms meningitis

Q.134 Most common cause of delayed puberty is :

A. Kallman's syndrome
B. Gonadal dysgenesis
C. Hypothalamic tumor
D. Constitutional

Q.135 Double vision while walking downstairs is seen with lesion of

A. Abducens nerve
B. Occulomotor nerve
C. Trochlear nerve

D. Medial longitudinal Fasciculus

Q.136 Postterm pregnancy is associated with all the following except

A. Transient tachypnea of the newborn
B. Oligohydramnios
C. Meconium aspiration
D. Intrauterine fetal demise

Q.137 A reduction in carotid sinus pressure would cause a decrease in which of the following?

A. Heart rate
B. Myocardial contractility
C. Total peripheral resistance
D. Venous Compliance

Q.138 A woman is found to have a unilateral invasive carcinoma of vulva that is 2 cm in diameter but not associated with evidence of lymph node spread. Initial management should consists of

A. Chemotherapy
B. Radiation therapy
C. Radical vulvectomy
D. Radical vulvectomy and bilateral inguinal lymphadenectomy

Q.139 Shift of medial temporal lobe medially towards tentorial hiatus is referred to as :

A. Sub falcine herniation
B. Uncal herniation
C. Tentorial herniation
D. None of the above

Q.140 Lanugo hair starts forming in which month of intrauterine life?

A. 3 **B.** 4 **C.** 5 **D.** 6

Q.141 Which one of the following test is used to detect malingering?

A. Stenger's test **B.** Bunge's test
C. Weber's test **D.** Rinne's test

Q.142 Which of the following is not a branch of Artery 'A' shown in the Figure?

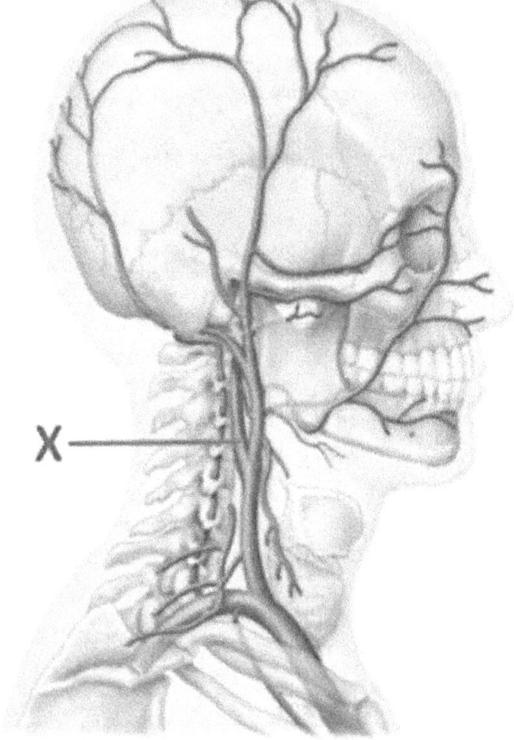

A. Posterior Communicating
B. Posterior Choroidal
C. Anterior Cerebral
D. Anterior Choroidal

Q.143 A 67-year-old man recently diagnosed with benign prostatic hyperplasia was scheduled for surgery. Which of the following drug classes would be absolutely contraindicated in this patient?

A. Alpha-1 blockers **B.** Antimuscarinics
C. Beta blockers **D.** Alpha-2 agonists

Q.144 Utero-placental blood flow at term in pregnancy is

A. 50 - 75 ml/min **B.** 150 - 200 ml/min
C. 350 - 400 ml/min **D.** 500 - 700 ml/min

Q.145 A 68-year-old man with a history of a previous myocardial infarction presents complaining of a painful lesion noted on his foot. He has been experiencing pain in his lower legs with ambulation over the last year. The most likely diagnosis is?

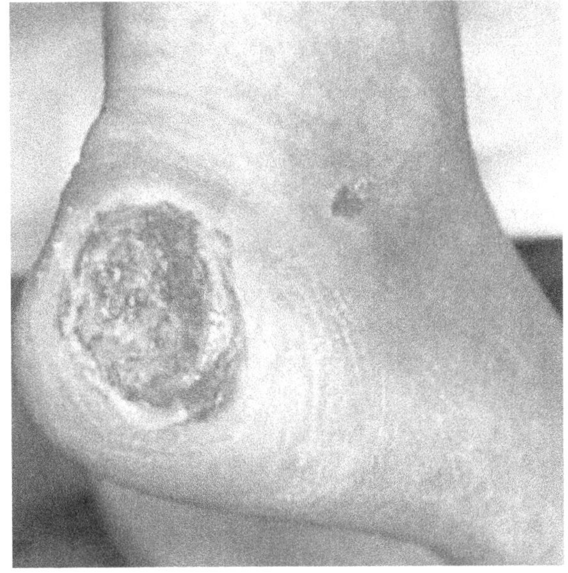

A. Venous stasis ulcer

B. Arterial ulcer

C. Basal cell carcinoma

D. Livedo reticularis

Q.146 During the delivery, it is necessary to do an episiotomy. The tear extends through sphincter of the rectum, but the rectal mucosa is intact. How would you classify this type of episiotomy ?

A. First- degree

B. Second-degree

C. Third-degree

D. Fourth-degree

Q.147 Auricular branch of vagus passes through

A. Mental foramen

B. Pterygoid canal

C. Zygomatic foramen

D. Mastoid canaliculi

Q.148 A patient presents with acute respiratory distress, stridor and inability to speak. Likely diagnosis is:

A. Asthma

B. Aspiration pneumonia

C. Foreign body aspiration

D. Pleural effusion

Q.149 Acrodermatitis enteropathica is:

A. Inherited disorder of excessive excretion of zinc from body

B. Inherited disorder of impaired uptake of zinc from body

C. Inherited disorder of excessive excretion of copper from body

D. Inherited disorder of impaired uptake of copper from body

Q.150 Which is known as Fifth disease:

A. Erythema infectiosum

B. Rubeolla infantum

C. Dukes disease

D. Measles

Part C

Q.151 Rising sun sign is seen in:

A. Glomus jugulare tumour

B. Low jugular bulb

C. Otosclerosis

D. Acoustic neuroma

Q.152 In a patient, serologic test results show HBsAg & anti-HBc as positive and IgM anti-HBc & anti-HBs as negative. What is the correct interpretation?

A. Acutely infected

B. Chronically infected

C. Susceptible

D. Interpretation unclear

Q.153 What is the mechanism of action of Botulinum toxin?

A. It blocks release of acetylcholine.

B. It inhibits glycine and GABA.

C. It is a lecithinase.

D. It is a superantigen.

Q.154 Which of the following malignancies is associated with the skin condition shown here?

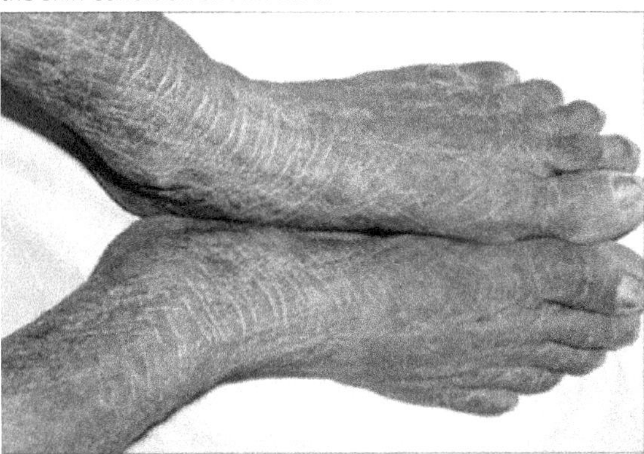

A. Diabetes

B. Gastric carcinoma

C. Malignant melanoma

D. Addison's disease

Q.155 The most common predisposing factor for placenta accrete among the following is

A. Tubal surgery

B. Recent curettage

C. Previous cesarean section

D. Placenta previa

Q.156 Which of the following roentgenographic findings is most commonly seen in infants with bronchiolitis caused by RSV?

A. Hyperinflation

B. Hilar adenopathy

C. Multilobar infiltrate

D. Pleural effusion

Q.157 Absent urobilinogen in urine with icterus indicates

A. Liver failure

B. Peri-hepatic obstruction

C. Hemolysis

D. Hepatitis

Q.158 Penetrating injury to NECK is defined as

A. More than 2 cm deep injury

B. Injury to any internal neck organ

C. Violation of platysma

D. Sharp instrument

Q.159 On T1-weighted and T2-weighted MRI, what are the signal characteristics of subacute hemorrhage?

A. Hypointense on T1-weighted and hypointense on T2-weighted images

B. Hyperintense on T1-weighted and hypointense on T2-weighted images

C. Hyperintense on T1-weighted and hyperintense on T2-weighted images

D. Hypointense on T1-weighted and hyperintense on T2-weighted images

Q.160 A 5 year old child presents with coarse facial features, hepatosplenomegaly & progressive loss of developmental milestones. Most likely cause is

A. Mucopolysacharidosis

B. Aminoaciduria

C. Urea cycle deficiency

D. Urea cycle enzyme deficiency

Q.161 Intracyctoplasmic inclusion bodies are pathognomonic of

A. Measles

B. Adenovirus

C. Poliovirus

D. Rabies

Q.162 Serum marker indicating active viral replication in hepatitis-B is :

A. HBsAg

B. HBeAg

C. HBcAg

D. Anti-HBs

Q.163 A 25-year-old man develops abrupt onset of hematuria and proteinuria, accompanied by azotemia and salt and water retention. Most likely diagnosis is

A. Nephrotic syndrome

B. Diabetic nephropathy

C. Nephrolithiasis

D. Acute glomerulonephritis

Q.164 Which of the following is the peritoneal ligament containing splenic vessels at the hilum of the spleen?

A. Hepatoduodenal ligament

B. Coronary ligament

C. Lienorenal ligament

D. Gastrolienal ligament

Q.165 A 44-year-old woman presents with a 3-cm breast mass of 4-month duration. On examination, mammography shows microcalcification and features are suggestive of malignancy. The diagnosis is confirmed by?

A. Needle biopsy

B. Open biopsy from the edge

C. Lymph node biopsy

D. Thermography

Q.166 Which of the following agents has good analgesic and sedative properties but does not cause skeletal muscle relaxation?

A. Enflurane

B. Nitrous oxide

C. Thiopental

D. Halothane

Q.167 Which of the following is the most likely cause of chronic granulomatous disease in a 7-year-old boy?

A. Defect in the enzyme NADPH oxidase

B. Defect in the enzyme adenosine deaminase (ADA)

C. Defect in the IL-2 receptor

D. Developmental failure of pharyngeal pouches 3 and 4

Q.168 Which of the following statements about venlafaxine is true?

A. It is a potent inhibitor of dopamine reuptake

B. It has been demonstrated to have the same percentage of response and completeness of response as fluoxetine in severely depressed individuals

C. It can be tapered during 1 to 2 weeks

D. It is approved for the treatment of generalized anxiety disorder

Q.169 Calcification is best detected by :

A. X - ray   **B.** USG   **C.** CT Scan   **D.** MRI

Q.170 Which of the following would you expect to find in a patient whose diet has been low in calcium for 2 months?

A. Increased formation of 24, 25-dihydroxycholecalciferol

B. Decreased amounts of calcium-binding protein in intestinal epithelial cells

C. Increased parathyroid hormone secretion

D. A high plasma calcitonin concentration

Q.171 An 8-month-old female presents with failure to thrive, constipation, fevers, and polydipsia. On evaluation, you find hypokalemia and hyperchloremic metabolic acidosis and suspect Fanconi syndrome. Which of the following would be the most likely inherited cause ?

A. Cystinosis

B. Cystic fibrosis

C. Glycogen storage disease

D. Tyrosinemia

Q.172 True regarding Marshall-Marchetti-Krantz procedure (MMK) for stress incontinence is

A. Urinary retention is very common after an MMK procedure and often requires long-term self-catheterization.

B. Patient has a 5% risk of enterocele formation.

C. The MMK procedure is highly effective, with greater than 90% long-term cure rate.

D. Osteitis pubis occurs in approximately 10% of patients after an MMK, but is easily treated with oral antibiotics.

Q.173 Gamma hemolytic gram positive cocci in chains grown in an ICU patient should be tested for sensitivity to

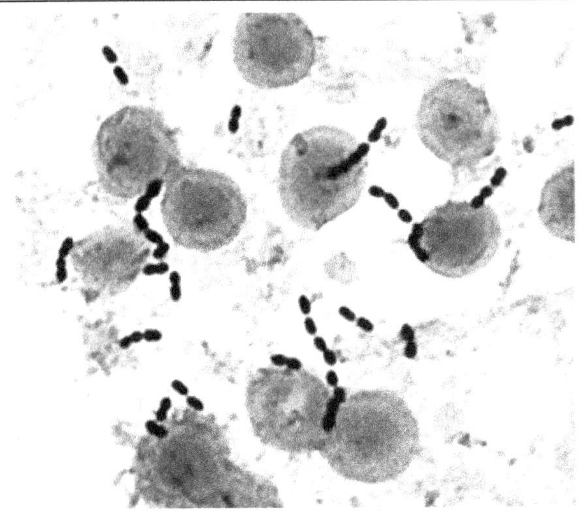

A. Cefepime
B. Vancomycin
C. Tigycycline
D. Imepenem

Q.174 A 4-year-old boy has a history of wheezing with colds, but presently suffering from persistent cough and is being given an albuterol MDI with some relief. He has symptoms at least one night out of the week and almost every day. What is the most appropriate medication regimen for this patient?

A. Over-the-counter cough medication
B. Albuterol twice daily
C. Inhaled corticosteroid twice daily plus albuterol as needed
D. Daily systemic corticosteroids

Q.175 All of the following are diagnostic features of neuroleptic malignant syndrome (NMS) EXCEPT:

A. Diaphoresis
B. Tachypnea
C. Mutism
D. Tachycardia

Q.176 Action which halts the progress of a disease at its incipient stage and prevents complications:

A. Primary prevention
B. Primordial prevention
C. Secondary prevention
D. Tertiary prevention

Q.177 Consent is required for:

A. Mass immunization
B. Medico-legal autopsy
C. Pathological autopsy
D. Treatment of unconscious patient

Q.178 All the following clostridia are predominantly saccharolytic except:

A. Clostridia septicum
B. Clostridia perfringens
C. Clostridia sporogenes
D. Clostridia acetobutylicum

Q.179 Which of the following is true for SIADH:

A. Hyponatremia with increased plasma osmolality
B. Hypernatremia with decreased plasma osmolality
C. Hyponatremia with decreased plasma osmolality
D. Hypernatremia with increased plasma osmolality

Q.180 Confirmatory diagnosis of rabies on postmortem:

A. Negri bodies in saliva
B. Negri bodies in corneal scrapings
C. Anti-rabies antibodies in blood
D. Negri bodies in brain

Q.181 Out of the following important events, which does not take place at the level of sixth cervical vertebra?

A. At this level lies the junction of larynx and trachea
B. The cricoid cartilage is located here
C. The common carotid artery bifurcates into external and internal carotid arteries
D. The junction of pharynx and esophagus lies at this level

Q.182 Which of the following is true regarding the diagnosis of Tourette disorder?

A. Motor and vocal tics must occur concurrently
B. Onset must be before the age of 21
C. Tics must be present every day consecutively for at least 1 year
D. Multiple motor tics must occur

Q.183 After being severely reprimanded by his employer, a man goes home and is extremely nasty to his wife. What is his behavior an example of?

A. Displacement
B. Dissociation
C. Rationalization
D. Conversion

Q.184 The weight of an adult eyeball is

A. 10 gms
B. 15 gms
C. 5 gms
D. 7 gms

Q.185 The eggs seen in the image are of

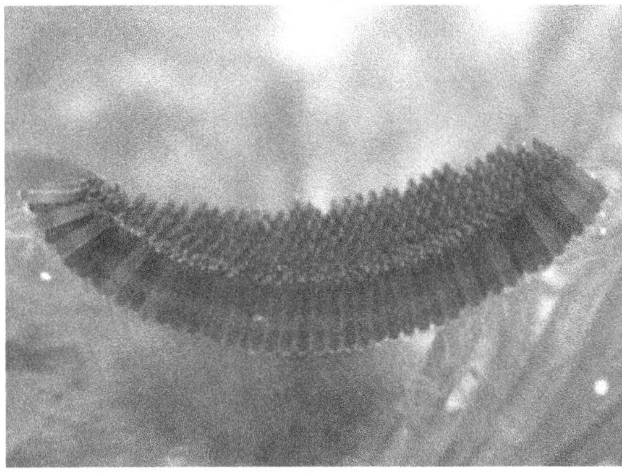

A. Culex
B. Aedes
C. Anopheles
D. Mansonia

Q.186 Xanthogranulomatous pyelonephritis shows the following features except :

A. Accumulation of fatty macrophages
B. Yellow nodules in kidney
C. Association with tuberculosis
D. Presence of plasma cells

Q.187 A 33-year-old man with coeliac disease presents with a blistering rash over the elbows and scalp. The most appropriate treatment is:

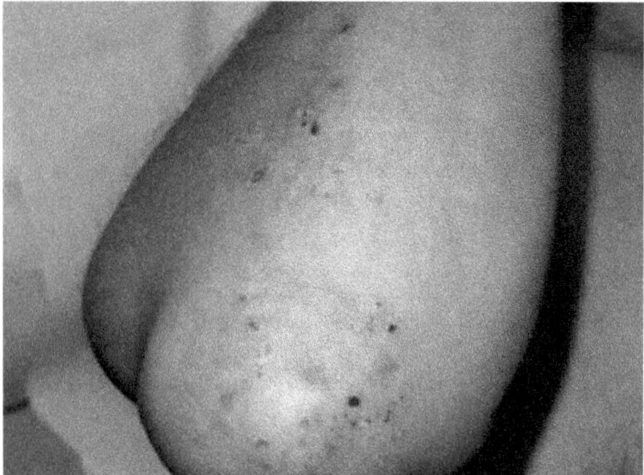

A. Oral prednisolone   **B.** Dapsone
C. NSAIDs   **D.** Aciclovir

Q.188 Raghu, a 5 year old child, came with scalds of approximately 10% TBSA. He is a known case of juvenile diabetes and has associated inhalation injury. Which of these is not a risk factor for susciptibility to systemic infections -

A. Age (age of children greater than adults)
B. Total burn surface area-TBSA
C. Premorbid diabetes mellitus
D. Inhalation injury

Q.189 Corneal scrapings were taken from a 67 yr old farmer presenting with a corneal ulcer of the right eye. A piece of vegetable matter was embedded in the cornea and scrapings were done. Gram stain (500x magnification) showed numerous narrow angled septate hyphae (figure). Which of the following is the likely etiologic agent?

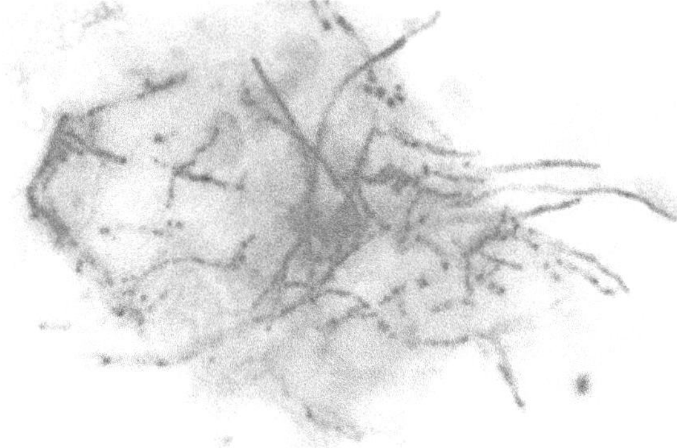

A. Candida   **B.** Aspergillus
C. Mucor   **D.** Histoplasma

Q.190 A 60-year-old woman experiences mild intermittent right hip pain after falling down a flight of stairs. A radiograph shows calcified, medium-sized arterial branches in the pelvis but no fractures. This radiographic finding most likely represents

A. An incidental observation
B. Benign essential hypertension
C. Long-standing diabetes mellitus

D. Unsuspected hyperparathyroidism

Q.191 Clostridia are implicated in the following except:

A. Botulism
B. Necrotising enterocolitis
C. Bacillary dysentery
D. Pseudomembranous colitis

Q.192 A 47-year-old woman develops headache and double vision. One of her midline sagittal MRIs is shown in figure. On examination, she may have all of the following except:

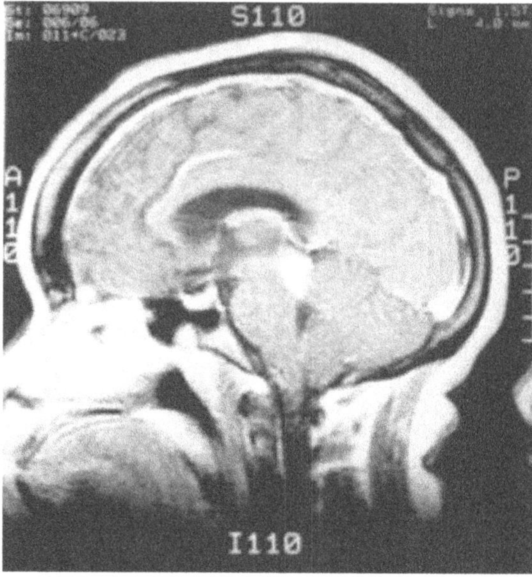

A. Sixth nerve palsy
B. Skew deviation
C. Lid retraction
D. Pupils that react well to a near stimulus but not to light

Q.193 What is the definition of premature ovarian failure?

A. Cessation of menstrual cycles occurring prior to 35 years
B. The start of irregular menstrual cycles at age 38
C. Cessation of menstrual periods prior to age 40
D. The start of irregular menstrual cycles at age 42

Q.194 Regarding investigations in hypospadias all are true except -

A. Urethroscopy and cystoscopy are of value to detect whether internal male sexual organs are developed normally or not
B. Buccal smear and karyotyping to establish genetic sex in penoscrotal and perineal hypospadias
C. Excretory urography to detect additional congenital abnormalities of kidney and ureter
D. Buccal smear and karyotyping to establish genetic sex in glanular hypospadias

Q.195 An 11 year old boy presents with mass in the abdomen and ascites. On imaging the para-aortic lymph nodes are enlarged. On biopsy starry sky appearance (figure) is seen. What is the underlying abnormality?

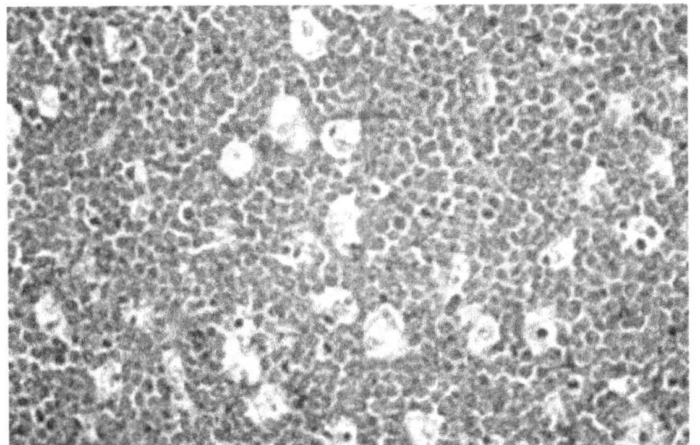

A. P53 gene mutation

B. RB gene mutation

C. Translocation involving BCR-ABL genes

D. Translocation involving MYC-gene

Q.196 The type of mutation shown in the image is known as

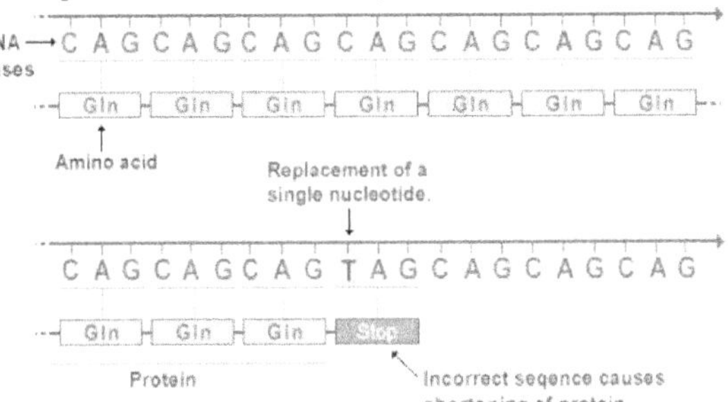

A. Nonsense mutation

B. Missense mutation

C. Frameshift mutation

D. Insertion

Q.197 On the basis of following findings, what is the diagnosis in a 2-year-old with seizures and left hemiparesis?

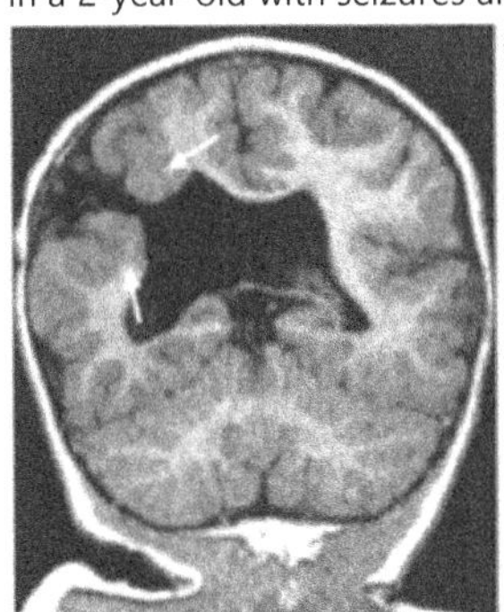 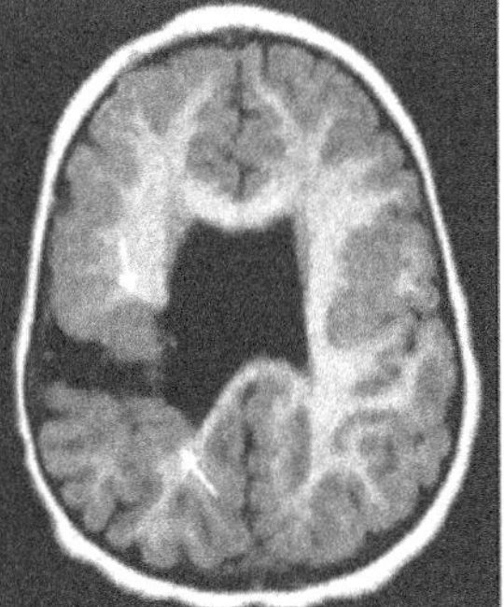

A. Subdural haemorrhage

B. Arnold-Chiari malformation

C. Schizencephaly

D. Lissencephaly

Q.198 False regarding von-Willebrand disease:

A. Normal prothrombin time

B. Normal bleeding time

C. Normal platelet count

D. Normal or slightly increased Partial thromboplastin time

Q.199 Following a right pneumonectomy, the postoperative recovery of a patient is complicated by bronchopleural fistula, which presents with pyrexia, expectoration of large amounts of purulent sputum and a high fluid level on chest radiograph. In addition to positioning the patient to lie on the operated side, what procedure is urgently required?

A. Bronchoscopy

B. Chest drain insertion

C. CT scan of the chest

D. Pulmonary function tests

Q.200 Which of the following is an early sign of prolonged grief?

A. Clinging behavior

B. Self-blame regarding the death

C. Brief hallucinations

D. Anxiety when reminded of loss

Q.201 Untrue about CVP monitoring -

A. Seldinger technique is utilized for cannulation

B. Tip of catheter should be in right atrium

C. Normal is 3 - 10 cm H_2O

D. During catheterization, direction of needle should be towards ipsilateral nipple.

Q.202 The test shown in the image is done for

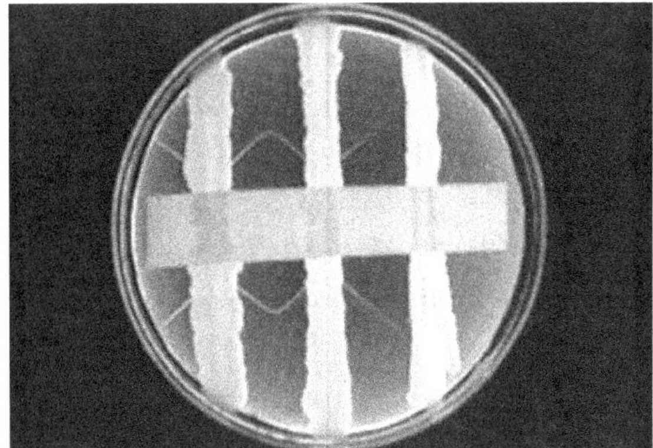

A. Cholera

B. Diptheria

C. Influenza

D. Brucellosis

Q.203 The smear of a patient's peripheral blood is shown in the image. Which of the following substances is most likely to be deficient in this individual?

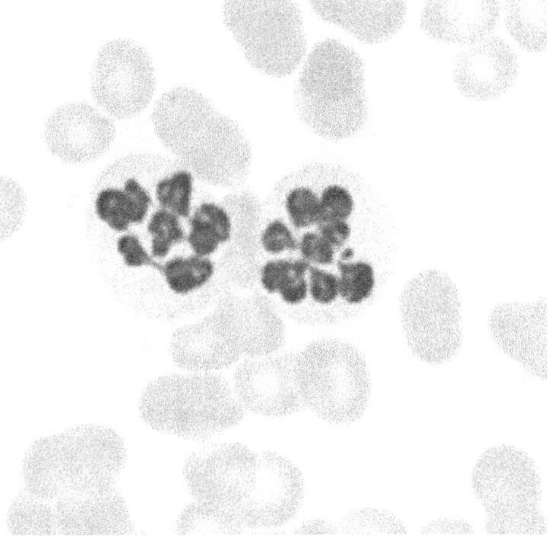

A. Ascorbic acid

B. Folic acid

C. Retinoic acid

D. Vanillylmandelic acid

Q.204 In comparing the secondary structure of proteins, which of the following descriptions applies to both the α-helix and the β-pleated sheet?

A. All peptide bond components participate in hydrogen bonding.

B. N-terminals of chains are together and parallel.

C. The structure is composed of two or more segments of polypeptide chain.

D. N- and C-terminal ends of chains alternate in an antiparallel manner.

Q.205 A patient presenting for evaluation of deafness is found to also have an elevated plasma renin, although his blood pressure is 118/75 mm Hg. Mutation of which of the following single gene would be likely to explain these findings?

A. The gene for barttin

B. The gene for Na+ channel

C. The gene for renin

D. The gene for tyrosine hydroxylase

Q.206 All of the following statements regarding keratoacanthoma are true, except:

A. It is histologically similar to a squamous cell carcinoma.

B. It might resolve spontaneously about subsequent 6 months.

C. It is a form of slowly growing solitary tumour.

D. It might be associated with visceral malignant tumours.

Q.207 The demyelinating disease multiple sclerosis is characterized by a loss of which lipids?

A. Phospholipids and ceramide

B. Sphingolipids and ceramide

C. Sphingolipids and gangliosides

D. Phospholipids and sphingolipids

Q.208 Which of the following pulmonary function tests may correspond to Idiopathic pulmonary fibrosis

A. Increased total lung capacity (TLC), decreased vital capacity (VC), decreased FEV1/FVC ratio

B. Decreased TLC, decreased VC, decreased residual volume (RV), increased FEV1/FVC ratio, normal

C. maximum inspiratory pressure (MIP)

D. Decreased TLC, increased RV, normal FEV1/FVC ratio, decreased MIP

Q.209 In ethylene glycol poisoning, ethanol is used as it is

A. Competitive inhibitor of NADPH oxidase

B. Competitive inhibitor of aldehyde dehydrogenase

C. Non-competitive inhibitor of aldehyde dehydrogenase

D. Competitive inhibitor of alcohol dehydrogenase

Q.210 Gangrene of intestine is seen in all the following conditions, except :

A. Tricuspid valve endocarditis

B. Shock

C. Mesenteric artery thrombosis

D. Volvulus

Q.211 Which of the following is the induction agent of choice in renal patients:

A. Vecuronium   **B.** Atracurium

C. Pancuronium   **D.** Rapacuronium

Q.212 Enzyme responsible for respiratory burst reaction is -

A. Peroxidase   **B.** Hydroxylase

C. NADPH - Oxidase   **D.** Dehydragenase

Q.213 Disease eradicated from world:

A. Small pox   **B.** Guineworm

C. Polio   **D.** Diphtheria

Q.214 Which of the following statements regarding cardiac imaging is correct?

A. Sestamibi imaging can be readily used to identify hibernating myocardium

B. Thallium cannot be readily used to identify hibernating myocardium

C. Dipyridamole stress testing is safe in patients with chronic obstructive pulmonary disease (COPD)

D. The effects of dipyridamole can be reversed with intravenous theophylline

Q.215 An elderly woman presented with a 3-month history of non-healing ulceration on the dorsal hand (image) that had not responded to antibiotics. Her past medical history includes rheumatoid arthritis. What is the diagnosis?

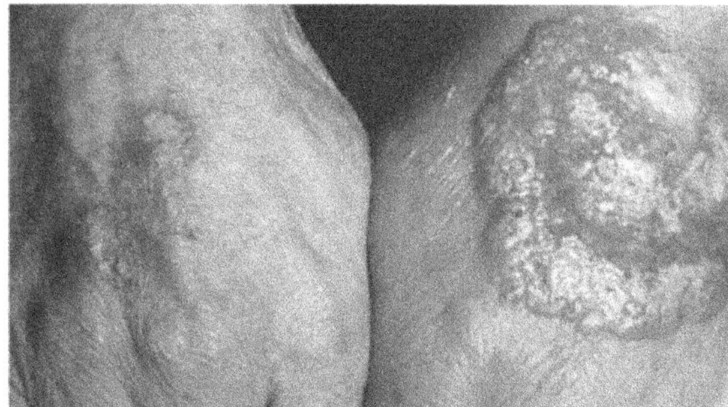

A. Rheumatoid vasculitis

B. Pyoderma gangrenosum

C. Squamous cell carcinoma

D. Keratoacanthoma

Q.216 Bacterial antibiotic resistance is frequently conveyed by

A. A temperate bacteriophage

B. An R-factor plasmid

C. A replicon

D. A lytic bacteriophage

Q.217 A 25-year-old homeless man presents to your office with reports of decreased vision and pain in his right eye for the past 2 days. Examination reveals marked conjunctival injection, a 2-mm hypopyon, and dense vitreous opacities on B-scan ultrasound. You suspect endogenous endophthalmitis, and on further questioning, the patient admits to IV drug abuse. Given the patient's history, which one of the following organisms is the least likely to be involved in this patient's endophthalmitis?

A. C. albicans

B. Staphylococcus species

C. Bacillus cereus

D. Haemophilus influenzae

Q.218 ECG findings of Ostium Secundum atrial septal defect includes all EXCEPT :

A. Left axis deviation

B. rSR′ pattern

C. Right ventricle hypertrophy

D. Right atrial hypertrophy

Q.219 Which of the following investigational research procedures can distinguish most clearly whether an isolated 1-cm pedunculated polyp in the sigmoid colon represents hyperplasia of the colonic mucosa or a tubular adenoma?

A. Flow cytometry to quantitate cells in the S phase

B. Histochemical staining for mucin

C. Immunohistochemical staining for keratin

D. Molecular marker of clonality

Q.220 In an outbreak of cholera in a village of 2000 population 20 cases have occurred and 5 have died. Case fatality rate is:

A. 1% **B.** 0.25% **C.** 5% **D.** 25%

Q.221 In sleep apnea syndrome, select the most likely sleep disturbance -

A. Most common cause of excessive daytime sleepiness in the elderly

B. Increased arousals during the night

C. Breakdown of normal temporal organization of sleep-wake cycling

D. Increased slow-wave sleep

Q.222 Montenegro test is done in:

A. Tetanus **B.** Trachoma

C. Kala azar **D.** AIDS

Q.223 A 35 year old woman develops hirsutism, deepening of voice and clitorimegaly. A pelvic examination reveals a left ovarian mass. Assuming appropriate diagnostic and staging tests are performed, given this clinical presentation, if the patient requires chemotherapy she should be treated in a fashion analogous to the management of

A. Epithelial ovarian cancer

B. Lymphoma

C. Soft tissue sarcoma

D. Testicular cancer

Q.224 90 percent sensitivity indicates :

A. 90 percent diseased people will give true positive results

B. Detection of positivity cases not in disease

C. It identify correctly those who have not in disease

D. None of the above

Q.225 A 75-year-old man was admitted to the hospital for hip replacement. Which of the following antibiotics would be an appropriate prophylactic agent to be given before surgery?

A. Metronidazole **B.** Tetracycline

C. Aztreonam **D.** Cefazolin

Q.226 False statement regarding conduct money

A. It is paid in civil cases

B. It is not paid in criminal cases

C. It is paid in both civil & criminal cases

D. None of the above

Q.227 Leishmania recidivans is seen in infection with:

A. L donovani **B.** L tropica

C. L braziliensis **D.** L mexicana

Q.228 Herniation of brain tissue with its dural covering into the nasal cavity is called as:

A. Glioma

B. Neurofibroma

C. Encephalocele

D. Olfactory neuroblastoma

Q.229 In a patient of colon cancer, recurrent perirectal masses compress the pelvic splanchnic nerves. This could affect the organs supplied by which of the following arteries?

A. Right colic artery **B.** Left colic artery

C. Renal arteries **D.** Lumbar arteries

Q.230 Conjugated hyperbilirubinemia is seen in

A. Criggler Najjar Syndrome-I

B. Criggler Najjar Syndrome-II

C. Gilbert syndrome

D. Dubin Johnson syndrome

Q.231 A 13-year-old boy is brought to the hospital by his mother after experiencing fever, malaise, and anorexia followed by tender swelling of his parotid glands. Which of the following is the most likely complication to occur in this patient?

A. Myocarditis

B. Orchitis

C. Oophoritis

D. Guillain-Barré syndrome

Q.232 A large retained stone impacted in the distal common bile duct is noted when T-tube cholangiography is performed after choledochostomy. The best management of the stone is :

A. Dissolution with sodium cholate

B. Dissolution with heparin

C. Catheter extraction via the tract of the T-tube

D. Transduodenal papillotomy with endoscopic stone extraction

Q.233 The drug of choice for hypoplastic left heart syndrome is

A. Digoxin **B.** Prostaglandin E1

C. Milrinone **D.** Nicardipine

Q.234 The following are imaging features of Renal lymphangiectasia :

A. Renal sinus and perinephric complex cysts seen

B. Kidneys show accentuation of cortico-medullary differentiation

C. Kidneys are usually small

D. Cysts are fluid density on CT scan

Q.235 A 19 year old patient develops intussusception. He was operated and a segment of intestine showing multiple polyps was resected. On the basis of following pathological images, what is the likely diagnosis?

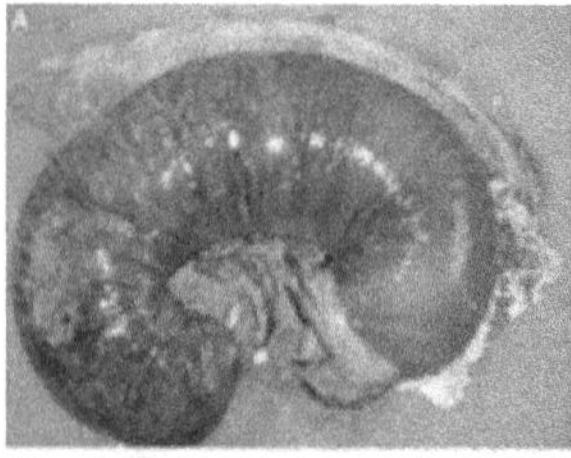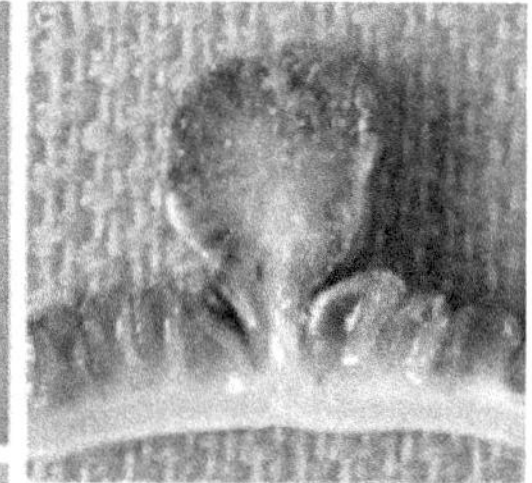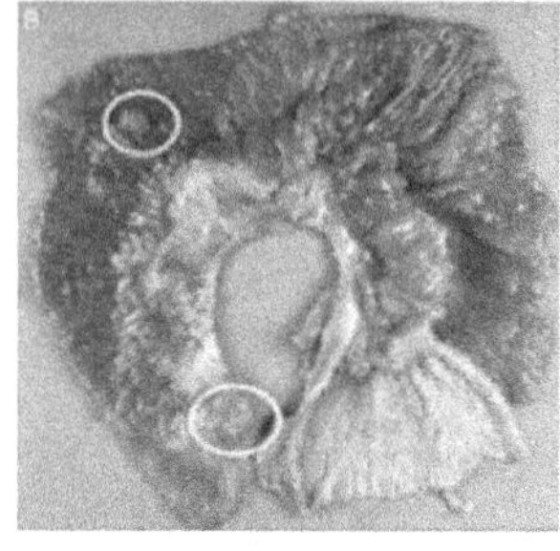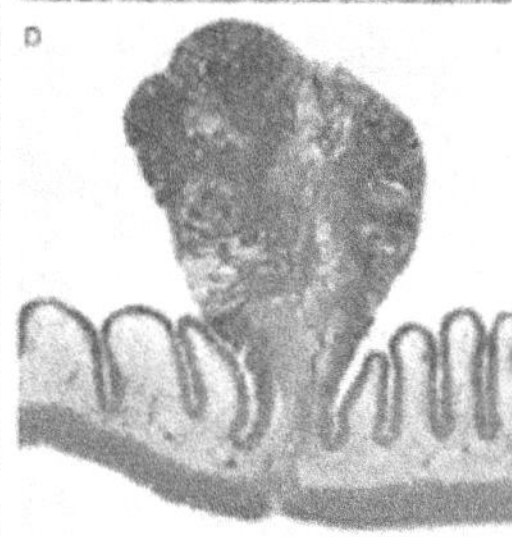

A. Adenocarcinoma
B. Tubulovilluus polyps
C. Hamartomatous polyps
D. Inflammatory polyps

Q.236 A 33-year-old woman, otherwise perfectly well, presents with recurrent episodes of hemoptysis, cough and infection. Her physical examination and lab tests are entirely normal. Which of the following is the most appropriate initial diagnostic test?

A. Gallium scan
B. CT scan of chest
C. Bronchoscopy
D. Pulmonary function tests

Q.237 During intubation of newborn to insert endotracheal tube the blade of laryngoscope is :
A. Curved blade with uncuffed tube
B. Straight blade with Cuffed tube
C. Straight blade with Uncuffed tube
D. Curved blade with cuffed tube

Q.238 Therapeutic gamma irradiation is given to a 50-year-old woman for treatment of a breast carcinoma. The treatments occur over 6 weeks. The neoplasm diminishes in size during this time. Which of the following mechanisms of cellular injury is most likely to account for the efficacy of this radiation therapy?

A. Hyperthermia
B. NK cell lysis
C. Free radical formation
D. Vascular thrombosis

Q.239 Pentameric antibody with a J chain is?

A. IgA　　**B.** IgG　　**C.** IgM　　**D.** IgE

Q.240 Main early complication of TIPSS is :-
A. Perforation of liver capsule

B. Hepatic encephalopathy
C. Shunt stenosis
D. None of the above

Q.241 Vidian neurectomy is done in:
A. Vasomotor rhinitis　　**B.** Rhinintis sicca
C. Allergic sinusitis　　**D.** Epistaxis

Q.242 Which of the following conditions is considered an AIDS defining illness?
A. Antibodies to HIV
B. Kaposi sarcoma
C. Oral candidiasis (thrush)
D. Herpes zoster (shingles)

Q.243 Which of the following is the most common presentation of hemophilia A ?
A. Pressure neuropathy　　**B.** Melera
C. Hematuria　　**D.** Hemarthrosis

Q.244 True regarding stratified sampling is
A. It is used for hidden population
B. In this method population under study is first divided into homogeneous groups
C. It is used when units of population are natural groups or clusters
D. In this method sampling procedure is carried out in several stages

Q.245 True about Cryoprecipitate?
A. Is prepared by thawing fresh frozen plasma
B. Is rich in fibrinogen
C. May reverse the platelet defect in uremic patients
D. All of the above

Q.246 Which of the following tests is most sensitive for the diagnosis of a pituitary adenoma?
A. Serum prolactin measurement
B. Visual field examination
C. CT scan with contrast injection
D. MRI with gadolinium injection

Q.247 R. Rickettsii causes:
A. Indian tick typhus
B. Rocky mountain spotted fever
C. Rickettsial pox
D. Trench fever

Q.248 Penicillinase resistant pencillin are all except
A. Dicloxacillin　　**B.** Oxacillin
C. Nafcillin　　**D.** Ampicillin

Q.249 Which of the following morphologic features is most likely to be present in the liver of a 50-year-old man with a history of chronic alcoholism, but has stopped drinking alcohol 10 years ago and has 35% hematocrit?
A. Concentric "onion-skin" bile duct fibrosis
B. Massive hepatocellular necrosis
C. Periportal PAS-positive globule deposition
D. Portal fibrosis with regenerative nodules

Q.250 A 56 year old woman present with hypertension, anxiety and depression was found to have an adrenal mass when being screened for an abdominal aortic aneurysm. Her 9 am cortisol was 565 nmo/L, 24-hour urine cortisol was normal and 24-hour urine catecholamines were elevated. Most Likely diagnosis is

A. Carcinoid syndrome

B. Conn's syndrome

C. Phaeochromocytoma

D. Metastatic liver disease

Q.251 Heart with the characteristic shape shown in the radiograph is found in?

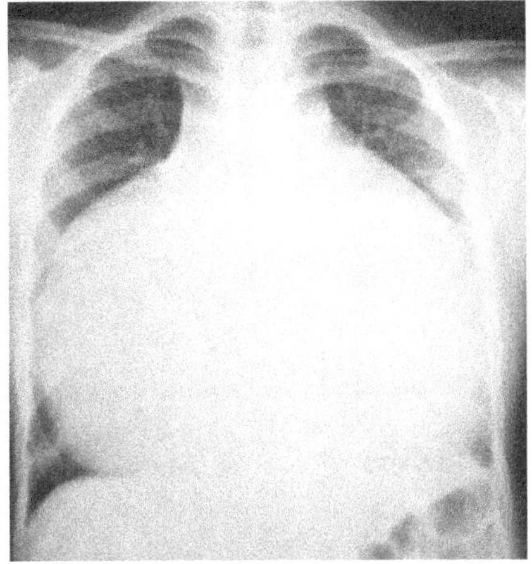

A. Ebstein anomaly   **B.** Truncus arteriosus

C. TOF   **D.** D-TGA

Q.252 Severity of the disease best assessed by:

A. Disease-specific mortality rate

B. Crude death rate

C. Age-specific mortality rate

D. Case fatality rate

Q.253 The method of female sterilization shown in the figure is known as

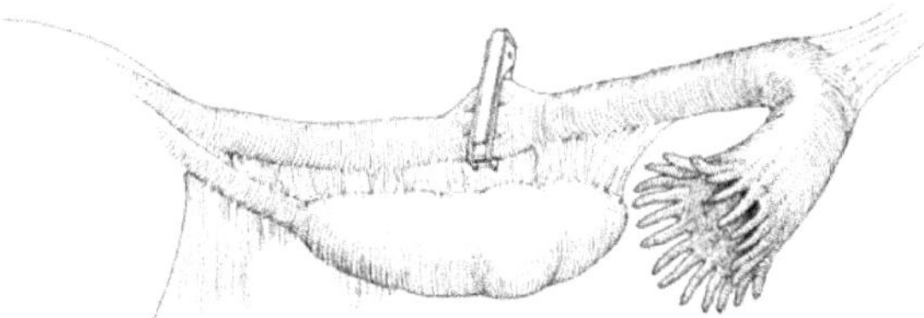

A. Hulka Method   **B.** Pomeroy Technique

C. Parkland Method   **D.** Adiana procedure

Q.254 Osteomalacia can be prevented by the administration of calcium and :

A. Vitamin A   **B.** Vitamin B

C. Vitamin C   **D.** Vitamin D

Q.255 Pandemics are caused by:

A. Hepatitis B   **B.** Influenza - A

C. Influenza - B   **D.** Influenza - C

Q.256 What is the preferred method to diagnose the infection with Chlamydia trachomatis?

A. Nucleic acid amplification

B. Cell culture

C. Cytology (Pap smear)

D. Serology

Q.257 The following sign is least likely to present with which of the following

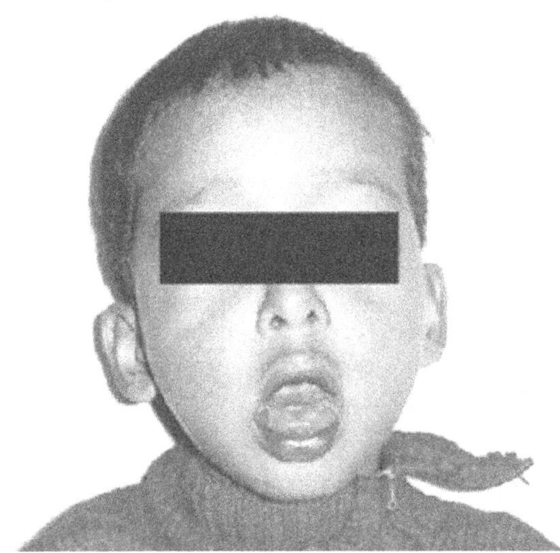

A. Severe anemia with PDA

B. Congenital heart disease

C. Bronchospasm

D. Empysema

Q.258 The commonest site for rheumatoid nodules is :

A. Olecranon process

B. Tendo - Achilles

C. Proximal interphalangeal joints

D. Distal interphalangeal joints

Q.259 What is FALSE about the instrument shown in the image?

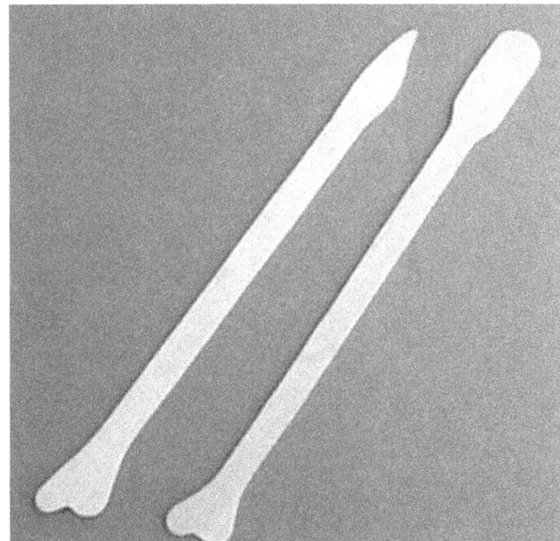

A. Ayre spatula

B. Wooden spatula

C. Long end inserted into cervical canal

D. Primary prevention for cervical cancer

Q.260 Which of the following are incorrectly paired?

A. Lesion of the parietal lobe of the representational hemisphere: unilateral inattention and neglect

B. Lesions of mamillary bodies: loss of recent memory

C. Lesion of the angular gyrus in the categorical hemisphere: nonfluent aphasia

D. Lesion of Broca's area in the categorical hemisphere: slow speech

Q.261 The PO_2 of the arterial blood is

A. 104 mm Hg   **B.** 159 mm Hg

C. 40 mm Hg   **D.** 95 mm Hg

Q.262 All of the following are true for hangman's fracture except?

A. It is a traumatic spondylolisthesis of C2 on C3 as a result of the bilateral fracture of C2 pars or pedicles.

B. The mechanism of injury is a primary hyperflexion of the neck.

C. Type I fracture has an intact C2/C3 disc.

D. A C2/C3 fusion is indicated for a type III fracture.

Q.263 Which of the following is the least likely first clinical presentation of respiratory distress syndrome?

A. Tachypnea   **B.** Cyanosis

C. Wheezing   **D.** Pallor

Q.264 A 36-year-old man receives amoxicillin for presumed bacterial sinusitis. One week later he presents with a diffuse itchy rash. His mucus membranes are normal. Which of the following is the most likely diagnosis?

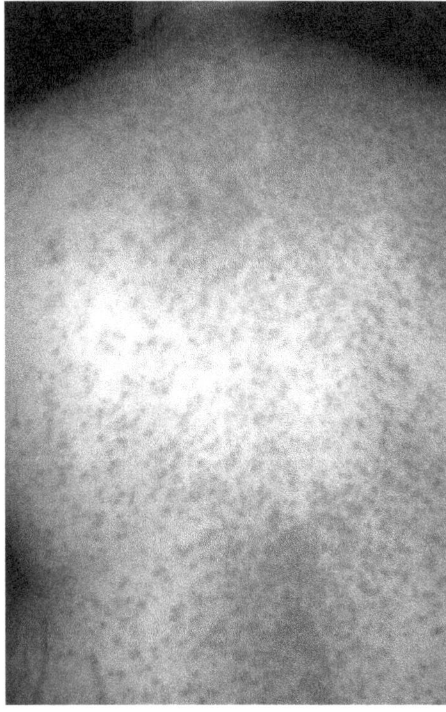

A. Morbilliform drug eruption

B. Stevens-Johnson syndrome

C. Toxic shock syndrome

D. Urticaria

Q.265 A 12-year-old boy has multiple skin lesions that are diagnosed as von Recklinghausen's syndrome (NF-1). What is TRUE of this condition?

A. It does not show other malignant lesions.

B. It is autosomal recessive.

C. It is associated with optic nerve gliomas.

D. It is characterized by atrioventricular (AV) malformation.

Q.266 The given skin condition (image) present at birth in an infant is most likely

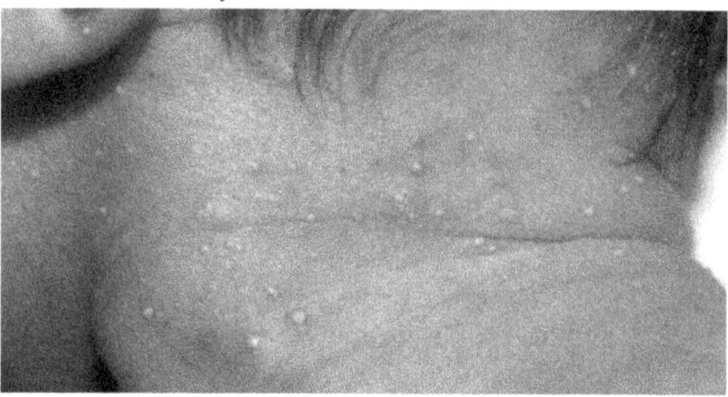

A. Erythema Toxicum Neonatorum

B. Transient Neonatal Pustular Melanosis

C. Neonatal Cephalic Pustulosis

D. Sclerema Neonatorum

Q.267 Features most consistent with a malignant eyelid lesion include:

A. Tenderness, erythema, alteration in pigment pattern

B. Disruption of tarsal architecture, raised pearly margins, pruritus

C. Lash loss, central ulceration, rapid growth

D. Ipsilateral lymph node metastasis, hyperkeratosis, dark pigmentation

Q.268 A 9-year-old girl presents for evaluation of regular vaginal bleeding. History reveals thelarche at age 7 and adrenarche at age 8. Which of the following is the most common cause of this condition in girls?

A. Idiopathic

B. Gonadal tumors

C. Hypothyroidism

D. Tumors of the central nervous system

Q.269 In case of Strychnine poisoning, which of the following should be additionally preserved during autopsy?

A. CSF   **B.** Lung

C. Spinal cord   **D.** Vitreous humor

Q.270 Chicken pox is infective

A. 2 days before and 2 days after rash appearance

B. 2 days before and 5 days after rash appearance

C. 4 days before and 4 days after rash appearance

D. 4 days before and 5 days after rash appearance

Q.271 Cocks peculiar tumor is:

A. Papilloma

B. Infected sebaceous cyst

C. Cylindroma

D. Squamous cell Ca

Q.272 Adverse effects of diphenhydramine can include all of the following except:

A. Dry mouth
B. Blurred vision
C. Bradycardia
D. Sedation

Q.273 You find a discrete, whitish polyp that extends through the tympanic membrane in a child with a history of recurrent otitis media. This most likely represents which of the following?

A. A cholesteatoma

B. Tympanosclerosis

C. Acute otitis media with perforation and drainage

D. Dislocation of the malleus from its insertion in the tympanic membrane

Q.274 The venom produced by the snake shown in the image is used to make which of the following drugs

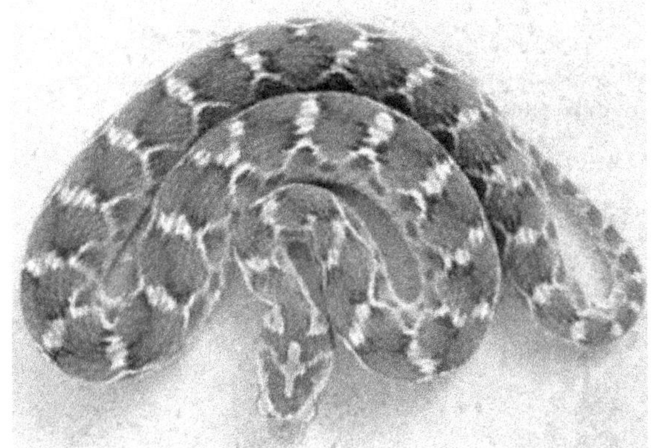

A. Analgesics
B. Anticoagulant drugs
C. Antimicrobial drugs
D. Anti-cancer drugs

Q.275 In relation to pregnant women with epilepsy, which of the following statements is incorrect?

A. The rate of congenital malformation is increased in the offspring of women with epilepsy

B. Seizure frequency increases in approximately 70% of women

C. Breastfeeding is safe with most anticonvulsants

D. Folic acid supplementation may reduce the risk of neural tube defect

Q.276 In the physical test illustrated below, the patient is asked to touch his buttocks with his heel while working against resistance. Which muscle group is being tested?

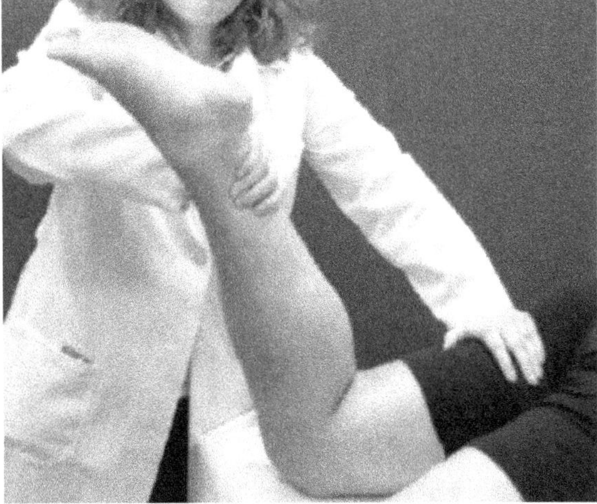

A. Quadriceps femoris
B. Hamstrings
C. Adductors
D. Triceps surae

Q.277 An 11-year-old child develops glomerulonephritis a week after he was treated for a sore throat. The causal agent is identified by serotyping of the

A. Capsule

B. M proteins

C. Outer membrane proteins

D. Pili

Q.278 Which of the following is an epimeric pair?

A. Glucose and fructose

B. Glucose and galactose

C. Galactose and mannose

D. Lactose and maltose

Q.279 Which of the following nerve palsy is responsible for the deformity as shown in the image?

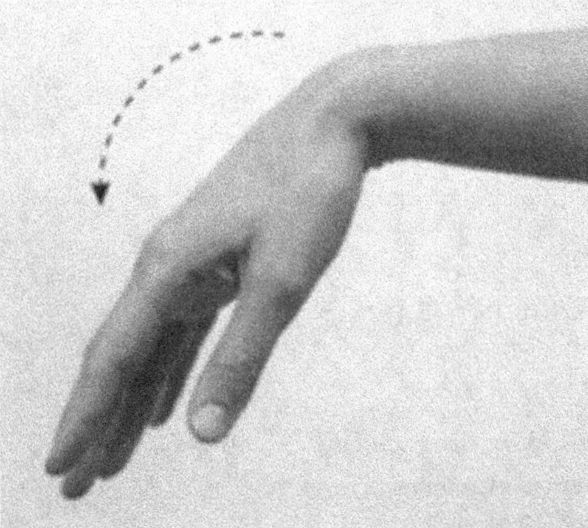

A. Ulnar nerve

B. Radial nerve

C. Musculocutaneous nerve

D. Median nerve

Q.280 A 6-month-old child has an iris lesion and recurrent anterior chamber bleeding. A biopsy of this mass was performed. A high-magnification image of the histology is shown in the figure. Which statement is correct?

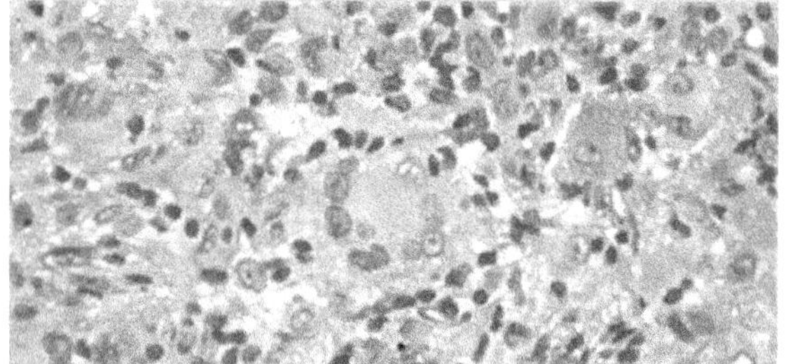

A. The lesion shows pleomorphic cells with a multinucleated tumor cell.

B. This is a benign cutaneous disorder rarely involving the eye.

C. Immunohistochemical stains for macrophages (histiocytes) are negative.

D. Most ocular lesions occur after 1 year of age in this disease entity.

Q.281 What is the mechanism of action of amiodarone?

A. It is a β-receptor antagonist

B. It decreases refractoriness

C. It interferes with outward potassium current

D. It has a relatively short half-life

Q.282 The following is true about prevalence and incidence:

A. Both are rates

B. Prevalence is a rate but incidence is not

C. Incidence is a rate but prevalence is not

D. Both are not rates

Q.283 In the treatment of hydatid cyst PAIR is contraindicated in -

A. Lung cyst

B. Size more than 5 cm

C. Not amenable to treatment with albendazole

D. Multiple cysts

Q.284 Name of mumps vaccine is:

A. Jeryl Lynn

B. Edmonston

C. Danish 1331

D. OKA

Q.285 The following findings in a newborn infant definitely require further workup :

A. A scrotal hydrocele

B. Breast enlargement

C. A shallow sacral dimple

D. Absent femoral pulses

Q.286 Glucosamine is an important constituent of

A. Homopolysaccharide

B. Heteropolysaccharide

C. Mucopolysaccharide

D. Dextran

Q.287 True regarding Tolazoline are all except

A. It is a competitive α-adrenergic receptor antagonist

B. It is more potent than phentolamine

C. It is a direct peripheral vasodilator

D. It can be used in the treatment of persistent pulmonary hypertension in newborns

Q.288 A 51-year-old man with increasing abdominal discomfort and abdominal enlargement for the past two years is found to have massive (estimated 3000 gm size) splenomegaly. Laboratory data include Hgb 9 g/dL, WBC count 5,000/microliter, and platelet count 50,000/microliter. Which of the following underlying conditions does he most likely to have?

A. Myelofibrosis

B. Portal hypertension

C. Infectious mononucleosis

D. Hemochromatosis

Q.289 Human leukocyte antigen B27 is associated with all except

A. Anterior uveitis

B. Systemic lupus erythematosus

C. Ankylosing spondylitis

D. Reactive arthritis

Q.290 Phase-4 depolarization of SA nodal cells is caused by which of the following -

A. An increase in the flow of sodium into the cell

B. A decrease in the flow of potassium out of the cell

C. An increase in activity of Na/Ca exchanger

D. A decrease in flow of chloride out of the cell

Q.291 Oral contraceptive of choice in a patient of epilepsy is:

A. Ultra low dose

B. Low dose

C. Standard dose

D. Sequential

Q.292 Drug not metabolized by liver is :

A. Penicillin G

B. Phenytoin

C. Erythromycin

D. Rifampicin

Q.293 A 26-yrs-old patient has had three consecutive spontaneous abortions early in the second trimester. As part of an evaluation for this problem, the least useful test would be:

A. Hysterosalpinogram

B. Chromosomal analysis of the couple

C. Endometrial biopsy in the luteal phase

D. Postcoital test

Q.294 Regarding Werdnig Hoffman syndrome

Assertion: The spinal muscular atrophies lead to muscle weakness

Reasoning: It is characterized by degeneration of nerve cells in lateral corticospinal tract

A. Both Assertion and Reason are true, and Reason is the correct explanation for Assertion

B. Both Assertion and Reason are true but Reason is not the correct explanation for Assertion

C. Assertion is true but Reason is false

D. Reason is true but Assertion is false

Q.295 Modified acid-fast stain is used for the diagnosis of

A. Entamoeba histolytica

B. Toxoplasma gondii

C. Cryptosporidium parvum

D. Leishmania donovani

Q.296 Neuroendocrine pathways of the stress response consist of the following except:

A. Spinal cord
B. Thyroid
C. Hypothalamus
D. Pituitary

Q.297 The epithelium tissue type shown in the image is found in

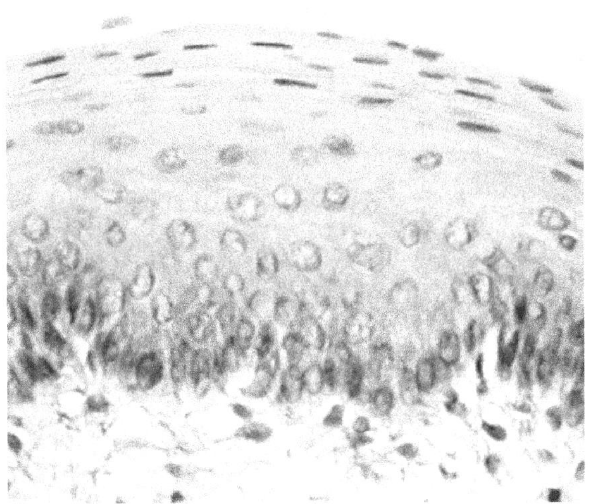

A. Mammary glands
B. Lining of small intestine
C. Inner lining of esophagus
D. Unicellular exocrine gland

Q.298 X-ray of a 47 year old patient presenting with pain and palpable mass in the femur is shown. The solitary tumor is seen with endosteal scalloping and presence of punctate calcification. The most likely diagnosis is

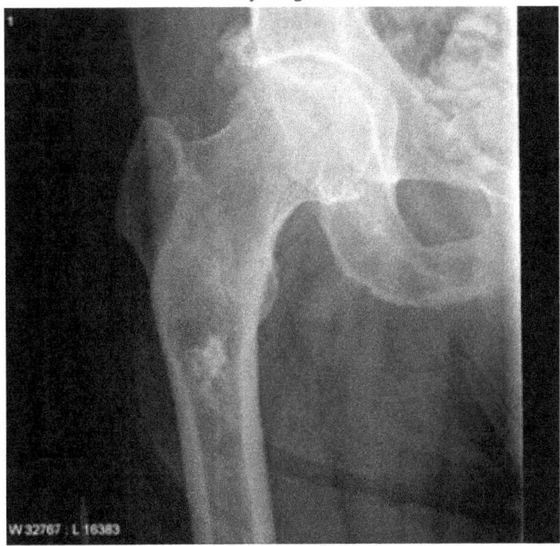

A. Osteosarcoma
B. Chondrosarcoma
C. Osteopetrosis
D. Fibrous dysplasia

Q.299 In Benign positional vertigo, semicircular canal involved is:

A. Anterior
B. Lateral
C. Posterior
D. Superior

Q.300 A 25-year-old man complains of 2 weeks of small volume loose, bloody stool. He has urgency to move his bowels. He occasionally has crampy abdominal pain. Barium enema finding is shown below. What is your diagnosis?

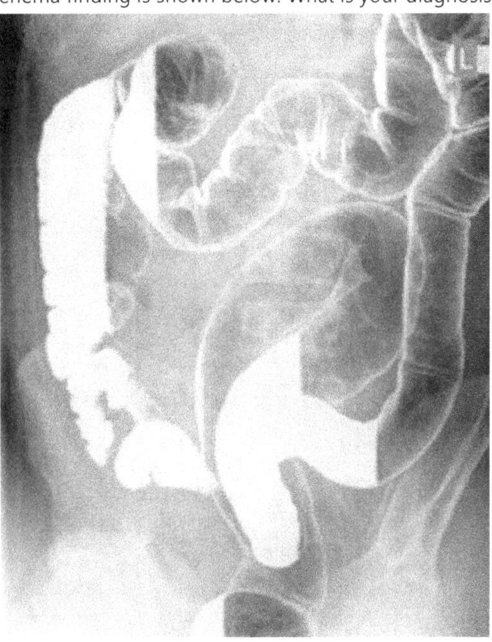

A. Diverticulosis
B. Crohn's disease
C. Ulcerative colitis
D. Irritable Bowel Syndrome

// Smart Answer Sheet //

Correct   Indicates percentage of students who answered questions correctly.

Skipped   Indicates percentage of students who skipped questions.

Q.	Ans.	Correct / Skipped	Q.	Ans.	Correct / Skipped	Q.	Ans.	Correct / Skipped	Q.	Ans.	Correct / Skipped	Q.	Ans.	Correct / Skipped
1	C	16.22 % / 21.62 %	17	A	37.84 % / 40.54 %	33	B	29.73 % / 40.54 %	49	B	43.24 % / 41.9 %	65	D	17.57 % / 52.7 %
2	C	44.59 % / 36.49 %	18	A	12.16 % / 43.25 %	34	D	39.19 % / 37.84 %	50	D	25.68 % / 44.59 %	66	C	12.16 % / 52.7 %
3	C	32.43 % / 41.89 %	19	C	22.97 % / 39.19 %	35	B	21.62 % / 44.6 %	51	B	28.38 % / 51.35 %	67	A	16.22 % / 52.7 %
4	A	25.68 % / 39.18 %	20	A	54.05 % / 27.03 %	36	C	40.54 % / 40.54 %	52	C	28.38 % / 48.65 %	68	A	10.81 % / 54.05 %
5	D	31.08 % / 41.89 %	21	A	25.68 % / 39.18 %	37	D	16.22 % / 41.89 %	53	C	13.51 % / 52.71 %	69	A	24.32 % / 52.71 %
6	B	27.03 % / 45.94 %	22	B	27.03 % / 37.83 %	38	C	33.78 % / 43.25 %	54	C	24.32 % / 50.0 %	70	D	40.54 % / 45.95 %
7	B	41.89 % / 41.89 %	23	B	6.76 % / 45.94 %	39	C	40.54 % / 41.89 %	55	B	28.38 % / 51.35 %	71	A	16.22 % / 51.35 %
8	A	43.24 % / 41.9 %	24	C	17.57 % / 37.84 %	40	C	24.32 % / 45.95 %	56	A	33.78 % / 51.36 %	72	D	32.43 % / 50.0 %
9	D	27.03 % / 41.89 %	25	A	24.32 % / 43.25 %	41	B	31.08 % / 47.3 %	57	C	14.86 % / 52.71 %	73	B	17.57 % / 51.35 %
10	C	29.73 % / 44.59 %	26	D	20.27 % / 47.3 %	42	C	13.51 % / 41.9 %	58	A	25.68 % / 51.35 %	74	D	37.84 % / 47.3 %
11	C	28.38 % / 41.89 %	27	A	48.65 % / 41.89 %	43	C	24.32 % / 41.9 %	59	A	12.16 % / 54.06 %	75	A	24.32 % / 51.36 %
12	D	27.03 % / 40.54 %	28	B	22.97 % / 37.84 %	44	D	14.86 % / 43.25 %	60	B	17.57 % / 51.35 %	76	C	12.16 % / 51.35 %
13	C	17.57 % / 41.89 %	29	D	43.24 % / 43.25 %	45	D	13.51 % / 45.95 %	61	A	29.73 % / 52.7 %	77	D	13.51 % / 51.35 %
14	A	50.0 % / 37.84 %	30	C	29.73 % / 41.89 %	46	B	31.08 % / 39.19 %	62	C	14.86 % / 51.36 %	78	D	27.03 % / 50.0 %
15	A	27.03 % / 41.89 %	31	A	32.43 % / 41.89 %	47	D	35.14 % / 43.24 %	63	A	27.03 % / 52.7 %	79	A	6.76 % / 52.7 %
16	C	39.19 % / 40.54 %	32	B	27.03 % / 40.54 %	48	D	16.22 % / 44.59 %	64	B	20.27 % / 50.0 %	80	D	8.11 % / 51.35 %

Q.	Ans.	Correct	Skipped	Q.	Ans.	Correct	Skipped	Q.	Ans.	Correct	Skipped	Q.	Ans.	Correct	Skipped	Q.	Ans.	Correct	Skipped
81	C	18.92 %	51.35 %	97	D	14.86 %	52.71 %	113	A	35.14 %	52.7 %	129	C	6.76 %	54.05 %	145	B	21.62 %	51.35 %
82	B	24.32 %	50.0 %	98	A	16.22 %	54.05 %	114	A	9.46 %	52.7 %	130	C	12.16 %	51.35 %	146	C	33.78 %	51.36 %
83	C	20.27 %	51.35 %	99	C	6.76 %	52.7 %	115	B	20.27 %	52.7 %	131	C	21.62 %	50.0 %	147	D	9.46 %	54.05 %
84	D	17.57 %	47.29 %	100	B	22.97 %	51.35 %	116	B	17.57 %	55.4 %	132	D	22.97 %	50.0 %	148	C	33.78 %	52.71 %
85	A	31.08 %	52.7 %	101	C	41.89 %	52.7 %	117	C	14.86 %	52.71 %	133	C	6.76 %	56.75 %	149	B	22.97 %	54.06 %
86	A	25.68 %	50.0 %	102	C	8.11 %	54.05 %	118	A	13.51 %	55.41 %	134	D	33.78 %	51.36 %	150	A	28.38 %	51.35 %
87	B	16.22 %	51.35 %	103	A	17.57 %	54.05 %	119	B	17.57 %	55.4 %	135	C	12.16 %	52.7 %	151	A	29.73 %	51.35 %
88	A	28.38 %	51.35 %	104	D	22.97 %	51.35 %	120	B	12.16 %	55.41 %	136	A	21.62 %	51.35 %	152	B	31.08 %	51.35 %
89	A	16.22 %	54.05 %	105	C	12.16 %	51.35 %	121	B	28.38 %	50.0 %	137	D	6.76 %	52.7 %	153	A	21.62 %	54.06 %
90	C	22.97 %	52.71 %	106	C	18.92 %	54.05 %	122	C	13.51 %	48.65 %	138	D	21.62 %	52.7 %	154	B	18.92 %	55.4 %
91	C	12.16 %	52.7 %	107	A	14.86 %	51.36 %	123	A	20.27 %	50.0 %	139	B	22.97 %	51.35 %	155	D	17.57 %	56.75 %
92	D	17.57 %	50.0 %	108	B	16.22 %	55.4 %	124	B	33.78 %	51.36 %	140	B	14.86 %	52.71 %	156	A	17.57 %	54.05 %
93	D	31.08 %	51.35 %	109	D	39.19 %	51.35 %	125	B	18.92 %	52.7 %	141	A	28.38 %	54.05 %	157	B	28.38 %	54.05 %
94	C	25.68 %	50.0 %	110	D	14.86 %	55.41 %	126	B	14.86 %	54.06 %	142	B	17.57 %	54.05 %	158	C	10.81 %	55.41 %
95	D	31.08 %	51.35 %	111	D	16.22 %	51.35 %	127	D	9.46 %	54.05 %	143	B	9.46 %	52.7 %	159	B	10.81 %	58.11 %
96	A	36.49 %	50.0 %	112	B	13.51 %	54.06 %	128	C	33.78 %	52.71 %	144	D	21.62 %	50.0 %	160	A	32.43 %	54.06 %

Q.	Ans.	Correct / Skipped	Q.	Ans.	Correct / Skipped	Q.	Ans.	Correct / Skipped	Q.	Ans.	Correct / Skipped	Q.	Ans.	Correct / Skipped
161	D	17.57 % / 54.05 %	177	C	22.97 % / 54.06 %	193	C	24.32 % / 54.06 %	209	D	12.16 % / 52.7 %	225	D	21.62 % / 55.41 %
162	B	21.62 % / 51.35 %	178	C	10.81 % / 56.76 %	194	D	13.51 % / 56.76 %	210	A	24.32 % / 52.71 %	226	C	25.68 % / 56.75 %
163	D	21.62 % / 54.06 %	179	C	16.22 % / 54.05 %	195	D	18.92 % / 54.05 %	211	B	25.68 % / 58.1 %	227	A	14.86 % / 56.76 %
164	C	22.97 % / 51.35 %	180	D	36.49 % / 51.35 %	196	A	17.57 % / 51.35 %	212	C	28.38 % / 55.4 %	228	C	28.38 % / 54.05 %
165	A	27.03 % / 54.05 %	181	C	17.57 % / 54.05 %	197	C	13.51 % / 54.06 %	213	A	41.89 % / 54.06 %	229	B	16.22 % / 55.4 %
166	B	20.27 % / 54.05 %	182	D	8.11 % / 55.4 %	198	B	13.51 % / 54.06 %	214	D	5.41 % / 56.75 %	230	D	29.73 % / 51.35 %
167	A	22.97 % / 56.76 %	183	A	25.68 % / 51.35 %	199	B	29.73 % / 56.76 %	215	B	20.27 % / 56.76 %	231	B	29.73 % / 51.35 %
168	D	10.81 % / 55.41 %	184	D	20.27 % / 52.7 %	200	A	6.76 % / 54.05 %	216	B	22.97 % / 54.06 %	232	D	20.27 % / 51.35 %
169	C	32.43 % / 52.71 %	185	A	18.92 % / 56.76 %	201	B	10.81 % / 55.41 %	217	D	8.11 % / 54.05 %	233	B	16.22 % / 56.75 %
170	C	20.27 % / 52.7 %	186	C	20.27 % / 54.05 %	202	B	32.43 % / 51.35 %	218	A	10.81 % / 56.76 %	234	D	6.76 % / 56.75 %
171	A	6.76 % / 51.35 %	187	B	24.32 % / 52.71 %	203	B	32.43 % / 54.06 %	219	D	2.7 % / 58.11 %	235	C	21.62 % / 55.41 %
172	B	4.05 % / 55.41 %	188	B	12.16 % / 55.41 %	204	A	6.76 % / 58.1 %	220	D	31.08 % / 54.06 %	236	B	21.62 % / 54.06 %
173	B	25.68 % / 54.05 %	189	B	27.03 % / 55.4 %	205	A	14.86 % / 54.06 %	221	A	21.62 % / 55.41 %	237	C	18.92 % / 55.4 %
174	C	32.43 % / 52.71 %	190	A	12.16 % / 56.76 %	206	C	8.11 % / 55.4 %	222	C	25.68 % / 54.05 %	238	C	16.22 % / 54.05 %
175	C	27.03 % / 55.4 %	191	C	16.22 % / 54.05 %	207	D	13.51 % / 56.76 %	223	D	17.57 % / 54.05 %	239	C	25.68 % / 56.75 %
176	C	18.92 % / 54.05 %	192	A	16.22 % / 55.4 %	208	B	22.97 % / 55.41 %	224	A	32.43 % / 54.06 %	240	A	10.81 % / 54.05 %

Q.	Ans.	Correct		Q.	Ans.	Correct		Q.	Ans.	Correct		Q.	Ans.	Correct		Q.	Ans.	Correct
		Skipped				Skipped				Skipped				Skipped				Skipped
241	A	32.43 %		253	A	13.51 %		265	C	18.92 %		277	B	27.03 %		289	B	22.97 %
		55.41 %				55.41 %				54.05 %				54.05 %				55.41 %
242	B	29.73 %		254	D	41.89 %		266	B	21.62 %		278	B	21.62 %		290	A	8.11 %
		55.41 %				54.06 %				55.41 %				52.7 %				55.4 %
243	D	27.03 %		255	B	29.73 %		267	C	13.51 %		279	B	32.43 %		291	C	17.57 %
		54.05 %				55.41 %				55.41 %				55.41 %				54.05 %
244	B	12.16 %		256	A	17.57 %		268	A	29.73 %		280	B	4.05 %		292	A	18.92 %
		55.41 %				55.4 %				51.35 %				54.06 %				51.35 %
245	D	29.73 %		257	A	18.92 %		269	C	21.62 %		281	C	17.57 %		293	D	17.57 %
		54.05 %				54.05 %				55.41 %				54.05 %				54.05 %
246	D	22.97 %		258	A	16.22 %		270	B	27.03 %		282	C	22.97 %		294	C	12.16 %
		52.71 %				52.7 %				51.35 %				54.06 %				56.76 %
247	B	33.78 %		259	D	13.51 %		271	B	32.43 %		283	A	12.16 %		295	C	25.68 %
		55.41 %				54.06 %				52.71 %				54.06 %				55.4 %
248	D	25.68 %		260	C	8.11 %		272	C	21.62 %		284	A	24.32 %		296	B	13.51 %
		54.05 %				55.4 %				54.06 %				55.41 %				51.35 %
249	D	18.92 %		261	D	21.62 %		273	A	20.27 %		285	D	27.03 %		297	C	10.81 %
		54.05 %				54.06 %				54.05 %				54.05 %				55.41 %
250	C	33.78 %		262	B	12.16 %		274	B	36.49 %		286	C	28.38 %		298	B	22.97 %
		52.71 %				55.41 %				54.05 %				54.05 %				52.71 %
251	A	18.92 %		263	C	12.16 %		275	B	12.16 %		287	B	6.76 %		299	C	18.92 %
		54.05 %				54.06 %				56.76 %				56.75 %				54.05 %
252	D	28.38 %		264	A	32.43 %		276	B	32.43 %		288	A	18.92 %		300	C	22.97 %
		54.05 %				52.71 %				54.06 %				52.7 %				54.06 %

Performance Analysis

Avg. Score (%)	14.67%
Toppers Score (%)	82.67%
Your Score	

Part A

Q.1 Which of the following has a function of protein synthesis and cell growth during the cell division cycle?

A. S phase   **B.** G1 phase

C. G2 phase   **D.** G0 phase

Q.2 Which nerve is involved in a patient suffering from defective adduction of the hip joint and pains in the hip and knee joint.

A. Saphenous nerve   **B.** Femoral nerve

C. Obturator nerve   **D.** Sciatic nerve

Q.3 Muscle(s) causing dorsiflexion of foot is/are -

a) Extensor digitorum longus

b) Extensor hallucis longus

c) Flexor digitorum longus

d) Flexor hallucis longus

e) Tibialis anterior

A. a,b,c   **B.** a,e,d   **C.** a,b,e   **D.** b,c,d

Q.4 Artery/arteries supplying occipital cortex is -

A. PCA   **B.** MCA

C. MCA + PCA   **D.** ACA

Q.5 Which artery is the main source of blood for the arm?

A. Ulnar artery   **B.** Radial artery

C. Brachial artery   **D.** Profunda branchii

Q.6 The diagram below shows the relationship between the esophagus, stomach, and duodenum. The area labeled A is the region that contains which of the following types of cells?

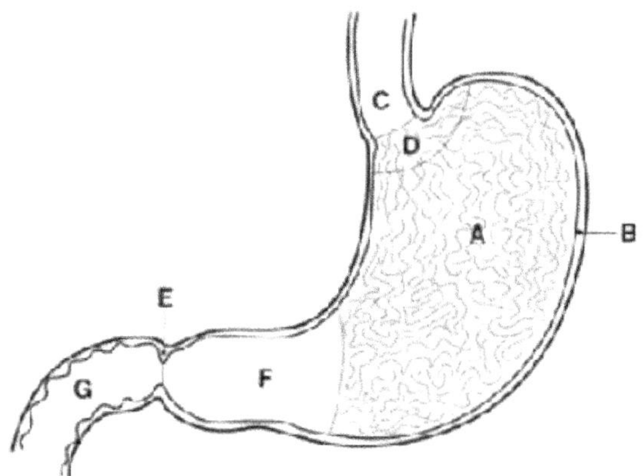

A. Cells that secrete gastric intrinsic factor

B. Most of the Paneth cells

C. Cells that secrete mucus and gastrin

D. Cells that secrete mucus and bicarbonate

Q.7 The arrow represents the dark structure in the midbrain, in this midsagittal MRI represents a passage for which of the following?

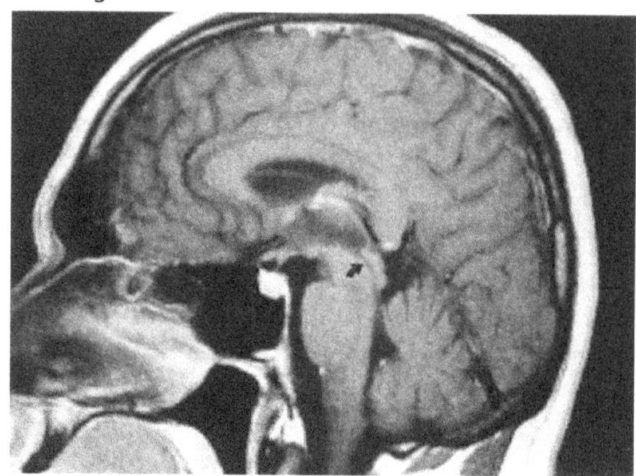

A. Venous blood

B. Cerebrospinal fluid

C. Neurons of the corticospinal tract

D. Arterial blood (in the basilar artery)

Q.8 The spinal nerve is related to

A. Glossopharyngeal   **B.** Vagus

C. Hypoglossal   **D.** Facial

Q.9 Name the muscle attached at point 'X' ?

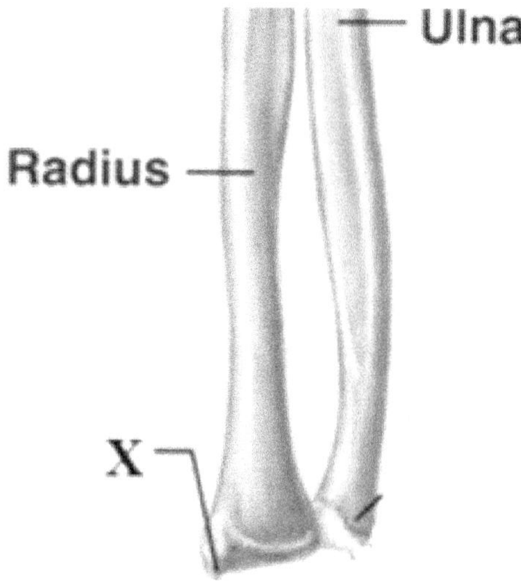

A. Brachioradialis

B. Pronator quadratus

C. Pronator teres

D. Lateral collateral ligament

Q.10 Rasmussen's aneurysm involves

A. Bronchial artery   **B.** Pulmonary artery

C. Intercostal artery   **D.** Aorta

Q.11 Hortega cells are:

A. Microglia

B. Modified macrophages

C. Astrocytes

D. Neutrophils

Q.12 End arteries occur in all of the following except :

A. Brain

B. Kidneys

C. Liver

D. The regions of the joints

Q.13 Most lateral deep cerebellar nucleus is:

A. Fastigial nucleus

B. Emboliform nucleus

C. Dentate nucleus

D. Globose nucleus

Q.14 Bed of tonsil is formed by -

A. Superior constrictor **B.** Middle constrictor

C. Inferior constrictor **D.** Platysma

Q.15 Depressor of Temporomandibular joint is

A. Temporal is muscle

B. Masseter muscle

C. Lateral pterygoid muscle

D. Medial pterygoid muscle

Q.16 A branch of Supraclinoid segment of Internal Carotid Artery is :

A. Ophthalmic artery

B. Medullary branches

C. Branches to pituitary

D. Anterior cerebral artery

Q.17 Which of the following structures does the fetal allantoic duct become in the adult ?

A. Cloaca

B. Medial umbilical ligament

C. Urachus

D. Ureter

Q.18 Collagen of which type is found in hyaline cartilage:

A. Type III **B.** Type IV **C.** Type II **D.** Type I

Q.19 Sorensess and pain in muscels after vigrous exercise is due to -

A. Hyperkalemia **B.** Hyperthermia

C. Lactic acidosis **D.** Hyponatremia

Q.20 Pulmonary vasoconstriction is caused by

A. Prostacyclin **B.** Alpha-2 stimulation

C. Hypoxia **D.** Histamine

Q.21 Hypopnea is a condition where:

A. The airway becomes partially obstructed.

B. The blood does not clot properly.

C. The lungs cannot eliminate the excess carbon dioxide from the body.

D. The blood oxygen levels are abnormally low.

Q.22 Find faulty statement regarding muscle spindle.

A. Central zone has no actin & myosin

B. Peripheral zone has no actin & myosin

C. Type 1 nuclear bag fibers has low myosin ATPase activity

D. Type 2 nuclear bag fiber has high level of myosin ATPase activity

Q.23 Which of the following is not the thermoreceptor.

A. Cold receptor & warm receptor

B. Pain receptor

C. Stretch receptor & pressure receptor

D. None of the above.

Q.24 Marey's Law states:

A. Relationship of HR with CO.

B. Relationship of HR with Stroke volume.

C. Relationship of HR with Presystolic pressure.

D. Relationship of HR with BP.

Q.25 Normal alveolar ventilation pressure on inspiration is

A. −1 cm water **B.** -1 cm Hg

C. +1 cm water **D.** +1 cm Hg

Q.26 Hormone that increases "Post Menopausal" is:

A. Progesterone **B.** Estrogen

C. FSH **D.** Androgens

Q.27 "Major Basic Protein" is secreted by:

A. Basophil **B.** Macrophage

C. Eosinophil **D.** Monocyte

Q.28 Which of the following is freely filtered by kidney across glomerular capillaries

A. Creatinine

B. Albumin (across glomerular capillaries)

C. Globulin

D. All of the above

Q.29 The mechanism involved in the absorption of glucose from the small intestine is

A. Passive diffusion

B. Facilitated diffusion

C. Secondary active co-transport with sodium

D. Actively by insulin dependent uptake

Q.30 The radiograph below was taken in a 36-year old man who presented to the ED with severe left flank pain and one episode of hematuria. Which of the following measures could cause another episode of this pathology?

C. Exocytosis **D.** Pinocytosis

Q.34 What is/are the effect(s) on membrane when extracellular concentration of K^+ is decreased

a) ↓magnitude of RMP

b) ↑negativity of the membrane

c) ↑magnitude of RMP

d) ↓negativity of membrane

A. b and c **B.** a and b **C.** b and d **D.** a and c

Q.35 Selenium is co-factor for

A. Glutathione peroxidase

B. Glutathione reductase

C. Glutathione synthetase

D. Glutathione dehydrogenase

Q.36 Which of the following is a functional enzyme:

A. Creatine kinase (CK)

B. Alkaline phosphatase

C. Lipoprotein lipase

D. Lactate dehydrogenase (LDH)

Q.37 In which of the following conditions a low/controlled glycemic index diet is preferred?

A. Diabetes **B.** Hypertension

C. Children **D.** Normal adults

Q.38 In beta-oxidation of fatty acids, carnitine is required for

A. Conversion of short chain fatty acids to long chain fatty acids

B. Transport of long chain fatty acid to mitochondrial inner layer

C. Transport of long chain fatty acid to cytoplasm

D. Conversion of long chain fatty acids to short chain fatty acids

Q.39 Find the amino acid which is justifiable to be found in the transmembrane region of a protein

A. Lysine **B.** Arginine

C. Leucine **D.** Aspartate

Q.40 Regarding glutathione which of the following is not true?

A. It helps in absorption of certain amino acids

B. It inactivates some enzymes

C. It helps in mebrane transport

D. It helps in conjugation reactions

Q.41 Absorption of iron is increased by?

A. Tea **B.** Coffee

C. EDTA **D.** Vitamin C

Q.42 All of the following abbreviations are true except

a) AMP-Adenosine monophosphate

b) CMP-Cytidine monophosphate

c) GMP-Guanosine monophosphate

d) TMP-Thymine monophosphate

e) UMP-Uracil monophosphate

A. a and b **B.** d and e **C.** c and d **D.** b and d

Q.43 True about DNA supercoiling is all except

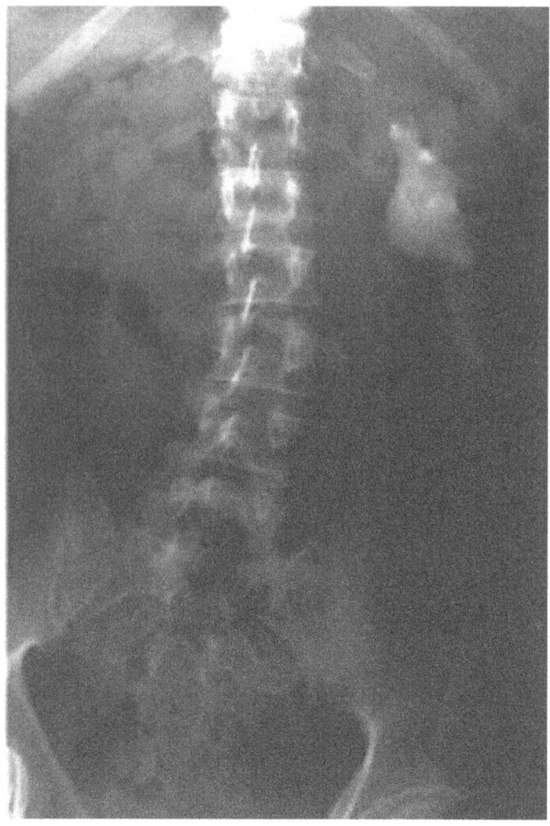

A. Calcium restriction

B. Increased fluid intake (> 2 L/d)

C. Protein restriction

D. Sodium restriction

Q.31 The action potentials shown in below figure represent which kind of cells?

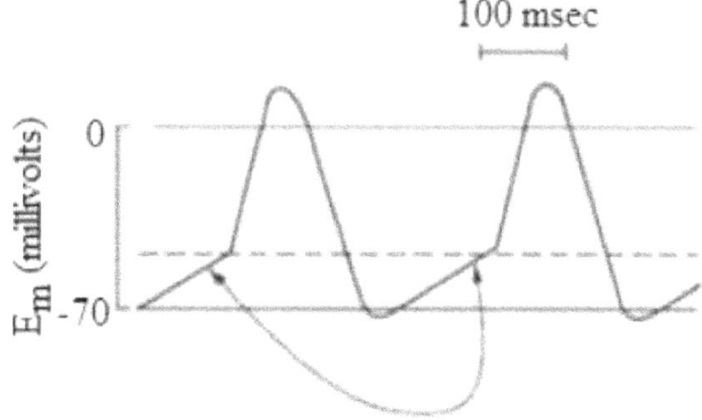

A. Cardiac nodal cells

B. Myelinated motor axons

C. Sensory neurons

D. Skeletal muscle cells

Q.32 What is an individual contractile unit known as?

A. Sarcomere **B.** Sarcolemma

C. Myofibril **D.** Sarcotubular system

Q.33 Transport of two substances in the same direction is called as?

A. Symport **B.** Antiport

A. Underwinding results in negative superhelical density & supercoiling

B. Underwinding strain is normally accommodated by strand separation

C. Topoisomerase II change linking number in increments of 2

D. Most cellular DNA is underwound

Q.44 True about polymorphism is

A. Single locus → multiple normal alleles

B. Single locus → multiple abnormal alleles

C. Single phenotype : Single locus → multiple normal alleles

D. Single phenotype : Single locus → multiple abnormal alleles

Q.45 Coenzyme associated with glycogen phosphorylase is -

A. Pyridoxal Phosphate

B. Tetrahydrofolate

C. Thiamine

D. FMN

Q.46 A 30-year-old man is diagnosed with type I familial dyslipidemia. He has had recent laboratory studies showing elevated triglycerides and normal cholesterol levels. Which of the following explains the pathophysiology of this disease?

A. Apolipoprotein E deficiency

B. LDL cholesterol receptor deficiency

C. Lipoprotein lipase deficiency

D. VLDL cholesterol clearance deficiency

Q.47 Heme synthesis occurs in the bone marrow and liver. Deficiency of δ-aminolevulinic acid hydrase would lead to the accumulation of which of the following

A. δ-Aminolevulinic acid

B. Coproporphyrinogen

C. Glycine

D. Porphobilinogen

Q.48 Rate limiting enzyme in heme synthesis

A. ALA dehydratase

B. Hmg coa reductase

C. ALA synthase

D. Uroporphyrinogen 1 synthase

Q.49 Hormone Synthesized from Tyrosine is:

A. Cortisol

B. Calcitonin

C. Calcitrol

D. Thyroxine

Q.50 Enzyme catalyzing reversible step in glycolysis is/are

A. Glucokinase / Hexokinase

B. Phosphofructokinase-I

C. Pyruvate kinase

D. Enolase

Part B

Q.51 Fat necrosis is seen in?

A. Breast **B.** Brain **C.** Kidney **D.** Spleen

Q.52 Central to apoptosis is the utilization of -

A. Nitrous oxide **B.** Adenyl cyclase

C. Caspases **D.** c-AMP

Q.53 Increased permeability in acute inflammation is due to

A. IL-2 **B.** Histamine

C. TGF-p **D.** FGF

Q.54 Mallory bodies are composed of -

A. Fat droplets

B. Microfilaments

C. Lysosomal enzymes

D. Intermediate filaments

Q.55 Identity the disease shown in photograph by its Granuloma

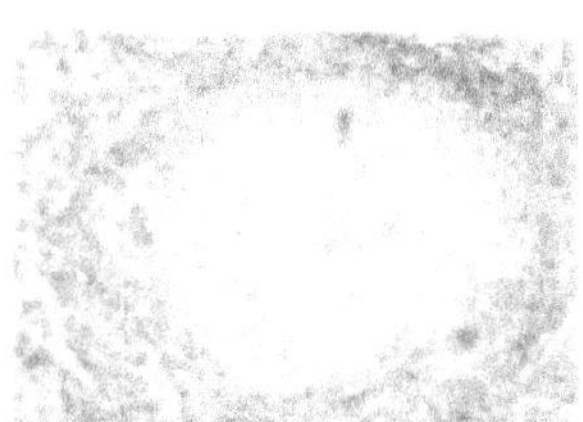

A. Brucellosis **B.** Syphilis

C. Leprosy **D.** TB

Q.56 Provisional matrix is made up of -

A. Fibrin **B.** Hemoglobin

C. Insulin **D.** Albumin

Q.57 HLA is present on –

A. Short arm of chromosomes 6

B. Short arm of chromosomes 3

C. Long arm of chromosomes 3

D. Long arm of chromosomes 6

Q.58 Function of CD4 is all except

A. Memory

B. Immunoglobulin production

C. Activation of macrophages

D. Cytotoxicity

Q.59 Comment on the diagnosis?

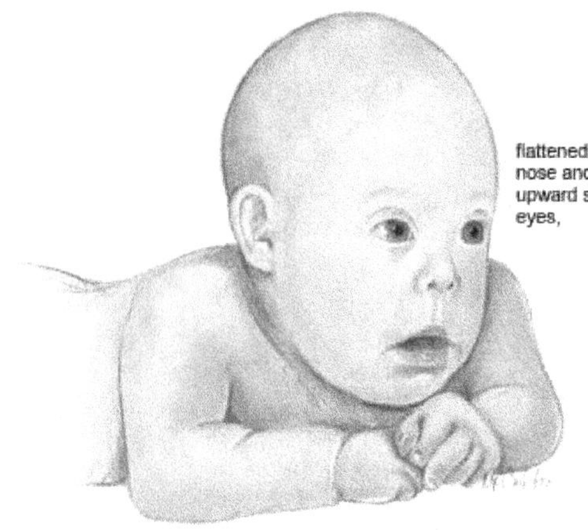

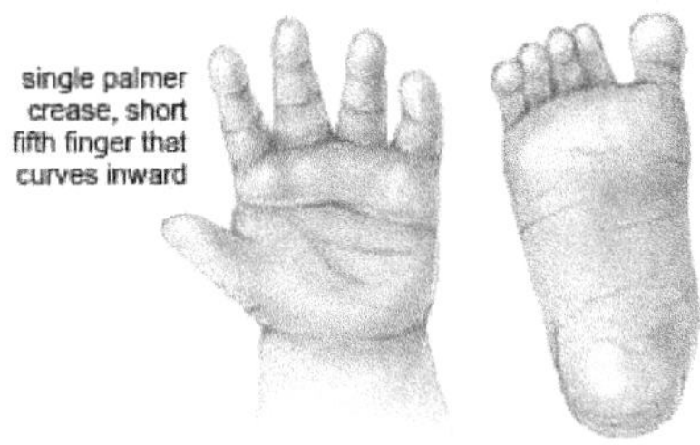

A. Turner Syndrome
B. Down syndrome
C. Prader-Willi syndrome
D. Patau syndrome

Q.60 Increased risk of cancer is seen in

A. Fibroadenoma of breast
B. Chronic ulcerative colitis
C. Bronchial asthma
D. Leiomyoma of the uterus

Q.61 Lynch syndrome is associated with cancers of the

A. Colon, endometrium, ovary
B. Breast, endometrium, ovary
C. Breast, colon, endometrium
D. Breast, colon, ovary

Q.62 In atherosclerosis, increased LDL in monocyte/macrophage is due to -

A. LDL receptors on macrophage
B. LDL receptors on endothelium
C. Lipids in LDL get oxidized
D. All of the above

Q.63 A 3-month-old infant is brought to the physician because of difficulty feeding, failure to thrive, and episodes of bluish pale skin during crying or feeding, Physical examination reveals a harsh systolic ejection murmur that is heard over the pulmonic area and left sternal border, A chest radiograph at shows a boot-shaped heart,

Which of the following events will most likely explain the embryologic mechanism responsible for the development of this condition?

A. Anterosuperior displacement of the infundibular septum
B. Failure of aorticopulmonary septum to divide

C. Failure of aorticopulmonary septum to spiral
D. Incomplete absorption of the sinus venosus into the right atrium

Q.64 Bite cells are seen in -

A. G6PD deficiency
B. SCA
C. Hereditary spherocytosis
D. Trauma

Q.65 A 9-year-old boy with elevation in both PT and APTT. What is the diagnosis?

A. Defect in extrinsic pathway
B. Defect in intrinsic pathway
C. Platelet function defect
D. Defect in common pathway

Q.66 If PTT is high in bleeding disorders then what will happen ?

a) Hemophilia A
b) Hemophilia B
c) Henoch-schonlein purpura
d) Bernard-soulier syndrome
e) Von-Willebrand disease

A. a,b,e   **B.** b,c,d   **C.** c,d,e   **D.** a,c,d

Q.67 Classical markers for Hodgkin's disease -

A. CD_{15} and CD_{30} **B.** CD_{15} and CD_{22}
C. CD_{15} and CD_{20} **D.** CD_{20} and CD_{30}

Q.68 Characteristic histopathological finding in shock lung-

A. Diffuse alveolar necrosis
B. Interstitial pulmonary edema
C. Diffuse interstitial inflammation
D. Intra-cellular debris

Q.69 Commonest histological type of carcinoma testis is -

A. Teratoma   **B.** Yolk sac tumor
C. Seminoma   **D.** Choriocarcinoma

Q.70 Chronic gastritis is caused by all except

A. H. Pylori
B. Pernicious anemia
C. Alcohol
D. Overuse of salicylates

Q.71 Which of the following is not true regarding viral hepatitis -

A. Raised transaminase level correlates well with hepatic injury
B. Variable elevation of transaminase in prodromal phase.
C. The first sign of liver damage is inflammation.
D. Liver failure.

Q.72 A 20 year old female is diagnosed with granulosa cell tumor of the ovary. Which of the following biomarkers would be most useful for follow-up of patient?

A. CA 19-9
B. CA 50

C. Inhibin

D. Neuron-specific -enolase

Q.73 Tophi in gout found in all regions except -

a) Joint capsule

b) Skin

c) Muscle

d) Articular cartilage

e) Synovial membrane

A. a,e   **B.** b   **C.** a,b   **D.** a,d

Q.74 Most common cause of Heridetary Spherocytosis is:

A. Glycophyrin   **B.** Spectrin

C. Band 4   **D.** Ankyrin

Q.75 Asteroid bodies are seen in :

A. Sarcoidosis

B. Both of them (Sarcoidosis and Sporotrichosis)

C. Sporotrichosis

D. Anaphylaxis

Q.76 This antihistaminic drug can cause cardiac arrhythmia at a high dose by blocking cardiac K+ channels. It is most likely to be :

A. Levocetirizine   **B.** Fexofenadine

C. Astemizole   **D.** Loratadine

Q.77 What did Pavlov conclude from his experiments with the dog?

A. Conditional response

B. Unconditioned response

C. Procedural memory

D. Familiarity

Q.78 Selective 5–$HT_{1B/1D}$ receptor agonist useful in acute migraine is :

A. Buspirone   **B.** Ondansetron

C. Frovatriptan   **D.** Ketanserin

Q.79 Mycobacterium lepree was discovered by:

A. Robert Koch   **B.** Hansen

C. Edward Jenner   **D.** Louis Pasteur

Q.80 Dr. Sunil used edrophonium for differentiating a myasthenic crisis from the cholinergic crisis. He preferred it over other anticholinesterase agents because of its :

A. Shorter duration of action

B. Longer duration of action

C. Direct action on muscle end plate

D. Selective inhibition of true cholinesterase

Q.81 All are true about starting of beta-blocker therapy in a patient with congestive heart failure except :

A. They should be started with optimum doses

B. They should be gradually increased over weeks

C. Special precautions should be taken in cases of NYHA class III and IV

D. Carvedilol and metoprolol are the preferred drugs.

Q.82 Drugs that have been found to be useful in compensated heart failure include all of the following except :

A. $Na^+ K^+$ ATPase inhibitors

B. Alpha blockers

C. Beta receptor agonists

D. Beta receptor antagonists

Q.83 A pregnant female Salma with thyrotoxicosis is planned for surgery. Before surgery can be done, her gland should be reduced in size and vascularity by administering :

A. Iodide ion   **B.** Propranolol

C. Propylthiouracil   **D.** Radioactive iodine

Q.84 Which of the following is not true :

A. If a drug is administered rectally it follow 1st order kinetics

B. If a drug is administered I.M. it follows zero order kinetics

C. If a drug is administered I.V. it follows 1st order kinetics

D. All of these

Q.85 A drug X is secreted through renal tubules, tubular secretion of this drug can be confirmed if renal clearance of drug X is :

A. More than the GFR

B. Equal to the GFR

C. Less than the GFR

D. More than volume of distribution

Q.86 In a patient of head injuries with rapidly increasing intracranial tension without hematoma, the drug of choice for initial management would be :

A. Furosemide   **B.** Steroids

C. 20% Mannitol   **D.** Glycine

Q.87 Amiloride can cause hyperkalemia due to its action on :

A. Electrogenic K^+ channels

B. Electrogenic Na^+ channels

C. Non electrogenic Na^+-$C1^-$ symporter

D. H^+-K^+ ATPase

Q.88 Busulfan

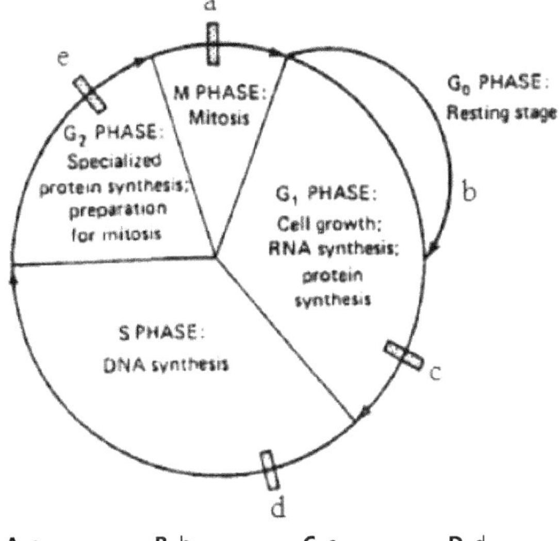

A. a   **B.** b   **C.** c   **D.** d

Q.89 The plasma concentration of drug Y is 50 mg/L, and it is eliminated at a rate of 2 mg/ min. Which of the following is the clearance rate of drug Y ?

A. 0.01 L/min   **B.** 0.04 L/min
C. 4 L/min   **D.** 10 L/min

Q.90 A 40-year-old man has been diagnosed with glioblastoma multiforme. The patient's neurologist must choose an appropriate cancer drug to treat this tumor. Which of the following can cross the blood–brain barrier for effective treatment of brain tumors ?

A. Cytarabine
B. Etoposide
C. Nitrosoureas
D. Selective estrogen receptor modulators

Q.91 If a drug is repeatedly administered at dosing intervals that are equal to its elimination half-life, the number of doses required for the plasma concentration of the drug to reach the steady state is

A. 2 to 3   **B.** 4 to 5   **C.** 6 to 7   **D.** 8 to 9

Q.92 Postoperative vomiting is uncommon with this intravenous anaesthetic agent and patients are able to ambulate sooner than those who receive other anaesthetic agents :

A. Ketamine   **B.** Enflurane
C. Propofol   **D.** Remifentanil

Q.93 Dissociative anaesthesia is seen on administration of :

A. Ether   **B.** Halothane
C. Enflurane   **D.** Ketamine

Q.94 All are true about cephalosporins, EXCEPT :

A. Ceftazidime is a 3rd generation cephalosporin.
B. Cefoperazone has got antipseudomonal effect.
C. Cefoxitin has got no activity against anaerobes.
D. Cephalosporins act by inhibiting cell wall synthesis.

Q.95 Biclutamide is a drug. True about it is:

A. Binds to androgen receptors
B. Given as montherapy in prostatic cancer
C. Causes gynaecomastia
D. All of the above

Q.96 Human fibroblast cell line is used for cultivation of -

A. Adenovirus   **B.** Poliovirus
C. HIV   **D.** Measles

Q.97 Lysogenic conversion is -

A. New properties in a bacterium due to integration of phage genome
B. Transfer of DNA from one bacterium to another by a bacteriophage
C. Transfer of free DNA
D. Transfer of genome during physical contact

Q.98 Which of the following is a bacteria taxonomically -

a) Chlamydia
b) Rickettsia
c) Mycoplasma
d) Prion
e) Bacteriophage

A. a,b   **B.** a,b,c   **C.** a,c,d   **D.** b,c,d

Q.99 Apart from T & B lymphocytes, the other class of lymphocytes is -

A. Macrophages   **B.** Astrocytes
C. NK cells   **D.** Langerhans cells

Q.100 A possible source of "second signal" to a B-cell bound by specific antigen include -

A. EB virus
B. Endotoxin
C. Antigen-specific T-cells
D. Plasma cells

Q.101 Which of the following is not a mechanism for resistance to MRSA -

A. Resistance is chromosomally mediated
B. Produced mainly by alteration in PBP's
C. MRSA resistance is absolutely beta lactamase dependent
D. Intrinsic resistance is known

Q.102 Reverse transcriptase polymerase chain reactions can aid in the diagnosis of all of the following viral infections except -

A. Adenovirus   **B.** Astrovirus
C. Rotavirus   **D.** Poliovirus

Q.103 All are true about Entamoeba Histolytica except -

A. Cyst are 4 nucleated
B. Trophozoites colonise in the colon
C. The chromatid bodies are stained by Iodides
D. None of the above.

Q.104 Which amongst the following biological agents carries the least potential for use as a biological weapon for microbial terrorism?

A. Plague (Yersinia pestis)
B. Small pox (Variola major)
C. Botulism (Clostridium botulinum)
D. Brucellosis (Brucella sp)

Q.105 A person gets infected in a hospital and clinical manifestation appear after he is discharged this is called -

A. Nosocomial infection
B. Opportunistic infection
C. Epizootic infection
D. Physician induced

Q.106 There is an outbreak of MRSA infection in a ward. What is the best way to control the infection-

A. Vancomycin given emperically to all the patients
B. Fumigation of ward frequently
C. Washing hand before & after attending patient
D. Wearing mask before any invasive procedure in ICU

Q.107 Correctly matched stain -

A. Mucicarmine - Cryptococcus

B. Giemsa - Candida

C. Gram's - Pneumocystis carinii

D. Fontana- Histoplasma

Q.108 The following figure represents :-

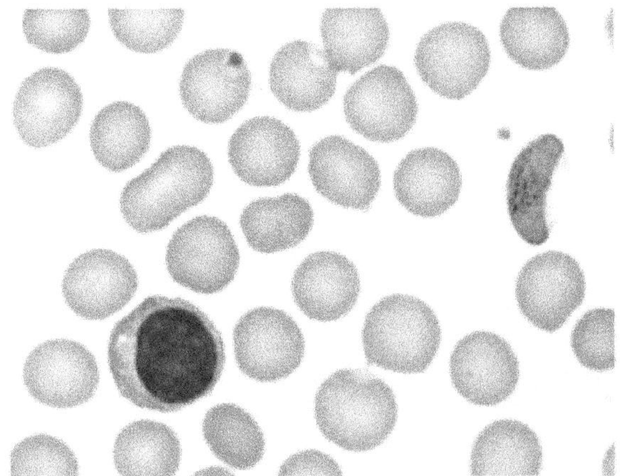

A. Gametocyte – Plasmodium malariae

B. Gametocyte – Plasmodium falciparum

C. Trophozoites – Plasmodium falciparum

D. Trophozoites – Plasmodium vivax

Q.109 The organism shown here is most likely :-

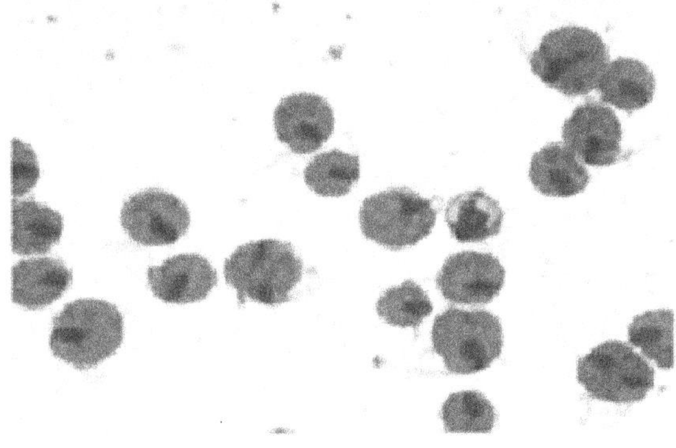

A. Giardia lambia

B. Trichomonas vaginalis

C. Leishmania donovani

D. None

Q.110 This image describes multiple, erythematous papules that develop at a site and progress to severely pruritic, serpinginous, dark skin lesions which elongate daily. This condition could be most likely due to :-

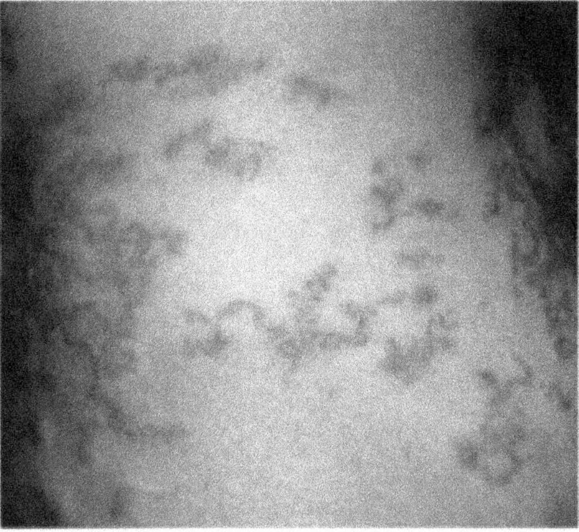

A. Ancylostoma caninum

B. Ancylostoma braziliense

C. Ancylostoma duodenale

D. Uncinaria stenocephala

Q.111 The following section describes a fungal organism obtained from nasal sinus of a neutropenic patient. The most likely organism is :-

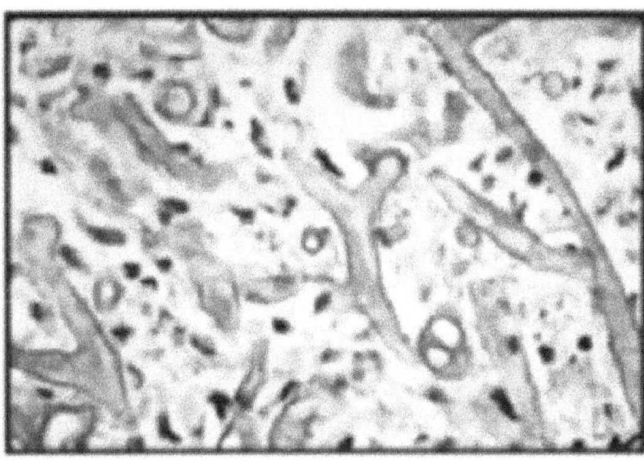

A. Aspergillus   **B.** Rhizopus

C. Candida   **D.** Histoplasma

Q.112 What is the correct order of reagents in the Gram stain?

A. Gentian violet → Iodine → Carbol fuchsin

B. Iodine → Gentian violet → Carbol fuchsin

C. Carbol fuchsin → Iodine → Gentian violet

D. Carbol fuchsin → Gentian violet → Iodine

Q.113 Stain is not taken by capsule in gram negative organisms because the capsule consist of -

a) Polysaccharides

b) Lipopolysaccharides

c) Lipids

d) Protein

A. b   **B.** c   **C.** ac   **D.** ad

Q.114 Electron microscopy is used for the following except -

A. To differentiate T & B lymphocytes

B. IgG deposits in kidney

C. TPI

D. Flagella

Q.115 Peptide binding site on class I MHC molecules for presenting processed antigens to CD_8 T cells is formed by -

A. Proximal domain of α subunits

B. Distal domain of α subunit

C. Proximal domains of α and β subunit

D. Distal domains of α and β subunit

Q.116 IPC 197 is related to –

A. Causing disappearance of evidence

B. Giving false evidence

C. Issuing false certificate by doctor

D. Examination of accused

Q.117 Punishment for issuing false certificate –

A. 7 years　　**B.** 5 years　　**C.** 3 years　　**D.** 20 years

Q.118 Injury by Lathi

A. Laceration　　　**B.** Stab wound

C. Abrasion　　　　**D.** Contusion

Q.119 Cadaveric spasm is -

A. Shows primary relaxation

B. Occurs immediately after death

C. It does not indicates the nature of death

D. Contraction of muscles involved in cadaveric sapsm is less pronounced than rigor mortis

Q.120 The MTP Act was introduced in -

A. 1961　　**B.** 1971　　**C.** 1974　　**D.** 1975

Q.121 Leaving (or forgetting) an instrument or sponge in the abdomen of the patient during a surgery and closing the operation is -

A. Contributory negligence

B. Civil

C. Corporate negligence

D. Criminal negligence

Q.122 Thanatology deals with the study of:

A. Snakes　　　　**B.** Poison

C. Finger prints　　**D.** Death

Q.123 All of the following are true about death by strangulation except -

A. Dribbling of saliva down the chin

B. Bleeding from nose is common

C. Hyoid fracture is common

D. Fracture dislocation of cervical ventebrae is rare

Q.124 Cephalic index is most useful in the identification of -

A. Age　　**B.** Sex　　**C.** Religion　　**D.** Race

Q.125 Post mortem staining in case of "CO" poisoning is:

A. Brown　　　**B.** Bright red

C. Cherry red　　**D.** Blue

Q.126 Due to an effective prevention program, the prevalence of an infectious disease in a community has been reduced by 90%. A physician continues to use the same diagnostic test for the disease that she has always used. How have the test's characteristics changed ?

A. Its sensitivity has increased

B. Its positive predictive value has increased

C. Its negative predictive value has increased

D. The test's characteristics have not changed

Q.127 The term 'Hidden Hunger' refers to:

A. Hunger amongst tribal communities

B. Hunger amongst war-torn area residents

C. Micronutrient deficiency

D. Severe malnutrition in young children

Q.128 Under the National Programme, NCD clinic is established at:

A. Anganwadi　　　**B.** Sub-centre

C. PHC　　　　　　**D.** CHC

Q.129 Kyasanur forest disease is transmitted by:

A. House fly　　**B.** Sand fly

C. Hard tick　　**D.** Soft tick

Q.130 Which of the following statements is true about the epidemiological determinants of measles -

A. Measles virus survives outside the human body for 5 days

B. Carriers are important sources of infection

C. Secondary attack is less than that of rubella

D. Incidence of measles is more in males than females

Q.131 MTP act allows abortion upto:

A. 10 weeks　　**B.** 12 weeks

C. 16 weeks　　**D.** 20 weeks

Q.132 Which of the following is primordial prevention for non communicable Disease [NCD]

A. Salt restriction in high NCD area

B. Smoking cessation in high NCD area

C. Preservation of traditional diet in low NCD area

D. Early diagnosis & Treatment

Q.133 Immunization is-

A. Primary prevention

B. Secondary prevention

C. Tertiary prevention

D. Disability limitation

Q.134 Following can be used as a yardstick for the assessment of standards of therapy -

A. Specific death rate

B. Case fatality rate

C. Proportional mortality rate

D. Survival rate

Q.135 Modifiable risk factors for hypertension is ?

A. Ethinicity　　**B.** Age

C. Sex　　　　　**D.** Obesity

Q.136 Which is most economical and best screening-

A. Mass screening

B. High risk screening

C. Multiphasic screening

D. Any of the above

Q.137 Body mass index (Quetelet's index) is:

A. Weight (Kg)/Height^2 (m)

B. Weight (Kg)/Height (m)

C. Weight^2 (Kg)/Height (m)

D. Weight^2 (Kg)/Height^2 (m)

Q.138 Which of the following is purification of water at large scale -

A. Disinfection of well

B. Rapid sand filter

C. Household purification

D. None of the above

Q.139 Human development index value ranges between:

A. 0 to 100   **B.** 0 to 10   **C.** 0 to 1   **D.** 0 to 0.5

Q.140 Chronological age 10 years, mental age 4 years. What that person called as?

A. Imbecile   **B.** Idiot   **C.** Normal   **D.** Genius

Q.141 Diagnostic power of the test is reflected by-

A. Sensitivity

B. Specificity

C. Predictive value

D. Population attributable risk

Q.142 Ergonomics –

A. Adjusting the Worker to his job

B. Study of human behavior

C. Study of social mobility

D. None

Q.143 Mercury is disposed by

A. Controlled combustion

B. Deep burial

C. Chemical treatment

D. Safely collect and re-use

Q.144 PERT type of system is used for –

A. Cost effective analysis

B. Cost benefit analysis

C. Network analysis

D. Input-Output analysis

Q.145 Under the National Programme for Control of Blindness in India, medical colleges are classified as eye care centers of –

A. Primary level   **B.** Secondary level

C. Tertiary level   **D.** None of the above

Q.146 A group of experts discussing and interacting about a particular topic in presence of audience is :

A. Panel discussion   **B.** Chalk and talk

C. Group discussion   **D.** Workshop

Q.147 Disease which does not come under Integrated Disease Surveillance Project is:

A. Tuberculosis

B. Meningoencephalitis

C. Herpes Zoster

D. Cholera

Q.148 National AIDS control Programme was started on –

A. 1977   **B.** 1985   **C.** 1986   **D.** 1990

Q.149 Occurrence in the community of a number of cases of disease that is unusually large or unexpected

A. Endemic   **B.** Epidemic

C. Pandemic   **D.** Infection

Q.150 The proportion of disease incidence that can be attributed to a specific exposure

A. Relative risk   **B.** Odds ratio

C. Attributable risk   **D.** Potential risk

Part C

Q.151 Which of the following is/are not the cause of hypopigmentation –

A. Leprosy   **B.** Pinta

C. Syphilis   **D.** Pytriasis alba

Q.152 Most common association with Acanthosis nigricans -

A. Hypertension   **B.** DM

C. Obesity   **D.** Hypothyroidism

Q.153 Glial cells are the most abundant cells in:

A. Lungs   **B.** Kidney

C. Gallbladder   **D.** Nervous system

Q.154 Caterpillar bodies are seen in

A. Dyskeratosis congenita

B. Amyloidosis

C. Porphyria cutanea tarda

D. Lipoid proteinosis

Q.155 Most common organism causing T. capitis is –

A. Trichoderma   **B.** Microsporum

C. Epidermophyton   **D.** Candida albicans

Q.156 Drug not causing exatithematous skin eruption –

A. Phenytoin   **B.** Hydrocortisone

C. Ampicillin   **D.** Phenylbutazone

Q.157 Which is not a connective tissue

A. Blood   **B.** Bone   **C.** Cartilage   **D.** Muscle

Q.158 A child is presenting with erythmatous follicular papules on trunk. There are areas of normal skin within the lesions. There is thickening of palms & soles. This child is suffering from –

A. Pityriasis rosea

B. Pityriasis rubra pilaris

C. Psoriasis

D. Seborrheic dermatitis

Q.159 A 50 years old man has a 2 year history of facial bullae & oral ulcers. Microscopic smear from skin lesions is most likely to disclose –

a) Tzanck cells

b) Acantholytic cells

c) Necrosis

d) Koilocytosis

A. c   **B.** d   **C.** ab   **D.** ac

Q.160 Thalidomide is drug of choice for .... , if two courses of glucocorticoids fail.

A. Lepra I reaction

B. Lepra II reaction

C. Both Lepra I & II reactions

D. Nerve abscess

Q.161 Incubation period of scabies is –

A. 7 days   **B.** 2 weeks   **C.** 4 weeks   **D.** 2–3 days

Q.162 In which of the following Palpable pupura is not seen –

A. Cryoglobulinuria

B. H.S. pupura

C. Gaint cell arteritis

D. Drug induced vasculitis

Q.163 In which of the following flaky paint dermatosis is observed

A. Dermatitis   **B.** Pellagra

C. Marasmus   **D.** Kwashiorkor

Q.164 Isolated 3rd nerve palsy is seen in-

A. Frontal lobe tumour

B. Diabetes

C. Webers syndrome

D. Lateral medullary syndrome

Q.165 Locus heterogeneity is a feature of which of the following?

A. Familial adenomatous polyposis

B. Turcot syndrome

C. Osteogenesis imperfecta

D. All of the above

Q.166 Which one of the following veins does not drain into coronary sinus?

A. Middle cardiac vein

B. Anterior cardiac vein

C. Oblique cardiac vein

D. Small cardiac vein

Q.167 Mayer–Rokitansky–Kuster–Hauser syndrome (MRKH) syndrome is associated with -

A. Ovarian agenesis

B. Absent fallopian tube

C. Vaginal atresia

D. Bicornuate uterus

Q.168 Duroziez's sign is seen in?

A. Aortic regurgitation   **B.** Aortic stenosis

C. Mitral stenosis   **D.** Mitral regurgitation

Q.169 The most common cause of Pulmonary thromboembolism

A. DIC

B. DVT

C. Coagulopathy

D. Venous hypertension

Q.170 In hyperkalemia with bradycardia treatment is -

A. Calcium gluconate   **B.** Steroid

C. Salbutamol   **D.** K+resin

Q.171 All are true regarding anaemia of chronic diseases, except

A. Decreased serum Fe

B. Decreased ferritin

C. Decreased total Fe binding capacity

D. Increased bone marrow Fe

Q.172 In which leukemia, autoimmune hemolytic anemia is most common in

A. Acute lymphoblastic leukemia (ALL)

B. Acute myeloid leukemia (AML)

C. Clinical manifestations of immediate hypersensitivity (CMIL)

D. Chronic lymphocytic leukemia (CLL)

Q.173 All of the following feature of hallucination EXCEPT-

a) Depends on will of observer and is under voluntary control

b) Occur in inner subjective space

c) It is vivid as sensory perception

d) It occurs in absence of perceptual stimulus

A. ac   **B.** a   **C.** ad   **D.** ab

Q.174 All are examples of cortical dementia except -

A. Alzheimer's disease

B. Multiple sclerosis

C. Creutzfeldt–Jakob disease (CJD)

D. Pick's disease

Q.175 A boy is having diarrhoea, rhinorrhoea, sweating & lacrimation, What is the most probable diagnosis -

A. Cocaine withdrawal   **B.** Heroin withdrawal

C. Alcohol withdrawal   **D.** LSD withdrawal

Q.176 Naltrexone is used in opioid dependence to -

A. Prevent respiratory depression

B. Treat withdrawal symptoms

C. Prevent relapse

D. Treatment of opioid overdose

Q.177 Secretion of growth hormone is stimulated by which of the following?

A. Increased plasma glucose levels

B. Deep sleep

C. Free fatty acids

D. Somatostatin

Q.178 The term "Dementia praecox" was coined by -

A. Freud **B.** Bleuler
C. Kraepelin **D.** Schneider

Q.179 Nihilistic delusions are seen in -
a) Endogenous depression
b) Double depression
c) Depression in involutional stage
d) Cyclothymia
e) Dysthymia

A. ab **B.** abc **C.** acd **D.** bce

Q.180 Delusion of Nihilism and Early morning insomnia are characteristic features of -

A. Mania **B.** Major depression
C. Personality disorder **D.** Schizophrenia

Q.181 Treatment of choice for the phobic disorder is -

A. Psychotherapy **B.** Behaviour therapy
C. SSRI **D.** Benzodiazepam

Q.182 Which of the following is false about somatization disorder -

A. Involves 2 sexual disturbance Symptoms
B. Two GI symptoms
C. Four pain symptoms
D. Multiple recurrent symptoms

Q.183 Hallucinations which arises when a patient is falling asleep -

A. Hypnagogic hallucination
B. Hypnopompic hallucination
C. Non specific hallucinations
D. Jactatio nocturna capitis

Q.184 How to differentiate between psychological and organic erectile dysfunction -

A. Nocturnal penile tumescence
B. PIPE therapy
C. Sildenafil induced erection
D. Stop-squeeze technique

Q.185 A young lady is present with repeated episode of overeating followed by purging using laxatives, she probably suffering from -

A. Bulimia nervosa
B. Schizophrenia
C. Anorexia nervosa
D. Binge eating disorders

Q.186 Following drugs are used in the treatment of ADHD ?

A. Amphetamine **B.** Modafinil
C. Methylphenidate **D.** All of the above

Q.187 Treatment of hyperkinetic syndrome include -
a) Imipramine
b) Methylphenidate
c) Haloperidol
d) Clozapine
e) Amphetamine

A. ab **B.** ad **C.** be **D.** ce

Q.188 Memory disturbance of ECT recovers in -
A. Few days to few weeks
B. Few weeks to few months
C. Few months to few year
D. Permanent

Q.189 All are true about RVF Except :
A. Hepatomegaly **B.** Nocturia
C. Normal JVP **D.** Ascites

Q.190 Schrimer's Test is used for evaluation of function of :
A. Optic nerve **B.** Abducent nerve
C. Occulomotor nerve **D.** Facial nerve

Q.191 Urinary VMA levels are increased in :
A. Carcinoid syndrome
B. Conn's syndrome
C. Phaeochromocytoma
D. Hepatocellular carcinoma

Q.192 Non-oliguric renal failure is seen with :
A. NSAID **B.** PSGN
C. Hypovolemia **D.** Gentamycin

Q.193 Not a cause of Diarrhea:
A. Hypercalcemia **B.** Diabetes mellitus
C. Carcinoid **D.** Hyperythyroidism

Q.194 N-myc gene is seen in:
A. Retinoblastoma **B.** Neuroblastoma
C. Williams tumor **D.** Nephroblastoma

Q.195 Hepatitis B is not transmitted through :
A. Semen **B.** Milk **C.** Blood **D.** Stool

Q.196 Barret's esophagus can lead to -
a) Stricture
b) Reflux esophagitis
c) Peptic ulcer
d) Achalasia

A. a and c **B.** b and c **C.** a and d **D.** b

Q.197 True about achalasia cardio, all except :
A. elevated resting LES tone
B. increased primary peristaltic waves in the esophagus
C. increased baseline intraesophageal pressure
D. pre malignant

Q.198 Artery to bleed in duodenal ulcer haemorrhage -
A. Splenic artery
B. Gastroduodenal artery
C. Left gastric artery
D. Superior mesenteric artery

Q.199 Anomaly associated with duodenal atresia is
A. Down syndrome
B. Duodenal adenomas
C. Limb defects

D. Autoimmune disorders

Q.200 Portal hypertension following portal vein thrombosis are guided by -

a) ↑ in splenic pulp pressure

b) ↑ in portal vein pressure

c) ↑ in hepatic vein pressure

d) Portal vein doppler study

A. abd   **B.** bcd   **C.** abc   **D.** ab

Q.201 Indication of aspiration in liver abscess is all, except:

A. Left lobe abscess

B. Deep & less than $5\ mm$ size

C. Multiple

D. Recurrent

Q.202 Which of the following is not an indication for cholecystectomy

A. 70-year-old male with symptomatic gallstones

B. 20-year-old male with sickle cell anaemia and symptomatic gallstones

C. 65-year-old female with a large gallbladder polyp

D. 55-year-old with an asymptomatic gallstone

Q.203 CBD stone may present with

A. decreased bilirubin

B. ↓WBC count

C. ↓serum alkaline phosphatase

D. cholangitis

Q.204 Which of the following parameters will fall the earliest in iron deficiency

A. MCV

B. MCH

C. MCHC

D. Red cell distribution width

Q.205 Raised MCV in pregnancy can be due to all except

A. Megaloblastic Anaemia

B. Iron Deficiency

C. Hypothyroidism

D. Alcohol use

Q.206 Meckels diverticulum represents which structure of the embryonic life ?

A. Vitellointestinal duct

B. Wolfian duct

C. Mullerian duct

D. Paramesonophric duct

Q.207 All of the following are significant risk factors for colonic carcinoma in an adenomatous polyp except

A. Pedunculated polyp   **B.** Villous histology

C. Size > 2 cm   **D.** Atypia

Q.208 Non-union is a complication of

A. Inter-trochanteric of hip

B. Colles' fracture

C. Supracondylar humerus

D. Scaphoid

Q.209 In anterior cruciate ligament tear, which of these tests are positive -

A. Lachman's test

B. McMuny's test

C. Posterior drawer test

D. Apley's test

Q.210 Increased alkaline phosphate in seen in -

A. Multiple myeloma

B. Chronic renal failure

C. Osteoporosis

D. All of the above

Q.211 The most visually disabling type of cataract is:

A. Cortical cataract

B. Nuclear cataract

C. Posterior subcapsular cataract

D. Anterior capsular cataract

Q.212 Housemaids knee is bursitis of -

A. Prepatellar bursa   **B.** Infrapatellar bursa

C. Olecranon   **D.** Ischial bursa

Q.213 The correct order of priorities in the initial management of head injury is -

A. Airway, Breathing, Circulation, treatment of extra cranial injuries

B. Treatment of extracranial injuries, Airway, Breathing, Circulation

C. Circulation, airway, Breathing, treatment of extra cranial injuries

D. Airway, circulation, breathing, treatment of extra cranial injuries

Q.214 Maximum weight for skin traction -

A. 1-2 kg   **B.** 4-5 kg   **C.** 10-15 kg   **D.** 15-20 kg

Q.215 Bone resorption markers are -

A. Serum propeptide of type I procollagen

B. Osteocalcin

C. Urine total free deoxypyridinoline

D. Free glutamic acid cross linkage

Q.216 A 20-years old male presents with anterior shoulder dislocation. This injury is usually caused as a combination of which of the following -

A. Abduction & external rotation

B. Adduction & external rotation

C. Abduction & internal rotation

D. Adduction & internal rotation

Q.217 Cubitus valgus is seen in

A. Intercondylar of humerus

B. Of the olecranon

C. Head of the radius

D. Lateral condyle of humerus

Q.218 Late complication of acetabular fracture

A. vascular necrosis of head of the femur
B. Avascular necrosis of lilac crest
C. Fixed deformity of the hip joint
D. None of the above

Q.219 Ratio of O_2 : N_2O in Entonox is –
A. 50 : 50   **B.** 60 : 40   **C.** 40 : 60   **D.** 25 : 75

Q.220 Circuit of choice for controlled ventilation
A. Magill circuit   **B.** Type B
C. Type C   **D.** Type D

Q.221 Identify the type of waves shown in the photograph.

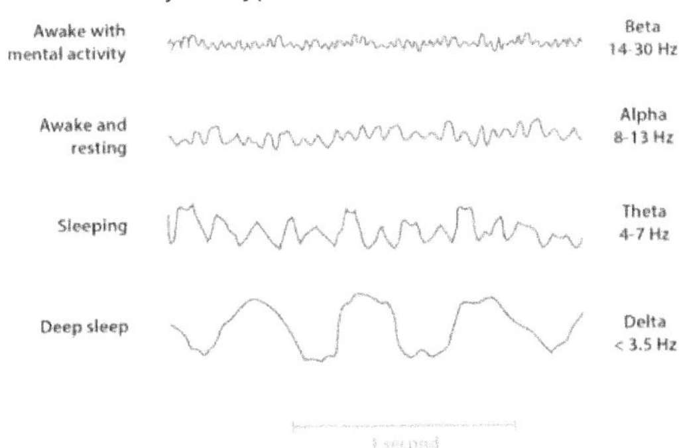

A. ECG   **B.** EEG   **C.** JVP   **D.** PCWP

Q.222 Capnography is useful for –
A. Determining vaporizer malfunction or contamination.
B. Determining circuit hypoxia.
C. Determining the appropriate placement of endotracheal tube.
D. Detecting concentration of oxygen in the anesthetic circuit.

Q.223 All are the complication of CVP line, except:
A. Airway injury   **B.** Haemothroax
C. Air embolism   **D.** Septicemia

Q.224 Pentothiol sodium should preferablay be injected into –
A. Femoral vein
B. Antecubital vein
C. Neck vein
D. Veins on outer aspect of fore arm

Q.225 Cerebral metabolism and O_2 consumption are increased by –
A. Propofol   **B.** Ketamine
C. Atracurium   **D.** Fentanyl

Q.226 Addition of epinephrine to lignocaine –
A. Increaseses distribution of LA
B. Decreases absorption of LA
C. Decreases duration of LA
D. Increases metabolism of LA

Q.227 Local anaesthetic with maximum ionized form at physiological pH –
A. Lidocaine   **B.** Etidocaine
C. Bupivacaine   **D.** Chloroprocaine

Q.228 Cocaine was first used as local anaesthetic by –

A. Carl Kollar   **B.** Horace Wells
C. Morton   **D.** None

Q.229 Upper respiratory tract infection is a common problem in children. All the following anaesthetic complications can occur in children with respiratory infections, except –
A. Bacteremia
B. Halothane granuloma
C. Increased mucosal bleeding
D. Larygospasm

Q.230 Right anterior oblique view of chest X-ray true is/are
A. Cassette near right shoulder
B. Cassette near the left shoulder
C. Arch of Aorta best seen
D. Mitral & tricuspid valves better seen

Q.231 Figure of 8 in chest X-ray is seen in –
A. Ebstein anomaly
B. Total anomalous pulmonary venous connection (TAPVC)
C. Tetrology of fallot
D. Transposition of great vessels

Q.232 Soap bubble appearance in X-ray is seen in –
A. Multiple cystic kidney
B. Neuroblastoma
C. Cystic lymphangiectasis
D. Meconium ileus

Q.233 Which of following is not a feature of renovascular hypertension on intravenous urography -
A. Delayed 'wash - out' of contrast
B. Filling defect in calyces
C. Ureteral kinking
D. Normal or small sized kidney

Q.234 76 year old man presents with a lytic lesion in the vertebrae. X-ray skull showed multiple punched out lesions. The diagnosis is –
A. Metastasis
B. Multiple myeloma
C. Osteomalacia
D. Hyperparathyroidism

Q.235 A 20 year female patient with 6th cranial nerve palsy on T_2 weighted MRI shows a hyperintense lesion in cavernous sinus which shows homogenous contrast enhancement. Most probable diagnosis is?
A. Schwannoma
B. Meningioma
C. Cavernous sinus hemangioma
D. Cavernous hemangioma

Q.236 In Radionuclide imaging the most useful radiopharmaceutical for skeletal imaging is –
A. Gallium 67 (^{67}Ga)
B. Technetium–sulphur-colloid (^{99m}Tc–Sc)
C. Technetium–99m linked to Methylene diphosphonate (^{99m}Tc–MDP)
D. None of the above

Q.237 Which of the following liver metastasis appear hypoechoic on Ultrasonography –

A. Breast cancer

B. Colon cancer

C. Renal cancer

D. Mucinous adenocarcinoma

Q.238 Tracheal bifurcation on X-ray corresponds to –

A. Thoracic inlet

B. $T_4 T_5$

C. $T_5 T_6$

D. None of the above

Q.239 A newborn presenting with intestinal obstruction showed on abdominal X-ray, multiple air-fluid levels. The diagnosis is not likely to be –

A. Pyloric obstruction

B. Duodenal atresia

C. Heal atresia

D. Ladd's bands

Q.240 Looser's zone is seen in –

A. Osteoporosis

B. Hyperparathyrodism

C. Osteomalacia

D. Both (B) and (C)

Q.241 All are used for contraception in sickle cell anaemia except

A. IUCD

B. Oral Pill

C. Progestin only pill

D. Progesterone Impants

Q.242 Rupture of membrane is said to be premature when it occurs at :

A. 38 weeks of pregnancy

B. 32 weeks of pregnancy

C. Prior to 1st stage of labour

D. II stage of labour

Q.243 Birth weight of a baby can be increased by :

A. Cessation of smoking

B. Aspirin

C. Ca++ and vitamin D supplement

D. Bed rest

Q.244 Cephalhematoma :

A. Is caused by oedema of the subcutaneous layers of the scalp

B. Should be treated by aspiration

C. Most commonly lies over the occipital bone

D. Does not vary in tension with crying

Q.245 The number of fontanelles present in a newborn child is:

A. 1　　B. 2　　C. 4　　D. 6

Q.246 Which of the following method is the best predictor for ovulation in a female infertility patient during a menstrual cycle

A. Basal body temperature

B. Hormonal Study

C. Endometrial biopsy

D. Fern study

Q.247 Not an indication for blood transfusion

A. Moderate anemia at 24-30 weeks

B. Severe anemia at 36 weeks

C. Blood loss anemia

D. Refractory anemia

Q.248 Postcoital test (PCT) is done for :

A. Cervical receptivity

B. Sperm motility

C. Absolute sperm count

D. Viable sperm count

Q.249 Type of maternal anaemia based on Photograph of the peripheral smear

A. Iron deficiency anemia

B. Thalassemia

C. Sickle cell anemia

D. Sideroblastic anemia

Q.250 The following statements are related to the therapy of iron deficiency anaemia except :

A. Oral iron can be given only if anemia is detected before 20 weeks of pregnancy

B. Parenteral iron therapy markedly increases the reticulocytic count within 7-14 days

C. Parenteral therapy is ideal during 30-36 weeks

D. Blood transfusion may be useful in severe anaemia beyond 36 weeks

Q.251 Drug given to reduce uterine contractions during preterm labour with least side effects :

A. Ritodrine

B. Nifidipine

C. Magnessium sulphate

D. Progesterone

Q.252 Blood will interfere with the nitrazine test for detecting ruptured membranes because :

A. It is acid

B. It is alkaline

C. It contains increased amounts of sodium chloride

D. It contains decreased amounts of sodium chloride

Q.253 Early date for detection of fetal heart :

A. 6.0-6.5 week

B. 6.5-7 week

C. 7.1-7.5 week

D. 8 week

Q.254 Diagnostic factor for choriocarcinoma is :

A. Hypoplastic trophoblasts

B. Lung Metastasis

C. HCG Level less than 35,000Miu/ml

D. None of them

Q.255 Late deceleration is due to :

A. Cord compression

B. Abdominal compression

C. Placental insufficiency

D. Head compression

Q.256 The triangular area bounded by clitoris, fourchette and labia minora is

A. Fossa navicularis

B. Fouchette

C. Vestibule

D. Vulva

Q.257 True about clomiphene citrate is :

A. Enclomiphene has antiestrogenic affect

B. Chance of pregnancy is three fold as compared to placebo

C. Risk of multiple pregnancy is 2-4%

D. It can also be used for male infertility with oligozoospermia

Q.258 Most common site of ectopic pregnancy is

A. Ovary

B. Peritoneum

C. Fallopian tube

D. Cervix

Q.259 Best prenatal treatment CAH is

A. Betamethasone

B. Prednisolone

C. Hydrocortisone

D. Dexamethasone

Q.260 Acute PID is treated by:

a) IV antibiotics (broad spectrum)

b) Drainage of TO mass

c) Abdominal hysterectomy

d) Laparoscopic exploration

A. acd

B. bcd

C. abd

D. ab

Q.261 Among the surgeries of stress incontinence, the long-term success rate is maximum with

A. Stamey's repair

B. Burch's colposuspension

C. Kelly's stitch

D. Aldridge surgery

Q.262 The fallopian tube

A. Is lined entirely by ciliated columnar epithelium

B. Has a submucous layer

C. Undergoes shedding during menstrual cycle

D. Surrounded by peritoneum on all sides except along the line of attachment of mesosalpinx

Q.263 Granulosa cells produces estrogen with the help of the enzyme:

A. Alkaline phosphatase

B. Aromatase

C. Acid phosphatase

D. Glucuronidase

Q.264 Which of the following infection affects fetal growth?

A. CMV

B. Rubella

C. Herpes simplex

D. All

Q.265 OCP gives protection against following cancers:

a) Endometrial

b) Ovary

c) Cervix

d) Breast

e) Liver

A. ac

B. a

C. ad

D. ab

Q.266 The drug which reduces the size of myoma include

A. Danazol

B. Progesterone

C. GnRH agonist

D. Mifepristone

Q.267 Submucosal fibroid is detected by

A. Hysteroscopy

B. Hysterosalpingography

C. USG(Transabdominal)

D. Laparoscopy

Q.268 Endometriosis is commonly associated with:

A. B/L chocolate cyst of ovary

B. Adenomyosis

C. Fibroid

D. Luteal cyst

Q.269 Causes of dysfunctional uterine bleeding can be:

a) Uterine polyp

b) Fibroid

c) Granulosa cell tumour

d) Irregular ripening of endometrium

e) Irregular shedding of endometrium

A. ab

B. bc

C. cd

D. be

Q.270 Long-term tamoxifen therapy may cause:

A. Endometrium Ca

B. Ovary Ca

C. Cervix Ca

D. Vagina Ca

Q.271 Child draws triangle at what age ?

A. 3 years

B. 5 years

C. 6 years

D. 7 years

Q.272 Newborn babies are able to breathe and suck at the same time due to –

A. Wide short tongue

B. Short soft palate

C. High larynx

D. Short pharynx

Q.273 Persistence of Moro's reflex is abnormal beyond the age of –

A. 3rd month

B. 4th month

C. 5th month

D. 6th month

Q.274 A child with central cyanosis and enlarged left ventricle the probable diagnosis is –

A. Tricuspid atresia

B. Eisenmenger's syndrome

C. tetralogy of fallot

D. Anomolous pulmonary artery

Q.275 The following is false about Atrial septal defect –

A. Ostium secundum most common

B. Right to Left Shunt

C. May be associated with TAPVC

D. CCF is very rare

Q.276 A most common cause of Bronchiolitis is?

A. RSV

B. Adenovirus

C. Parainfluenza

D. Mycoplasma

Q.277 Glioma of the optic nerve is usually –

A. Gemistocytic

B. Pilocytic

C. Fibrillary

D. Lamellar

Q.278 Most important cause of abdominal distension in intestinal obstruction –

A. Cases produced by bacterial activity

B. Cases diffused from blood

C. Swallowed air

D. Products of digestion

Q.279 What is the probable diagnosis for a cyst in a child which is located at and associated with vertebral defects –

A. Myelocele

B. Bronchogenic cyst

C. Neuroenteric cyst

D. Neuroblastoma

Q.280 Potter's syndrome is associated with –

A. Renal anomalies

B. Severe oligohydramnios

C. Flattened nose

D. All the above

Q.281 Paranasal sinus opening in middle meatus includes all except-

A. Maxillaly

B. Anterior ethmoid

C. Frontal

D. Sphenoid

Q.282 Percentage of newborn with deviation of nasal septum -

A. 2%   **B.** 10%   **C.** 20%   **D.** 50%

Q.283 The highest frequency of palpable metastasis in neck on presentation is -

A. Carcinoma tongue

B. Buccal mucosa

C. Alveolus

D. Lip

Q.284 Surgery on eardrum is done using

A. Operative microscope

B. Laser

C. Direct vision

D. Blindly

Q.285 Tympanic membrane develops from:

A. Ectoderm

B. Mesoderm

C. Endoderm

D. All the three germinal layers

Q.286 Stapes superstructure develops from:

A. Meckel's cartilage

B. Reichert's cartilage

C. Both (A) and (B)

D. Both (A) and (B) plus bony otic capsule

Q.287 Intratemporal lesion of chorda tympani nerve result in -

A. Loss of taste sensations from papilla of tongue

B. Loss of taste sensations from anterior 2/3rd of tongue

C. Loss of secretomotor fibres to the submandibular salivery gland

D. Loss of taste sensations from posterior 1/3rd of tongue

Q.288 Which one of the following statements is correct in facial paralysis -

A. The nasolabial fold is obliterated on same side

B. The nasolabial fold is obliterated on opposite side

C. The face deviates to the opposite side

D. Both (A) and (C)

Q.289 Maxillary sinus epithelium is

A. Squamous

B. Non ciliated columnar

C. Non-Keratinized squamous

D. Ciliated columnar

Q.290 All of the following are true about retropharyngeal abscess except -

A. Confined to one side of the midline

B. Can be palpable per orally by pressing the finger on posterior pharyngeal wall

C. Lies behind the prevertebral fascia

D. Presents with dysphagia & difficulty in breathing

Q.291 Treatment of Phylenticular conjunctivitis is:

A. Miotics

B. Mydriatics

C. Antibiotics

D. Steroid

Q.292 A soft contact lens wearer developed pain and itching of the eye and showed a reticular pattern on the corneal epithelium. The cause could be –

A. Corneal dystrophy

B. Acanthamoeba

C. Pseudomonas

D. Virus

Q.293 All of the following may lead to corneal opacity in newborn except –

A. Endothelial dystrophy

B. Sclerocornea

C. Mucopolysaccharidosis

D. Droplet keratopathy

Q.294 Vogt Koyanagi–Harada (VKH) syndrome is –

A. Chronic granulomatous uveitis

B. Chronic non-granulomatous uveitis

C. Acute purulent uveitis

D. None

Q.295 Cataract in diabetic patients is because of the accumulation of sorbitol in the lens. The enzyme responsible for this is –

A. Hexokinase

B. $NADPH^+$ dependant aldolase reductase

C. Glucokinase

D. Phosphofructo isomerase

Q.296 Treatment of acute congestive glaucoma includes all except –

a) Sclerectomy

b) Trabeculectomy

c) Trabeculoplasty

d) Vitrectomy

e) Iridotomy

A. ab   **B.** bc   **C.** ed   **D.** cd

Q.297 Diabetes mellitus can lead to –

A. Vitreous haemorrhage

B. Rubeosis iridis

C. Retinal detachment

D. All of the above

Q.298 A child presents with sudden loss of vision with painful ocular movements. The eye is white and there are no obvious signs on ophthalmoscopy. The most likely diagnosis is -

A. Optic nerve glioma   **B.** Retrobulbar neuritis

C. Craniopharyngioma   **D.** Papillitis

Q.299 Which is the commonest cause of occular morbidity in the community -

A. Cataract

B. Refractive error

C. Occular injury

D. Vitamin A deficiency

Q.300 The condition shown in Figure may be associated with which one of the following choices?

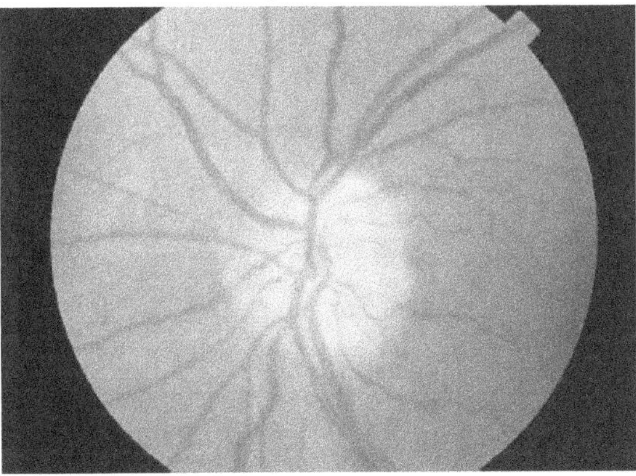

A. Visual loss

B. Papilledema

C. Autosomal recessive inheritance

D. Bilaterality in 25%

// Smart Answer Sheet //

Correct   Indicates percentage of students who answered questions correctly.

Skipped   Indicates percentage of students who skipped questions.

Q.	Ans.	Correct / Skipped
1	C	44.96 % / 3.95 %
2	C	30.79 % / 15.12 %
3	C	38.42 % / 20.71 %
4	A	21.25 % / 23.98 %
5	C	40.05 % / 27.39 %
6	A	25.75 % / 25.34 %
7	B	39.65 % / 27.24 %
8	C	19.75 % / 28.07 %
9	A	17.98 % / 29.98 %
10	B	20.16 % / 31.34 %
11	A	11.85 % / 32.43 %
12	D	22.34 % / 31.34 %
13	C	22.48 % / 32.56 %
14	A	21.12 % / 32.42 %
15	C	31.47 % / 32.97 %
16	A	16.21 % / 35.56 %
17	C	24.39 % / 34.33 %
18	C	27.93 % / 33.92 %
19	C	44.41 % / 34.2 %
20	C	23.84 % / 34.61 %
21	A	15.8 % / 36.92 %
22	B	17.71 % / 38.15 %
23	C	26.7 % / 37.47 %
24	D	14.17 % / 38.28 %
25	A	18.39 % / 38.01 %
26	C	23.43 % / 36.65 %
27	C	16.08 % / 37.73 %
28	A	25.2 % / 36.65 %
29	C	31.88 % / 37.33 %
30	A	16.76 % / 39.23 %
31	A	20.84 % / 40.06 %
32	A	33.79 % / 38.55 %
33	A	48.37 % / 38.41 %
34	A	14.03 % / 39.92 %
35	A	21.8 % / 40.33 %
36	C	17.57 % / 40.6 %
37	A	44.69 % / 39.78 %
38	B	22.62 % / 41.82 %
39	C	14.17 % / 41.28 %
40	B	15.4 % / 42.37 %
41	D	41.55 % / 40.33 %
42	B	19.75 % / 42.1 %
43	B	9.81 % / 44.28 %
44	C	18.26 % / 43.05 %
45	A	21.8 % / 42.51 %
46	C	16.62 % / 42.92 %
47	A	23.43 % / 41.97 %
48	C	20.44 % / 42.09 %
49	D	28.61 % / 41.83 %
50	D	11.17 % / 41.83 %
51	A	42.1 % / 35.83 %
52	C	28.61 % / 41.83 %
53	B	27.11 % / 44.14 %
54	D	11.72 % / 45.36 %
55	D	22.21 % / 46.73 %
56	A	27.11 % / 48.09 %
57	A	25.48 % / 47.68 %
58	B	16.35 % / 47.41 %
59	B	37.33 % / 47.55 %
60	B	29.84 % / 47.68 %
61	A	15.26 % / 48.64 %
62	C	7.49 % / 50.41 %
63	A	11.72 % / 50.41 %
64	A	20.3 % / 50.41 %
65	D	20.44 % / 50.95 %
66	A	20.3 % / 52.04 %
67	A	19.75 % / 50.96 %
68	A	13.22 % / 51.09 %
69	C	32.29 % / 50.95 %
70	D	9.67 % / 50.82 %
71	A	9.54 % / 52.99 %
72	C	14.17 % / 52.04 %
73	A	8.99 % / 52.73 %
74	D	13.62 % / 51.64 %
75	B	21.93 % / 52.46 %
76	C	14.03 % / 53.27 %
77	A	21.8 % / 52.18 %
78	C	22.21 % / 52.18 %
79	B	4.9 % / 53.96 %
80	A	15.53 % / 53.54 %

Q.	Ans.	Correct / Skipped	Q.	Ans.	Correct / Skipped	Q.	Ans.	Correct / Skipped	Q.	Ans.	Correct / Skipped	Q.	Ans.	Correct / Skipped
81	A	10.22 % / 53.68 %	97	A	10.63 % / 56.4 %	113	D	4.5 % / 58.44 %	129	C	17.03 % / 59.4 %	145	C	24.66 % / 59.54 %
82	C	20.57 % / 54.91 %	98	B	21.66 % / 55.72 %	114	C	11.44 % / 59.0 %	130	C	9.54 % / 60.62 %	146	A	22.21 % / 59.13 %
83	C	22.34 % / 52.86 %	99	C	24.93 % / 54.77 %	115	B	5.18 % / 60.9 %	131	D	16.21 % / 59.4 %	147	C	17.44 % / 59.54 %
84	D	17.98 % / 55.32 %	100	C	19.75 % / 56.82 %	116	C	19.75 % / 59.41 %	132	C	13.35 % / 58.18 %	148	C	15.4 % / 59.67 %
85	A	15.4 % / 55.04 %	101	C	15.53 % / 57.22 %	117	A	12.26 % / 58.18 %	133	A	29.84 % / 58.17 %	149	B	20.44 % / 58.85 %
86	C	34.74 % / 53.68 %	102	A	8.45 % / 57.63 %	118	D	25.75 % / 57.36 %	134	D	8.72 % / 59.81 %	150	C	20.3 % / 59.13 %
87	B	10.63 % / 55.17 %	103	C	10.76 % / 58.31 %	119	B	15.94 % / 57.63 %	135	D	32.97 % / 58.17 %	151	C	21.53 % / 47.82 %
88	B	12.53 % / 56.95 %	104	D	12.4 % / 57.35 %	120	B	23.16 % / 58.18 %	136	B	17.98 % / 59.54 %	152	C	17.71 % / 51.23 %
89	B	17.3 % / 56.54 %	105	A	30.25 % / 56.53 %	121	D	17.71 % / 57.9 %	137	A	24.11 % / 58.18 %	153	D	19.75 % / 53.68 %
90	C	8.58 % / 56.95 %	106	C	18.53 % / 57.22 %	122	D	25.2 % / 57.36 %	138	B	17.98 % / 58.45 %	154	C	12.53 % / 53.96 %
91	B	15.8 % / 56.54 %	107	A	10.63 % / 58.85 %	123	A	9.26 % / 57.77 %	139	C	11.99 % / 59.26 %	155	B	10.76 % / 54.77 %
92	C	17.71 % / 54.77 %	108	B	16.35 % / 58.99 %	124	D	21.39 % / 57.49 %	140	A	21.93 % / 58.86 %	156	B	14.71 % / 56.27 %
93	D	24.25 % / 54.5 %	109	B	15.67 % / 58.31 %	125	C	29.02 % / 57.63 %	141	C	10.63 % / 58.85 %	157	D	14.03 % / 54.36 %
94	C	19.21 % / 56.27 %	110	B	15.8 % / 58.59 %	126	C	9.67 % / 59.68 %	142	A	17.44 % / 59.4 %	158	B	13.9 % / 55.99 %
95	D	20.98 % / 56.27 %	111	B	14.99 % / 57.76 %	127	C	21.53 % / 59.53 %	143	D	10.9 % / 60.08 %	159	C	20.84 % / 56.0 %
96	B	11.85 % / 56.0 %	112	A	16.89 % / 57.63 %	128	D	11.99 % / 60.49 %	144	C	14.17 % / 60.63 %	160	B	18.53 % / 55.18 %

Q.	Ans.	Correct / Skipped	Q.	Ans.	Correct / Skipped	Q.	Ans.	Correct / Skipped	Q.	Ans.	Correct / Skipped	Q.	Ans.	Correct / Skipped
161	C	11.58 % / 55.86 %	177	B	15.94 % / 56.95 %	193	A	11.72 % / 59.12 %	209	A	13.35 % / 60.76 %	225	B	11.85 % / 61.31 %
162	C	12.4 % / 56.81 %	178	C	12.4 % / 58.99 %	194	B	15.12 % / 58.72 %	210	B	3.27 % / 58.72 %	226	B	13.08 % / 60.63 %
163	D	12.94 % / 55.86 %	179	B	11.04 % / 60.49 %	195	D	22.07 % / 57.9 %	211	C	13.9 % / 59.53 %	227	D	2.72 % / 61.18 %
164	B	8.17 % / 56.27 %	180	B	17.85 % / 59.13 %	196	A	5.04 % / 58.58 %	212	A	18.39 % / 59.68 %	228	A	9.54 % / 60.49 %
165	C	5.04 % / 57.49 %	181	B	19.21 % / 57.63 %	197	B	11.58 % / 59.26 %	213	A	22.62 % / 58.72 %	229	B	10.08 % / 60.36 %
166	B	9.4 % / 58.58 %	182	A	11.72 % / 60.35 %	198	B	20.57 % / 58.86 %	214	B	14.03 % / 60.36 %	230	A	5.86 % / 61.58 %
167	C	11.72 % / 57.35 %	183	A	15.53 % / 59.13 %	199	A	18.53 % / 58.58 %	215	C	8.04 % / 60.35 %	231	B	20.44 % / 59.26 %
168	A	17.3 % / 58.04 %	184	A	12.67 % / 58.45 %	200	A	8.72 % / 59.81 %	216	A	14.99 % / 59.4 %	232	D	9.81 % / 59.94 %
169	B	26.57 % / 56.4 %	185	A	23.84 % / 57.22 %	201	B	14.44 % / 59.67 %	217	D	15.94 % / 59.4 %	233	B	5.31 % / 61.86 %
170	C	10.35 % / 56.82 %	186	D	21.39 % / 58.31 %	202	D	20.16 % / 59.54 %	218	A	9.95 % / 59.67 %	234	B	26.02 % / 59.54 %
171	B	9.81 % / 57.08 %	187	C	7.9 % / 59.54 %	203	D	20.44 % / 58.99 %	219	A	9.81 % / 60.76 %	235	B	4.36 % / 60.9 %
172	D	5.72 % / 57.77 %	188	B	9.4 % / 59.95 %	204	A	11.58 % / 59.26 %	220	D	5.59 % / 61.03 %	236	C	18.8 % / 60.36 %
173	D	7.08 % / 58.18 %	189	C	23.02 % / 59.13 %	205	B	14.58 % / 58.99 %	221	B	17.85 % / 62.67 %	237	A	6.68 % / 60.89 %
174	B	11.44 % / 58.04 %	190	D	13.08 % / 58.99 %	206	A	26.16 % / 58.31 %	222	C	17.03 % / 59.81 %	238	B	20.98 % / 59.95 %
175	B	10.9 % / 57.49 %	191	C	27.52 % / 58.72 %	207	A	12.94 % / 60.22 %	223	A	13.9 % / 59.81 %	239	A	10.49 % / 59.95 %
176	C	8.58 % / 56.82 %	192	D	8.58 % / 59.68 %	208	D	9.26 % / 59.54 %	224	D	6.27 % / 61.58 %	240	D	14.31 % / 60.08 %

Q.	Ans.	Correct / Skipped	Q.	Ans.	Correct / Skipped	Q.	Ans.	Correct / Skipped	Q.	Ans.	Correct / Skipped	Q.	Ans.	Correct / Skipped
241	B	9.54 % / 60.49 %	253	A	17.98 % / 60.09 %	265	D	10.22 % / 60.35 %	277	B	10.76 % / 61.99 %	289	D	12.94 % / 60.77 %
242	C	13.76 % / 59.4 %	254	D	4.77 % / 60.76 %	266	C	12.13 % / 61.03 %	278	C	13.49 % / 60.9 %	290	C	10.49 % / 62.4 %
243	A	11.17 % / 59.54 %	255	C	13.76 % / 60.76 %	267	A	9.13 % / 60.08 %	279	C	8.86 % / 61.3 %	291	D	15.26 % / 61.31 %
244	D	5.31 % / 59.27 %	256	C	14.71 % / 59.81 %	268	A	19.62 % / 59.81 %	280	D	23.16 % / 61.04 %	292	B	17.17 % / 60.9 %
245	D	12.67 % / 59.54 %	257	A	5.99 % / 61.31 %	269	D	9.13 % / 61.17 %	281	D	14.85 % / 60.76 %	293	D	5.31 % / 62.26 %
246	B	16.21 % / 59.27 %	258	C	33.79 % / 59.13 %	270	A	19.21 % / 60.35 %	282	B	8.99 % / 61.58 %	294	A	9.67 % / 61.72 %
247	A	19.89 % / 60.08 %	259	D	9.81 % / 60.9 %	271	B	16.08 % / 59.81 %	283	A	11.44 % / 61.45 %	295	B	18.53 % / 60.9 %
248	A	14.17 % / 60.08 %	260	C	13.76 % / 60.35 %	272	C	17.03 % / 59.95 %	284	A	23.3 % / 61.17 %	296	D	5.72 % / 62.26 %
249	C	31.34 % / 59.4 %	261	B	11.44 % / 61.45 %	273	D	12.67 % / 60.08 %	285	D	22.34 % / 60.77 %	297	D	26.7 % / 59.95 %
250	A	14.03 % / 61.17 %	262	D	11.44 % / 60.36 %	274	A	4.5 % / 60.21 %	286	B	8.45 % / 61.44 %	298	B	15.12 % / 61.72 %
251	B	11.72 % / 60.49 %	263	B	19.21 % / 60.49 %	275	B	11.04 % / 60.89 %	287	C	6.81 % / 62.4 %	299	B	16.08 % / 59.94 %
252	B	9.95 % / 61.85 %	264	D	26.29 % / 59.81 %	276	A	20.84 % / 59.81 %	288	D	21.39 % / 61.04 %	300	A	5.18 % / 59.53 %

Performance Analysis

Avg. Score (%)	12.25%
Toppers Score (%)	75.92%
Your Score	

Q.1 Nerves of Branchial arch derived from:

A. Mesoderm   **B.** Endoderm

C. Neural crest   **D.** Neuroectoderm

Q.2 Hard palate contains:

A. Keratinised, submucosa, minor salivary gland

B. Keratinised, absent submucosal layer, minor salivary gland

C. Non keratinised, submucosal layer, minor salivary gland

D. Non keratinised, absent submucosa, minor salivary gland

Q.3 What is the tensor of vocal cords?

A. Cricothyroid

B. Lateral Cricoarytenoid

C. Thyroarytenoids

D. Posterior cricoarytenoids

Q.4 Ureteric bud develops from:

A. Mesonephros   **B.** Metanephros

C. Pronephros   **D.** Genital sinus

Q.5 About Weber's syndrome which is incorrect:

A. Contralateral hemiplegia

B. Ipsilateral Oculomotor nerve palsy

C. Contralateral Parkinsonism

D. Anterior cerebral peduncle

Q.6 About Sibson's fascia which is incorrect:

A. Attached to the inner border of 2nd rib

B. Covers apical part of lung

C. Part of scalenus anterior muscle

D. Vessel pass above the fascia

Q.7 Thrombosis of posterior inferior cerebellar artery causes:

A. Lateral medullary syndrome

B. Weber syndrome

C. Medial medullary syndrome

D. None of these

Q.8 Broca's area situated in:

A. Inferior frontal gyrus

B. Superior temporal gyrus

C. Angular gyrus

D. None of the above

Q.9 Acute tonsillitis affects which nerve:

A. Glossopharyngeal Nerve

B. Facial Nerve

C. Trigeminal nerve

D. Vagus Nerve

Q.10 Structures not passing through Aortic opening:

A. Azygos vein   **B.** Aorta

C. Thoracic duct   **D.** Vagus

Q.11 What should be the value of BMI to be considered as "Lethal" in men?

A. 12   **B.** 18   **C.** 13   **D.** 14

Q.12 Which receptors are blocked in Myasthenia Gravis?

A. Ach receptors   **B.** Ca^{++} receptors

C. Na^{2+} receptors   **D.** Opioid receptors

Q.13 What is the characteristic pattern seen in Brown sequard syndrome:

A. C/L loss of joint sense and position

B. C/L loss of pain

C. I/L loss of complete sensory functions

D. C/L motor functions

Q.14 When Va/Q is infinity?

A. Partial pressure of O_2 becomes zero

B. No exchange of O_2 & CO_2

C. Partial pressure of CO_2 alone becomes zero

D. Partial pressure both CO_2 and O_2 remain normal

Q.15 C wave is seen in:

A. Iso-volumetric contraction

B. Slow filling at end of diastole

C. End of systole

D. Start of diastole

Q.16 Alpha waves are seen during?

A. Sleep   **B.** REM movements

C. Relaxed state   **D.** Active state

Q.17 In hypovolemic shock there is:

A. Afferent arteriolar constriction

B. Efferent arteriolar constriction

C. Increased blood flow to kidney

D. Normal cardiac output

Q.18 Components responsible for counter current mechanism in kidney are all except:

A. Sodium outflow in thick ascending limb

B. Water outflow in thin descending limb

C. Sodium outflow in thin ascending limb

D. Flow of tubular fluid from PCT to DCT

Q.19 Glucose is absorbed in intestine by?

A. Secondary active transport

B. Facilitated diffusion

C. Simple diffusion

D. Primary active transport

Q.20 Insulin like growth factor is secreted by:

A. Liver   **B.** Pituitary gland

C. Pancreas   **D.** Adrenal glands

Q.21 What is Prosopagnosia?

A. Impairment of consciousness

B. Being unaware of one's problems

C. Difficulty in identifying known faces

D. Failure to identify objects

Q.22 Tyrosinosis is caused due to deficiency of which enzyme?

A. Fumarylacetoacetate hydrolase

B. p-hydroxy phenylpyruvate dehydrogenase

C. Tyrosine transaminase

D. Tyrosine ligase

Q.23 Lesch-Nyhan syndrome is caused by deficiency of which enzyme?

A. Orotate Phosphoribosyltransferase

B. Uracil phosphoribosyltransferase

C. Quinolinate Phosphoribosyltransferase

D. Hypoxanthine-guanine phosphoribosyltransferase (HGPRT)

Q.24 Fish odor syndrome is caused by deficiency of which enzyme?

A. Fumarylacetoacetate hydrolase

B. Methane monooxygenase

C. Monooxygenase 3(FMO$_3$)

D. D-amino acid oxidase

Q.25 Galactosemia is due to deficiency of which enzymes?

A. Galactose-1-phosphate uridyltransferase

B. HGPRT

C. Galactokinase

D. Epimerase

Q.26 Which of the following is most abundant end product of fatty acid synthesis?

A. Oleic acid

B. Palmitic acid

C. Arachidonic acid

D. Glucose

Q.27 About DNA polymerase I which one is correct?

A. Not required in bacteria

B. Repair any damage with DNA

C. Involved in okazaki fragment

D. Participate in DNA replication

Q.28 What does chaperones assist in?

A. Protein Cleavage

B. Protein Folding

C. Protein Degradation

D. Protein Modification

Q.29 Fishy odour occurs due to deficiency of this vitamin from diet:

A. Biotin

B. Thiamine

C. Riboflavin

D. Vit. A

Q.30 VMA is excreted in urine in which condition?

A. Alkaptonuria

B. Phenylketonuria

C. Pheochromocytoma

D. Diabetic ketoacidosis

Q.31 In Cystinuria all of the following aminoacids reabsorption defect is present, except:

A. Lysine

B. Citrulline

C. Arginine

D. Ornithine

Q.32 Fibrinopeptide A and fibrinopeptide B are acidic due to the presence of which amino acids in its structure:

A. Serine and threonine

B. Glutamate and aspartate

C. Histidine and lysine

D. Glutamine and valine

Q.33 HIAA in urine present in?

A. Alkaptonuria

B. Albinism

C. Carcinoid

D. Phenylketonuria

Q.34 Warthin finkeldey cells are seen in:

A. Measles

B. Rubella

C. Rabies

D. Typhoid

Q.35 CD59 marker of which disease?

A. PNH

B. PTEN

C. BRR

D. Cowden syndrome

Q.36 Opsonin is:

A. C_3a

B. C_3b

C. C_5a

D. C_6

Q.37 Bernard–Soulier syndrome due to deficiency of:

A. Gp 2b/3a

B. Gp 1b

C. vWf

D. TNF

Q.38 Cowden syndrome:

A. P53

B. PTEN

C. Rb

D. Ras

Q.39 Chromosome involved in myotonic dystrophy is:

A. Chromosome 19

B. Chromosome 20

C. Chromosome 21

D. Chromosome 22

Q.40 TRALI occurs within how many hours of transfusion?

A. 48 Hrs

B. 72 Hrs

C. 6 Hrs

D. 12 Hrs

Q.41 Kidney responds to shock by:

A. Decreases renal blood flow

B. Increases afferent arteriole resistance

C. GFR remains unaltered

D. Perfusion of kidney increases

Q.42 Which of the following is epithelial tumour of stomach?

A. Carcinoid

B. Lymphoma

C. GIST

D. Gastric adenocarcinoma

Q.43 Identify an X linked disorder?

A. Colour blindness

B. Thalassemia

C. Azoospermia

D. Retinitis Pigmentosa

Q.44 H and L variety seen in:

A. Mixed cellularity hodgkin

B. Lymphocyte depleted

C. Lymphocyte predominance

D. Nodular sclerosis

Q.45 Stellate granuloma seen in:

A. Sarcoidosis **B.** Cat scratch disease

C. Cryptococcosis **D.** Histoplasmosis

Q.46 Which best explains "Flipping effect"?

A. LDH-1 > LDH-2 **B.** LDH-2 > LDH-1

C. LDH-2 > LDH-3 **D.** LDH-3 > LDH-2

Q.47 Nude mice is not resistant to xenograft due to absence of:

A. B cell **B.** T cell

C. Both B and T cell **D.** None of these

Q.48 Anaplasia is:

A. Changing one type of epithelium to another

B. Nuclear chromatin

C. Lack of differentiation

D. Morphological changes

Q.49 Which level of prolactin definitely suggest prolactinoma?

A. 300 ng/ml **B.** 150 ng/ml

C. 200 ng/ml **D.** 100 ng/ml

Q.50 Laxative abuse causes which of the following renal stones?

A. Uric acid **B.** Ammonium urate

C. Struvite **D.** Ca oxalate

Q.51 Which of the following can result in dactylitis?

A. Hemophilia

B. Von willebrand disease 1

C. Measles

D. Sickle Cell Anemia

Q.52 Which chromosome is responsible for the production of MIF?

A. Chromosome 16 **B.** Chromosome 22

C. X Chromosome **D.** Y chromosome

Q.53 Site of action of amphotericin B is:

A. Ribosomes **B.** Cell wall

C. Plasma membrane **D.** Protein

Q.54 Which antiretroviral drug also has anti hepatitis activity?

A. Abacavir **B.** Tenofovir

C. Nevirapine **D.** Emtricitabine

Q.55 Drug of choice for resistant rheumatic chorea?

A. Valproate **B.** Haloperidol

C. Diazepam **D.** Probenecid

Q.56 At pKa=pH:

A. Conc. of drug is 50% ionic and 50% non-ionic

B. Absorption of drug is 50% ionic and 50% ionic

C. Conc of drug is 75% ionic and 25% non-ionic

D. Conc of drug is 25% ionic and 75% non-ionic

Q.57 Physiological dose of hydrocortisone (mg/kg/day) is:

A. 5 mg/kg/day **B.** 10 mg/kg/day

C. 15 mg/kg/day **D.** 20 mg/kg/day

Q.58 What is mechanism of action of colchicine in acute gout?

A. Inhibition of purine metabolism

B. Inhibition of uric acid conversion

C. Migration of leukocytes

D. Leukocytes, lymphocytes inhibition & microtubular inhibitor

Q.59 Basiliximab is an:

A. IL-1 receptor antagonist

B. Anti-CD3 antibody

C. IL-2 receptor antagonist

D. TNF inhibitor

Q.60 Pirenzepine is used:

A. Gastric ulcer

B. Glaucoma

C. Hypertension

D. Congestive cardiac failure

Q.61 Which of the following antipsychotic have increased prolactin secretion?

A. Olanzapine **B.** Ziprasidone

C. Clozapine **D.** Risperidone

Q.62 Which of the following is glucocorticoid synthesis inhibitor?

A. Mifepristone **B.** Flutamide

C. Finasteride **D.** Metyrapone

Q.63 Which of the following statements isincorrect w.r.t Prasugrel?

A. Not a prodrug

B. P2Y purinergic receptor blocker

C. Has a strong antiplatelet activity

D. Causes intracranial hemorrhage in TIA patients.

Q.64 Q-T elongation is seen in which drug?

A. Quinidine **B.** Amiodarone

C. Magnesium Sulfate **D.** Lignocaine

Q.65 Sacubitril is:

A. ACE inhibitor

B. Neutral endopeptidase inhibitor

C. Calcium channel inhibitor

D. Beta adrenergic blocker

Q.66 Niacin therapy is contraindicated in diabetes because:

A. Increases the blood sugar levels

B. Causes scleroderma

C. Difficult to give injection

D. Increases the metabolism of oral hypoglycemic drugs

Q.67 Endothelin acts through which receptors?

A. cAMP **B.** cGMP

C. Na+ receptors **D.** Calcium receptos

Q.68 Which is the centrally acting alpha 2 agonist muscle relaxant:

A. Diazepam **B.** Bromocriptine
C. Tizanidine **D.** Methocarbamol

Q.69 Apixaban is:
A. Antithrombin inhibitor
B. Direct Xa inhibitor
C. Platelet activator
D. Clotting Factor XII

Q.70 Anaerobes are resistant intrinsically against:
A. Beta lactam antibiotics
B. Aminoglycosides
C. Azithromycin
D. Metronidazole

Q.71 Which is not bacteriostatic antibiotic:
A. Clindamycin **B.** Vancomycin
C. Tetracycline **D.** Cephalosporins

Q.72 Which of the following causes melanosis coli?
A. Senna
B. Sorbitol
C. Magnesium Sulphate
D. Bisacodyl

Q.73 Which among the following will the choiceof antibiotic for a bedridden patient withcatheter-related UTI and pneumonia.
A. Amoxicillin
B. Beta-Lactam antibiotics with beta lactamase
C. 3rd gen cephalosporins
D. 2nd gen cephalosporins

Q.74 Mycoplasma is resistant to:
A. Ceftriaxone **B.** Cephalosporins
C. Aminoglycosides **D.** Fluoroquinolones

Q.75 Tadalafil should not be given with:
A. Vasodilator **B.** Antibiotics
C. Vasoconstrictors **D.** Valproate

Q.76 Estimate volume of ringer lactate in first 8 hrs for 40% burns in 50 kg male with $2°$ burns?
A. 8 litre **B.** 4 litre **C.** 2 litre **D.** 6 litre

Q.77 Posthumous child is:
A. Child delivered after death of biological mother
B. Child delivered after death of biological father
C. Born after death of parents
D. Has been abandoned by parents

Q.78 M'naghten rule comes under which section of IPC?
A. CRPC 84 **B.** CRPC 48
C. IPC 84 **D.** IPC 48

Q.79 Bluish discoloration of gastric mucosa seen in which poisoning?
A. Mercury **B.** Cadmium
C. Amytal sodium **D.** Arsenic

Q.80 Muscle pain, nephropathy caused by which metal poisoning:
A. Arsenic **B.** Cadmium
C. Mercury **D.** Lead

Q.81 Which is the first organ to putrefy?
A. Brain **B.** Heart **C.** Prostate **D.** Kidney

Q.82 Locard is famous for:
A. Theory of exchange
B. Fingerprint study
C. Formula for estimation of stature
D. System of personal identification using the body measurement

Q.83 When does basiocciput fuses with basisphenoid?
A. 18 to 22 **B.** 22 to 25 **C.** 14-16 **D.** 12-14

Q.84 What is the smell of mummified body?
A. Odourless **B.** Putrid
C. Pungent **D.** Offensive

Q.85 Patient presented with proximal tubuleproteinuria. Which metal is likely to beassociated with it?
A. Cadmium **B.** Mercury
C. Gold **D.** Lead

Q.86 Which of the following constitutionalarticle is not related to children:
A. 23 **B.** 21-A **C.** 42 **D.** 24

Q.87 Which of the statement regarding Factory act is correct ?
A. Child age less than 14 carrying serious work earn more money
B. Less than 14 yr not done for factory act
C. More than 72 hour work per week
D. More than 82 hours a week

Q.88 Burkholderia cepacia is resistant to whichof the following drugs?
A. Ceftazidime
B. Trimethoprim-sulfamethoxazole
C. Temocillin
D. Cefotetan

Q.89 Shingles is caused by which of the following?
A. Varicella-zoster **B.** Herpes simplex
C. CMV **D.** None

Q.90 Urea breath test is used for diagnosis of:
A. H.pylori
B. Campylobacter jejuni
C. E. co
D. Lactobacillus

Q.91 Hyperacute graft rejection occurs after how much time?
A. 24 hours **B.** 2 weeks right
C. In minutes **D.** Years

Q.92 Australian antigen for hepatitis B is?
A. HBsAg **B.** HBeAg **C.** HBsAg **D.** HBvDna

Q.93 Which fungus is most commonly associated with orbital cellulitis in patients with diabetic ketoacidosis.

A. Candida

B. Mucor

C. Aspergillus

D. Rhizopus

Q.94 Sabin Feldman dye test is used for diagnosis of which of the following condition?

A. Botulism

B. Toxoplasmosis

C. Sarcoidosis

D. Yellow fever

Q.95 Acute Hemorrhagic Conjunctivitis is caused by which of enterovirus type?

A. 69

B. 68

C. 70

D. 71

Q.96 Echinococcus granulosus are commonly seen in which of the given animals?

A. Dog

B. Cat

C. Fox

D. Pig

Q.97 An anaerobe causing multiple abscesswith discharging sinuses, demonstratingsulphur granules in pus is?

A. Actinomycetes

B. Nocardia

C. Salmonella

D. Tularemia

Q.98 Whole blood is used as a sample for which test?

A. Bacteria

B. IGRA

C. Genexper

D. Virus

Q.99 Which organism causing acute bacterialprostatitis?

A. Enterococcus

B. Streptococcus viridans

C. Peptostreptococcus

D. E.coli

Q.100 Which of the following organismreleases histamine and cause scombroidfish poisoning?

A. Salmonella

B. Staphylococcus

C. P. aeruginosa

D. Weissella

Q.101 Who is the father of microbiology?

A. A. V. L. hook

B. Robert brown

C. J.C Bose

D. Pasteur

Q.102 Cutaneous larva migrans caused bywhich organism?

A. Strongyloides

B. Toxocara canis

C. Ancylostoma braziliense

D. Necator americanus

Q.103 After kidney transplantation whichorganisms infection is more likely tohappens:

A. CMV

B. Klebsiella

C. Streptococcus

D. Staphylococcus

Q.104 Incidence of a disease is 4 per 1000 ofpopulation with duration of 2 years.Calculate the prevalence?

A. $\frac{8}{1000}$

B. $\frac{4}{1000}$

C. $\frac{2}{1000}$

D. $\frac{6}{1000}$

Q.105 Cytotoxic and expired drug disposal is done by which method?

A. Dumping

B. Autoclave

C. Landfill

D. Burning

Q.106 For NRR to be 1 couple protection rateshould be?

A. 50%

B. 60%

C. 55%

D. 75%

Q.107 New RNTCP software online to monitorTB control programme is:

A. NIKSHAY

B. NICHAY

C. E- DOTS

D. NIRBHAI

Q.108 Study unit of ecological study is:

A. Population

B. Patient

C. Community

D. Case

Q.109 In a screening test for DM out of 1000 population, 90 were positive. Then thegold standard test was done in which 100 were positive. Calculate thesensitivity?

A. $\frac{90}{100}$

B. $\frac{100}{110}$

C. $\frac{80}{100}$

D. $\frac{100}{100}$

Q.110 What is the mass chemoprophylaxis formeningococcal meningitis?

A. Rifampicin

B. Chloramphenicol

C. Tetracycline

D. Penicillin

Q.111 Which among the following is an active form of chlorination?

A. Hypochlorite ion

B. Hydrogen chloride

C. Hypochlorous acid

D. Chloride ion

Q.112 Kala-Azar is found in all endemic areasexcept.

A. West Bengal

B. UP

C. Bihar

D. Assam

Q.113 Risk among exposed to risk among nonexposed is defined to be:

A. Relative risk

B. Odds ratio

C. Attributable risk

D. None of the above

Q.114 Pasteurization is done at:

A. 73°C For 20 min

B. 63°C For 30 min

C. 72°C For 30 seconds

D. 63°C For 30 seconds

Q.115 Ideal time gap between 2 live vaccination:

A. 2 weeks

B. 4 weeks

C. 8 weeks

D. 12 weeks

Q.116 Susceptible person developed diseasewithin range of IP after coming in contactwith primary case:

A. Secondary attack rate

B. Case fatality rate

C. Primary attack rate

D. Tertiary attack rate

Q.117 Out of 100 women who were offered ocp for contraception 10 women got pregnant when followed for 24 months. What is Pearl's index?

A. 10

B. 5

C. 4

D. 2

Q.118 Which of the following do not causehardness of water?

A. Calcium carbonate

B. Calcium sulphate

C. Calcium bicarbonate

D. Magnesium bicarbonate

Q.119 Which of the following is not an exampleof direct transmission in communicablediseases?

A. Transplacental (vertical)

B. Soil

C. Respiratory

D. STD

Q.120 Water's view is used to obtain diagnosticinformation of:

A. Maxillary sinus
B. Ethmoidal sinuses

C. Frontal sinus
D. Sphenoid sinus

Q.121 Tracheostomy indication is:

A. Vocal cord replacement

B. Pharynx replacement

C. Tracheomalacia

D. Foreign body obstructing airway

Q.122 Caldwell's view is used for:

A. Maxillary sinus
B. Frontal sinus

C. Ethmoidal sinus
D. All of the above

Q.123 Astigmatism in emmetropic eye of elderly person contribute to:

A. +1D   **B.** +2D   **C.** +3D   **D.** +4D

Q.124 100 day Glaucoma seen in which of thefollowing condition:

A. Central retinal vein occlusion (CRVO)

B. Neovascular glaucoma

C. Central retinal artery occlusion (CRAO

D. Steroid induced Glaucoma

Q.125 Q Roth spots is seen in:

A. Uveal melanoma
B. Acute leukaemia

C. Both (A) & (B)
D. None of the above

Q.126 Yoke muscle of right lateral rectus:

A. Lt medial rectus
B. Lt superior rectus

C. Lt lateral rectus
D. Lt inferior oblique

Q.127 Severe Conjunctivitis caused by:

A. Neisseria
B. Staphylococcus

C. Streptococcus
D. Haemophilus

Q.128 Which is example of the Simple MyopicAstigmatism among the prescriptionsgiven below:

A. Rx (+) sphere

B. Rx will be plano (-)

C. Rx will be (-) sphere

D. (-)(+) (+)(-) on both 90 and 180 degree axis

Q.129 Blow out fracture of orbit involves:

A. Floor
B. Medial wall

C. Lateral wall
D. Roo

Q.130 Which of the following is endogenouspyrogen?

A. PG E2
B. PG D2

C. PGF2 alpha
D. PG I2

Q.131 In Bartter syndrome defect is seen in:

A. Defect in PCT

B. Defect in DCT

C. Defect in thick ascending limb of loop of Henle

D. None

Q.132 Not seen in allergic pulmonaryaspergillosis is:

A. High IgE level

B. Recurrent pneumonia

C. Occurrence in patients with old cavitary lesions

D. Pleural effusion

Q.133 Pseudo P Pulmonale:

A. Hypokalemia
B. Hyponatremia

C. Hypocalcemia
D. Hypercalcemia

Q.134 Automatic Implantable CardioverterDefibrillator, (AICD) implantation is donefor which of following conditions:

A. Brugada syndrome

B. Ventricular fibrillation

C. Acute coronary syndrome with low EF

D. All of the above

Q.135 What is the line of treatment forintractable Sydenham chorea?

A. Haloperidol
B. Valproate

C. Warfarin
D. Risperidone

Q.136 Neurofibromatosis 1 criteria except:

A. Brain tumor
B. Acoustic neuromas

C. Pseudoarthrosis
D. Cafe-au-lait spots

Q.137 Most common site of chronic gastric ulcer.

A. Pyloric antrum

B. Upper part of lesser curvature

C. Lower part of lesser curvature

D. Segment of large intestine

Q.138 Approximate time interval between HIVinfection & manifestation of AIDS is?

A. 7.5 yr   **B.** 10 yr   **C.** 12 yr   **D.** 11 yr

Q.139 Heller's myotomy is done for:

A. Zenker's diverticulum

B. Achalasia cardia

C. Bunions

D. Knee arthroscopy

Q.140 Myocardial stunning pattern notmatching the ECG. What is thediagnosis?

A. Takotsubo cardiomyopathy

B. Restrictive cardiomyopathy

C. Brigade's cardiomyopathy

D. Pericardial something

Q.141 Alternative drug for cardiac arrest inplace of epinephrine is?

A. Amiodarone infusion

B. Atropine

C. High dose vasopressin

D. Adenosine

Q.142 Patient presenting with cutaneousvasculitis, glomerulonephritis, peripheralneuropathy, Which investigation is to beperformed next that will help youdiagnose the condition?

A. ANCA

B. RA factor

C. Hbsag

D. MIF

Q.143 Cryoglobulinemia:

A. Hepatitis C

B. Ovarian cancer

C. Diabetes

D. Leukemia

Q.144 Causes of hypokalemic metabolicalkalosis with hypertension:

A. Liddle syndrome

B. Bartter syndrome

C. Gitelman syndrome

D. Renal tubular acidosis

Q.145 Gold criteria for very severe COPD:

A. Fev1/Fvc <70 and Fev1 < 30

B. Fev1/Fvc <70 and Fev1 < 70

C. Fev1/Fvc <70 and Fev1 < 50

D. Both (A) and (C)

Q.146 ABPI increases artificially in:

A. Arteriosclerosis calcified arteries

B. Ischemic ulcers

C. Intermittent claudication

D. DVT

Q.147 Minimal brain dysfunction syndrome seen in:

A. Dyslexia

B. Attention deficit hyperactivity disorder(ADHD)

C. Mental subnormality

D. Down's syndrome

Q.148 Van Nuys prognostic index is not basedon:

A. Age

B. Microcalcification

C. Size

D. ER status

Q.149 Common cause of chronic pancreatitis:

A. Chronic alcohol

B. Chronic pancreatic calculi

C. Pancreas divisum

D. Gall bladder stones

Q.150 The following statement about Keloid istrue:

A. It contain growth factor

B. Extended excision is the treatment of choice

C. It do not extend beyond the wound

D. None of the above

Q.151 Which of the following layers are cutduring fasciotomy?

A. Skin

B. Skin+subcutaneous fascia

C. Skin+subcutaneous tissue+Superficial fascia

D. Skin+subcutaneous tissue+Superficial fascia+deep fascia

Q.152 Which statement is not true regardingcrohn's disease?

A. Rectum is not involved

B. Continuous lesion visualized in endoscopy

C. Non caseating granulomas

D. Cobblestone appearance

Q.153 Which is the best investigation for carcinoma head of pancreas:

A. Guided biopsy

B. ERCP

C. Transduodenal/transperitoneal sampling

D. EUS

Q.154 An abdominal mass is bestdemonstrated in congenital hypertrophicpyloric stenosis by:

A. In palpation over the epigastrium

B. In left hypochondriac

C. Right iliac fossa

D. During feeding

Q.155 Calculate GCS of 25 year old head injurypatient with following parametersconfused, opening eyes in response topain, localizing pain will be:

A. 6

B. 11

C. 12

D. 7

Q.156 RET proto-oncogene is associated withthe development of:

A. Medullary carcinoma thyroid

B. Astrocytoma

C. Paraganglioma

D. Hurthle cell tumor thyroid

Q.157 Cutoff for surgery in an abdominal aorticaneurysm in asymptomatic patients:

A. 5.5cm

B. 6.5cm

C. 7.5cm

D. 8.5cm

Q.158 Which of the fontanelle is the last to close?

A. Anterolateral

B. Anterior

C. Lateral

D. Occipital

Q.159 Which enzyme deficiency causes Lesch-Nyhan syndrome?

A. Hypoxanthine-guanine phosphoribosyltransferase (HGPRT)

B. Xanthine oxidase

C. Adenine phosphoribosyltransferase (APRT)

D. AMP deaminase

Q.160 Which vaccine is not include inIndra Dhanush mission?

A. Tuberculosis

B. Measles

C. Japanese Encephalitis

D. Diphtheria

Q.161 Which among the following is the mostcommon cause for neonatal blindness?

A. Neisseria gonorrhoeae

B. Chlamydia trachomatis

C. Klebsiella

D. Enterobacter

Q.162 Muscles affected in De quervaintenosynovitis:

A. Abductor pollicis longus and extensor pollicis brevis

B. Adductor pollicis longus and extensor pollicis brevis

C. Abductor pollicis longus and Flexor pollicis brevis

D. Adductor pollicis longus and Flexor pollicis brevis

Q.163 What is meant by Perilunate dislocations?

A. Lower radius, scaphoid and lunate and capitate all in same plane

B. Lower radius, scaphoid and capitate in alignment, lunate aloneout of plane

C. Lower radius, scaphoid and Lunate in alignment ,capitate alone is out of plane

D. Both lunate and capitate are out of plane

Q.164 Fallen fragment sign:

A. Simple bone cyst

B. Osteosarcoma

C. Adamantinoma

D. Aneurysmal bone cyst

Q.165 You are posted as an intern incausality. Which among the followingpatients with fracture will be your 1stpriority to call ortho PG and inform?

A. Patient's finger is blackening

B. Patient can't extend his arm

C. A 10 cm abrasion

D. Intra articular fracture of Elbow Joint

Q.166 In Rheumatoid arthritis, which type ofcells are prominently present?

A. B cells

B. T cells

C. Macrophages

D. Dendritic cells

Q.167 8th and 9th rib costal cartilage formswhich type of joint?

A. Costochondral joint

B. Interchondral joint

C. Synovial joint

D. Costovertebral joint

Q.168 Tom smith septic arthritis is:

A. Acute Gonococcal arthritis

B. Smallpox arthritis

C. Septic arthritis of infancy

D. Chronic pyogenic arthritis

Q.169 Which of the following is correct regarding placenta?

A. Placental artery provides nutrients through umbilical cord to baby

B. Placenta has Wharton's jelly

C. Placenta has 2 veins and 1 artery

D. Estrogen is secreted by placenta

Q.170 Acute fatty liver commonly seen inpregnancy at:

A. 3rd trimester

B. 1st trimester

C. Immediate postpartum

D. Intrapartum

Q.171 Establishment of fetoplacentalcirculation seen at:

A. 11 to 13 days

B. 20 to 22 days

C. 7 days

D. 25 to 26 days

Q.172 Fimbriectomy procedure is known as:

A. Uchida method

B. Irving method

C. Madlener technique

D. Kroener method

Q.173 RDA of iodine in lactation in microgram:

A. 150

B. 220

C. 100

D. 250

Q.174 Which one of the following is not acause of secondary PostpartumHaemorrhage?

A. Placenta previa

B. Retained bits of placenta

C. Endometritis

D. Polyp

Q.175 Best time to do quadruple test:

A. 8-12 weeks

B. 11-15 weeks

C. 15-20 weeks

D. 18-22 weeks

Q.176 Drug that is used for fetal lung maturity is:

A. Dexamethasone

B. Folic acid

C. Beclomethasone

D. None of these

Q.177 In Uterine prolapse how to know if ring is in place?

A. If not expelled after increased abdominal pressure

B. If Bleeding does not occur

C. If patient feels discomfort

D. None of these

Q.178 HT indicated in menopausal women:

A. Hot flash

B. Ca breast

C. Endometriosis

D. Uterine bleeding

Q.179 Dilatation & curettage (D&C) iscontraindicated in:

A. Pelvic inflammatory disease (PID)

B. Endometriosis

C. Ectopic pregnancy

D. None of these

Q.180 Which of these steps is followed first forthe management of shoulder dystociaafter McRoberts maneuver?

A. Sharp flexion of hip joints towards abdomen

B. Supra pubic pressure

C. 90 degree rotation of posterior shoulder

D. Emergency c-section

Q.181 True hermaphroditism karyotype:

A. 45 X0 streaked gonads

B. 46 XX Ovotestis

C. 47 XY+9

D. 47 XX

Q.182 Peripartum cardiomyopathy occurs at:

A. Within 7 days

B. Within 6 weeks

C. Within 24 months

D. Within 5 months

Q.183 Nerve mostly compressed in pregnancypuerperium:

A. Radial nerve

B. Median nerve

C. Femoral nerve   **D.** Facial nerve

Q.184 In pregnancy which of the following levelis altered mostly:

A. Total T3   **B.** Free T3   **C.** Free T4   **D.** TSH

Q.185 Paget's is associated with which othercancer:

A. Vulva   **B.** Vagina   **C.** Cervix   **D.** Uterus

Q.186 What is meant by Superfecundation?

A. Fertilization of two or more ova in one intercourse

B. Fertilization of two or more ova in different intercourses in samemenstrual cycle

C. Fertilization of ova and then it's division

D. Fertilization of second ovum first being implanted

Q.187 Fetal heart starts contracting at:

A. 10-12 days   **B.** 10-12 weeks

C. 3-5 weeks   **D.** 3- 5 month

Q.188 Anesthesia of choice for cesarean section insevere pre-eclampsia:

A. Spinal   **B.** GA

C. Epidural   **D.** Spinal+epidural

Q.189 Which of the following is not a high-riskpregnancy?

A. Previous history of manual removal of placenta

B. Anemia

C. Diabetes

D. Obesity

Q.190 Which of the following is not used in preeclampsia?

A. Methyldopa   **B.** Atenolol

C. Labetalol   **D.** Hydralazine

Q.191 Cutis marmorata occurs due to exposureto:

A. Cold temperature   **B.** Dust

C. Hot temperature   **D.** Humidity

Q.192 Murphy's eye is seen in:

A. Macintosh laryngoscope

B. Endotracheal tube

C. LMA

D. Flexible laryngoscope

Q.193 Modified MallamPati grading is used inassessment of:

A. Difficult intubation

B. Airway obstruction

C. Death due to aspiration

D. Intubation

Q.194 Which nerve is tested for adequacy of anaesthesia?

A. Median Nerve   **B.** Ulnar Nerve

C. Radial nerve   **D.** Mandibular nerve

Q.195 Most effective circuit in spontaneousanaesthesia is:

A. Mapleson A   **B.** Mapleson B

C. Mapleson C   **D.** Mapleson D

Q.196 What is mechanism of action ofCuranium drugs as muscle relaxant?

A. Persistently depolarizing at Neuromuscular junction

B. Act competitively on Ach receptors blocking post-synaptically

C. Repetitive stimulation of Ach receptors on muscle end plate

D. Inhibiting the calcium channel on presynaptic membrane

Q.197 Dye used in diagnosis of esophageal perforation:

A. Iohexol   **B.** Barium sulphate

C. Gadolinium   **D.** Iodine dye

Q.198 Bragg peak effect pronounced in:

A. X ray   **B.** Proton   **C.** Neutron   **D.** Electron

Q.199 Salt and Pepper pot appearance of skull seen in:

A. Hyperparathyroidism

B. Multiple myeloma

C. Hyperthyroidism

D. Pseudo hyperparathyroidism

Q.200 Imaging techniques used in Uterus anomalies except:

A. HSG   **B.** MRI guided HSG

C. CT guided HSG   **D.** USG

Q.201 Semen squeeze:

A. Erectile dysfunction

B. Premature ejaculation

C. Retrograde ejaculation

D. Antegrade ejaculation

Q.202 A patient with a history of RTA before 2months presents with complaints ofdreams of accidents. He is able tovisualize the same scene whenever hevisits the place. Hence is afraid to goback to the accident site. Identify thetype of disorder that he might besuffering from?

A. Adjustment disorder

B. PTSD

C. Anxiety disorder

D. OCD

Q.203 Freud's theory of dream includes allexcept:

A. Displacement   **B.** Condensation

C. Symbolisation   **D.** Correlation

Q.204 Expression and consequent release ofpreviously repressed emotion is calledas:

A. Regression   **B.** Dissociation

C. Abreaction   **D.** All of the above

Q.205 All are habit disorder except:

A. Nail biting   **B.** Thumb sucking

C. Temper tantrum   **D.** Tics

Q.206 New name of mental retardationaccording to American Association ofMental Retardation:

A. Feeble Mindedness

B. Madness

C. Intellectual disability

D. Mentally unstable

Q.207 Now-a-days Down syndrome Is referredto as:

A. Submental disorder   **B.** Oligophrenia
C. Madness   **D.** Mentally unstable

Q.208 A 55 years aged chronic alcoholic male, presented with irrelevant talks, tremorand sweating. He had his last drink 3days back. What will the probablediagnosis?

A. Delirium tremens
B. Korsakoff psychosis
C. Post-Acute withdrawal syndrome
D. Discontinuation syndrome

Q.209 Identify the type of muscle shown in theimage below.

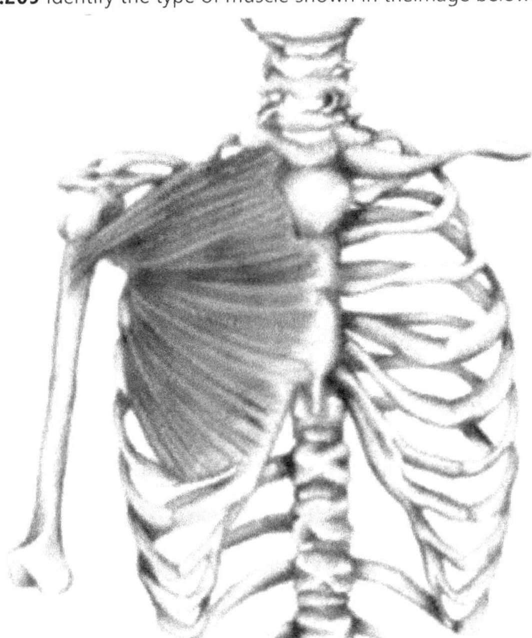

A. Cruciate   **B.** Multipennate
C. Parallel   **D.** Unipennate

Q.210 Function of the muscle shown in picture:

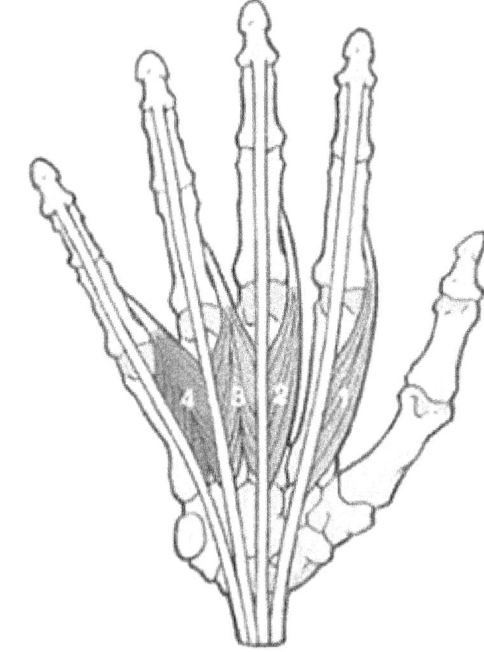

A. Flexion   **B.** Extension
C. Adduction   **D.** Abduction

Q.211 Following image is also known as?

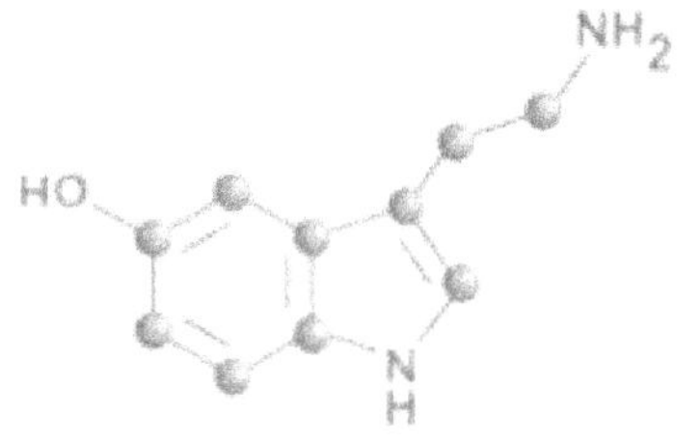

A. 5-hydroxytryptamine (5-HT)
B. N-methyl phenylamine
C. 3-Methoxytyramine
D. Phenethylamine

Q.212 Choose the best method of diagnosis forthe clinical sign represented in theimage.

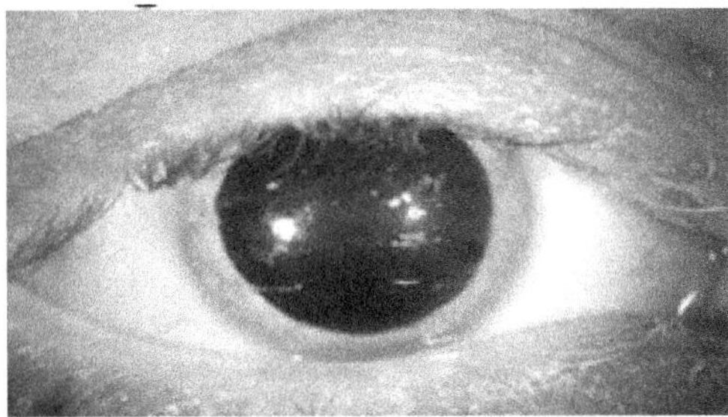

A. Serum copper
B. Serum ceruloplasmin
C. Karyotyping
D. PCR

Q.213 Identify the condition represented in the image.

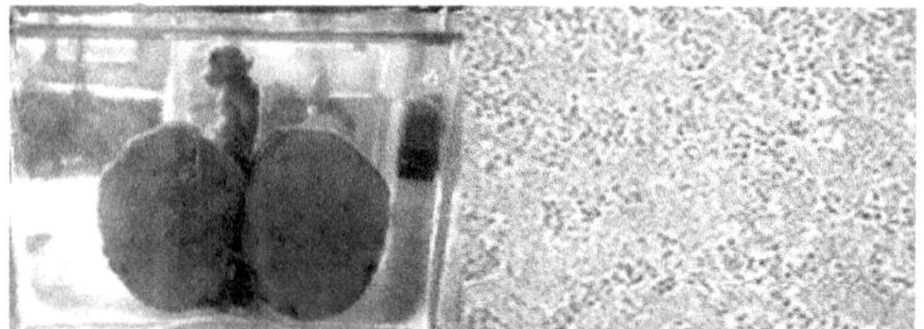

A. Seminoma
B. Germ cell differentiate tumor
C. Non-seminoma
D. Teratoma

Q.214 Identify the condition shown in theimage.

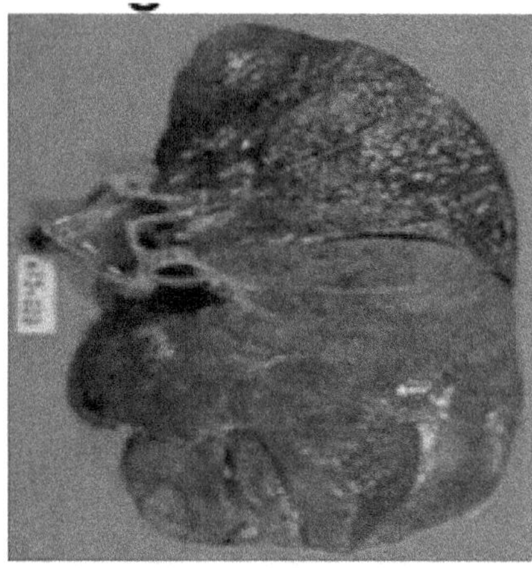

A. Lobar Pneumonia
B. Bronchopneumonia
C. Acute glomerulonephritis
D. Congested kidney

Q.215 Identify the condition represented in below image:

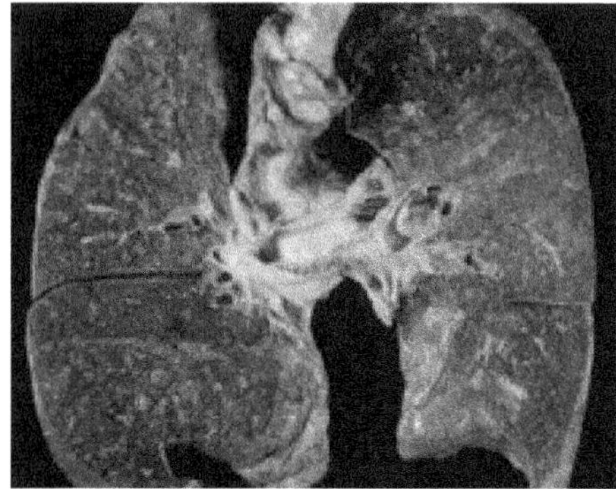

A. Miliary tuberculosis   B. Bronchiectasis
C. COPD   D. Lung cancer

Q.216 Identify the organism related to blood smear image:

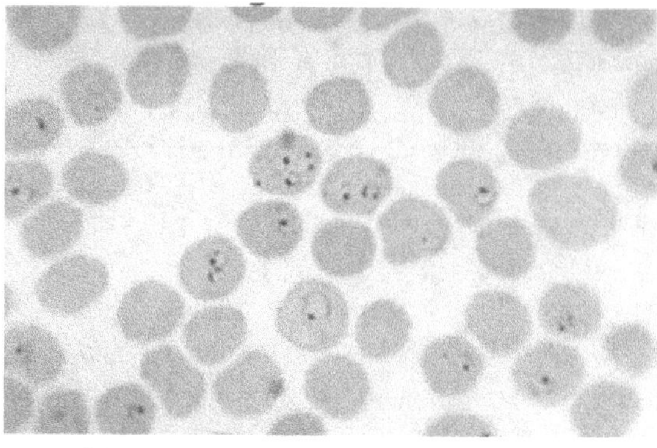

A. P. falciparum
B. S. Typhi
C. Treponema pallidum
D. Toxoplasma gondii

Q.217 Which is thickened nerve shown here:

A. Facial Nerve
B. Greater auricular nerve
C. Vagus Nerve
D. Glossopharyngeal Nerve

Q.218 Which type of retractor is shown in the image:

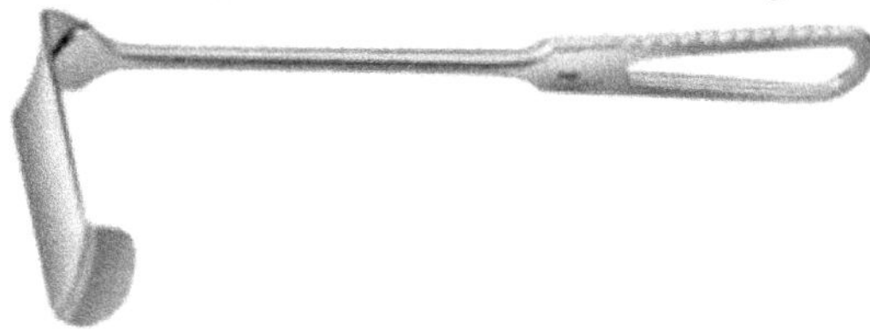

A. Morris retractor
B. Czerny retractor
C. Richardson retractor
D. Lower lid retractor

Q.219 Which of the following statement is trueabout suture material in the image:

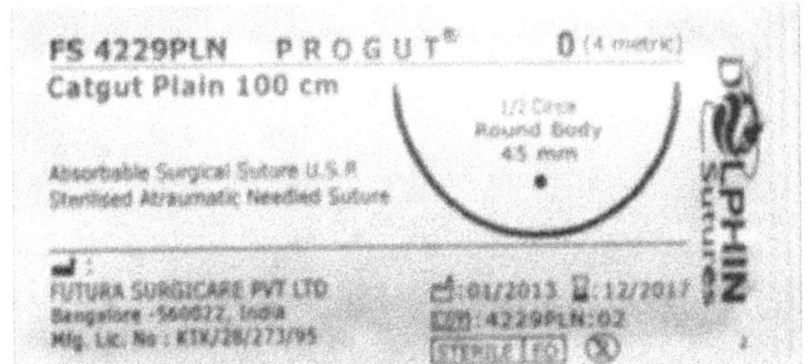

A. Made of rabbit submucosa
B. Made of cat submucosa
C. Not degraded
D. Degraded by enzymatic degradation

Q.220 A Patient has history of RTA 2 yearsback, at the same sight he developedpain and swelling. X-ray shows thefollowing features. What will be thediagnosis?

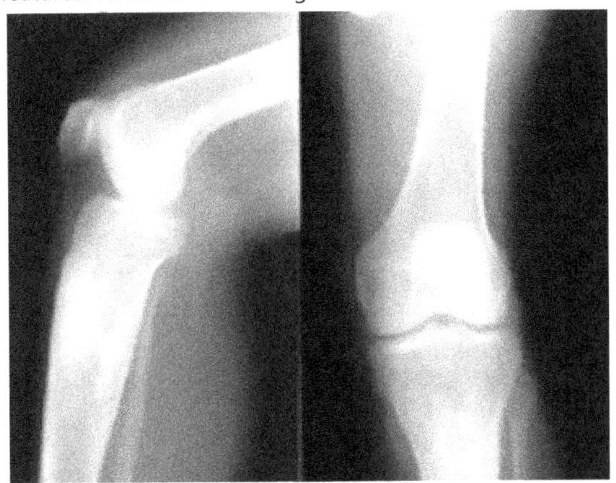

A. Osteogenic sarcoma
B. Ewing's sarcoma
C. Chronic osteomyelitis
D. Multiple myeloma

Q.221 Identify the bone numbered in the X-raybelow that most commonly fracturewhen a person falls on outstretchedhands?

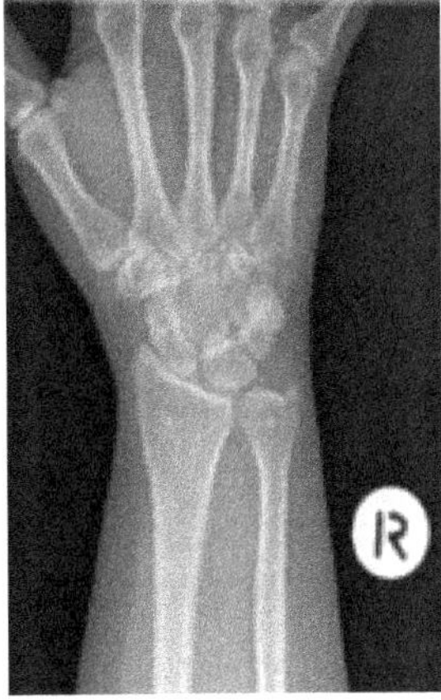

A. 1   **B.** 2   **C.** 3   **D.** 4

Q.222 Identify the condition shown in the CTScan image below.

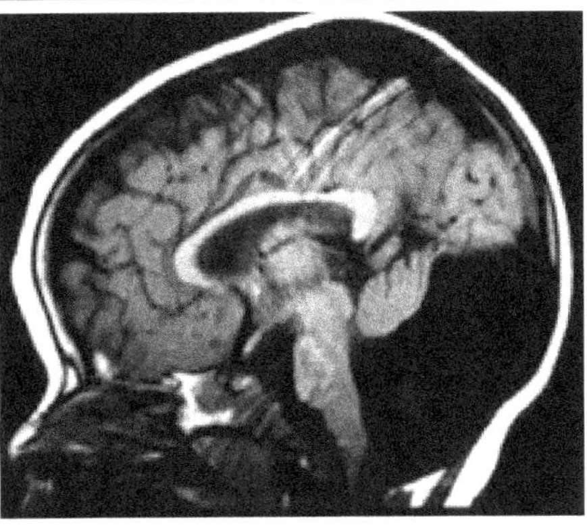

A. Dandy walker malformation
B. Cerebellar vermis hypoplasia
C. Mega cisterna magna
D. None of these

Q.223 Identify the X ray HSG Shown below:

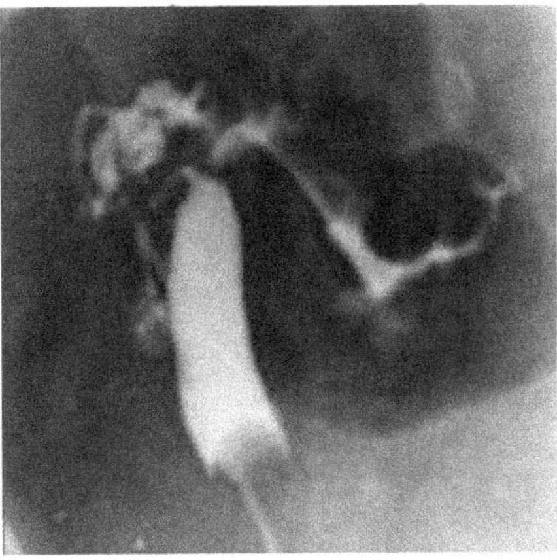

A. Septate uterus   **B.** Uterus didelphys
C. Unicornuate uterus   **D.** Bicornuate uterus

Q.224 In a woman complaining of AUB following image was seen in endoscopicexamination of uterus. What will be thediagnosis?

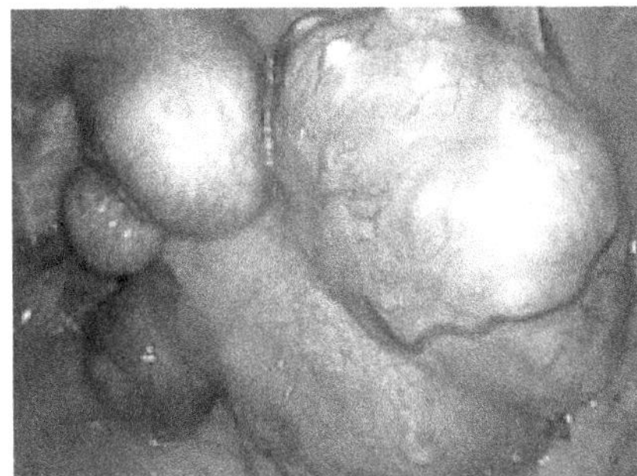

A. Leiomyoma   **B.** Adenomyosis
C. Ovarian neoplasm   **D.** Carcinoma of uterus

Q.225 Identify the following lesion:

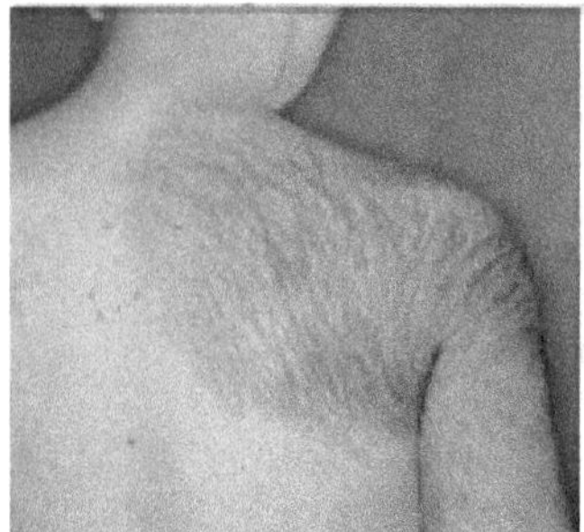

A. Becker nevus
B. Hypopigmented macule
C. Spitz nevus
D. Epidermal nevus

Q.226 A child has a rash as shown in thepicture. His family history is positive forasthma. What could be the mostprobable diagnosis?

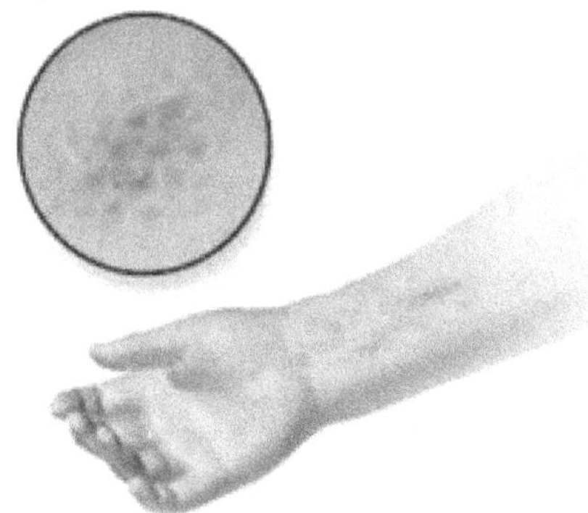

A. Seborrheic dermatitis
B. Atopic dermatitis
C. Allergic contact dermatitis
D. Erysipelas

Q.227 Spot radiography from a double contrast esophagram. Image represents:

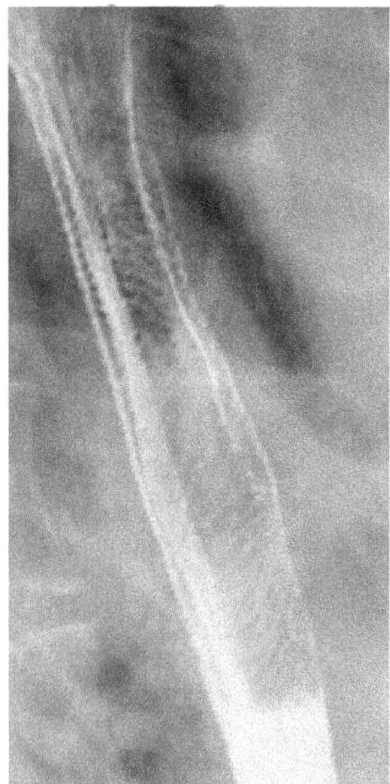

A. Esophageal atresia
B. Esophageal stenosis
C. Feline oesophagus
D. Tracheoesophageal fistula

Q.228 MRI of skull represents:

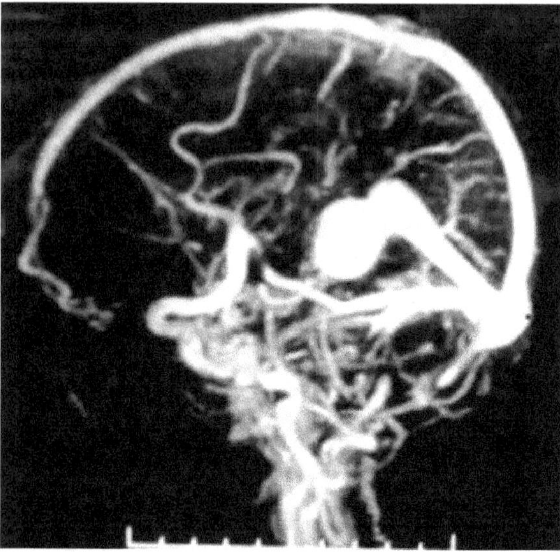

A. Vein of Galen
B. Dandy walker Syndrome
C. Pneumocephalus
D. Crouzon syndrome

Q.229 What is a diagnosis based on a given image:

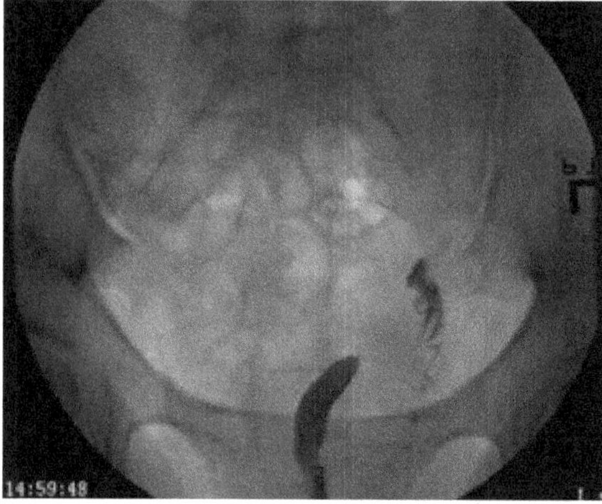

A. Uterus didelphys   B. Bicornuate Uterus
C. Unicornuate Uterus   D. Septate uterus

Q.230 X-ray of skull showing which lesions inthe brain:

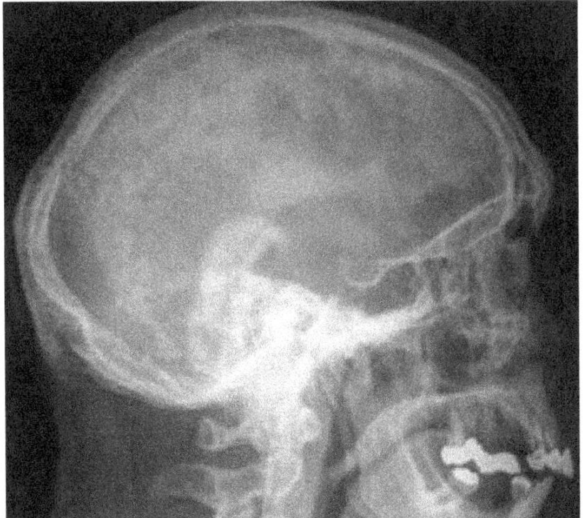

A. Paget's disease   **B.** Multiple myeloma
C. Osteosarcoma   **D.** Osteomyelitis

Q.231 CT of Thorax represents:

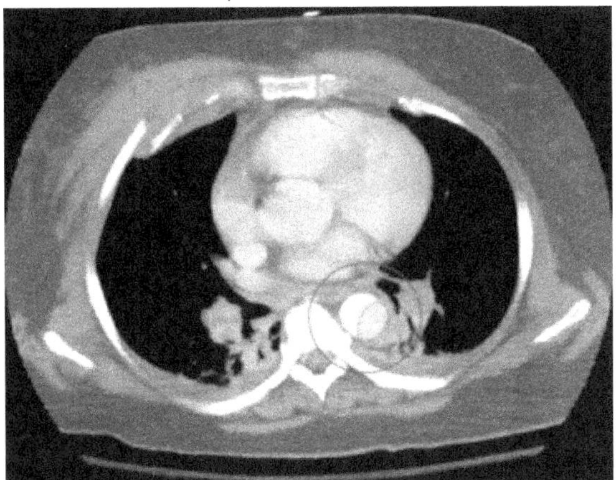

A. Ascending Aortic dissection
B. Descending Aortic dissection
C. Aortic aneurysm
D. Cystic fibrosis

Q.232 CT scan of abdomen showing an areathat branching into the liver. Identify thestructure?

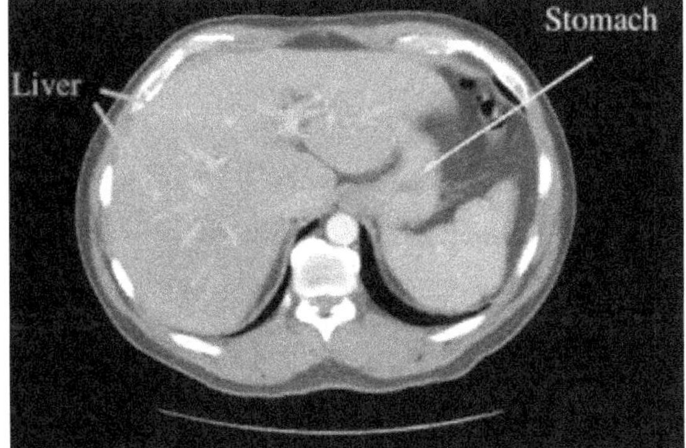

A. SVC   **B.** IVC
C. Portal vein   **D.** Splenic vein

Q.233 Identify artery 'X' in the givenangiography anatomy image:

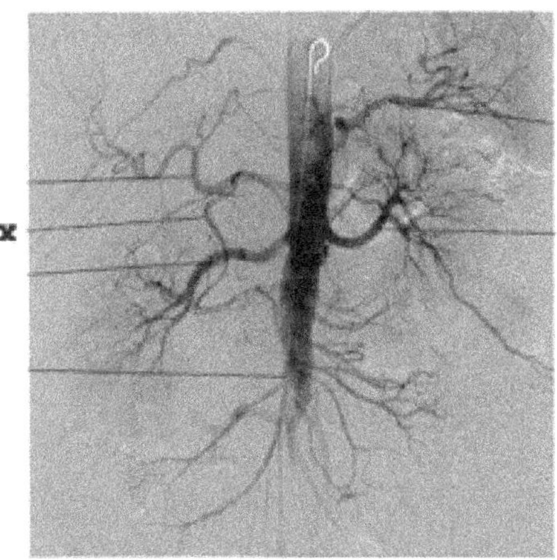

A. Superior mesenteric artery
B. Subclavian artery
C. Celiac artery
D. Brachiocephalic artery

Q.234 A woman shows symptoms of massivepulmonary thromboembolism.The grossappearance of liver autopsy is shown.Which of the following statement bestcharacterizes the patient's condition?

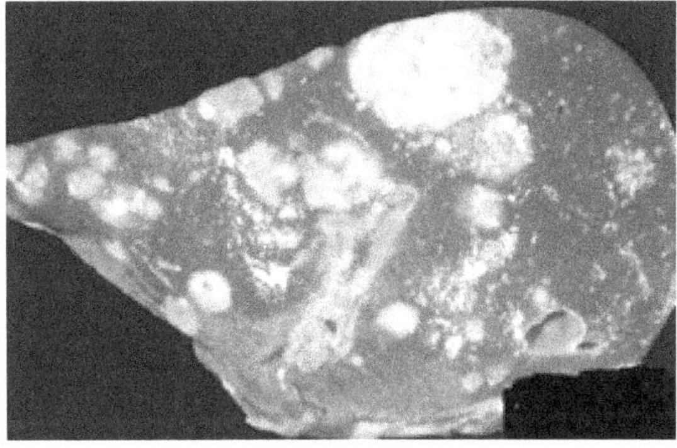

A. Metastasis from PE
B. Angiosarcoma
C. Colonic adenocarcinoma with metastasis
D. Locally invaded hepatocellular carcinoma

Q.235 What is the structure seen in the given X-ray below?

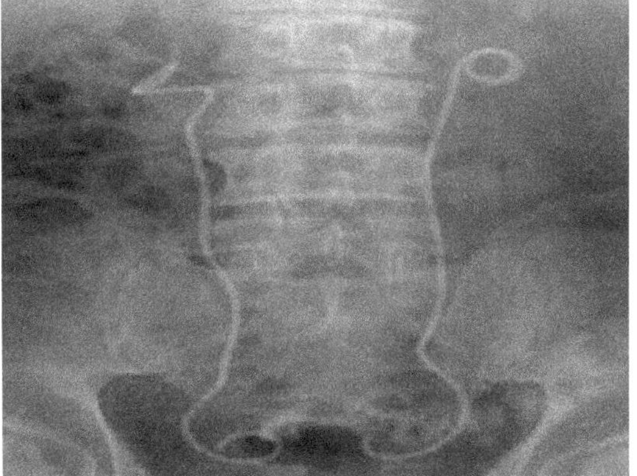

A. Stent

B. Surgical clips

C. Foley catheter

D. Intravesical wire

Q.236 What is the diagnosis based on thefollowing X-ray?

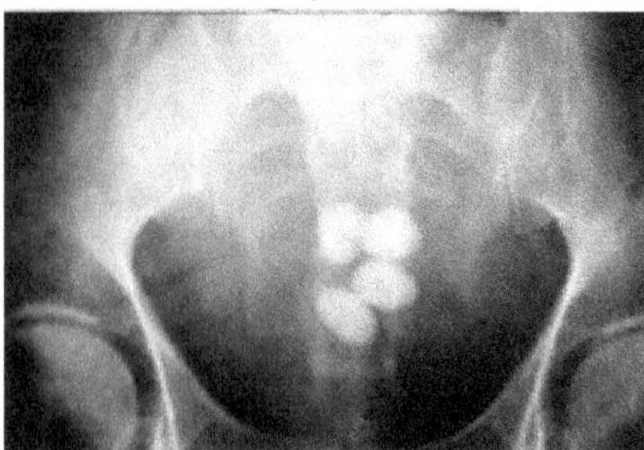

A. Uterine Fibroid

B. Bladder Carcinoma

C. Bladder stone

D. Renal Tuberculosis

Q.237 A red soft to firm swelling on sternumthat on biopsy shows followinghistology. What is the diagnosis?

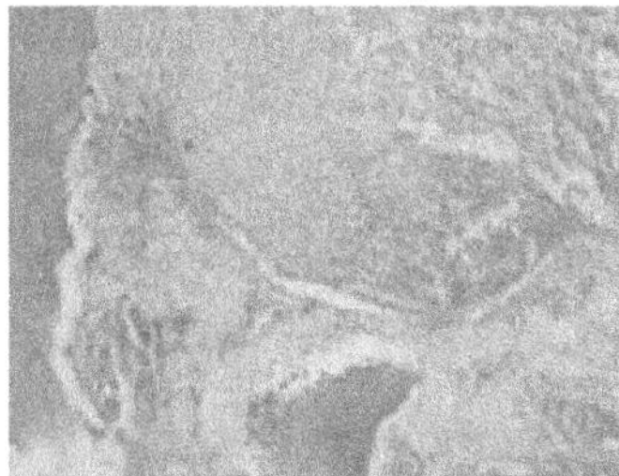

A. Hemangioma

B. Osteochondroma

C. Osteoid osteoma

D. Paget disease

Q.238 Which of the following is carrying agentfor the disease with given characteristicon polarized microscopy?

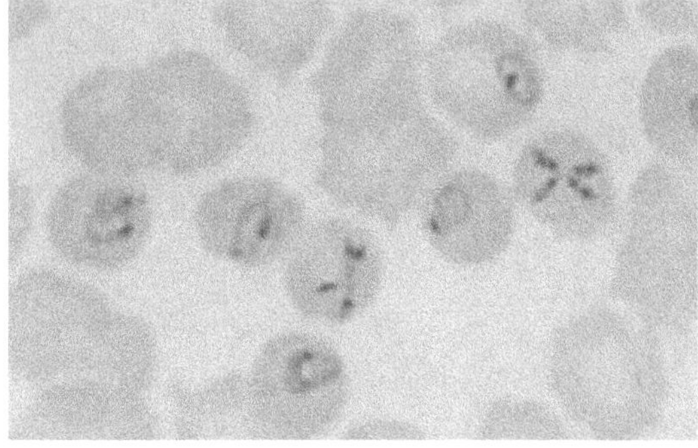

A. Anopheles

B. Ixodes scapularis ticks

C. Louse

D. Rat flea

Q.239 Chordoma arises from:

A. Pharyngeal bursa

B. Notochord

C. Rathke's pouch

D. Luschka's bursa

Q.240 What is the effect of Progesterone only pills?

A. Completely suppresses ovulation

B. Thin lining of uterus

C. Thick cervical mucus

D. All of the above

Q.241 Which metal results in "Saturnine gout" formation?

A. Cadmium

B. Lead

C. Beryllium

D. Mercury

Q.242 Which drug decreases the boneresorption in osteoporosis?

A. Teriparatide

B. Risedronate

C. Cortisone

D. Cimetidine

Q.243 Phenylketonuria is due to deficiency of:

A. Phenylalanine

B. Phenylalanine hydroxylase(PAH)

C. Phenylene

D. All of these

Q.244 Which is not correct:

A. MRI needed to access haemorrhage

B. GCS assessment helps in prognosis

C. Haematoma must be operated

D. All of the above

Q.245 Maastricht classification of donationafter cardiac death. What category isstage 3?

A. Awaiting cardiac arrest

B. Brought in dead

C. Unsuccessful resuscitation

D. Cardiac arrest after brain-stem death

Q.246 What is the cause of myocardial shockother than MI?

A. acute mitral regurgitation

B. ventricular septal rupture

C. isolated right ventricular shock

D. All of the above

Q.247 Nitric oxide acts by increasing?

A. BRCA 1

B. BRCA 2

C. Interleukin

D. cGMP

Q.248 Positive acid schiff macrophages seen in?

A. Whipples disease

B. Crohns disease

C. AIDS

D. None of the above

Q.249 A boy presented with multiple nonsuppurative osteomyelitis with sickle cellanaemia. What will be the causativeorganism?

A. Salmonella

B. S. aureus

C. H. influenzae

D. Enterobacter species

Q.250 Term pathology refers to:

A. Work

B. Function

C. Details

D. Explains

Q.251 1 yr child weighing 6 kg is suffering fromAcute Gastroenteritis along with signs ofsunken eyes & skin pinch going back tonormal very rapidly. What will be yourmanagement?

A. RL infusion 120 ml in the first hour followed by 360 ml in thenext 5 hours

B. RL INFUSION 180 ml in the first hour followed by 420 ml in thenext 5 hours

C. RL INFUSION 180 ML IN the first hour followed by 480 ml in thenext 5 hours

D. RL INFUSION 240 ml in the first hour followed by 360 ml in thenext 5 hours

Q.252 What constitute malpighian layer?

A. Corneum lucidum

B. Corneum spinosum

C. Spinosum and basale

D. Basale granulosum

Q.253 Mechanism of action colchicine in acutegout:

A. Uric acid nephrolithiasis

B. Deficiency of enzyme Xanthine oxidase

C. Increase in serum urate concentration

D. Renal disease involving interstitial tissues

Q.254 Oxygen therapy may not be useful in:

A. Asthma

B. Pneumonia

C. Subglottic stenosis

D. Pulmonary fibrosis

Q.255 New born baby with heart rate less than 60 beats per minute can be resuscitated by all except:

A. chest compression

B. oxygen therapy

C. tactile stimulati

D. slapping the back

Q.256 Mobitz type 2 second degree AV block isseen in all except:

A. Hypothyroidism

B. Coronary Artery Disease

C. Sarcoidosis

D. Cushing syndrome

Q.257 When can one diagnose acuterespiratory distress in a child?

A. Within 7 days of known clinical insult

B. Respiratory failure not fully explained

C. Left ventricular dysfunction

D. All of the above

Q.258 A 6-year-old boy experienced lifethreatening shock, his CT scan showedlarge amount of ascites, bowel wallthickening and poor or absentenhancement of the strangulated bowelsegment, showing gangrenous bowel onsurgical exploration.True about anastomosis is:

A. Should be done by continuous layers as it takes less time

B. Should be Done with catgut

C. Should be Done by single layer seromuscular lembert sutures

D. Should be Done by Single layer taking submucosa

Q.259 In ACLS which drug can be givenfollowing ventricular fibrillation aftercardiac arrest other than epinephrine?

A. Amiodarone

B. Dopamine

C. Adenosine

D. Atropine

Q.260 Which of the following statement is falseabout MR vaccination campaignlaunched by WHO?

A. Children from 9 months to less than 15 vaccinated

B. Congenital rubella syndrome (CRS), responsible for irreversiblebirth defects

C. India has not yet launched this campaign

D. Will replace routine immunization for measles vaccine

Q.261 Which of the following true regarding Hemophilia A?

A. Serum levels of factor VIII are decreased

B. Deficiency of factor IX

C. PT increased

D. FIT decreased

Q.262 Marked bleeding is seen in which offollowing conditions?

A. VMA disease

B. Haemophilia A

C. Haemophilia B

D. All of the above

Q.263 Reed Sternberg cells are found in:

A. Hodgkin's disease

B. Sickle cell anaemia

C. Thalassemia

D. CML

Q.264 By which method foreign DNA isintroduced into a cell by a virus or viralvector?

A. Transduction

B. Transcription

C. Lysogenic conversion

D. Transformation

Q.265 Which one of the following showsallosteric inhibition?

A. Malonic acid & succinate

B. 2,3-BPG

C. Amino acid alanine & pyruvate kinase

D. Citrate

Q.266 Which of the following is seen inseropositive rheumatoid arthritis?

A. Multiple joints affected

B. Symmetrical joint symptoms

C. Joint pain and swelling

D. All of the above

Q.267 Which of the following is not seen inAnterior mediastinum?

A. Thyroid tumour

B. Thymoma

C. Lymphoma

D. Neurogenic tumor

Q.268 Struvite stone is caused by which metal?

A. Magnesium

B. Calcium

C. Sodium & potassium

D. Both (A) & (B)

Q.269 Which of the following statements aboutGraves disease is false?

A. Results in hyperthyroidism

B. Autoimmune disorder

C. Common in Male

D. Referred as Toxic diffuse goitre

Q.270 Aldosterone synthesis is stimulated by which of thefollowing?

A. ACTH
B. Hyperkalemia
C. Hypernatremia
D. Exogenous steroids

Q.271 Which of the following is false aboutAlzheimer's disease?

A. One in 10 people age 65 and older has Alzheimer's disease
B. Alzheimer's disease is curable
C. Cause dementia
D. All of the above

Q.272 Which of the following is true aboutvitamin K?

A. Anticoagulant
B. Prolong use of antimicrobial leads to deficiency
C. Dietary allowance is 15-20 mg
D. All of the above

Q.273 Which drugs needs continuousmonitoring of prothrombin time?

A. Aspirin
B. Lepirudin
C. Digoxin
D. Coumadin

Q.274 Which of the following are the risk factorfor cutaneous lymphoma?

A. Age
B. Gender
C. Weakened immune system
D. All of the above

Q.275 Which is not included in AIDS relatedcomplex?

A. Ectopic pregnancy
B. Recurrent genital candidiasis
C. Generalised lymphadenopathy
D. Chronic diarrhea

Q.276 Which is the treatment of choice forirradiation in Chordoma?

A. Protons
B. Electrons
C. Gamma radiation
D. 3D-CRT

Q.277 What differentiates delirium fromdementia?

A. Confusion
B. Difficulty in communicating
C. Hallucination
D. Sudden change

Q.278 Genital warts are caused by which virus?

A. Herpes simplex
B. Human papilloma
C. Cytomegalovirus
D. Varicella zoster

Q.279 Which drug regimen is given in apregnant woman with HIV infection?

A. Tenofovir disoproxil fumarate with emtricitabine
B. Tenofovir disoproxil fumarate with lamivudine
C. Abacavir with lamivudine
D. All of the above

Q.280 Which of the following structure develops from dorsal mesentery?

A. Greater omentum
B. Lesser omentum
C. Liver
D. Diaphragm

Q.281 Which of the following is the best Stentfor Femoropopliteal Bypass?

A. Dacron
B. Reversed saphenous
C. PTFE
D. None of these

Q.282 Trilene is degraded by:

A. Enzymatic Degradation
B. Non Enzymatic degradation
C. Chemical Degradation
D. None of these

Q.283 The earliest feature of 3rd cranial nerveinvolvement in diabetes mellitus patientis:

A. Normal light reflex
B. Abnormal light reflex
C. Normal light and accommodation reflex
D. Abnormal light and accommodation reflex

Q.284 During squint surgery, anesthesiologistsees the machine and see the bpsuddenly drops to 40. What will be bestimmediate management:

A. Give atropine
B. Increase level of anesthesia
C. Ask the surgeon to stop the surgery
D. Give adrenaline

Q.285 All are special visceral efferent columnexcept:

A. Glossopharyngeal n
B. Nucleus ambiguus
C. Vagus nerve
D. Trigeminal nerve

Q.286 Which of the following condition is NOT caused by Parvovirus B19?

A. Roseola infantum
B. Aplastic anemia in sickle cell disease
C. Fetal hydrops
D. Erythema infectiosum

Q.287 Which of the following statements is nottrue about iliolumbar ligament?

A. Upper fibres attached to iliac crest
B. Lower fibres attached to base of sacrum
C. Help in maintaining lumbosacral joint stability
D. Upper attachment to transverse process of T12

Q.288 Where will be the placement location for Auditory Brainstem Implant?

A. Scala tympani
B. Recess of 4th ventricle
C. IAC
D. Back of ear

Q.289 Which condition is associated with Congenital adrenal hypoplasia?

A. Male pseudohermaphroditism
B. Female pseudohermaphroditism
C. True pseudohermaphroditism
D. Sequential pseudohermaphroditism

Q.290 Which is true regarding ataxiatelangiectasia:

A. Increase in AFP

B. Increases the risk of squamous cell carcinoma

C. Autosomal dominant

D. None of above

Q.291 A diabetic patient 2 days after postcataract surgery develops developshypopyon. What will be themanagement?

A. Intravitreal antibiotics

B. Eye drops

C. Surgery

D. No treatment required

Q.292 What is the thinnest part of neuro-retinal rim according to ISNT rule?

A. Inferior

B. Superficial

C. Temporal

D. Medial

Q.293 Leiden thrombophilia is caused bymutational deficiency of which of thefollowing factors?

A. Factor V

B. Factor VII

C. Factor IX

D. Factor X

Q.294 Anteversion of uterus is maintained by?

A. Cardinal ligament

B. Uterosacral ligament

C. Pubocervical ligament

D. Round ligament

Q.295 Long-standing pelvic inflammation maylead to which of the followingconditions?

A. Pyometra

B. Uterine polyposis

C. Pseudopregnancy

D. Cystic endometrial hyperplasia

Q.296 Ether was first used as an anaesthetic by?

A. Priesly **B.** Morton **C.** Wells **D.** Simpson

Q.297 The following increases Intraocular pressure:

A. Thiopentone

B. Althesin

C. Ketamine

D. Barbiturate

Q.298 All of the following are correct about ketamine, EXCEPT:

A. It functionally "dissociates" the thalamus

B. It increases arterial blood pressure

C. It is a potent bronchoconstrictor

D. It inhibits polysynaptic reflexes in the spinal cord

Q.299 All of the following statements about neuromuscular blockage produced by succinylcholine are true, except:

A. No fade on Train of four stimulation

B. Fade on tetanic stimulation

C. No post tetanic facilitation

D. Train of four ratio > 0.4

Q.300 Heller's operation is done for:

A. Achalasia Cardia

B. A hiatus hernia

C. Diaphragmatic

D. Reflux esophagitis

// Smart Answer Sheet //

Correct — Indicates percentage of students who answered questions correctly.

Skipped — Indicates percentage of students who skipped questions.

Q.	Ans.	Correct / Skipped
1	C	66.76 % / 30.05 %
2	A	67.61 % / 31.49 %
3	A	84.3 % / 11.2 %
4	A	48.73 % / 33.22 %
5	D	64.89 % / 30.38 %
6	A	63.71 % / 31.17 %
7	A	68.05 % / 31.95 %
8	A	17.29 % / 69.87 %
9	A	13.44 % / 84.19 %
10	D	51.38 % / 45.35 %
11	C	62.28 % / 37.09 %
12	A	84.04 % / 15.62 %
13	D	77.59 % / 20.67 %
14	B	83.41 % / 11.99 %
15	A	77.29 % / 22.23 %
16	C	81.94 % / 11.45 %

Q.	Ans.	Correct / Skipped
17	A	61.6 % / 37.1 %
18	C	18.89 % / 69.13 %
19	B	80.95 % / 18.62 %
20	A	46.87 % / 48.78 %
21	C	69.78 % / 30.0 %
22	A	64.07 % / 35.19 %
23	D	43.64 % / 40.09 %
24	C	88.87 % / 10.79 %
25	A	83.15 % / 16.72 %
26	B	62.25 % / 30.04 %
27	A	77.08 % / 15.28 %
28	B	49.92 % / 38.96 %
29	C	47.77 % / 34.84 %
30	C	59.69 % / 36.29 %
31	B	56.26 % / 31.99 %
32	B	78.25 % / 20.68 %

Q.	Ans.	Correct / Skipped
33	C	47.8 % / 38.77 %
34	A	69.21 % / 30.15 %
35	A	45.15 % / 48.39 %
36	B	69.57 % / 30.38 %
37	B	65.14 % / 31.97 %
38	B	21.91 % / 71.26 %
39	A	80.35 % / 12.46 %
40	C	85.32 % / 10.8 %
41	B	25.47 % / 73.09 %
42	D	57.89 % / 31.36 %
43	A	17.46 % / 70.47 %
44	C	51.25 % / 37.25 %
45	B	87.15 % / 12.61 %
46	A	88.4 % / 10.72 %
47	B	54.96 % / 39.38 %
48	C	42.18 % / 39.13 %

Q.	Ans.	Correct / Skipped
49	C	86.42 % / 10.32 %
50	B	85.3 % / 13.51 %
51	D	82.72 % / 11.75 %
52	D	64.84 % / 30.96 %
53	B	48.56 % / 32.25 %
54	D	47.8 % / 51.76 %
55	A	61.78 % / 33.53 %
56	A	84.83 % / 12.72 %
57	B	51.66 % / 38.47 %
58	D	11.69 % / 85.77 %
59	C	68.25 % / 31.02 %
60	A	61.94 % / 37.03 %
61	D	42.27 % / 40.32 %
62	D	63.13 % / 35.61 %
63	A	61.12 % / 36.9 %
64	A	87.67 % / 11.89 %

Q.	Ans.	Correct / Skipped
65	B	60.33 % / 31.84 %
66	A	46.06 % / 52.14 %
67	A	85.98 % / 11.9 %
68	C	69.78 % / 30.16 %
69	B	77.39 % / 21.81 %
70	B	67.08 % / 30.5 %
71	B	59.47 % / 30.9 %
72	A	86.75 % / 11.87 %
73	B	78.45 % / 19.74 %
74	A	77.06 % / 17.79 %
75	A	61.65 % / 37.58 %
76	B	89.18 % / 10.0 %
77	B	80.63 % / 18.05 %
78	C	16.62 % / 76.19 %
79	C	49.25 % / 31.33 %
80	A	40.01 % / 53.48 %

Q.	Ans.	Correct / Skipped
81	A	42.5 % / 42.92 %
82	A	84.27 % / 10.82 %
83	A	42.42 % / 52.11 %
84	A	51.16 % / 47.55 %
85	A	80.38 % / 13.19 %
86	C	55.7 % / 36.93 %
87	B	52.26 % / 46.48 %
88	D	63.48 % / 30.22 %
89	A	57.06 % / 36.15 %
90	A	89.85 % / 10.15 %
91	C	60.5 % / 38.57 %
92	A	88.14 % / 10.02 %
93	C	26.51 % / 71.51 %
94	B	82.06 % / 13.38 %
95	C	19.52 % / 69.74 %
96	A	59.45 % / 30.16 %

Q.	Ans.	Correct / Skipped
97	A	88.73 % / 10.23 %
98	B	85.22 % / 14.11 %
99	D	48.36 % / 40.5 %
100	C	68.72 % / 30.74 %
101	A	65.44 % / 32.98 %
102	C	40.21 % / 45.69 %
103	A	49.38 % / 49.93 %
104	A	52.79 % / 40.98 %
105	C	63.15 % / 31.95 %
106	B	49.57 % / 40.72 %
107	A	81.62 % / 17.69 %
108	A	89.14 % / 10.59 %
109	A	64.84 % / 32.75 %
110	A	44.1 % / 32.85 %
111	C	79.19 % / 14.29 %
112	D	66.22 % / 32.81 %

Q.	Ans.	Correct / Skipped
113	A	83.51 % / 12.99 %
114	B	50.29 % / 37.54 %
115	B	59.86 % / 31.68 %
116	A	84.93 % / 10.12 %
117	B	61.08 % / 30.3 %
118	A	86.75 % / 10.85 %
119	C	54.54 % / 37.73 %
120	A	62.09 % / 37.0 %
121	D	83.37 % / 11.7 %
122	B	51.58 % / 37.83 %
123	C	58.03 % / 36.76 %
124	A	85.8 % / 10.27 %
125	B	64.18 % / 34.07 %
126	A	65.15 % / 33.77 %
127	A	30.14 % / 67.22 %
128	B	15.23 % / 78.08 %

Q.	Ans.	Correct / Skipped
129	A	59.37 % / 37.66 %
130	A	63.69 % / 30.55 %
131	C	68.43 % / 31.42 %
132	B	57.88 % / 32.6 %
133	A	67.12 % / 30.68 %
134	D	15.88 % / 79.78 %
135	B	41.37 % / 30.11 %
136	B	15.68 % / 81.74 %
137	A	89.19 % / 10.3 %
138	B	43.87 % / 41.99 %
139	B	57.22 % / 39.81 %
140	A	67.31 % / 31.52 %
141	C	54.64 % / 43.37 %
142	A	58.77 % / 31.22 %
143	A	48.64 % / 46.22 %
144	A	80.42 % / 11.08 %

Q.	Ans.	Correct / Skipped
145	A	66.82 % / 31.17 %
146	A	54.82 % / 31.21 %
147	A	87.1 % / 10.14 %
148	D	65.49 % / 34.26 %
149	A	57.75 % / 33.27 %
150	A	86.34 % / 13.46 %
151	D	68.28 % / 31.47 %
152	B	64.46 % / 35.0 %
153	D	86.59 % / 10.48 %
154	D	29.54 % / 67.12 %
155	B	53.42 % / 30.86 %
156	A	60.87 % / 38.53 %
157	A	10.15 % / 81.07 %
158	B	80.31 % / 18.1 %
159	A	18.82 % / 77.02 %
160	C	89.5 % / 10.29 %

Q.	Ans.	Correct / Skipped	Q.	Ans.	Correct / Skipped	Q.	Ans.	Correct / Skipped	Q.	Ans.	Correct / Skipped	Q.	Ans.	Correct / Skipped
161	A	47.73 % / 31.01 %	177	A	48.79 % / 30.2 %	193	A	23.43 % / 73.34 %	209	B	58.93 % / 36.99 %	225	A	57.9 % / 41.05 %
162	A	46.81 % / 40.32 %	178	A	52.35 % / 31.85 %	194	A	61.3 % / 33.21 %	210	A	88.71 % / 10.55 %	226	C	85.5 % / 11.41 %
163	B	51.8 % / 45.01 %	179	A	77.24 % / 19.87 %	195	A	32.59 % / 67.4 %	211	A	57.8 % / 38.2 %	227	C	43.45 % / 45.36 %
164	A	63.49 % / 33.34 %	180	B	26.07 % / 72.16 %	196	B	67.99 % / 31.16 %	212	B	69.09 % / 30.83 %	228	A	68.46 % / 30.31 %
165	A	61.83 % / 36.93 %	181	B	89.25 % / 10.02 %	197	B	16.91 % / 74.47 %	213	A	40.16 % / 37.12 %	229	C	88.12 % / 10.89 %
166	C	52.62 % / 33.65 %	182	D	49.56 % / 37.05 %	198	B	57.69 % / 40.51 %	214	A	86.83 % / 11.34 %	230	A	61.44 % / 31.45 %
167	C	64.47 % / 34.68 %	183	C	17.8 % / 71.92 %	199	A	57.87 % / 36.73 %	215	A	40.19 % / 42.3 %	231	B	67.03 % / 31.5 %
168	C	87.94 % / 11.93 %	184	A	40.86 % / 36.82 %	200	C	31.76 % / 68.11 %	216	A	44.19 % / 42.68 %	232	C	61.86 % / 37.44 %
169	B	85.71 % / 13.94 %	185	A	60.48 % / 35.14 %	201	B	84.25 % / 14.63 %	217	B	67.77 % / 31.4 %	233	A	49.56 % / 49.08 %
170	A	53.85 % / 43.76 %	186	B	69.83 % / 30.1 %	202	B	80.52 % / 18.55 %	218	A	83.98 % / 10.99 %	234	C	57.68 % / 41.09 %
171	B	30.32 % / 68.25 %	187	C	56.15 % / 30.48 %	203	D	51.65 % / 35.1 %	219	D	18.99 % / 77.45 %	235	A	52.53 % / 30.91 %
172	D	23.19 % / 76.26 %	188	C	62.96 % / 36.92 %	204	C	57.75 % / 41.09 %	220	C	61.07 % / 32.44 %	236	C	59.84 % / 36.07 %
173	D	64.12 % / 34.56 %	189	A	12.03 % / 78.41 %	205	C	42.66 % / 40.48 %	221	A	68.74 % / 30.21 %	237	A	42.67 % / 32.28 %
174	A	27.27 % / 68.81 %	190	B	59.26 % / 34.67 %	206	C	69.58 % / 30.0 %	222	A	77.42 % / 10.28 %	238	B	29.96 % / 69.99 %
175	C	67.66 % / 30.03 %	191	A	64.39 % / 32.16 %	207	A	79.72 % / 13.35 %	223	C	65.35 % / 34.14 %	239	B	53.3 % / 43.49 %
176	A	62.03 % / 31.63 %	192	B	43.29 % / 45.32 %	208	A	46.45 % / 43.16 %	224	A	52.44 % / 36.02 %	240	D	84.38 % / 14.59 %

Q.	Ans.	Correct / Skipped	Q.	Ans.	Correct / Skipped	Q.	Ans.	Correct / Skipped	Q.	Ans.	Correct / Skipped	Q.	Ans.	Correct / Skipped
241	B	48.43 % / 49.53 %	253	B	47.86 % / 42.33 %	265	B	85.4 % / 13.42 %	277	D	44.43 % / 32.41 %	289	B	11.98 % / 78.82 %
242	B	21.75 % / 67.3 %	254	D	43.34 % / 50.8 %	266	D	41.03 % / 40.87 %	278	B	47.3 % / 33.88 %	290	A	25.86 % / 70.38 %
243	B	84.83 % / 12.95 %	255	D	51.06 % / 48.27 %	267	D	54.23 % / 44.53 %	279	D	63.51 % / 35.19 %	291	A	44.84 % / 47.56 %
244	C	83.36 % / 13.44 %	256	D	86.15 % / 12.56 %	268	A	43.74 % / 42.98 %	280	A	79.51 % / 16.79 %	292	C	63.11 % / 31.44 %
245	A	89.38 % / 10.39 %	257	D	86.71 % / 11.51 %	269	C	89.57 % / 10.31 %	281	C	54.24 % / 36.28 %	293	A	83.2 % / 15.6 %
246	D	87.51 % / 11.47 %	258	C	48.74 % / 48.67 %	270	B	28.62 % / 71.24 %	282	A	45.89 % / 50.04 %	294	D	88.69 % / 10.08 %
247	D	82.27 % / 14.56 %	259	A	61.72 % / 31.83 %	271	B	11.08 % / 77.06 %	283	A	88.91 % / 10.01 %	295	A	88.99 % / 10.37 %
248	A	57.65 % / 34.88 %	260	C	61.32 % / 35.73 %	272	B	55.01 % / 36.65 %	284	D	28.91 % / 68.88 %	296	B	58.91 % / 31.38 %
249	A	10.49 % / 88.05 %	261	A	23.27 % / 68.24 %	273	D	53.26 % / 35.14 %	285	B	52.76 % / 32.08 %	297	C	89.14 % / 10.54 %
250	A	57.29 % / 38.27 %	262	D	86.52 % / 11.46 %	274	D	60.98 % / 31.29 %	286	A	53.62 % / 36.53 %	298	C	64.05 % / 30.48 %
251	B	60.75 % / 38.97 %	263	A	44.5 % / 34.97 %	275	A	22.02 % / 68.01 %	287	D	86.87 % / 11.32 %	299	B	87.94 % / 11.15 %
252	C	82.71 % / 15.9 %	264	A	63.48 % / 30.21 %	276	A	83.26 % / 14.33 %	288	B	77.42 % / 17.88 %	300	A	84.33 % / 11.47 %

Performance Analysis

Avg. Score (%)	71.42%
Toppers Score (%)	74.0%
Your Score	

Q.1 Which syndrome is associated with posterior inferior cerebellar artery thrombosis?

A. Wallenberg syndrome
B. Medial medullary syndrome
C. Inferior alternating syndrome
D. Dejerine syndrome

Q.2 Space of Disse is in:

A. Spleen
B. Lymph node
C. Liver
D. Bone

Q.3 What are Gitter cells?

A. Macroglia
B. Modified macrophages in CNS
C. Astrocytes
D. Oligodendrocytes

Q.4 Cholecystocaval line separates:

A. Right & Left liver lobe
B. Liver with Gall Bladder
C. Right Lobe of Liver with Gall Bladder
D. Left Lobe of Liver with Gall Bladder

Q.5 Which of the following exocrine glandular ducts are not obstructed in cystic fibrosis?

A. Pancreas
B. Lung
C. Sweat gland
D. All of above

Q.6 Boot shape of heart in TOF is due to:

A. Left atrial enlargement
B. Right atrial enlargement
C. Right ventricular hypertrophy
D. Biventricular hypertrophy

Q.7 Which of the following structure is not derived from external oblique muscle?

A. Inguinal ligament
B. Lacunar ligament
C. Cooper ligament
D. Linea Semilunaris

Q.8 Contralateral loss of pain and temperature is due to injury to:

A. Anterior spinothalamic tract
B. Lateral spinothalamic tract
C. Fasciculus gracilis
D. Fasciculus cuneatus

Q.9 Duct of Bellini are present in:

A. Pancreas
B. Liver
C. Kidney
D. Salivary gland

Q.10 Structure derived from first pharyngeal arch:

A. Levator palatini
B. Buccinator
C. Stylohyoid
D. Anterior belly of digastric

Q.11 Joint involved in movement of head from left to right:

A. Atlanto axial
B. Atlanto occipital
C. C_2 - C_3 Joint
D. C_3 - C_4 Join

Q.12 What is the nerve supply of Submandibular gland?

A. Auriculotemporal nerve
B. Lingual nerve
C. Glossopharyngeal nerve
D. Inferior alveolar nerve

Q.13 Parathyroid gland is implanted in which muscle?

A. Sartorius
B. Supinator
C. Deltoid
D. Brachioradialis

Q.14 Right coronary artery arises from:

A. Right Aortic Sinus
B. Left Aortic Sinus
C. Posterior coronary sinus
D. Anterior coronary sinus

Q.15 Bainbridge reflex causes:

A. Bradycardia
B. Increased cardiac output
C. Decreased venous return
D. Increased heart rate

Q.16 Golgi tendon organ responsible for:

A. Tension
B. Length
C. Pressure
D. Proprioception

Q.17 Hormone predominantly secreted after 14 day on endometrium is:

A. Progesterone
B. Estrogen
C. LH
D. FSH

Q.18 Peripheral chemoreceptors respond to hypoxia using which channel?

A. Calcium channel
B. Sodium channel
C. Potassium channel
D. Chloride channel

Q.19 With increase in age which of the following is true for lungs?

A. Pulmonary compliance increases
B. Residual volume decreases
C. Mucocillary clearance increases
D. Fibrous of interstitium decreases

Q.20 Functional residual volume is:

A. After normal inspiration
B. After normal expiration
C. After forceful expiration
D. After forceful inspiration

Q.21 Polyuria is:

A. 70ml/kg   **B.** 60ml/kg   **C.** 50ml/kg   **D.** 40ml/kg

Q.22 Tubuloglomerular feedback control is useful for which one of the following?

A. GFR

B. Plasma sodium

C. Plasma volume

D. Determining tubular secretion

Q.23 Calcitonin levels increased in:

A. Hyperthyroidism

B. Hyperparathyroidism

C. Hypoparathyroidism

D. Cushing Syndrome

Q.24 When the values of Fev1=1.3 & FCV=3.9. Which of the following does this signify?

A. Normal lung function

B. Obstructive lung disease

C. Restrictive lung disease

D. Both

Q.25 Antegrade peristalsis due to:

A. Ach   **B.** Serotonin

C. Substance P   **D.** VIP

Q.26 C-peptide seen in:

A. In Pre-proinsulin

B. In Proinsulin

C. As a combined entity with insulin after secretion

D. A gastrointestinal proactive molecule

Q.27 In forceful expiration, which of the following neurons gets fired?

A. VRG   **B.** DRG

C. Pneumotaxic centre   **D.** Chemoreceptors

Q.28 Slow conduction velocity is seen with which of the following nerve fibers?

A. Preganglionic autonomic nerve fibers

B. Postganglionic autonomic nerve fibers

C. Motor nerves

D. Sympathetic nerve fibers

Q.29 Testosterone secreted by:

A. Leydig's cells   **B.** Somatotropic cells

C. Acidophilic cells   **D.** Gonadotropic cells

Q.30 Vasopressin acts through which channels in collecting duct?

A. Aquaporin 1   **B.** Aquaporin 2

C. GLUT – 3   **D.** GLUT – 4

Q.31 True about decorticate rigidity:

A. Removal of cerebral cortex and basal ganglia

B. Flexion of lower limbs & extension of upper limbs

C. Rigidity is less pronounced than decerebrate rigidity

D. None of the above

Q.32 Zewellger syndrome is due to absence of:

A. Lysosomal   **B.** Mitochondria

C. Peroxisome   **D.** Nucleus

Q.33 Urea, creatinine, nitric oxide formed bywhich amino acid?

A. Histidine   **B.** Glycine   **C.** Cysteine   **D.** Arginine

Q.34 Which of the following is not the source ofcytosolic NADPH?

A. Isocitrate dehydrogenase

B. ATP citrate lyase

C. Malic enzyme

D. G6PD

Q.35 All are true regarding mitochondrial DNA,EXCEPT?

A. Double stranded

B. Inherited from mother

C. High mutation rate

D. All respiratory proteins are synthesized within mitochondriaitself

Q.36 Which apolipoprotein is responsible for Alzheimer's disease?

A. ApoE4   **B.** ApoE3   **C.** ApoE2   **D.** ApoE1

Q.37 Hyperammonemia inhibit TCA cycle by depleting?

A. Succinate   **B.** α -ketoglutarate

C. Malate   **D.** Fumarate

Q.38 Which amino acid is used to synthesis Nitric oxide?

A. Glycine   **B.** Arginine

C. Tyrosine   **D.** Threonine

Q.39 Menkes disease is associated with whichenzyme deficiency?

A. lysyl oxidase

B. Methionine synthase

C. Glutamyl aminopeptidase

D. Lysyl hydroxylase

Q.40 LCAT deficiency increases the following.

A. HDL   **B.** LDL

C. VLDL   **D.** Chylomicron

Q.41 A 25 year old alcoholic presented with edema, hypertension, ocular disturbance, and changes in mental state was observed, diagnosis of high output cardiac failure was made with Wet Beri Beri, this is due to deficiency of?

A. Vitamin B_3 **B.** Vitamin B_6

C. Vitamin B_9 **D.** Vitamin B_1

Q.42 Glutamine is Increase in CSF, blood andurine, this is due to deficiency of:

A. CPS-I

B. Arginase

C. OTC

D. Argininosuccinate synthetase

Q.43 True about type 1 diabetes mellitus.

A. Decreased protein catabolism

B. Decreased hepatic Glucose output

C. Increased lipolysis

D. Increase glucose uptake

Q.44 Protein which is not synthesised In liver is:

A. Phase protein   **B.** Immunoglobulins
C. Albumin   **D.** Plasma hormone

Q.45 Type of cholesterol present in gallstones?

A. Amorphous cholesterol monohydrate.
B. Amorphous cholesterol dihydrate.
C. Crystalline Cholesterol dihydrate.
D. Crystalline cholesterol monohydrate.

Q.46 Collagen present in skin is:

A. Type II   **B.** Type I   **C.** Type III   **D.** Type IV

Q.47 Which of the following is not Ribozyme?

A. Ploy A polymerase
B. Ribonuclease
C. Transpeptidase
D. Peptidyl Transferase

Q.48 Type-I hyperlipoproteinemia ischaracterized by:

A. Elevated LDL
B. Elevated HDL
C. Elevated chylomicrons
D. Elevated lipoprotein lipase

Q.49 In Kreb's cycle and Urea cycle the linking amino acid is:

A. Fumarate   **B.** Alanine
C. Arginine   **D.** Aspartate

Q.50 Vitamin A is stored in:

A. Cells of Ito   **B.** Hepatocyte
C. Endothelial cell   **D.** Kupffer cell

Q.51 Glanzmann thrombasthenia is due to:

A. Decreased GpIb
B. Decreased GpIIb/IIIa
C. Anti-GpIIb/IIIa antibodies
D. Inhibition or deficiency of ADAMTS 13

Q.52 Apoptotic gene is:

A. Bax   **B.** Bcl2   **C.** Bclx   **D.** Mcl

Q.53 Alpha one anti trypsin works by:

A. Inhibition of trypsin
B. Inhibition of trypsinogen
C. Inhibition of elastase
D. Inhibition of chymotrypsin

Q.54 Which one of the following is anautosomal recessive disorder?

A. Albinism
B. Huntington's syndrome
C. Marfan's syndrome
D. Neurofibromatosis-1

Q.55 Fish mouth appearance of valve in RHD isdue to:

A. Rupture of valve
B. Calcification & fibrosis

C. Hypertrophy of ventricular wall
D. None of the above

Q.56 Follicular lymphoma________ positivity.

A. Bcl-1   **B.** Bcl-6
C. Bcl- 2   **D.** None of the above

Q.57 What is the histological differencebetween them in Ulcerative colitis &Crohn's disease?

A. Diffuse distribution of pseudopolyps
B. Mucosal edema
C. Crypt abscess
D. Lymphoid aggregates in the mucosa

Q.58 What is the cause of intracorpuscular defects in hemolysis?

A. Uremic syndrome   **B.** PCH
C. PNH   **D.** Portal hypertension

Q.59 Type of necrosis seen in blood vesselsdue to immune reactions:

A. Coagulation   **B.** Liquefaction
C. Fibrinoid   **D.** None

Q.60 In a patient with lipoprotein lipase deficiency, which of the following is increased following a fatty meal?

A. Chylomicron   **B.** LDL
C. HDL   **D.** Apo-A

Q.61 In Wilson's disease, there is less urinaryexcretion of:

A. Phosphorus   **B.** Methyl- Histidine
C. Phosphotyrosine   **D.** Serine

Q.62 What is the function of IL1?

A. Enhances hematopoiesis
B. Stimulates mast cells
C. Has antiviral properties
D. Endogenous pyrogen

Q.63 CEAP score indicates:

A. Atrial disorders
B. Venous disorder
C. Neurological disorder
D. Trauma disorder

Q.64 IL- 1 activated by:

A. Capsase 1   **B.** Capsase 3
C. Capsase 8   **D.** Capsase 5

Q.65 Parotid mass mixed consistency:

A. Pleomorphic adenoma
B. Sebaceous cyst
C. Dermoid cyst
D. All of the above

Q.66 Krabbe's disease is:

A. Deficiency of Beta- galactosylceramidase
B. Deficiency of aryl sulphatase
C. Alpha galactosidase
D. Acid lipase

Q.67 What is the choice of treatment for idiopathic thrombocytopenia purpura (ITP)?

A. Blood transfusion

B. Spontaneous recovery

C. IV infusion

D. Splenectomy

Q.68 Fluoroquinolones with maximumbioavailability is:

A. Moxifloxacin

B. Gatifloxacin

C. Levofloxacin

D. Ciprofloxacin

Q.69 Mechanism of action of buspirone is:

A. 5 HT$_{1A}$ partial agonism.

B. 5 HT$_{1B}$ antagonism.

C. 5 HT$_{1B}$ partial agonism.

D. 5 HT$_{2C}$ antagonism.

Q.70 Which statement best describes mechanism of action of azole?

A. Synthesis of ergosterol

B. Thymidylate synthase

C. Targeting Beta-1,3 – glucan

D. Disruption of cell wall.

Q.71 Which is the following is orally active direct Xa inhibitor?

A. Rivaroxaban

B. Agrataban

C. Dabigatran

D. Bilverudin

Q.72 Which among the following is most probable reason for preference of Cisatracurium over atracurium?

A. Decreased histamine release

B. Increased histamine release

C. Due to elimination by Hofmann elimination

D. Increased CNS toxicity

Q.73 Which of the following drug is used in SIADH?

A. Tolvaptan

B. Desmopressin

C. Vwb factor

D. Terlipressin

Q.74 Drug acting on K$^+$ channels include which of the following?

A. Spironolacton

B. Amiloride

C. Nicorandil

D. Methyldopa

Q.75 Imipenem, a newer antibiotic with a broad antibacterial spectrum, is co administered with cilastatin. Which of the following is the best reason for the same?

A. Combination of antibiotics is synergistic against Pseudomonasspecie

B. Cilastatin aids gastrointestinal absorption of active moiety,imipenem

C. Cilastatin inhibits beta=lactamase enzyme destroying imipenem

D. Cilastatin inhibits an enzyme in kidney destroying imipenem

Q.76 DOC for smoking cessation?

A. Acamprosate

B. Varenicline

C. Thalidomide

D. Tryptophan

Q.77 DOC for Cyclosporiasis:

A. Trimethoprim sulfamethoxazole combination

B. Paromomycin

C. Metronidazole

D. Cyclosporin

Q.78 Mechanism of action of curare like drugs?

A. Blocks ACh synthesis

B. Blocks ACh receptors

C. Blocks ACh receptors

D. Agonistic with Ach receptors

Q.79 A drug with high plasma binding protein property has which of the following properties?

A. Less GFR

B. Less drug interaction

C. Higher volume of distribution

D. Less tubular secretion

Q.80 Mechanism of action of Oseltamivir?

A. Protein synthesis inhibitor

B. Thymidylate synthetase inhibitor

C. Neuraminidase inhibitor

D. Pyrimidine analogs.

Q.81 True about colchicines is/are:

A. Acts by neutrophil recruitment

B. Causes metaphase arrest

C. Useful in urate-lowering therapy

D. All of the above

Q.82 Which of the following drug is alpha 2agonist?

A. Apraclonidine

B. Timolol

C. PG analogues

D. Verampamil

Q.83 Drug to differentiate Myasthenia gravisfrom cholinergic crisis?

A. Pyridostgmine

B. Edrophonium

C. Methacholine

D. Clonidine

Q.84 Conversion of Norepinephrine toepinephrine is mainly by:

A. S-adenosyl methionine

B. Arginine

C. Phenylalanine

D. Dehydrogenease

Q.85 Carbapenem which has tendency to causemaximum seizures?

A. Imipenem

B. Ertapenem

C. Doripenem

D. Meropenem

Q.86 DOC for diphtheria carrier state is:

A. Penicillin

B. Antitoxin

C. Penicillin Or erythromycin

D. Ciprofloxacin

Q.87 Healthy Human volunteers part of which clinical trial phase?

A. Phase 1

B. Phase 0

C. Phase 3

D. Phase 4

Q.88 DOC for scorpion sting bite is:

A. EDTA   **B.** Neostigmine

C. N-acetylcysteine   **D.** Prazosin

Q.89 MOA of Teduglutide in short bowel syndrome?

A. GLP-2 inhibitor   **B.** HT1a inhibitor

C. GLP-1 analogs   **D.** C-peptide analogs

Q.90 DOC for chemotherapy induced vomitingis:

A. Granisetron   **B.** Prazosin

C. Clonidine   **D.** Dimenhydrinate

Q.91 What is the advantage of fixed-dose combination of drugs?

A. Increases efficacy of drug

B. Decreases adverse effects

C. Patient compliance improved

D. All of the above

Q.92 DOC for digitalis is induced tachycardia:

A. Lidocaine

B. Reducing dosage of digoxin itself, reverses the condition

C. Verapamil

D. Beta blockers

Q.93 Antiretroviral therapy is to be given in HIVinfected patients irrespective of presenceof symptoms if CD4 count is less than?

A. 100   **B.** 150   **C.** 200   **D.** 350

Q.94 Filgrastim is used in the treatment of:

A. Anemia   **B.** Neutropenia

C. Malaria   **D.** Filarial

Q.95 True about treatment of early breast carcinoma:

A. Aromatase inhibitors are replacing tamoxifen in premenopausal women.

B. Post mastectomy radiation therapy is given when 4 or morelymph nodes are positive.

C. Tamoxifen is not useful in post-menopausal women.

D. In premenopausal women, multidrug chemotherapy is given inselected patients.

Q.96 A patient of RA is taking methotrexate,steroids and NSAIDs since 4 months butactivity of disease progression is same.What should be the next probable step?

A. Start monotherapy with anti TNF alpha drugs

B. Continue methotrexate and steroids

C. Stop oral methotrexate and start parenteral methotrexate

D. Add sulfasalazine

Q.97 IV Mannitol is used for treatment of:

A. Acute congestive glaucoma

B. Pulmonary edema

C. Acute renal failure

D. CHF

Q.98 Variation in sensitivity of response todifferent doses of a drug in differentindividual is obtained from:

A. Dose response curve

B. Therapeutic index

C. Bioavailability

D. Phase 1 clinical trials

Q.99 Which one of following is functions ofPGI2?

A. Inhibits platelet aggregation

B. Is a vasodilator

C. Is pyrogenic like PGE2

D. All of the above

Q.100 Degloving skin involves removal of:

A. Skin, subcutaneous fat, fascia, muscle

B. Skin, subcutaneous fat, fascia

C. Skin only

D. Skin subcutaneous fat

Q.101 Sexual perversions(Exhibitionism) isunder section:

A. Section 290   **B.** Section 294

C. Section 230   **D.** Section 291

Q.102 1st affected in rigor mortis:

A. Eyelids   **B.** Myocardium

C. Jaw   **D.** Neck

Q.103 Punishment for perjury is under which section IPC?

A. Sec 193   **B.** Sec 191   **C.** Sec 197   **D.** Sec 190

Q.104 Gastric lavage is not contraindicatedafter ingestion of which acid?

A. HCL   **B.** H_2SO_4

C. Carbolic acid   **D.** Nitric acid

Q.105 Viscera in toxicology stored in:

A. Glycerine

B. Rectified spirit

C. Formalism

D. Saturated salt solution

Q.106 Two identical twins will not have same:

A. Fingerprints   **B.** DNA copies

C. Iris color   **D.** Blood group

Q.107 In Alleged history of gun shotinjury.there is burning, blackening, tattooing around the wound Dirt collar,the injury is:

A. Close shot entry wound

B. Close shot exit wound

C. Distant shot entry wound

D. Distant shot exit wound

Q.108 A child is having Battered babysyndrome how will you identify:

A. Stab wound

B. Gunshot wound

C. Bruise of different ages

D. None of these

Q.109 A patient is having gastrointestinalproblems including abdominal pain anddistension, bloody or mucus-filleddiarrhea, and tenesmus,with rectalprolapse, A stool, ova and parasitesexam reveals the presence of typicalBarrel-shaped eggs, possible causativeagent is?

A. Campylobacter

B. Clostridium difficile

C. Giardia lamblia

D. Trichuris

Q.110 Contact isolation is done for:

A. MRSA   **B.** Mumps

C. Diphtheria   **D.** Asthama

Q.111 A child is suffering from recurrentchronic infections with encapsulatedbacteria is due to deficiency of subclass.

A. IgG1   **B.** IgG2   **C.** IgG3   **D.** IgG4

Q.112 D.O.C for isospora:

A. Penicillin G

B. Benzathine penicillin

C. Co-trimoxazole

D. Albendazole

Q.113 Coxsackievirus A16 causes:

A. Yellow fever

B. Hand-foot-mouth disease

C. Rocky mountain spotted fever

D. Encephalomyocarditis

Q.114 Pneumocystis jerovici is:

A. Associated with CMV

B. Diagnosis is by sputum microscopy

C. Seen only in immunocompromised patients

D. Always associated with pneumatocele

Q.115 All are true about congenitalToxoplasmosis EXCEPT:

A. Chorioretinitis

B. Conjunctivitis

C. Hydrocephalus

D. Cerebral calcification

Q.116 True about TRIAD congenital rubellasyndrome:

A. PDA, cataract and deafness is seen

B. Hepatosplenomegaly, mental retardation, deafness

C. Chorioretinitis, multiorgan failure, pneumonitis

D. None of these

Q.117 Disc diffusion method is also known as:

A. Kirby Bauer

B. VDRL

C. Dark field microscopy

D. None of these

Q.118 Rubella virus belongs to which family?

A. Rheovirus   **B.** Togavirus

C. Picornavirus   **D.** Orthomyxo

Q.119 Which of the following infection resembles erythroblastosis?

A. EBV

B. CMV

C. HSV

D. STAPHYLOCOCCUS

Q.120 Diagnostic test for neurosyphilis:

A. VDRL   **B.** RPR

C. TPI   **D.** FTA-ABS

Q.121 Flask shaped ulcers in intestine causedby:

A. Giardia lamblia

B. Entamoeba histolytica

C. Helicobacter pylori (H. pylori)

D. E. vermicularis

Q.122 What type of culture media is used forLegionella?

A. (BCYE) agar media

B. MacConkey agar

C. Baird–Parker agar

D. Sabouraud's agar

Q.123 Special Stain for cryptococcus:

A. ZN stain   **B.** Gram stain

C. Mucicarmine stain   **D.** Malachite green

Q.124 A 36 yrs old male patient c/,o cough coldfever/rusty sputum / sputum neg for tb, h/o of travel in china & eaten crab,Name the infection.

A. Paragonimus westermani

B. Faciola hepatica

C. Fasciolopsis buski

D. Entamoeba histolytica

Q.125 Microbiological test for diagnosingleptospira infection?

A. Cold agglutination

B. Standard agglutination

C. Microscopic agglutination test (MAT)

D. None of these

Q.126 Green colour of triage is for whichpatient?

A. Low priority   **B.** Morbidity

C. Ambulatory   **D.** High priority

Q.127 Concurrent list of Indian Constitutionincludes which of the following?

A. International immigration rule for quarantine.

B. Prevention of extension of communicable disease from one unitto another.

C. Mines and oilfield workers rules.

D. Establishment and maintenance of drug standards.

Q.128 Last point where reproductive and childhealth programme are include:

A. Sub-centre   **B.** Anganwadi

C. District   **D.** Taluka

Q.129 Health center in remotest area for planning and management of schemes:

A. Anganwadi   **B.** Block centre

C. Sub-centre   **D.** PHC

Q.130 Diagnostic power of a test to correctlydiagnose a disease is:

A. Negative predictive value

B. Positive predictive value

C. Sensitivity

D. Specificity

Q.131 Paradoxical carriers are:

A. A person who acquires the microorganism due to his contactwith the patient.

B. A person who acquires the microorganism another carrier.

C. A person who is clinically recovered from an infectious diseasebut still capable of transmitting the infectious agent to others.

D. None of these

Q.132 According to IMNCI, a baby of 6 month age, criteria for fast breathing is more than ____/min

A. 60   **B.** 50   **C.** 40   **D.** 30

Q.133 All of the following are examples ofDietary fibre except:

A. Pectin   **B.** Lignin

C. Cellulose   **D.** Gums

Q.134 Cross product ratio is determined bywhich study?

A. Case control   **B.** Cohort

C. Cross sectional   **D.** RCT

Q.135 In a normal curve what is the area thatcomes under 1 standard deviation:

A. 50%   **B.** 68%   **C.** 95%   **D.** 100%

Q.136 2 year old boy of weight 12 kg with vitamin A deficiency. What will be oral dose of vitamin A.

A. 50, 000 I.U   **B.** 1 lakh I.U

C. 1.5 lakh I.U   **D.** 2 lakh I.U

Q.137 Not a personal protective equipment:

A. Goggles

B. Badges for detecting radiation

C. Gloves

D. Lab coat

Q.138 Confounding factor is defined as:

A. Factor associated with both the exposure and the disease andis distributed unequally in study and control groups.

B. Factor associated with exposure only and is distributedunequally in study and control groups.

C. Factor associated with both the exposure and the disease andis distributed equally in study and control groups.

D. Factor associated with the disease and is distributed equally instudy and control groups.

Q.139 The significance of difference betweenproportions can also be tested by:

A. 'T' test

B. Chi square test

C. ANOVA

D. Correlation and regression

Q.140 Paired T test is defined as:

A. Test used to assess quantitative observations before and afteran intervention

B. Test that is used when the observation are in the form ofproportions (for qualitative data)

C. Test applied when separate observations are made onindividuals of two separate groups, and these need to becompared

D. None of these

Q.141 Best representative of incidence ofdisease in different timeline.

A. Histogram   **B.** Line diagram

C. Scattered diagram   **D.** Bar diagram

Q.142 For trench type of sanitary filling theamount of land required for 2 meter deeptrench for 10000 population is:

A. 1 acre   **B.** 2 acre   **C.** 3 acre   **D.** 4 acre

Q.143 Risk of genetic diseasesin consanguineous marriage betweenfirst cousins:

A. 1-2%   **B.** 4-8%   **C.** 8-10%   **D.** 12-14%

Q.144 Which is not a epidemiologicalindicator?

A. ABER

B. Annual parasite index

C. Annual falciparum incidence

D. None of the Above

Q.145 Dose of diphtheria antitoxin is:

A. 1000 to 5000 IU   **B.** 10000 to 100000 IU

C. 1000 to 2000 IU   **D.** None of these

Q.146 Vertical transmission of HIV is highestwith:

A. Elective caesarean section

B. High viral RNA load

C. Breast feeding

D. Term delivery

Q.147 The most common site of the branchialcyst is:

A. Posterior border of sternocleidomastoid

B. Anterior border of sternocleidomastoid

C. Digastric muscle

D. Omohyoid muscle

Q.148 Inspiratory stridor is found in what kindof lesions:

A. Supraglottic   **B.** Subglottic

C. Trachea   **D.** Bronchus

Q.149 In Retinitis pigmentosa decreased levelof:

A. Arachidonic

B. Trielonic

C. Thromboxane

D. Docosahexaenoic acid

Q.150 What is against the rule correction inastigmatism?

A. -1.25 cyl 90   **B.** -2 spherical 180

C. -3 cyl 180   **D.** +2 cyl 180

Q.151 Morbid fear of darkness known as:

A. Claustrophobia   **B.** Xenophobia

C. Mysophobia   **D.** Nyctophobia

Q.152 A child has ptosis and poor levatorfunction. What surgery will you do?

A. Levator muscle resection

B. Mullerectomy

C. Fasanella Servat surgery

D. Frontalis suspension surgery

Q.153 Which drug causes ocular hypotensionwith apnea in an infant?

A. Latanoprost   **B.** Timolol

C. Brimonidine   **D.** Dorzolamide

Q.154 Chemotherapy agents forretinoblastoma:

A. vincristine, carboplatin and etoposide

B. vinblastine, etoposide and bleomycin

C. vinblastine, vincristine and etoposide

D. vinblastine, vincristine and cisplatin

Q.155 Drug used in acute congestive glaucomaare:

A. Atropine   **B.** Pilocarpine

C. Acetazolamide   **D.** Both (B) and (C)

Q.156 Which is the Most common ocularfinding in myasthenia gravis?

A. Ptosis   **B.** Lagophthalmos

C. Proptosis   **D.** Enophthalmos

Q.157 Esotropia is usually associated with:

A. Myopia   **B.** Hypermetropia

C. Astigmatism   **D.** Presbyopia

Q.158 Which wall of heart enlargement can beseen on barium swallow in patient withmitral stenosis?

A. Left atrium   **B.** Right atrium

C. Left ventricle   **D.** Right ventricle

Q.159 Which of the following statements is trueabout the bundle of kent?

A. Abnormal pathway between two atria

B. It is muscular or nodal pathway between the atria and ventriclein WPW syndrome

C. It is slower than the AV nodal pathway

D. None

Q.160 Deep venous thrombosis which isincorrect?

A. Clinical assessment highly reliable

B. Mostly bilateral

C. Most common clinically presents as pain and tenderness in calf

D. Some cases may directly present as pulmonarythromboembolism

Q.161 Punched out ulcer in esophagus is seenin:

A. Herpes   **B.** Cmv

C. Oesophagitis   **D.** Candida

Q.162 Type of sensation lost on same side ofBrown Sequard syndrome:

A. Pain   **B.** Touch

C. Proprioception   **D.** Temperature

Q.163 Achondroplasia shows which typeinheritance:

A. XLR

B. XLD

C. Autosomal recessive

D. Autosomal dominant

Q.164 MELD score includes:

A. Serum creatinine

B. Transaminase

C. Albumin

D. Alkaline phosphatase

Q.165 Infarcts involving which portion of themyocardium cause aneurysm as a post MI complication:

A. Subendocardial

B. Anterior transmural

C. Posterior transmural

D. Inferior wall

Q.166 Risk factors for alzheimer's diseaseinclude:

A. Klinefelter syndrome

B. Low BP

C. Down's syndrome

D. None of these

Q.167 A female patient of 26 years, presentswith oral ulcers, photosensitivity andskin malar rash in face sparing thenasolabial folds of both side:

A. Sturge weber syndrome

B. SLE

C. Dermatitis

D. Psoriasis

Q.168 Most characteristic cardiovascular defectseen in Rubella:

A. Pulmonary artery stenosis

B. Coarctation of aorta

C. Ankylosis spondylitis

D. Rheumatic fever

Q.169 Osborn J waves is seen in:

A. Hypothermia   **B.** Hyperkalemia

C. Hypocalemia   **D.** Hypokalemia

Q.170 Alcoholic shows which type ofcardiomyopathy?

A. Hyper cardiomyopathy

B. Dilated cardiomyopathy

C. Pericarditis

D. Myocarditis

Q.171 Which is not related to HIV?

A. Primary CNS lymphoma

B. Tertiary syphilis

C. Oesophageal candidasis

D. None of these

Q.172 Essential major blood culture criteria forinfective endocarditis.

A. Single positive culture of hacek

B. Single positive culture of coxiella

C. Single positive culture of cornybacterium

D. Both (A) and (B)

Q.173 Respiratory centres are stimulated by:

A. Oxygen   **B.** Lactic acid
C. Carbon dioxide   **D.** Calcium

Q.174 Which murmur increases on standing?

A. HOCM   **B.** MR   **C.** MS   **D.** VSD

Q.175 Most common indication for livertransplant in children:

A. Biliary atresia   **B.** Cirrhosis
C. Hepatitis   **D.** Drug reactions

Q.176 Most common type of gallstone is:

A. Mixed stones
B. Pure cholesterol stones
C. Pigment stones
D. Calcium bilirubinate

Q.177 Serpiginous ulcer distal esophagus:

A. CMV   **B.** Herpes
C. Pill   **D.** Corrosive

Q.178 Omphalocele is caused by:

A. Duplications of intestinal loops
B. Abnormal rotation of the intestinal loop
C. Failure of gut to return to the body cavity from its physiologicalherniation
D. Reversed rotation of the intestinal loop

Q.179 Dohlman procedure for:

A. Meckel's diverticulum
B. Zenker's diverticulum
C. Dermatomyositis
D. Menetrier's disease

Q.180 If a mother is donating kidney to her sonis an example:

A. Isograft   **B.** Allograft
C. Autograft   **D.** Xenograft

Q.181 Uvula vesicae is produced by whichprostate lobe?

A. Anterior lobe   **B.** Post lobe
C. Median lobe   **D.** Lateral lobe

Q.182 True about Barrett's esophagus are all ofthe following except:

A. Causes adenocarcinoma
B. Patient is usually asymptomatic
C. Histology of the lesion shows mucus secreting goblet cells
D. Chronic gastroesophageal reflux is a predisposing factor

Q.183 Parathyroid autoimplantation takes placein which of the muscle?

A. Biceps   **B.** Triceps
C. Brachioradialis   **D.** Sartorius

Q.184 Bell's palsy is associated with the lesionin which of the nerve?

A. 11th cranial nerve   **B.** 7th cranial nerve
C. 9th cranial nerve   **D.** 3rd cranial nerve

Q.185 Cushing ulcer is seen in case of:

A. Burns   **B.** Head injury
C. Cell necrosis   **D.** Stress

Q.186 Gasless abdomen seen in:

A. Ulcerative colitis
B. Acute pancreatitis
C. Intussusception
D. Necrotising enterocolitis

Q.187 Bidextrous grip is seen at what age?

A. 4 months   **B.** 5 months
C. 6 months   **D.** 7 months

Q.188 Which vaccine to be given every year?

A. Hepatitis A   **B.** Hepatitis B
C. Influenza   **D.** Chicken pox

Q.189 APGAR score of 3 at 1 minute indicates:

A. Mildly depressed
B. Further resuscitation not needed
C. Severely depressed
D. Normal

Q.190 Severe acute malnutrition as per WHOcriteria:

A. Weight for age less than median plus – 2 SD
B. Weight for height less than median plus 2 SD
C. Weight for age less than median plus 3 SD
D. Weight for height less than median minus -3 SD

Q.191 Where to look for pre-ductal O_2saturation in PDA in a 3 minute borninfant?

A. Fetal left Upper limb
B. Fetal left lower limb
C. Fetal right Upper limb
D. Fetal right lower limb

Q.192 True about Fragile X syndrome is:

A. Triple nucleotide CAG Sequence mutation
B. 10% Female carriers mentally retarded
C. Males have IQ 20-40
D. Gain of function mutation

Q.193 Foot drop is caused by injury to whichnerve involvement?

A. Femoral nerve
B. Tibial nerve
C. Common peroneal nerve
D. Sciatic nerve

Q.194 Which part of scaphoid fracture is mostsusceptible to avascular necrosis?

A. Distal 1/3rd   **B.** Middle 1/3rd
C. Proximal 1/3rd   **D.** Scaphoid Tubercle

Q.195 Pott's puffy tumor:

A. Subperiosteal abscess of frontal bone
B. Subperiosteal abscess of ethmoid bone
C. Mucocele of frontal bone
D. Mucocele of ethmoid bone

Q.196 Scissor gait is seen in which of thefollowing condition?

A. Polio   **B.** Cerebral palsy

C. Hyperbilirubinemia   **D.** Hyponatremia

Q.197 Which statement is incorrect about thepathology shown in the image:

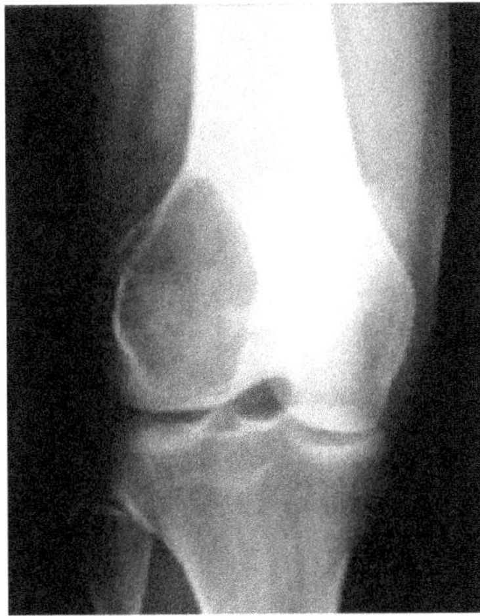

A. Tumor arise from epiphyseal to metaphyseal region
B. Tumor has distinct margin
C. Eccentric lesion
D. Chemotherapy is the treatment of choice

Q.198 What should be the most likely diagnosisof this 65 year old lady presents withbackache and following radiograph ofthe spine shown in image?

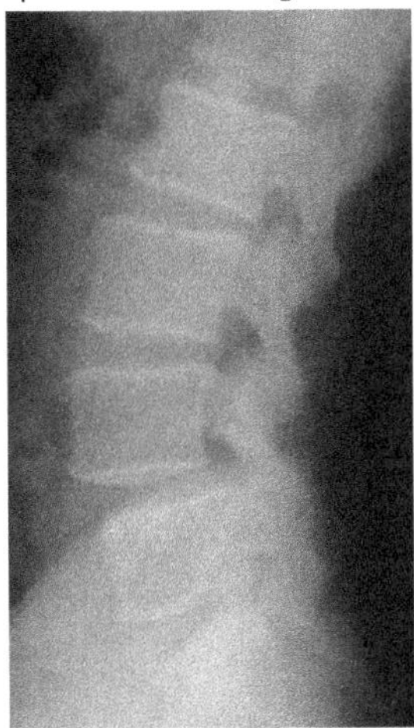

A. Osteoporosis   **B.** Spondylolisthesis
C. Spondylolysis   **D.** Discitis

Q.199 Which of the following attitude will be seen in a patient with posteriordislocation of hip?

A. Flexion, Abduction, Internal rotation
B. Flexion, Adduction, Internal rotation
C. Flexion, Abduction, External rotation
D. Flexion, Adduction, External rotation

Q.200 True about Tenosynovitis of finger?

A. Fingers held in mild extension / Extension deformity at theinvolved fingers.
B. Tenosynovitis of little finger will spread to thumb rather than ringfinger.

C. With involvement of little finger the infection can spread to theindex finger.
D. Treatment is conservative.

Q.201 Most common joint involved in septicarthritis:

A. Knee   **B.** Hip   **C.** Shoulder   **D.** Elbow

Q.202 Painful arc syndrome pain is felt during?

A. Mid abduction
B. Initial abduction
C. Full range of abduction
D. Overhead abduction

Q.203 Which of the following is false asphysiological change in pregnancy?

A. Increase cardiac output
B. Increase total protein
C. Increase residual volume
D. Increase GFR

Q.204 Overt gestational diabetes is defined asblood glucose more than________.

A. >200 mg/dl   **B.** >126 mg/dl
C. >100 mg/dl   **D.** >180 mg/dl

Q.205 $MgSO_4$ have no role in prevention of:

A. Seizures in severe pre-eclampsia
B. Recurrent seizures in eclampsia
C. RDS in premature baby
D. Bradycardia

Q.206 Green frothy vaginal discharge isproduced by:

A. Herpes simplex
B. Candida albicans
C. Trichomonas vaginalis
D. Normal vaginal flora

Q.207 Which of the following is an absoluteCONTRAINDICATION to OCP use?

A. Chronic renal disease
B. DVT
C. Diabetes mellitus
D. History of amenorrhea

Q.208 Which of the following statement iscorrect about acute fatty liver ofpregnancy?

A. Occurs in 1 in 1000 pregnancy
B. Mostly seen in last trimester
C. Common if female fetus is present
D. May be associated with decreased uric acid

Q.209 Female with 41 wk gestation confirmedby radiological investigation, very sureof her LMP, no uterine contractions, noeffacement and no dilatation. Whatshould not be done?

A. Intracervical foley's   **B.** PGE1 tab
C. PGE2 gel   **D.** PGF2α

Q.210 Double decidual sign is seen during:

A. 1st trimester   **B.** 2nd early trimester
C. 2nd late trimester   **D.** 3rd trimester

Q.211 60 year woman comes with 3rd degreeuterine prolapse. What will be themanagement?

A. Vaginal hysterectomy with pelvic floor repair

B. Pelvic floor repair

C. Sacrospinous fixation

D. Pessary

Q.212 Day 20 of menstrual cycle falls underwhich phase?

A. Menstrual phase

B. Follicular phase

C. Ovulation phase

D. Luteal phase

Q.213 Chromosome number of partialhydatidiform mole is:

A. 46 XX

B. 45 XO

C. 46 XXY

D. 69 XXX

Q.214 Vulvar atrophy and itching are treatedby:

A. Estrogen ointment

B. Antihistamines

C. Tamoxifen

D. None of these

Q.215 Premature ejaculation is a part of which phase ofsexual disorders?

A. Excitement phase

B. Plateau phase

C. Orgasm phase

D. Refractory phase

Q.216 Nuchal translucency in USG can bedetected at _____ weeks of gestation.

A. 11-13 weeks

B. 18-20 weeks

C. 8-10 weeks

D. 20-22 weeks

Q.217 First line of treatment of mastitis in alactating mother is:

A. Dicloxacillin

B. Cefazolin

C. Ceftriaxone

D. Ampicillin

Q.218 Patient with recurrent abortiondiagnosed to have antiphospholipidsyndrome. What will be the treatment?

A. Aspirin only

B. Aspirin + Low molecular weight Heparin

C. Aspirin + Low molecular weight Heparin + Prednisolone

D. No Treatment

Q.219 Gestational Trophoblastic neoplasmdoes not include:

A. Choriocarcinoma

B. Placental site trophoblastic tumour

C. Invasive mole

D. Partial mole

Q.220 Which vaccine is contraindicated inpregnancy?

A. Chickenpox

B. Rabies

C. Tet toxoid

D. Hepatitis B

Q.221 45 years female with 3 monthsmenorrhagia. USG showing 2 cmsubmucosal fibroid. Treatment options:

A. Ocp for 3 months

B. Progesterone for 3 months

C. Endometrial sampling

D. Hysterectomy

Q.222 In low ovarian reserve, anti mullerianhormone level will be:

A. <1

B. 1-4

C. >7

D. >10

Q.223 Presenting diameter of full flexed head:

A. Suboccipito-bregmatic diameter

B. Suboccipito-frontal diameter

C. Occipito-frontal diameter

D. Occipito-posterior position

Q.224 What is the dose of ulipristal acetate?

A. 300mg

B. 30mg

C. 300µg

D. 30µg

Q.225 The major contribution of the amnioticfluid after 20 weeks of gestation:

A. Ultrafiltrate and maternal plasma

B. Fetal urine

C. Fetal lung fluid

D. Fetal skin

Q.226 PGF2α maximum dose in PPH is:

A. 2000 µg

B. 200 µg

C. 2 mg

D. 20 mg

Q.227 All are true about skin except:

A. Both dermis & ectoderm are derived from ectoderm

B. Skin accounts for total of 15% of body weight

C. Most of the cells in skin are keratinocytes derived fromectoderm

D. Dermis is made up of type1 and type 3 collagen in 3:2 ratio

Q.228 Anaesthetic gas with maximumrespiratory irritation:

A. Halothane

B. Enflurane

C. Desflurane

D. Sevoflurane

Q.229 IV administration of which anestheticdrug is most painful among thefollowing?

A. Methohexital

B. Ketamine

C. Propofol

D. Etomidate

Q.230 Which of the following is notcardiodepressive?

A. Propofol

B. Thiopentone

C. Ketamine

D. Etomidate

Q.231 Which of the following is the mostcommon method used to know depthof anaesthesia?

A. BIS

B. Oesophageal contractility

C. Depressed responses

D. Hypotension

Q.232 MRP 2 associated with which of thefollowing?

A. Rotor syndrome

B. Dubin - Johnson syndrome

C. Crigler-Najjar syndrome

D. Gilbert syndrome

Q.233 Which of the following is water solublecontrast?

A. Barium

B. Iodine

C. Bromium

D. Calcium

Q.234 Solitary lytic lesions seen in:

A. Atherosclerosis

B. Multiple myeloma

C. Mitral stenosis

D. Osteoblast

Q.235 Not true about somnambulism amongthe following is:

A. Sleep walking

B. Patient consciousness is preserved.

C. Disorder of sleep arousal.

D. Low level motor skill/function is present

Q.236 Confusion assessment scale used forwhich of the following?

A. Schizophrenia   **B.** Delirium

C. Dementia   **D.** Depression

Q.237 Which of the following is the poorprognostic factor for OCD?

A. Magical thinking   **B.** Dirt contamination

C. Pathological doubt   **D.** Hoarding

Q.238 Test based on the principle of suspect'sreaction, if he witnesses an event thenhe behaves in a certain way is:

A. Narcoanalysis   **B.** Brain mapping

C. Truth serum testing   **D.** Polygraph

Q.239 Intense depression & misery without anycause is:

A. Melancholia

B. Major depressive disorder

C. Mania

D. Schizophrenia

Q.240 Which of the following is not trueregarding delusional disorder?

A. Held with absolute conviction

B. Usually false

C. Not amenable to reasoning

D. Occurs at early age

Q.241 Identify the condition shown in the imagebelow.

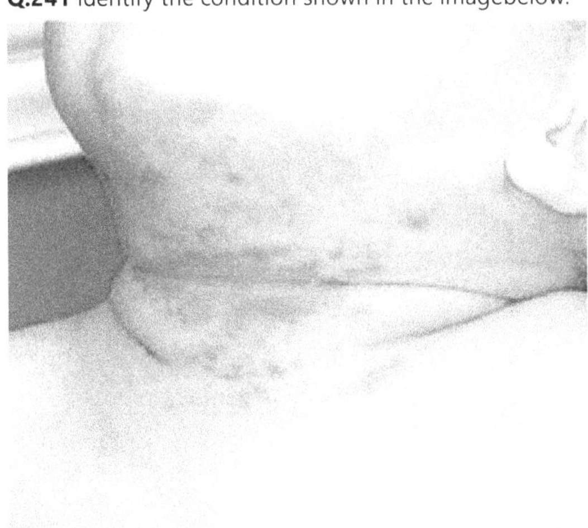

A. Intertrigo   **B.** Heat rash

C. Eczema   **D.** Impetigo

Q.242 Identify the infection from the chest Xray of a patient with low-grade fever?

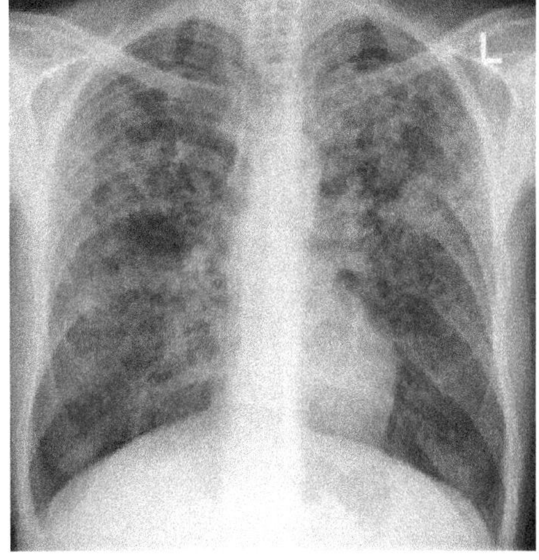

A. ILD   **B.** Bronchopneumonia

C. Miliary TB   **D.** Consolidation

Q.243 Identify the condition given in theimage?

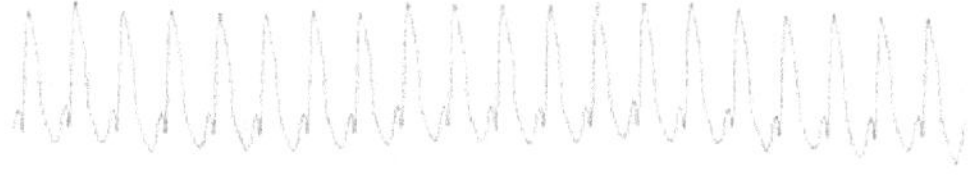

A. Atrial fibrillar

B. Atrial flutter

C. Ventricular tachycardia

D. SVT

Q.244 A patient presented with history ofdiplopia and restricted eye movements.A clinical image and CT image is shownbelow. What will be the diagnosis?

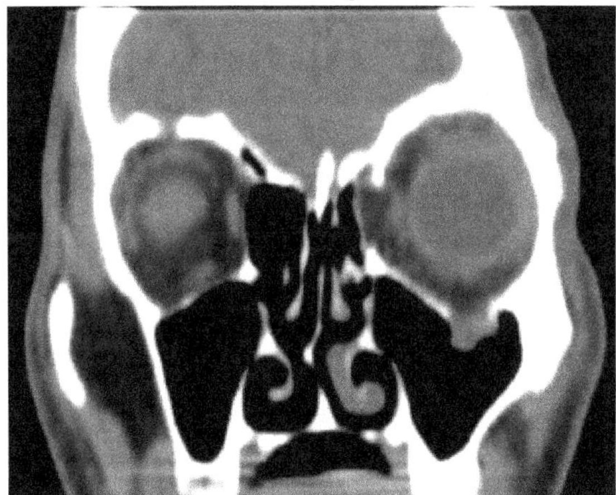

A. Le- fort fracture   **B.** Fracture maxilla

C. Fracture zygomatic   **D.** Blow out fracture

Q.245 Identify the radiological procedureshown below?

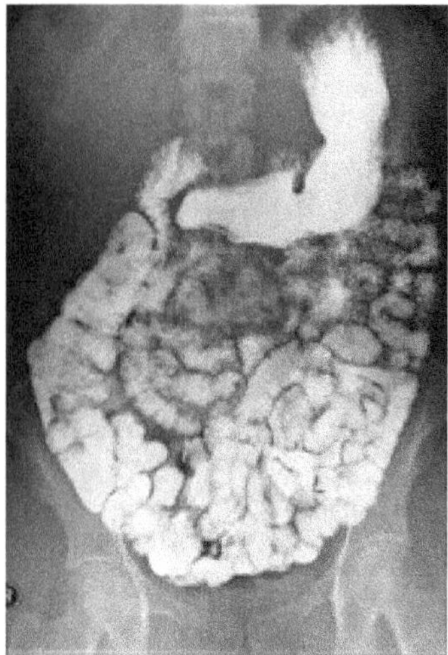

A. Barium meal follow through
B. Barium enema
C. Enteroclysis
D. Proctography

Q.246 Identify the condition in the belowimage?

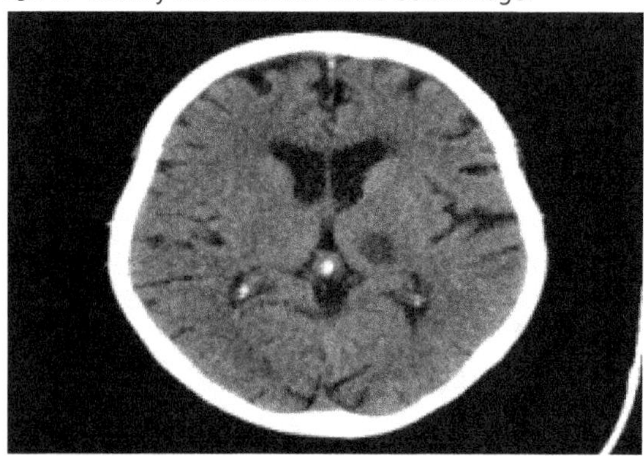

A. Lacunar infarct
B. Embolic infarct
C. Thrombotic infarct
D. Intracerebral hemorrhage

Q.247 A child with history of fever,photosensitivity, rash sparing nasolabialfold presents to OP. Identify thecondition?

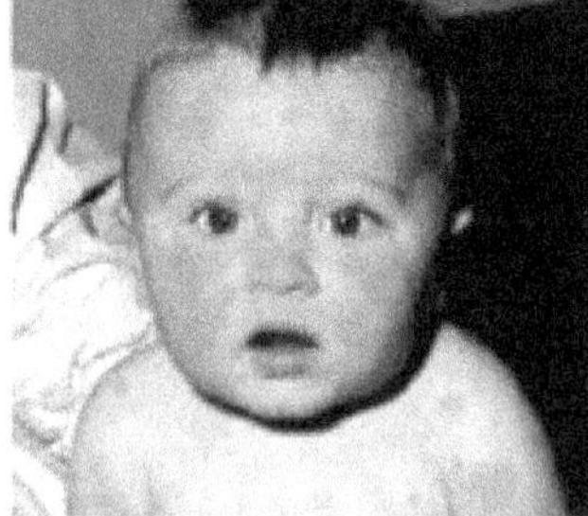

A. SLE
B. Polymorphous light eruption
C. Discoid lupus
D. Skin tuberculosis

Q.248 Patient presents with purities of interdigits of left hand as shown in the image.Identify the condition?

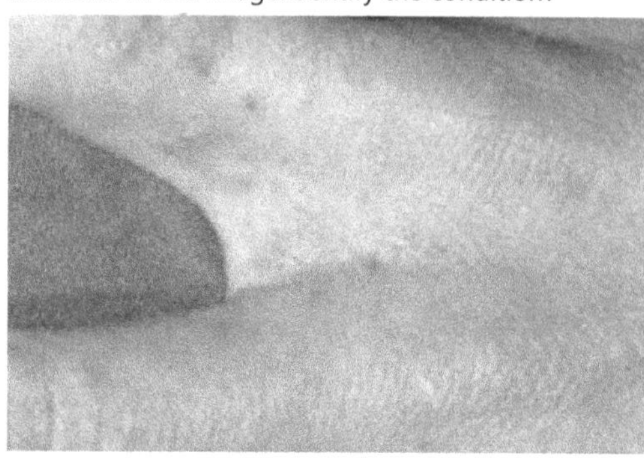

A. Sarcoptes scabis
B. Dermatitis herpetiformis
C. Xerotic dermatitis
D. Erythema multiforme

Q.249 Identify the condition. This is child withasthmatic mother.

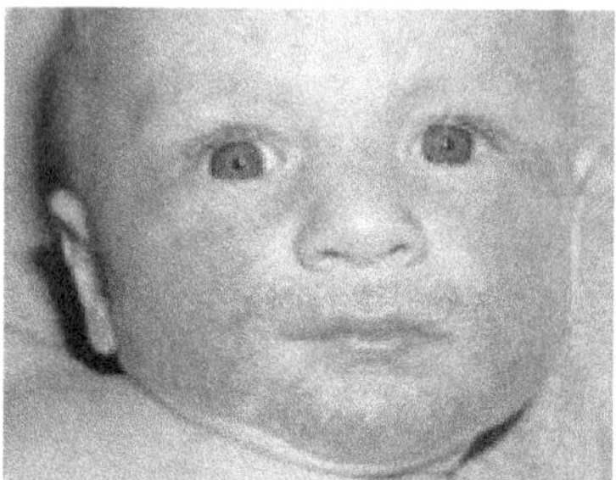

A. Atopic dermatitis   B. SLE
C. Erythema   D. TEN

Q.250 Identify the condition shown in theimage?

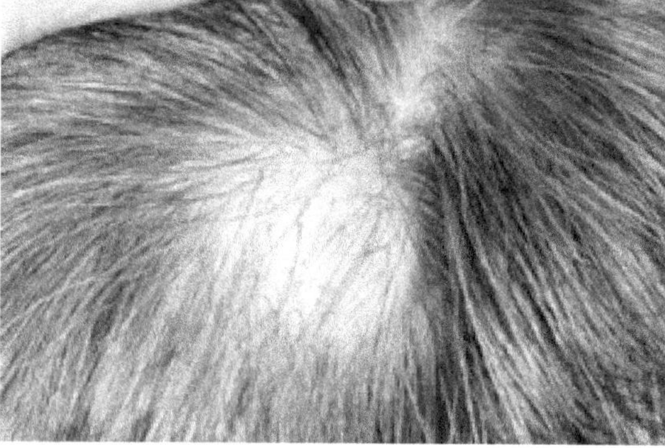

A. Sebaceous cyst   B. Alopecia areta
C. Trichotillomania   D. Tinea capitis

Q.251 Identify the condition in the image?

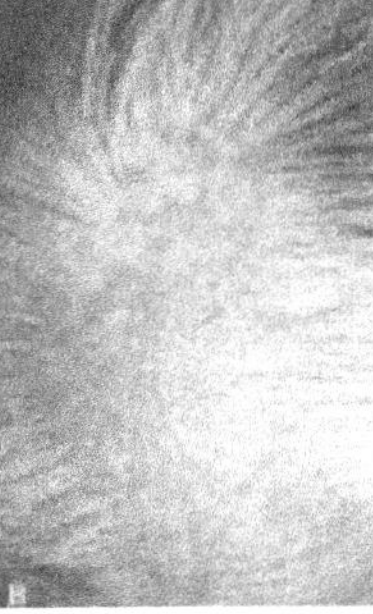

A. Leukoderma
C. Vitiligo
B. Piebaldism
D. DLE

Q.252 Which of the following regarding thecondition depicted in the image?

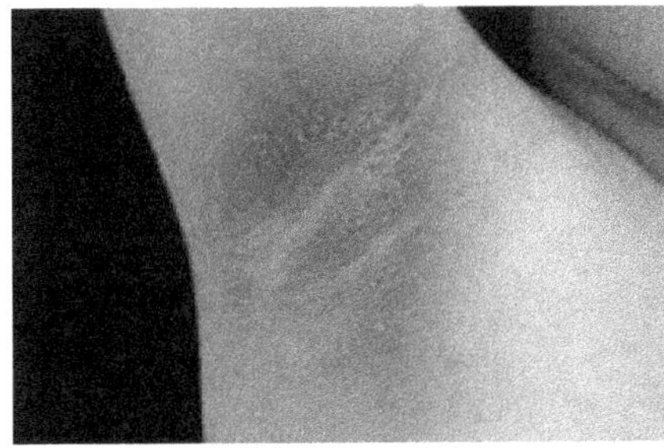

A. May be an indication of skin malignancy
B. Hypopigmentation
C. May be associated with Insulin resistant diabetes mellitus
D. Commonly occurs in lean and thin

Q.253 The causative organism for the conditiondepicted in image is:

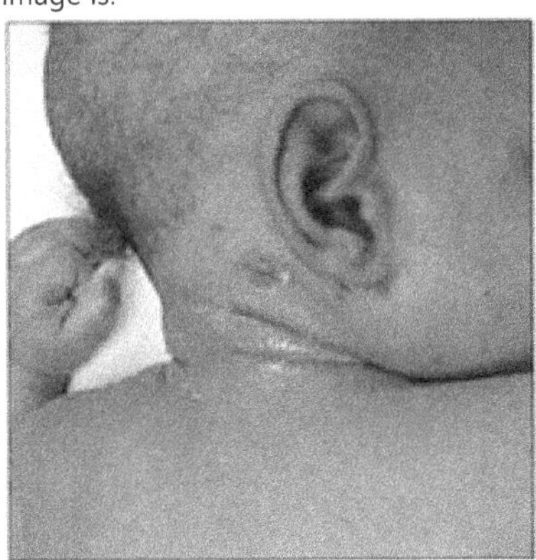

A. Staphylococcus
C. Streptococcus
B. Candidal infection
D. Actinomycetes

Q.254 Identify the condition as shown:

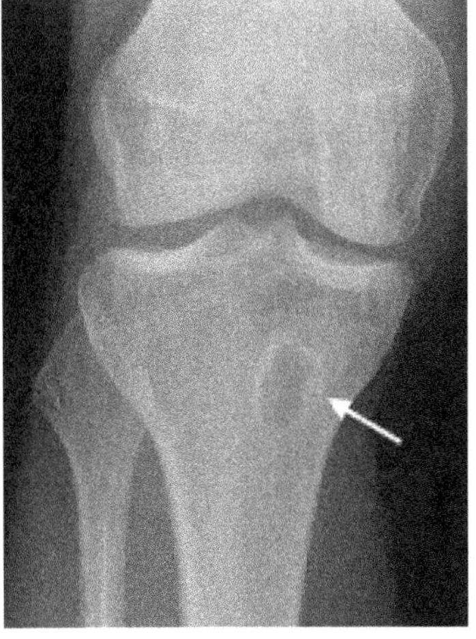

A. Brodie abscess
B. Osteoid osteoma
C. Intracortical hemangioma
D. Chondromyxoid fibroma

Q.255 14 yr old child with Naive RheumatoidArthritis patient as shown in image.What should be the correct treatment ofgiven condition:

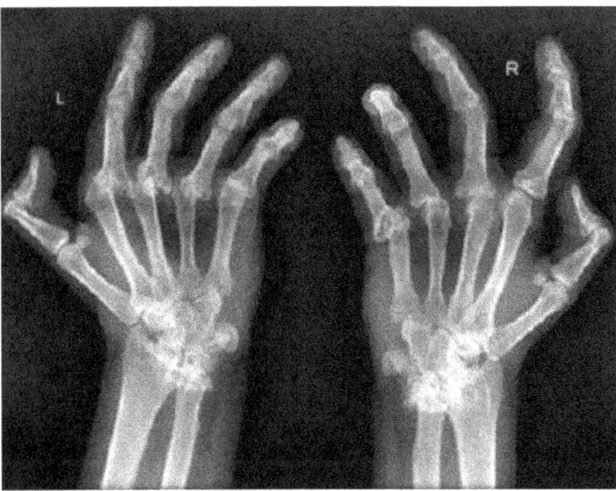

A. DMARD with short course of Steroids
B. Only NSAID'S
C. DMARD after initial 3 months of NSAID'S
D. Monotherapy with TNF drugs

Q.256 In 34 weeks gestation the weight of babywas 3kg.The child shows followingfeatures may indicate associatedcondition:

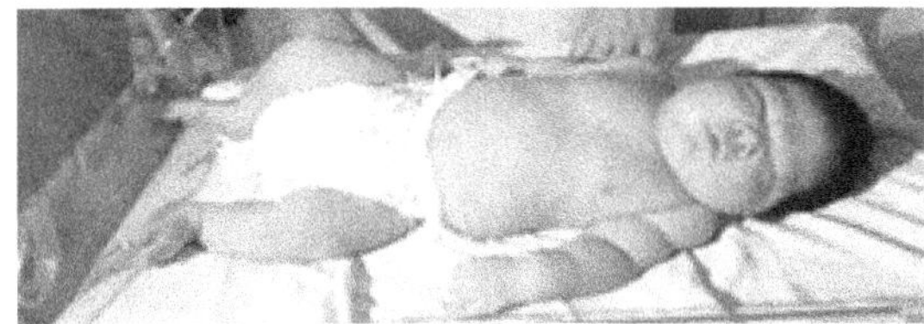

A. Anemia
B. Diabetes
C. APH
D. None

Q.257 30 year old woman with complaint ofdysmenorrhoea, dyspareunia with chronicpelvic pain undergoes hysterectomy.

Fromthe cut section of hysterectomy specimenbelow identify the condition.

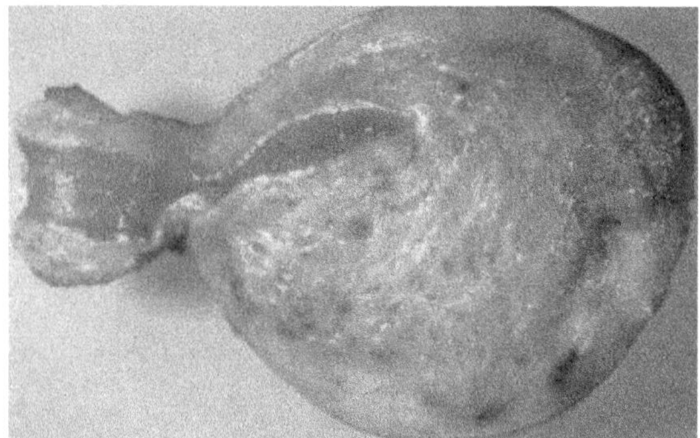

A. Adenomyosis

B. Fibroids

C. Leiomyoma

D. Endometriosis

Q.258 Identify the type of placenta praevia asshown in the picture below?

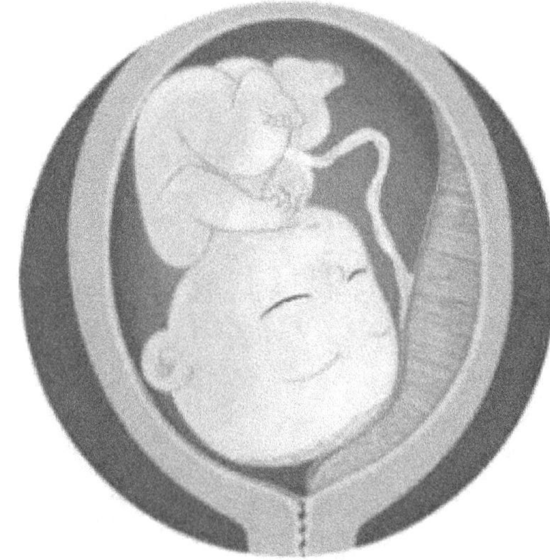

A. I **B.** II **C.** III **D.** IV

Q.259 A female patient presented withrecurrent Urinary tract infections.Imaging shows the following picture.What can be the most probablediagnosis?

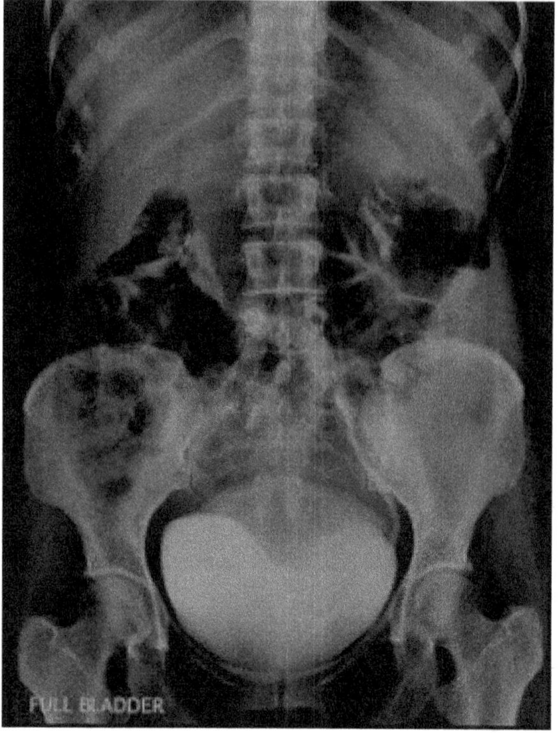

A. Duplication of Ureter

B. Congenital Megaureter

C. Ureterocele

D. Urinary Stones

Q.260 Identify the triangle in the image below:

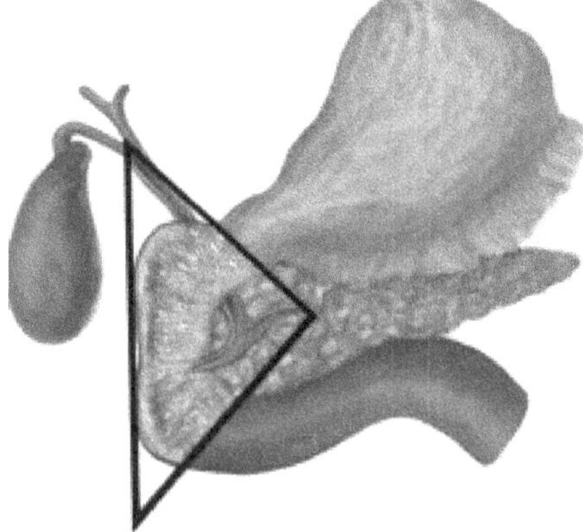

A. Koch's triangle

B. Gastrinoma triangle

C. Hesselbach's triangle

D. Sherren's triangle

Q.261 Identify the instrument:

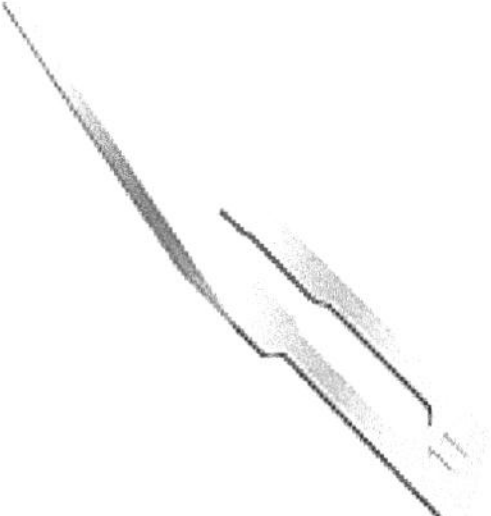

A. Blade no. 15   **B.** Blade no. 10
C. Blade no. 11   **D.** Blade 12

Q.262 Identify the type of knot in the image:

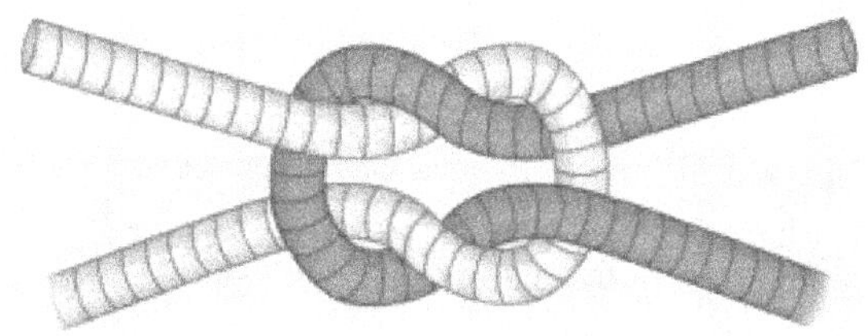

A. Granny knot   **B.** Surgeon's knot
C. Reef knot   **D.** None of these

Q.263 Identify the condition in the ECG:

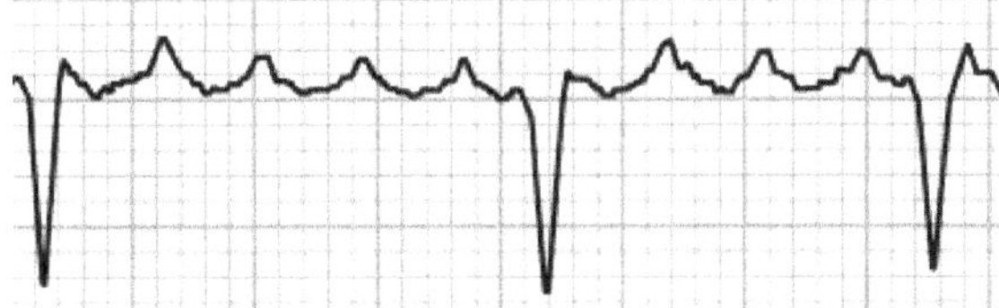

A. Atrial fibrillation   **B.** Arrhythmia
C. Atrial flutter   **D.** Cardiomyopathy

Q.264 A patient is a known case of acutepancreatitis develops breathlessness,bilateral basal crepitation on day 4 andchest radiography as shown in the imagebelow. What will be the diagnosis?

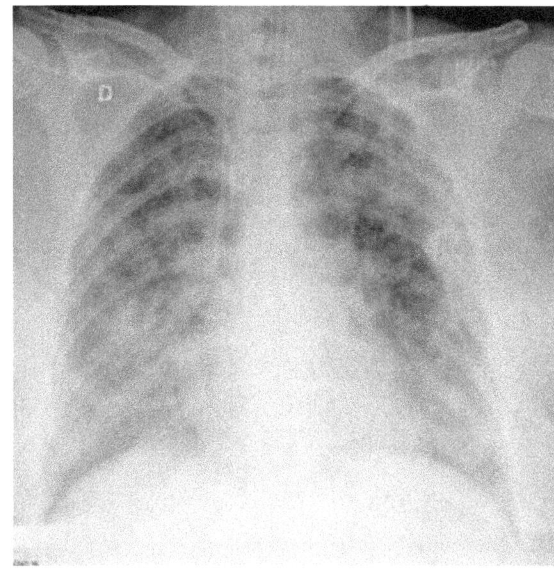

A. Bilateral pneumonia
B. ARDS
C. Carcinogenic PE
D. Collapse

Q.265 Identify the image with the diagnosis:

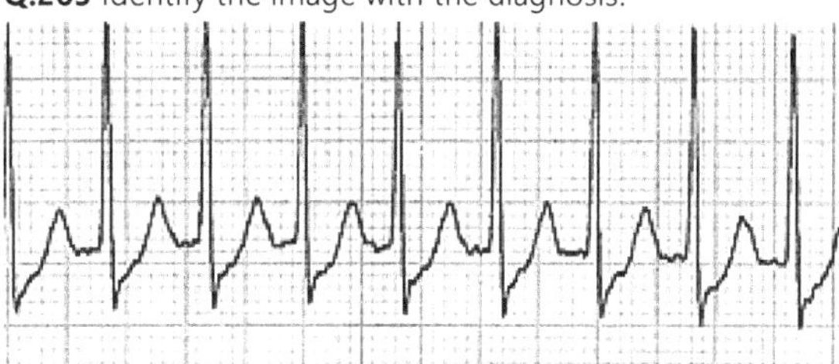

A. VT
B. PSVT
C. AT
D. Ventricular fibrillation

Q.266 A patient came in emergency with severeabdominal pain pulse 112/ minute andsystolic BP 80 mm/Hg with the chest Xray shown below. What will be the nextappropriate step to be taken for thepatient?

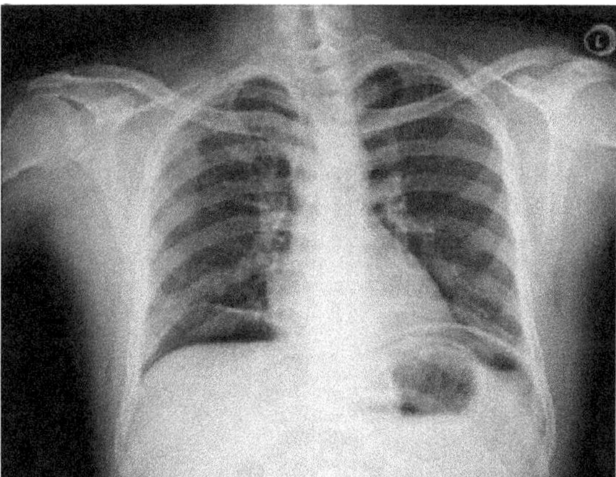

A. Exploratory laprotomy

B. Saline Wash of stomach

C. Intercostal tube drainage

D. None

Q.267 True statement about given condition ofeye except:

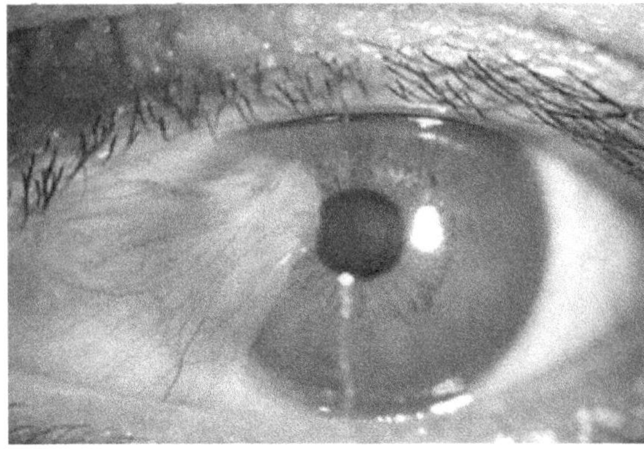

A. Arise from any part of conjunctiva

B. Can cause Astigmatism

C. Surgery is treatment of choice

D. UV exposure is risk factor

Q.268 Following test is used to diagnose whichocular condition as shown in image:

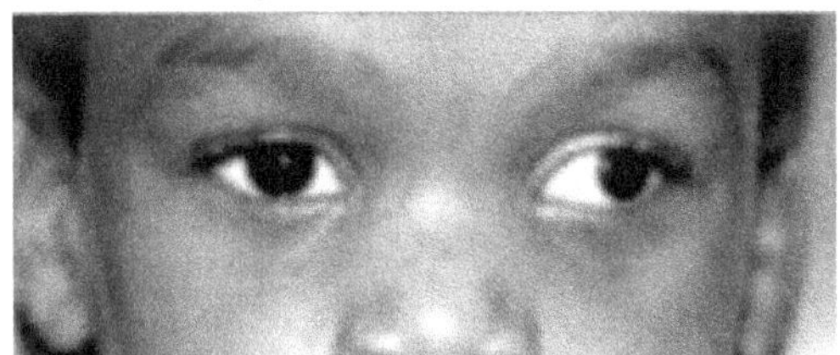

A. Strabismus   **B.** Heterophoria

C. Both (A) & (B)   **D.** None of the above

Q.269 Name the maneuver shown in the image:

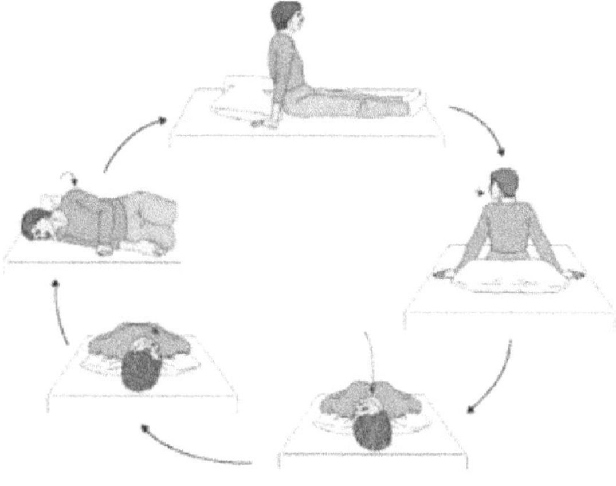

A. Brandt daroff   **B.** Epley

C. Foster   **D.** Semont

Q.270 Identify the condition of the given image:

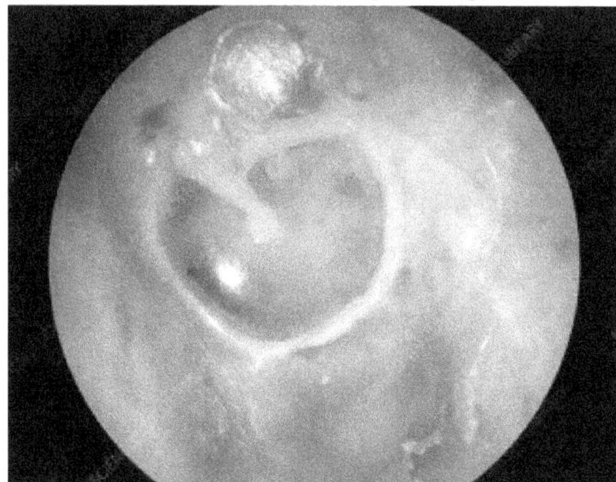

A. Acquired cholesteatoma

B. Congenital cholesteatoma

C. Rupture of tympanic membrane

D. Keratosis obturans

Q.271 CT image of left maxilla with history ofallergic rhinitis?

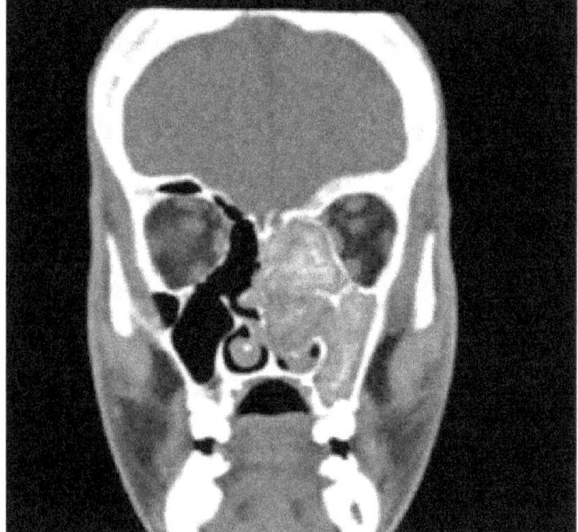

A. Ground glass appearance

B. Double densities

C. Honey comb

D. Onion Peel Appearance

Q.272 Identify the instrument:

A. Maddox rod   B. Maddox wing

C. Maddox glass   D. Red glasses

Q.273 Identify the lesion of vocal cord in theimage given below:

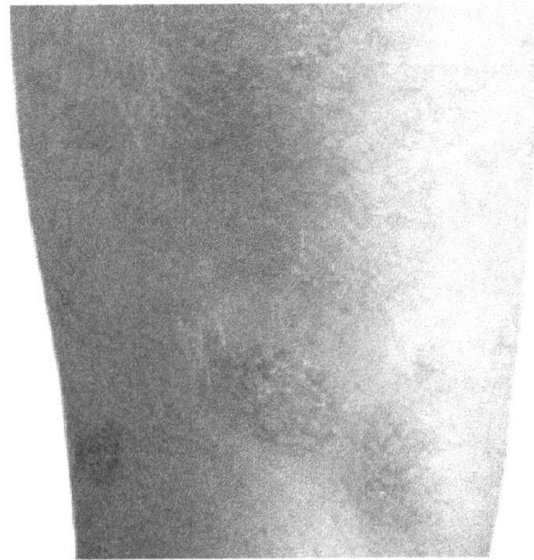

A. Reinke's edema

B. Laryngeal Papillomatosis

C. Malignancy

D. Tracheomalacia

Q.274 A patient gives H/o hoarseness in voice& presenting with clinical condition asshown in the image. Identify the lesion:

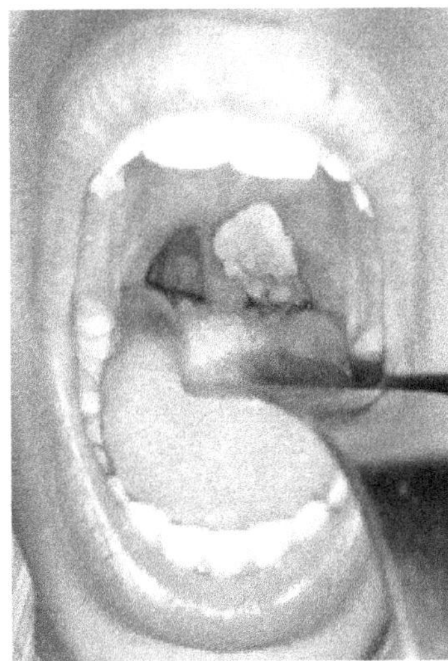

A. Membranous tonsillitis

B. Follicular tonsillitis

C. Diphtheria

D. Aphthous ulcer

Q.275 A patient presented with the followingpicture of Tympanic Membrane. MostProbable diagnosis (marked with arrow):

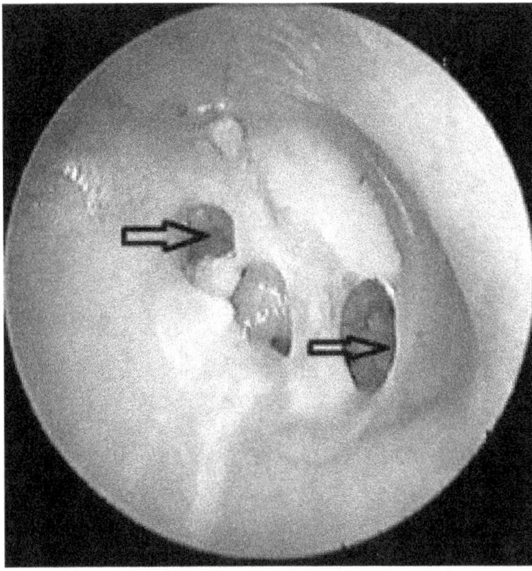

A. Tubercular Otitis Media

B. Syphilitic Otitis Media

C. Pseudomonas infection

D. Fungal Otitis Media

Q.276 Which method is used to study thefollowing timeline?

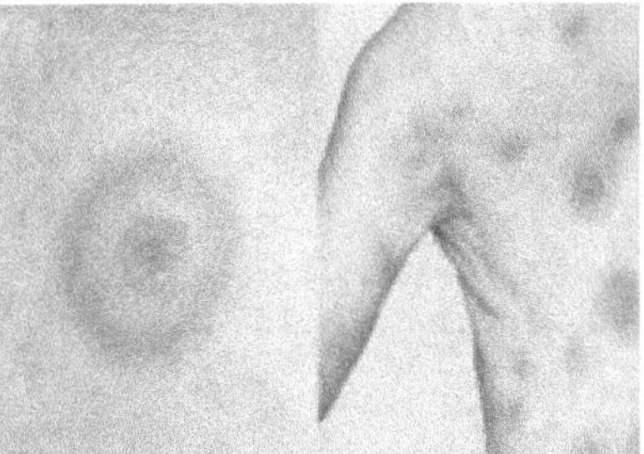

A. Cohort Study

B. Cross sectional study

C. Randomized Control Trials

D. Interventional Studies

Q.277 A 6 year old boy is having symptomssuch as fever and chills, cough, rapidbreathing, difficulty breathing, and chestpain, culture from a sample shows Gram-positive culture, Identify theimage:

A. Streptococcus pneumoniae

B. Staphylococcus

C. Propionibacterium

D. Mycobacterium

Q.278 Identify the picture:

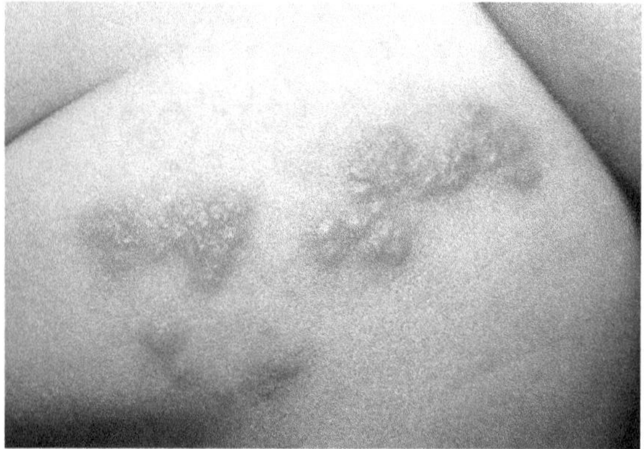

A. Herpes zoster pic
B. Small pox
C. Chicken pox
D. Atopic dermatitis

Q.279 Identify the image:

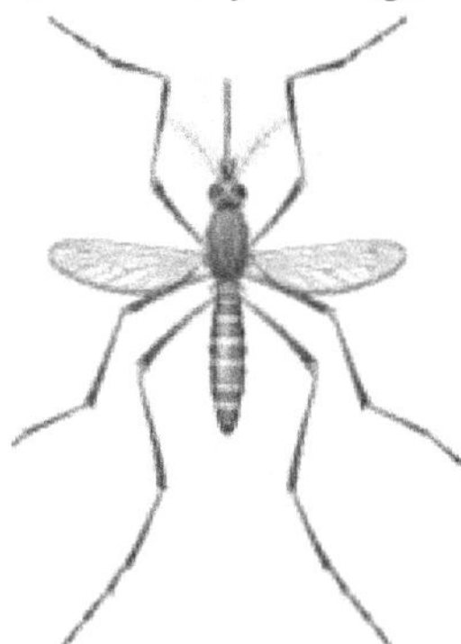

A. Malaria
B. Plague
C. Japanese encephalitis
D. Paragonimus

Q.280 What is the cause of death according to the below death certificate?

1	Cause of death*		Time interval between onset and death
Report disease or condition directly leading to death on line a	a	Direct cause of death **Cerebral haemorrhage**	4 hours
Report chain of events i due to order (if applicable)	b	Due to **Metastasis of the brain**	4 months
State the underlying cause on the lowest used line	c	Due to **Breast cancer**	5 years
	d	Due to	
2 Other singificant conditions contributing to death (time intervals can be included in brackets after the condition)	Arterial hypertension (3 years); Diabetes mellitus (10 years)		

*This does not mean the mode of dying. e.g. heart failure, respiratory failure. It means the disease, injury, or complication that caused death.

A. Breast Cance
B. Secondaries
C. Cerebral Hemorrhage
D. All of the above

Q.281 Identify the blood grouping process done here. Slide given with: AB no clumps, Clumping in O & No clumps in control. Which group does this signify?

A. A-ve
B. B+ve
C. O+ve
D. Rh group

Q.282 Identify the condition as shown in the image given below:

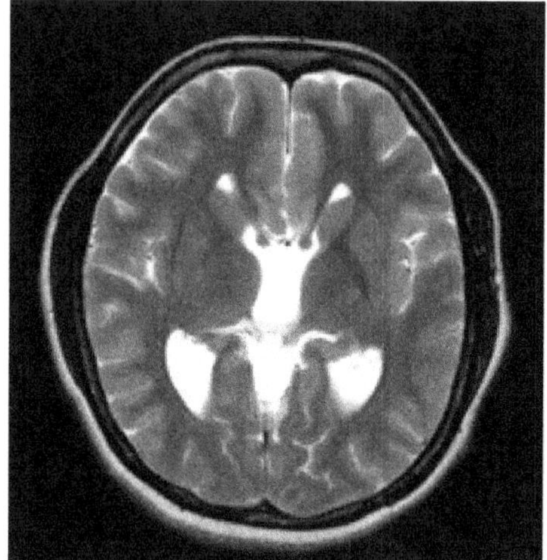

A. Callosal dysgenesis
B. Dandy walker syndrome
C. Aicardi syndrome
D. Septo optic dysplasia

Q.283 Which nerve supplies to the area marked as 'Area B' in the image?

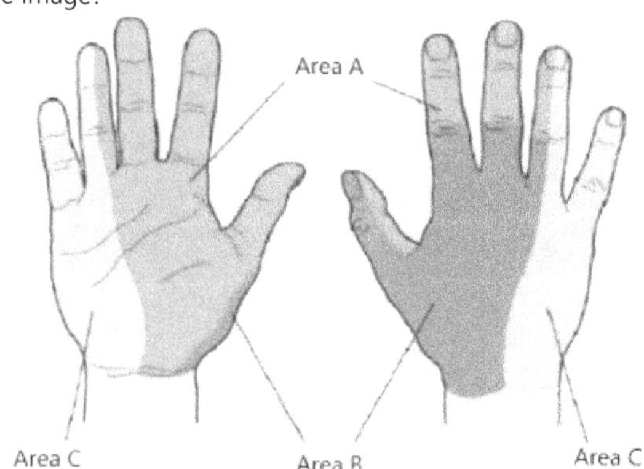

A. Ulnar nerve
B. Median nerve
C. Radial nerve
D. Posterior interosseous nerve

Q.284 Which of the following is not a boundary of given image?

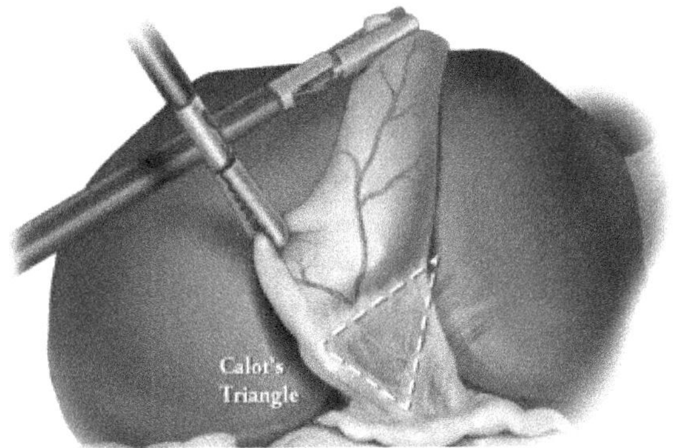

A. Common hepatic duct
B. Cystic duct
C. Inferior surface of the liver
D. Gall bladder

Q.285 Marked area in the given image is supplied by which dermatome?

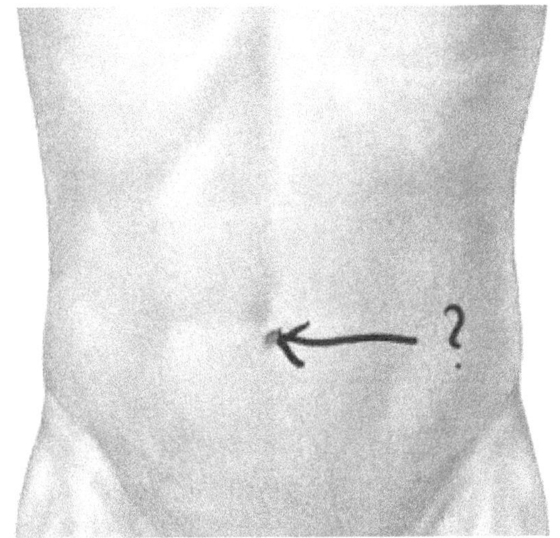

A. T8   B. T9   C. T10   D. T11

Q.286 Identify the type of the fibre marked in the image of internal capsule:

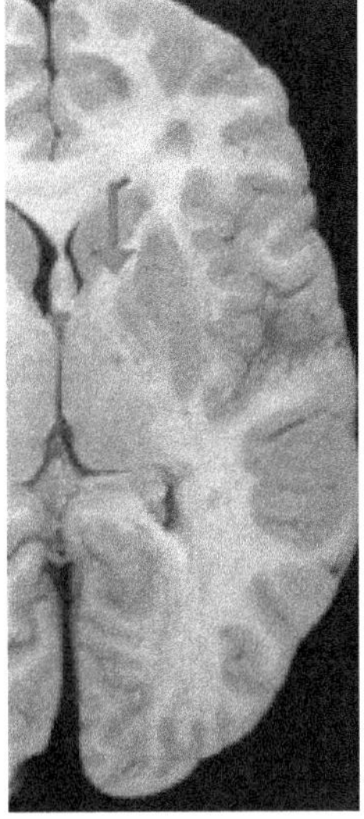

A. Projection fibres
B. Short association fibres
C. Long association fibres
D. Commissural fibres

Q.287 Identify the structure marked by a red arrow in the given image:

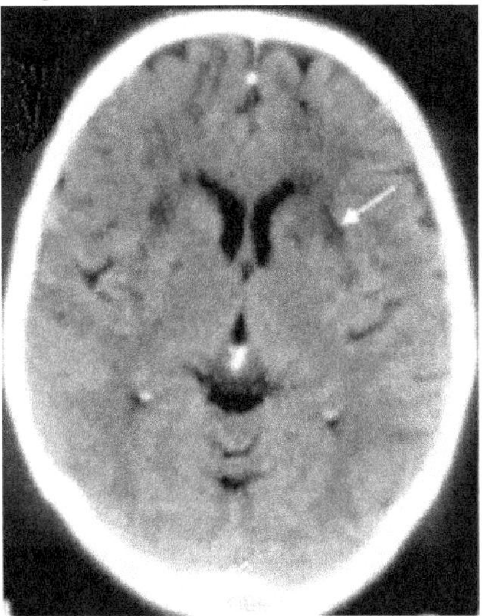

A. Great vein of galen   B. Pineal gland
C. Fornix   D. Falx cerebri

Q.288 What is the Nerve Supply of marked structure in the given image?

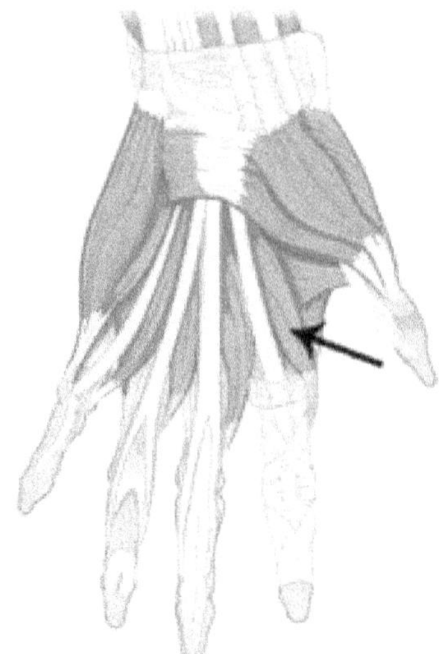

A. Anterior interosseous nerve
B. Posterior interosseous nerve
C. Ulnar nerve
D. Median nerve

Q.289 Identify the marked structure in theimage:

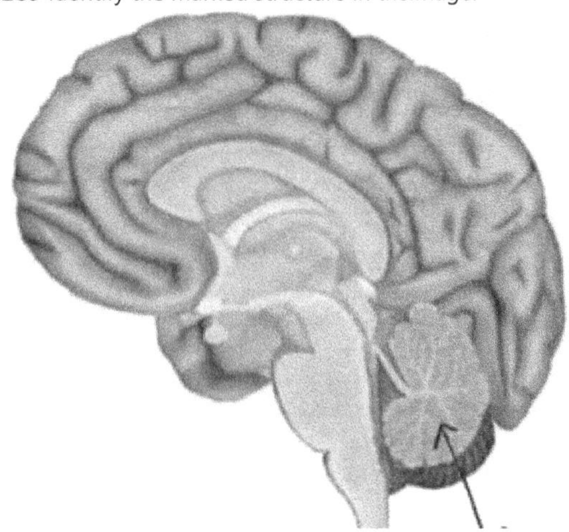

A. Cerebrum   B. Brain stem
C. Corpus callosum   D. Cerebellum

Q.290 Nerve injured in Frey's syndrome is:

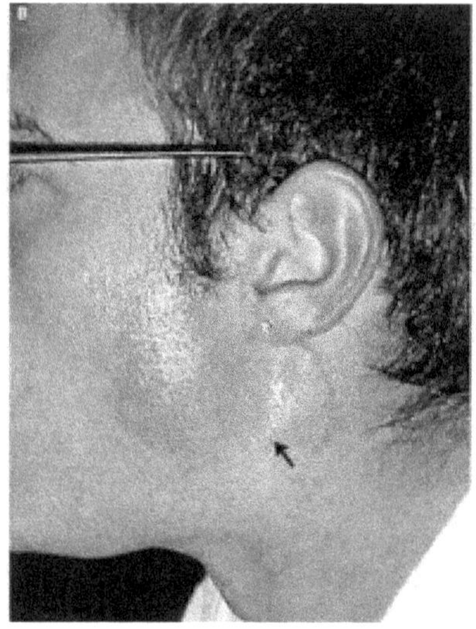

A. Auriculotemporal Nerve
B. Great auricular nerve
C. Lingual Nerve
D. Inferior alveolar nerve

Q.291 Which nerve passes through the markedforamen in the given image?

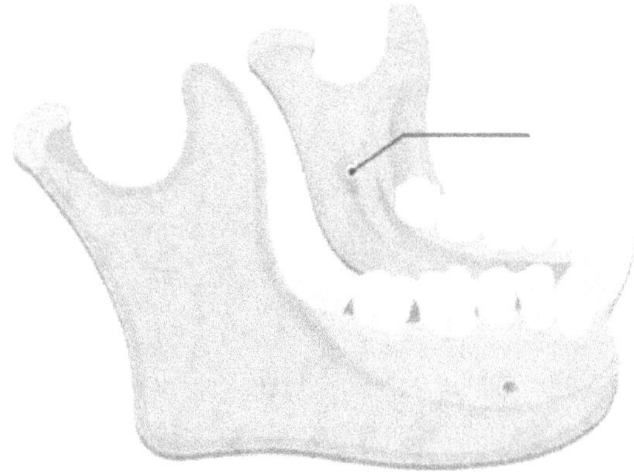

A. Lingual nerve
B. Mandibular nerve
C. Chorda tympani nerve
D. Inferior alveolar nerve

Q.292 Identify the marked muscle 'A' in thediagram:

A. Brachioradialis
B. Extensor carpi radialis longus
C. Flexor carpi radialis
D. Extensor carpi ulnaris

Q.293 Which of the following nail findings isseen in the condition shown below?

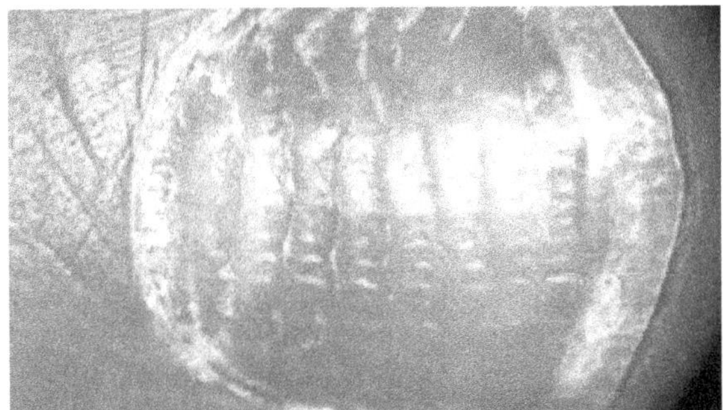

A. Pterygium B. Pigmentation
C. Pitting D. Ridges

Q.294 The COC-2 inhibitor is not to be given if patient is already taking:
A. Anti-allergic drug
B. Anti hypertensive drug
C. Anxiolytic drug
D. Oral anti-diabetic drug

Q.295 When the number of sperm falls below ____________ the male is likely to be infertile.
A. 20 million/ml B. 200 million/ml
C. 50-150 million/ml D. 100 million/ml

Q.296 Carbohydrates are precursors for many ______________ compound.
A. Organic B. Inorganic
C. Both (A) and (B) D. None of these

Q.297 ____________ receptor is useful for color vision.
A. Rod B. Cone
C. Muscarinic D. Nicotinic

Q.298 Identify the metabolite of prontosil responsible for its antibacterial activity.
A. Sulphacetamide
B. Sulphanilamide
C. p-Amino benzoic acid
D. Probenecid

Q.299 Which one of the following properties is characteristic of microemulsions?
A. These are transparent systems with droplet size less than 1 MICRO METER
B. These are transparent systems with droplet size less than 10 MICRO METER
C. These are non-transparent systems with droplet size less than 1 MICRO METER
D. These are transparent systems with droplet size less than MICRO METER

Q.300 The pouch of Douglas with vaginal wall prolapse of the uterus is known as:
A. Cystocele B. Urethrocele
C. Enterocele D. Rectocele

// Smart Answer Sheet //

Correct — Indicates percentage of students who answered questions correctly.

Skipped — Indicates percentage of students who skipped questions.

Q.	Ans.	Correct / Skipped	Q.	Ans.	Correct / Skipped	Q.	Ans.	Correct / Skipped	Q.	Ans.	Correct / Skipped	Q.	Ans.	Correct / Skipped
1	A	52.79 % / 41.14 %	17	A	69.0 % / 30.64 %	33	D	77.41 % / 16.52 %	49	D	83.75 % / 15.61 %	65	A	84.38 % / 13.05 %
2	C	57.28 % / 41.27 %	18	C	62.66 % / 31.74 %	34	B	65.32 % / 32.47 %	50	A	82.07 % / 12.19 %	66	A	87.89 % / 10.67 %
3	B	31.11 % / 68.78 %	19	A	22.25 % / 71.03 %	35	D	88.32 % / 10.16 %	51	B	86.03 % / 13.88 %	67	D	86.35 % / 10.86 %
4	A	78.91 % / 10.42 %	20	A	84.08 % / 11.05 %	36	A	78.43 % / 16.56 %	52	B	53.3 % / 37.28 %	68	C	87.25 % / 10.87 %
5	C	18.31 % / 72.03 %	21	C	83.43 % / 12.17 %	37	B	82.88 % / 11.54 %	53	C	88.27 % / 11.51 %	69	A	84.08 % / 11.12 %
6	C	78.06 % / 17.86 %	22	A	56.42 % / 38.76 %	38	B	78.18 % / 18.06 %	54	A	79.74 % / 20.12 %	70	A	81.04 % / 11.21 %
7	D	69.96 % / 30.03 %	23	B	81.99 % / 10.26 %	39	A	66.72 % / 30.45 %	55	B	86.22 % / 12.66 %	71	A	84.98 % / 12.92 %
8	B	83.49 % / 11.22 %	24	B	45.81 % / 42.26 %	40	A	63.36 % / 36.01 %	56	C	79.08 % / 15.34 %	72	A	79.68 % / 17.99 %
9	C	44.84 % / 30.76 %	25	D	89.06 % / 10.23 %	41	D	21.89 % / 68.89 %	57	C	63.32 % / 31.78 %	73	A	31.99 % / 67.63 %
10	D	50.69 % / 47.36 %	26	B	59.02 % / 38.53 %	42	A	52.82 % / 36.84 %	58	D	49.4 % / 49.71 %	74	C	86.91 % / 11.99 %
11	A	84.71 % / 15.28 %	27	A	30.45 % / 68.86 %	43	C	85.14 % / 11.06 %	59	C	86.34 % / 10.73 %	75	D	54.52 % / 44.94 %
12	B	12.53 % / 68.32 %	28	B	67.01 % / 31.64 %	44	B	11.56 % / 85.1 %	60	A	84.89 % / 13.12 %	76	B	87.04 % / 12.13 %
13	D	82.83 % / 13.99 %	29	A	88.89 % / 10.96 %	45	D	68.37 % / 30.93 %	61	B	76.75 % / 17.83 %	77	A	88.32 % / 10.35 %
14	A	78.75 % / 14.55 %	30	B	84.49 % / 13.68 %	46	B	85.03 % / 10.21 %	62	D	79.37 % / 16.64 %	78	B	59.51 % / 35.36 %
15	D	82.43 % / 14.25 %	31	C	88.34 % / 10.04 %	47	A	88.24 % / 10.97 %	63	B	78.86 % / 19.6 %	79	A	62.9 % / 35.81 %
16	A	40.98 % / 37.53 %	32	C	43.19 % / 54.66 %	48	C	20.68 % / 68.87 %	64	A	89.41 % / 10.55 %	80	C	82.86 % / 13.3 %

Q.	Ans.	Correct / Skipped	Q.	Ans.	Correct / Skipped	Q.	Ans.	Correct / Skipped	Q.	Ans.	Correct / Skipped	Q.	Ans.	Correct / Skipped
81	D	58.81 % / 33.67 %	97	A	80.39 % / 19.24 %	113	B	45.86 % / 51.38 %	129	C	55.33 % / 33.76 %	145	B	83.86 % / 14.34 %
82	A	51.95 % / 32.61 %	98	A	84.51 % / 10.33 %	114	B	58.31 % / 34.05 %	130	B	40.18 % / 33.71 %	146	B	25.23 % / 73.46 %
83	B	87.6 % / 11.29 %	99	D	88.4 % / 10.23 %	115	B	30.06 % / 69.91 %	131	B	88.24 % / 10.28 %	147	B	69.22 % / 30.1 %
84	A	85.38 % / 13.79 %	100	D	44.38 % / 48.07 %	116	A	27.92 % / 70.04 %	132	B	84.31 % / 15.3 %	148	A	29.22 % / 70.34 %
85	A	81.83 % / 13.61 %	101	B	78.85 % / 15.12 %	117	A	49.18 % / 40.08 %	133	D	17.39 % / 72.98 %	149	D	83.2 % / 10.71 %
86	C	68.3 % / 31.12 %	102	B	62.56 % / 36.47 %	118	B	88.09 % / 10.02 %	134	A	86.66 % / 12.81 %	150	D	31.76 % / 67.76 %
87	A	79.48 % / 13.26 %	103	A	65.71 % / 32.24 %	119	B	76.93 % / 16.9 %	135	B	82.94 % / 10.46 %	151	D	77.01 % / 13.73 %
88	D	43.17 % / 53.8 %	104	C	68.18 % / 31.48 %	120	A	88.78 % / 10.88 %	136	D	85.24 % / 11.11 %	152	D	10.51 % / 76.75 %
89	A	84.3 % / 13.29 %	105	D	78.85 % / 16.32 %	121	B	25.75 % / 70.85 %	137	B	64.45 % / 34.64 %	153	C	82.37 % / 14.27 %
90	A	89.05 % / 10.2 %	106	A	54.74 % / 38.98 %	122	A	63.13 % / 34.88 %	138	A	56.08 % / 31.44 %	154	A	26.28 % / 68.22 %
91	D	66.97 % / 30.51 %	107	A	31.39 % / 67.38 %	123	C	80.73 % / 18.06 %	139	B	62.61 % / 33.51 %	155	D	15.4 % / 69.67 %
92	A	29.04 % / 68.06 %	108	C	16.34 % / 81.1 %	124	A	20.88 % / 70.65 %	140	A	84.4 % / 12.62 %	156	A	78.46 % / 18.46 %
93	C	54.36 % / 42.65 %	109	D	44.32 % / 32.95 %	125	C	76.26 % / 17.52 %	141	B	89.84 % / 10.13 %	157	B	51.31 % / 43.38 %
94	B	60.28 % / 34.83 %	110	C	81.46 % / 17.36 %	126	C	28.16 % / 70.93 %	142	A	84.45 % / 10.01 %	158	D	77.58 % / 10.15 %
95	B	15.77 % / 75.21 %	111	B	49.53 % / 35.42 %	127	B	24.8 % / 73.77 %	143	B	58.16 % / 33.31 %	159	B	79.44 % / 14.37 %
96	D	88.9 % / 10.49 %	112	C	77.18 % / 18.62 %	128	C	80.1 % / 14.81 %	144	A	86.35 % / 13.45 %	160	B	30.27 % / 68.11 %

Q.	Ans.	Correct / Skipped	Q.	Ans.	Correct / Skipped	Q.	Ans.	Correct / Skipped	Q.	Ans.	Correct / Skipped	Q.	Ans.	Correct / Skipped
161	C	85.65 % / 14.1 %	177	A	79.54 % / 19.3 %	193	C	11.97 % / 86.28 %	209	D	83.05 % / 12.73 %	225	B	82.95 % / 13.78 %
162	C	88.41 % / 10.3 %	178	C	68.45 % / 31.37 %	194	C	60.88 % / 32.65 %	210	A	50.85 % / 47.54 %	226	C	43.71 % / 33.54 %
163	D	87.46 % / 11.06 %	179	B	59.11 % / 32.8 %	195	A	48.95 % / 35.99 %	211	A	26.62 % / 69.19 %	227	A	76.0 % / 14.59 %
164	A	32.09 % / 67.47 %	180	B	45.49 % / 49.52 %	196	B	88.58 % / 11.18 %	212	D	50.43 % / 39.0 %	228	C	56.37 % / 35.54 %
165	D	78.34 % / 20.78 %	181	C	80.58 % / 14.08 %	197	D	29.56 % / 68.49 %	213	D	49.1 % / 46.68 %	229	C	84.72 % / 10.69 %
166	C	50.16 % / 45.12 %	182	A	63.7 % / 35.35 %	198	B	16.83 % / 78.39 %	214	A	58.26 % / 39.14 %	230	D	82.69 % / 10.08 %
167	B	58.17 % / 35.66 %	183	C	86.03 % / 12.55 %	199	B	89.13 % / 10.52 %	215	C	19.33 % / 77.8 %	231	A	61.43 % / 36.71 %
168	A	85.07 % / 10.21 %	184	B	87.13 % / 10.05 %	200	B	60.48 % / 35.03 %	216	A	47.08 % / 45.3 %	232	B	76.67 % / 22.49 %
169	A	77.21 % / 15.85 %	185	B	62.32 % / 34.21 %	201	A	13.67 % / 73.56 %	217	A	48.07 % / 31.3 %	233	B	85.43 % / 13.59 %
170	B	79.18 % / 15.37 %	186	B	48.35 % / 38.29 %	202	A	25.36 % / 71.44 %	218	B	52.31 % / 42.32 %	234	B	56.82 % / 42.98 %
171	B	81.57 % / 16.33 %	187	A	12.07 % / 80.66 %	203	C	42.14 % / 45.05 %	219	D	81.92 % / 14.09 %	235	D	61.28 % / 34.99 %
172	A	67.89 % / 30.15 %	188	C	41.4 % / 35.75 %	204	B	84.66 % / 11.45 %	220	A	84.81 % / 12.25 %	236	B	13.53 % / 70.77 %
173	C	61.01 % / 37.08 %	189	C	51.43 % / 46.61 %	205	C	44.73 % / 33.17 %	221	D	81.6 % / 18.26 %	237	B	19.89 % / 76.3 %
174	A	80.67 % / 12.49 %	190	D	25.25 % / 72.86 %	206	C	77.58 % / 12.24 %	222	A	41.56 % / 30.24 %	238	D	81.85 % / 16.76 %
175	A	82.05 % / 12.58 %	191	C	46.42 % / 40.28 %	207	B	86.38 % / 10.81 %	223	A	29.33 % / 70.12 %	239	A	87.39 % / 11.5 %
176	A	67.24 % / 32.72 %	192	C	50.44 % / 31.26 %	208	B	56.12 % / 40.42 %	224	B	60.02 % / 33.36 %	240	D	83.95 % / 10.91 %

Q.	Ans.	Correct / Skipped	Q.	Ans.	Correct / Skipped	Q.	Ans.	Correct / Skipped	Q.	Ans.	Correct / Skipped	Q.	Ans.	Correct / Skipped
241	A	69.21 % / 30.65 %	253	A	80.45 % / 19.28 %	265	B	60.23 % / 34.13 %	277	A	62.67 % / 30.96 %	289	D	25.02 % / 70.37 %
242	C	49.86 % / 48.01 %	254	A	56.08 % / 41.58 %	266	A	41.35 % / 31.28 %	278	A	65.8 % / 32.05 %	290	A	53.3 % / 36.22 %
243	C	81.43 % / 17.45 %	255	D	24.73 % / 72.7 %	267	A	10.48 % / 85.42 %	279	C	81.25 % / 12.18 %	291	B	83.35 % / 10.97 %
244	D	88.19 % / 11.02 %	256	B	77.28 % / 10.4 %	268	C	47.84 % / 31.64 %	280	D	54.43 % / 41.9 %	292	B	53.85 % / 34.29 %
245	A	55.79 % / 43.64 %	257	A	58.98 % / 38.25 %	269	B	48.82 % / 40.65 %	281	D	83.08 % / 11.85 %	293	C	53.96 % / 33.11 %
246	A	66.12 % / 31.22 %	258	B	52.82 % / 32.0 %	270	D	83.84 % / 12.92 %	282	A	43.32 % / 40.14 %	294	B	64.6 % / 34.33 %
247	A	78.82 % / 19.82 %	259	C	59.24 % / 34.93 %	271	B	10.77 % / 88.93 %	283	C	44.2 % / 46.56 %	295	A	31.88 % / 67.45 %
248	A	62.0 % / 31.57 %	260	B	82.45 % / 15.61 %	272	A	52.15 % / 34.39 %	284	D	84.3 % / 11.28 %	296	A	21.52 % / 78.17 %
249	A	44.89 % / 31.83 %	261	C	76.93 % / 13.23 %	273	B	49.45 % / 47.02 %	285	C	11.3 % / 80.62 %	297	B	79.65 % / 13.92 %
250	B	76.85 % / 23.14 %	262	A	53.14 % / 36.53 %	274	C	69.05 % / 30.67 %	286	A	13.4 % / 72.59 %	298	B	84.54 % / 13.06 %
251	A	83.83 % / 11.64 %	263	C	45.09 % / 52.53 %	275	A	59.29 % / 31.06 %	287	C	19.04 % / 74.23 %	299	A	17.03 % / 79.43 %
252	C	45.57 % / 31.69 %	264	B	51.72 % / 32.77 %	276	A	86.44 % / 11.67 %	288	D	29.9 % / 70.08 %	300	C	78.01 % / 10.63 %

Performance Analysis

Avg. Score (%)	39.08%
Toppers Score (%)	64.0%
Your Score	

Q.1 Upward movement of the thyroid gland is prevented due to:

A. Berry ligament

B. Pretracheal fascia

C. Sternothyroid muscle

D. Thyrohyoid membrane

Q.2 The reason for the long left recurrrentlaryngeal nerve is due to the persistence ofwhich arch artery?

A. 3rd arch **B.** 4th arch **C.** 5th arch **D.** 2nd arch

Q.3 Ligation of the hepatic artery will impair blood supply in:

A. Right gastric and Right gastroepiploic artery

B. Right gastric and Left gastric artery

C. Right gastroepiploic and short gastric vessels

D. Right gastric and short gastric vessels

Q.4 Wolffian duct remnant in female is:

A. Pouch of Douglas **B.** Uterovesical pouch

C. Gartner's cyst **D.** Broad ligament

Q.5 Nerve supply of the extraocular muscles is constituted by all except:

A. Ophthalmic nerve **B.** Oculomotor nerve

C. Trochlear nerve **D.** Abducent nerve

Q.6 Claudication due to popliteal femoral incompetence is primarily seen in:

A. Thigh **B.** Calf **C.** Buttocks **D.** Feet

Q.7 Which muscle is paralyzed if there ishyperextension of metacarpophalangealjoint and flexion of the interphalangealjoint?

A. Extensor digitorum

B. Interossei and lumbricals

C. Adductor pollicis

D. Pronator quadratus muscle

Q.8 Tumour of the uncinate process of thepancreas will compress which artery?

A. Portal vein

B. Superior mesenteric artery

C. Inferior mesenteric artery

D. Common hepatic artery

Q.9 A boy met with a motorbike accident. CTbrain shows injury to the posterior end ofthe superior temporal gyrus. He is likely tosuffer from:

A. Fluent aphasia **B.** Non-fluent aphasia

C. Conduction aphasia **D.** None of these

Q.10 A 65-year-old lady presents with avascular injury to the inferior frontalgyrus. Which functional area wouldmostly be affected:

A. Visual **B.** Auditoryss

C. Wernicke **D.** Motor speech

Q.11 Where is the highest oxygenconcentration presents in fetal circulation?

A. SVC **B.** IVC

C. Right ventricle **D.** Aorta

Q.12 When the value of $\dfrac{V}{q}$ is infinity, itmeans:

A. No O_2 goes from alveoli to blood and no CO_2 goes from blood to alveoli

B. Dead space

C. The PO_2 of alveolar air is 159 mmHg and PCO_2 is 40 mmHg

D. Partial pressure of O_2 and CO_2 are equal

Q.13 Proteoglycan present in the glomerularbasement membrane is:

A. Keratan sulphate 1

B. Keratan sulphate 2

C. Heparan sulphate

D. Chondroitin sulphate

Q.14 35 year old female was watching TV for longhours with hands under her head. Shecomplains of tingling sensation over herarm. Which type of nerve fibers is mostlikely to be affected?

A. Fibers

B. B - fibers

C. C - Fibers

D. Sympathetic nerve fibers

Q.15 The reflex in which there is inhibition ofgastric emptying when there is acid andhypertonic solution in the duodenum?

A. Enterogastric **B.** Gastroileal

C. Gastrocolic **D.** Myenteric

Q.16 In multiple sclerosis, slow conduction ofmotor and the sensory pathways is dueto:

A. Defect in the node of Ranvier

B. Loss of myelin sheath

C. Leaking of sodium channels

D. Leaking calcium channels

Q.17 Which of the following clotting factor in a patient onWarfarin therapy, would have decreased gammacarboxyglutamate residue?

A. Factor 2 **B.** Factor 11

C. Tissue factor **D.** Factor 5

Q.18 Blood stored in citrate-phosphate-dextrose is better forhypoxic patients than acidic-citrate-dextrose because:

A. It has less P_{50}

B. It is less acidic

C. The fall in 2, 3 DPG is less

D. None of the above

Q.19 Which of the following is referred to as the "Window of thelimbic system"?

A. Hypothalamus

B. Amygdala

C. Hippocampus

D. Thalamus

Q.20 Cerebral blood flow is regulated by allexcept:

A. Blood pressure

B. Arterial PCO_2

C. Potassium ions

D. Both (A) and (C)

Q.21 Hepcidin inhibits:

A. Absorption of cobalamine

B. Transfer of iron into enterocytes

C. Folic acid synthesis

D. Respiratory oxidase

Q.22 Which of the following technique is usedto study current flow across a single ionchannel?

A. Patch-clamp

B. Voltage clamp

C. Iontophoresis

D. Galvanometry

Q.23 A 4-year-old boy of a first-degreeconsanguineous couple was noted by theparents to have darkening of the urine toan almost black color when it was leftstanding. He has a normal sibling, andthere are no other medical problems.Growth and development to date arenormal. Which of the following is mostlikely to be elevated in this patient?

A. Methylmalonate

B. Homogentisate

C. Phenylpyruvate

D. α-Ketoisovalerate

Q.24 Which of the following is true aboutdifferent structures of protein?

A. Secondary structure is the three-dimensional structure ofprotein

B. Secondary structure is stabilized by disulfide bonds

C. Primary, secondary and tertiary structures destroyed duringdenaturation

D. Secondary and tertiary structure depends on the sequence ofamino acids

Q.25 The insulin glucagon ratio decreased. Theenzyme is active at this time is:

A. Glucokinase

B. Hexokinase

C. Phosphofructokinase

D. Glucose 6 phosphatase

Q.26 Ochronosis is due to the accumulationof:

A. Homogentisic acid

B. Homogentisic acid

C. Xanthurenate

D. Glyoxylate

Q.27 Bilirubin in serum can be measured by:

A. Van den Bergh reaction

B. Ehrlich's Reaction

C. Schlesinger's Reaction

D. Fouchet's Reaction

Q.28 If a sample of DNA if adenine is 28%. Whatwill be the amount of Cytosine present?

A. 23%

B. 25%

C. 46%

D. 22%

Q.29 Which of the following vitamin at higherdoses causes cystoid macular edema?

A. Vitamin A

B. Vitamin D

C. Vitamin E

D. Niacin

Q.30 True statement regarding Huntington'schorea is:

A. There is a loss of function type of mutation.

B. It is an autosomal recessive.

C. It is a trinucleotide repeat expansion type of disorder.

D. Increased number of CAA repeats.

Q.31 Addition of which Amino Acid willincrease UV absorption?

A. Tryptophan

B. Leucine

C. Proline

D. Arginine

Q.32 Richest source of vitamin B12 is:

A. Meat

B. Green leafy vegetables

C. Corn oil

D. Sunflower oil

Q.33 Which amino acid is used to synthesizeNitric oxide?

A. Glycine

B. Arginine

C. Tyrosine

D. Threonine

Q.34 True About Noncompetitive antagonist:

A. K_m remains same, V_{max} decreases

B. K_m remains same, V_{max} decreases

C. K_m decreases, V_{max} increases

D. K_m increases, V_{max} increases

Q.35 Werner syndrome associated withpremature aging is caused due to a defectin which of the following?

A. Telomerase

B. Caspase

C. DNA topoisomerase

D. DNA helicase

Q.36 Which of the following dietary fiber isinsoluble in water?

A. Pectin

B. Lignin

C. Hemicellulose

D. Cellulose

Q.37 According to NCEP-ATP III, which amongthe following have not been included inmetabolic syndrome?

A. High LDL

B. Hypertriglyceridemia

C. Central Obesity

D. Hypertension

Q.38 Which of the following is the basis for theintestine-specific expression ofapoprotein B-48?

A. DNA rearrangement and loss

B. DNA rearrangement and loss

C. RNA alternative splicing

D. RNA editing

Q.39 A 30-year-old male came with complaintsof swelling around the knee joint.Histopathological examination of theswelling demonstrated many giant cellsinterspersed with mononuclear cells.What is the probable diagnosis?

A. Osteosarcoma

B. Ewing's sarcoma

C. Giant cell tumour

D. Chondrosarcoma

Q.40 30 years old came with complaints of easyfatigability, exertional dyspnea, andweight loss. She also complains offrequent falls. physical examinationrevealed there was a bilateral decrease invibration sense. Her hemoglobin levelswere 8.2g%. She was treated with folate.Her anemia improved but neurologicalsymptoms worsened. Which of thefollowing is the most probable reason forher condition?

A. Folate not absorbed

B. Unmasked pyridoxine deficiency

C. Deficiency of folate reductase in CNS

D. Folate therapy caused rapid use of vitamin B12 stores aggravatingsymptoms

Q.41 A 45-year-old man who is a chronicsmoker came to the clinic with acomplaint of cough. The physicianexamines the patient and takes a biopsy,the picture in the biopsy was as thedescription below. Which of the followingcellular changes has happened to thispatient?

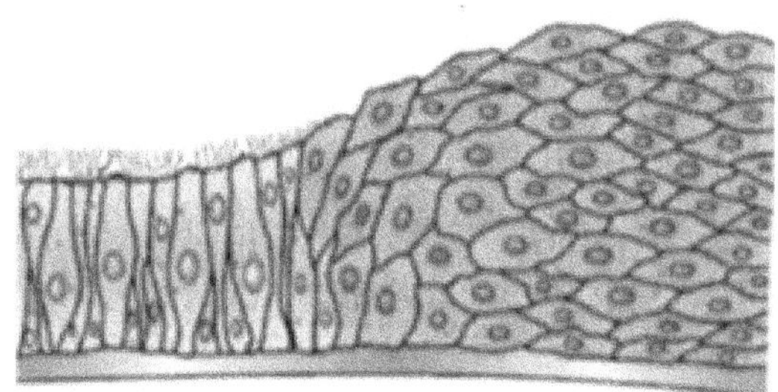

A. Hyperplasia

B. Dysplasia

C. Metaplasia

D. CIN3

Q.42 A 30-year-old woman presents withthyroid swelling. On investigations, herTSH levels are found to be elevated.Postoperative reports showedlymphocytic infiltration and hurthle cells.A most probable diagnosis is:

A. Graves disease

B. Hashimoto's thyroiditis

C. Follicular carcinoma

D. Medullary carcinoma thyroid

Q.43 Which of the following will be seen oncardiac biopsy of a patient who had a postMI reperfusion injury?

A. Waviness of fibres

B. Eosinophilic contraction bands

C. Neutrophils in cardiac cells

D. Swelling of cells

Q.44 Loss of foot process is classical in caseof:

A. Membranous glomerulitis

B. Segmental glomerulosclerosis

C. IgA nephropathy

D. Diabetic nephropathy

Q.45 Which of the following factors play amajor role in the initiation of thrombusformation?

A. Vasoconstriction

B. Coagulation cascade activation

C. Platelets activation

D. Endothelial injury

Q.46 A 33-year-old man presents with a 5-weekhistory of calf pain, swelling, and lowgrade fever. Serum levels of creatininekinase are elevated. A muscle biopsyreveals numerous eosinophils also shehad peripheral blood eosinophilia. Whichof the following interleukins is primarilyresponsible for the increase ineosinophils in this patient?

A. IL2   **B.** IL4   **C.** IL1   **D.** IL6

Q.47 Which of the following is true about PAN?

A. Microscopy shows fibrinoid necrosis in large arteries

B. ANCA is positive

C. 30% of people have HbsAg positive

D. Patient have hypogammaglobulinemia

Q.48 A 23-year-old male presented with ahistory of fatigue and tiredness. Oninvestigation, he was found to have Hbvalues of 9gm%, MCV of 101 FL.peripheral smear examination showedmicrocytic RBC and hypersegmentedneutrophils. Which is most probableetiology?

A. Lead poisoning

B. Iron deficiency anemia

C. Chronic alcoholism

D. Hemolytic anemia

Q.49 What is the main feature of chemotaxis asobserved in white blood cells?

A. Increased random movement of neutrophils

B. Increased adhesiveness to intima

C. Increased phagocytosis

D. Unidirectional locomotion of neutrophils

Q.50 Which of the following anticancer drugsare competitive inhibitors of tyrosinekinase?

A. Imatinib and sunitinib

B. Letrozole

C. Bicalutamide

D. Fulvestrant

Q.51 Which is not a prokinetic agent?

A. Dopamine antagonist

B. 5HT4 agonist

C. Macrolides

D. Diphenylmethane

Q.52 Which of the following drugs act byinhibiting DNA replication?

A. 6 Mercaptopurine   **B.** Actinomycin D

C. Mitomycin C   **D.** Asparaginase

Q.53 DOC for Onychomycosis is:

A. Terbinafine   **B.** Fluconazole

C. Nystatin   **D.** Itraconazole

Q.54 Theophylline by what mechanism causesdiuresis?

A. PDE3 inhibition

B. PDE4 inhibition

C. Beta 2 agonist action

D. Adenosine A1 receptor antagonism

Q.55 Which of the following antimicrobialsshould not be given to a chronicasthmatic patient managed ontheophylline therapy?

A. Erythromycin **B.** Amoxicillin
C. Cefotaxime **D.** Cotrimoxazole

Q.56 DOC of prophylaxis for motion sickness is:

A. Promethazine **B.** Prochlorperazine
C. Metoclopramide **D.** Itopride

Q.57 Which of the following antihypertensivedrug is avoided in patients with highserum uric acid levels?

A. Hydrochlorothiazide
B. Enalapril
C. Prazosin
D. Atenolol

Q.58 Mechanism of resistance to penicillins viabeta-lactamase is:

A. Altered penicillin-binding proteins
B. Drug efflux
C. Breaks drug structure
D. Alteration in 50S ribosome structure

Q.59 A patient on lithium therapy developedhypertension. He was started on Thiazidefor hypertension. After a few days, hedeveloped coarse tremors and othersymptoms suggestive of lithium toxicity.What is the probable mechanism ofinteraction?

A. Thiazide increases the tubular reabsorption of lithium
B. Thiazide inhibits the metabolism of lithium
C. Thiazides act as an add on the drug to lithium
D. All of the above

Q.60 Which drug acts via the tyrosine kinasereceptor?

A. Insulin **B.** TSH **C.** LH **D.** MSH

Q.61 Pegloticase is used for the treatment of anAnkylosing spondylosis:

A. Reactive Arthritis
B. CPPD
C. Chronic tophaceous gout
D. Refractory Rheumatoid arthritis

Q.62 Fluoroquinolone contraindicated in liverdisease is:

A. Levofloxacin **B.** Pefloxacin
C. Ofloxacin **D.** Lomefloxacin

Q.63 At a high altitude of 3000 m, a personcomplains of breathlessness. All of thefollowing can be used for themanagement of this person except:

A. Intravenous digoxin
B. Oxygen supplementation
C. Immediate descent
D. Acetazolamide

Q.64 A patient with diabetes and COPDdeveloped postoperative urinaryretention. Which of the following drugscan be used for short term treatment torelieve the symptoms of this person?

A. Bethanechol **B.** Methacholine

C. Terazosin **D.** Tamsulosin

Q.65 Drug of choice for invasive aspergillosis is:

A. Posaconazole **B.** Voriconazole
C. Liposomal AMB **D.** Caspofungin

Q.66 Which of the following drugs acts byinhibiting the transcription of DNA toRNA?

A. Rifampicin **B.** Nitrofurantoin
C. Ciprofloxacin **D.** Novobiocin

Q.67 A patient was recently started onFluphenazine. A few weeks later, hedeveloped tremors, rigidity, bradykinesia,and excessive salivation. The first line ofmanagement for this patient is:

A. Selegiline **B.** Trihexyphenidyl
C. Pramipexole **D.** Amantadine

Q.68 A person was given a muscle relaxant thatcompetitively blocks nicotinic receptors.Which of the following drugs is used forreversal of muscle relaxation aftersurgery?

A. Neostigmine **B.** Carbachol
C. Succinylcholine **D.** Physostigmine

Q.69 Zero-order kinetics is otherwise known as saturation kinetics. It is independent of:

A. Plasma concentration
B. Clearance
C. Volume of distribution
D. Half life

Q.70 Which of the following anticancer drugsare competitive inhibitors of tyrosinekinase?

A. Imatinib and sunitinib
B. Letrozole
C. Bicalutamide
D. Fulvestrant

Q.71 Which of the following is the law on childsexual abuse in India?

A. Child Sexual Abuse Prevention Act
B. Protection Of Children from Sexual Offences Act (POCSO)
C. Child Welfare Act
D. Sexual Offences Act

Q.72 Punishment of perjury comes under IPCsection?

A. IPC 191 **B.** IPC 192 **C.** IPC 193 **D.** IPC 197

Q.73 When civil negligence is brought upagainst a doctor, the onus of proof liesupon:

A. Judicial first-degree magistrate
B. Police not below the level of sub-inspector
C. Doctor
D. Patient

Q.74 Relatives of a patient told duringpostmortem examination that the personhad a tattoo - which was now invisible.How to identify?

A. Examine the Lymph node
B. Spectrophotometer

C. Ordinary light

D. X-ray

Q.75 True about hymen in Child rape is:

A. Hymen easily tears because it is thin

B. Hymen easily tears because it is in the front

C. Hymen hardly tears because it is highly elastic

D. Hymen hardly tears because it is situated deep

Q.76 Magnan's symptoms are related to:

A. Cocaine poisoning

B. Cannabis

C. Both (A) and (B)

D. Alcohol

Q.77 Parents of the Child complains ofassaulted by one of their relatives andanal pain in a child, On investigation testshows yellow iodine crystals with picricacid. What is the name of the test?

A. Florence test

B. Barberio's test

C. Acid phosphatase test

D. Creatine Phosphokinase

Q.78 The Magistrate can detain the maximumnumber of days for a mentally ill personas per mental health care is:

A. 30 days

B. 90 days

C. 50 days

D. 100 days

Q.79 Vector for zika virus is:

A. Aedes

B. Culex

C. Anopheles

D. None of these

Q.80 All are true regarding Japaneseencephalitis except:

A. Caused by flavivirus

B. Humans are dead-end hosts

C. Transmitted by culex

D. Cattles are amplifier hosts

Q.81 All of the following is/are having superantigen Property Except:

A. Vibrio cholera

B. Streptococcal pyrogenic

C. Staphylococcal enterotoxins

D. None of these

Q.82 Type A bioterrorism Agent is:

A. Chikungunya

B. Anthrax

C. Hendra

D. Influenza

Q.83 Culture media used for E.coli 0157:H7 is:

A. SMAC

B. Wilson and Blair medium

C. Potassium tellurite in Mcleod's medium

D. Deoxycholate citrate agar (DCA)

Q.84 Donovanosis is Caused By:

A. H. ducreyi

B. Leishmania donovani

C. K. granulomatis

D. Treponema pallidum

Q.85 Fungal Infection which is acquired bytraumatic inoculation is:

A. Sporothrix

B. Blastomycosis

C. Coccidioides

D. Paracoccidioides

Q.86 Which of the following is not involved inurethritis?

A. Trichomonas

B. H.ducreyi

C. Chlamydia

D. Gonococcus

Q.87 A patient complains about nausea,vomiting and stomach cramps afterattending a social gathering party, whichcausative organism is likely responsiblefor Food Poisoning within 3 hours?

A. Staphylococcus aureus

B. Salmonella

C. Clostridium botulinum

D. Clostridium perfringens

Q.88 A 46-year-old woman with HIV complainssevere persistent diarrhea, HistologicalInvestigation was performed, Identify theorganism causing diarrhea in HIV Patient.

A. Cryptosporidium

B. Staphylococcus aureus

C. Salmonella

D. Clostridium botulinum

Q.89 Organism Causing LGV is:

A. Chlamydia trachomatis

B. Neisseria gonorrhoeae

C. Treponema pallidum

D. Haemophilus ducreyi

Q.90 Which interleukin responsible forproducing IgE from B cells?

A. IL 1

B. IL 3

C. IL 4

D. Both (B) and (C)

Q.91 HbsAg is based on which principle?

A. Immunochromatography assays

B. Chemiluminescence

C. ELISA

D. Immunofluorescence

Q.92 Nosocomial Infection occurs within:

A. 48

B. 72

C. 24

D. 50

Q.93 Which of the following cell componentsproduced by Neisseria gonorrhoeae isresponsible for attachment to host cells?

A. Lipooligosaccharide

B. Pili (fimbriae)

C. IgA1 protease

D. Outer membrane porin protein

Q.94 Where will you put chemical liquidbiomedical waste?

A. White

B. Yellow

C. Blue

D. Red

Q.95 Maximum work hours for a personincluding overtime under the factories act is:

A. 48

B. 50

C. 60

D. 100

Q.96 The vaccine to be given after disaster is:

A. vaccination against typhoid

B. vaccination against cholera

C. vaccination against typhoid and cholera

D. vaccination against tetanus

Q.97 What is the MONICA project?

A. Multinational monitoring of trends and determinants inCardiovascular Disease

B. Multinational of trends and determinants in cerebrovasculardisease

C. Multinational monitoring of trends and determinants in diabetes

D. Multinational monitoring of trends and determinants incongenital heart disease

Q.98 Extended sickness benefit fortuberculosis under the ESI Act is:

A. 91 days   **B.** 1-year   **C.** 2 years   **D.** 4 years

Q.99 A person reports 4 hours after having aclean wound without laceration. He hadtaken TT 10 years before. The next step inmanagement is:

A. Full course Tetanus vaccine to be given

B. Full dose TT with TIG

C. Single-dose TT

D. No need for any vaccine

Q.100 Recent Influenza Pandemic was due to:

A. H1N1   **B.** H5N1   **C.** H7N7   **D.** H3N2

Q.101 Mission Indradhanush is for:

A. Non-communicable diseases

B. Universal immunization

C. Family planning

D. Safe water and sanitation

Q.102 A study had a normal distribution withthe median value as 200 and standarddeviation 20.68 % will fall between:

A. 160-240   **B.** 170-230   **C.** 180-220   **D.** 190-210

Q.103 Which of the following is atechnique/method based on behaviouralsciences?

A. Management by objectives

B. Network analysis

C. Systems analysis

D. Decision making

Q.104 As per the sustainable developmentgoals, The target for MMR is to achievematernal deaths of:

A. < 70 / Lac live births

B. < 100 / lac live births

C. < 7 / 1000 live births

D. < 10 / 1000 live births

Q.105 The best method for routine monitoringof air pollution is:

A. Sulphur dioxide, smoke, and particulate matter

B. Sulphur dioxide, Hydrogen sulphide, carbon monoxide

C. Carbon dioxide, hydrogen sulphide, lead

D. Sulphur dioxide, Lead and particulate matter

Q.106 The variation in data is compared withanother data set by:

A. Variance

B. Coefficient of variation

C. The standard error of mean

D. Standard deviation

Q.107 In which of the following methods ofmanagement is the benefit measured innatural units?

A. Program budgeting system

B. Network analysis

C. Cost-effective analysis

D. Cost-benefit analysis

Q.108 The difference between the incidence inthe exposed and non-exposed group isbest given by:

A. Relative risk

B. Attributable risk

C. Population attributable risk

D. Odds ratio

Q.109 If one variable is given then you can findanother variable by:

A. Coefficient of variation

B. Coefficient of correlation

C. Coefficient of regression

D. Coefficient of determination

Q.110 Prospective screening is done in caseof:

A. Neonate for thyroid diseases

B. Immigrant screening

C. Pap smear for 45-year female

D. Diabetes mellitus for 40-year male

Q.111 A researcher wanted to prove therelation between COPD and smoking. Hecollected patients records fromgovernment hospitals and records ofcigarette sales from the finance andtaxation department. This is an exampleof which study design?

A. Cross-sectional

B. Posological study

C. Ecological study

D. Operations research

Q.112 A study was done to assess malnutritionamong young children. 100 children wereselected each from rural and urbanareas. Out of these, 30 among rural and20 among urban were found to bemalnourished. Which of the followingstatistical test is used to compare thedata sets?

A. Paired t-test

B. Chi-square

C. The standard error of mean

D. ANOVA

Q.113 The active disinfectant property ofbleaching powder is due to:

A. Chlorine   **B.** Hypochloric acid

C. Hypochlorous acid   **D.** Chloramines

Q.114 Mother does not transmit what antibodyto the baby?

A. Polio
B. Diphtheria
C. Both (A) and (B)
D. Tetanus

Q.115 Voluntary admission can be donemaximum up to how much timeaccording to MHA 2017?

A. 48 hours **B.** 7 Days **C.** 30 Days **D.** 90 Days

Q.116 Blood bags are disposed of in:

A. Yellow bag
B. Black bag
C. Red bag
D. White bag

Q.117 Absolute contraindication for IUD (IntraUterine Contraceptive Device) are allexcept:

A. Pregnancy
B. Undiagnosed vaginal bleeding
C. Pelvic inflammatory disease
D. Uterine malformation

Q.118 Which of the following is water-relateddisease?

A. Yellow fever
B. Scabies
C. Cholera
D. Dysentery

Q.119 In Vision 2020, the target for SecondarySevice center is for how muchpopulation?

A. 10000 **B.** 50000 **C.** 1 lac **D.** 5 lac

Q.120 CA- 125 is a marker for the screening ofovarian cancer. To characterize this test,histopathological confirmation of ovariancancer was done in a cohort of patients. $\frac{60}{100}$ women who tested positive forthis test had ovarian cancer and $\frac{20}{100}$ women who tested negative had ovariancancer. What is the negative predictivevalue of this test?

A. $\frac{20}{100}$ **B.** $\frac{40}{100}$ **C.** $\frac{60}{100}$ **D.** $\frac{80}{100}$

Q.121 Screening is not useful in whichcarcinoma?

A. Carcinoma prostate
B. Carcinoma colon
C. Carcinoma breast
D. Testicular tumor

Q.122 Admission rate bias is:

A. Reporting bias
B. Response bias
C. Berkesonian bias
D. None of these

Q.123 Stimulation of the external auditory canalleads to cough due to which nerve?

A. Auricular branch Vagus
B. Greater auricular nerve
C. Auriculotemporal nerve
D. Facial Nerve

Q.124 Widening of the cartilaginous part of the extraauditory canal called:

A. Otoplasty
B. Myringoplasty
C. Tympanoplasty
D. Meatoplasty

Q.125 Tubercular Otitis media is characterizedby all except:

A. Painful otorrhea
B. Multiple perforations
C. Pale granulations
D. Foul-smelling ear discharge

Q.126 Partial and full closure done in:

A. Atrophic rhinitis
B. Allergic rhinitis
C. Vasomotor rhinitis
D. Occupational rhinitis

Q.127 Occipitomental view of PNS X-ray calledas:

A. Caldwell view
B. Water view
C. Town view
D. Pine view

Q.128 What causes shifting fluid?

A. Exudative Retinal detachment
B. Tractional Retinal Detachment
C. Rhegmatogenous retinal detachment
D. Retinodialysis

Q.129 Conjunctival injection, pharyngealinjection, polymorphic rash, cervicallymphadenopathy can be seen in:

A. Kawasaki syndrome
B. Measles
C. Thrombocytopenia
D. Mumps

Q.130 Incongruous Homonymous hemianopiawith Wernicke's hemianopia pupil is seenwith the lesion of:

A. Optic radiation
B. Lateral geniculate body
C. Optic tract
D. Anterior occipital cortex

Q.131 The patient came with proptosis,restriction of eye movements, and wasEuthyroid. What could this be from?

A. Orbital Cellulitis
B. Orbital Lymphoma
C. Orbital pseudotumor
D. Thyroid ophthalmopathy

Q.132 Prerequisite for sympatheticophthalmitis is:

A. Penetrating injury to the eye
B. Blunt ocular tumor
C. Chemical injury
D. Urinary tract infection

Q.133 Photostress test to differentiate:

A. Lens and cornea
B. The macula and Optic nerve diseases
C. Cataract and glaucoma
D. Retinal and vitreous diseases

Q.134 Which layer of cornea helps in thehydration of stroma of cornea?

A. Endothelium
B. Epithelium
C. Descemet membrane
D. Stroma

Q.135 A 65 old male with a history ofhypertension and diabetes, presents tothe OPD with complaints of diplopia andsquint. On examination, the secondarydeviation is more

than the primarydeviation. Which of the following is mostlikely diagnosis?

A. Concomitant squint
B. Paralytic squint
C. Restrictive squint
D. Pseudo squint

Q.136 Esotropia is common in:

A. Myopia
B. Hypermetropia
C. Emmetropia
D. Astigmatism

Q.137 An extra row of cilia posterior to the greyline is:

A. Distichiasis
B. Tylosis
C. Madarosis
D. Trichiasis

Q.138 The patient came with unilateralProptosis and bilateral Abducent nervepalsy. This could be from:

A. Cavernous sinus
B. Orbital cellulitis
C. Orbital pseudotumor
D. Orbital lymphoma

Q.139 The characteristic finding of fungalulcers is:

A. Satellite lesions
B. Dendritic ulcer
C. Ring abscess
D. White hypopyon

Q.140 A drug used in a patient with increasedIOP and optic disc changes, ciliarycongestion for decrease IOP acts byincreasing uveoscleral outflow is:

A. Latanoprost
B. Pilocarpine
C. Dorzolamide
D. Timolol

Q.141 A patient diagnosed with Rheumatoidarthritis was on medications. After 2years, he developed a blurring vision andwas found to have corneal opacity.Which drug is most likely to cause this?

A. Sulfasalazine
B. Chloroquine
C. Methotrexate
D. Leflunomide

Q.142 For Nutcracker esophagus the correctstatement is:

A. There is extremely forceful peristaltic activity leading toepisodes of chest pain and dysphagia
B. There is no medical t/t available
C. Type of oesophageal Malignancy
D. None of these

Q.143 Which of the following criteria is used toassess the prognosis of the livercondition.

A. Child pugh score
B. Milan score
C. Meld score
D. Alvarado score

Q.144 Sudden onset headache with neckrigidity is:

A. Intraparenchymal hemorrhage
B. Sah
C. Meningitis
D. None of the these

Q.145 Vegetation in mitral valve seen in whichcondition?

A. Libman sacks
B. Infective endocarditis
C. NBTE
D. Rheumatic fever

Q.146 Water hammer pulse is seen in:

A. Aortic regurgitation
B. Mitral stenosis
C. Aortic stenosis
D. Left ventricular failure

Q.147 What will you do when 3 years old childparents come to phc with fever, coughsince 5 days with chest indrawingpresent under mnci classification?

A. Give antipyretics only
B. Give antibiotics and follow up
C. Refer urgently to tertiary care
D. Give antibiotics and refer to tertiary care

Q.148 What poison will you detect in skeletoneven after emaciation?

A. Lead
B. Arsenic
C. Mercury
D. Cadmium

Q.149 Ph7.2, HCO_3 - (10 or 12), pco$_2$-35 ,metabolic acidosis due to:

A. K^+ excretion by the kidney
B. CO_2 expiration by lungs
C. H^+ excretion by the kidney
D. HCO_3 loss by kidney

Q.150 Impaired function of Aquaporin results in:

A. Liddel syndrome
B. Nephrogenic DI
C. Cystic fibrosis
D. Barter syndrome

Q.151 Most serious complication of measles is:

A. Croup
B. Meningo-encephalitis
C. Otitis media
D. Pneumonia

Q.152 The most common cause of death in SLEin children is:

A. Lupus nephritis
B. Lupus cerebritis
C. Libman sacks endocarditis
D. Anemia and infections

Q.153 A patient having multiple Gall stones andshows 8 mm dilation and 4 stones inCBD, best treatment modalities are:

A. Cholecystectomy with choledocholithotomy at the same setting
B. ESWL
C. Cholecystectomy and wait for ERCP
D. All of the above

Q.154 Pulmonary plethora is seen with allexcept:

A. TGS
B. Ebstein anomalies
C. Hypoplastic left heart syndrome
D. Double outlet right ventricle

Q.155 20 years old man presented with thecomplaint of swelling of the wrist for thelast two years. Histopathologicalexamination showed spindle-shapedcells and verocay bodies. What is thediagnosis?

A. Lipoma
B. Dermoid cyst
C. Neuro fibroma
D. Schwannoma

Q.156 Hemodynamically unstable patient withSVT is:

A. IV IBUTILIDE
B. IV DILTIAZEM
C. Cardioversion
D. Iv beta-blockers

Q.157 A Female patient was on lithium forbipolar disorder for 6 months. She fastedfor some days due to religious conditionand later presented withseizures,tremors, confusion andweakness. What investigations have to be done to diagnose her condition?

A. Serum electrolytes
B. Serum lithium
C. ECG
D. MRI

Q.158 Lithium causes:

A. Hypokalemia
B. Hyperkalemia
C. Hypocalcemia
D. Hypercalcemia

Q.159 A 50-year-old man presents withparesthesia. HB-6.8g/dl. Peripheralsmear shows macrocytosis andneutrophils with hypersegmentednuclei. Endoscopy reveals atrophicgastritis. A most probable diagnosis is:

A. Folate deficiency
B. Vitamin B12 deficiency
C. Riboflavin deficiency
D. Iron deficiency

Q.160 All trans retinoic acid is used in thetreatment of tumour associated with:

A. BCR-ABL
B. PML-RARA
C. CMYC
D. CEBPA

Q.161 Renal tubular acidosis with ABG valuepH = 7.24 PO$_2$=80; PaCO$_2$= 36 Na = 131;HCO$_3$ = 14 Cl= 90; BE = -13 Glucose =135 above ABG picture suggest:

A. Respiratory acidosis
B. Respiratory alkalosis
C. Metabolic acidosis
D. Metabolic alkalosis

Q.162 Patient with pulmonary fibrosis. Whichantiarrhythmic drug should not be given?

A. Amiodarone
B. Flecainide
C. Iv ibutilide
D. lidocaine

Q.163 A 42-year-old patient with obstructivejaundice. Alp, Ggt, haptoglobin allincreased. The most likely cause is:

A. Alcohol
B. Lead
C. Chronic rf
D. None of the these

Q.164 The differentiating feature between IBSand organic GI disease is:

A. Diarrhea
B. Stool calprotectin
C. Pain abdomen
D. Mucus in stools

Q.165 A patient has fatigue. But not gainingweight. Body was warm. Investigationwill show:

A. Low TSH with more t3 or t4
B. High TSH with normal t3 or t4
C. High TSH with euthyroid
D. Increased uptake of t3, but decrease t4

Q.166 Warming in Frost frostbite should bedone at what temperature?

A. 37 degree
B. 42 degree
C. 44 degree
D. 46 degree

Q.167 Which of the following is not seen inPituitary apoplexy?

A. Headache
B. Hypertension
C. Hypotension
D. Vomiting

Q.168 Loss of pain/temperature sensation onipsilateral face & C/L body due tothrombosis in:

A. PICA
B. Posterior cerebellar artery
C. Superior cerebellar artery
D. None of the these

Q.169 All found in LVF except:

A. Lung oligemia
B. Kerley b lines
C. Rales
D. Pedal edema

Q.170 All of the following show low glucose inpleural fluid, EXCEPT:

A. Empyema
B. Malignant pleural effusion
C. Rheumatoid arthritis
D. Dressler's syndrome

Q.171 A 25 years old lady with a history of feverfor 1 month presents with headache andataxia. Brain imaging shows dilatedventricles and significant basalexudates. Which of the following will bethe most likely CSF finding?

A. Lymphocytosis, Low Glucose, High protein
B. Lymphocytosis, Normal Glucose, High protein
C. Lymphocytosis, Low Glucose, Normal protein
D. Neutrophilia, Low glucose, Low Protein

Q.172 Which of the following drug can be givenin patients of primary pulmonaryhypertension?

A. Icatibant
B. Bosentan
C. Labetolol
D. Sodium nitroprusside

Q.173 A patient arrived in ER following an RTAwith hypotension, respiratory distressand subcutaneous emphysema with noentry of air on one side. What will be thebest management?

A. Needle decompression in 5th intercostal space in themidaxillary line
B. Continue PPV
C. Shift to ICU and incubate
D. Secure IV line and start fluid resuscitation after insertion of thewide-bore IV line

Q.174 Treatment of Renal cell carcinoma ofless than 4 cm will be:

A. Partial nephrectomy
B. Radical nephrectomy

C. Radical nephrectomy + postoperative radiotherapy

D. Radical nephrectomy + chemotherapy

Q.175 Which is not seen in Asepsis score?

A. Erythema

B. Induration

C. Serous discharge

D. Purulent exudate

Q.176 Esophageal manometry was performed -it revealed panesophageal pressurizationwith distal contractile integrity as>450mm Hg pressure in the body. Whatwill be the diagnosis?

A. Type I achalasia

B. Type II achalasia

C. Type III achalasia

D. Jackhammer esophagus

Q.177 What will be the appropriatemanagement for Abdominal aorticaneurysm?

A. Monitor till size reaches 55mm

B. Immediate surgery

C. USG monitoring till >70mm asymptomatic

D. No treatment

Q.178 What is the T stage of a $2.5cm$ lungcarcinoma, not involving the pleura?

A. T_{1a}

B. T_2

C. T_{1b}

D. T_{1c}

Q.179 In the primary survey which is notincluded?

A. CECT to look for bleeding

B. Exposure of the whole body

C. ABC

D. Recording BP

Q.180 MC location of gastrinoma in MEN-1syndrome is:

A. Duodenum

B. Jejunum

C. Pancreas

D. Ileum

Q.181 Patients have precancerous lesions withabdominal swelling and inguinal nodesare seen. On examination,lymphadenopathy was found. The mostprobable carcinoma related to thiscondition will be:

A. ca penis

B. CaTestis

C. ca prostate

D. ca bladder

Q.182 A man under alcohol intoxication hadfallen into a manhole and had a perinealinjury with swollen scrotum and upperthigh along with blood at meatus. Thepatient is having difficulty passing urineas well. What will be the injuryassociated due to this trauma?

A. Bladder rupture

B. Penile fracture

C. Bulbar urethra

D. Membranous urethra

Q.183 Patient with a history of carcinomabladder presenting with dyspnoea withclinical signs of DVT and tachycardia.The risk for the patient to developPulmonary embolism according toWELL's score is:

A. High

B. Medium

C. Low

D. Cannot comment without d-dimer values

Q.184 After 4 months of renal transplantation, apatient can likely to develop whichinfection?

A. EBV

B. CMV

C. Candida

D. Histoplasma

Q.185 The patient is present with fecalperitonitis and during laparotomy, adiverticular perforation is seen. Whichstage is classified according toHinchey's stage?

A. I

B. II

C. III

D. IV

Q.186 A young man met with a motorbikeaccident and had injuries to ileum andjejunum. Therefore the entire ileum andpartial jejunum were resected. Which ofthe following would the patient sufferfrom?

A. Vitamin B12 deficiency

B. Atrophic gastritis

C. Constipation

D. None of these

Q.187 A patient after a heavy meal comes withepigastric pain. On examinationtenderness and rigidity in the upperabdomen. X-ray showingpneumomediastinum. What can be thecause?

A. Spontaneous esophageal rupture

B. Penetrating foreign body injury to esophagus

C. Perforated peptic ulcer

D. Rupture of emphysematous bulla

Q.188 Transplantation between identical twins is:

A. Isograft

B. Allograft

C. Autograft

D. Xenograft

Q.189 Thoracoscore, what is not thecomponent?

A. ASA classification

B. Surgery priorities

C. Performance status

D. Expected complications post-surgery

Q.190 For Retrosternal goiter which is true?

A. All patients should undergo CT chest

B. All patients require a median sternotomy

C. It receives blood supply from thoracic vessels

D. Majority of retrosternal goitres should be operated immediately

Q.191 True for King's Criteria with acutefulminant liver failure except:

A. Age

B. Jaundice <7days

C. Serum bilirubin >17.5 mg/dl

D. INR >3.5

Q.192 A patient who was posted for electiveinguinal hernia surgery has history MI forwhich he underwent CABG. What willyou do in pre operative assessment?

A. History + c/e + routine labs + angiography to look for stentpatency

B. History + c/e + routine labs

C. History + c/e + routine labs + stress test
D. History +c/e + routine labs + V/Q scan

Q.193 History of trauma with a stab injury tothe right lower chest with low BP and lowpulse rate. It can be improved with IVfluids and after resuscitation in thetrauma center patient's BP becomesnormal. A chest X-ray showed clear lungfields. What will be the next step?

A. EFAST
B. Keep immediate chest tube
C. CECT abdomen
D. CECT chest

Q.194 In a patient with parathyroid adenoma,how do we confirm the removal of thecorrect gland after surgery?

A. 50% reduction in PTH after 10mins
B. 50% reduction in PTH after 5mins
C. 25% reduction in PTH after 10mins
D. 25% reduction in PTH after 5mins

Q.195 Flap commonly used in breastreconstruction is:

A. DIEP based on deep inferior epigastric vessels
B. TRAM based on superior gluteal vessels
C. Gluteal flap based on thoracodorsal artery
D. Latissimus dorsi flap based on the inferior epigastric artery

Q.196 A 30-year-old man is presented withcramping gluteal pain after walking500m. Which is the vessel involvedduring this?

A. Arterial disease with aortoiliac involvement
B. Arterial disease with femoral artery involvement
C. Femoral venous insufficiency
D. None of these

Q.197 Which is the most common pancreaticendocrine neoplasm?

A. Insulinoma
B. Gastrinoma
C. VIPoma
D. Glucagonoma

Q.198 An elderly man with a long-standingmole over the face which is increasing insize and showing irregular borders. Whatwill be the diagnosis?

A. Superficial spreading melanoma
B. Lentigo maligna
C. Acral melanoma
D. Nodular melanoma

Q.199 Which parameter conclusively rules outmalnutrition?

A. Edema
B. Lean body mass
C. Skinfold thickness
D. Normal ECF volume

Q.200 A 2 years baby with 6.7 kg, Hb%- 6 mg/dltotal protein 3mg/dL, low albumin withdistended stomach but no proteinuria.What will be the diagnosis?

A. Marasmus
B. Kwashiorkor
C. Indian childhood cirrhosis
D. None of these

Q.201 In RDS in a child, which cells are founddefective?

A. Type 1 pneumocytes
B. Type 2 pneumocytes
C. Bronchial epithelium
D. None of these

Q.202 Cause of greenish-black stool in aneonate is:

A. Meconium
B. Biliverdin
C. Bilirubin
D. Urochrome

Q.203 A term baby on breastfeeding withbilirubin 14mg/dL. Which of the followingis true?

A. Exchange transfusion
B. Continue to breastfeed
C. Phototherapy
D. None of these

Q.204 True hermaphroditism karyotype:

A. 45 X0 streaked gonads
B. 46 XX Ovotestis
C. 47 XY+9
D. 47 XX

Q.205 APGAR score 3 at 1 minute indicates:

A. Mildly depressed
B. Further resuscitation not needed
C. Severely depressed
D. Normal

Q.206 A woman developed pain and crawlingsensation on her legs at night. Clinicalhistory of restless leg syndrome. Drug ofchoice is:

A. Pramipexole
B. Gabapentin
C. Vitamin B12
D. Iron tablets

Q.207 History of Arthritis involving 1st MCPjoint, other PIP & DIP joints, spares wristand ankle. What could be the diagnosis?

A. Osteoarthritis
B. Rheumatoid arthritis
C. Psoriatic arthritis
D. Gout

Q.208 12 year old Child admitted to ICU with blunttrauma and femur fracture- Pao2 60%despite 100%o2 and rebreather mask,CXR shows lung fields clear but thepatient remains confused. What is mostlikely the diagnosis?

A. Pulmonary contusion
B. Fat embolism syndrome
C. Hypovolaemic shock
D. Pulmonary embolism

Q.209 A 4 year old child while playing suddenlyspun around his elbow from her servantmaid's hand and now continuouslycrying not allowing anyone to touch hiselbow. He is keeping his elbow extended. What is most likely the diagnosis?

A. Radial head fracture
B. Pulled elbow
C. Supra condylar fracture

D. Elbow dislocation

Q.210 A sexually active female with the profusefrothy foul-smelling discharge withintense itching. Strawberry cervixrevealed on examination. What will bethe diagnosis?

A. Trichomonas vaginalis
B. Bacterial vaginosis
C. Candidiasis
D. None of these

Q.211 33 year old female with heavy menstrualbleeding for 6 months comes to thegynaecology OPD. On examination, noabnormality was seen. USG alsoappeared normal. The patient was triedto be managed on non-hormonaltreatment but it failed. What will be thenext management step?

A. Hormonal therapy
B. Endometrial sampling
C. Hysterectomy
D. Hysterectomy

Q.212 Postmenopausal women 1st line of drugfor osteoporosis is:

A. OCP | **B.** Bisphosphonates
C. Raloxifene | **D.** Strontium

Q.213 Prolactin secreted maximum at:

A. 24 hours after delivery
B. REM
C. 2 hours running
D. 24 hour after Ovulation

Q.214 All are used for postcoital contraceptionexcept:

A. CuT | **B.** Ru 486
C. High dose estrogen | **D.** Danazol

Q.215 A patient delivered at home with acomplete perineal tear came to thehospital after 2 weeks. Whatmanagement will you prefer?

A. Immediate repair
B. Repair 3 weeks post-delivery
C. Repair 6 weeks post-delivery
D. Repair 3 months post-delivery

Q.216 In Modern obstetrics, for sensitized Rhnegative mother what should be done toevaluate the condition of the mother?

A. MCA doppler peak systolic volume
B. Fetal blood
C. Amniocentesis
D. Biophysical profile

Q.217 A 7 weeks pregnant lady has 1 accidentalexposure to x-ray. Which of the followingshould be done?

A. Continue pregnancy
B. Terminate pregnancy
C. Chromosome analysis
D. Pre invasive diagnostic testing

Q.218 A 32-year-old woman complains of amenorrhea since the delivery of a baby 15 months previously, despite the fact that she did not breastfeed her baby. The delivery was complicated by excessive hemorrhage that required a transfusion of 2.5 liters of blood. She has also been fatigued and has gained an additional 4.5Kg since the baby was born. Laboratory data show the following:

Serum LH < 1 IU/L (normal, 4-24 IU/L)
Serum estradiol 5 pg/mL (normal, 20 - 100 pg/mL)
Serum TSH 0.1 mU/L (normal, 0.5 - 5 mU/L)
Serum GH 3 ng/mL (normal, < 5 ng/mL)
Serum ACTH 28 pg/mL (normal, 10 - 50 pg/mL)
Serum prolactin 2 ng/mL (normal, Injection of 500 µg of TRH failed to produce the expected rise in both serum TSH and prolactin.

Which of the following diagnoses most likely explains the findings in this patient?

A. Hashimoto's thyroiditis
B. Isolated gonadotropin deficiency
C. Primary amenorrhea
D. Sheehan's syndrome

Q.219 Meiosis occurs in:

A. Adult ovary | **B.** Prepubertal testis
C. At birth in ovary | **D.** All of the above

Q.220 DCDA twins, 38wks, first twin breechmother has BP 140/96, 1+ proteinuria. What's the management?

A. Immediate LSCS
B. Induction at 40 weeks
C. Immediate induction and delivery
D. Induction if signs of preeclampsia

Q.221 A 36-week old pregnant lady withprevious twin delivery. What is theOvarian score?

A. G2P1 | **B.** G2P2 | **C.** G3P2 | **D.** G3P3

Q.222 Misoprostol used in the induction oflabour is an analogue of which of thefollowing type of prostaglandin?

A. PGE1 | **B.** PGE2
C. PGI2 | **D.** PGF2alpha

Q.223 In early pregnancy clinical signs offeeling the cervix and the body of bulkyuterus separated because of softenedisthmus at 6 - 8 weeks of gestation is:

A. Goodell's sign | **B.** Chadwick's sign
C. Piskacek's sign | **D.** Hegar's sign

Q.224 13 yr old child visit gynaecology OPDwith a complaint of not attainingmenarche with karyotype 46XX. Onexamination, clitoromegaly is seen.Which enzyme is most likely to bedeficient in the above condition?

A. 21 alpha-hydroxylase
B. 11 beta-hydroxylase
C. 17 alpha-hydroxylase
D. 3 beta-hydroxysteroid dehydrogenase

Q.225 A mother brought her 16-year-olddaughter to Gynaecology OPD with acomplaint of not attending menarche.She gives H/O cyclic abdominal pain. Onfurther examination midline, abdominalswelling seen. Per rectal examinationreveals a bulging mass in the vagina.Which of the following can be mostcommonly seen?

A. Imperforate hymen

B. Transvaginal septum

C. Vaginal agenesis

D. MRKH

Q.226 Which of the following is not anestrogen-dependent pubertal change?

A. Hair growth

B. Menstruation

C. Vaginal Cornification

D. Cervical mucus

Q.227 A 22-year-old primigravida visits ANCOPD with 20 weeks POG. On examinationuterine height reveals a 16-weeksize. USG shows reduced liquor. Whatwill be the diagnosis?

A. Renal agenesis

B. Fetal anemia

C. Barter's syndrome

D. Liddle syndrome

Q.228 Most common site for Fertilization is:

A. Ampulla

B. Isthmus

C. Intramural

D. Fimbriae

Q.229 Distension media used for hysteroscopywith bipolar cautery is:

A. Glycine

B. NS

C. CO_2

D. Dextran 70

Q.230 Best treatment option for septate uterus is:

A. Tompkins Metroplasty

B. Jones metroplasty

C. Strassmann metroplasty

D. Transcervical hysteroscopic resection of the septum

Q.231 A pregnant female had Meconiumstained liquor and underwent emergencyLSCS. A few days later her conditiondeteriorated. USG showed edematousbowels. What's the cause?

A. Meconium peritonitis

B. Paralytic ileus

C. Adhesive intestinal obstruction

D. Intra-abdominal abscess

Q.232 18-year-old girl presents with 6 monthsof amenorrhea with h/o low-grade fever,weight loss, pain abdomen, generalizedweaknesses. On PR examination,palpable left-sided pelvic mass felt. Diagnosis is:

A. Fibroid with degeneration

B. TB pelvis with Tubo ovarian mass

C. Ectopic pregnancy

D. Granulosa cell tumour

Q.233 A Child is born, covered with a thickmembranous coat, what could be thepossible diagnosis?

A. Lamellar ichthyosis

B. X-linked ichthyosis

C. Ichthyosis Vulgaris

D. Ichthyosis acquista

Q.234 Mouth to mouth respiration provideswhat percentage of oxygen?

A. 10%   **B.** 16%   **C.** 21%   **D.** 100%

Q.235 Cancer patient undergoes radiotherapy,pick the true statement forradiosensitivity of tissues.

A. Rapidly dividing cells are resistant to radiation

B. GI mucosa is one of the most radioresistant tissues in the body

C. The intensity of radiation is inversely proportional to the squareof distance from the source

D. Small blood vessels are least resistant to radiation

Q.236 Most common DRUG causingdependence is:

A. Cannabis

B. Cocaine

C. Heroin

D. Amphetamine

Q.237 MBBS student she was choking withdyspnea, chest tightness, anxiety and animpending sense of doom onexamination all systemic conditions werefound normal, then she went topsychiatry. What is the probablediagnosis of the condition?

A. Panic disorder

B. Depression

C. Epilepsy

D. Asthma

Q.238 A patient with depression was givenImipramine for 2 weeks. Relativesnoticed increased excitement, colourfulclothes, increased talking. What is thenext step in management?

A. Antipsychotic with Imipramine continued

B. Discontinue Imipramine and start Valproate

C. Continue Imipramine alone

D. Manage with Valproate alone

Q.239 A Patient falls down often withbehavioral change and enuresis. What isthe condition associated with him?

A. Frontotemporal dementia

B. Normal pressure hydrocephalus

C. Parkinson's disease

D. Alzheimer's disease

Q.240 A Patient with depressive symptoms for6 months and associated withauditory hallucinations for 2 weeks. Whatis the probable diagnosis of thecondition?

A. Psychotic depression

B. Schizoaffective disorder

C. Mania depressive illness

D. Schizophrenia

Q.241 Identify the type of joint in the givenpicture.

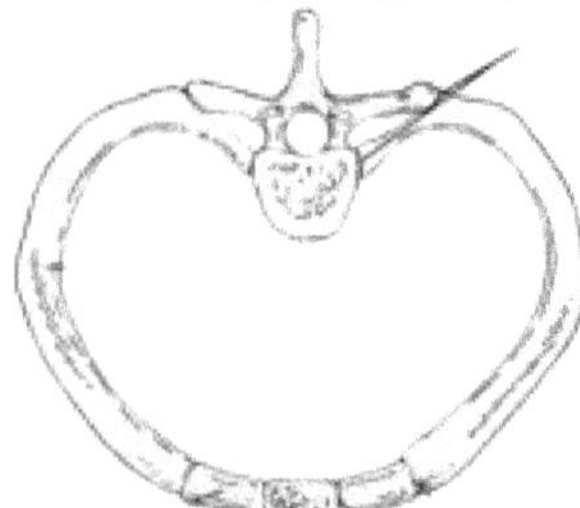

A. Syndesmosis

B. Synarthrosis

C. Synovial joint

D. Symphysis

Q.242 Identify the muscle. What is its nervesupply?

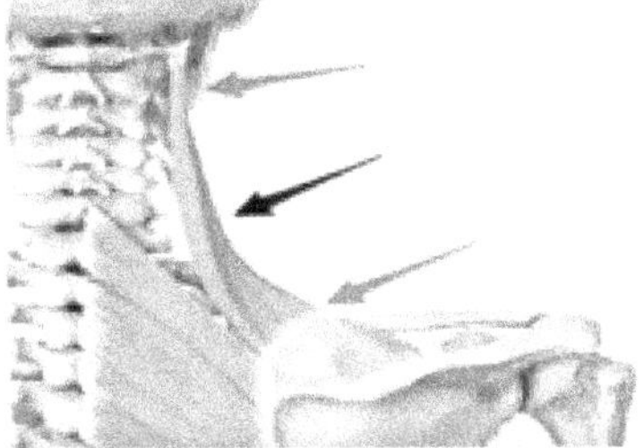

A. Dorsal scapular nerve
B. Thoracodorsal nerve
C. Spinal accessory nerve
D. Suprascapular nerve

Q.243 Identify the cartilage.

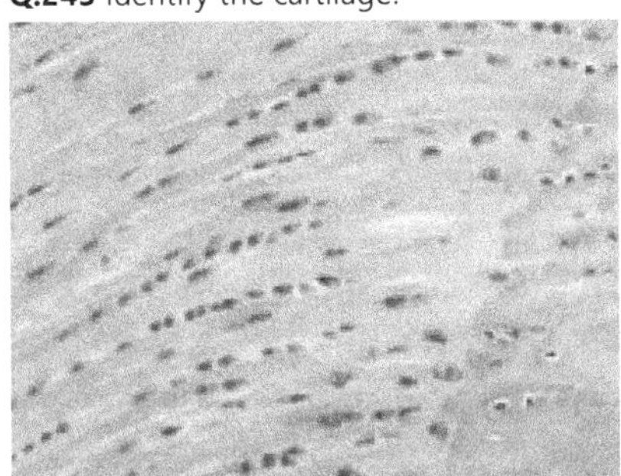

A. Hyaline cartilage
B. Elastic cartilage
C. Articular cartilage
D. Fibrocartilage

Q.244 Identify the boundaries of the anatomicalstructure in the image.

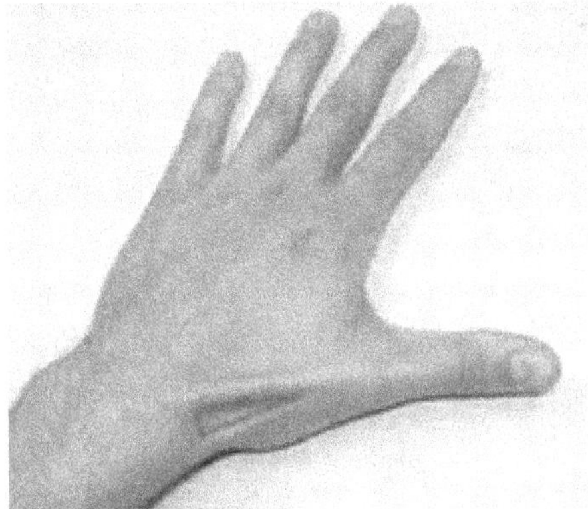

A. Extensor pollicis longus
B. Abductor pollicis longus
C. Styloid process of the radius
D. All of the above

Q.245 Identify the cell type marked in thecerebellum?

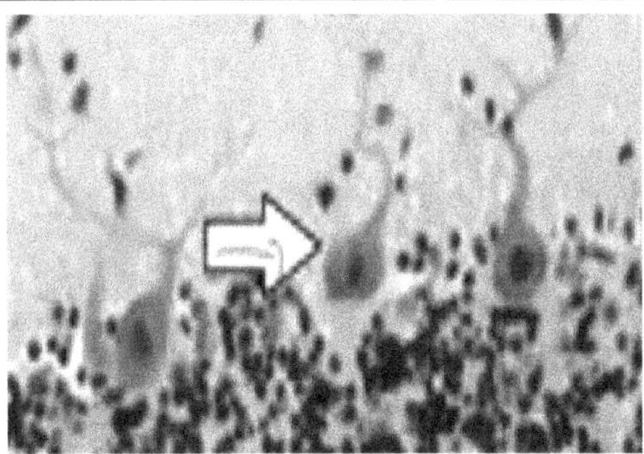

A. Basket cells
B. Granule cells
C. Golgi cells
D. Purkinje cells

Q.246 Identify the sleep wave marked in theEEG during the sleep-wake cycle?

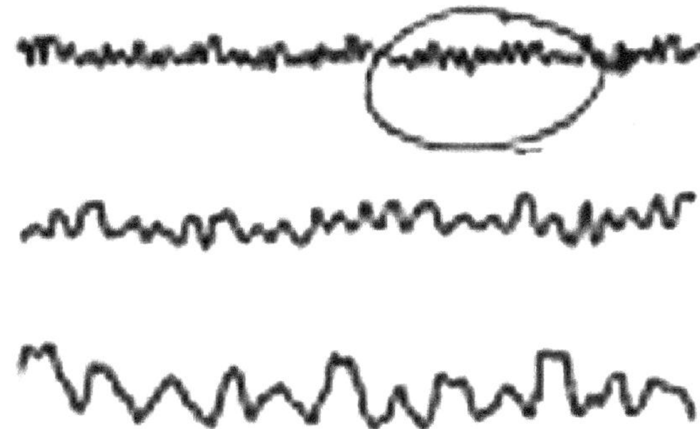

A. Stage 1 sleep
B. REM sleep
C. Stage 2 sleep
D. Stage 3 sleep

Q.247 Casal's necklace is seen in deficiency of:

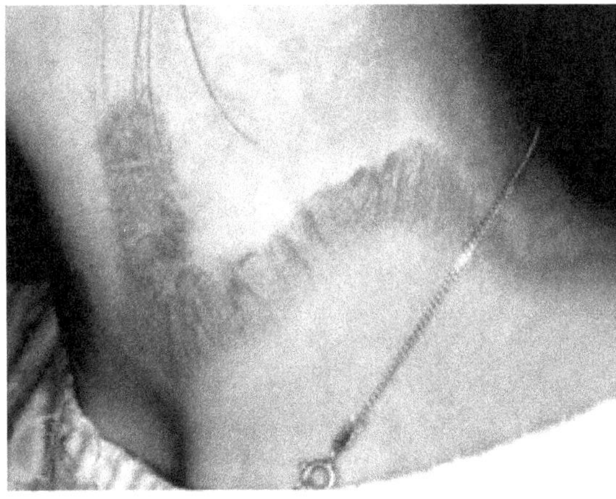

A. Vitamin A deficiency
B. Niacin
C. Iron deficiency anemia
D. Vitamin B12 deficiency

Q.248 An Hiv positive patient with a CD4COUNT OF 300/Cumm presents withmucosal lesions in the mouth as shownin the figure. on microscopy buddingyeasts and pseudohyphae are seen. Amost probable diagnosis is:

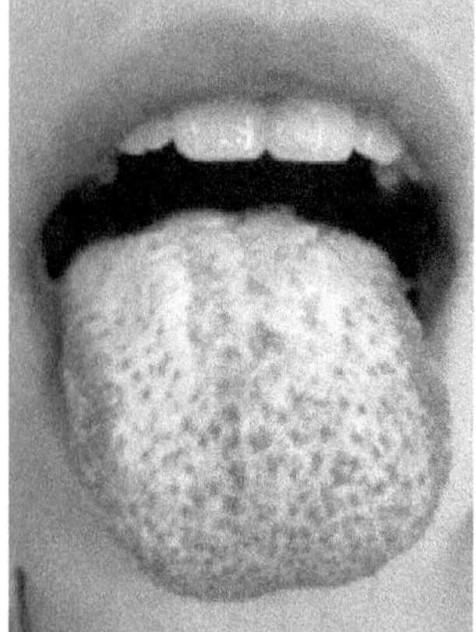

A. Candidiasis
B. Hairy leukoplakia
C. Lichen planus
D. Diphtheria

Q.249 A 25-Year-old male presented with a 2cmthyroid nodule. A thyroidectomy wasdone. The histology picture is givenbelow. What could be the diagnosis?

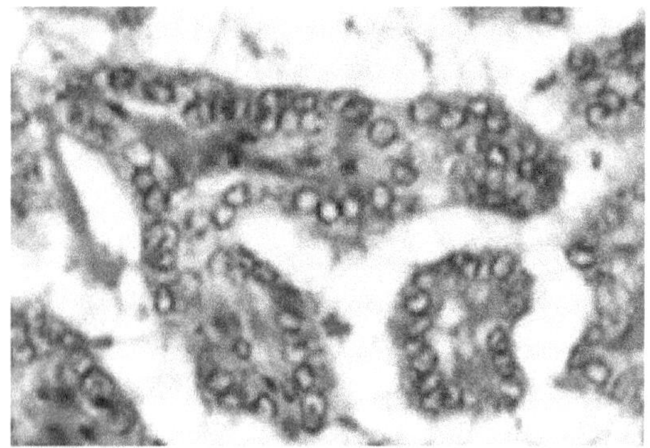

A. Papillary carcinoma thyroid
B. Follicular adenoma
C. Graves disease
D. Adenomatous goitre

Q.250 A 5-year-old child presented with ahistory of blood in the stools. Onexamination, there was a polypoid massin the rectum, a biopsy of which showedas below. A most probable diagnosis is:

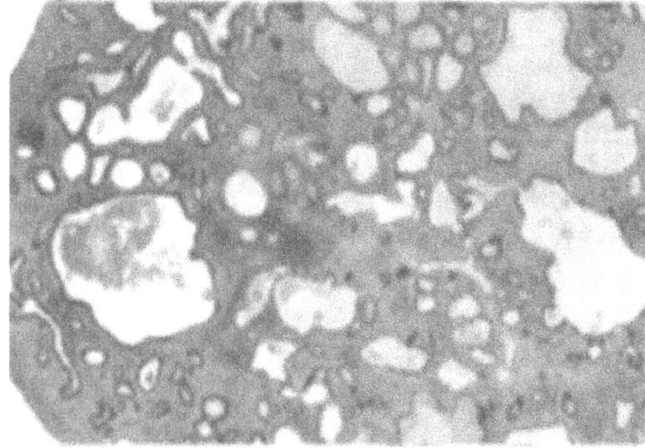

A. Villous adenoma
B. Juvenile polyp
C. Vascular malformation
D. Serrated adenoma

Q.251 25-year-old man presents for a routinephysical examination. The patient is talland on examination, he was found tohave an early diastolic murmur. Hisfamily pedigree is given below. Which ofthe following is the mode of inheritanceby which the disease is likely to betransmitted?

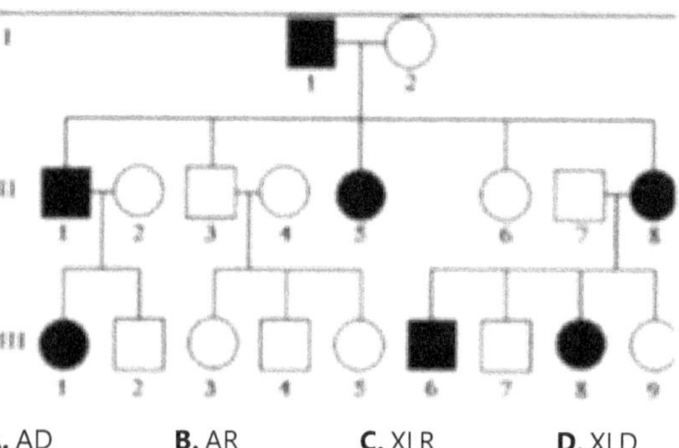

A. AD
B. AR
C. XLR
D. XLD

Q.252 A 51-year-old person came with acomplaint of hematuria. On examination,he was normotensive and had pedaledema. Investigations revealed thepatient had no glucosuria and had acreatinine value of 9mg%. Renal biopsyis as shown below which of the followinginvestigations one should do to identifythe etiology of the disease?

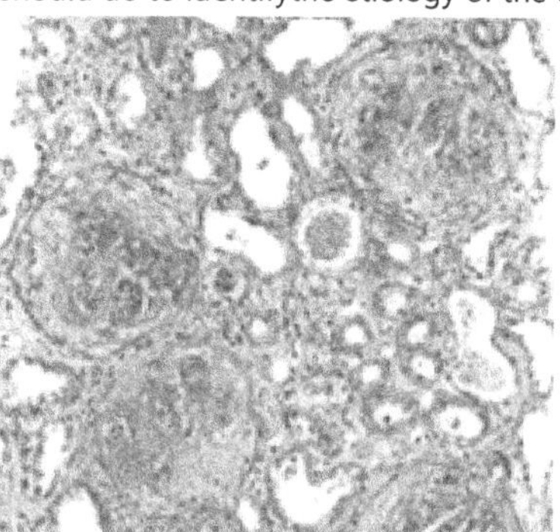

A. ANA
B. ANTI GBM antibodies
C. HIV RNA
D. Urine immunoelectrophoresis

Q.253 A 35-year-old heterosexual patientdiagnosed with HIV had a history ofchronic watery diarrhea. A colonoscopicbiopsy is shown below. A most probablediagnosis is:

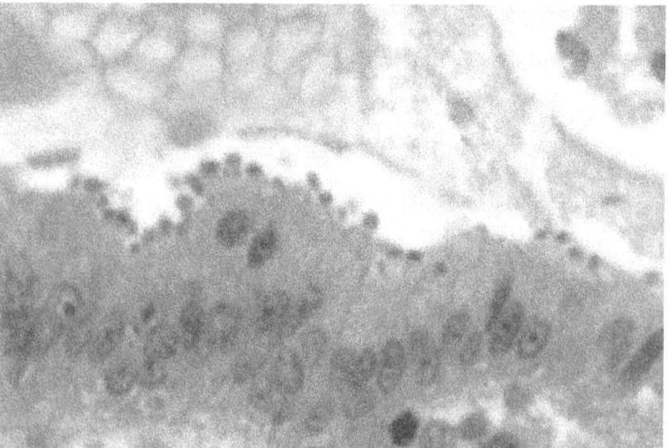

A. Giardia
B. CMV
C. Microspora
D. Cryptosporidium

Q.254 An 11-year boy presented with cough for15 days on examination he was found tohave cervical lymphadenopathy. lymphnode examination showed below findingwhat could be the diagnosis?

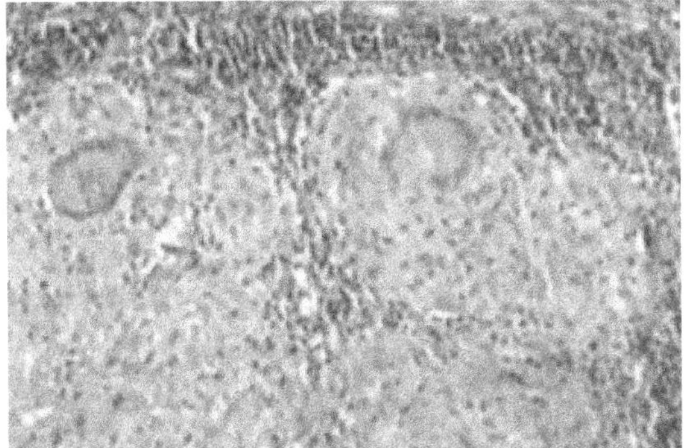

A. Leprosy
C. TB
B. Sarcoidosis
D. Syphilis

Q.255 A 40year old person presented with 10 ×8swelling in a retroperitoneal,biopsy fromthe lesion is as shown below. Molecularanalysis demonstrated t(12,16). A mostprobable diagnosis is:

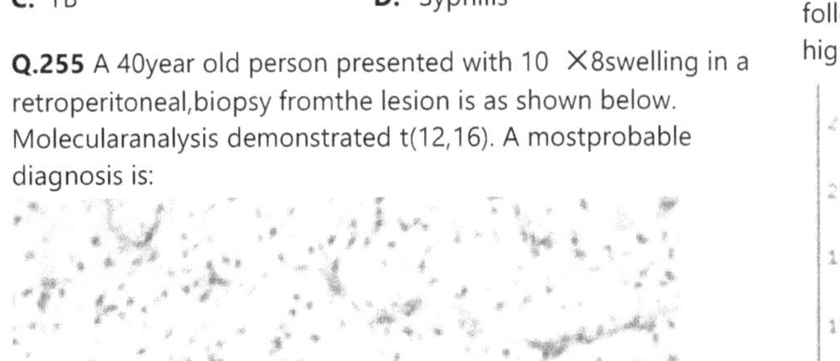

A. Myxoid liposarcoma
B. Lipoma
C. Synovial sarcoma
D. Pleomorphic sarcoma

Q.256 35-year-old woman with a longhistory of dyspnea, chronic cough,sputum production, and wheezing diesof respiratory failure following a bout oflobar pneumonia. She was not a smokeror an alcoholic. The lung autopsy isshown in the image. Which of thefollowing underlying condition was mostlikely associated with the pathologicchanges shown here?

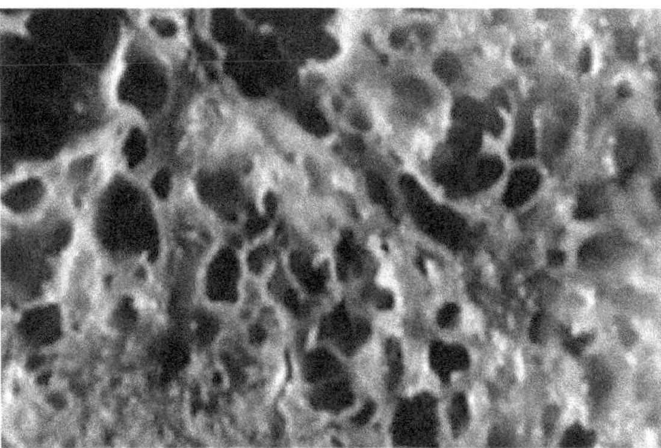

A. Mutation in dynein arms
B. Cystic fibrosis
C. Alpha 1 antitrypsin deficiency
D. Antibodies against type 4 collagen

Q.257 Graph showing three drugs A, B & C.Which of the following drugs shown inthe graph below has the highestpotency?

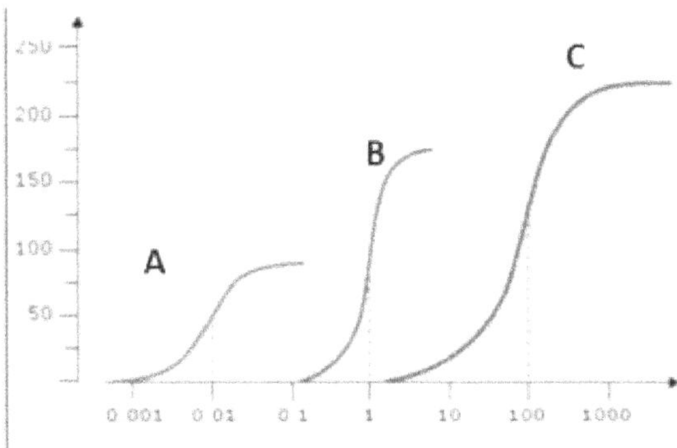

A. Drug A
C. Drug C
B. Drug B
D. Both (A) and (B)

Q.258 In the following X-ray of the wrist, what isthe exact age?

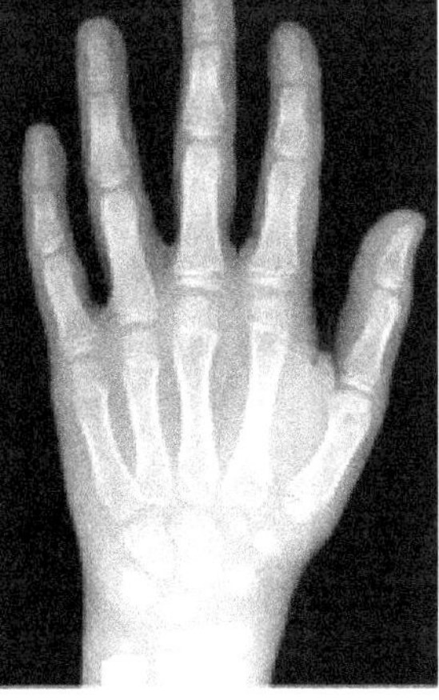

A. 2 years **B.** 8 years **C.** 6 years **D.** 9 years

Q.259 Identify the phenomena.

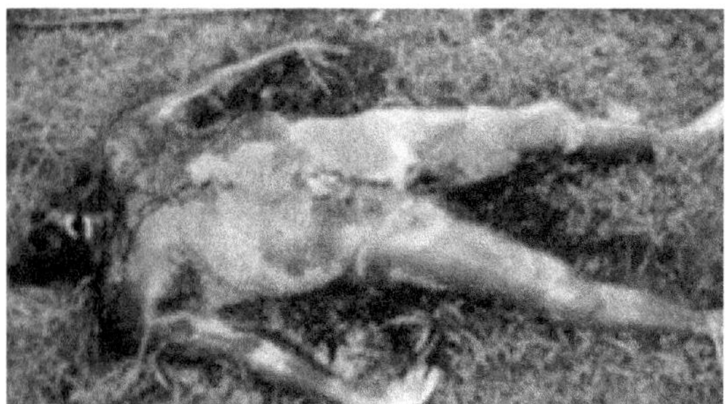

A. Electric Burn   **B.** Crocodile Burn
C. Scalds   **D.** Putrefaction

Q.260 Identify the following Image.

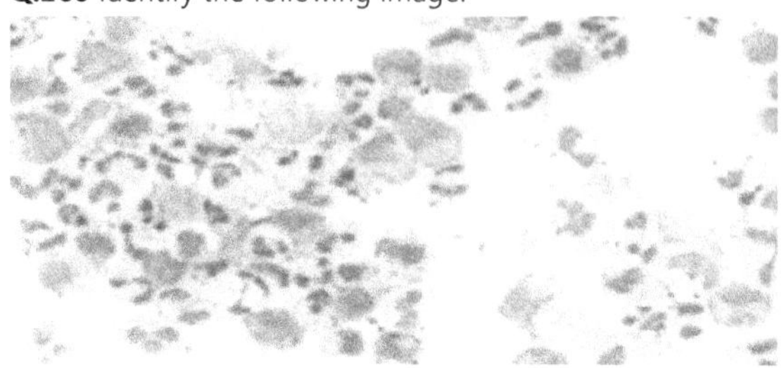

A. Neisseria meningitidis
B. Neisseria cinerea
C. Neisseria gonorrhoeae
D. Neisseria polysaccharea

Q.261 Identify the Image.

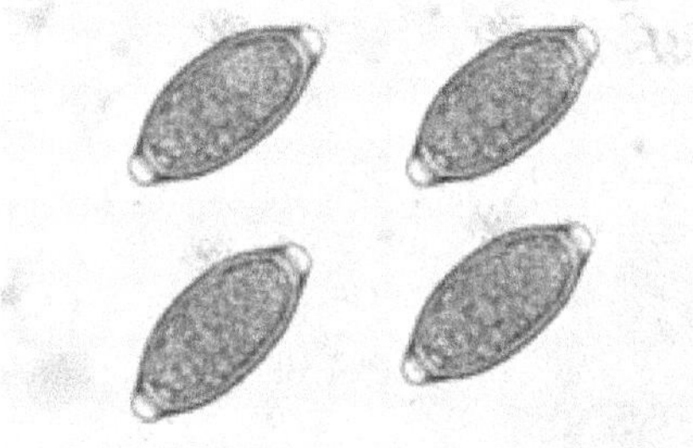

A. Trichuris trichiura
B. Ancylostoma duodenale
C. Paragonimus
D. Strongyloides

Q.262 Identify the organism causing aninfection on the upper arm.

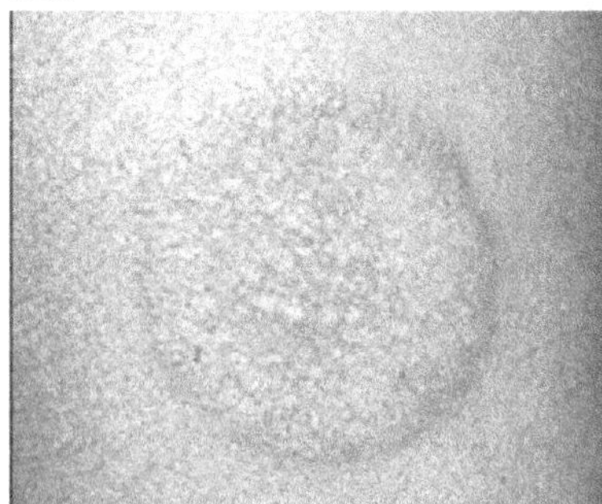

A. Tinea corporis   **B.** Tinea capitis
C. Tinea cruris   **D.** Tinea manus

Q.263 Immunoglobulin Image shown below isof:

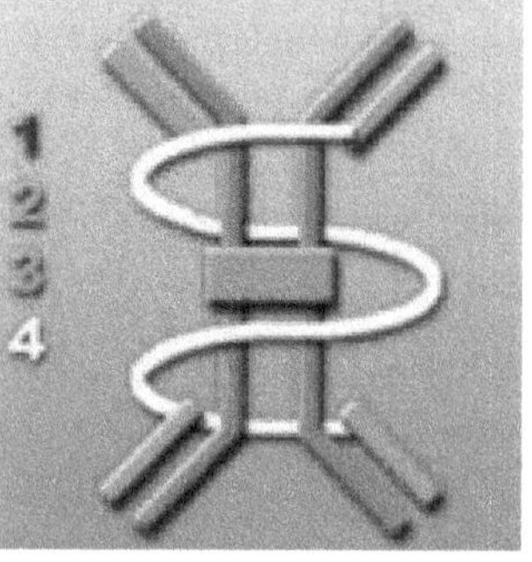

A. IgA   **B.** IgG   **C.** IgM   **D.** IgE

Q.264 A 15 years old boy presented with feverand chills for 3 days. On examination, hewas found to have delayed skin pinchtime and dry oral mucosa. A peripheralblood smear revealed the followingpicture. Identify the pathogen involved?

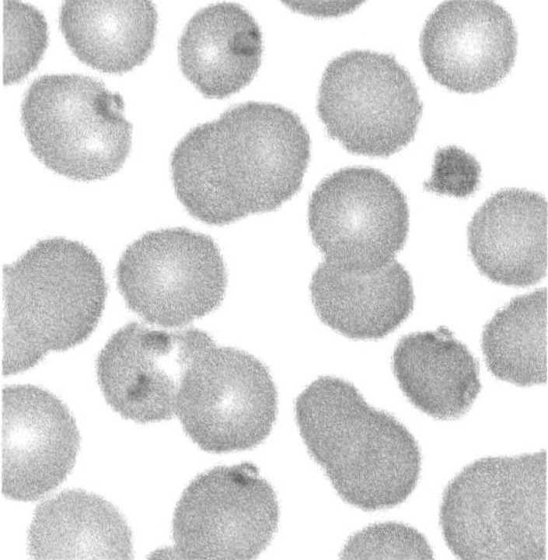

A. Babesia
B. Plasmodium vivax
C. Plasmodium falciparum
D. Salmonella typhi

Q.265 A patient complains about painfulblisters around the angle of mouthidentify the pathogen.

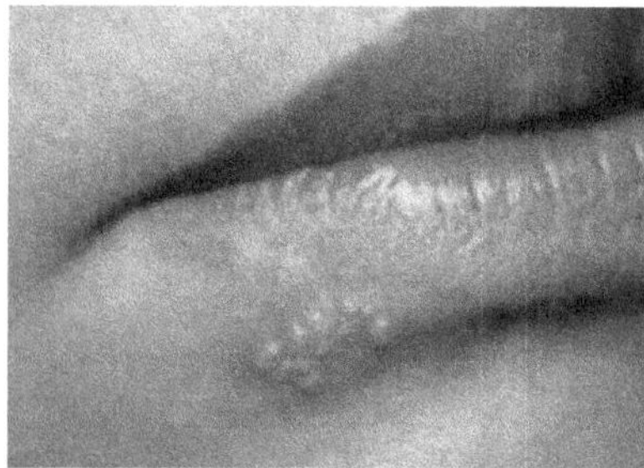

A. Herpes Labialis   **B.** Herpangina
C. Herpes zoster   **D.** Epstein - Barr

Q.266 A patient with the following featureshown in the image. The patient reportshaving another 3-year-old sibling athome, who is fully immunized as per theimmunization schedule. what is the bestmeasure to prevent diphtheria in thesibling of the diphtheria case child.

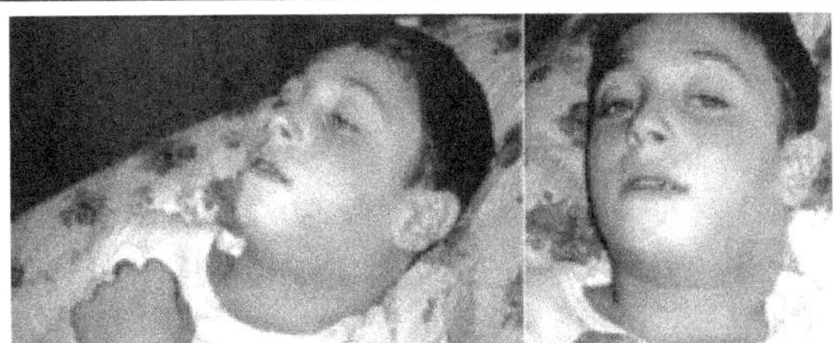

A. Give diphtheria toxoid booster
B. Give a full course of DPT vaccine
C. Give prophylactic erythromycin
D. Nothing is required to be done

Q.267 The most common site of origin of thediverticulum of the pharynx seen in thebarium swallow given below is:

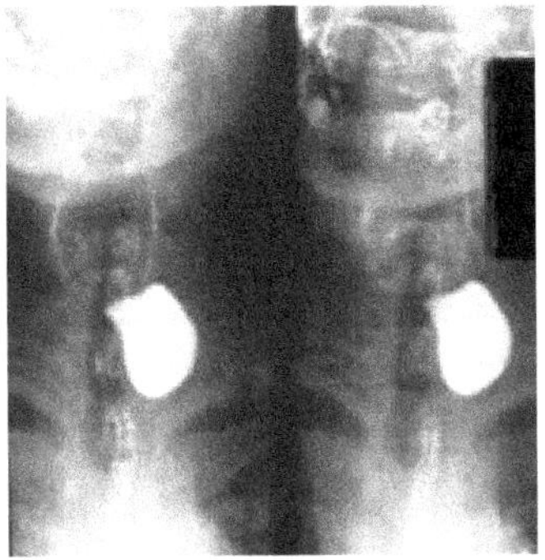

A. Between stylopharyngeus and palatopharyngeus
B. Between middle and inferior constrictor
C. Between inferior constrictor and esophagus
D. Between thyropharyngeus and cricopharyngeus

Q.268 Battle sign image Bluish Purple colourbehind mastoid is:

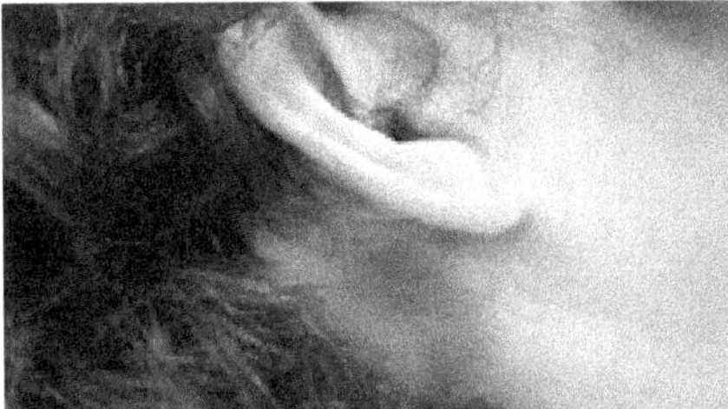

A. Battle sign
B. Bezold abscess
C. Both (A) and (B)
D. None of these

Q.269 The patient presents with, fever,dysphagia. Image showing pushingtonsil. what is the diagnosis?

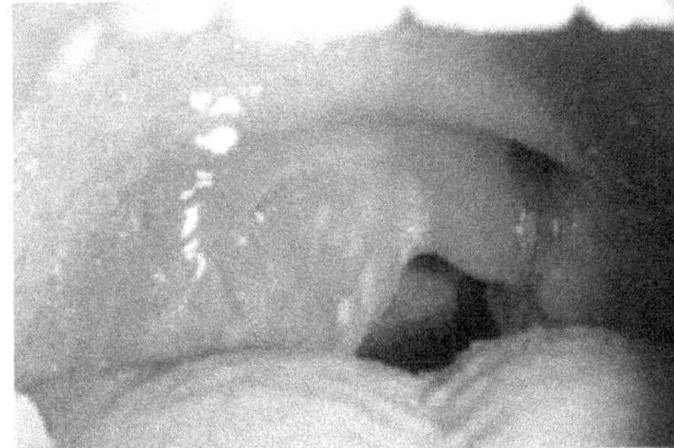

A. Parapharyngeal abscess
B. Retropharyngeal abscess

C. Peritonsillar abscess
D. Ludwig's angina

Q.270 This patient gives a history of toothachefor one week. What is the diagnosis.

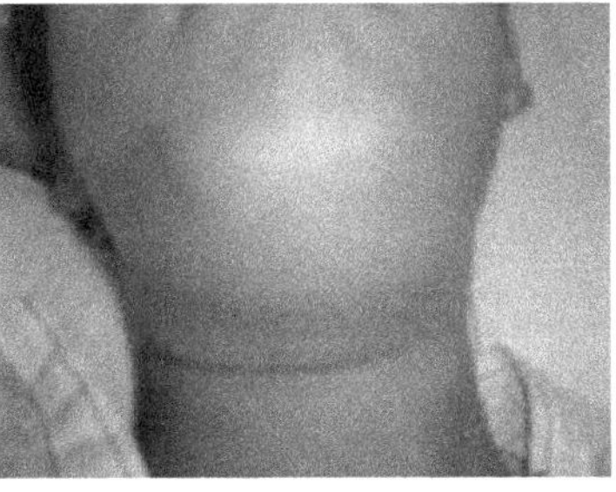

A. Acute parotitis
B. Angioneurotic edema
C. Ludwig's angina
D. Parapharyngeal abscess

Q.271 The movement is lost in:

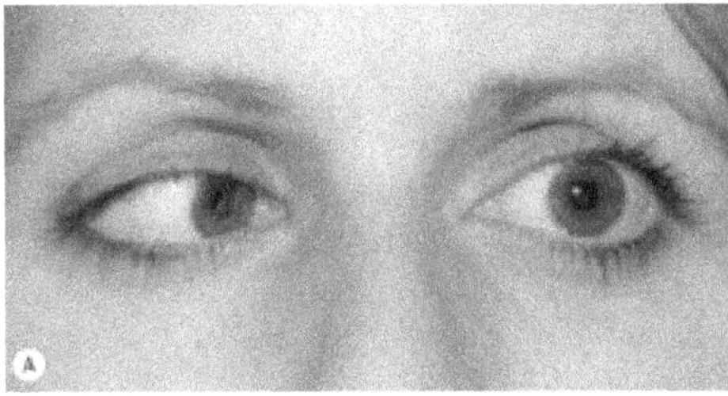

A. Third nerve palsy
B. Trochlear palsy
C. Sixth nerve palsy
D. Facial nerve palsy

Q.272 Identify the condition given below in theimage.

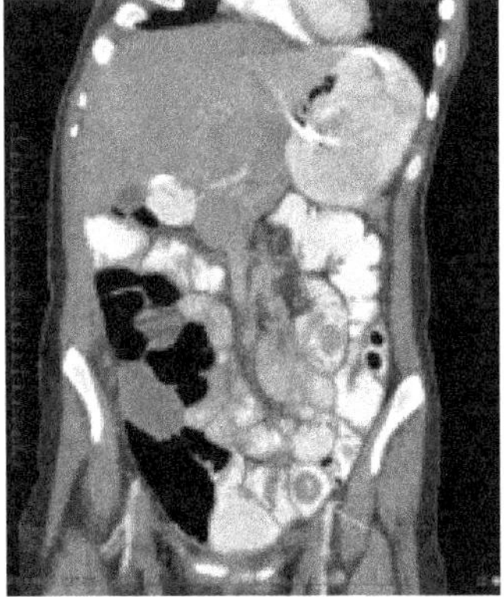

A. Peutz jeghers
B. Juvenile polyp
C. Villous adenoma
D. Hyperplastic polyp

Q.273 Barium Swallow examination is shown.What can be the most probablediagnosis?

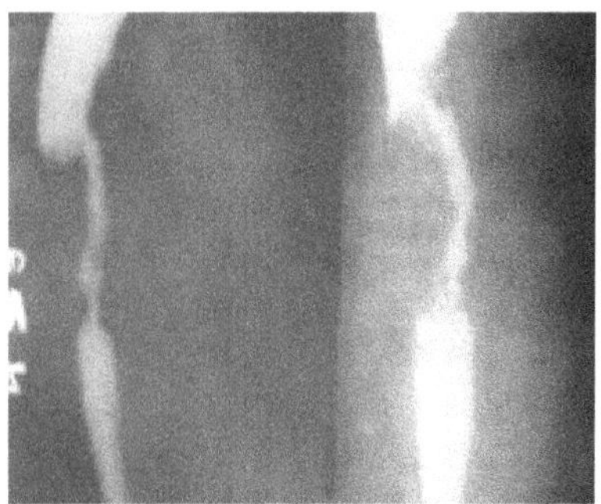

A. Esophageal Ca **B.** Esophageal Ring
C. Esophageal Tear **D.** Achalasia Cardia

Q.274 Identify the condition given in the imagebelow.

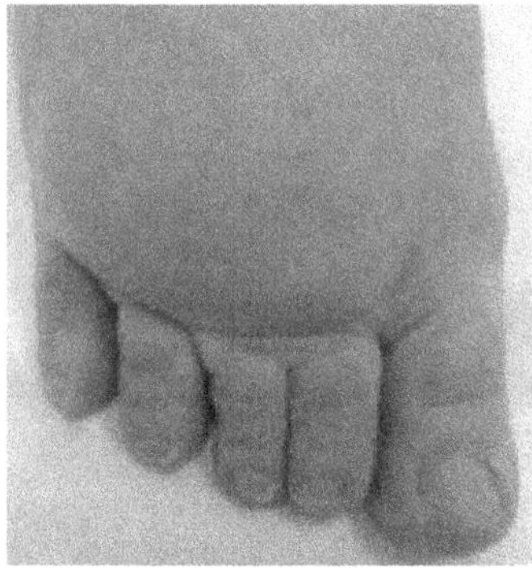

A. Chronic lymphedema
B. Cushing syndrome
C. Osteoporosis
D. None of these

Q.275 Identify the condition given below.

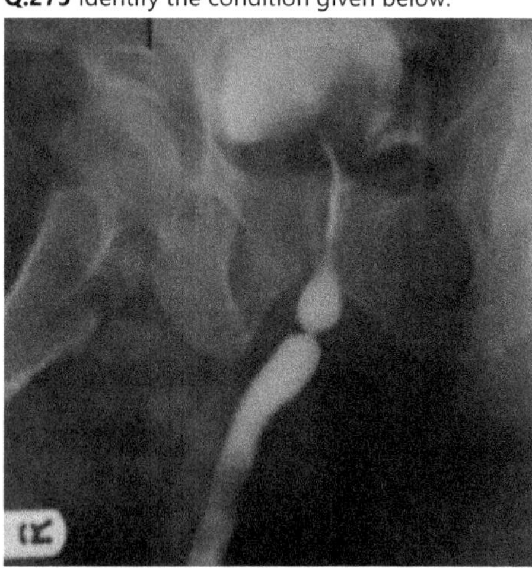

A. MCU with Bulbar urethral stricture
B. MCU with penile stricture
C. RGU with membranous stricture
D. RGU with prostatic stricture

Q.276 What is the use of the instrument givenin the image below?

A. Laparoscopic sterilisation
B. Removal of ectopic pregnancy
C. Termination of pregnancy
D. Laparoscopic procedures to create pneumoperitoneum

Q.277 Identify the image below.

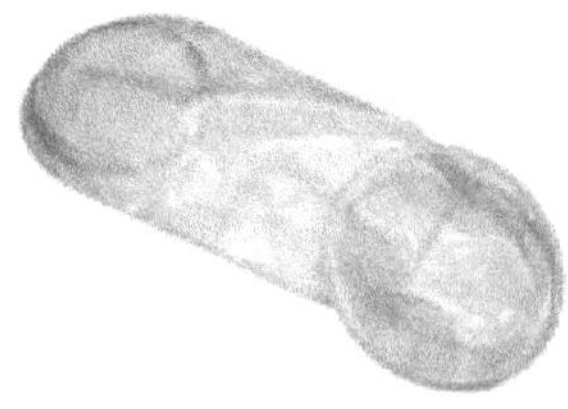

A. Female condom **B.** Male condom
C. Chaaya **D.** Today

Q.278 What condition of the mother isassociated with the following fetalanomaly?

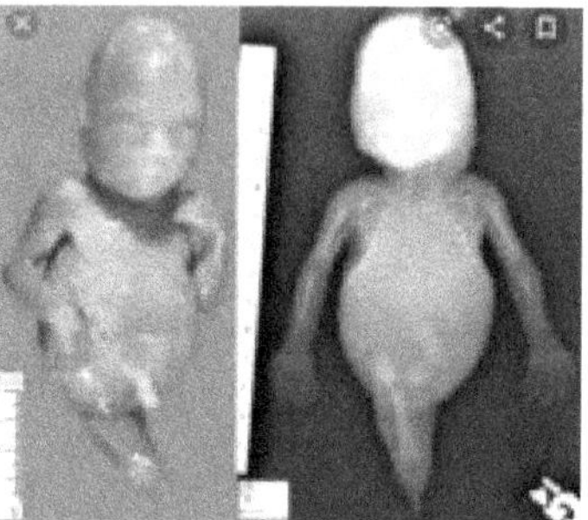

A. ACE inhibitor **B.** GDM
C. Pregestational DM **D.** Valproate

Q.279 Interpret the partogram.

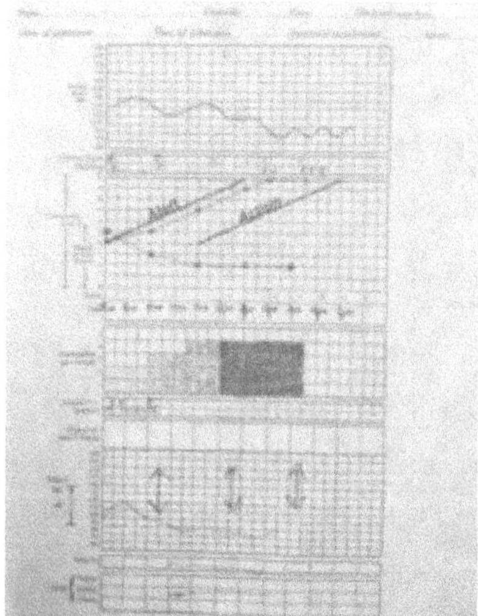

A. CPD
B. Maternal exhaustion
C. Inadequate uterine contractions
D. Rupture uterus

Q.280 60 year female with a history of intermittentbleeding with USG pic shown below.What is the diagnosis?

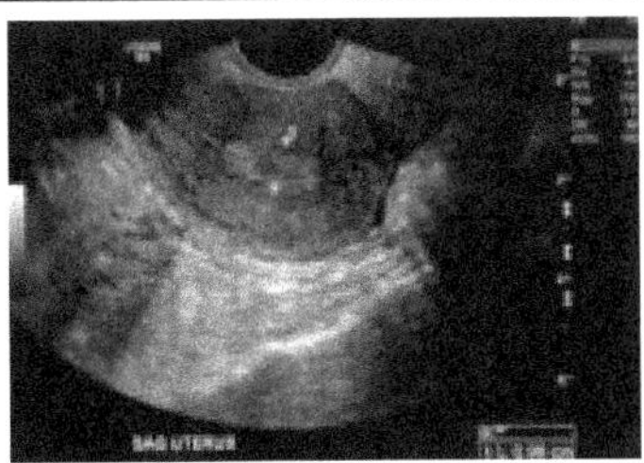

A. Endometrial polyp   **B.** Ca endometrium
C. Submucosal fibroid   **D.** None of these

Q.281 What will be the Hysteroscopic finding inthe given image?

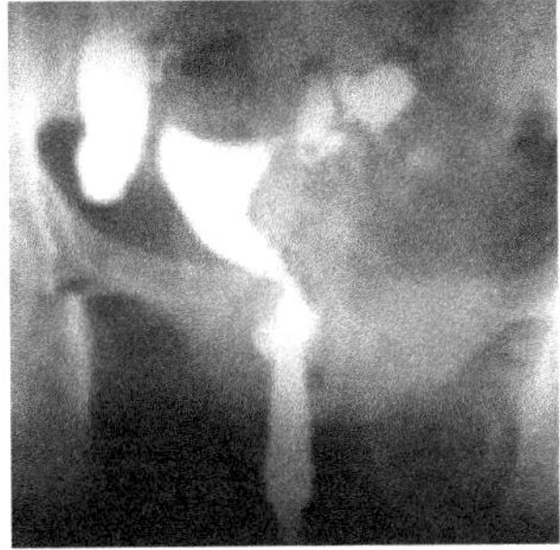

A. Bilateral Hydrosalpinx
B. Bilateral cornual block
C. Normal HSG
D. Bicornuate uterus

Q.282 A lady on treatment for infertilitydeveloped ascites, abdominal pain &dyspnea. USG of the patient was done shownbelow. What will be the diagnosis?

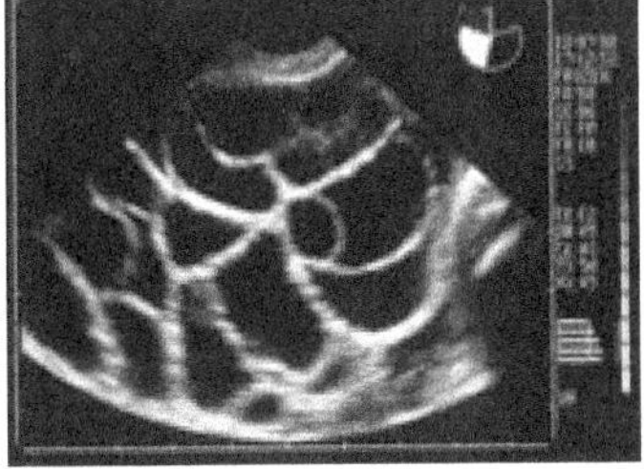

A. PCOS
B. OHSS
C. Theca lutein cyst
D. Mucinous cystadenomas

Q.283 5-year male child present to the clinicwith H/O recurrent infection Onexamination he was found to haverashes shown below in the image. Onroutine blood investigation, low plateletcount was found what will be thediagnosis?

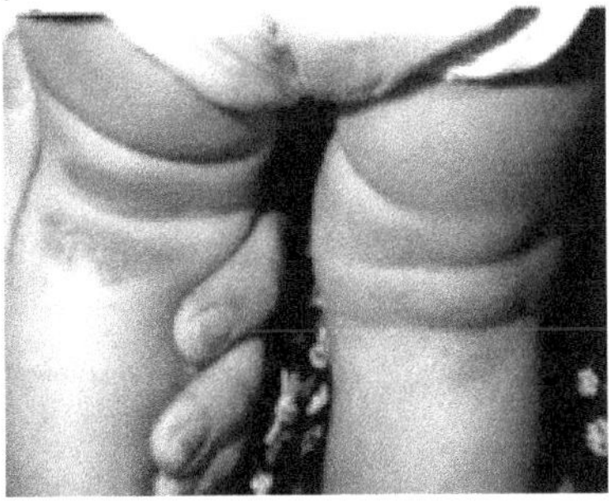

A. Wiskott Aldrich syndrome
B. Job's syndrome
C. Chediak Higashi syndrome
D. None of these

Q.284 The patient is presenting with thedeformity of the finger as shown. The PIPis involved but the DIP is spared:

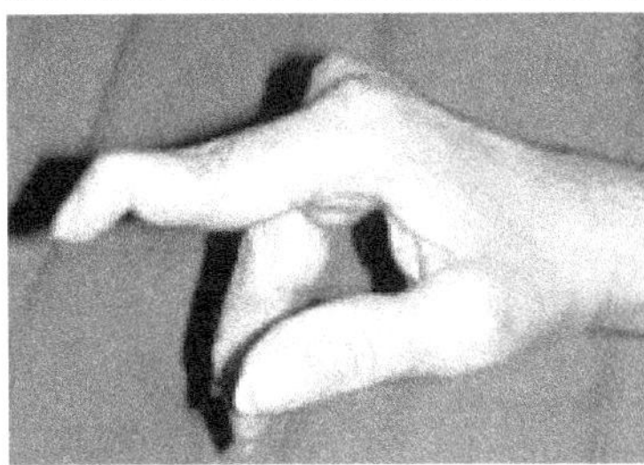

A. Osteoarthritis
B. Rheumatoid arthritis
C. Psoriatic Arthritis
D. Ankylosing spondylitis

Q.285 What is the most likely diagnosis givenin the image?

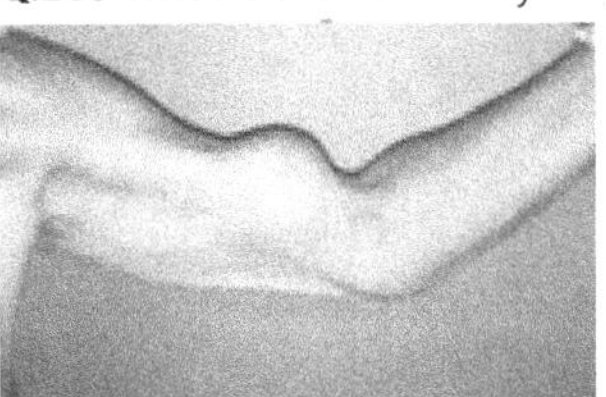

A. Popeye's sign   **B.** Griesinger sign
C. Rising sun sign   **D.** Winner sign

Q.286 The patient is presenting with painaround the base of the thumb, tendonsinvolved:

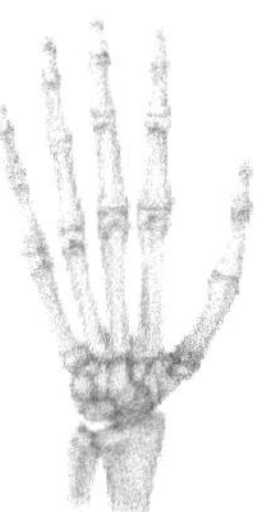

A. APB & EBL   **B.** APL & EPB
C. APB & EPB   **D.** APL & EPL

Q.287 The shown angle in the image is knownas:

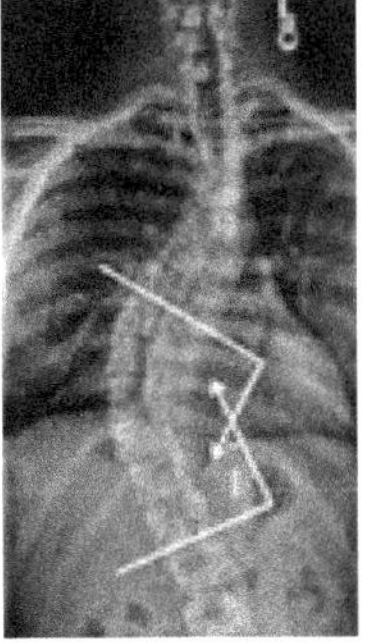

A. Cobb's angle   **B.** Bohler's angle
C. Ferguson angle   **D.** Baumann's angle

Q.288 What is the diagnosis of 55 old womenwith a chronic low backache?

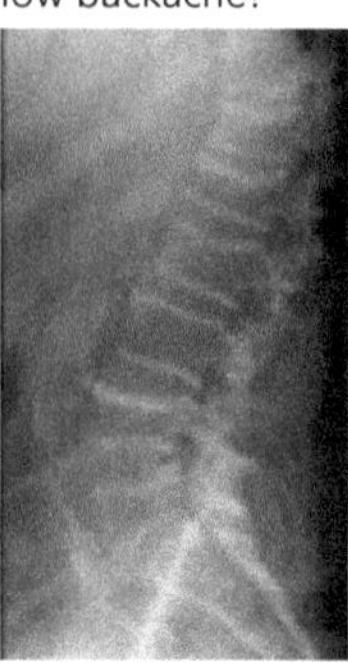

A. Osteoporosis
B. Hurler's syndrome
C. Paget's disease
D. Renal osteodystrophy

Q.289 Identify the condition shown in theimage?

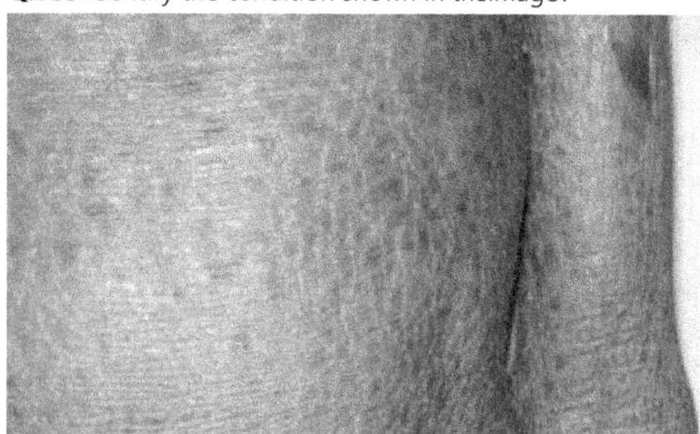

A. Ichthyosis Vulgaris
B. Syndromal ichthyosis
C. Leprosy
D. Sarcoidosis

Q.290 The patient came with history of bullaeinvolving >30 "A, body surface areaalong with erosions of the lips and othermucosae for the past 7 days. What is themost probable underlying etiology?

A. Bacterial infection   **B.** Viral infection
C. Drugs   **D.** Malignancy

Q.291 Which of the following does the image ofCapnograph below depicts?

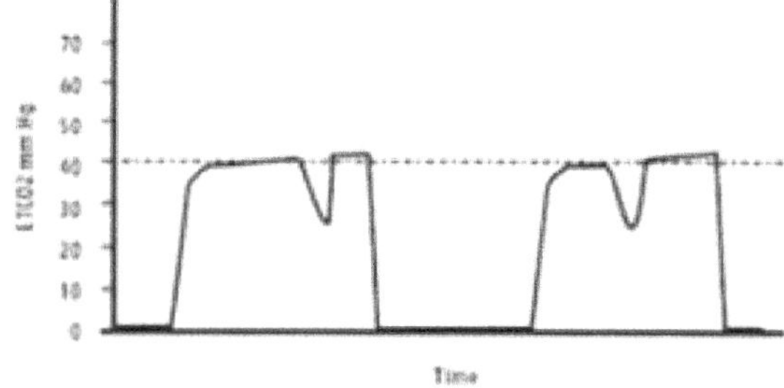

A. During inspiration

B. Inspiration with cardiac oscillations
C. During expiration
D. Spontaneous respiration

Q.292 Identify the device shown in the image.

A. Nasopharyngeal Airway
B. Endotracheal Tube(Cuffed)
C. Guedel Airway
D. Laryngeal Mask Airway

Q.293 Identify the condition in the X-ray givenbelow.

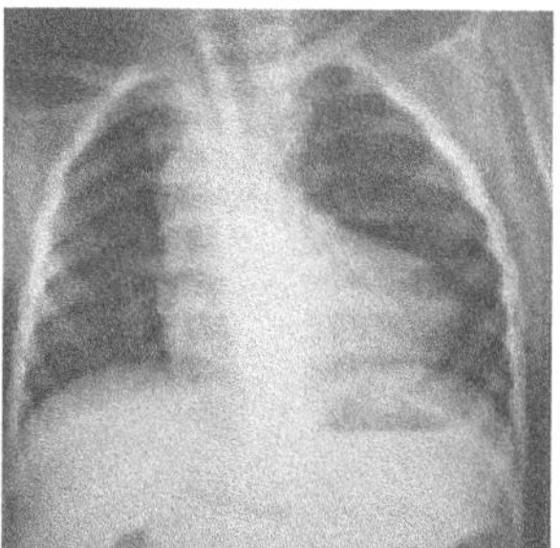

A. TGA   **B.** TAPVC
C. TOF   **D.** Ebstein's anomaly

Q.294 A chest radiograph obtained a male withhypertension. What will be thediagnosis?

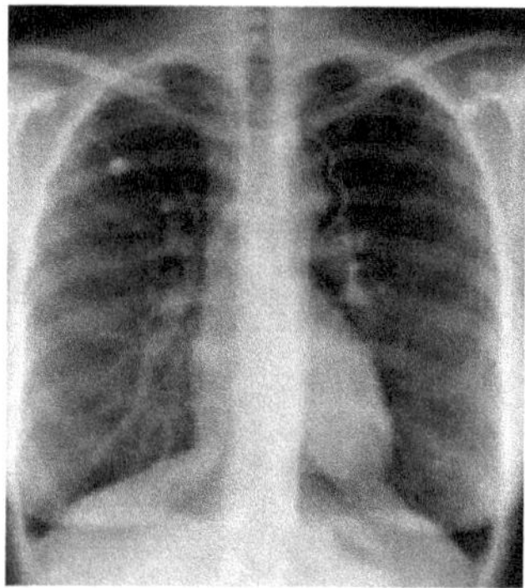

A. Tetralogy of Fallot
B. Ebstein's Anomaly
C. TAPVC
D. Coarctation of Aorta

Q.295 Steeple sign is seen in which of thefollowing condition?

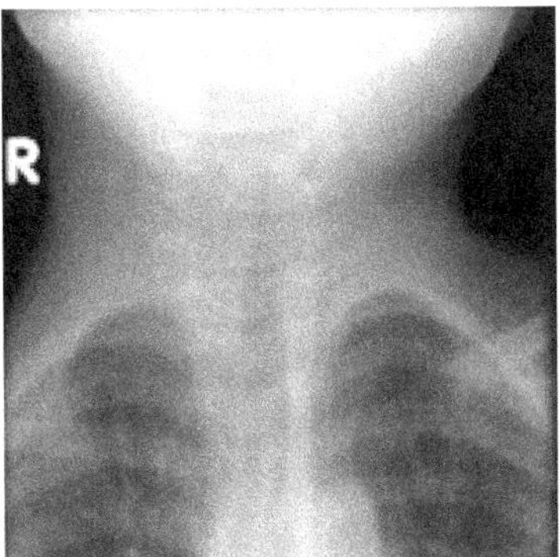

A. Acute epiglottitis
B. Acute laryngotracheobronchitis
C. Laryngeal papillomatosis
D. Bilateral abductor paralysis

Q.296 Identify the radiological sign givenbelow.

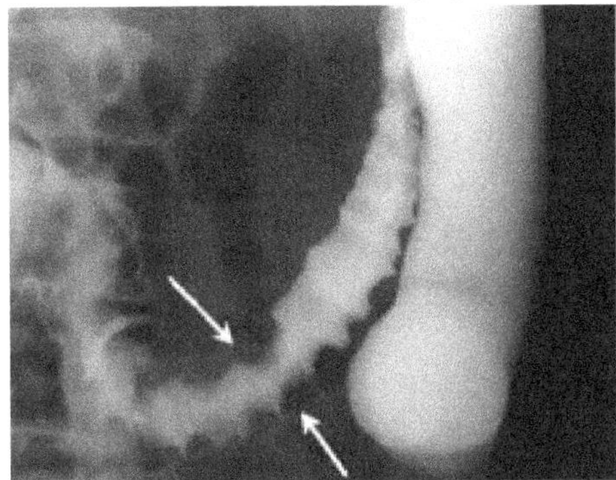

A. Diverticulitis
B. Ischaemic colitis
C. Appendicitis
D. None of these

Q.297 A middle-aged man with a swelling overthe neck since childhood with theoverlying skin not intact which had a bagor worm-like appearance with a blackspot in the middle. What will be thediagnosis?

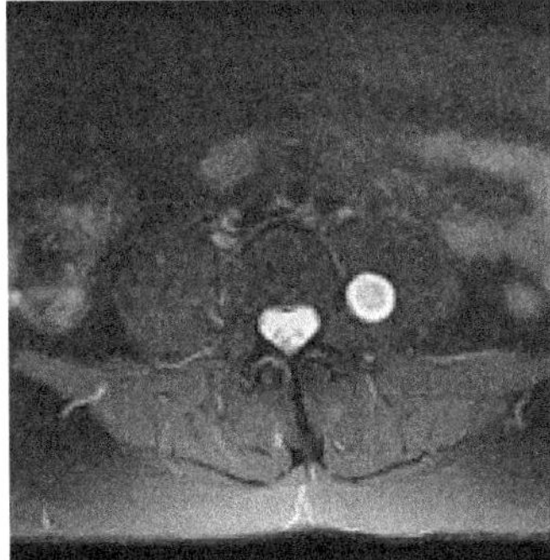

A. Cirsoid aneurysm
B. Varicocele
C. Plexiform neurofibroma
D. Lymphangioma

Q.298 Identify the radiological image givenbelow.

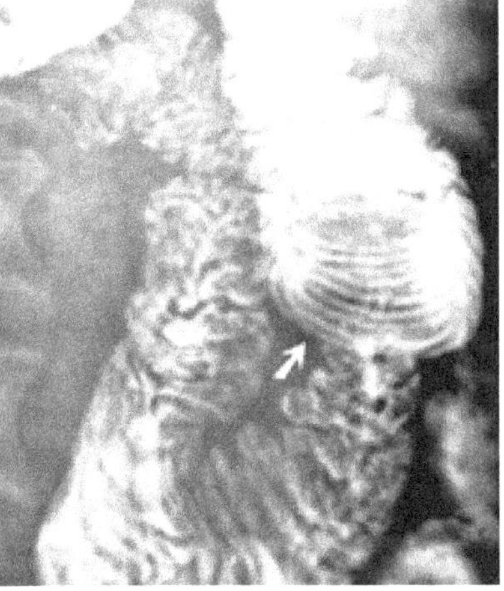

A. Intussusception
B. Carcinoma colon
C. Sigmoid volvulus
D. Sigmoid volvulus

Q.299 Name the sign seen in the given belowimage represents.

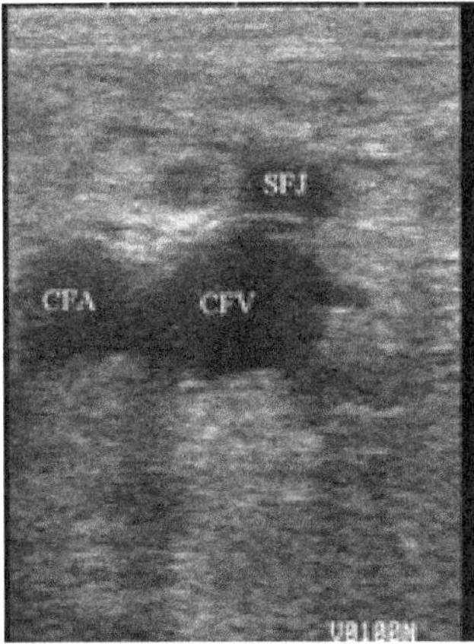

A. Mickey mouse sign
B. String sign
C. Tillaux sign
D. Stemmer's sign

Q.300 A 35-year-old male presents withrecurrent episodes of abdominal pain,jaundice, and fatigue and underwentMRCP. What will be the most likelydiagnosis?

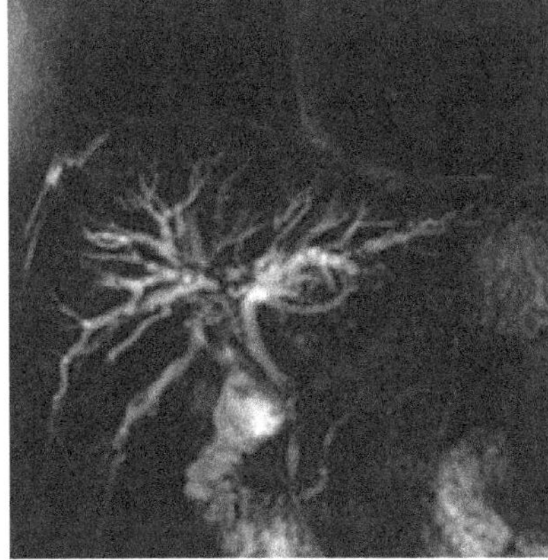

A. Primary biliary cirrhosis
B. Caroli's disease
C. Primary sclerosing cholangitis
D. Oriental cholangitis

// Smart Answer Sheet //

Correct — Indicates percentage of students who answered questions correctly.

Skipped — Indicates percentage of students who skipped questions.

Q.	Ans.	Correct / Skipped	Q.	Ans.	Correct / Skipped	Q.	Ans.	Correct / Skipped	Q.	Ans.	Correct / Skipped	Q.	Ans.	Correct / Skipped
1	B	78.96 % / 16.42 %	17	A	44.31 % / 42.57 %	33	B	31.25 % / 68.58 %	49	D	87.24 % / 12.1 %	65	B	55.21 % / 39.1 %
2	B	63.45 % / 35.08 %	18	C	55.76 % / 37.93 %	34	A	47.47 % / 39.08 %	50	A	45.58 % / 38.99 %	66	A	44.79 % / 31.57 %
3	A	78.6 % / 12.99 %	19	B	57.24 % / 34.28 %	35	D	46.61 % / 32.62 %	51	D	48.85 % / 41.84 %	67	B	52.23 % / 46.73 %
4	C	43.28 % / 40.82 %	20	D	55.79 % / 35.72 %	36	B	67.25 % / 31.7 %	52	A	60.0 % / 39.17 %	68	A	45.76 % / 45.26 %
5	A	14.29 % / 85.19 %	21	B	65.58 % / 34.28 %	37	A	57.67 % / 41.79 %	53	A	48.92 % / 36.74 %	69	A	57.41 % / 42.02 %
6	B	47.23 % / 50.79 %	22	A	56.3 % / 32.47 %	38	D	61.63 % / 31.29 %	54	D	44.45 % / 38.13 %	70	A	49.93 % / 48.7 %
7	B	44.48 % / 48.13 %	23	B	65.3 % / 30.62 %	39	C	22.92 % / 67.33 %	55	A	64.07 % / 34.92 %	71	B	65.17 % / 30.15 %
8	B	44.06 % / 31.51 %	24	D	61.74 % / 35.93 %	40	D	60.1 % / 36.22 %	56	A	52.52 % / 43.85 %	72	C	85.33 % / 12.83 %
9	A	66.19 % / 30.6 %	25	D	55.58 % / 34.71 %	41	C	63.9 % / 35.8 %	57	A	60.52 % / 31.94 %	73	D	65.46 % / 34.32 %
10	D	17.07 % / 71.14 %	26	A	83.44 % / 10.24 %	42	B	46.36 % / 36.98 %	58	C	68.87 % / 30.35 %	74	A	76.04 % / 20.65 %
11	B	45.34 % / 30.33 %	27	A	59.69 % / 39.31 %	43	B	64.37 % / 34.06 %	59	A	59.31 % / 33.52 %	75	D	69.35 % / 30.02 %
12	B	23.29 % / 69.42 %	28	D	58.95 % / 34.95 %	44	B	52.8 % / 30.66 %	60	A	48.41 % / 41.92 %	76	A	57.82 % / 34.63 %
13	C	68.26 % / 31.67 %	29	D	50.52 % / 43.5 %	45	D	42.22 % / 56.33 %	61	C	44.66 % / 37.03 %	77	B	62.05 % / 36.92 %
14	A	46.41 % / 45.72 %	30	C	17.04 % / 82.7 %	46	B	50.36 % / 39.75 %	62	B	43.75 % / 35.17 %	78	A	69.08 % / 30.65 %
15	A	49.45 % / 49.76 %	31	A	55.46 % / 32.92 %	47	C	57.93 % / 41.63 %	63	A	44.19 % / 54.62 %	79	A	50.47 % / 49.39 %
16	B	62.69 % / 31.11 %	32	A	69.01 % / 30.17 %	48	A	69.17 % / 30.16 %	64	A	59.31 % / 34.41 %	80	D	58.13 % / 30.58 %

Q.	Ans.	Correct / Skipped	Q.	Ans.	Correct / Skipped	Q.	Ans.	Correct / Skipped	Q.	Ans.	Correct / Skipped	Q.	Ans.	Correct / Skipped
81	A	69.07 % / 30.6 %	97	A	42.63 % / 51.35 %	113	C	47.55 % / 42.43 %	129	A	26.79 % / 69.05 %	145	B	57.87 % / 38.13 %
82	B	61.99 % / 35.13 %	98	C	61.29 % / 38.61 %	114	A	48.06 % / 45.76 %	130	C	66.05 % / 31.02 %	146	A	68.8 % / 30.98 %
83	A	46.12 % / 46.82 %	99	C	49.34 % / 50.59 %	115	D	59.52 % / 36.24 %	131	C	62.6 % / 34.11 %	147	D	49.97 % / 42.78 %
84	C	53.37 % / 34.42 %	100	A	57.85 % / 37.43 %	116	C	68.38 % / 31.11 %	132	A	48.1 % / 51.5 %	148	B	40.22 % / 31.46 %
85	A	40.2 % / 36.79 %	101	B	54.85 % / 37.04 %	117	D	85.42 % / 10.92 %	133	B	57.19 % / 38.9 %	149	D	66.64 % / 30.35 %
86	B	65.12 % / 34.01 %	102	C	44.96 % / 50.08 %	118	A	55.91 % / 40.95 %	134	A	53.29 % / 32.86 %	150	B	41.5 % / 40.28 %
87	A	55.18 % / 36.19 %	103	A	65.71 % / 33.14 %	119	D	84.7 % / 14.76 %	135	B	79.48 % / 12.66 %	151	B	50.15 % / 30.27 %
88	A	57.6 % / 34.38 %	104	A	62.09 % / 36.48 %	120	D	62.96 % / 36.5 %	136	B	51.03 % / 30.96 %	152	A	66.17 % / 33.63 %
89	A	64.19 % / 30.27 %	105	D	59.26 % / 40.6 %	121	D	64.04 % / 34.46 %	137	A	64.57 % / 35.16 %	153	A	30.25 % / 69.46 %
90	C	64.92 % / 33.57 %	106	B	67.81 % / 30.6 %	122	C	49.44 % / 30.12 %	138	A	47.48 % / 49.17 %	154	B	53.93 % / 38.91 %
91	A	42.59 % / 55.28 %	107	C	69.51 % / 30.23 %	123	A	53.17 % / 31.06 %	139	A	65.26 % / 30.18 %	155	D	41.35 % / 30.52 %
92	A	50.2 % / 33.36 %	108	B	43.27 % / 46.13 %	124	D	54.76 % / 43.81 %	140	A	46.77 % / 45.96 %	156	C	76.47 % / 15.78 %
93	B	24.45 % / 70.11 %	109	C	68.16 % / 30.48 %	125	A	63.53 % / 35.15 %	141	B	45.06 % / 35.02 %	157	B	64.26 % / 30.37 %
94	B	53.36 % / 35.96 %	110	B	32.71 % / 67.08 %	126	A	32.2 % / 67.07 %	142	A	44.38 % / 53.38 %	158	A	65.85 % / 31.65 %
95	C	61.18 % / 35.37 %	111	C	84.27 % / 10.63 %	127	B	89.46 % / 10.52 %	143	A	55.45 % / 33.96 %	159	B	88.57 % / 10.04 %
96	D	63.99 % / 32.07 %	112	B	54.59 % / 45.38 %	128	A	46.39 % / 33.01 %	144	B	69.38 % / 30.54 %	160	B	80.55 % / 14.74 %

Q.	Ans.	Correct	Skipped	Q.	Ans.	Correct	Skipped	Q.	Ans.	Correct	Skipped	Q.	Ans.	Correct	Skipped	Q.	Ans.	Correct	Skipped
161	C	53.95 %	32.21 %	177	A	68.54 %	31.09 %	193	A	88.49 %	10.2 %	209	B	81.05 %	16.58 %	225	A	78.53 %	13.52 %
162	A	48.93 %	49.19 %	178	D	78.97 %	16.4 %	194	A	85.55 %	10.57 %	210	A	80.07 %	12.77 %	226	B	78.88 %	16.45 %
163	A	86.01 %	13.64 %	179	A	83.21 %	14.39 %	195	A	84.28 %	15.26 %	211	B	77.39 %	18.77 %	227	A	85.49 %	11.69 %
164	B	66.16 %	30.04 %	180	A	86.67 %	12.57 %	196	A	84.4 %	13.06 %	212	B	82.26 %	16.2 %	228	A	80.11 %	13.42 %
165	A	60.77 %	36.97 %	181	A	41.52 %	38.18 %	197	A	89.29 %	10.26 %	213	A	79.78 %	14.19 %	229	B	78.86 %	19.18 %
166	A	86.26 %	13.13 %	182	C	76.71 %	15.78 %	198	A	47.5 %	37.79 %	214	D	86.12 %	13.59 %	230	D	89.45 %	10.12 %
167	C	56.88 %	37.0 %	183	B	59.21 %	37.37 %	199	B	79.45 %	13.67 %	215	D	83.62 %	12.09 %	231	B	79.37 %	13.87 %
168	A	29.65 %	68.39 %	184	B	48.57 %	40.66 %	200	B	89.83 %	10.15 %	216	A	84.55 %	14.56 %	232	B	87.63 %	11.55 %
169	A	89.09 %	10.85 %	185	D	88.19 %	10.09 %	201	B	81.51 %	12.08 %	217	A	84.29 %	11.28 %	233	A	79.36 %	17.17 %
170	D	89.42 %	10.03 %	186	A	86.05 %	11.65 %	202	B	50.09 %	45.9 %	218	D	81.5 %	11.01 %	234	B	86.19 %	12.49 %
171	A	88.61 %	10.75 %	187	A	89.33 %	10.36 %	203	B	79.62 %	13.08 %	219	A	76.16 %	22.94 %	235	C	78.52 %	11.51 %
172	B	87.52 %	11.31 %	188	A	85.86 %	10.66 %	204	B	85.51 %	10.26 %	220	A	85.07 %	11.04 %	236	A	84.05 %	10.24 %
173	A	81.23 %	18.41 %	189	B	88.44 %	11.35 %	205	C	81.82 %	15.23 %	221	A	80.77 %	15.09 %	237	A	80.74 %	18.06 %
174	A	77.5 %	14.24 %	190	A	76.68 %	21.45 %	206	A	58.3 %	35.94 %	222	A	78.51 %	10.19 %	238	A	48.83 %	38.82 %
175	B	56.7 %	41.18 %	191	B	57.37 %	35.37 %	207	A	85.68 %	13.57 %	223	D	76.32 %	17.5 %	239	B	50.99 %	37.78 %
176	C	78.57 %	19.57 %	192	C	84.6 %	12.23 %	208	B	87.32 %	11.22 %	224	A	86.82 %	10.69 %	240	A	41.06 %	57.93 %

Q.	Ans.	Correct / Skipped	Q.	Ans.	Correct / Skipped	Q.	Ans.	Correct / Skipped	Q.	Ans.	Correct / Skipped	Q.	Ans.	Correct / Skipped
241	C	69.53 % / 30.4 %	253	D	82.37 % / 11.24 %	265	A	85.58 % / 11.07 %	277	A	82.81 % / 14.11 %	289	A	87.42 % / 10.58 %
242	A	77.23 % / 21.18 %	254	C	88.09 % / 10.62 %	266	D	67.03 % / 30.15 %	278	C	85.05 % / 13.45 %	290	C	67.38 % / 31.86 %
243	D	84.69 % / 14.05 %	255	A	76.34 % / 11.85 %	267	D	56.44 % / 40.62 %	279	A	57.02 % / 32.99 %	291	D	80.29 % / 17.05 %
244	D	89.7 % / 10.29 %	256	C	43.6 % / 35.37 %	268	A	85.94 % / 10.15 %	280	A	45.84 % / 40.7 %	292	D	58.55 % / 38.41 %
245	D	54.97 % / 40.89 %	257	A	81.3 % / 18.44 %	269	C	80.36 % / 13.11 %	281	A	79.64 % / 18.63 %	293	C	87.53 % / 11.32 %
246	B	40.16 % / 43.36 %	258	C	84.55 % / 14.33 %	270	C	84.33 % / 10.84 %	282	B	81.64 % / 16.82 %	294	D	80.4 % / 14.43 %
247	B	82.68 % / 11.09 %	259	D	84.4 % / 15.42 %	271	B	88.27 % / 11.29 %	283	A	56.44 % / 37.58 %	295	B	47.62 % / 51.67 %
248	A	79.66 % / 20.02 %	260	A	78.61 % / 11.04 %	272	B	68.48 % / 31.03 %	284	B	86.72 % / 12.4 %	296	B	80.68 % / 13.32 %
249	A	89.89 % / 10.05 %	261	A	49.64 % / 39.42 %	273	A	88.39 % / 11.08 %	285	A	80.12 % / 14.28 %	297	C	82.54 % / 17.01 %
250	B	84.94 % / 11.02 %	262	A	49.03 % / 50.95 %	274	A	82.05 % / 13.9 %	286	B	84.0 % / 14.18 %	298	A	65.63 % / 30.94 %
251	A	76.0 % / 12.68 %	263	A	77.09 % / 13.89 %	275	A	88.78 % / 10.67 %	287	A	67.5 % / 30.96 %	299	A	80.02 % / 12.74 %
252	B	77.67 % / 13.29 %	264	C	85.19 % / 13.82 %	276	A	57.07 % / 30.4 %	288	A	85.62 % / 10.72 %	300	C	46.11 % / 51.86 %

Performance Analysis

Avg. Score (%)	45.17%
Toppers Score (%)	68.0%
Your Score	

// Notes //

// Notes //